Lecture Notes in Computer Science 866

Edited by G. Goos, J. Hartmanis and J. van Leeuwen

Advisory Board: W. Brauer   D. Gries   J. Stoer

Yuval Davidor   Hans-Paul Schwefel
Reinhard Männer (Eds.)

Parallel Problem Solving from Nature – PPSN III

International Conference on Evolutionary Computation
The Third Conference on
Parallel Problem Solving from Nature
Jerusalem, Israel, October 9-14, 1994
Proceedings

Springer-Verlag

Berlin Heidelberg New York
London Paris Tokyo
Hong Kong Barcelona
Budapest

Series Editors

Gerhard Goos
Universität Karlsruhe
Postfach 69 80, Vincenz-Priessnitz-Straße 1, D-76131 Karlsruhe, Germany

Juris Hartmanis
Department of Computer Science, Cornell University
4130 Upson Hall, Ithaka, NY 14853, USA

Jan van Leeuwen
Department of Computer Science, Utrecht University
Padualaan 14, 3584 CH Utrecht, The Netherlands

Volume Editors

Yuval Davidor
Schema – Evolutionary Algorithms Ltd.
61a Hadar Street, Herzelia 46326, Israel

Hans-Paul Schwefel
Fachbereich Informatik, Lehrstuhl für Systemanalyse, Universität Dortmund
D-44221 Dortmund, Germany

Reinhard Männer
Fakultät für Mathematik und Informatik, Lehrstuhl für Informatik V
Universität Mannheim, D-68131 Mannheim, Germany

CR Subject Classification (1991): C.1.2, D.1.3, F.1-2, I.2.6, I.2.8, J.0

ISBN 3-540-58484-6 Springer-Verlag Berlin Heidelberg New York

CIP data applied for

© Springer-Verlag Berlin Heidelberg 1994
Printed in Germany

Typesetting: Camera-ready by author
SPIN: 10479007   45/3140-543210 - Printed on acid-free paper

Preface

The history of the conference

In October 1994, the international conference on parallel problem solving from nature (PPSN) was held for the third time.

The first event of this series took place at Dortmund, Germany, in 1990. It had originally been planned as a small workshop with about 30 participants. To the big surprise of the organizers, the interest was so high that PPSN 1 became an international conference with more than 100 participants. The topics covered were, among others, genetic algorithms, evolution strategies, simulated annealing, neural networks, classifier systems, immune networks, adaptation processes in general, and other natural paradigms and their application to solve real-world problems.

Due to the unexpected success of PPSN 1 in 1990 the organizers were encouraged to plan a follow-up conference, PPSN 2, two years later. Many of the participants from the USA supported this idea although the biennial international conference on genetic algorithms (ICGA) had already been established in the USA in 1985. However, ICGA focused primarily on aspects of genetic algorithms whereas PPSN allowed a broader scope of problem solving paradigms adopted from natural models. Thus, both conferences supplement each other, and it was agreed that ICGA and PPSN should be held alternately, ICGA on odd years in America, PPSN on even years on the other side of the Atlantic.

Accordingly, the PPSN 2 conference was held in 1992 at Brussels, Belgium. Compared to the Dortmund conference, the number of participants increased to about 150. Unfortunately, however, the scope of submitted papers narrowed down. Most of them dealt with evolutionary algorithms and only a few with other biological metaphors. Since 1991, the scope of ICGA also changed a little. Whereas earlier conferences dealt nearly exclusively with "US type" genetic algorithms (characterized, for example, by binary encodings of the decision variables and fixed application rates for the genetic operators), extensions and modifications to include aspects of the "European type" evolution strategies (floating point or integer representation of variables, dynamic adaptation of parameters, etc.), were adopted. Evolutionary programming, a contemporary third way of simulating organic evolution with its own annual conference series at San Diego since 1992, has also been integrated now within the broader stream of evolutionary computation. A witness of that fact was the recent first world congress on computational intelligence (WCCI) at Orlando, Florida, in June/July 1994, where proponents of all three kinds of evolutionary algorithms met.

To ensure continuity in planning further PPSN conference series and to coordinate them with conferences like ICGA, a PPSN steering committee has been set up. Currently, it consists of the following members:

Y. Davidor (Israel)   B. Manderick (The Netherlands)
K. De Jong (USA)   H. Mühlenbein (Germany)
H. Kitano (Japan)   H.-P. Schwefel (Germany)
R. Männer (Germany)

One of the first decisions the PPSN steering committee took was to empha-size the diverse evolutionary aspects covered by the PPSN conference series and to change the conference name into one more indicative of its scope, "interna-tional conference on evolutionary computation" with the running subtitle "the third international conference on parallel problem solving from nature" and the acronym "ICEC/PPSN 3".

Invited and contributed talks and posters

Some years ago, theoreticians and practitioners working in the field of evolution-ary computation and other biologically motivated paradigms could be found in conferences on physics, biology, computer science, economics, and many others. The PPSN conference series was initiated because there was a need to bring these people together to facilitate interdisciplinary cross-fertilization of ideas. At the first PPSN conference in 1990, this could be achieved in the usual style of a small conference. However, even the relatively small number of oral presentations and long poster sessions did not seem to leave enough time for discussions.

For PPSN 2 in 1992, therefore, the style of the conference was changed radi-cally. It was a nearly poster-only conference, designating only the invited talks as plenary sessions. The success of this programme structure led the PPSN steering committee to repeat the same conference structure for this ICEC/PPSN 3 event.

The conference scope

To increase the theoretical and empirical understanding of algorithms based on natural paradigms, ICEC/PPSN 3 brings together an international community from academia, industry, business, and government. Examples of such algorithms are genetic algorithms (GA), evolutionary programming (EP), and evolution strategies (ES) that are inspired by the organic processes of mutation, recom-bination, and natural selection in biology; classifier systems (CS), evolving rule based systems; cellular automata (CA), evolving according to local "laws" like physical entities; artificial neural networks (NN); and combinations of the above.

Although PPSN focuses on *problem solving* using such algorithms, ample room is given to contributions advancing the understanding of basic concepts, their extensions and combination. Additional emphasis is put on practical aspects: How can these computing-intensive algorithms be implemented on parallel computers? How can they be applied to real-world problems? What kind of tools ease their application?

Review of submitted papers

To identify the high-quality contributions, all submissions were reviewed anonymously by three independent reviewers who are recognized experts in the relevant fields. Papers whose reviewers disagreed on some important aspect of the submission were reviewed again by the programme and conference chairs to resolve the disagreements. Finally, 61 out of 115 papers, which resulted from this careful filtering process, were selected for inclusion in the conference proceedings and for presentation at the conference. We are confident that this process has ensured that ICEC/PPSN 3 presents original, high-quality contributions to the field of evolutionary computation. Since this is absolutely vital for the success of the PPSN conference series, the help of all reviewers on the Programme Committee listed below is gratefully acknowledged:

Emile H. L. Aarts	Philips Research Labs., Eindhoven	The Netherlands
Jarmo T. Alander	University of Vaasa	Finland
Thomas Bäck	Informatik Centrum Dortmund at the University of Dortmund	Germany
Wolfgang Banzhaf	University of Dortmund	Germany
Peter Bock	The George Washington University, Washington D.C.	U.S.A.
Lashon Booker	The MITRE Corporation, McLean, VA	U.S.A.
Paul Bourgine	CEMAGREF, Antony	France
Michael Conrad	Wayne State University, Detroit, MI	U.S.A.
Yuval Davidor	Schema - Evolutionary Algorithms Ltd., Herzelia	Israel
Kenneth A. De Jong	George Mason University, Fairfax, VA	U.S.A.
Werner Ebeling	Humboldt University at Berlin	Germany
Terence C. Fogarty	University of the West of England, Bristol	U.K.
David Fogel	Natural Selection, Inc., La Jolla, CA	U.S.A.

It should be noticed that many of the reviewers received considerable help from colleagues. Unfortunately, there is not enough space to mention all of them here. We are very grateful for their important contribution to the quality of the conference and the proceedings. All authors were provided with the reviewers' comments and had the chance to improve their contributions accordingly.

Acknowledgements

Although the work of the reviewers is essential, many more people are required for organizing a successful conference and for editing the proceedings. We want to stress that all PPSN conferences have been and will be non-profit events. Neither the organizers, nor the reviewers, neither the editors of the proceedings, nor the many helpful persons involved in the local organization get any benefits from their work — except the satisfaction of being involved in such an interesting and important activity.

It is therefore a great pleasure for us to thank all those who have worked so hard to make ICEC/PPSN 3 a success and to prepare the proceedings in time. On behalf of all others we want to thank particularly Thomas Bäck and Frank Kursawe from the University of Dortmund, Germany.

Jerusalem,
Mannheim,
Dortmund,
July 1994

Yuval Davidor, Conference Chair
Reinhard Männer, Programme Co-Chair
Hans–Paul Schwefel, Programme Co-Chair

Contents

Modifications and Extensions to Evolutionary Algorithms

Classifier Systems

Hybrid Methods

Evolutionary Algorithms for Neural Networks

Parallel Implementations of Evolutionary Algorithms

Applications

Software Tools for Evolutionary Computation

Subject Index   639

Introduction

Only a few years ago, terms like *genetic algorithms, evolution strategies, classifier systems, genetic programming*, etc. did not mean anything to most scientists let alone practitioners in industry, business, and the general public. However, these research fields, which are united now under the name *evolutionary computation*, have existed for a long time. Three of its most important roots are generally recognized. One is the work of John Holland[1] in the USA, the second the work of Ingo Rechenberg[2] in Germany, and the third is the work of Lawrence Fogel[3], again in the USA. Fogel, Rechenberg, Holland, and some others started already 30 years ago to investigate systems that evolve artificially. Some remarkable theoretical and practical results were achieved already at that time, but they had to wait for their broad acknowledgement.

Today, the scene has changed considerably. Even some newspapers have reported on artificially evolving systems and their application to solve practical problems. There are two main reasons for this change: the apparent simplicity of evolutionary algorithms coupled with the availability of powerful computers, which allow to handle more realistic and thus more complex models now. The basic idea of such algorithms is easily described: *For any optimization problem, generate a number of solutions. Repeatedly, let the worst die out and modify the others at random, until a sufficiently good solution has been found.* Since anybody can understand such algorithms immediately, David Goldberg called them once CP–easy[4]. However, large evolving populations of solutions combined with a long evolution time require high computing power. Nowadays, computers providing that power are available nearly everywhere, in every lab, at home, at school, etc. It is thus very easy to write a short program and have first success.

Yet, artificial evolution is far from being well understood. Until now, there is no comprehensive theory for any type of evolutionary algorithm — only the most simple ones have been analyzed thoroughly, and even that for very simple problem situations only. For most practical applications, the algorithms' parameters have to be crafted manually. In contrast to this lack of understanding, evolutionary algorithms and algorithms based on other natural paradigms have been practically applied with remarkable success. One reason for that is the very high robustness of such algorithms and the fact that they can be applied in many situations, also where classical algorithms fail.

Within the last years, we see an explosion of interest in evolutionary computation and the application of other natural metaphors like neural networks, simulated annealing, and so forth. The at first relatively small communities of

---

[1] Holland, J.H.: Adaptation in Natural and Artificial Systems. University of Michigan Press, Ann Arbor, Michigan, 1975

[2] Rechenberg, I.: Evolutionsstrategie — Optimierung technischer Systeme nach Prinzipien der biologischen Evolution. Frommann–Holzboog, Stuttgart, Germany, 1973

[3] Fogel, L.J. et al.: Artificial Intelligence through Simulated Evolution. Wiley, New York, 1966

[4] Cocktail Party easy — can be explained during small–talk.

researchers in the USA and Europe who made progress in these fields during the last decades have grown exponentially, and new ones have been formed, such as the one in Japan. After many very difficult years, governments and industry have recognized the potential behind such algorithms, and funding sources for research have become available. Nonetheless, in all aspects there are so many open questions that every progress made could increase the efficiency and effectivity of such algorithms dramatically and thus open up new fields of application.

ICEC/PPSN 3 tries to advance the state-of-the-art by presenting high–quality original research papers in a number of different topics. Five papers were selected that discuss general aspects of Darwinian and Lamarckian evolution, the relations between genotype and phenotype, the control of population diversity, and co-evolution. Since theory can best improve the applicability of new algorithms, considerable space was allocated to it. Eleven papers were selected that present new theoretical results. They consider either a specific type of algorithm and try to cover as many applications as possible, or focus on a specific aspect of a general class of algorithms. Examples are the convergence rate of evolutionary algorithms and the optimal population size. Despite of the lack of a complete theoretical understanding, researchers have altered the basic algorithms, either by incorporating application specific knowledge or introducing new ideas, and reported improved performance. PPSN 3 presents nine papers of this type. Classifier systems and genetic programming have received less attention than genetic algorithms and evolution strategies, although very promising results have been reported recently. Three papers concentrate on learning in these rule-based systems, one of them in combination with fuzzy logic. Four papers focus on various theoretical and practical aspects of genetic programming. Unfortunately, only a few of the submitted papers deal with other natural metaphors. Four have been selected that have been subsumed under the term "emergent computation", even if this is a little arbitrary. They range from aspects of artificial life to cellular automata. Two papers compare different algorithms or different parameter settings with each other. They are of particular interest to practitioners that want to get a feeling for the behaviour of such algorithms under various conditions. A further topic relates to the combination of different paradigms. Two of the three papers accepted deal with parallel simulated annealing guided by the application of genetic operators. Here and in the following section, at least a few other natural metaphors are presented. Six papers deal with various aspects of the combination of neural networks with evolutionary algorithms.

Whereas the former sections are more on the theoretical side, the following sections relate directly to practical applications. One section considers the parallel implementation of evolutionary algorithms. The four papers presented concentrate on the efficiency gain obtained by implementing genetic algorithms on parallel processors of various type or on a cluster of distributed processors. In one of them a hardware implementation of an evolutionary algorithm is described that increases the processing speed dramatically. The last large section is devoted to specific applications. Up to now, evolutionary computation has been applied to a great variety of optimization problems, and this variety is mirrored in the selected eight papers. The applications range from optimization of VLSI chips over time tables to the bi-partitioning problem. Finally, one paper presents a software tool that facilitates the application of evolutionary algorithms.

Here is a short list of the topics covered:

- Basic concepts of evolutionary computation
- Theoretical aspects of evolutionary computation
- Modifications and extensions to evolutionary algorithms
- Classifier systems
- Genetic programming
- Emergent computation
- Comparison of different evolutionary algorithms
- Hybrid methods
- Evolutionary algorithms for neural networks
- Parallel implementations of evolutionary algorithms
- Applications
- Software tools for evolutionary computation

We are sure that these papers presented at ICEC/PPSN 3 are of interest to many of the conference participants, the researchers, and the users of evolutionary computation.

Jerusalem,   Yuval Davidor, Conference Chair
Mannheim,   Reinhard Männer, Programme Co-Chair
Dortmund,   Hans–Paul Schwefel, Programme Co-Chair
July 1994

Basic Concepts of
Evolutionary Computation

Lamarckian Evolution, The Baldwin Effect and Function Optimization

Darrell Whitley, V. Scott Gordon and Keith Mathias

Computer Science Department, Colorado State University, Fort Collins, CO 80523
whitley@cs.colostate.edu

Abstract. We compare two forms of hybrid genetic search. The first uses Lamarckian evolution, while the second uses a related method where local search is employed to change the fitness of strings, but the acquired improvements do not change the genetic encoding of the individual. The latter search method exploits the Baldwin effect. By modeling a simple genetic algorithm we show that functions exist where simple genetic algorithms without learning as well as Lamarckian evolution converge to the same local optimum, while genetic search utilizing the Baldwin effect converges to the global optimum. We also show that a simple genetic algorithm exploiting the Baldwin effect can sometimes outperform forms of Lamarckian evolution that employ the same local search strategy.

1 Introduction

A "hybrid genetic algorithm" combines local search with a more traditional genetic algorithm. The most common form of hybrid genetic algorithm uses local search to improve the initial population as well as the strings produced by genetic recombination. The resulting improvements are then coded onto the strings processed by the genetic algorithm. This is equivalent to a form of Lamarckian evolution.

Local search in this context can be thought of as being analogous to a kind of learning that occurs during the lifetime of an individual string. But there is another way in which learning (i.e., local search) and evolution can interact. Instead of coding the improvements back onto the string, the fitness value of the improvement can be transferred to the individual. This has the effect of changing the fitness landscape, but the resulting form of evolution is still "Darwinian" in nature. Various phenomena associated with this form of combining learning and evolution are collectively known as the *Baldwin effect* [2] [7] [1].

In this paper we compare a form of Lamarckian evolution and a simple genetic algorithm that exploits the Baldwin effect. We also compare these approaches to a simple genetic algorithm without learning. Our empirical and analytical tests look specifically at function optimization problems. We use a binary encoding for these problems; thus, local search in this context involves changing each of the L bits in a string encoding. Local search is limited to one step in the search space. When transferring fitness from one string to another under the Baldwinian strategy, we would like each string to have a unique evaluation. We therefore use steepest ascent as our local search instead of next ascent. [1]

Our analytical and empirical results indicate that Lamarckian strategies are often an extremely fast form of search. However, functions exist where both the simple genetic algorithm without learning and the Lamarckian strategy used in this paper converge to local optima while the simple genetic algorithm exploiting the Baldwin effect converges to a global optimum. We study this phenomenon using exact models of a simple genetic algorithm developed by Whitley [10] which are a special case of the Vose and Liepins models [8]. We also show that equivalence classes exist for functions, such that the functions in an equivalence class are processed in an identical fashion under specific forms of Lamarckian and Baldwinian search strategies.

1.1 Lamarckian Evolution versus the Baldwin Effect

Many of the "hybrid genetic algorithms" that combine local search and genetic search use what is in effect a form of Lamarckian evolution. Another way that learning and evolution can interact is to allow learning (i.e., local optimization) to change the fitness of an individual without altering the individual's genetic code. Local search, or learning, will have the effect of changing the fitness landscape. This is part of what is known as the *Baldwin effect* [7] [1]. Gruau and Whitley [5] have found that when evolving Boolean neural networks using grammar trees, genetic search that used learning to change the fitness function was just as effective as Lamarckian strategies: both Lamarckian strategies and search exploiting the Baldwin effect were more efficient and effective than genetic search alone.

This paper explores the combination of local and genetic search in the domain of function optimization for problems that have been encoded as binary strings. Our local search algorithm uses one iteration of steepest ascent. Given a current solution, flip each of the L bits; if the current solution is not a local optimum, then the *improved solution* is the best of the L possible neighbor states. If the improved solution is coded back onto the chromosome, we will refer to this as a Lamarckian search strategy. In this case, the next state replaces the current state. If the improved solution is merely used to change the fitness of the current state, then the search strategy will be referred to as Baldwinian.

Figure 1, taken from Gruau and Whitley [5], illustrates how local search can alter the fitness landscape. Taking N steps deepens the basin of attraction, thus

---

[1] In next ascent, the first improvement found is taken; if the neighbors of a string are checked in random order, next ascent does not yield a unique solution. For steepest ascent, all L bit changes are tested and the best improvement is taken.

8

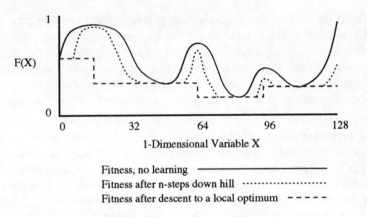

Figure 1: *The effect of local search on the fitness landscape of a one dimensional function. Improvements move downhill on the fitness landscape.*

making the function flatter around the local optimum. If local search is done to convergence, then the fitness function becomes flat in each basin of attraction. Note that each basin of attraction, however, has a potentially different evaluation corresponding to the evaluation of the local optimum. Changing the fitness landscape in this way creates the potential for impacting genetic search by increasing the likelihood of allocating more samples in certain basins of attraction.

Hinton and Nolan [7] were the first researchers to explore the *Baldwin effect* using genetic algorithms. They illustrate the Baldwin effect using a genetic algorithm and a simple random learning process that develops a simple neural network. The genetic encoding specifies a neural network topology by indicating which of 20 potential connections should be used to connect a given set of artificial neurons. The objective function (without learning) is such that the "correct" network results in increased fitness, and all other networks have the same, inferior fitness. This creates a spike at the "correct" solution in an otherwise flat fitness landscape. The genetic encoding uses a 3 character alphabet (0, 1, ?) which specifies the existence of a connection (i.e., 1), the absence of a connection (i.e., 0) or the connection can be unspecified (i.e., ?). If the connection is unspecified it can be set randomly or set via learning. Learning in this case is merely a random search of possible assignments to unspecified connections denoted by the ? symbol.

Hinton and Nolan found that the "?" symbol never fully disappeared from their genetic code when the search got close enough to the global optimum that it could be reached via learning. This appears to be a by-product of genetic drift coupled with premature convergence. Harvey [6] provides a good explanation for the anomalous results of Hinton and Nolan with respect to the "puzzle of the persistent questions marks." Belew [3] also offers a review and a critique of Hinton and Nolan.

2 Analytical Results

To better understand Lamarckian and Baldwinian search strategies an exact model of the simple genetic algorithm was used to study both approaches for solving small test problems. The model was used to track the expected representation of strings in an infinitely large population.

To model the effect of the Baldwinian strategy, only the fitness function needs to be changed. For each string i we will refer to evaluation-A as the value returned by the evaluation function used by the simple genetic algorithm without learning. When a Baldwinian search strategy is used, a second evaluation function is constructed. For each string i we define the evaluation-B for string i as the maximum evaluation-A value among the set of strings composed of string i and it's L neighbors in Hamming space. Running a simple genetic algorithm on function evaluation-B produces results identical to running a simple genetic algorithm on function evaluation-A and using one iteration of steepest ascent to change the evaluation of the current string.

An example function illustrates the effect of modeling the Baldwinian search strategy. The following 4 bit function was created by sorting the binary strings of length four according to their integer value. The string 0000 is given the value 28; as the integer value of the strings increases by 1 the value assigned to the string is decremented by 2. String 1110 has value 0. String 1111 is then assigned value 30. The following function will be denoted Function 1:

e(0000) = 28	e(0100) = 20	e(1000) = 12	e(1100) = 4
e(0001) = 26	e(0101) = 18	e(1001) = 10	e(1101) = 2
e(0010) = 24	e(0110) = 16	e(1010) = 8	e(1110) = 0
e(0011) = 22	e(0111) = 14	e(1011) = 6	e(1111) = 30

The function is posed as a maximization problem. This function is not fully deceptive [4] [9] since $\mu(* * *1) > \mu(* * *0)$ and $\mu(* * 11) > \mu(* * 00)$, where $\mu(\xi)$ is the average evaluation of all strings in hyperplane ξ. However, it does have a significant amount of deception. The following function $eb(i)$ represents evaluation-B constructed from Function 1.

eb(0000) = e(0000) = 28	eb(1000) = e(0000) = 28
eb(0001) = e(0000) = 28	eb(1001) = e(0001) = 26
eb(0010) = e(0000) = 28	eb(1010) = e(0010) = 24
eb(0011) = e(0001) = 26	eb(1011) = e(1111) = 30
eb(0100) = e(0000) = 28	eb(1100) = e(0100) = 20
eb(0101) = e(0001) = 26	eb(1101) = e(1111) = 30
eb(0110) = e(0010) = 24	eb(1110) = e(1111) = 30
eb(0111) = e(1111) = 30	eb(1111) = e(1111) = 30

Note that the basins of attraction are made deeper and flatter around each local minimum.

Under the Lamarckian strategy used here, the string with the best value in the local neighborhood of string i would always replace string i unless i has the best value, in which case string i is a local optimum. In this implementation of the Lamarckian search strategy the string distributions are altered at the beginning of each generation to model the effects of one iteration of steepest ascent. A string residing at a local optimum, for example, increases its own distribution by the sum of the distributions of all of its immediate L neighbors. However, these neighbor points do not necessarily end up with zero representation. Neighbors at a Hamming distance of two from the local optimum will also move downhill one step (assuming they are in the same basin of attraction), thus creating new representations for some strings that are one step closer to the local optimum.

Let $P(i,t)$ be the representation of string i in the population at time t. At the beginning of each generation the proportional representation of strings are changed by doing one iteration of steepest ascent. In the following equations, $P'(i,t)$ represents the distribution of strings after steepest ascent. Note that the redistribution of string representations will usually be different for functions that are different. For function 1, those changes are

```
P'(0000,t) = P(0000,t) + P(0001,t) + P(0010,t) + P(0100,t) + P(1000,t)
P'(0001,t) = P(0011,t) + P(0101,t) + P(1001,t)
P'(0010,t) = P(0110,t) + P(1010,t)
P'(0100,t) = P(1100,t)
P'(1111,t) = P(1111,t) + P(1110,t) + P(1101,t) + P(1011,t) + P(0111,t)
P'(0011,t) = 0
P'(0101,t) = 0
P'(0110,t) = 0
P'(0111,t) = 0
P'(1000,t) = 0
P'(1001,t) = 0
P'(1010,t) = 0
P'(1011,t) = 0
P'(1100,t) = 0
P'(1101,t) = 0
P'(1110,t) = 0.
```

Strings which lie on a saddle between basins of attraction have no representation after one iteration of steepest ascent. The number of points falling on the saddle between local optima is quite high in a small 4 bit function. What about larger functions? Obviously, a 100 bit function with two local optima will have a smaller percentage of saddle points as compared to the size of the search space; it follows that fewer strings will have zero representation in an infinite population genetic algorithm. However, two issues are worth considering.

1. As the number of local optima increase, generally the number of saddle points will also increase. When the maximal number of local optima exists in a binary coded space, then exactly half the points in the space are local optima and half are saddle points between the local optima. More

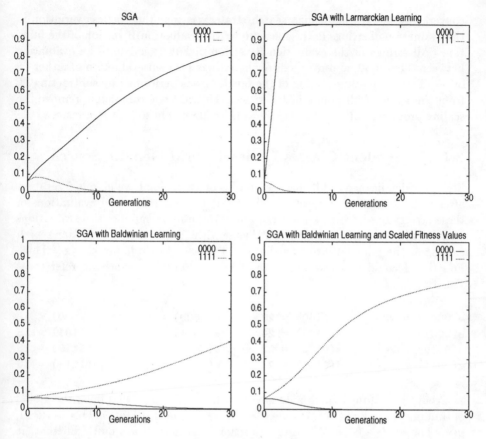

Figure 2: SGA behavior with and without Lamarckian and Baldwinian Learning. The string 0000 is a local optimum and 1111 the global optimum.

generally, when the basins of attraction have a radius greater than 1, the number of saddle points for each local optima will grow as a function of the Hamming distance from the local optima to the nearest saddle point.

2. In any finite population genetic algorithm, many points that have representation in the population before local search is applied may have no representation after local search is applied.

Figure 2 illustrates the results obtained using the exact model of a simple genetic algorithm to process Function 1. Figure 2 also includes the results of executing the evaluation-B version of Function 1 which models the behavior of the Baldwinian search strategy, as well as the results of the Lamarckian search strategy. The crossover rate was 0.6 and the mutation rate was 0 for all experiments. Both the simple genetic algorithm without learning and the Lamarckian search strategy converge to a local optimum. The Baldwinian search strategy converges to the global optimum, but does so slowly. One reason for the slow convergence of the Baldwinian search strategy is that there is less variation in the evaluation of strings in the space under the evaluation-B version of the function. All strings in the evaluation-B version of Function 1 have an evaluation between 20 and 30, and over half of the strings have an evaluation of either 28 or 30. Thus a one-time scaling of the function was performed by subtracting 20 from the value of all points in the space. This did not completely remove the scaling problem, but it did cause the genetic algorithm to converge faster.

2.1 Equivalent Classes Under Hybrid Genetic Search

Strings which lie on a saddle between basins of attraction have no representation after one iteration of steepest ascent; it follows that the actual evaluations of these strings are in some sense irrelevant. To be more specific, the evaluations of strings that are saddle points can change without effecting Lamarckian search as long as the gradient directions induced by local search do not change. Thus, Function 1 could be converted to the following function, which we refer to as Function 2:

```
e(0000) = 28      e(0100) = 20      e(1000) = 18      e(1100) = 18
e(0001) = 26      e(0101) = 24      e(1001) = 24      e(1101) = 18
e(0010) = 24      e(0110) = 22      e(1010) = 22      e(1110) = 18
e(0011) = 24      e(0111) = 22      e(1011) = 22      e(1111) = 30
```

About half of the hyperplanes now have fitness averages that favor the global optimum 1111 (e.g., $\mu(**1*) > \mu(**0*)$, $\mu(***1) > \mu(***0)$, $\mu(*1*1) > \mu(*0*0)$, $\mu(**11) > \mu(**00)$). While this function is in many ways quite different, it behaves identically to Function 1 under the Lamarckian search strategy defined here. This is because the set of equations describing the redistribution of strings under Lamarckian search remains exactly the same. Also note that any string in Function 1 which has representation after one iteration of steepest ascent does not change its evaluation in Function 2. Only saddle points change their evaluation. Thus, the same moves occur in both functions when one iteration of steepest ascent is applied. This implies that Function 1 and Function 2 are processed in an identical fashion under the Baldwinian search strategy as well, since all saddles points acquire their evaluation from other points in the space. Since the actual values of these saddle points are irrelevant, it is clear that there are sets of functions that are equivalent under the Lamarckian and Baldwinian search strategies; however, the different functions within these sets are still unique to the simple genetic algorithm without learning.

When a simple genetic algorithm without learning is executed on Function 2, the search again converges to the same local minimum. The results of using either the Lamarckian or Baldwinian strategy are identical to the results obtained for Function 1.

3   Empirical Function Optimization Tests

We tested the effects of adding Baldwinian and Lamarckian search strategies to a simple genetic algorithm on the following numerical optimization problems:

$$Rastrigin:\ f(x_i|_{i=1,20}) = 200 + \sum_{i=1}^{20} x_i^2 - 10cos(2\pi x_i), \qquad x_i \in [-5.12, 5.11]$$

$$Schwefel:\ f(x_i|_{i=1,20}) = V + \sum_{i=1}^{20} -x_i sin(\sqrt{|x_i|}), \qquad x_i \in [-512, 511]$$

$$Griewank:\ f(x_i|_{i=1,20}) = \sum_{i=1}^{20} \frac{x_i^2}{4000} - \prod_{i=1}^{20} cos(\frac{x_i}{\sqrt{i}}) + 1, \qquad x_i \in [-512, 511]$$

For Schwefel's function V is the negative of the global minimum, which is added to the function so as to move the global minimum to zero. The exact value of V depends on system precision; for our experiments $V = 8379.65723$.

In these experiments, we used an elitist form of the standard simple genetic algorithm ($ESGA$). The probability of crossover was set to 0.7 and the mutation rate was 0.003. Tournament selection (with tournaments of size 2) and Gray coding were used in every case. The string length was 200 for all three problems. Local optimization is employed in the form of *steepest ascent*.

Table 1 shows performance data for each algorithm on each of the functions for a variety of population sizes. In particular, we consider population sizes of 50 and 100 for all three functions, as well as a population size of 400 for Griewank (since it is the hardest of the three functions for the genetic algorithm to solve). Table 1 shows how many times the genetic algorithm finds the global solution (out of 30 runs) within 1000 generations. (Note that these are *minimization* problems; the problems in section 2 were *maximization* problems.)

	Rastrigin		Schwefel		Griewank		
popsize =	50	100	50	100	50	100	400
ESGA	0	0	0	0	2	1	1
ESGA+Baldwin	30	30	19	30	6	8	15
ESGA+Lamarckian	30	30	9	25	14	16	30

Table 1: Performance of *ESGA* on three numeric functions. The number of times that the GA finds the optimal solution, out of 30 runs, is shown.

If one wishes to obtain results quickly, the Lamarckian strategy is consistently the best. However, if one is interested in the long term effects of these search strategies, then Lamarckian search appears to work better on the Rastrigin and Griewank functions, while Baldwinian learning works better on the Schwefel function. Figure 3 shows convergence graphs for the Rastrigin and Schwefel

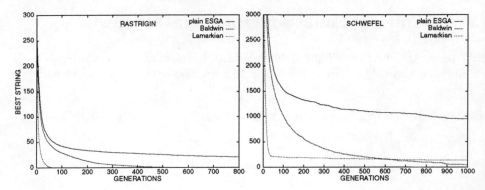

Figure 3: Baldwin vs. Lamarckian learning in two numeric optimization functions.

functions; the value of the best string in the population (averaged over 30 runs) is plotted for each genetic algorithm, using a population size of 50. Similar results are observed for larger population sizes. In all cases Lamarckian search results in faster improvement. However, on the Schwefel function the average best solution is poorer for Lamarckian search than Baldwinian learning after an extended period of time.

4   Conclusions

The results presented here are largely exploratory in nature. However, the results clearly indicate that a Baldwinian search strategy as defined in this paper can sometimes be more effective than a Lamarckian strategy using the same form of local search. It should be noted that by more effective, we mean that the Baldwinian search strategy will sometimes converge to a global optimum when the Lamarckian strategy converges to a local optimum. However, in all of the cases presented here, the Baldwinian search strategy is much slower than the Lamarckian search.

It is also clear that there exist equivalence classes of functions for Lamarckian and Baldwinian search strategies. An equivalence class in this case is defined such that all functions in the equivalence class are processed in an identical fashion under either a Lamarckian or a Baldwinian search strategy.

One notable difference between the results reported here and the results obtained by Gruau and Whitley [5] is that the Baldwinian search strategy did not prove to be as efficient as the Lamarckian search strategy on all of the function optimization problems studied in this paper. That may be due in part to the fact that these test problems are too easy. For the Rastrigin and Schwefel functions, the evaluation subfunction associated with each parameter is nonlinear, but the subfunctions applied to each parameter are simply summed together. Thus there are no non-linear interactions between the individual parameters. We have found that all three of these problems are relatively easy to solve using stochastic hill-climbing methods and thus it is not surprising that Lamarckian search is so effective on these problems. Ideally, the effectiveness of a Baldwinian search strategy should be evaluated in more complex domains. It should also be noted that Gruau and Whitley used a type of genetic algorithm based on the steady state genetic algorithm model rather than a simple genetic algorithm; this too could impact their results.

5   Acknowledgement

The original idea for using local search to change the fitness landscape was communicate to us by Rik Belew. This work was supported in part by NSF grant IRI-9312748.

References

[1] D.H. Ackley and M. Littman, (1991) Interactions between learning and evolution. In, *Proc. of the 2nd Conf. on Artificial Life*, C.G. Langton, ed., Addison-Wesley, 1991.

[2] J.M.Baldwin, (1896) A new factor in evolution. *American Naturalist*, 30:441-451, 1896.

[3] R.K. Belew, (1989) When both individuals and populations search: Adding simple learning to the Genetic Algorithm. In *3th Intern. Conf. on Genetic Algorithms*, D. Schaffer, ed., Morgan Kaufmann.

[4] D. Goldberg, (1989) Genetic algorithms and walsh functions: Part II, deception and its analysis. *Complex Systems 3*:153-171.

[5] F. Gruau and D. Whitley, (1993) Adding learning to the cellular development of neural networks: evolution and the Baldwin effect. *Evolutionary Computation* 1(3):213-233.

[6] I. Harvey, (1993) The puzzle of the persistent question marks: a case study of genetic drift. In *5th Intern. Conf. on Genetic Algorithms*, S. Forrest, ed., Morgan Kaufmann.

[7] G.E. Hinton and S.J. Nolan, (1987) How learning can guide evolution. *Complex Systems*, 1:495-502.

[8] M. Vose and G. Liepins, (1991) Punctuated equilibria in genetic search. *Complex Systems* 5:31-44.

[9] D. Whitley, (1991) Fundamental principles of deception. *Foundations of Genetic Algorithms*. G. Rawlins, ed. Morgan Kaufmann.

[10] D. Whitley, R. Das, C. Crabb, (1992) Tracking primary hyperplane competitors during genetic search. *Anals of Mathematics and Artificial Intelligence*, 6:367-388.

Control of Parallel Population Dynamics by Social-Like Behavior of GA-Individuals[*]

Dirk C. Mattfeld[1], Herbert Kopfer[2] and Christian Bierwirth[2]

[1] LRW Computing Center, 28334 Bremen, Germany
[2] Department of Economics, University of Bremen

Abstract. A frequently observed difficulty in the application of genetic algorithms to the domain of optimization arises from premature convergence. In order to preserve genotype diversity we develop a new model of auto-adaptive behavior for individuals. In this model a population member is an active individual that assumes social-like behavior patterns. Different individuals living in the same population can assume different patterns. By moving in a hierarchy of "social states" individuals change their behavior. Changes of social state are controlled by arguments of plausibility. These arguments are implemented as a rule set for a massively-parallel genetic algorithm. Computational experiments on 12 large-scale job shop benchmark problems show that the results of the new approach dominate the ordinary genetic algorithm significantly.

1 Introduction

A major topic of recent research in genetic algorithms (GA) focuses on the ability to control population dynamics. The difficulty in reaching this goal is caused by the complex mechanisms of selection. Optimal balancing of selection pressure means to adjust it as sharply as possible without destroying genotype diversity. In this paper we consider a new approach to control convergence by means of social-like behavior patterns (SBP). The phenomena of social hierarchies and individual behavior can be found in many natural populations. Thus it seems worthwhile to explore the power of social mechanisms within the GA paradigm.

Section 2 gives a brief survey on related approaches. Section 3 introduces our metaphor of social-like behavior. We show how to translate SBP into a local recombination strategy and how to implement it in massively-parallel GA's. Section 4 presents the test platform which is a standard model of job shop scheduling. The job-shop specific components of local recombination are briefly described. Finally we report our computational results.

2 Controlled Convergence

The most frequently observed difficulty in the application of standard GA's to large-scale optimization problems results from premature convergence. While GA heuristics perform well for small problems they often suffer from strong sub-

[*] Supported by the Deutsche Forschungsgemeinschaft (Project Parnet)

optimality in larger ones. Population dynamics of standard GA's is known to be responsible for premature convergence. In order to improve the average fitness of a population the best individuals are given the highest selection rates for reproduction. Hence a dynamic is enforced that decreases genotype diversity continuously. Thus the reproduction scheme's ability to build new solutions becomes smaller and smaller and eventually the GA converges.

Several approaches of maintaining a population's diversity were proposed. Some direct approaches focus on genetic operators. Obviously, a more disruptive crossover delays the reduction of genotype diversity. The success of these strategies is considered to be highly problem specific. More general strategies are going by the term of controlled convergence.

2.1 Mating Strategies

Whenever proportional mate selection leads to premature convergence more sophisticated mating strategies can be used to slow down convergence. Due to this analogy mates practice incest if their genotypes are too similar. Some attempts were made to avoid such constellations. Goldberg introduced a mechanism into mate selection called sharing functions. In this approach the fitness of individuals is used as an indicator for genotypical similarity. More direct approaches of incest prevention are based on the measure of similarity between genotypes by means of the hamming distance. A brief survey of such techniques can be found in a paper of Davidor [4]. Another approach proposed by Eshelman and Schaffer controls mate selection by a threshold [7]. The threshold forbids mating if it dominates the hamming distance of mating candidates. Whenever a population cannot progress, the threshold value is decremented in the next generation.

2.2 Structured Populations

Further approaches to control convergence result from structuring the entire population. This is either reached by splitting up population into islands (migration model) or by defining overlapping neighborhoods which cover it entirely (diffusion model). Both models restrict immediate data flow between individuals to local areas of the population. Thereby the nature-like feature of ecological niches is introduced into population dynamics. This feature is expected to preserve genotype diversity within useful bounds.

Since 1988, when Mühlenbein and Gorges-Schleuter developed the diffusion model [11] this kind of population structure received increasing attention. The probably most exciting feature of neighborhood structures is the explicit introduction of parallelism. It enables individuals to act without centralized control. Mate-selection and offspring-replacement are done locally. For this reason the diffusion model fits the restrictions of massively-parallel environments. A combined approach of traditional GA's and diffusion models is shown by the ECO-framework of Davidor [4]. A brief outline of other local mating strategies proposed is published in a recent paper of Gorges-Schleuter [8].

3 Incorporating Patterns of Social Behavior

In structured populations derived from diffusion models mating is restricted to a small number of nearby individuals. Hence global premature convergence is alleviated at the expense of incest in the neighborhood.

While the environment changes constantly at a slow pace for the individuals, evolution from generation to generation works well. If locality is introduced, the evolutionary process is too fast to solve some of the problems faced by individuals of the population. Our approach extends the global GA adaptation towards the adaptation of a single individual to its neighborhood. Each individual must respond to its own specific environmental conditions. Thus individuals are able to change behavior usefully as a function of immediate changes of the environment.

The psychologist school of Behaviorism became important in the early days of the 20th century. Staats gives a comprehensive survey in [12]. He emphasizes that complex functional behavior of an individual is learned and that environmental events can affect the individuals behavior. Thorndike laid the foundations in 1898 with his "law of effect": One effect of successful behavior is to increase the probability that it will be used again in similar circumstances. Rewards granted in case of success lead to patterns of behavior, called habits. In 1947 Doob extended the formal learning theory to the consideration of attitudes. He suggested that attitudes are anticipatory responses which can mediate behavior. An attitude can be seen as a disposition to react favorably or unfavorably to a class of environmental stimuli. Staats notes that in social interactions attitudes are formed by social rewards which stimulate reinforcement on a certain behavior.

3.1 The Metaphor

We borrowed the basic ideas of our metaphor from the Behaviorists. As shown in figure 1 we classify individual behavior by three general cases. The initial attitude of individuals is an established one, i.e. they all act cooperatively within their environments. Secondly, the elitist attitude follows a conservative behavior pattern. The last attitude is a more critical one, which tends to be risk-prone. The actual behavior of each pattern is rewarded in terms of social interaction. Again we classify three simple responses which are defined by reinforcements. An individual can be pleased, satisfied or disappointed. The success of the actual behavior carried out may change its attitude and therefore changes its habit in a similar situation within the near future. The individual will react differently and may receive a different reinforcement on the same environmental situation.

In most cases a cooperative individual will be satisfied and therefore does not change its attitude. If pleased by success of its habit, next time it will tend to act conservative trying to keep its previous performance level. With this elitist attitude an individual can only be satisfied or disappointed by the success of its habit. In case of disappointment it will change back to the established attitude. Failing on cooperative behavior brings up a critical attitude of the individual towards its neighborhood environment. It will then tend towards a more risk-prone behavior. The critical attitude is kept so long as a disappointing response

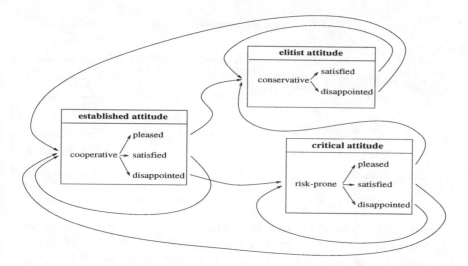

Fig. 1. Scheme of social behavior patterns.

is still received. If the individual is satisfied by the result of its behavior, it may change to the established pattern again. In rare cases a risk-prone individual will receive a pleasing response. Then it changes towards the elitist attitude.

Don't expect figure 1 to be a blueprint of the complete transition structure of the attitude changes. In fact the response on a certain behavior gives only a rough idea of which attitude may be suitable for the next trial. In general, attitudes are changed only after a number of identical reinforcements. Strong reinforcements can lead to immediate attitude changes, while, in general, weak and moderate reinforcements lead to memory adjustments only.

3.2 Translating the Metaphor into the Model

In our population model individuals reside on a torodial square grid. Mating of individuals is restricted to the North, South, West and East neighbors. Selection is carried out locally by the ranking scheme of 40%, 30%, 20% and 10% from the best to the worst-fit neighbor. An individual is replaced in the population if the fitness of its offspring is at most 2.5% worse.

In order to implement social behavior patterns we transform our metaphor into a local recombination strategy. The established attitude corresponds to co-operation with one of the neighbors by crossover. The critical attitude corresponds to a mutation. The conservative behavior tries to save the reached state. The individual performs no active operation (i.e. is sleeping) to avoid replacement by offspring. Figure 2 show these operations in boldface.

First an individual compares its fitness with the neighborhood. If the fitness is superior to all neighbors, the conservative behavior will cause the individual to sleep. If several best individuals exist in one neighborhood none of them will be superior. For this reason incorporating SBP does not introduce an elitist strategy into PGA. An inferior individual determines its attitude. The actual behavior

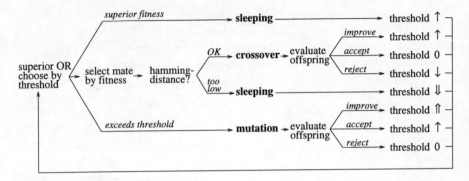

Fig. 2. Control model of local recombination.

is drawn probabilistically from a threshold. Initially the threshold is set to 1, which enforces crossover. Decreasing the threshold increases the probability of mutations. In case of crossover, the hamming distance to the selected mate is evaluated. If mates differ in less than 1% of their genes it is not worthwhile to try a crossover. Again, the individual sleeps, but now because of a different reason. If crossover or mutation is carried out, the offspring is evaluated. Either an offspring dominates its parents (improve), or the acceptance rule decides whether to replace the individual (accept/reject).

Summing up all distinct operations we count 8 responses which are tied to reinforcements of the threshold. We modify the threshold by rules of plausibility. The symbols "⇑⇓↓↑" express the degree of change of the threshold. This rule set attempts to adjust the behavior of each single individual towards the environment of its actual neighborhood. In our implementation the threshold vector $(+0.02, +0.05, 0, -0.02, -0.20, +0.15, +0.05, 0)$ performed well. This setting reacts adaptively on incest occurrence with a strong decrease of the threshold. It favors risky behavior by mutations in further generations. If a mutation succeeds, the threshold is increased which in turn leads to crossover.

4 Job Shop Scheduling

Job shop scheduling is known to be a difficult combinatorial optimization problem. It has become a popular platform for comparison of modern heuristics, e.g. Simulated-Annealing (Laarhoven et. al. [9]) and Tabu-Search (Taillard [13], Dell'Amico et. al. [6]). Furthermore many GA approaches were proposed, e.g. the Giffler-Thompson-GA (Davidor et. al. [4]). Nevertheless, concerning scheduling Simulated-Annealing and especially Tabu-Search perform better than GA's.

The standard problem of job shop scheduling can now be described roughly. A production program containing n jobs is released. Each job is split into m operations that must be processed by m dedicated machines in a predefined technological order. The processing times of operations are known and considered as tasks on machines. While several assumptions concerning the way of processing tasks are made (e.g. no preemption of operations) a schedule has to be found that optimizes a certain measure of performance. In order to compare computational results we consider the measure that is predominantly used in literature: To minimize of the total completion time, i.e the makespan.

PGA uses a genetic representation of the job shop problem described in [3]. In this approach a solution's genotype is defined by a permutation with repetition. The permutation contains $n \times m$ genes from the alphabet $\{J_1, \ldots J_n\}$, where J_k denotes job k. Within a chromosome each gene is repeated exactly m times. E.g., if $n = 2$ and $m = 3$ the chromosome "$J_2 J_1 J_1 J_2 J_2 J_1$" represents a feasible genotype. The i-th occurrence of a gene in the string refers to the i-th operation of the named job. Crossover is done by a generalized order-crossover technique [3]. It preserves the n/m permutation-structure and inherits nearly half of the relative gene-order from both parents to the offspring. Mutation results from a position-based random-change of an arbitrary gene.

An elegant way of modeling the job shop problem via a disjunctive graph is given by Adams et. al. [1]. Each oriented acyclic graph in the disjunctive graph represents a feasible solution. The cost of the longest-path in such a graph gives the makespan of the represented solution. Solving a job shop problem means to find the acyclic oriented graph with the minimal longest-path.

Evaluation of genotypes is done in three steps. First we transform a chromosome into an acyclic graph and calculate its longest path. Second we apply local-search to reduce makespan by exchanging adjacent operations on the longest path as described by Taillard [13]. Finally the reoptimized graph is transformed back into a genotype.

5 Computational Results and Analysis

Two versions of PGA were run on a suite of 12 problems. It includes the famous "10 × 10" and "20 × 5" Muth-Thompson benchmarks and 10 other difficult problems, see Applegate and Cook [2]. In version 1 PGA was running alone whereas version 2 incorporates the SBP model (parameterized as described in 3.2). All routines are written in C++ by massively use of the LEDA-library [10]. The algorithms run on a SUN/10 workstation.

5.1 The Muth-Thompson Benchmarks

PGA and PGA+SBP were run for a total of 200 iterations. The population size was set to 100, termination occurred after 150 generations. Experimental results appear in table 1. The column "Trials" refers to the average number of genotype evaluations of a single run. A single evaluation requires about 1 millisecond

Problem	Opt	PGA+SBP				PGA			
		Average	Best	Var	Trials	Average	Best	Var	Trials
mt (10x10)	930	947	930	8.2	10935	950	934	9.2	15000
mt (20x5)	1165	1188	1165	10.3	11738	1190	1173	10.7	15000

Table 1. Comparison of results (makespan) on the Muth-Thompson problems.

PGA+SBP PGA

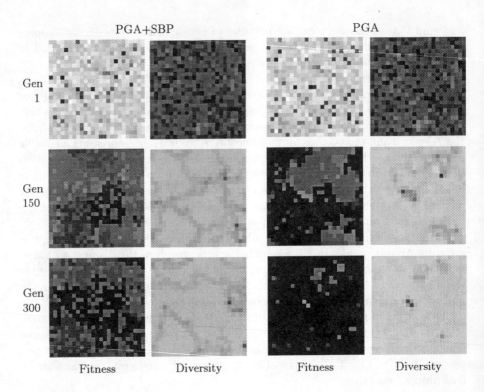

Fig. 3. Convergence process of arbitrary PGA and PGA+SBP runs.

for both problems, thus PGA solves a problem in less than 3 minutes. The computational amount arising from incorporating SPB increases evaluation time by approximately 5%. But the smaller number of genotype evaluations leads to a shorter runtime of 2.3 minutes in average for PGA+SBP.

Figure 3 illustrates the evolution of 625 individuals solving the "mt10x10" problem. Snapshots on the initial, the medium and the final generation show the distribution of fitness and diversity on the torodial grid. We calculate the diversity of individuals by the average hamming distance to 4 neighbors. Greyscale refers to levels of fitness and diversity by using darker colors to indicate larger values (min makespan ≡ max fitness).

It can be seen that in the PGA-run as well as in the PGA+SBP-run average fitness increases at the expense of decreasing diversity. PGA permits highly fit individuals to spread rapidly into areas of lower fitness in their vicinity. After 150 generations the population is dominated by two large fitness plateaus. Moderate genotype diversity exclusively remains in the lower plateau. This niche is completely driven out by the upper plateau after another 150 generations. Uniformity of genotypes inside the dominating plateau prevents further progress. Promising search is limited to the borderlines of plateaus.

To the contrary, PGA+SBP evolves different regions of similar genotypes simultaneously. Borderlines between such regions can be seen clearly on the diversity map after 150 generations. The corresponding fitness map still shows

Problem(Size)	Known	PGA+SBP			PGA		
		Average	Best	Trials	Average	Best	Trials
la21 (15x10)	1048 [6]	1061.5	1053	24956	1064.9	1053	30000
la24 (15x10)	*935 [2]	948.0	938	25335	954.2	938	30000
la25 (15x10)	*977 [2]	989.1	977	25733	990.8	984	30000
la27 (20x10)	1242 [6]	1265.7	1236	24797	1266.7	1256	30000
la29 (20x10)	1180 [13]	1214.4	1184	25013	1222.9	1185	30000
la38 (15x15)	1203 [6]	1222.4	1201	24026	1234.1	1206	30000
la40 (15x15)	*1222 [2]	1243.5	1228	47881	1254.1	1233	57600
abz7 (15x20)	667 [13]	684.6	672	45812	685.4	675	57600
abz8 (15x20)	670 [9]	697.9	683	44664	698.7	687	57600
abz9 (15x20)	691 [9]	712.6	703	45004	715.8	704	57600

*optimal.

Table 2. Results for 10 "tough" job shop problems (see [2], table V).

heterogeneity, i.e. SBP prevents the building of rigid fitness plateaus. Even after 300 generations the situation has hardly changed. Although regions of higher fitness have grown the population is still active. Summing up, both versions of PGA lead to optimal or near-optimal solutions of the Muth-Thompson benchmarks. Although both versions come along different population dynamics, the reached quality of solutions differs insufficiently in order to allow general statements.

5.2 Large-Scale Benchmarks

The application of SBP to moderate job shop problems (up to 100 operations) cannot show all properties of the SBP model. The improvement by genetic search is so fast that the decreasing diversity does not prevent the algorithms from finding good solutions. Therefore we focus on the 10 most difficult problems of the 53 benchmark-suite provided by Applegate and Cook.

Now, PGA and PGA+SBP were run for a total of 30 iterations on each problem. The population size was set to 100 in 6 instances and to 144 in 4 even more difficult cases. Termination was set to 300 and 400 generations respectively. Experimental results appear in table 2. The computation time for a single evaluation scales up dramatically with problem size. E.g. we need a total computation time of 30 minutes to solve a 20 × 10 problem on a single workstation. It can be seen from the table, that PGA+SBP decreases the number of trials by 20%.

For all problems the average makespan generated by PGA+SBP is significantly better than the corresponding PGA result. For the relatively small 15 × 10 problems the best found solutions are similar in both strategies. The best of all found solutions were always generated by PGA+SBP. These solutions are within a 13-unit range of the best known solutions. For the problems "la27" and "la38" new best solutions were found. Notice that "la27" is solved by a makespan of 1236. This value differs only one unit from the theoretical lower bound, thus we assume the problem to be solved to optimality.

Figure 4 compares arbitrary runs of PGA and PGA+SBP solving "la27". The upper pictures show fitness progress for the population's average and for the best

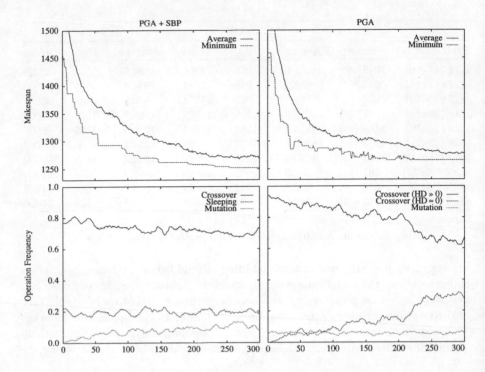

Fig. 4. Population dynamics of PGA and PGA+SBP.

individual. Compared with PGA the PGA+SBP strategy slows convergence in early generations and retains average fitness longer. PGA stagnates in generation 200 whereas PGA+SBP generates improvements continuously.

The lower pictures report the operation frequency over time. PGA uses only two genetic operators which are crossover and mutation. The probability of mutation is fixed at 5%. Exemplary crossover operations are divided into two classes. A crossover falls into the first class if the mates differ by at least 1% of their genes. This class is shown in the upper curve. It can be seen that the condition to match class one decreases approximately linear in time. To the contrary, the increasing lower curve documents the incest rate. This rate refers to mating of individuals inside dominating fitness plateaus (compare figure 3).

The corresponding picture of PGA+SBP indicates a totally different population dynamic. Whereas the crossover frequency decreases slowly with increase of mutations, sleeping frequency is fixed at about 20%. Whenever incest occurs the affected individual sleeps in this generation and increases the probability of mutations in future generations. Actually, sleeping has two distinct reasons: Sleeping caused by incest trials and, secondly, by superior fitness within a neighborhood (see figure 2). During the initial phase of algorithm sleeping is mainly caused by superior fitness, whereas during later phases sleeping is mainly triggered by incest trials. Amazingly, adding both cases leads to a nearly constant frequency of sleeping during the whole process. This seemly stationary sleeping process is conjectured to be the most important condition for SBP to work successfully. Bear in mind that solely local adjustment of genetic operators leads to this overall balance of population dynamics.

6 Summary

This paper presents a first approach to incorporate individual behavior into genetic algorithms. Applying our approach to job shop scheduling enabled us to find some new best solutions for a suite of difficult benchmark problems. We do not claim that incorporating SBP into GA's can be a successful strategy for all kinds of optimization problems, e.g. the emulation of our "risk-prone" behavior pattern by mutations might fail. This is the case if a mutation/hill-climbing strategy performs poorly on the problem. Furthermore our parameterizing of reinforcements of attitudes might seem arbitrary. Of course, its evidence is derived from plausibility but the setting requires at least some computational experience from the domain of the optimization problem. In conclusion, our results encourage the combination of long-term learning by inheritance and short-term learning by behavior in further research of simulated evolution.

References

1. Adams, J., Balas, E., Zawack, D.: The Shifting Bottleneck Procedure for Job Shop Scheduling. Management Science **34** (1988) 391–401
2. Applegate, D., Cook, W.: A Computational Study of the Job-Shop Scheduling Problem. ORSA Journal on Computing **2** (1991) 149–156
3. Bierwirth, C.: A Generalized Permutation Approach to Job Shop Scheduling with Genetic Algorithms. OR Spektrum (to appear)
4. Davidor, Y.: A Naturally Occurring Nice & Species Phenomenon: The Model and First Results. Proc. of ICGA **4**, Morgan Kaufmann (1991) 257–263
5. Davidor, Y., Yamada, T., Nakano, R.: The ECOlogical Framework II, Improving GA Performance at Virtually Zero Cost. Proc. of ICGA **5**, Morgan Kaufmann (1993) 171–176
6. Dell'Amico, M., Trubian, M.: Applying Tabu-Search to the Job Shop Scheduling Problem. Annals of Operations Research **41** (1993) 231–252
7. Eshelman, L.J., Schaffer, J.D.: Preventing Premature Convergence in Genetic Algorithms by Preventing Incest. Proc. of ICGA **4**, Morgan Kaufmann (1991) 115–122
8. Gorges-Schleuter, M.: Comparison of Local Mating Strategies in Massively Parallel Genetic Algorithms. Proc. of PPSN **2**, North-Holland (1992) 553–562
9. van Laarhoven, P.J., Aarts, E.H., Lenstra, J.K.: Job Shop Scheduling by Simulated Annealing. Operations Research **40** (1993) 113–125
10. Mehlhorn, K., Näher, S.: LEDA, A Library of Efficient Data Types and Algorithms. TR **A 05/89** University of Saarbrücken (1989)
11. Mühlenbein, H., Gorges-Schleuter, M.: Die Evolutionsstrategie: Prinzip für parallele Algorithmen. GMD Annual Report (1988)
12. Staats, A.W.: Social behaviorism. The Dorsey Press, Illinois (1975)
13. Taillard, E.: Parallel Taboo Search Techniques for the Job Shop Problem. TR **ORWP 89/11**, Ecole Polytechnique de Lausanne (1989)

Studying Genotype-Phenotype Interactions: a Model of the Evolution of the Cell Regulation Network

Emmanuel Chiva and Philippe Tarroux

Groupe de BioInformatique
Laboratoire de Biologie et Physiologie du Développement – URA 686 CNRS
Département de Biologie, Ecole Normale Supérieure
46 rue d'Ulm, 75230 PARIS Cedex 05 – FRANCE

Abstract. A new model of the interactions between genotype and phenotype is presented. These interactions are underlied by the activity of the cell regulation network. This network is modeled by a continuous recurrent automata network, which describes both direct and indirect interactions between proteins. To mimic evolutionary processes, a particular genetic algorithm is used to simulate the environmental influences on the interactions between proteins. The fitness function is designed to select systems that are robust to transient environmental perturbations, thus exhibiting homeostasy, and that respond in an adapted way to lasting perturbations by a radical change in their behavior. We show that by evaluating the phenotypic response of the system, one can select networks that exhibit interesting dynamical properties, which allows to consider a biological system from a global prospect, taking into account its structure, its behavior and its ontogenetic development. This model provides a new biological metaphor in which the cell is considered as a cybernetic system that can be programmed using a genetic algorithm.

1 Introduction

The use of metaphors in science allows the researcher to focus on problems that cannot be easily investigated by other means, and Nature provides a great number of such problems [1]. This approach – that eventually leads to modeling – is particularly useful in biology since most biological systems are integrated systems, the behavior and structure of which are complex [2].

In this work, we focused on the problem of the relations between genotype and phenotype, since this problem has not been deeply investigated so far. Because these relations are underlied by a complex, integrated system, the emergent behavior of which cannot be anticipated by superposing its subparts ("the whole is greater than the sum of its parts", as it is classically said), one has to find new ways both to understand and to describe the problem *globally* [3]. We propose here to combine evolutionary considerations and a connectionist approach to examine this question.

We considered the genotype-phenotype relations to be underlied by the behavior of a large regulation network, describing the interactions between proteins, both direct (*e.g.,* enzyme/substrate) and indirect (gene-mediated) [4]. In this view, the *phenotype* of the cell is defined from a global prospect, by the responses the cell presents to environmental variations, if the cell is considered *as a whole*. The phenotype is thus determined by the complex dynamics of the protein regulation network, possibly consisting of particular attractors. The idea in itself is not new: some authors have either studied the genes interaction network, modeling it by random autonomous boolean networks [5,6], or focused on the principles of gene regulation [7]. Still, a global picture of this problem has not yet been found.

Because biological systems inherently depend on the way they are encoded, that is, the structure of their genomes, one can expect genetic algorithms (GA) to provide biologically realistic tools to study both the evolution of the system and the conditions that allow specific behaviors to emerge. More than being only optimization methods, they mimic natural mechanisms, and make it possible to investigate specific aspects of evolutionary processes: *e.g,* the effect of crossover, the balance between crossover and mutation, the constraints imposed by the genome structure, and the emergence of mechanisms such as gene duplication and gene amplification. Besides, genetic search for automata networks architectures provides alternative perspectives in the study and the modeling of a cell [8], considering it as a kind of complex system the efficacy of which is related to the way it implements a particular calculus procedure.

In the present work, we intend to associate a modeling of the genome evolution with a realistic model of the regulation network that it encodes. We use a continuous recurrent automata network as a model of the cell regulation network. In this new metaphor, the cell is considered as a particular kind of heteroassociative memory [9,10], and its phenotypic responses are identified with the responses a cybernetic system presents to its environmental context. We show that a GA can be used to program this system, and that the resulting network presents interesting dynamical properties. We observe that under the constraint of the GA, the system structurates hierarchically. Especially, the emergence of units implementing canalyzing functions, thus playing a determinant part in the network dynamics, enables the system to maintain itself "at the edge of chaos", according to the value of an interactivity parameter, acting as the phase transition parameter of the system. We assume these properties to compare favorably with the properties that can be encountered in real biological systems.

2 The Model

In order to obtain a realistic model of the genotype-phenotype interactions we designed a model of the protein regulation network in the cell. We started from the fact that in a first approximation the interactions between proteins are achieved through their conformations and that these conformations are determined by the gene sequence coding for each protein. The response of the cell to variations of the external environment is mediated by the dynamics of the regulation network.

2.1 Network Specifications

Each unit of the network represents a protein, and its activity defines the concentration of the protein. The activation of unit i is simply given by the equation $v_i(t) = \sum_j w_{ij} x_j(t)$

where $x_j(t)$ represents the state of unit j at time t and w_{ij} the interaction strength between units i and j. It is thus possible to model the protein regulation network as a deterministic, recurrent and synchronous connectionist system. The dynamics of the network is then defined by the following vector equations:

$$v(t) = Wx(t - 1)$$
$$x(t) = F[v(t)/T]$$

where W is a weight matrix, $v(t)$ the network activation vector ($v_i(t) \in \mathbb{R}$), $x(t)$ the state vector ($x_i(t) \in [0, 1]$) and $1/T$ the slope of the activation function. F is defined as a non linear mapping: $\mathbb{R}^n \xrightarrow{F} [0, 1]^n$, here $x_i(t) = \dfrac{1}{1 + e^{-v_i(t)/T}}$ In the following we will use $I = 1/T$ defined as the interactivity between units.

2.2 Weight Matrix Generation Method

A genomic control of the regulation network dynamics is achieved by using a genome to define the weights in the following way:
Each unit i is associated with a vector $G_i \in \{-1, 1\}^\nu$ defining the gene coding for this unit. We are thus able to define the genome as a set of genes or more formally as a finite family of G_i vectors ($((G_i)_{i \in [1:n]})$). The expression of each gene is defined as the projection of G_i onto two linearly independent conformation subspaces:

$$P_i^+ = \Phi^+ \, G_i$$
$$P_i^- = \Phi^- \, G_i$$

where Φ^+, Φ^- are two constant $\mu_1 \times \nu$, $\mu_2 \times \nu$ matrices (here $\mu_1 = \mu_2 = \nu/2$), the elements of which belong to $\{-1, 0, 1\}$. These matrices define the physico–chemical interactions within the system. Their connectivity (the number of non-null elements in each row) defines the contribution of each element of a gene to the resulting conformation subspaces. To achieve a uniform distribution of these contributions the connectivity was set identical in each row. The elements of the P_i^+, P_i^- code for the conformations of the expressed protein i. This method leads to individualize two conformation subfields respectively describing the conformations of i potentially involved in the regulation of the other proteins (P_i^+), and the conformations of i potentially accepting regulations from the other proteins (P_i^-). The network weight w_{ij} between units i and j is then computed from P_i^+ and P_j^- by the equation $w_{ij} = \dfrac{1}{\varkappa} \sum_p \sum_q (P_i^+(p) - P_j^-(q))$

where $\varkappa$ is an appropriate normalization factor, so that $|w_{ij}| \leq 1$. Similarly, w_{ji} is computed from P_j^+ and P_i^-. Thus, the resulting weight matrix is non-symmetrical. This method in which a linear genome is used to compute the conformations which will eventually determine the interactions between proteins, has been chosen as an abstract model that mimics protein folding. Each P_i^+ and P_i^- set, initially random, is allowed to evolve according to the evolution of the genome.

2.3 GA Specifications

2.3.1 Principles and Implementation

It must be emphasized that here the genetic algorithm is not only used for its ability to find the optimal structure it codes for but also as a realistic model of genome evolution. However, in order to avoid the problem of genetic drift, there is only one copy of each solution in the population, and among the new solutions generated by mutation or crossover only those which are not already present in the population are allowed to survive. The time is discretized in such a way there is only one mutation or recombination event at a time. We have found that if mutation is allowed on each individual instead of on new offsprings the convergence of the algorithm is increased.

The recombination and selection steps are similar to those of conventional GAs [11]. The "parents" are randomly chosen within the population with the probability p_c, and undergo uniform crossover [12] with a swap probability p_s. Two "bad" chromosomes are chosen, with a probability $\dfrac{\mathcal{F}_{min} - \mathcal{F}}{\mathcal{F}_{min} - \mathcal{F}_{max}}$, where $\mathcal{F}$ is the fitness of the chromosome, with respect to the maximal and minimal fitnesses of the population. The offsprings issued from the crossover are allowed to replace these individuals only if their fitnesses are higher than those of the "bad" individuals.

A mutation event can occur with the probability p_m, independently of the offspring production step. It is not necessarily followed by and immediate evaluation of the chromosome in order to let mutations accumulate. The probability of evaluation after mutation is p_e. This feature implements a way to exploit epistatic effects where the simultaneous presence of two defavorable alleles at different loci can give rise to an adapted phenotype.

When we consider actual protein regulation networks, we observe that there is a dramatic exponential change in complexity when the size of the genome, i.e. the number of proteins, increases. On the other hand, there is a constant increase in DNA content during species evolution and gene duplication phenomena seem to play a major role in the appearance of new functionalities. This is why we implement mechanisms that lead to an increase of genetic material. The first way is to add a new gene at random. The second is properly speaking a duplication mechanism, in which a gene is reproduced with a given probability. However, to simplify the implementation, duplication simultaneously occurs in every chromosome of the population. Thus all chromosomes have always the same length.

2.3.2 The Fitness Function

To compute the fitness function, a set of input vectors is applied to the network. The components of these vectors are submitted to transient and lasting perturbations according to the following equations:

$$x_j^{(p)}(t) = F(w_j^\tau \cdot x^{(p)}(t-1)) \quad j \in N \setminus K \qquad p \in [1; m] \qquad (1)$$
$$x_j^{(p)}(t) = x_j^{(p)}(t-1) \quad j \in K \subset N \qquad (2)$$

where $x_j^{(p)}(t)$ is the state of the unit j at time t according to the pth initial condition among m, K the subset of indices of clamped units among N, and w_j^τ the jth row of the connection matrix W. A transient perturbation of the network is obtained by clamping the K units during a certain period of time (t_s) (eq. (2)), in such a way that $K = \emptyset \quad \forall t > t_s$.

For a lasting perturbation, the clamp is applied throughout the entire simulation $(t = t_s)$ (eq. (1)). Thus, we define the final $n \times m$ matrix $X_t = \left(x^{(1)}(t)...x^{(m)}(t)\right)$, where $x_t^{(p)}(t)$ is the vector state of the system at time t for the pth initial condition. Similarly, for transient perturbations ($t_s < t$), we define the matrix X'_t. Then, given $\Delta_t = X_t - \frac{1}{m} X_t u \ u^\tau$ where $u^\tau = (1...1)$, the fitness of the genome is computed as the difference between the normalized short- and long-term variances of the network states according to the following equation $\mathcal{F} = \frac{1}{\Gamma} tr(\Delta^\tau_t \Delta_t - (\Delta'_t)^\tau \Delta'_t)$, where Γ is a normalizing factor that ensures $\mathcal{F} \in [0; 1]$. Maximizing this difference enables to select networks that are robust with respect to transient perturbations, and diverging facing lasting perturbations.

Our aim is to account for the ability of real cells to usually respond to perturbations only when they are applied for a long time, though exhibiting a certain level of homeostasis. Our system, like most biological systems, is selected to respond to the duration of the stimulus rather than to its amplitude. There are indeed several evidences that in such nonlinear systems, small perturbations can give rise to extremely divergent asymptotic behaviors, provided they are applied during a sufficiently long period of time.

The environmental induction is mimicked by clamp units the activities of which represent the concentrations of external inducers. Their fan-in (the connections they receive) is zero since the network has no effect on its environment. The other units are initially set to zero.

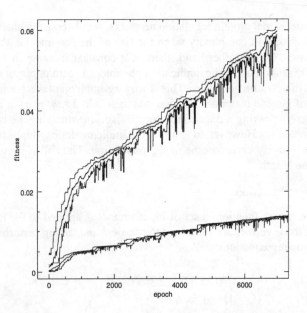

Fig.1. Evolution of the fitness of the network. The upper curve shows the results obtained with the settings 0.25/0.5/0.2/0.7/35/40. Settings for the lower curve are 1.0/0.5/0.5/0.7/35/40. The interactivity parameter is set to 1.0. Gene size is 20. The expression matrix connectivity is 0.8. Each curve presents the max, mean and min fitness values.

To simplify the notations, each simulation is labeled $p_c/p_s/p_m/p_e/n/s$ where p_c stands for the crossover rate, p_s is the crossover swap rate, p_m is the mutation rate, p_e is the selection rate after mutation, n is the size of the network and s the size of the population. Unless otherwise specified, all simulations are obtained with the following settings: 10000 steps are evaluated. At each step, 10 runs are performed to evaluate the fitness, 5 units being clamped. Each run consists of 75 iterations. Transitory clamp is exerted during 25 iterations, and continuous clamp during 75 iterations.

3. Results

3.1 Dynamics of Random Continuous Networks

We studied the dynamics of the network, especially focusing on the presence of attractors, and investigating the stability of the system once it has reached an attractor. It appeared that a random initialization of the matrix does not enable the system to present complex dynamics at low interactivity. Indeed, when I is low ($T>1.0$), the units take truly continuous values, the system exhibits orderly behavior and is highly homeostatic: it is always driven to a single small attractor (low-frequency limit cycle or fixed point). As I increases, the number of attractors increases (and possibly their size), and thus the system exhibits more and more complex behavior. When I is very high ($T<0.05$) the units behave like binary units and the network can exhibit "pseudo-chaotic" behavior. In the following, we will speak of chaotic behavior when the attractors are very large [6]. Randomly initialized networks never exhibit such behavior at low interactivity. I is thus a critical parameter that conditions the whole dynamics of the system.

a   b

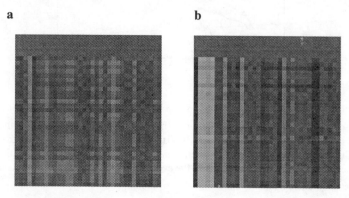

Fig.2. Evolution of the weight matrix structure. a/ after 109 time steps b/ after 6987 time steps. Each square in the image corresponds to a weight in the interaction matrix. Dark (resp. light) elements correspond to highly positive weights (resp. highly negative). The first five rows correspond to clamped units (their fan-in is zero).

3.2 Evolution of the Fitness

The evolution of the fitness is presented in Figure 1. One notices that the convergence speed can be improved by adjusting the crossover rate and the mutation rate in a balanced way. The two curves show a comparison between the fitness evolution for different values of the crossover and mutation parameters. It is obvious that an appropriate choice for these rates allows to greatly improve the fitness of the system. We have observed that both crossover and mutation shall be present to allow the fitness to increase.

3.3 Structure of the Weight Matrix

Figure 2 presents the evolution of the structure of the weight matrix in relation to the evolution of the fitness. As the fitness increases, homogeneous vertical stripes appear in the matrix image while no such stripes can be found horizontally. These vertical stripes represent homogeneously intense weights that correspond to units which fan-out is greater than their fan-in. These units send almost homogeneous connections to the other units, that is to say "they give more than they receive". Furthermore, the increase in fitness seems to be correlated with an increase in the absolute values of the weights.

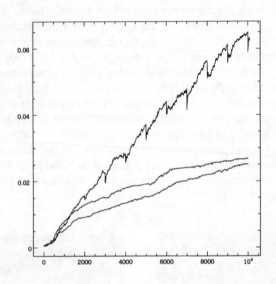

Fig. 3. Effect of gene addition on the evolution of the fitness. The upper curve shows the evolution of the fitness when a new gene is added every 1000 time steps. The size of the network varies from 20 to 30 units during the simulation. The intermediate curve shows the evolution of the fitness of a 30-units network. The lower curve presents the evolution of the fitness of a 20-units network. Settings: 0.2/0.5/0.3/0.7/-/25

3.4 Complexification of the Network

The effect of adding a new gene in every chromosome was investigated, and the results are plotted on Figure 3. Starting from a 20-units network, a new randomly initialized gene was added every 1000 steps, in every chromosome, so that at the end of the simulation, the network was composed of 30 units. As we see from the figure, the variable size network outperforms the 30-units and 20-units networks.

3.5 Dynamics of the Fittest Networks

It appears that the fittest networks can exhibit complex behavior (with stable oscillations) at higher values of I while, at such interactivity, low-fitness networks are driven to a single attractor. As it was previously said, for randomly initialized networks, rich dynamic landscapes appear at $I \gtrsim 20.0$, while under this threshold, the networks exhibit only a single, low-dimensional attractor. The GA structurates the network so that it enables it to exhibit rich dynamics at $I \gtrsim 2.0$.

4 Discussion

Traditionally, the phenotype of a cell is only defined with regards to the morphological and molecular characteristics of the cell. It is determined by analyzing the molecules the cell expresses when placed in a given environment, in the presence of various inducers (*e.g.,* growth factors). It is a static definition because it only focuses on the "being" of the system, rather than describing its global properties [1]. In addition, it does not account for the fact that a cell is a complex dynamical system. In this paper, we present a new model in which the phenotype is defined as the responses the cell regulation network presents to environmental perturbations, these responses consisting of particular dynamics arising from protein interactions.

This model addresses questions related to cybernetics, genetic programming and automata networks analysis. Especially, it allows to investigate a new definition of the phenotype which efficiently takes into account at one and the same time the state of the system, its organization and its behavior (*i.e.,* its dynamical properties).

The analogy between the dynamical properties of a cell and the behavior a cybernetic system can exhibit in relation to its environmental conditions suggests that a cell can implement powerful computational processes. In this prospect, the regulation network is metaphorically viewed as a particular kind of connectionist system that can learn complex dynamics and which can possibly be genetically programmed. The learning algorithm presented here is more general than the classical learning procedures used for recurrent networks. Most of these procedures are indeed based on correlation methods [10], that result in symmetrical connections. Only methods in which the modifications of weights are independent (the adaptations of GBP to recurrent networks and GA-based methods) lead to non-symmetrical connections.

Different implementations of genetic algorithms have been proposed for the design of formal automata networks. The simplest ones directly encode the weights of the connection matrix into a bit string to which genetic operators are applied [13]. Others code a development program in each solution. Coding development rules can indeed be achieved by using formal grammars (e.g. L-systems) [14,8] or graph-growing rules [15]. The GA is thus able to search not only for a suitable weight matrix but also for an optimal architecture.

However, all these approaches lack of biological realism when compared with the actual effect of the genome. In biological systems as in our model, the interactions (represented here by the weights) are not directly encoded. Each of them results from the mutual contact between two conformations. We can assume that with such a drastically different coding, a different search of the solution space will be achieved by the GA. One advantage of this implementation is obvious when one considers that a direct coding of the weights is $O(n^2)$, while a conformation coding is $O(n)$ (n being the number of units in the network). Another interest is due to the fact that in such an implementation, the effect of a point change in a gene is largely pleiotropic, since, affecting the conformation this gene is coding for, it modifies all the weights this conformation is involved in. Since during learning, there are usually no local changes in the weights, some of them being modified together, a moving target problem [16] is not likely to occur. A last advantage is the easy, natural and progressive way a new unit can be introduced through duplication.

Indeed, we have shown that to rapidly adapt, it is better to start from a simple system and progressively complexify it rather than starting from a complex system which optimal configuration is much longer to find (*cf* Fig. 3). Variable size networks implement an incremental search for the optimum, while static networks have to explore the whole search space from the beginning in order to adapt. This observation can be related to the evolution of biological systems which implement several features to limit the exploration of an exponentially growing search space. Indeed, there are evidences that a process such as gene duplication leads to the production of new genes without affecting the organization of the genetic material already present in the cell. Here, the basic properties of the system are conserved, but the addition of a new unit allows to improve the efficacy of a well-adapted system by increasing its complexity [17].

It appears that adapted networks have particular hierarchized architectures, which are materialized by the emergence of units that homogeneously send connections to the whole network. These units can be considered as *command units*, since their activities condition the global activity of the system. They map to receptors that are sensitive to the environmental conditions, and which orient the whole phenotypic response, thus implementing *canalyzing functions*. Such functions, that are often described in boolean networks [5], play a determinant part in the propagation of perturbations inside the system: they make percolation possible. The cell is thus viewed as a system that can be genetically programmed to acquire specialized functions, consequently specific dynamics.

Indeed, we have shown that such genetically designed systems tend to exhibit rich behavior, according to the interactivity parameter. The critical value of the interactivity can thus be viewed as a "phase transition parameter" of the system, since it acts as a threshold which determines its dynamic behavior. Under the assumption that fitness is related to the long-term responses variability of the cell, the evolution process we investigated leads to a system "at the edge of chaos". This property is related to the emergence of canalyzing functions inside the network [18, 19]. As Langton described, such systems have powerful computational possibilities [20], hence they can adapt more easily than other systems.

One can assume that such an adaptive system, which evolves in a finite state space of variable dimensions [21] –since the number of units is allowed to increase– gives new insights into the study of the complex interactions between genotype and phenotype.

Acknowledgements. The authors would like to thank Philippe Andrey, Anne Brelet and Eric Granjeon for their interest and for inspiring discussions at various stages in the conducting of the present work. The research was partially supported by a grant from the DGA–DRET (93/070).

References

1. R.C. Paton , H.S. Nwana, M.J.R. Shave, T.J.M. Bench–Capon and S. Hughes: Transfer of Natural Metaphors to Parallel Problem Solving Applications. In: Schwefel H.P, Männer R (eds.): Parallel Problem Solving from Nature I, Berlin: Springer-Verlag 1990, pp. 363-372

2. H.A. Simon: Architecture of complexity, Proc.Am.Philo.Soc. 106, 467-482 (1962)

3. S. Forrest: Emergent computation: self–organizing, collective, and cooperative phenomena in natural and artificial computing networks. In: Forrest S. (ed.) : Emergent Computation, Cambrige: MIT Press 1991: pp. 1–12

4. Z. Agur and M. Kerszberg : The emergence of phenotypic novelties through progressive genetic change, American Naturalist 129, 6, 862-875 (1987)

5. S.A. Kauffman: Requirement for evolvability in complex systems, orderly dynamics and frozen components, Physica D 42, 135-152 (1990)

6. S.A. Kauffman: Principles of adaptation in complex systems. In: Stein D. (ed.): Lectures in the science of complexity, 1, New York:Addison-Wesley 1989, pp. 619-712

7. M. Huynen and P. Hogeweg: Genetic algorithms and information accumulation during the evolution of gene regulation. In: Schaffer J.D. (ed.): Proceeding of the Third International Conference on Genetic Algorithms, San Mateo, CA: Morgan Kauffman 1989, pp. 225-230

8. R.K. Belew, J. McInerney and N.N. Schraudolph: Evolving networks: using the genetic algorithm with connectionist learning. In: C.G Langton, C. Taylor, J.D. Farmer, S. Rasmussen (eds.): Artificial Life II, New York: Addison-Wesley 1992, pp. 511-547

9. J.J. Hopfield: Neural networks and physical systems with emergent collective computational abilities, Proc.Natl.Acad.Sci.USA 79, 2554-2558 (1982)

10. M.H. Hassoun: Dynamic associative memories, In: Sethi I.K. and Jain A.K. (eds.): Artificial Neural Networks and Statistical Pattern Recognition, Old and New Connections, Amsterdam: North–Holland 1991, pp. 195-218

11. D.E. Goldberg: Genetic algorithms in search, optimization and machine learning, Addison–Wesley, Reading, MA (1989).

12. G. Syswerda : Uniform crossover in genetic algorithms. In: Schaffer J.D. (ed.): Proceeding of the Third International Conference on Genetic Algorithms, San Mateo, CA.:Morgan Kauffman 1989, pp. 2-9

13. G.F.Miller, P.M. Todd and S.U.Hegde: Designing neural networks using genetic algorithms. In: Schaffer J.D. (ed.): Proceeding of the Third International Conference on Genetic Algorithms, San Mateo, CA: Morgan Kauffman 1989, pp. 379–384

14. H.Kitano: Designing neural networks using genetic algorithms with graph generation system. Complex Systems 4: 461-476 (1992)

15. F. Gruau: Genetic synthesis of modular neural networks. In : Forrest S. (ed.): Proceeding of the Fifth International Conference on Genetic Algorithms, San Mateo, CA.:Morgan Kauffman 1993: pp. 318–325

16. S. Fahlman and C. Lebiere: The Cascade-Correlation Learning Architecture, Tech. Rep.CMU-CS-90-100 (1990)

17. H. Jacobson: Information, reproduction and the origin of life, American Scientist 43, 119-127 (1955)

18. B. Derrida and D. Stauffer: Phase-transitions in two–dimensional Kauffman cellular automata, Europhys.Lett. 2, 739-745 (1986)

19. G.Weisbuch and D. Stauffer : Phase transition in cellular random Boolean nets, J.Phys 48, 11-18 (1987)

20. C.G. Langton: Computation at the edge of chaos, phase transitions and emergent computation, Physica D 42, 12-37 (1990)

21. R.J.Bagley, J.D.Farmer, S.A. Kauffman, N.H. Packard, A.S. Perelson and I.M. Stadnyk : Modeling adaptive biological systems, BioSystems 23, 113-138 (1989)

A Diploid Genetic Algorithm for Preserving Population Diversity — pseudo-Meiosis GA

YOSHIDA Yukiko and ADACHI Nobue

Institute for Social Information Science, Fujitsu Laboratories Ltd.
9–3, Nakase 1-chome, Mihama-ku, Chiba-shi, Chiba 261, Japan

Abstract. This paper proposes a diploid genetic algorithm, which is named the pseudo-Meiosis Genetic Algorithm (psM GA), that preserves population diversity. The psM GA has a meiosis-like procedure to generate a phenotype from a pair of functionally different chromosomes, unlike a conventional diploid GA with dominance. Another new feature is a procedure for re-pairing two chromosomes for the next generation. The psM GA is applied to a non-stationary traveling salesman problem (TSP), which conventional diploid GAs can hardly cope with. The psM GA preserved population diversity and adapted the population quickly to the problem changes.

1 Introduction

If a genetic algorithm (GA) loses population diversity, its genetic operations, such as crossover, become almost ineffective. The GA then has difficulty escaping from a local optimum where the population has converged into. Avoiding such traps is crucial particularly with multi-modal or non-stationary problems.

One way to preserve population diversity is to increase population randomness, for example, high mutation and immigration of new random individuals [1, 2]. Mutation is understood to improve extensive searches, but not fine searches. Another way is to control the population diversity, for example, using a sharing function or niche to prevent the population from crowding at one near-optimum [3, 4].

Another popular method is to introduce redundancy into the representation of the solution. An example is using a plural number of chromosomes (or polyploid chromosomes) to represent a solution (phenotype). Generally speaking, since a solution can be expressed with different polyploid genotypes, the population diversity is preserved even if the population converges at the phenotypic level. Conventional GAs use a single self-contained chromosome (or haploid chromosome) that represents uniquely one solution. Therefore population diversity decreases as the GA search proceeds.

Some researchers have studied diploid chromosomes, i.e., pairs of chromosomes [5]. Dominance is widely used to generate a phenotype (or an intermediate haploid chromosome) from diploid chromosomes. Methods based on dominance assign a dominant-and-recessive property to possible values (or alleles) for each chromosome position (or locus), and dominant values are chosen for each position to generate a haploid chromosome.

This kind of dominance method cannot be always used for various problems. Previous studies on diploid and dominance GAs have focused mainly on bit-coding problems, such as function optimization problems and knapsack problems. With bit-coding problems, a solution is coded as a bit string and loci have no strong inter-dependency. But, order-coding problems often have strong constraints among loci. Consider a traveling salesman problem (TSP) and assume that each chromosome represents a tour in the form of a permutation of cities. The TSP has the constraint that every city must appear only once in a tour. If dominant cities are chosen independently of each other from a pair of chromosomes (tours) to form a new tour, most resulting tours would violate the constraint. Also, it is often difficult to define dominant-and-recessive relations among cities.

Another dominance method for diploid GAs, which differs from nature, is to select one of a pair of chromosomes according to some criterion, for example, choosing one randomly, or the better (or higher-fitness) one. This method never generates illegal (or lethal) haploid chromosomes, and can therefore be used for order-coding problems. But, it has the drawback that one of two chromosomes does not contribute to the GA search.

In this paper we propose a new type of diploid GA, that we call the pseudo-Meiosis GA (psM GA). Our GA preserves population diversity effectively. Diploid-to-haploid mapping is based on meiosis [6]. Our method avoids generating lethal haploid chromosomes and makes both homologous chromosomes contribute to a haploid. Also, haploid-to-diploid re-pairing procedure forms diploid chromosomes in the next generation. The following section describes our psM GA with meiosis-like mapping and re-pairing. We applied our GA to a non-stationary TSP, and discussed the results from various points of view, including adaptability to problem changes and population diversity.

2 Pseudo-Meiosis GA

2.1 Designing the pseudo-Meiosis GA

Before describing the details of our psM GA, we should understand some of the considerations behind its design.

a) Producing a single chromosome from a pair of chromosomes is analogous to meiosis in biology. Meiosis involves genetic recombination between homologous chromosomes and cell division producing haploid gametes. As the metaphor from nature, we named our diploid-to-haploid mapping pseudo-meiosis (psM). By "pseudo-" we mean that throughout mapping the chromosome pair is kept intact, unlike real meiosis. We gave the name *post-meiosis* to haploid chromosomes produced by psM mapping.

b) To avoid lethal haploids and to make both homologous chromosomes contribute to a (post-meiosis) haploid, we use an ordinary crossover operator as psM mapping. Pseudo-meiosis mapping and crossover are the same from an algorithmic point of view. We distinguish between psM mapping and

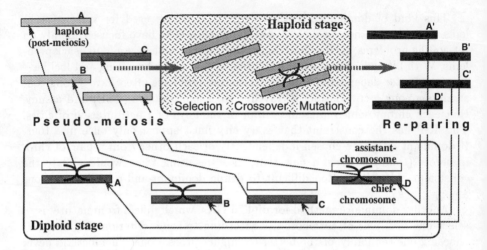

Fig. 1. Genetic operations of the pseudo-Meiosis GA.

crossover, because psM occurs inside an individual whereas crossover occurs between individuals. We can design original psM mapping, but crossover is regarded as a first approximation. Some crossover operators over two parent chromosomes yield two offspring chromosomes. In psM mapping, we assume that one of the two is selected according to some criterion (i.e., the one inheriting more properties of the chief chromosome, or the higher-fitness one).

c) One chromosome of a diploid does not undergo selection. If, during selection, both chromosomes of a diploid become extinct, and a clone offspring of a diploid is reproduced, the population diversity decreases, like with haploid GAs. Because one of the two chromosomes bypasses selection, the population retains its diversity.

d) Haploid-to-diploid re-pairing procedure builds a diploid from the one chromosome that survived selection, and another chromosome which bypassed selection. If both chromosomes of a diploid are processed as one body, re-pairing is not necessary.

Each of these ideas may not be new, but collectively they give an interesting search method at the cost of the complex construction.

2.2 Algorithm

The psM GA has several steps. Below is a detailed explanation of each step (Fig. 1).

1. (Initialization) All chromosomes are created according to some rule, as in other GAs. We assume that each individual has two *slots* to hold a pair of

chromosomes; a *chief* slot and an *assistant* slot. The chromosome in a chief slot is called a chief chromosome, and the one in an assistant slot is called an assistant chromosome. Chief and assistant properties do not change during generation.

2. (Pseudo-meiosis) Pseudo-meiosis mapping is applied to each diploid with probability p_{meio} in order to generate a post-meiosis (haploid) chromosome. For individuals that bypass pseudo-meiosis, a copy of the chief chromosome is treated as a post-meiosis one.

3. (Selection, crossover and mutation) This step is very similar to that of ordinary haploid GAs, except that GA operations are applied only to the post-meiosis chromosomes' population. The post-meiosis chromosomes are first evaluated and then selected and reproduced based on their fitness values. The offspring chromosome undergoes crossover, with probability p_c, and mutation, with probability p_m.

4. (Re-pairing) Each offspring chromosome is pulled back to the chief slot of its parent individual. The chief slot of an individual whose post-meiosis chromosome became extinct because of selection is filled with reproduced, and therefore promising, offspring.

   Each assistant chromosome undergoes mutation with probability p_{mA}. Note that, apart from mutation, there is no destructive operation for assistant chromosomes.

5. (Generation cycle) Steps 2 to 4 form one generation cycle. The generation is repeated until some terminating condition is satisfied.

The names, chief and assistant, come from their functions. The chief chromosome is related to the principal search cycle of the GA, whereas the assistant one works only for its chief pair inside the individual.

One of the unusual features of the psM GA is that assistant chromosomes vary independently of chief ones, and therefore continuously maintain population diversity. Assistant chromosomes work as follows during a search: Copies of the better (or higher-fitness) post-meiosis chromosome will migrate to many individuals, and be psM-mapped with different assistant chromosomes in the next generation cycle. In other words, random local searches are performed around the better chief chromosomes. Because a variety of assistant chromosomes are retained independent of chief ones, local searches function continuously. In contrast, variation in population of typical haploid GAs tends to decrease as generation proceeds. The chances of having better chromosomes for crossover with different chromosomes also decrease.

If the psM GA is applied to non-stationary problems, it behaves differently. When the problem changes at some generation, more of post-meiosis chromosomes no longer survive, and consequently more of chief slots are filled with successor chromosomes of the other individuals. Assistant chromosomes therefore meet a wider variety of chief chromosomes. Hence a large number of combinations of various chromosomes, which are essential in transient situations, are examined quickly. We can say that a random local search is done around the assistant chromosome, because the assistant chromosome walks relatively slowly on the fitness landscape, while the chief one changes much more frequently.

In short, the psM GA has different search mechanisms and chooses a suitable mechanism autonomously to adapt to changing situations.

3 Simulation Experiments

As an example of an order-coding problem, we chose a non-stationary TSP in which the distances between two cities vary with time, but not cyclically. One reason for this choice is that ordinary diploid GAs with dominance can hardly cope with TSPs because an order-coding chromosome for TSPs has strong restrictions among loci, as stated before. Another reason is that, in general, non-stationary problems need population diversity more than stationary ones. A non-stationary TSP seems more realistic since it can, for example, reflect a traffic jam in the real world.

We used a 50-city problem created randomly in a 100×100 square area. The distance between two cities is the Euclidean distance between them. The cities are assumed to shift position every 100 generations, i.e., one *phase*. The shift in magnitude is a maximum of 5 in the x- and y-directions respectively, according to a probability distribution.

3.1 Comparison with Simple GA

We compared our GA with a well-known Simple GA (SGA) [4]. Simulation conditions were as follows: Population size was 100 for the psM GA, and 200 for the SGA, so that the total number of chromosomes was 200 for both GAs. Fitness value was tour length scaled with a ranking over the population. Selection was a hybrid of roulette wheel and *elitism*: N_e copies of the best chromosome are always reproduced. The copies undergo crossover and mutation, as well as the other offspring chromosomes that are selected according to a roulette wheel. Partially matched crossover (PMX) [4] is used for both psM mapping and crossover. For both algorithms, *elitist size* $N_e = 3$, and crossover probability $p_c = 0.6$. For the psM GA, pseudo-meiosis probability (of PMX, in this case) $p_{meio} = 0.1$, swap mutation probability over (post-meiosis) haploid chromosomes $p_m = 0.2$, and swap mutation probability over assistant chromosomes $p_{mA} = 0.1$. For SGA, swap mutation probability $p_m = 0.5$. These parameter values were the best combination found in preliminary simulations.

Fig. 2 shows the best, the median, and the worst tour lengths in the population. Note that the shorter the length, the better tour. After a few hundred generations, the psM GA finds the better near-optima in most phases, and quickly adapts the population to TSP phase changes. The best lengths are kept within a slight variation at each phase. The averages of worst lengths are widely separated from the best lengths and are almost constantly kept, unlike with the SGA where the worst length fluctuates with each generation. This implies that the psM GA maintains a large population diversity. With the SGA, the median

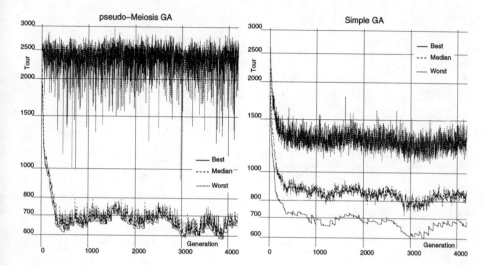

Fig. 2. Best, median, and worst tour lengths with a pseudo-Meiosis GA and a Simple GA.

lengths are further from the best lengths. This is probably because of the high mutation rate.

Pseudo-meiosis has a partly destructive effect, like mutation, and therefore looks like a Simple GA with high mutation. These are not, however, equivalent. Although the mutation rate p_m of the SGA is higher and $p_m = 0.5$ is the best choice, the best tour lengths are not good. Fig. 3 shows the best lengths of SGA with different mutation probabilities $p_m = 0.01$, 0.4, 0.5, and 0.6. Unlike the psM GA, the best lengths have spike-like fluctuations and slowly trace TSP phase changes. At higher probabilities, the gap between the best and median lengths tended to be larger, and that the best lengths fluctuated more.

Elitist ensures that the best chromosome is passed to the next generation and thereby reduces the best length monotonically. However, elitist seems to have less effect with the SGA. We can explain this as follows. Consider the extreme cases. A low mutation rate makes elitists lead the population to local optima, but cannot cause the population to escape from the local optima. A high mutation rate helps the population reach global optima, but disturbs keeping near-optima by means of elitists, that is, making fine searches around near-optima. Fig. 3 shows those effects at a low mutation rate ($p_m = 0.01$) and a high mutation rate ($p_m = 0.6$).

To quantify population diversity, we calculated standard deviations of the population at genotypic and phenotypic levels. At the genotypic level, we examined the frequency distribution $f_{i,j}$ of connections between two cities, c_i and c_j. Here, the number of connections is counted over the whole population. With the psM GA, the population of post-meiosis chromosomes is taken into account. Let C be the total number of cities and P be the population size. The number of possible connections is, then, $C \times (C - 1)/2$, and the overall sum of $f_{i,j}$'s is

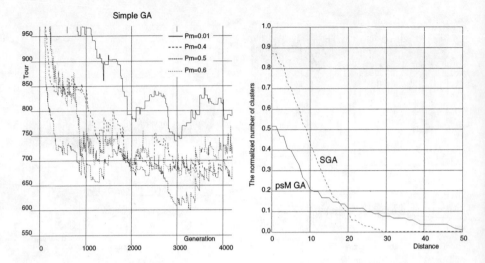

Fig. 3. Best tour lengths with different mutation probabilities for a Simple GA.

Fig. 4. The normalized number of clusters for a Simple GA and a pseudo-Meiosis GA.

$C \times P$. The normalized average of $f_{i,j}$'s is $2/(C \times (C-1))$. If every tour in the population contains the connection between c_i and c_j, $f_{i,j}$ is P. The normalized $f_{i,j}$ is $1/C$. At the other extreme, $f_{i,j}$ is zero if no tour contains that connection. If tours are created at random, most $f_{i,j}$'s are close to the average. Therefore, the standard deviation of $f_{i,j}$'s is close to zero. In other words, a small deviation gives a large population diversity. With the psM GA, the normalized standard deviation starts at 0.0204, then stabilizes at 0.176. With the SGA, standard deviation reaches 0.165 after starting at 0.0138. This suggests that the SGA case has a slightly larger population diversity. At the phenotypic level, however, the psM GA has larger diversity. Here standard deviation of tour length distribution in the population was calculated. With the psM GA, the standard deviation is about 338 after the initial value 130, compared with about 127 after 139 with the SGA. This implies that the genotypic diversity of the SGA was insufficiently reflected in phenotypic diversity.

We made a cluster analysis with hamming distance between chromosomes. In Fig. 4, horizontal axis is the distance that separates clusters from each other, and vertical axis is the normalized number of clusters, that is, the number of clusters divided by the population size. With the SGA, many individuals were about 5–15 distant from each other. The number of clusters decreased rapidly with an increase in the distance, and the population formed one cluster at a distance of 29, as shown in Fig. 4. Compared with the SGA, the psM GA had a smaller number of clusters at a short distance, and a larger number of clusters at a long distance. Roughly speaking, an individual was either near to others, or far from others. Therefore we can draw the following conclusion: With the psM GA, individuals are not uniformly distributed over the chromosome landscape measured by hamming distance between chromosomes. Individuals are grouped into a number of clusters that consist of similar individuals, probably grouped around better individuals.

3.2 Parameters of the psM GA

The psM GA has some new parameters: pseudo-meiosis probability p_{meio}, mutation probability of assistant chromosome p_{mA}, and elitist size N_e. We experimented with different parameter values.

Fig. 5 shows the best tour lengths for $p_{meio} = 0.01, 0.1$, and 0.3. As stated before, pseudo-meiosis contributes to random local search at the population level and acts as a mutation at the individual level. The best tour length fluctuates more in the $p_{meio} = 0.3$ case. This fluctuation is similar to high-mutation with the SGA. However, a low $p_{meio} = 0.01$ retains less population variety, since variation of assistant chromosomes is not effectively reflected in post-meiosis chromosomes. $p_{meio} = 0.1$ case seems the best choice in this simulation.

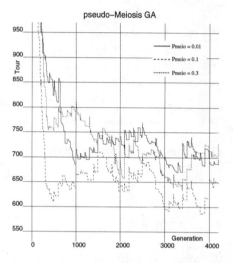

Fig. 5. Best tour lengths with different pseudo-meiosis probabilities.

Fig. 6 shows the best tour lengths under $N_e = 0, 2, 3$ and 4. As described above, elitist avoids accidentally losing the best tour because of GA operators, and thereby makes a series of the best lengths more stable. But, too many elitists are unnecessary and risk losing population diversity. In fact, $N_e = 4$ in Fig. 6 shows a variety of chief chromosomes are maintained at a low level and prevent the population from adapting to TSP changes. With $N_e = 0$, the best tour length has little chance to survive destructive GA operations, as shown by the many downward spike-like fluctuations. The series of best tour lengths is, therefore, unstable and quality is low.

Fig. 7 shows the best tour lengths for $p_{mA} = 0.01, 0.1, 0.3$, and 0.6, with fixed parameters $p_{meio} = 0.1$, $p_m = 0.2$, and $N_e = 3$. A high p_{mA} rate has a similar effect to a p_{meio} rate. A low rate weakens the effect of a local search as if there were no pseudo-meiosis. As a result, both extremes $p_{mA} = 0.01$ and 0.6 behave like the SGA.

Needless to say, these parameters are strongly related to other parameters, such as crossover and mutation rates of post-meiosis chromosomes. The discussion above is based on limited preliminary simulations.

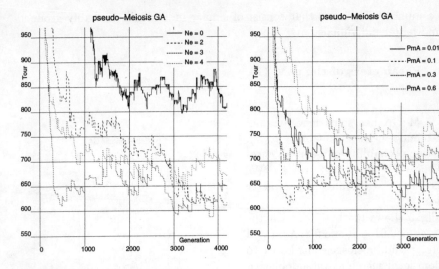

Fig. 6. Best tour lengths with different elitist size.

Fig. 7. Best tour lengths with different mutation probabilities of assistant chromosomes.

4 Summary

We proposed a diploid GA named the pseudo-Meiosis GA (psM GA). In the psM GA, diploid chromosomes have different functions during a search. Chief chromosomes participate in the main search course. An assistant chromosome mutates inside the individual and contributes to producing a variant of its chief chromosome via pseudo-meiosis diploid-to-haploid mapping. We found that assistant chromosomes are important to preserving population diversity and to improving local searches around better solutions.

We applied our psM GA to a non-stationary TSP and studied how it adapted to changes in the problem. Simulation showed that the psM GA quickly adapted the population to changes. We also discussed the effects of various GA parameters, particularly the pseudo-meiosis probability and the elitist size that are important to the psM GA. We have not yet applied the psM GA to optimizing a changing function, but we expect the psM GA to work because the framework of the psM GA is the same.

In our experiments, we used PMX for both pseudo-meiosis mapping and crossover, for convenience. Previous studies have devised various crossover operators for order-coding, some of which have been examined with the SGA [7]. Since pseudo-meiosis mapping affects the behavior of the psM GA, we need to study various crossover mechanisms for pseudo-meiosis mapping.

To solve a non-stationary problem with a GA, someone may consider to monitor the problem changes through the behavior of the population. The psM GA, however, can choose a suitable search mechanism automatically, even though appropriate setting of additional parameters may be difficult.

The results in this paper are preliminary, and more detailed investigation is needed. Application of the psM GA to various problems, including bit-coding problems, has been left for future study.

References

1. John J. Grefenstette. Genetic algorithms for changing environments. In *Parellel Problem Solving from Nature II*, pages 137–144. Elsevier Science Publishers, 1992.
2. Helen G. Cobb and John J. Grefenstette. Genetic algorithms for tracking changing environments. In *Proc. of the Fifth International Conference on Genetic Algorithms*, pages 523–530, 1993.
3. David E. Goldberg and John Richardson. Genetic algorithms with sharing for multimodal function optimization. In *Proc. of the Second International Conference on Genetic Algorithms*, pages 41–49, 1987.
4. David E. Goldberg. *Genetic Algorithms in Search, Optimization and Machine Learning*. Addison-Wesley Publishing Company, Inc., 1989.
5. David E. Goldberg and Robert E. Smith. Nonstationary function optimization using genetic algorithms with dominace and diploidy. In *Proc. of the Second International Conference on Genetic Algorithms*, pages 59–68, 1987.
6. Robert H. Tamarin. *Principles of Genetics*. PWS Publishers, A Division of Wadsworth, Inc., 1986.
7. Bernard Manderick, Mark de Weger, and Piet Speissens. The genetic algorithm and the structure of the fitness landscape. In *Proc. of the Fourth International Conference on Genetic Algorithms*, pages 143–150, 1991.
8. Yukiko Yoshida and Nobue Adachi. A dominance-wise genetic algorithm (in Japanese). In *Proc. of the 47-th IPSJ Annual Conference*, pages (2) 241–242, 1993.

Co-evolutionary Constraint Satisfaction

Jan Paredis

Research Institute for Knowledge Systems
Postbus 463, NL-6200 AL Maastricht, The Netherlands
e-mail: jan@riks.nl

Abstract. This paper introduces CCS, a Co-evolutionary approach to Constraint Satisfaction. Two types of objects - constraints and solutions - interact in a way modelled after predator and prey relations in nature. It is shown that co-evolution considerably focuses the genetic search. In addition, the new technique of life-time fitness evaluation (LTFE) is introduced. Its partial but continuous nature allows for efficient fitness evaluation. Moreover, co-evolution and LTFE nicely complement each other. Hence, their combined use further improves the performance of the evolutionary search.

CCS also provides a new perspective on the problems associated with high degrees of epistasis and the use of penalty functions.

Keywords: co-evolution, constraint satisfaction, epistatic problems, genetic algorithms, life-time fitness evaluation, predator-prey systems.

1. Introduction

Arms races constitute an important evolutionary driving force leading towards highly complex adaptations. These races occur, for example, in predator-prey relations. There is a strong evolutionary pressure for prey to defend themselves better (e.g. by running quicker, growing bigger shields, better camouflage ...) in response to which future generations of predators develop better attacking strategies (e.g. stronger claws, better eye-sight ...). In arms races, success on the one side is felt by the other side as a failure to which must be "responded" in order to maintain one's chances of survival. This, in turn, calls for a reaction of the other side. This inverse fitness interaction leads towards a stepwise increase in complexity of both: predator and prey. Hence, both populations are said to co-evolve.

Recent research by Hillis (92) has shown the use of the principles behind arms races to boost the performance of evolutionary algorithms (EAs). Hillis used the design of sorting hardware as a test domain for his technique. Paredis (94a) has adapted this approach to evolve classification neural networks. It combines another biologically inspired technique, called life-time fitness evaluation (LTFE), with co-evolution. Here we show that this combination can be used successfully to solve constraint satisfaction problems as well.

Constraint Satisfaction Problems (CSPs) typically consist of a set of n variables x_i ($i \leq n$) which have an associated domain D_i of possible values. There is also a set of constraints, called C, which describe relations between the values of the x_i. (e.g. the value of x_1 should be different from the value of x_3). A *solution* consists of an assignment of values to the x_i such that all constraints in C are satisfied, i.e. the solution is valid.

Typically, highly constrained CSPs have a high *degree of epistasis*: the choices made during the search are closely coupled. In general, highly epistatic problems are characterised by the fact that no decomposition in independent subproblems is possible. In that case, it is difficult to combine subparts of two valid solutions into another valid solution. This is bad news for GAs which typically search by combining features of different "solutions".

The last couple of years a number of methods for constraint handling have been proposed within the GA community. The first one - genetic repair (Mühlenbein 92) - removes constraint violations in invalid solutions generated by the genetic operators (such as mutation and crossover). The second one uses decoders such that all possible representations give rise to a valid solution (Davis 88). A third one uses penalty functions, see for example (Richardson et al 89). This approach defines the fitness function as the objective function one tries to optimize minus the penalty function which represents the "degree of invalidity" of a solution. Hence, the search process is allowed to wander around in portions of the search space containing only invalid solutions. The rationale being that it might be easier to find a solution if one is allowed to reach it from both sides of the valid/invalid border.

All three approaches mentioned above, have a major disadvantage: they are all problem specific. For every CSP one has to determine a good decoder, a good genetic repair method or a penalty function which balances between convergence towards suboptimal valid solutions (when the penalty function is too harsh) or towards invalid solutions (too tolerant a penalty function is used).

Recently, Paredis (93) proposed GSSS, a general method for introducing domain knowledge - through the use of constraint programming - to guide the evolutionary search when solving constraint problems. Now, an alternative approach - called Co-evolutionary Constraint Satisfaction (CCS) - is presented. Both CCS and GSSS are specifically designed to solve constraint problems. The explicit focus on this class of problems brings several advantages with it. A first one is that it allows for a natural problem specification in terms of constraints. Moreover, these constraints explicitly represent the epistatic interactions. This information can be used to guide the evolutionary search. Paredis (93) also shows the use of the constraints as domain elements in a general, abstract, genetic repair method.

In contrast with GSSS, CCS only checks whether a proposed solution satisfies the constraints. No active knowledge on how to enforce the constraints is required. Hence CCS relies on less domain knowledge than GSSS. Or in other words, GSSS is more knowledge-rich than CCS. Hence, the choice between both approaches depends on issues such as the availability of knowledge and its quality (i.e. do the constraints focus the search enough to overcome the computational overhead created by the use of the additional knowledge?).

The structure of this paper is as follows. The next section describes the bench-mark problem on which CCS will be tested. Section three describes the algorithm. Empirical results and comparison with other algorithms are given in section four. The paper closes with conclusions and a discussion.

2. The Test Problem

In this section, we describe the bench-mark problem on which our approach will be tested empirically. The n-queens problem consists of placing n queens on a n×n chess board so that no two queens attack each other (i.e. they are not in the same row, column, or diagonal). A frequently used representation of this problem - which we use as well - consists of n variables x_i. Each such variable represents one column on the chess board. The assignment $x_2=3$, for example, indicates that a queen is positioned in the third row of the second column. Hence, the x_i take a value from the set $\{1,2, ...,n\}$. The constraints for this problem are simple:

- $x_i \neq x_j$ $i \neq j$; row-constraint
- $|x_i - x_j| \neq |i-j|$ $i \neq j$; diagonal-constraint

The first line above prohibits two queens to be placed in the same row. The second line ensures that no two queens are on a same diagonal. Note that the column constraint (only one queen is allowed per column) is implicit in the representation. Here, we test our approach on a 50-queens CSP. Hence, a solution consists of 50 variables. Each of which has to be assigned a value from the set $\{1,2, ..., 50\}$.

3. The Algorithm

The algorithm involves two populations. The first one contains the constraints. The second population contains potential - possibly invalid - solutions to the CSP to be solved. Just as in predator-prey models the selection pressure on members of one population depends on the fitness of the members of the other population. Or, in other words, there is an inverse fitness interaction between both populations.

Figure 1 depicts the data structures used in CCS. The "genetic representation" of both types of individuals is quite simple. The solutions are represented as 50-dimensional vectors containing integers from the set {1,2,3 ..., 50}. A constraint, on the other hand, is an à priori defined piece of LISP-code which checks whether it is violated by a given solution. The constraints can be taken directly from the problem specification. For each xi two constraints are used. A first one checks whether any of the other columns have a queen positioned at the same row as xi. The second one checks the diagonal constraint. Or, in a more formal way: for each i ∈ {1,2,3 ..., 50} the following two constraints are present in the constraint population:

$$\forall j \in \{1,2,3 ..., 50\}: i=j \text{ or } x_i=x_j$$
$$\forall j \in \{1,2,3 ..., 50\}: i=j \text{ or } abs(x_i-x_j)=abs(i-j).$$

As we discuss in more detail below, the constraint population contains all the time the same hundred constraints. This in contrast to the population of solutions in which new solutions - created through reproduction - gradually replace older ones. Hence, the constraints do not form a real population in a strict sense.

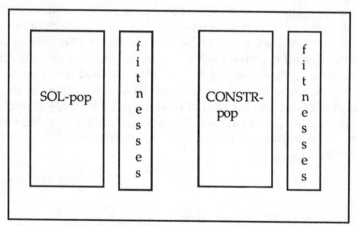

Figure 1: Co-evolving solutions and constraints

CCS uses GENITOR (Whitley 1989a; 1989b) as its core evolutionary algorithm. An important novelty, however, is the notion of an *encounter* between a solution and a constraint. During such an encounter the solution is checked with respect to the constraint it encounters. The solution receives a reward when it satisfies the constraint, it receives a penalty in case the constraint is violated. For the constraint involved in an encounter the result of an encounter is opposite: it gets a penalty when the solution encountered satisfies it and a reward in case of violation. In our implementation rewards have the value of 1 and penalties -1. Both can be interpreted as the *pay-off* resulting from an encounter. Each individual - whether constraint or solution - has an associated history containing the rewards and penalties it received during its most recent encounters. Here we use a history of length 25. Hence, the fitness of an individual is defined as the sum of the pay-off it received during the 25 most recent encounters it was involved in. This is a clear example of the use of life-time fitness evaluation (LTFE). A continuous series of tests during the life-time is used to approximate the fitness of an individual. This in contrast with the traditional "once and for all" fitness calculation. The limited length of the histories ensures that only the most recent encounters are taken into account. That is why LTFE is said to provide a partial fitness measure.

The pseudo-code below describes the basic cycle of the algorithm. First 20 - this number is rather arbitrarily chosen - constraint-solution encounters are executed. The function which SELECTs the individuals to be involved in an encounter is biased towards highly ranking individuals: the most fit individual is 1.5 times more likely to be selected than the individual with median fitness. This way, fit solutions and constraints are often involved in an encounter. Or in other words, good solutions have to prove themselves more often. At the same time, the algorithm concentrates on satisfying difficult, i.e. not yet solved, constraints. This is because constraints have a high fitness when they are violated by many members of the solution population. The function ENCOUNTER returns 1 if the solution satisfies the constraint. In the other case, -1 is returned. Next, the histories of the solution and constraint involved in the encounter are UPDATEd. This is done by pushing the pay-off associated with the current encounter on the history of the individuals. At the same time the pay-off associated with the least recent encounter is removed from these histories. Finally, the fitness of an individual - which is defined as the sum of rewards in its history - is updated. As the populations are continually kept sorted on fitness, this change of fitness might move the individual up or down in its population.

```
DO 20 TIMES
    sol:= SELECT(sol-pop)
    constr:= SELECT(constr-pop)
    res:= ENCOUNTER(sol,constr)
    UPDATE-HISTORY-AND-FITNESS(sol,res)
    UPDATE-HISTORY-AND-FITNESS(constr,-res)
  sol1:= SELECT(sol-pop)                    ; parent1
  sol2:= SELECT(sol-pop)                    ; parent2
  child:= MUTATE-CROSSOVER(sol1,sol2)
  f:= FITNESS(child)
INSERT(child,f,sol-pop)
```

After the execution of the 20 encounters one new solution is created using one-at-a-time reproduction (cf. GENITOR): 1) two parent solutions are SELECTed. This selection is - again - biased towards fitter individuals. 2) a new solution is generated from these parents through the application of MUTATION (which replaces a value by a randomly drawn member from the set {1,2, ..., 50}) and CROSSOVER (two-point crossover is used here), 3) the initial FITNESS of this child is calculated by having it to encounter 25 SELECTed constraints. The rewards associated with these encounters are pushed on the history. Again, the fitness of the newly created solution is the sum of these rewards, 4) if this fitness is higher than the minimum fitness in the population then the child is INSERTed into the appropriate rank location in the NN population. At the same time, the individual with the minimum fitness is removed. As mentioned above the members of the constraint population do not change. Hence, no selection and reproduction operates on the constraint population.

Just as in (Hillis 92), the fitness interaction between solutions and constraints keeps both populations in constant flux. As soon as the solutions are becoming successful on a certain set of constraints then these constraints get a lower fitness. As a consequence, other, not yet satisfied constraints, move up in the population and will be selected more often. This forces the solutions to concentrate on these "more difficult" constraints (because of the fitness proportional selection of the individuals involved in an encounter). In our test problem, for example, the diagonal-constraints rapidly move up in the population. This is because they check both diagonals. Hence, for every occupied board location, they constrain 2×49 other locations. The row-constraints, on the other hand, only constrain the 49 board locations in one row.

Let us now look at the benefits gained from the use of LTFE. Its continuous partial nature allows for an early detection of good and bad solutions: the solutions need not evaluate all 100 constraints at once. A few, well chosen, i.e. highly informative, constraint-checks provide sufficient information. This is true during different stages of the genetic search. Initially, all solutions are rather bad. In this case, one does not need extensive testing. A rough indication of their quality is sufficient. Even if - due to an unlucky choice of constraints in its initial encounters - the fitness is rated a bit too low then future encounters will certainly raise this fitness. At later stages - during which more mutation occurs[1] - LTFE is advantageous as well: it immediately weeds out clearly inferior offspring at minimal computational expense. When almost all solutions have a high fitness, e.g. they satisfy more than 80% of the constraints, then clearly inferior solutions can be spotted quite easily. Here too, one does not need to check all constraints. In addition, the biased selection of constraints allows to focus on the most relevant ones. In

---

[1] The probability of mutation is linearly proportional to the "genetic similarity" of the parents. This is known as adaptive mutation [Whitley 1989b].

this way, LTFE and the negative fitness interaction of the co-evolution nicely complement each other.

Obviously the fitness of an individual - based on 25 encounters - is only approximate. The continuous life-time fitness feedback together with the limited history length limits the effect of unrepresentative pay-off. Moreover, the same mechanisms allow the individuals to keep up with the changing individuals or rankings in the other population. This is the role of the 20 encounters executed in the DO-loop in the pseudo-code given above. As the empirical results of the next section show, the combined use of co-evolution and LTFE considerably focuses the genetic search.

4. Empirical Results

In this section we compare CCS with two other genetic approaches. The first one, called TRAD, is a traditional GENITOR-like algorithm. This algorithm uses only a population of solutions. The fitness of a solution is defined as the number of constraints (out of 100) it satisfies. Hence, TRAD uses the traditional once-and-for-all fitness evaluation (instead of LTFE) and no co-evolution. The code of the basic cycle of TRAD is given below (compare this with the code in section 3)

The second one, called CCS-, is identical to CCS except for the population structure of the constraints. In CCS- the constraints do not have any fitness. Hence, the selection of constraints involved in an encounter is not biased towards "difficult" constraints. Or, in other words, the constraints form a set instead of a sorted "population". The main difference between CCS- and TRAD is that the former uses LTFE. CCS-, however, does not use co-evolution. In this way an empirical comparison of these three systems can point out the relative merits of LTFE, co-evolution, and their combination.

All three approaches were run 10 times. Each run used a population size of 250. A run is stopped after the creation of 200000 offspring. In terms of solution quality both, CCS- and TRAD, are poor performers. On the 10 runs, TRAD never found a global solution satisfying all constraints. CCS- found such a solution only once. CCS, on the other hand, was seven out of ten times successful. And this after having created, on average, 125000 offspring which is significantly less than the maximally allowed 200000. In the three other runs CCS found solutions which satisfy 98 out of the 100 constraints. This is also consistently higher than the quality obtained by TRAD and CCS-. Even after the generation of 200000 offspring TRAD and CCS-, on average, only found solutions satisfying 95.7 and 97.2 constraints, respectively. For CCS this average is 99.4. This comparison between TRAD, CCS-, and CCS gives a good indication of the contribution of the successive introduction of LTFE and co-evolution.

5. Conclusions and Discussion

To our knowledge, CCS is the first system using co-evolution for solving constraint satisfaction problems. Earlier work (Paredis 94a) showed that the integrated use of LTFE and co-evolution clearly boosts the performance of genetic neural net search. Here, we have illustrated the power of the combination of these same techniques in the completely different field of constraint satisfaction. The empirical results presented in both papers confirm the potential of the approach. The observed performance increase can be attributed to two factors. Primo, the partial nature of life-time fitness evaluation allows for early detection of particularly good or bad solutions. Secundo, co-evolution concentrates its effort on the constraints which are most relevant at a given moment of the search. Furthermore, the combination of LTFE and co-evolution has a clearly beneficial effect. The partial and continuous nature of LTFE - which only takes into account the most recent encounters - is well suited when dealing with coupled fitness landscapes. Here the fitnesses of solutions and constraints are coupled because changes in one population (through a different ranking or through the introduction of new individuals) clearly affect the fitness of the members of the other population. For this reason only the pay-off resulting from the most recent encounters provides an up-to-date approximation of the fitness of an individual. Moreover the use of LTFE makes the steady-state evolutionary algorithm more robust and adaptive. This is a consequence of the relation between LTFE, noise and steady-state reproduction as discussed in more detail in (Paredis 94a).

CCS also provides an interesting approach towards some well-known research issues of EAs. The first one relates to the notion of building blocks. Holland showed that for problems with a low degree of epistasis, operators that splice together parts of two different individuals might yield good solutions. For such problems, sets of functionally dependent genes are relatively small. In that case, it becomes possible to use a string representation in which the "correlated" genes are placed near to each other. Once the EA finds good values for these genes, they are unlikely to be split apart during sexual reproduction. Analogously, independent genes should be located far apart from each other on the string. Otherwise there will be too little exploration: suboptimal values for these genes are unlikely to get disrupted. This last case typically results in premature convergence. In general, a linear string might not be sufficient to place interacting bits near to each other, and to place non-interacting bits far apart. This is particularly the case when addressing problems with a high degree of epistasis, such as tightly constrained CSPs.

In CCS each constraint checks the consistency between a number of "genes" (here constraint variables). Good values for such a set of correlated genes should then be combined in order to obtain a global solution. As is the case in other approaches, crossover tends to disrupt genes which are located far apart from each other. But on the other hand, the constraints checking such "difficult genes" will rapidly become fit. In this way, more search effort will be devoted to these genes. This is particularly relevant for problems consisting of too many dependencies to be packed on a linear string. The n-queens problem used here is an example of this: each variable is related to each other variable. The uniformity of the constraints does not allow to say which variables are most tightly coupled. As a matter of fact, the degree of interaction between two variables is not constant over the search space. It strongly depends on the assignment of the other variables. LTFE together with co-evolution enables CCS to concentrate on the relevant difficult (sets of) genes.

A second important issue is the relation between CCS and approaches using penalty functions. As discussed in the introduction of this paper, the success of these approaches critically depends on the choice of a good penalty function. In CCS, on the other hand, the co-evolution gives rise to an "auto-adjusting" penalty function. This is because the fitness evaluation is a kind of a penalty function, i.e. it counts the number of constraint violations. The changing ranking of the constraints and the biased selection of constraints on which the solutions are tested, allows CCS to focus on the more difficult - not yet satisfied - constraints. Or, in other words, the penalty function becomes more and more harsh as better solutions are found. Informally, one could say that the penalty function co-evolves in step with the quality of the solution population. Various researchers already observed that gradually adding constraints during the evolutionary search improves the results obtained. CCS automatically performs such a gradual tightening of the problem.

The research reported here can be extended in multiple directions. A first extension is to tackle constrained optimization problems. In these problems one has to find a valid solution to a CSP which at the same time maximizes a given objective function. Constraint relaxation is another interesting line of future research. The goal is then to delete constraints from an over-constrained problem such that the problem is no longer over-constrained, i.e. a valid solution exists. Two observations of CCS's mode of operation are relevant here. Primo, the ranking of the constraints during the search reflects the difficulty of a constraint. This information may be used to determine which constraints to delete or relax. Secundo, each individual in the solution population is a valid solution with respect to some less constrained version of the problem to be solved.

Further research will concentrate on the application of the method proposed here to other tasks. Here we addressed constraint satisfaction problems. Paredis (94a) applies LTFE and co-evolution on a classification task using neural nets. Path finding is another application area currently under investigation. Undoubtedly, many other tasks are still waiting for exploration.

In addition to the application to other tasks the current framework can be extended in yet another way. All examples discussed above have used predator-prey relations to improve the power of artificial search. Obviously, many other mechanisms - not necessarily based on inverse fitness interaction - exist in nature. Symbiosis is such an important and widely occurring counter example. It consists of a positive fitness feedback in which a success on one side improves the chances of survival of the other. As far as we know, the use of symbiosis to enhance the power of evolutionary search is as yet unexplored. Paredis (94b) describes a first investigation into the symbiotic evolution of solutions and their genetic representation (i.e. the ordering of the genes). A representation adapted to the solutions currently in the population speeds up the search for even better solutions which in their turn might progress optimally when yet another representation is used.

Finally, we hope that this paper may prove instrumental in further stimulating research in the computational use of co-evolution and its combination with LTFE.

Acknowledgements

The author is indebted to Desiree Baaten for proofreading this paper.

References

Davis, L., (1988), *Applying Adaptive Algorithms to Epistatic Domains*, Proc. IJCAI-88.

Hillis, W.D., (1992), *Co-evolving Parasites Improve Simulated Evolution as an Optimization Procedure*, in Artificial Life II, Langton, C.G.; Taylor, C.; Farmer, J.D., and Rasmussen, S., (eds), Addison-Wesley, California.

Mühlenbein, H., (1992), *Parallel Genetic Algorithms in Combinatorial Optimization*, Proc. Computer Science and Operations Research: New Developments in Their Interfaces, ORSA, Pergamon Press.

Paredis, J., (1993), *Genetic State-Space Search for Constrained Optimization Problems*, Proc. Thirteenth International Joint Conference on Artificial Intelligence (IJCAI 93), Morgan Kaufmann Publishers.

Paredis, J., (1994a), *Steps towards Co-evolutionary Classification Neural Networks*, Proc. Artificial Life IV, R. Brooks, P. Maes (eds), MIT Press / Bradford Books.

Paredis, J., (1994b), *The Symbiotic Evolution of Solutions and their Representation*, (in preparation).

Richardson, J.T. ; Palmer, M.R. ; Liepins, G.; Hilliard M., (1989), *Some Guidelines for Genetic Algorithms with Penalty Functions*. Proc. Third Int. Conf. on Genetic Algorithms, Morgan Kaufmann.

Whitley, D., (1989a), *The Genitor Algorithm and Selection Pressure: Why Rank-Based Allocation of Reproductive Trails is Best*. Proc. Third Int. Conf. on Genetic Algorithms, Morgan Kaufmann.

Whitley, D., (1989b), *Optimizing Neural Networks using Faster, more Accurate Genetic Search*. Proc. Third Int. Conf. on Genetic Algorithms, Morgan Kaufmann.

Theoretical Aspects of
Evolutionary Computation

Towards a Theory of 'Evolution Strategies': Results for $(1 \dagger \lambda)$-Strategies on (Nearly) Arbitrary Fitness Functions*

Hans-Georg Beyer**

University of Dortmund, Department of Computer Science, Chair of Systems Analysis, D-44221 Dortmund, Germany

Abstract. Recent findings in the local $(1 \dagger \lambda)$ ES-theory for (nearly) arbitrary continuous fitness functions are presented and compared to ES-experiments. Two approaches will be considered: The probability theory approach and an extension of the spherical model theory by Riemannian geometry.

1 Introduction and Notations

The theoretical understanding of the ES performance in an N-dimensional continuous parameter space $\mathbb{R}^N$ ($N \geq 30$) is strongly connected to the description of the local behavior of the $(1 \dagger \lambda)$ ES. This behavior depends on the local structure of the *fitness landscape*. It is assumed that the fitness function $F(\mathbf{y})$, $\mathbf{y}^T := (y_1, y_2, \ldots y_N)$, to be maximized can be locally approximated by the *local quality function* $Q(\mathbf{x})$, $\mathbf{x}^T := (x_1, x_2, \ldots x_N)$. I. e. the transition from the parental state $\mathbf{y}^{(t)}$ at time (t) to $(t+1)$ by the mutation $\mathbf{x}$

$$\mathbf{y}^{(t+1)} := \mathbf{y}^{(t)} + \mathbf{x} \tag{1}$$

induces a fitness change

$$F(\mathbf{y}^{(t+1)}) - F(\mathbf{y}^{(t)}) = F(\mathbf{y}^{(t)} + \mathbf{x}) - F(\mathbf{y}^{(t)}) =: Q^{(t)}(\mathbf{x}) \tag{2}$$

expressed by the local quality function $Q(\mathbf{x}) := Q^{(t)}(\mathbf{x})$. The mutations $\mathbf{x}$ are assumed to be normally distributed with standard deviation σ and zero mean, the density reads

$$p(\mathbf{x}) = \left(\frac{1}{\sqrt{2\pi}\,\sigma}\right)^N \exp\left(-\frac{1}{2\sigma^2}\sum_{i=1}^{N} x_i^2\right) \tag{3}$$

---
* This work was funded by DFG grant Be 1578/1-1
** e-mail: beyer@LS11.informatik.uni-dortmund.de

1.1 The Quality Gain and the Progress Rate

The performance of the ES can be described by the quality gain and the progress rate, respectively. The *quality gain* $\langle Q \rangle$ is defined as the expectation of the fitness change induced by the mutation $\mathbf{x}$

$$\langle Q \rangle_{(1\dagger\lambda)} := E\{Q\} = \int p_{(1\dagger\lambda)}(\mathbf{x}) Q(\mathbf{x}) \, d\mathbf{x} = \int p_{(1\dagger\lambda)}(Q) \, Q \, dQ, \qquad (4)$$

i. e., $\langle Q \rangle$ is the generational change of the fitness. Local evolutionary learning aims at maximizing $\langle Q \rangle$ by tuning the mutation width σ (cf. section 3.1).

Another way of describing the ES performance is given by the *progress rate* φ. Assuming the optimum of $F(\mathbf{y})$ at $\mathbf{y} = \hat{\mathbf{y}}$, then φ is the expectation of the distance change from generation (t) to $(t+1)$

$$\varphi := E\left\{ \|\hat{\mathbf{y}} - \mathbf{y}^{(t)}\| - \|\hat{\mathbf{y}} - \mathbf{y}^{(t+1)}\| \right\}. \qquad (5)$$

This is a quite different view of ES performance expressing the global approach to the optimum point $\hat{\mathbf{y}}$. From the theoretical point of view this definition should be the preferred ES performance measure. Unfortunately, the determination of φ is difficult and tractable for simple fitness functions only [Bey93]. From a practical point of view it should be mentioned that both performance measures can lead to different - sometimes contradictory - σ-control policies, indicating the limits of local learning rules (cf. section 3.1).

1.2 Model Quality Functions

The tractability of the progress rate concept strongly depends on the use of simple model functions. Up until now, only the so-called *corridor model* [Rec73], [Sch81], the *sphere* [Rec73], [Sch81], [Bey93], and the *discus* [Bey89] have been treated successfully. Some progress extending the spherical model to an elliptical was reported (without proof) by RECHENBERG [Rec89]. Recently [Rec93] he postulates this *elliptical* model to be the 'general quality function' expressing the so-called 'strong causality' of the optimization problem necessary for the working of the ES. The argumentation mainly stems from the TAYLOR expansion of (2) neglecting higher order terms:

$$Q(\mathbf{x}) = \sum_i \frac{\partial F}{\partial y_i} x_i + \frac{1}{2} \sum_{i,j} \frac{\partial^2 F}{\partial y_i \partial y_j} x_i x_j + \cdots \qquad (6)$$

After transformation to the principal axes his general Q reads [Rec93]

$$Q(\mathbf{y}) = \sum_{K=1}^{N} c_k y_k - \sum_{K=1}^{N} d_k y_k^2, \qquad d_k \geq 0. \qquad (7)$$

Eq. (7) suggests that each fitness function $F(\mathbf{y})$ could be approximated locally by a negative definite quadratic form. However, this does not hold, e. g. for a saddle point and its vicinity. Therefore the author proposes the quadratic quality function

$$Q(\mathbf{x}) = \sum_i a_i x_i - \sum_{i,j} b_{ij} x_i x_j = \mathbf{a}^T \mathbf{x} - \mathbf{x}^T \mathbf{B} \mathbf{x}, \qquad b_{ij} = b_{ji}. \tag{8}$$

In the case of vanishing second order derivatives $\frac{\partial^2 F}{\partial y_i \partial y_j} = 0$ it even will be necessary to use higher order model functions, e. g.

$$Q(\mathbf{x}) = \sum_i a_i x_i - \sum_i c_i x_i^4. \tag{9}$$

The theory to be presented here is a quality gain theory and applicable to a wide range of Q-functions. An attempt extending the results to the progress rate will be discussed in section 3.

2 Results from the Quality Gain Theory

2.1 The $(1, \lambda)$-Theory

The Quality Gain The success of the quality gain theory approach arises from the second integral in (4). The problem reduces to a one-dimensional one: The mutation density $p(\mathbf{x})$ (3) is transformed by the quality function $Q(\mathbf{x})$ to the density $p(Q)$ from which the density of the best offspring $p_{(1+\lambda)}(Q)$ can be determined easily. The quality gain for the $(1, \lambda)$ ES reads

$$\langle Q \rangle_{(1,\lambda)} = \int_{-\infty}^{Q(\hat{\mathbf{y}})} Q \, \lambda p(Q) [P(Q)]^{\lambda-1} \, dQ, \qquad P(Q) = \int_{-\infty}^{Q} p(Q') \, dQ'. \tag{10}$$

In general, there exist no closed expressions for $p(Q)$ and $P(Q)$. The basic idea for a suitable approximation of $p(Q)$ is given by standardization $z := (Q - m)/s$, with $m := \langle Q \rangle$ and $s := \sqrt{\langle Q^2 \rangle - \langle Q \rangle^2}$ (standard deviation of Q), and expanding $p(z)$ in a series of Hermite polynomials He_k. Thus, the distribution function $P(z) = P(\frac{Q-m}{s})$ can be expressed by the series

$$P(z) = \frac{1}{2} + \Phi_0(z) - \frac{e^{-\frac{1}{2}z^2}}{\sqrt{2\pi}} \left[\frac{\kappa_3}{3!} He_2(z) + \left(\frac{\kappa_4}{4!} He_3(z) + \frac{\kappa_3^2}{72} He_5(z) \right) + \cdots \right], \tag{11}$$

with the Gauß-integral $\Phi_0(z)$ and the He_k-polynomials

$$\Phi_0(z) := \frac{1}{\sqrt{2\pi}} \int_0^z e^{-\frac{1}{2}t^2} \, dt \quad , \quad He_k(z) := (-1)^k e^{\frac{1}{2}z^2} \frac{d^k}{dz^k} \left(e^{-\frac{1}{2}z^2} \right). \tag{12}$$

The κ_k-coefficients are the so-called cumulants $\kappa_k\{z\}$ of the variate $(Q - m)/s$. Using this approach one will get for the quality gain

$$\langle Q \rangle_{(1,\lambda)} = m + s \, c_{1,\lambda} \left(1 + \frac{4\kappa_3^2 - 3\kappa_4}{24} \right)$$

$$- s \left[(d_{1,\lambda}^{(2)} - 1) \frac{\kappa_3}{36} (\kappa_3 - 6) + d_{1,\lambda}^{(3)} \frac{4\kappa_3^2 - 3\kappa_4}{72} + \cdots \right]. \tag{13}$$

$c_{1,\lambda}$ is the well known progress coefficient [Bey93]: $c_{1,\lambda} \equiv d_{1,\lambda}^{(1)}$, a special case of the higher order progress coefficients $d_{1,\lambda}^{(k)}$

$$d_{1,\lambda}^{(k)} := \frac{\lambda}{\sqrt{2\pi}} \int_{-\infty}^{\infty} z^k e^{-\frac{1}{2}t^2} \left[\frac{1}{2} + \Phi_0(z) \right]^{\lambda-1} dz. \tag{14}$$

The coefficients m, s, and κ_k depend on the quality function $Q(\mathbf{x})$. For the general quadratic case one finds from (3) and (8)

$$m = -\sigma^2 Tr\{\mathbf{B}\}, \qquad s = \sigma\sqrt{\mathbf{a}^T\mathbf{a} + 2\sigma^2 Tr\{\mathbf{B}^2\}}, \tag{15}$$

$$\kappa_3 = -\frac{\sigma^4}{s^3}\left(6\mathbf{a}^T\mathbf{B}\mathbf{a} + 8\sigma^2 Tr\{\mathbf{B}^3\}\right), \quad \kappa_4 = 48\frac{\sigma^6}{s^4}\left(\mathbf{a}^T\mathbf{B}^2\mathbf{a} + \sigma^2 Tr\{\mathbf{B}^4\}\right) \tag{16}$$

(NB.: $Tr\{\mathbf{B}\}$ is the trace of $\mathbf{B}$: $Tr\{\mathbf{B}\} := \sum_i b_{ii}$) and for the biquadratic (9)

$$m = -3\sigma^4 \sum_{i=1}^{N} c_i, \qquad s = \sigma\sqrt{\sum_{i=1}^{N} a_i^2 + 96\sigma^6 \sum_{i=1}^{N} c_i^2},$$

$$\kappa_3 = -36\frac{\sigma^6}{s^3}\left(\sum_i a_i^2 c_i + 264\sigma^6 \sum_i c_i^3\right). \tag{17}$$

Normalization and Comparison with Experiments In order to compare the theory with experimental results it is worth normalizing the quality gain and the mutation width σ. For the quadratic case (8) the normalized quantities σ^* and $\langle Q \rangle_{(1\dagger\lambda)}^*$ are defined by

$$\sigma^* = \sigma\,2\sqrt{N}\,\sqrt{\frac{Tr\{\mathbf{B}^2\}}{\mathbf{a}^T\mathbf{a}}} \quad \text{and} \quad \langle Q \rangle_{(1\dagger\lambda)}^* = \langle Q \rangle_{(1\dagger\lambda)}\,2\sqrt{N}\,\frac{\sqrt{Tr\{\mathbf{B}^2\}}}{\mathbf{a}^T\mathbf{a}}, \tag{18}$$

and for the biquadratic case (9) the normalization is

$$\sigma^* = \sigma\,2\sqrt[6]{N}\,\sqrt[6]{\frac{\sum_i c_i^2}{\sum_i a_i^2}} \quad \text{and} \quad \langle Q \rangle_{(1\dagger\lambda)}^* = \langle Q \rangle_{(1\dagger\lambda)}\,2\sqrt[6]{N}\,\frac{(\sum_i c_i^2)^{\frac{1}{6}}}{(\sum_i a_i^2)^{\frac{2}{3}}}. \tag{19}$$

Two examples using a $(1,5)$ ES will be discussed. The experimental settings for the quadratic case are:

$$N = 100, \quad b_{ii} = i, \quad b_{ij} = 0 \;\; \forall i \neq j, \quad a_i = 1, \quad (i,j = 1\ldots N), \tag{20}$$

and for the biquadratic case

$$N = 100, \quad c_i = 1, \quad a_i = 1, \quad (i = 1\ldots N). \tag{21}$$

For each σ^*-value 40,000 trials have been performed/averaged, depicted in Fig. 1.

One observes an excellent agreement between experiment and theory. From the series (13) only the third order approximation has been used, i. e.,

$$\langle Q \rangle_{(1,\lambda)} = m + s\,c_{1,\lambda} + s\,(d_{1,\lambda}^{(2)} - 1)\frac{\kappa_3}{6}, \quad c_{1,5} = 1.163, \quad d_{1,5}^{(2)} = 1.8. \tag{22}$$

It should be mentioned that the RECHENBERG-theory to be investigated in the next subsection yields comparable results for the quadratic case.

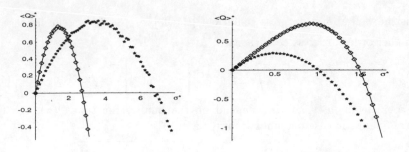

Fig. 1.: The $(1,5)$ ES. Left picture: the quadratic example. Right picture: the bi-quadratic example. The $\diamond$-points depict the averaged quality gain whereas the $\star$-points represent the corresponding (normalized) progress rate to be discussed in section 3.1. The solid curve is the graph of the quality gain theory.

Limits of Rechenberg's Approach In [Rec93] a progress rate theory is proposed which is mainly based on the quality function (7) and a quality gain formula derived by plausibility arguments

$$\langle Q \rangle_{(1,\lambda)} = \sigma\, c_{1,\lambda} \sqrt{\sum_i a_i^2} - \sigma^2 \sum_i d_i. \tag{23}$$

It can be shown, under certain limiting conditions, that (23) can be derived from (22). If these conditions are violated the Rechenberg formula fails. This violation can easily be simulated by an experiment:

$$N = 100,\; d_1 = 200,\; d_i = 1\,(i = 2\ldots N),\; a_i = 1\,(i = 1\ldots N). \tag{24}$$

Fig. 2 displays the results. As can be seen the third order approximation (22) yields better results than (23). Note, for large σ^*-values (22) deviates from the experiment. Using higher order terms (e. g. (13)) will decrease this deviation.

2.2 The $(1 + \lambda)$ Theory

Quality Gain and Success Probability The method used for the $(1, \lambda)$ theory can be applied to the $(1 + \lambda)$ ES as well. The only difference will be the lower limit in the Q-integral (10). Because in (+) strategies parents can survive, a successful mutation has to obey the condition $Q > 0$, thus the lower limit becomes zero

$$\langle Q \rangle_{(1+\lambda)} = \int_0^{Q(\hat{\mathbf{y}})} Q\, \lambda p(Q)[P(Q)]^{\lambda-1}\, dQ, \qquad P(Q) = \int_{-\infty}^Q p(Q')\, dQ'. \tag{25}$$

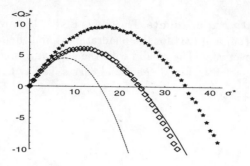

Fig. 2.: Limits of Rechenberg's quality gain formula for a $(1,5)$ ES: $\diamond$ - quality gain experiment, $\star$ - corresponding progress rate, dashed line - Rechenberg theory, solid line - third order approximation.

After some tricky calculations one gets

$$
\begin{aligned}
\langle Q \rangle_{1+\lambda} = & \left[m + s \frac{\kappa_3}{36}(\kappa_3 - 6) + \cdots \right] P_{s\lambda} \\
& + s \left(1 + \frac{4\kappa_3^2 - 3\kappa_4}{24} + \cdots \right) d_{1+\lambda}^{(1)} \left(\Phi_0^{-1} \left(P_0 - \frac{1}{2} \right) \right) \\
& - s \left(\frac{\kappa_3}{36}(\kappa_3 - 6) + \cdots \right) d_{1+\lambda}^{(2)} \left(\Phi_0^{-1} \left(P_0 - \frac{1}{2} \right) \right) \\
& - s \left(\frac{4\kappa_3^2 - 3\kappa_4}{72} + \cdots \right) d_{1+\lambda}^{(3)} \left(\Phi_0^{-1} \left(P_0 - \frac{1}{2} \right) \right) - \cdots ,
\end{aligned} \tag{26}
$$

$$
P_0 = \frac{1}{2} - \Phi_0(\frac{m}{s}) - \frac{e^{-\frac{1}{2}(\frac{m}{s})^2}}{\sqrt{2\pi}} \left[\frac{\kappa_3}{3!} He_2(\frac{m}{s}) + \left(\frac{\kappa_4}{4!} He_3(\frac{m}{s}) + \frac{\kappa_3^2}{72} He_5(\frac{m}{s}) \right) + \cdots \right]. \tag{27}
$$

The $d_{1+\lambda}^{(k)}(x)$ are the so-called progress functions introduced by the author [Bey93]

$$
d_{1+\lambda}^{(k)}(x) := \frac{\lambda}{\sqrt{2\pi}} \int_x^\infty z^k e^{-\frac{1}{2}t^2} \left[\frac{1}{2} + \Phi_0(z) \right]^{\lambda-1} dz. \tag{28}
$$

$\Phi_0^{-1}(x)$ is the inverse function to the Gauß-integral (12). The probability $P_{s\lambda}$ is the so-called success probability expressing the survival of the best offspring [3]

$$
P_{s\lambda} = 1 - [P_0]^\lambda. \tag{29}
$$

---

[3] sometimes known as parental death probability [Bey93]

Comparison with Experiments The $(1+1)$ ES has been tested by the experimental settings (20) and (21) for the quadratic (8) and the biquadratic quality function (9), respectively. The results with the normalization (18) and (19), respectively, are depicted in Fig. 3. The solid curves display the quality gain (26)

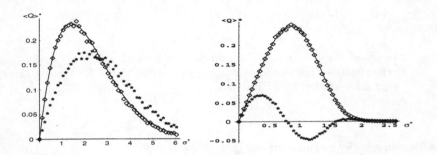

Fig. 3.: The $(1 + 1)$ ES. Left picture: the quadratic example. Right picture: the biquadratic example. The $\diamond$-points depict the averaged quality gain whereas the $\star$-points represent the corresponding (normalized) progress rate to be discussed in section 3.1. The solid curve is the graph of the quality gain theory.

using terms up to the third order (neglecting κ_3^2 and κ_4 in (26, 27)) and the progress functions

$$d_{1+1}^{(1)}(x) = \frac{e^{-\frac{1}{2}x^2}}{\sqrt{2\pi}} \qquad \text{and} \qquad d_{1+1}^{(2)}(x) = \frac{1}{2} - \Phi_0(x) + x\frac{e^{-\frac{1}{2}x^2}}{\sqrt{2\pi}}. \qquad (30)$$

As can be seen, one observes a good agreement between theory and experiment.

3 The Progress Rate

3.1 Rechenberg's Definition

Probably, because of the difficulties arising from the 'hard' definition (5), Rechenberg [Rec93] prefers a locally defined progress rate that measures the distance from the hypersurface $Q(\mathbf{x}) = 0$ at $\mathbf{x} = \mathbf{0}$ to the hypersurface $Q(\mathbf{x}) = \langle Q \rangle_{(1\dagger\lambda)}$ in gradient direction $\nabla Q(\mathbf{x})|_{\mathbf{x}=\mathbf{0}}$. We will call this the Rechenberg *normal progress* φ_R (because the gradient direction of $Q(\mathbf{x})$ is normal to the hypersurface $Q(\mathbf{x}) = 0$). Taylor expansion delivers

$$\langle Q \rangle_{(1\dagger\lambda)} \approx \nabla Q(\mathbf{x})|_{\mathbf{x}=\mathbf{0}} \, \delta\mathbf{x}_n =: \nabla Q(\mathbf{x}) \left(\frac{\nabla Q(\mathbf{x})}{\|\nabla Q(\mathbf{x})\|} \varphi_R \right) \quad \Rightarrow \quad \varphi_R := \frac{\langle Q \rangle_{(1\dagger\lambda)}}{\|\nabla Q(\mathbf{x})\|}. \qquad (31)$$

Using (23) one gets for the normal progress in the case of $(1, \lambda)$ strategies

$$\varphi_R = c_{1,\lambda}\sigma - \sigma^2 \frac{\sum_i d_i}{\sqrt{\sum_i a_i^2}}. \tag{32}$$

Due to this simple definition one should not expect a 'higher information' content than given by the quality gain $\langle Q \rangle_{(1\dagger\lambda)}$. Only for nearly symmetric success domains the φ_R concept delivers results comparable with the 'hard' progress definition (5).

One can interpret (31) as a special normalization of $\langle Q \rangle$, and indeed, the normalizations (18) and (19) include this factor (actually $\varphi_R^\star = \langle Q \rangle_{(1\dagger\lambda)}^\star$ holds). Thus, it is possible to compare the hard definition (5) with φ_R. Figs.1 to 3 contain the experimental progress rates (normalized like $\sigma^\star$ and displayed by "$\star$"). In all cases one observes large differences between the $\varphi_R \propto \langle Q \rangle$ definition and the hard definition (5).

The observed differences are also interesting for the ES practice. Evolutionary progress by simple $(\mu \dagger \lambda)$-strategies is achieved by selection of the best offspring. Self-adaptation [Sch81] of the mutation width σ by inheriting the σ-values of the best offspring necessarily relies on the quality gain.[4] This is a local learning behavior. Switching to the hard progress definition shows, however, that the optimum σ for a maximum quality gain and for the optimum progress rate can be quite different. Thus, it can be possible (but only locally) that a high quality gain corresponds to a negative progress rate (cf. the right pictures in Figs. 1 and 3)! A practicable solution to this dilemma may be *meta ES*, i. e. selection of strategy parameters on the population level with isolation periods [5] [Her92].

3.2 A Differential Geometry Approach

In a certain sense the normal progress φ_R (32) lies in the 'realm' of the simple spherical model. As conjectured by the author ([Bey92], p. 10) the applicability of the spherical model should be extendible to non-spherical success domains, if it is possible to approximate the local behavior of the quality hypersurface $Q(\mathbf{x}) = 0$ by a hypersphere.

From the viewpoint of Riemannian geometry $Q(\mathbf{x}) = 0$ is an $(N - 1)$-dimensional hypersurface ∂Q immersed in the flat $\mathbb{R}^N$. The local properties of ∂Q are given by the covariant metric tensor $g_{\alpha\beta}$, $(\alpha, \beta = 1 \ldots N - 1)$. If there is a representation of ∂Q by a set of (contravariant) coordinates $u^1, \ldots u^{N-1}$, i. e., $\partial Q : Q(\mathbf{x}) = 0 \Rightarrow \mathbf{x} = \mathbf{x}(u^1, \ldots u^{N-1})$, then the fundamental tensor reads (see e. g. [Kre68])

$$g_{\alpha\beta} = \mathbf{x}_{u^\alpha}^T \mathbf{x}_{u^\beta}, \qquad \mathbf{x}_{u^\alpha} := \frac{\partial}{\partial u^\alpha} \mathbf{x}. \tag{33}$$

---

[4] This kind of self-adaptation working on the individual's level should be called *implicit adaptation* (of the strategy parameters, e. g. σ) on the same level.

[5] In contrast to the self-adaptation (implicit adaptation) the meta ES performs an *explicit adaptation* (of the strategy parameters) on the lower level.

The curvature of a (one-dimensional) curve on ∂Q is closely connected to the so-called second fundamental form established by the $b_{\alpha\beta}$-tensor

$$b_{\alpha\beta} = \mathbf{n}^T \mathbf{x}_{u^\alpha u^\beta} \tag{34}$$

with the normal vector $\mathbf{n} := \nabla Q / \|\nabla Q\|$. The eigenvalues of $b_{\alpha\beta}$ are known as the principal curvatures κ_p (not to be mixed with the cumulants from section 2). Due to the tensor calculus the sum M of κ_p is a scalar invariant, called *mean curvature*, to be obtained by contraction of $b_{\alpha\beta}$: $M := b_{\alpha\beta} g^{\alpha\beta}$ (EINSTEIN's summation convention used). Therefore, the reciprocal value of $M/(N-1)$ may be called *mean radius* $\overline{R}$ of ∂Q. For the Rechenberg model (7) one obtains

$$\overline{R} = \frac{N-1}{b_{\alpha\beta} g^{\alpha\beta}} = \frac{N-1}{2} \frac{(\sum_{i=1}^N a_i^2)^{3/2}}{\sum_{i=1}^N d_i \left[\sum_{j=1}^N a_j^2 - a_i^2 \right]} \tag{35}$$

The introduction of $\overline{R}$ into the spherical model [Bey93] by substitution

$$\sigma = \sigma^\star \overline{R}/N \qquad \text{and} \qquad \varphi = \varphi^\star \overline{R}/N \tag{36}$$

(assuming $N/(N-1) \to 1$) yields for the $(1, \lambda)$ ES

$$\varphi = c_{1,\lambda} \sigma - \frac{\sigma^2}{2} b_{\alpha\beta} g^{\alpha\beta}. \tag{37}$$

With the assumption $\sum a_j^2 \gg a_i^2$, $\forall i = 1 \ldots N$, one can recover the Rechenberg formula (32) from (35 – 37). In this case the 'quadratic complexity' $\Omega = \sum_k d_k / \sqrt{\sum_i a_i^2}$ [Rec89] is nothing but half the mean curvature of ∂Q at $\mathbf{x} = 0$.

The $\overline{R}$-approach can also be used for (+)-strategies. If applied to 'moderate' problems it yields results with good agreement to the probability theory approach (26/27). E. g., the $(1 + 1)$ ES with quadratic quality and parameter setting (20) shows an excellent agreement between theory and experiment

$$\langle Q \rangle^\star_{(1+1)} = \varphi^\star_{(1+1)} = \frac{\sigma^\star}{\sqrt{2\pi}} e^{-\frac{1}{8}(\sigma^\star)^2} - \frac{(\sigma^\star)^2}{2} \left[\frac{1}{2} - \Phi_0 \left(\frac{\sigma^\star}{2} \right) \right] \tag{38}$$

(taking (31, 35, 36) into account, and cp. [Bey93]), as can be seen from Fig. 4.

The advantage of the approach is twofold: first, simpler expressions for the quality gain, and secondly, extendibility of results gathered from the relatively well developed ES theory of the spherical model. The second point is a strong argument for focusing investigations concerning recombinative $(\mu \dagger \lambda)$ ES first to the spherical model.

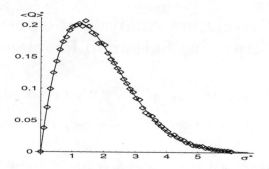

Fig. 4.: $(1 + 1)$ ES experiment and differential geometric $\overline{R}$ theory. The normalized quality gain (equal to the normalized normal progress $\varphi_R^\star$) is displayed versus the normalized mutation strength.

References

[Bey89] H.-G. Beyer. *Ein Evolutionsverfahren zur mathematischen Modellierung sta-tionärer Zustände in dynamischen Systemen.* Dissertation, Hochschule für Architektur und Bauwesen, Weimar, Germany, 1989. Reihe: HAB-Dissertationen, Nr. 16.

[Bey92] H.-G. Beyer. Towards a Theory of 'Evolution Strategies'. Some Asymptotical Results from the $(1, +\lambda)$-Theory. Technical Report SYS-5/92, Department of Computer Science, University of Dortmund, 1992.

[Bey93] H.-G. Beyer. Toward a theory of evolution strategies: Some asymptotical results from the $(1, +\lambda)$-theory. *Evolutionary Computation,* 1(2):165–188, 1993.

[Her92] M. Herdy. Reproductive isolation as strategy parameter in hierarchically organized evolution strategies. In R. Männer and B. Manderick, editors, *Parallel Problem Solving from Nature, 2,* pages 207–217. Elsevier, Amsterdam, 1992.

[Kre68] E. Kreyszig. *Differentialgeometrie.* AVG Geest & Portig K.-G., Leipzig, 1968.

[Rec73] I. Rechenberg. *Evolutionsstrategie: Optimierung technischer Systeme nach Prinzipien der biologischen Evolution.* Frommann–Holzboog Verlag, Stuttgart, 1973.

[Rec89] I. Rechenberg. Artificial evolution and artificial intelligence. In R. Forsyth, editor, *Machine Learning: Principles and Techniques,* pages 83–103. Chapman and Hall, London, 1989.

[Rec93] I. Rechenberg. Evolutionsstrategie '93. manuscript of a forthcoming book, 1993.

[Sch81] H.-P. Schwefel. *Numerical Optimization of Computer Models.* Wiley, Chichester, 1981.

Advanced Correlation Analysis of Operators for the Traveling Salesman Problem

John Dzubera and Darrell Whitley

Computer Science Department, Colorado State University, Fort Collins, CO 80523

Abstract. An extension to the correlation analysis of Manderick et al. and Mathias and Whitley used to study TSP operators is introduced. Part correlation and partial correlation further refine the relationship between an operator's preservation of genetic information and its overall fitness. The fitness landscapes of ten genetic operators are studied in isolation and in conjunction with the *2-opt* local improvement technique in a GENITOR environment. Five variables (parent fitness, child fitness, child failure rate, insertion rate and increased tour length due to failure) are considered in the analyses. Results suggest that certain operators (Edge Family, MPX and Schleuter crossover (SCHX)) maintain higher correlations over several *interesting* variable relations, especially the parent to child (PC) relation, than do other genetic operators.

1 Introduction

With their introduction of correlation analysis, Manderick et al. [3] have provided a useful metric for determining the fitness of a genetic operator. Borrowing from statistics theory, Manderick proposed the *correlation coefficient, ρ_{op}*, as a method of analyzing the correlation between parent and child strings.

$$\rho_{op}(P, C) = \frac{Cov(P, C)}{\sigma(P)\sigma(C)}$$

where *op* is the genetic operator, P and C are variables that represent the fitnesses of the parent and child respectively, $Cov(P, C)$ is the covariance between P and C and σ represents the standard deviation. With respect to most non-flat landscapes, a larger value of ρ_{op} implies a greater preservation of genetic material between parents and offspring as well as an increased ability to exploit the fitness landscape [4]. The goal of this research is to extend this work by introducing the concepts of *part correlation* and *partial correlation* as more accurate metrics for genetic operator analysis. Unlike traditional correlation methods which determine the simple relationship between two variables, part and partial correlation consider the degree of association between two variables *while the effects of other variables are held constant*. This "parting out" or "partialling out" of possible extraneous influences allows the true relationship of the variables to be ascertained. Although computationally explosive as the number of variables is increased, part and partial correlation supply the means by which mathematically stronger statements about these relationships may be made. To facilitate this analysis, ten genetic operators were examined in isolation and in conjunction with the *2-opt* local improvement operator on the Padberg 532 city TSP. In addition to the primary research, two other issues considered were *statistical inference* and *statistical significance*. Manderick [3] neglects to address whether his results, which are based on sample data, are applicable to the entire population. Although his conclusions may be correct primarily due to adequate sample size [5], significance tests add additional rigor to findings based on sample data. All differences presented in this work have been tested and found to be statistically significant at a .05 level.

2   Fundamental Concepts

Genetic algorithms, in their purest form, may be thought of as *blind* search methods. That is, they do not exploit any local information to construct solutions. Several researchers [4] [8] have recently explored combinations of genetic algorithms and local improvement techniques (*hybridized genetic algorithms.*) In the work reported here, the *2-Opt* algorithm was utilized as the local search operator. Given a TSP tour, 2-Opt chooses two edges to remove from the string. One of the two segments is then reversed. If the fitness of the modified tour is "better" than the original, the change is kept; otherwise it is discarded. 2-Opt continues in this manner for all $\frac{(n)(n-1)}{2}$ edge pairings. To limit the expense of 2-Opt, a *single-pass* of 2-Opt was used. Since more improvement occurs during the first pass than subsequent passes [4], *one-pass 2-Opt* provided a suitable balance between performance and expense.

With respect to partial correlation analysis, several variables were studied in both hybridized and non-hybridized environments. In addition to parent fitness (P) and child fitness (C), *insertion rate* (R), *failure rate* (F), and *accumulated length due to failures* (L) were also considered. Insertion rate refers to offspring insertion frequency, or how often the newly constructed child fitness is greater than the least fit member of the population. This provides insight into the ability of the genetic algorithm to find improved points in the solution space [4]. Failure rate denotes the number of *foreign edges* introduced into the offspring during recombination. A failure or foreign edge occurs when an edge (e.g. city A - city B) is present in the child, but does not appear in either of its parents. Closely related to failure rate is accumulated length due to failures. This variable records the additional tour length added to the child because failures have occurred. Both failure rate and accumulated length due to failures measure how well the crossover operator preserves information from parent to child and how serious a penalty is incurred when a foreign edge is introduced.

3   Part and Partial Correlation

In this paper, part correlation (or *semi-partial correlation*) theory will be developed from an arithmetic perspective with some references to linear regression interpretations [5] [7]. Consider a sample of strings from a random population that is measured according to three variables which are considered important in understanding how an underlying genetic operator functions. These variables are the parents' fitness (P)[1], the child's fitness (C), and the failure rate (F). Suppose that one area of interest is to determine the extent of the relationship between P and C when variation in F, which is related to variation in C, is held constant. The technique for solving this problem is called *part correlation,* as the area of interest is the relationship between two variables (P and C) with the effect of a third (F) "parted out" of *one* of the other two, in this case C. Symbolically:

$$r_{P(C \cdot F)} = \frac{r_{PC} - r_{PF}\,r_{CF}}{\sqrt{1 - r_{CF}^2}},$$

where r_{PC} is the regular correlation coefficient between P and C. An informal way to think about part correlation is as follows. Consider a plot of the distribution of F on a single axis. *Group* the data into significantly different clusters, with all points in a cluster fitting a normal curve (this could be inferred by choosing a large enough cluster (≥ 30) and applying the *Central Limit Theorem*). Next construct a set of plots, one for each F cluster, consisting of raw C scores. Finally, suppose that the C graphs are constructed on transparencies and that they are merged to form a single plot. This last graph represents C's *deviation scores* with F held constant, denoted $(C \cdot F)$. Thus, to calculate the part correlation of P and C with the influence of F removed from C, one would correlate P's raw scores with C's deviation scores.

While the use of part correlation may provide greater insight into the nature of data relationships than simple correlation, its power is limited. Not only does it lack the ability to "part out" a third variable from both of the variables under consideration, but it also does not admit higher-order relationships. *Partial correlation* addresses both of these shortcomings.

3.1   First-Order Partial Correlation

In the previous example, a relationship was determined between the variables of parent fitness (P) and child fitness (C) with the effect of failure rate (F) removed from C. Now suppose that one wishes to find the relationship between P and C when any association between P and F, as well as between C and F, is removed. Unlike part correlation, *partial correlation* removes the effects of a third variable from both variables under consideration ("F partialled out of P and C"), rather than just one. The formula for the above relationship is:

$$r_{PC \cdot F} = \frac{r_{PC} - r_{PF}\,r_{CF}}{\sqrt{1 - r_{PF}^2}\sqrt{1 - r_{CF}^2}}$$

where, again, each r on the right side of the equation is a normal correlation.

---

[1] Since two parents are used in the construction of an offspring, P corresponds to the *average* of the parents' fitness.

3.2 Second- and Higher-Order Partial Correlation

Although the above example considered only three variables, there is no theoretical need for such limits. Suppose now that a fourth variable is introduced, accumulated length due to child failures (L). Assume that the area of interest is to determine the relationship between P and C when the effects of variation in F and L are removed from both P and C. Again, a theoretically simple equation solves the problem:

$$r_{PC \cdot FL} = \frac{r_{PC \cdot F} - r_{PL \cdot F}\, r_{CL \cdot F}}{\sqrt{1 - r_{PL \cdot F}^2}\,\sqrt{1 - r_{CL \cdot F}^2}}.$$

However, each r term on the right side of the equation is now a *first-order* partial correlation, not a normal correlation as before.

The partial correlation concept is not limited to any finite number of variables; one could add the child's insertion rate R into the calculation, producing a *third-order partial correlation*:

$$r_{PC \cdot FRL} = \frac{r_{PC \cdot FR} - r_{PL \cdot RF}\, r_{CL \cdot RF}}{\sqrt{1 - r_{PL \cdot RF}^2}\,\sqrt{1 - r_{CL \cdot RF}^2}},$$

where each correlation on the right hand side is now a *second-order* partial correlation. Indeed, one might consider fourth, fifth, or even higher partials; however, such partials are not usually studied due to computational expense.

3.3 Significance Tests

The Fisher z-transformation [1] will be utilized to convert the calculated correlation coefficient to a statistical form which possesses a normal distribution. This is necessary because the significance tests used in this research depend upon normally distributed data. The formula for the z-transform is:

$$z_f = (1.1513)\ log[(1 + r)/(1 - r)].$$

To complete the conversion of the correlation to a normal form, the converted data must be divided by the standard error of the z-transform corresponding to the given partial. Thus, the calculated partial z-transform is:

$$pz_f = \frac{(1.1513)\ log[1 + r/1 - r]}{[1\,/\,\sqrt{N - (m + 3)}]},$$

where N is the sample size and m is the number of variables "partialled out." The calculated value of pz_f is then tested at a .05 level of significance to determine the relationship (if any) between the sample value and population value.

The other significance test needed is one which determines if two different population partial correlation coefficients derived from two sets of sample data are significantly different. The following formula calculates the relevant statistic d, which is then tested at a .05 level of significance:

$$d = \frac{z1_f - z2_f}{\sqrt{\frac{1}{(N_1 - m - 3)} + \frac{1}{(N_2 - m - 3)}}}, \qquad N_1, N_2 > m + 3.$$

4 Edge-4 And Schleuter Crossover (SCHX)

Most of the operators studied in this research have been previously described [3] [4] [6] except for Edge-4 and SCHX. Edge-4 is a new operator presented here for the first time, while SCHX has been considered in only brief detail [2]. Both operators give good results with respect to several *interesting* correlations, but neither perform consistently as well as MPX in the context of hybridized search.

4.1 Edge Crossover

The Edge family of operators emphasizes adjacency information of the cities in the tour [6]. Briefly, Edge works by collecting the edge information contained in both parents in an *edge table*. The rows of the table consist of a city (e.g. A) followed by a list of cities which are connected to A in the two parent tours.

To construct an offspring, the original Edge algorithm first chooses a random starting city (e.g. A) and removes all instances of A from the "link" lists in the edge table. The next city is then chosen by finding the city connected to the current city with the least number of remaining connections. If all connecting cities have the same number of links, the next city is chosen randomly. This city is now removed from all of the remaining cities' link lists, and the algorithm proceeds as before. If at any time, a city is chosen such that its link list is empty, a *failure* occurs. In this case, the original Edge operator does not attempt to fix the failure, but instead chooses a new city, adds it to the child, and continues the method described above. The algorithm halts when all cities have been included in the offspring.

Successive versions of Edge have attempted to improve the amount of genetic information preserved between parent and child by limiting the number of failures. Edge 2 added the ability to preserve common subtours between parents by "flagging" duplicate link list entries with a minus (-) sign and giving priority to those entries when the next city in the tour is chosen. Although a minor change, the flagging operation improved the Edge algorithm's performance [6].

Edge-3 and Edge-4 enhanced the algorithm further by attempting to minimize failures (the primary source of increased tour length) through intelligent failure resolution methods. Unlike its ancestors, when Edge-3 encounters a failure it does not randomly choose a new city. Instead, it reverses the current tour segment and attempts to extend the tour by adding cities to the other end of the segment. The algorithm continues to add cities until another failure is reached, at which point a true failure occurs. Since the tour cannot be reversed again, the default behavior of choosing a random city to continue the tour is employed.

Edge 4 takes this idea still further by considering the end cities after failures have occurred on both ends. Since the end city has resulted in a failure, it must be the case that all of its links are already contained in the partially built tour. Edge 4 now attempts to reverse *only part* of the tour such that the end city will be adjacent to one of its original links, thereby postponing and possibly averting random failure resolution. For example, suppose that the original edge table entry for A contains edges to B, C, D, and E, where the partial tour consists of

Q X B̲ Y Z C̲ W D̲ R E̲ A.

Both A and Q are failure cities. The Edge 4 algorithm then inspects the link lists of the cities adjacent to the cities in A's link list. For example, the link lists of Y, W, and R would be examined and the one with the smallest number of entries would be chosen. Suppose Y is picked using this criteria. Edge 4 now reverses the subtour Y Z C W D R E A to produce

Q X B̲ A E R D̲ W C̲ Z Y.

The effect of this reversal is twofold. First, A is no longer a failure city as the edge BA was present in one of the original parents. Second, the tour may now be extended if Y still contains cities in its link list. If this reversal does not admit any extension of the tour, another A link will be chosen and a different reversal will be attempted. For example, if C is chosen, the tour would then be

Q X B̲ Y Z C̲ A E R D̲ W

and the algorithm would try to extend the tour from W. Backtracking would continue until an extension is found or all other edge swaps (excluding the adjacent edge E) produce no extension. Next, the algorithm would use the same method starting from the other end of the tour. If extensions still could not be constructed, the algorithm chooses a random city and proceeds as before.

4.2 Schleuter Crossover

The Schleuter crossover operator (SCHX) [2], is a variation on Mülenbein's MPX operator, although it has features similar to those found in Davis' order crossover [4] and it includes partial tour reversals. (The source code of Schleuter Crossover was derived from Pascal code received from E. Pesch.) SCHX begins by denoting the two selected parent strings as the *donor* and the *receiver*. A random city and a random segment length ($3 \leq |segment| \leq (\frac{1}{3})tourlength$) are then chosen in the donor. For example, suppose the randomly chosen donor city is A (at position 10) and the length of the segment is 81 cities, ending in B (at position 90). Expressing the cities between A and B as $x_1, x_2, \cdots, x_{79}$, the donor is then

$$(\cdots A(10) \ x_1(11) \ x_2(12) \ \cdots \ x_{79}(89) \ B(90) \ \cdots)$$

where the number in parentheses represents the position of that city in the donor. The algorithm then finds the cities on either end of the segment (A and B) and locates them in the receiver. Suppose A and B are found in the receiver at positions 25 and 245 respectively. The receiver can be represented as:

$$(\cdots A(25) \ y_1(26) \ y_2(27) \ \cdots \ y_{219}(244) \ B(245) \ \cdots).$$

Next two copies of the receiver are made (temp1 and temp2), but they are altered in the following way. In temp1, the partial tour $y_1 \ y_2 \cdots y_{219} \ B$ is reversed to relocate city B adjacent to city A:

$$(\cdots A(25) \ B(26) \ y_{219}(27) \ \cdots \ y_2(244) \ y_1(245) \ \cdots).$$

Similarly, in temp2 the tour is reversed to move city A adjacent to city B:

$$(\cdots \ y_{219}(25) \ y_{218}(26) \ \cdots \ y_1(243) \ A(244) \ B(245) \ \cdots \ ).$$

Finally, two offspring are constructed as follows. First, copy the donor segment into the first offspring at the position where city A was located in the receiver:

$$(\cdots \ A(25) \ x_1(26) \ x_2(27) \ \cdots \ x_{79}(104) \ B(105) \ \cdots \ ).$$

The remainder of the first child is constructed by examining each city after the AB edge in temp1 and adding it to the child after B if the city is not already contained in the tour. Similarly, the second offspring receives the donor segment such that city B from the donor corresponds to city B in the receiver:

$$(\cdots \ A(165) \ x_1(166) \ x_2(167) \ \cdots \ x_{79}(244) \ B(245) \ \cdots \ ).$$

To complete the construction of the second child, each city after the AB edge in temp2 is examined and added to the child after city B if it does not exist in the offspring. In both cases, the *relative order* of the temporary strings is preserved. Finally, both children are evaluated and the more fit child is retained.

5 Experimental Method and Data Collection

To examine the part and partial correlation behavior and the fitness landscapes of the ten genetic operators with and without the *2-opt* local improvement operator[2], the following experimental setup was devised. First, four areas of interest were selected: ordinary GENITOR (called PC), GENITOR with an initially 2-opted population (P2C), GENITOR with 2-opt performed on the resulting child (PC2), and GENITOR with an initially 2-opted population and 2-opt performed on the resulting child (P2C2). For each interest area, two different sets of runs were performed. One set was used to generate correlations over 30 independent runs of 2500 recombinations each from an initial population. This provided insight into how each of the operators work when the population is diverse. The other set generated correlations over 2 independent runs of 250,000 recombinations each. This showed how the operators and their associated correlations performed *over time* as the population became more homogeneous and converged toward a solution. Each sample run began with the same initial population. For each pair of parents in the sample, 2-opt was performed on the parents (if applicable), followed by the recombination of two parents to produce offspring. 2-opt was then applied to the resulting child (if applicable), and statistical data was collected. This data included both parents' fitness, child fitness, the number of failures in the child, whether or not the resulting child was inserted in the GENITOR population, and the total TSP tour length increase due to failures in the child. Finally, the part and partial correlations were calculated and significance tests were performed on the *interesting* relations.

---

[2] 2-opt in this case means *one-pass 2-opt*, not *2-opt to convergence*. For an in-depth discussion of the differences among 2-opt operators, as well as the workings of MPX and Edge, see [4].

Correlation	MPX	SCHX
PC	0.299089	0.423785
$P(C \cdot F)$	0.493316	0.454906
$C(P \cdot F)$	0.275070	0.382705
$PC \cdot FRL$	0.634582	0.431662

Table 1. P2C Correlation Performance / 2500 Recombinations

5.1 Utility of Part and Partial Correlation

Part and partial correlation justify their expense over a series of related correlations, as can be seen from Table 1. When simple correlation is considered, SCHX appears to admit the greater correlation. A calculation of d (see Section 3.3) would show that the difference is significant and therefore SCHX possesses a higher PC correlation than MPX does for this environment. However, this conclusion would be misleading. Under the $P(C \cdot F)$ relation, MPX exhibits greater correlation than SCHX. Clearly, the failure rate in the child negatively masks part of the PC correlation and once that effect is removed, a much different picture develops. Conversely, the $C(P \cdot F)$ relationship demonstrates a different masking effect. Both operators' correlations are decreased when failure rate is removed from the parents; however, the effect is greater in MPX than in Schleuter crossover. Finally, when all other variables are "partialled out," MPX exhibits the greater correlation. From this analysis, two important pieces of information are obtained. First, the true correlation between parents and child is much higher in MPX than in SCHX, even though simple correlation analysis would have shown the reverse. Also, by examining a series of part and partial correlations, the masking effects of other variables on the correlation relationship may be determined.

5.2 Results

From the sample data collected, several significant trends are uncovered. As seen from Table 2, MPX appears to be the best overall genetic operator with respect to preserving information from parent to child. Not only does MPX perform well with respect to ρ_{op} in environments with no local optimization over a short initial sample (PC, 2500), but MPX is also the operator of choice when the initial population has been locally optimized (P2C, P2C2). There are two reasons for MPX's success. First, the operator performs a straight copy of one-third of the donor into the final child. This results in a correlation of one for all variables over the subtour domain. Second, MPX does not rely on simple relative order to complete offspring tours, but instead looks in both the donor and receiver to preserve edge and order information, thereby maximizing genetic preservation.

The Edge family, on the other hand, exhibits comparable or superior performance on the PC relation when no local optimization is performed. While the

Relation	# Recom.	Correlation	Rank
PC	2500	0.634582	1
PC	250000	0.996977	3
P2C	250000	0.951699	1
P2C2	250000	0.646876	1

Table 2. MPX $PC \cdot FRL$ correlation performance

Edge Corr. / $PC \cdot FRL$/ 250K Recom.			
Operator	PC Correlation	PC Rank	P2C Correlation	P2C Rank
Edge-4	0.998321	1	0.434894	6
Edge-3	0.997705	2	0.528044	4
Edge-2	0.996653	4	0.531802	3

Table 3. Edge family performance in local and non-local environments.

Edge family is superior in non-local environments, Edge-4's correlations may suggest that the point of diminishing returns has been reached. Edge-4 consumes greater resources than Edge-3, yet as Table 3 shows, Edge-4 provides only an .001 gain (the difference is statistically significant, however).

Still, there is room for improvement in the Edge family as seen by their performance under local optimization. For the P2C relation, Edge's best correlation is 0.531802. This pales in comparison to MPX's correlation of 0.951699 and SCHX's 0.894806 in the same environment. One reason for Edge-4's poor execution may be its "decomposing" of the parent tours into component edge parts. Unlike MPX, Edge-4 possesses no direct copy mechanism from parent to child. Such a deficiency does not make a difference in the PC case, but when local optimization is used the absence of direct copy may severely hamper parent-child correlation. This suggests that a direct copy mechanism added to Edge-4 might improve its performance when used with optimized initial populations. The other possible cause for Edge-4's inferiority in hybridized environments may be the operator's exclusive emphasis on edge information instead of relative order information. It may be that after a failure occurs, relative order can help determine which city should be chosen to start the next tour segment.

Although not shown, SCHX's performance is comparable to MPX's. Whereas SCHX is ranked behind Edge in non-local environments, it performs better than Edge when 2-Opt is used. While not an optimal genetic operator, SCHX's combination of direct copy, internal swapping and relative order child completion allows it to distance itself performance-wise from the less fit genetic operators.

Although the above results highlight the importance of partial correlation, a central question remains: "Does PC correlation imply greater performance?" The answer is a qualified "yes." Mathias and Whitley [4] have shown the superiority of Edge in a environment without 2-opt and of MPX when 2-opt is used. Their results support the findings of this work. However, caution must be taken not to assume that a greater preservation of genetic material *always* corresponds to improved performance. Consider the genetic operator (Unity) that constructs a child by cloning one parent. Under correlation analysis, most relations would be unity since no change has occurred from parent to child. Yet no improvement would be obtained beyond the fitness of the best parent in the initial population. Thus, while correlation analysis provides insight into performance, it is clearly not the only feature to consider when choosing a genetic operator.

Another comparison concerns the third order FL correlations. Without exception, MPX exhibits a greater correlation between the number of failures and the accumulated length due to failures than the Edge family. While this implies that a certain number of failures will almost always map to the same failure length, it does not provide any insight into the magnitude of the length. For example, suppose that MPX exhibits a characteristic such that, for 99% of the time, when five failures are present in the child, length due to failure is 100K. For another operator, the length might be 10 for 5 failures. In either case, the correlations themselves would be equivalent. Thus, this relationship shows only that MPX's failures and failure length are more correlated than Edge's, not that this characteristic is necessarily positive or negative.

The other genetic operators (OrderDav, OrderSyz, Pmx, Cycle, Position) [6] considered in this work do not compare very well to SCHX, MPX or Edge. Under the PC relation, for example, these operators almost never rank higher than sixth, with the occasional exception of Davis' order operator. Overall, the results of this work tend to reinforce Manderick's and Mathias and Whitley's conclusion of the superiority of Edge and MPX over other genetic operators.

References

1. M. Fogiel. (1991) *The Statistics Problem Solver*. Research and Education Assoc.
2. Martina Gorges-Schleuter. (1989) "ASPARAGOS An Asynchronous Parallel Genetic Optimization Strategy." In *Proceedings of the Third International Conference on Genetic Algorithms*. J. David Schaffer, ed. Morgan Kaufmann.
3. B. Manderick, M De Weger, and P. Spiessens. (1991) "The Genetic Algorithm and the Structure of the Fitness Landscape." In *Proceedings of the Fourth International Conference on Genetic Algorithms.* R. Belew and L.Booker, ed. Morgan Kaufmann.
4. K. Mathias and D. Whitley. (1992) "Genetic Operators, The Fitness Landscape and the Traveling Salesman Problem." In *Parallel Problem Solving from Nature, 2* R. Manner and B. Manderick, ed. Elsevier Science Publishers.
5. D. F. Morrison. (1967) *Multivariate Statistical Methods*. McGraw-Hill.
6. T. Starkweather, S. McDaniel, K. Mathias, D. Whitley, and C. Whitley. (1991) "A Comparison of Genetic Sequencing Operators." In *Proc. of the Fourth Intl. Conf. on Genetic Algorithms*. R. Belew and L.Booker, ed. Morgan Kaufmann.
7. R. M. Thorndike. (1978) *Correlational Procedures for Research*. Gardner Press.
8. N. Ulder, E. Aarts, H. Bandelt, P. van Laarhoven, E. Pesch. (1991) "Genetic Local Search Algorithms for the Traveling Salesman Problem." In *Parallel Problem Solving from Nature* H.P. Schwefel and Reinhard Manner, ed. Springer/Verlag.

Genetic algorithms with multi-parent recombination

A.E. Eiben, P-E. Raué, Zs. Ruttkay

Artificial Intelligence Group
Dept. of Mathematics and Computer Science
Vrije Universiteit Amsterdam
De Boelelaan 1081a
1081HV Amsterdam
e-mail: {gusz, peraue, zsofi}@cs.vu.nl

Abstract We investigate genetic algorithms where more than two parents are involved in the recombination operation. We introduce two multi-parent recombination mechanisms: gene scanning and diagonal crossover that generalize uniform, respectively n-point crossovers. In this paper we concentrate on the gene scanning mechanism and we perform extensive tests to observe the effect of different numbers of parents on the performance of the GA. We consider different problem types, such as numerical optimization, constrained optimization (TSP) and constraint satisfaction (graph coloring). The experiments show that 2-parent recombination is inferior on the classical DeJong functions. For the other problems the results are not conclusive, in some cases 2 parents are optimal, while in some others more parents are better.

1 Introduction

In nature, new individuals are always created through either asexual (one parent) or sexual (two parents) reproduction. People hardly ever wonder why the number of parents is restricted to one or two. For a mathematician or computer scientist, however, this restriction should not be self-evident. Still, almost no GA publications report on recombination mechanisms based on more than two parents, we are aware of only two, namely [Müh89, Ser92], and in the context of Evolution Strategies that of [Bäc93]. Here we examine whether multi-parent recombination should be avoided for practical reasons or it offers advantages and is just overlooked.

Aside from this motivation we have another argument for investigating multi-parent recombination. Namely, one would expect that by biasing the recombination operator the performance of the GA would improve. A problem indepedent way to incorporate a bias into the recombination operator can be based on selecting n parents and applying some limited statistical analysis on the allele distribution within the parents. A very slight bias is introduced when choosing an allele from the parents uniform randomly. Looking at the number of occurrences of a certain allele at a position and choosing the most common allele introduces a stronger bias. Inheriting the number of alleles proportional to the fitness-value of the parents is a more sophisticated, but still problem-independent mechanism. In the next section we give detailed descriptions of a number of multi-parent recombination operators. In section 3 we present test results on 6 different problems. An evaluation of the test results is presented in section 4. Open issues and future work are discussed in section 5.

2 Multi-parent genetic operators

A multi-parent operator uses two or more parents to generate children. In this section we define two multi-parent recombination mechanisms: gene scanning and diagonal crossover that generalize uniform, respecively n-point crossovers. In this paper we concentrate on the gene scanning mechanism, we describe and investigate five versions of scanning that differ in the type of bias applied when creating children.

2.1 Gene scanning techniques

Gene scanning, as introduced in [Eib91], is a general mechanism that produces one child from n > 1 parents in the following way. First, a number of markers are assigned, one for each of the parents and one for the child. The child-marker traverses all the positions in the child from left to right, one at a time. For each position, the markers for the parents are updated so that when choosing a value for the gene currently marked in the child, the parent markers indicate the choices. This algorithm is shown in pseudo-code in figure 2.1.

```
1   Initialize parent markers
2
3   FOR child_marker = 1 TO CHROMOSOME_LENGTH DO
4       update parent markers
5
6       child.allele[child_marker] = choose from values indicated by
                                      the parent markers
7   END_FOR
```

Figure 2.1. The general gene scanning mechanism

The two characterizing features of all gene scanning procedures are the (parent) marker update mechanism (line 4) and the mechanism that chooses the value to be inherited by the child (line 6). By changing this latter mechanism we have defined three specific scanning techniques, namely: uniform, occurrence-based and fitness-based scanning. The marker update mechanism is discussed at the end of this section.

Uniform scanning The classical uniform crossover traverses two parents and the two children from left to right, and for each position in child 1 chooses randomly whether to inherit from parent 1 or parent 2 (the second child is created by reversing the decisions). U-Scan uses a mechanism with is basically the same, the difference is that only one child is created and instead of only 2 parents any number of parents can be used. Each parent has an equal chance of contributing an allele to be inherited by the child, which means that the probability to inherit an allele from parent i, P(i), and the expected number of genes to inherit from parent i, E(i), are defined as follows:

$$P(i) := \frac{1}{number\ of\ parents}, \ E(i) := P(i) \times CHROMOSOME\_LENGTH$$

Occurrence-based scanning Occurrence-based scanning (OB-Scan) is based on the premise that the value which occurs most often in a particular position in the parents (which are selected based on their fitness) is probably the best possible value to choose. Choosing one of the marked values is thus done by applying a majority function. If no value occurs more than any other one (the majority function is undecided), then the value which is encountered first is chosen in our implementation Another way of doing this would be to break ties randomly, proportionally to the number of occurrences. Note, that the distrubution used should not be uniform, since it that case this randomized occurrence-based scanning would yield uniform scanning.

Fitness-based scanning Fitness-based scanning (FB-Scan) uses roulette wheel selection when deciding from which parent an allele will be inherited. This means that if parent i has a fitness value of f(i) the probability that a value for a position in the child is inherited from this parent is:

$$P(i) := \frac{f(i)}{\sum f(i)}$$

Using this mechanism the child will inherit more alleles from fitter parents, since the number of alleles inherited from parent i is $E(i) = P(i) \times CHROMOSOME\_LENGTH$.

Adapting scanning to different representation types It is possible to define scanning procedures for different representation types by changing the marker update mechanism. For representations where all positions are independent (no epistasis), the marker update mechanism is simple, the parent markers are all initialized to the first position in each of the parents, and each step the markers are all increased by one (thus traversing the parents from left to right). Problems where epistasis occurs may need a more sophisticated marker update mechanism. In particular, for other order-based representation one needs a marker update mechanism which ensures that no value is added to the child twice. This can be obtained by increasing the marker in each parent until it marks a value which has not been added to the child yet. An example of how this marker update mechanism works is shown in figure 2.2.

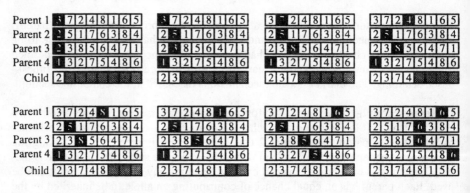

Figure 2.2. OB-Scan on order-based representation

2.2 Adjacency-based crossover

The adjacency-based crossover (ABC) is a special case of scanning, designed for order-based representations where relative positioning of values is important, e.g. the TSP. The main differences between the scanning procedures described above and ABC are the way in which the first value is selected and the marker update mechanism. The first gene value in the child is always inherited from the first gene value in the first parent. The marker update mechanism is as follows: for each parent its marker is set to the first successor of the previously selected value which does not occur in the child yet. (For this mechanism each individual is seen as a cycle).

A crossover similar to ABC was proposed in [Whi91]. Whitley's crossover differs from ABC in the number of parents applied (Whitley uses 2 parents) and the choice of a value to inherit when all the immediate successors to a city have already been inherited by the child. For example, suppose that the successors to city D are cities A, E, F and H (in parents 1, 2, 3 and 4 respectively), and furthermore that these four cities have already been incorporated into the child. Whitley's crossover would randomly choose a city not already included in the child. ABC will check the successors of city A in parent 1, city E in parent 2, city F in parent 3 and city H in parent 4 (and if any of these have already been included in the child, their successors), the city to be added to the child will be chosen from among these successors.

We define two types of ABC, namely occurrence-based (OB-ABC) and fitness-based (FB-ABC) similarily to occurrence-based and fitness-based scanning. The difference is the marker update mechanism. OB-ABC is shown in figure 2.3.

Parent 1	3 7 2 4 8 1 6 5	3 7 2 4 8 1 6 5	3 7 2 4 8 1 6 5	3 7 2 4 8 1 6 5
Parent 2	2 5 1 7 6 3 8 4	2 5 1 7 6 3 8 4	2 5 1 7 6 3 8 4	2 5 1 1 6 3 8 4
Parent 3	2 3 8 5 6 4 7 1	2 3 8 5 6 4 7 1	2 3 8 5 6 4 7 1	2 3 8 5 6 4 7 1
Parent 4	1 3 2 7 5 4 8 6	1 3 2 7 5 4 8 6	1 3 2 7 5 4 8 6	1 3 2 7 5 4 8 6
Child	3	3 8	3 8 1	3 8 1 2

Parent 1	3 7 2 4 8 1 6 5	3 7 2 4 8 1 6 5	3 7 2 4 8 1 6 5	3 7 2 4 8 1 6 5
Parent 2	2 5 1 7 6 3 8 4	2 5 1 7 6 3 8 4	2 5 1 7 6 3 8 4	2 5 1 1 7 6 3 8 4
Parent 3	2 3 8 5 6 4 7 1	2 3 8 5 6 4 7 1	2 3 8 5 6 4 7 1	2 3 8 5 6 4 7 1
Parent 4	1 3 2 7 5 4 8 6	1 3 2 7 5 4 8 6	1 3 2 7 5 4 8 6	1 3 2 7 5 4 8 6
Child	3 8 1 2 5	3 8 1 2 5 7	3 8 1 2 5 7 4	3 8 1 2 5 7 4 6

Figure 2.3. OB-ABC

2.3 Diagonal multi-parent crossover

Diagonal crossover is a generalization of n-point crossover, which creates 2 children from 2 parents. Diagonal crossover uses $n \geq 1$ crossover points and creates $n+1$ children from $n+1$ parents as the following figure illustrates.

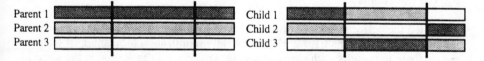

Figure 2.4: The diagonal crossover operator for 3 parents.

As mentioned before, in this paper we concentrate on scanning. We will report on the effect of the number of parents for diagonal crossover in forthcoming publications

3 The experiments

We decided to study multi-parent recombination within the framework of scanning by testing and comparing the three basic versions of scanning (uniform, occurrence-based and fitness-based) together with the scanning-like ABC which is tailored to routing problems. We were mainly interested in the following issues:

- Is scanning better than classical crossover?
- Which version of scanning is the best?
- What is the optimal number of parents?
- Does a relation exist between the type of the problem and
  - the optimal version of scanning (as a refinement of the second question),
  - the optimal number of parents (as a refinement of the third question)?

We have tested five numerical functions to be optimized and two 'real' problems. For numerical optimization we have chosen four well-known DeJong functions (the formulas were taken from [Gol89]) and a function from [Mic92] because these functions provide a test-bench with variously shaped functions. The first 'real' problem is the TSP because it is well known constrained optimization problem in the GA community and is important in practice. We use an instance concerning 30 cities from [Oli87] to keep running times down. For the second 'real' problem we have chosen graph 3-coloring: the nodes of a graph must be colored using three colors so that no neighboring nodes have the same color. This is known to be a very tough constraint satisfaction problem. (Note that this problem is different from the graph coloring problem discussed in [DavL91].) We considered 'difficult, but solvable' graphs: graphs which can be colored with 3 colors, but for which solutions are difficult to construct [Che91]. In other papers we report on heuristic GAs that outperformed the applicable classical deterministic search methods, [Eib94a, Eib94b].

For the DeJong functions and the function from [Mic92] we applied the standard binary representation. For the TSP and graph coloring we used order-based representation, furthermore we tested graph coloring with a representation based on a ternary alphabet. As for the number of parents we tested every multi-parent version of our crossovers for any number of parents from 2 to 10. The results shown here were obtained by running the GA 100 or 200 times and calculating performance averages for each number of parents. We used the generational GA model with 100% crossover rate and 50% mutation rate (per individual, not per position). The maximum number of generations was set to 500 (with earlier termination if the optimum was reached).

3.1 The test results

We tested the performance of uniform, occurrence-based and fitness-based scanning on the DeJong functions F1, F2, F3 and F4 (all minimization problems). In section 4 we compare the results with classical 1-point crossover. (The legend is the same for each graph.)

———— OB-Scan - - - - - - FB-Scan ⋯⋯⋯⋯ U-Scan

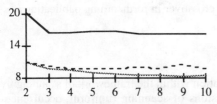

Figure 3.1. The average nr. of generations needed to find the optimum for OB/FB/U-Scanning on F1 (chrom. length = 30)

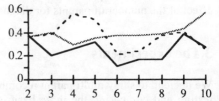

Figure 3.2. The best f-value after 500 generations for OB/FB/U-Scanning on F2 (chrom. length = 22)

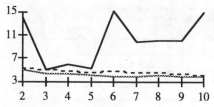

Figure 3.3. The average nr. of generations needed to find the optimum for OB/FB/U-Scanning on F3 (chrom. length = 50)

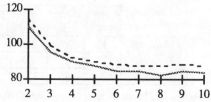

Figure 3.4a. The average nr. of generations needed to find the optimum for FB/U-Scanning on F4 (chrom. length = 240)

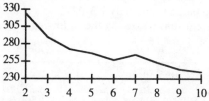

Figure 3.4b. The average nr. of generations needed to find the optimum for OB-Scanning on F4 (chrom. length = 240)

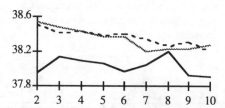

Figure 3.5. The best f-value after 500 generations for OB/FB/U-Scanning on the function from [Mic92], pg. 34 (maximization problem, chrom. length = 33)

For the graph coloring problem we applied primarily order-based representation, decoding permutations similar to the way in which it is done for scheduling problems, [Eib94b]. We tested two graphs with 90 nodes and 5 edges per node. This is known to be approximately the toughest topology for graph coloring.

	number of parents								
	2	**3**	**4**	**5**	**6**	**7**	**8**	**9**	**10**
OB-Scan	32	10	18	14	4	6	6	2	4
FB-Scan	40.5	34	28	27	28.5	21	29	26	28
U-Scan	46	29	34	36.5	34.5	36	28.5	32.5	33
OB-ABC	36	22	8	10	6	8	4	16	4
FB-ABC	20	16	10	18	20	16	24	14	20

Figure 3.6. Percentage of cases when a solution was found for graph coloring with 90 nodes (order based representation, chrom. length = 90, population size = 180)

Besides order-based representation of colorings we also tested a representation with a ternary alphabet, each symbol denoting one color. In this case we looked at the performance of the 'standard' scanning mechanisms.

	number of parents								
	2	**3**	**4**	**5**	**6**	**7**	**8**	**9**	**10**
OB-Scan	31	2.5	4.5	2	5.5	1.5	1	0	1.5
FB-Scan	35	26	34	34.5	33	32.5	33.5	31.5	29
U-Scan	42.5	35	32.5	28.5	27	26	32.5	30	27

Figure 3.7. Percentage of cases when a solution was found for graph coloring with 30 nodes (ternary alphabet, chrom. length = 30, population size = 100)

When testing the TSP we found that the best 'traditional' order-based crossover was order1, which we used to compare our results against. For TSP only occurrence-based scanning and ABC had an optimal number of parents higher than two, the other scanning techniques performed best with two parents, and only FB-ABC was able to outperform the order1 crossover. The results are summarized in the following figure showing the effectivity of the GA.

	number of parents								
	2	**3**	**4**	**5**	**6**	**7**	**8**	**9**	**10**
OB-Scan	514.2	500.3	501.7	506.6	500.6	504.5	504.6	504.8	500.0
FB-Scan	492.6	492.6	493.4	493.7	497.3	499.9	499.0	497.3	500.7
U-Scan	491.6	492.2	500.3	494.5	493.4	497.7	498.3	495.1	500.7
OB-ABC	509.1	486.6	484.8	477.4	475.6	478	474.9	472.5	476.6
FB-ABC	453.2	458.7	457.9	459.5	461.7	457.3	462.8	463.6	461.6
order1	461.6								

Figure 3.8. The length of the best route after 500 generations (order based representation, chrom. length = 30, population size =100).

4 Evaluation of the tests

In this part we review the test results grouped around three main questions: advantages of scanning with respect to classical recombination mechanisms, different types of bias in scanning and the effect of different numbers of parents.

4.1 Scanning and classical recombination

Considering the five numerical optimization problems we have tested, we observed that in 4 out of the 5 cases (fitness-based) scanning outperformed 1-point crossover. On the DeJong functions it outperformed 1-point crossover by respectively, 42%, 19%, 40% and 59%. On the function from [Mic92] fitness-based scanning was 1.3% worse than 1-point crossover. Let us remark that on the function F2 OB-Scan proved to be better than FB-Scan and outperformed 1-point crossover by as much as 70%.

For the TSP we first tested the classical order based crossovers order1, order2, position, cycle, PMX and uox (provided by our test environment LibGA, [Cor93]) and observed that order1 outperformed the rest. Then we ran tests to compare different versions of scanning with order1. Here, the fitness-based version of ABC (a multi-parent operator designed specifically for the TSP) turned out to be the best scanning mechanism, and was slightly (1.8%) better than order1.

4.2 Different types of bias in scanning

On 4 out of the 5 numerical optimization problems fitness-based scanning was superior to the uniform and occurrence-based versions. The exception was F2, where OB-Scan was better, even though on the other 4 functions it was the worst of the three. In section 5 we give a possible explanation for this. For graph coloring we found that choosing genes uniform randomly proved to be better than choosing fitness- or occurrence-based. On the TSP, performance for the uniform and fitness-based scanning was approximately the same, OB-Scan was inferior to both. As for the adjacency-based crossover operators, FB-ABC clearly outperformed OB-ABC.

4.3 The effect of different number of parents

The results on the DeJong functions show that the performance increases as the number of parents is raised above 2. The tests, however, provide no real insight into the optimal number of parents. For instance, the optimal number of parents for fitness-based scanning was respectively, 9, 4, 6-10, 10 for F1, F2, F3 and F4. We also observed that the different versions of scanning show different behaviour, i.e. reach optimal performance at different numbers of parents. Nevertheless, on all of the DeJong functions we tested the optimal number was higher than 2. For the function from [Mic92] 2 parents proved to be optimal, although the difference in performance between different numbers of parents remained below 1%. This suggests that for this function the number of parents does not really matter.

The TSP shows a somewhat similar picture. We have tested 5 multi-parent recombination mechanisms and each of them has shown little variance in performance for different numbers of parents. For three of them the results became worse (by at most 2.3%) when the number of parents was raised above 2; for the two occurrence-based recombination mechanisms the optimal number of parents was 10, respectively 9, but the gain with respect to 2 parents did not exceed 7.2%. For graph coloring the data clearly shows that 2 parents are superior.

When increasing the number of parents extra costs are introduced. These costs occur due to the extra time needed to select additional parents and the time needed to identify the gene to be inherited. Gene inheritance costs are almost negligible on binary strings. In the worst case (e.g. order-based representation), the increase can be quadratic, for instance for OB-Scan. However, even in this case, the decrease in the number of generations may compensate the time increase per generation.

5 Open questions and future work

In spite of the 23.000 runs in total, we are aware of the limitations of the present investigation. Thus, instead of general conclusions we discuss some questions that can only be answered reliably if more knowledge is collected on the phenomenon of multi-parent reproduction.

5. 1 When is the optimal number of parents larger than 2?

Using a greater number of parents, the child creation is biased based on a larger sample from the search space. If a function has many (almost) optimal points separated by 'gaps' of poor points then sampling might not help. The different good elements in a population may very well belong to the 'gravity field' of different solutions. Hence, the larger number of parents does not provide information about the *same* solution, and the generated child will most likely be somewhere in-between the (different) gravity fields of the parents, instead of getting closer to one of them. Hence, one might not expect improvement by increasing the number of parents for 'hedgehog-like' functions. This was justified for FB-Scan and U-Scan on the function taken from [Mic92], and we expect similar results for the F5 DeJong function.

If there are relatively few (optimal) solutions, OB-Scan is expected to be the most effective (as was shown for F2), since in this case the fit parents close to different solutions differ on many bits, and the occurrence-based inheritance of genes is likely to produce children close to that solution which is close to many of the parents.

Obviously, the number of parents which can be used in the recombination mechanism is limited by the number of individuals in the pool. The question is whether increasing the number of parents always improves the performance of the GA. Our experiments support two kinds of conclusions. In some cases, increasing the number of parents improves the performance, though the degree of improvement becomes smaller and smaller. This was observed for FB-Scan and U-Scan for F3, and roughly for all multi-parent crossovers for F1 and F4. In other cases, the performance improves up to a certain number of parents and decreases, or oscillates afterwards. This was observed for the OB-Scan for F2 and F3.

The largest improvement when increasing the number of parents was achieved in the case of OB-Scan, independently from the problem. This is not surprising, as a larger sample provides more reliable information on strong gene patterns, and the two-parent OB-Scan in our implementation always reproduced the first parent.

In most of the cases we experienced a much larger improvement when the number of parents was changed from 2 to 3 than in the successive steps. We do not have a sound explanation for this phenomenon, though from the practical point of view it would be very useful to know that it is not worth while to go beyond 3-4 parents.

Another interesting question is whether the type of (the bias in) a crossover is the decisive factor with respect to the performance. In other words, if a 2-parent crossover is better than another crossover, does the same apply for the n-parent version for any $n > 2$ as well? (For the optimization problems we tested this was approximately true, with the exception of F2.)

5.2 Other issues

In our first experiments, we were interested whether the increase in the number of parents results in better performance. The optimal number of parents obviously depends on the length of the individuals and on the alphabet, or in general, on the size of the search space (in addition to its topology). A further investigation could aim at deciding the optimal number of parents in different stages of the GA, especially, in the case of premature convergence. By introducing incest prevention the performance of the multi-parent crossovers may improve.

Another aspect which needs to be investigated is the number of children generated from a given number of parents. So far, we have only studied n-parents-1-child versions of scanning-like crossovers, whereas more children can be created easily.

Looking at the performance as we have done here is the most common way in which to compare different genetic operators or genetic algorithms. Nevertheless, to get a better understanding of this novel phenomenon of multi-parent recombination we need a 'higher resolution' picture of the behaviour of our GAs. This can be obtained by a theoretical schema survival analysis, or monitoring extra features along the evolution, such as:

- uniformity within the population measured by the average Hamming distance of randomly chosen pairs of individuals;
- power of sexual reproduction measured by the child fitness - parent fitness ratio.

Acknowledgements

We wish to thank A.L. Corcoran who provided us the LibGA library that we used for our experiments.

References

[Bäc93]   T.-B. Bäck and H.-P. Schwefel, An Overview of Evolutionary Algorithms for parameter Optimization, Journal of Evolutionary Computation 1(1), 1993, pp. 1-23.

[Che91]   P. Cheeseman, B. Kenefsky and W.M. Taylor, Where the really hard problems are, Proc. of IJCAI-91, 1991, pp. 331-337.

[Cor93]   A.L. Corcoran and R.L. Wainwright, LibGA: A User Friendly Workbench for Order-Based Genetic Algorithm Research, Proc. of Applied Computing: Sates of the Art and Practice, 1993, pp. 111-117.

[DavY91]   Y. Davidor, Epistasis Variance: A View-point on GA-Hardness, Proc. of FOGA-90, 1991, pp. 23-35.

[DavL91]   L. Davis, Handbook of Genetic Algorithms, Van Nostrand Reinhold, New York, 1991.

[Eib91]   A.E. Eiben, A Method for Designing Decision Support Systems for Operational Planning, PhD Thesis, Eindhoven University of Technology, 1991.

[Eib94a]   A.E. Eiben, P.-E. Raué and Zs. Ruttkay, Solving Constraint Satisfaction Problems Using Genetic Algorithms, proceedings of the 1st IEEE World Conference on Computational Intelligence, to appear in 1994.

[Eib94b]   A.E. Eiben, P.-E., Raué, Zs. Ruttkay, GA-easy and GA-hard Constraint Satisfaction Problems, Proc. of the ECAI'94 Workshop on Constraint Processing, LNCS Series, Springer-Verlag, to appear in August, 1994.

[Gol89]   D.E. Goldberg, Genetic Algorithms in Search, Optimization and Machine Learning, Addison-Wesley, 1989.

[Gre85]   J. Grefenstette, R. Gopal, B. Rosmaita and D. Van Gucht, Genetic Algorithms for the Travelling Salesman Problem, Proc. of ICGA-85, 1985, pp.160-168.

[Mic92]   Z. Michalewicz, Genetic Algorithms + Data Structures = Evolution Programs, Springer-Verlag, 1992.

[Müh89]   H. Mühlenbein, Parallel Genetic Algorithms, Population Genetics and Combinatorial Optimization, Proc. of ICGA-89, 1989, pp. 416-421.

[Oli87]   I.M. Oliver, D.J. Smith and J.R.C. Holland, A study of permutation crossover operators on the travelling salesman problem, Proc. of ICGA-87, 1987, pp. 224-230.

[Ser92]   G. Seront and H. Bersini, In Search of a Good Evolution-Optimization Crossover, Proc. of PPSN 2, 1992, pp. 479-488.

[Whi91]   D. Whitley, T. Starkweather and D. Shaner, The traveling salesman and sequence scheduling: quality solutions using genetic edge recombination, In: [DavL91], pp. 350-372.

On the Mean Convergence Time of Evolutionary Algorithms without Selection and Mutation

Hideki Asoh* and Heinz Mühlenbein

German National Research Center for Computer Science (GMD)
Schloss Birlinghoven, D-53754 Sankt Augustin, Germany
E-mail: asoh@etl.go.jp, muehlen@gmd.de
(* Permanent address: Electrotechnical Laboratory, Tsukuba, Ibaraki 305 Japan)

Abstract. In this paper we study random genetic drift in a finite genetic population. Exact formulae for calculating the mean convergence time of the population are analytically derived and some results of numerical calculations are given. The calculations are compared to the results obtained in population genetics. A new proposition is derived for binary alleles and uniform crossover. Here the mean convergence time τ is almost proportional to the size of the population and to the logarithm of the number of the loci. The results of Monte Carlo type numerical simulations are in agreement with the results from the calculation.

1 Introduction

Two opposite tendencies operate on natural populations: *natural selection*, or the propensity to adapt to a given environment; and *polymorphism*, or the propensity to produce variation to cope with changing environments. With the explosion of data reporting polymorphism on the biochemical level, the long-standing problem of the relative importance of nonrandom and random processes in the genetic structure of populations has revived in the form of a selectionist-neutralist controversy. The most prominent neutralist is Kimura[8].

The controversy has stimulated the study of many stochastic models including the infinite alleles model and the sampling formula. Later Kimura and many others extensively applied diffusion analysis to the study of stochastic genetic models[7]. The problems considered include the analysis of random sampling effects due to small populations, the balance in small populations of recurrent mutation and random genetic drift, the expected time of fixation of a mutant gene.

Random genetic drift is also important for *evolutionary algorithms*. It is a source of reducing the variation of the population. But if the variation is reduced then the response to selection i.e. the increase of the mean fitness becomes less in the next generation [10]. In this paper we will compute the expected time until convergence for different genetic models. Convergence means that all genotypes in the population become equal. The most complex genetic model deals with recombination by uniform crossover. For this model the genetic drift has not been investigated before. We derive exact formulae for calculating the mean convergence time and compare them with the results from Monte Carlo type simulations. These results show that uniform crossover recombination increases the convergence time only slightly.

The outline of the paper is as follows. In the next section we analyze the classical simple sampling case as a preparation for treating the case with uniform crossover. In section 3 we present the main result. It is compared with simulations in section 4. Section 5 is for discussion and conclusion.

2 Random drift with simple sampling

2.1 One gene with two alleles

Let the population consist of N individuals. Assume that each individual has only one gene (one locus) in which there are two different alleles termed "A" and "a". There is no mutation, crossover, and selection. The generations are discrete and the size of the population is fixed, that is, in each new generation we sample N offspring from the gene pool of N ancestors with replacements. This model is approximately equivalent with the classical diploid model with $N/2$ individuals which is usually treated in the literatures of quantitative genetics.

We can describe the status of the population by the number of individuals which have genotype "A". Let the set of possible states be $\Theta = \{0, 1, ..., N\}$. The development of the state of the population can be described by a simple Markov chain[2][6]. We denote the probability of the population to be in state $i \in \Theta$ at time t as $P_i(t)$. Then the transition probability of the Markov chain from the state i to the state j is denoted as $q(j|i)$ $i, j \in \Theta$.

The product law leads us to the following formula for $q(j|i)$

$$q(j|i) = \binom{N}{j} \left(\frac{i}{N}\right)^j \left(\frac{N-i}{N}\right)^{N-j}, \tag{1}$$

and the relation

$$P_j(t) = \sum_{i=0}^{N} q(j|i) P_i(t-1) \tag{2}$$

holds.

In vector-matrix notation, we denote the transition probability matrix as $Q = (q_{ji})$, where $q_{ji} = q(j-1|i-1)$ and the probability vector as $\mathbf{P}(t)$. The i-th element of $\mathbf{P}(t)$ is $P_{i-1}(t)$. Then we can write the equation (2) as

$$\mathbf{P}(t) = Q\mathbf{P}(t-1) \tag{3}$$

By iteration we obtain

$$\mathbf{P}(t) = Q^t \mathbf{P}(0). \tag{4}$$

Here Q^t is the power t of the matrix Q.

If the population is in the state 0 or N, the population is homogeneous. Hence, the probability of the population converging by time $t = k$ can be expressed as

$$s(k) = P_0(k) + P_N(k). \tag{5}$$

The probability of convergence just at time $t = k > 0$ is

$$c(k) = s(k) - s(k-1). \tag{6}$$

We can calculate the mean convergence time τ using $c(k)$ as

$$\tau = \sum_{k=1}^{\infty} k\, c(k). \tag{7}$$

If k is large enough, $kc(k)$ decreases as k increases and converges to 0 quickly. By taking a large enough K we can approximately calculate τ as

$$\tau \approx \sum_{k=1}^{K} k\, c(k) = Ks(K) - \left(\sum_{k=0}^{K-1} s(k)\right). \tag{8}$$

Table 1 shows some results of numerical calculations using equation (8). We tested values of K and found that $K = 1000$ is large enough for obtaining the given results.

p_A	$N = 2$	$N = 4$	$N = 8$	$N = 16$	$N = 32$	
1/2	2.00	4.55	9.89	20.76	42.71	$\tau \approx 1.4N$
3/4	—	3.69	7.94	16.71	34.48	$\tau \approx 1.0N$
7/8	—	—	5.26	11.02	22.85	$\tau \approx 0.7N$

Table 1. Mean convergence time τ for simple sampling for 2 alleles (1)

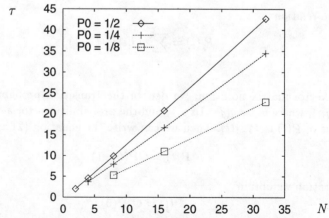

Figure 1. Population size versus mean convergence time (1)

Here the value of p_A means that in the initial population $p_A * N$ individuals have genotype "A" and the rest $((1 - p_A) * N)$ have genotype "a". We can summarize the results in the following proposition.

Proposition 1 *Let each individual have one gene with two alleles "A" and "a". Then in a population of size N with random sampling, the mean convergence time τ increases almost proportionally with the population size N. For $p_A = 1/2$ (half of the initial population has allele "A") the mean convergence time is given by $\tau \approx 1.4N$.*

Kimura et al. approximately analyzed the equivalent genetic model using the diffusion equations. The first order approximation of $s(k)$ is[7]

$$s(k) \approx 1 - 6p_A(1 - p_A)e^{-t/2N}. \tag{9}$$

From this formula one can calculate τ as $\tau = 12p_A(1 - p_A)N$. This gives $\tau = 3N$ for $p_a = 1/2$. If more terms are used $\tau = 2.8N$ is obtained for $p_A = 1/2$[5]. Considering that in their model each individual has two chromosomes (diploid organisms), their results and the above exact calculation are consistent.

If $p_A > 1/2$, the initial population is biased and has a greater tendency to converge to genotype "A" and a lesser tendency to converge to genotype "a". We call these cases as "all A" and "all a" respectively. For these cases, we can calculate the conditional mean of the convergence time under the condition of "all A" or "all a". The results are shown in the following table.

p_A	Final State	$N = 4$	$N = 8$	$N = 16$	$N = 32$	
3/4	all A	2.99	6.43	13.60	28.16	$\tau \approx 0.9N$
3/4	all a	5.78	12.47	26.06	53.45	$\tau \approx 1.7N$
7/8	all A	—	4.08	8.55	17.83	$\tau \approx 0.6N$
7/8	all a	—	13.57	28.30	57.98	$\tau \approx 1.9N$
15/16	all A	—	—	5.26	10.89	$\tau \approx 0.35N$
15/16	all a	—	—	29.34	60.10	$\tau \approx 1.92N$

Table 2. Mean convergence time for simple sampling for 2 alleles (2)

Let $P_A(\infty)$ and $P_a(\infty)$ denote the probability of the population converging to "all A" and "all a" respectively. Then the following theorem holds.

Theorem 1 *Let the size of the population be N. Let each individual have only one gene with two alleles "A" and "a". Let in the initial state, $p_A N$ individuals have allele "A", the rest has allele "a". Then in a randomly mating population,*

$$P_A(\infty) = p_A, \quad P_a(\infty) = 1 - p_A. \tag{10}$$

Proof Every individual chromosome in the initial population has the same probability to survive till the convergence of the population. Hence it is intuitively clear that the probability of converging to "all A" ($P_A(\infty)$) is proportionate to the ratio of genotype "A" in the initial population (p_A). ∎

That is, if the initial population has n times more individuals with genotype "A" at the initial stage, then the probability of the population converging to "all A" is also n times larger.

2.2 One gene with many alleles

With more than two alleles the Markov chain describing the evolution of the population becomes rather complicated. If we have $m \geq 2$ alleles, we must consider a Markov chain with $(\sum_{i_m=0}^{N} \sum_{i_{m-1}=0}^{i_m} \cdots \sum_{i_2=0}^{i_3} 1)$ states. Each state is characterized by the number of each genotype included in the population. Although we can calculate the mean convergence time in principle, it is practically impossible to do the calculation. However, if the number of alleles is very large and we can assume that all individuals have a different genotype at the initial stage, there is a simple trick to calculate the mean convergence time.

Let each different genotype be a_i ($i = 1, ..., N$). The probability of the convergence to a genotype a_i is equal for all i and is $1/N$. We denote this probability as $P_{a_i}(\infty)$. The conditional mean convergence time τ_{a_i} under the condition that the population converges to a_i is also equal for all i. Let this conditional mean be τ_c. The "unconditional" mean convergence time τ can be calculated as

$$\tau = \sum_{a_i} \tau_{a_i} P_{a_i}(\infty) = \sum_{a_i} \frac{1}{N} \tau_c, \tag{11}$$

and is equal to τ_c in this case.

Now a fact worth noticing is that τ_c is equal to the conditional mean convergence time in the two alleles case under the condition of converging to the state "all A" from the initial state $p_A = 1/N$. Therefore we can calculate τ for a very large number of alleles by the same formula as for the case with two alleles. The results are shown in the following table 3. We also show results from Monte Carlo type simulations.

	$N = 2$	$N = 4$	$N = 8$	$N = 16$	$N = 32$	
Exact	2.00	5.78	13.57	29.34	61.12	$\tau \approx 2.0N$
Simulation	—	—	13.6	29.4	60.3	

Table 3. Mean convergence time for simple sampling with many alleles

The remarkable fact is that τ is still proportional to N and only slightly larger than for the case with two alleles. Now we can state the following proposition.

Proposition 2 *Let the number of alleles be sufficiently large. Then in a population of size N with random sampling the mean convergence time τ increases almost proportionally with the population size N, and $\tau \approx 2.0N$ holds approximately.*

Note that in this case τ is mathematically equivalent to the the mean fixation time of a mutant gene introduced in a population. In Crow and Kimura[1] $\tau \approx 4.0N$ is derived for diploid organisms using the diffusion equation model. Our results are consistent with theirs.

3 Genetic drift with uniform crossover

In this section we investigate how much recombination by uniform crossover will reduce the influence of genetic drift. Uniform crossover is an adaptation of Mendel's chance model to haploid organisms. It is used in many genetic algorithms.

We assume that each individual has one chromosome and each chromosome has n loci. We denote the set of alleles for the i-th locus as Θ_i.

Let the chromosome of parents be $\mathbf{x} = (x_1, ..., x_n)$ and $\mathbf{y} = (y_1, ..., y_n)$. Here $x_i, y_i \in \Theta_i$. Then the offspring $\mathbf{z} = (z_1, ..., z_n)$ is computed by the uniform crossover operation according to the following probability;

$$Prob[z_i = x_i] = 0.5, \quad Prob[z_i = y_i] = 0.5.$$

In the following we assume that all Θ_i are the same. Then the probability of fixing (converging) each locus till time $t = k$ is identical for all i and we denote it as $r(k)$. Because each locus behaves statistically independent, the probability of fixing all n loci till the time $t = k$ is easily calculated as $r(k)^n$. This proves the following theorem,

Theorem 2 *Let the number of loci be n. Then the mean convergence time τ of the population with uniform crossover operation is*

$$\tau = \sum_{k=1}^{\infty} k \left(r(k)^n - r(k-1)^n \right). \tag{12}$$

If we assume that each locus has two alleles, we have $r(k) = s(k)$, where $s(k)$ was introduced in the previous section. If k is large enough, $kc_n(k) = k(s(k)^n - s(k-1)^n)$ is decreasing for k and converges to 0 very rapidly. By taking a large enough K we can approximately calculate τ as

$$\tau \approx \sum_{k=1}^{K} k\, c_n(k) = Ks(K)^n - \left(\sum_{k=0}^{K-1} s(k)^n \right). \tag{13}$$

Table 4 and figure 2 show the result of numerical calculations using the above equation. We tested some value of K and found that $K = 5000$ is large enough. The horizontal axis of the figures are scaled by $\log_2$.

n	$N = 2$	$N = 4$	$N = 8$	$N = 16$	$N = 32$
1	2.00	4.55	9.89	20.76	42.71
2	2.67	6.32	13.72	28.71	58.90
4	3.50	8.35	18.10	37.80	77.38
8	4.42	10.55	22.86	47.63	97.38
16	5.37	12.86	27.82	57.91	118.24
32	6.36	15.21	32.90	68.41	139.56
64	7.34	17.60	38.03	79.03	161.07
128	8.34	19.99	43.19	89.71	182.62
256	9.34	22.39	48.37	100.42	204.03
512	10.33	24.80	53.55	111.14	225.05
1024	11.33	27.21	58.74	121.87	245.17

Table 4. Mean convergence time with uniform crossover ($p_A = 1/2$)

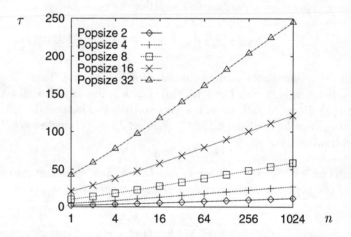

Figure 2. Number of loci versus mean convergence time τ ($p_A = 1/2$)

As one can see from the figure, the mean convergence time τ increases almost proportionally to $\log n$.

In figure 3 the relation between the convergence time τ and the population size N is shown. The figure shows that τ increases proportionally to N.

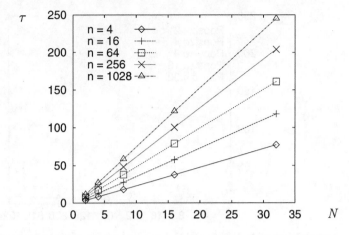

Figure 3. Population size versus mean convergence time ($p_A = 1/2$)

To maintain consistency with the results in the previous section, we approximate the above numerical results by a simple formula

$$\tau \approx C_0 N \left(a \log_e n + 1.0\right)^b. \tag{14}$$

Here C_0 is a constant which depends on p_A. The optimal values of a and b which minimize the squared error have been computed and we got the following approximative formulae for some values of p_A.

Proposition 3 *Let the number of loci be n. Let each gene have two alleles. Then the mean convergence time τ of the population with uniform crossover is approximately*

$$\tau \approx 1.4N \left(0.5 \log_e n + 1.0\right)^{1.1} \text{ for } p_A = 1/2, \tag{15}$$

$$\tau \approx 1.0N \left(0.7 \log_e n + 1.0\right)^{1.1} \text{ for } p_A = 3/4, \tag{16}$$

$$\tau \approx 0.7N \left(0.8 \log_e n + 1.0\right)^{1.2} \text{ for } p_A = 7/8. \tag{17}$$

4 Comparison with simulations

Proposition 3 has been compared to simulations with our Parallel Genetic Algorithm Simulator "PeGAsuS". For the simulation the initial population is generated randomly, that is, each locus has a probability $1/2$ to have the value 0 and $1/2$ to have the value 1. In the simulations self-fertilization is prohibited. This is different from the theoretical analysis. However these differences are not essential here.

In figure 4 the results of simulations are shown, and in figure 5 the calculation is compared to the simulation results.

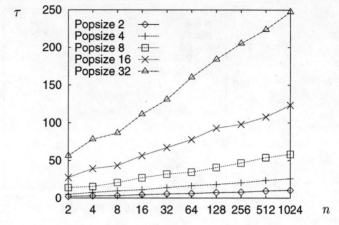

Figure 4. Number of loci versus mean convergence time
(Averages of 1000 runs)

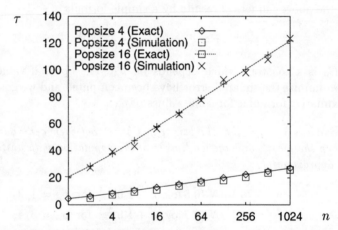

Figure 5. Comparison between exact calculation and simulation

The agreement between the analytical fit and the simulations are very good.

5 Discussion and conclusion

We have derived some formulae for calculating the mean convergence time of random genetic drift in a random mating population without selection and mutation. Exact numerical calculations using the formulae show that in all cases treated here, the mean convergence time τ is approximately proportional to the size of the population N and to the logarithm of the number of loci n. Thus τ is surprisingly small. This means that genetic drift is an important factor for reducing the variance of the population, especially if weak selection is used. But the reduction of the variance will reduce the increase of of the average fitness of the population [11]. Therefore it becomes very unlikely that one gets the optimum with weak selection.

The above results have been compared with the results from simulations. The agreement between the results is very good. The simulation results show in addition that the standard deviation of the convergence time increases rather rapidly with population size N. Although in this paper we evaluate only the mean of convergence time, the extension for calculating the variance is straightforward.

An analytical derivation of the proposition 3 and its extension to the case with n genes and a large number of alleles are left for future work. Furthermore it would be interesting to include mutation. In this case the first passage time has to be investigated. Many topics remain to be investigated in the future.

Acknowledgments

The Monte Carlo type simulation results in section 2 and section 4 are from Andreas Reinholtz. Dirk Schlierkamp-Voosen helped to use PeGAsuS. Byoung-Tak Zhang and Bill Buckles carefully read the manuscript and gave us useful comments. This work was done while one of the authors (Hideki Asoh) was at GMD as a guest researcher. He thanks GMD and Electrotechnical Laboratory (ETL) for that opportunity, and also to the Science and Technology Agency of the Japanese government for supporting his stay. This work is a part of the SIFOGA project funded by Real World Computing Partnership.

References

1. Crow,J.F. and Kimura,M. *An Introduction to Population Genetics Theory*, Harper and Row, New York, 1970.
2. Feller,W. *An Introduction to Probability Theory and its Applications. vol.1* (3rd ed.), John Wiley & Sons, New York, 1957.
3. Fisher,R.A. On the dominance ratio. Proc. Roy. Soc. Edinburgh **42**, 321-341, 1922.
4. Goldberg,D.E. *Genetic Algorithms in Search, Optimization and Machine Learning*, Addison-Wesley, Readin, 1989.
5. Hartl,D.L. *A Primer of Population Genetics*, Sinauer Associates, Sunderland, 1981.
6. Karlin,S. and Taylor H.M. *A First Course in Stochastic Processes.* (2nd ed.), Academic Press, New York, 1975.
7. Kimura,M. Diffusion Models in Population Genetics, *J. Appl. Prob.* **1**, 177-232, 1964.
8. Kimura,M. *The Neutral Theory of Molecular Evolution*, Cambridge Univ. Press, 1983.
9. Mühlenbein,H. Evolutionary algorithms: Theory and applications, in E.Aarts and J.K.Lenstra (eds.) *Local Search in Combinatorial Optimization*, Wiley, 1993.
10. Mühlenbein,H.and Schlierkamp-Voosen,D. Predictive models for the Breeder Genetic Algorithm, *Evolutionary Comptation* **1**, 25-49, 1993.
11. Mühlenbein,H. and Schlierkamp-Voosen,D. The science of breeding and its application to the breeder genetic algorithm BGA, *Evolutionary Comptation* **1**, 335-360, 1994.
12. Wright,S. Evolution in Mendelian populations, *Genetics* **16**, 97-159, 1931.

Estimating the Heritability by Decomposing the Genetic Variance

Hideki Asoh* and Heinz Mühlenbein

German National Research Center for Computer Science (GMD)
Schloss Birlinghoven, D-53754 Sankt Augustin, Germany
E-mail:asoh@etl.go.jp, muehlen@gmd.de
(* Permenent address: Electrotechnical Laboratory, Tsukuba, Ibaraki 305 Japan)

Abstract. Population genetics succeeded in recasting the macroscopic phenotypic Darwinian theory as formalized by Galton and Pearson into the microscopic genetic chance model initiated by Mendel. In order to do this the concept of genetic variance of a population was introduced. This concept and its application is one of the most difficult parts of population genetics. In this paper we define precisely how the genetic variance can be decomposed and how the method can be applied to haploid organisms. A fundamental theorem is proven which allows estimation of the heritability from microscopic genetic information of the population. It is indicated how the theorem can be used in the breeder genetic algorithm BGA.

1 Introduction

Genetics represents one of the most satisfying applications of statistical methods. Galton and Pearson found at the end of the last century a striking empirical regularity. On the average a son's height is halfway between that of his father and the overall average height for sons. They used data from about 1000 families. In order to see this regularity Galton and Pearson invented the scatter diagram, regression and correlation[4]. The regression coefficient between parent and offspring provides useful information for estimating the response of the population to selection[6].

Independently Mendel found some other striking empirical regularities like the reappearance of a recessive trait in one-fourth of the second generation hybrids. He conceived a chance model involving what are now called *genes* to explain his rules. He conjectured these genes by pure reasoning – he never saw any.

At first sight, the Galton–Pearson's results look very different from Mendel's, and it is hard to see how they can be explained by the same biological mechanism. Indeed Pearson wrote an article in 1904 claiming that his results cannot be derived from Mendel's laws. About 1920 Fisher, Wright and Haldane more or less simultaneously recognized the need to recast the Darwinian theory as described by Galton and Pearson in Mendelian terms. They succeeded in this task, but unfortunately much of the original work is very abstruse and difficult to follow. The difficulty lies in the concept of *additive genetic variance* and its connection to *heritability*.

Several researchers in theoretical biology have tried to calculate the heritability and the correlation between relatives[2][3] using the Mendelian chance model. However, the cases analysed in the literature of quantitative genetics are closely related to diploid organisms. In the context of evolutionary algorithms, haploid virtual organisms are used most of the time. In this paper we will make the classical analysis more precise and extend the analysis to haploid organisms.

The key idea of the analysis is to decompose the genetic variance into an additive part and non-additive parts. The same method is used to decompose the covariance between parent and offspring. The outline of the paper is as follows. In section 2 some definitions and notations are given. In section 3 the fitness function is decomposed into an additive part and its interacting parts. For this decomposition several lemmas are proven, which will be used in section 4 for the main results. Because of the space limitations we only sketch some of the proofs. In section 5 some applications of estimating heritability by the fundamental theorem are given. Furthermore comparisons to experimental results are done. The importance of this theorem and its connection to Fisher's fundamental theorem of natural selection are discussed in section 6.

2 Regression and heritability

Consider a population of N haploid individuals. The generations are discrete and the size of the population is fixed at N. The mating scheme is random, that is, two parents are selected randomly from the population. The chromosomes of the parents are recombined giving an offspring. Self-fertilization is allowed. Neither selection nor mutation takes place. In the following discussion we assume that the population size N is large enough that the sample mean variance of interesting statistical values are near to theoretical mean and variance.

We assume that each individual has one chromosome of n loci. We denote the set of alleles for the i-th locus as Θ_i. Let the chromosomes of two parents be denoted by $\mathbf{x} = (x_1, ..., x_n)$ and $\mathbf{y} = (y_1, ..., y_n)$. Here $x_i, y_i \in \Theta_i$. Recombination is done by uniform crossover. The offspring $\mathbf{z} = (z_1, ..., z_n)$ is computed according to the following probability:

$$Prob[z_i = x_i] = \frac{1}{2}, \quad Prob[z_i = y_i] = \frac{1}{2}. \qquad (1)$$

Recombination by uniform crossover is an adaptation of Mendel's chance model to haploid organisms.

Let the quantitative feature (fitness) of the individual with chromosome $\mathbf{x}$ be $f(\mathbf{x})$ and the relative frequency of the chromosome $\mathbf{x}$ in the population be $p(\mathbf{x})$. If we select two parents $\mathbf{x}$ and $\mathbf{y}$, then uniform crossover can generate 2^n offspring with equal probability of $1/2^n$. Note that the possible chromosomes of the offspring depend on the chromosomes of the parents and uniform crossover. If for instance the alleles at some loci are equal, then this allele remains fixed in the chromosome of all possible offspring. We denote the chromosome of the

i-th possible offspring of parents $\mathbf{x}$ and $\mathbf{y}$ by $\mathbf{z}_i$. Then the midparent–offspring covariance is defined as

$$Cov_{\bar{p}o} = \sum_{\mathbf{xy}} p(\mathbf{x})p(\mathbf{y}) \left(\frac{f(\mathbf{x}) + f(\mathbf{y})}{2} - \bar{f} \right) \frac{1}{2^n} \sum_{i=1}^{2^n} (f(\mathbf{z}_i) - \bar{f}). \tag{2}$$

Here $\bar{f}$ is the mean of the fitness value of the population.

$$\bar{f} = \sum_{\mathbf{x}} p(\mathbf{x})f(\mathbf{x}). \tag{3}$$

The midparent fitness is just the average of the parent's fitness. We assume that mean and variance of the parent population are equal to the offspring population because there is no selection.

From the covariance the midparent–offspring correlation $Cor_{\bar{p}o}$ and the regression coefficient $b_{\bar{p}o}$ for midparent and offspring can be easily obtained. Using the well known formula $Var_{\bar{p}} = Var_p/2$ and the relation $Var_o = Var_p$ we get

$$Cor_{\bar{p}o} = \frac{\sqrt{2}Cov_{\bar{p}o}}{Var_p} \quad \text{and} \quad b_{\bar{p}o} = \frac{Cov_{\bar{p}o}}{Var_{\bar{p}}} = \sqrt{2}Cor_{\bar{p}o}. \tag{4}$$

Galton and Pearson called the regression coefficient the *heritability*. The heritability can be used to estimate the *response to selection* in breeding experiments.

In [10] the response to selection equation was introduced

$$R(t) = b_t S(t), \tag{5}$$

where $R(t) = M(t+1) - M(t)$ is called the response and $S(t) = M_s(t) - M(t)$ is called the *selection differential*. $M(t)$ and $M(t+1)$ are the mean fitness of generation t and $t+1$, and $M_s(t)$ is the mean fitness of selected parents. b_t is called the *realized heritability*.

The following theorem was proven in [11].

Theorem 1 *If the regression equation*

$$(f'_{ij} - \bar{f}) = b_{\bar{p}o}\left(\frac{f_i + f_j}{2} - \bar{f}\right) + \varepsilon_{ij}$$

with $E[\varepsilon_{ij}] = 0$ is valid between the fitness value of selected parents (f_i, f_j) and the offspring generated from them (f'_{ij}), then

$$R(t) = b_{\bar{p}o}S(t).$$

The above theorem connects the regression coefficient with the *realized heritability* $R(t)/S(t)$ in selection experiments. For applications of this theorem see [11]

In the following we will describe a method for calculating the regression coefficient $b_{\bar{p}o}$ from the microscopic information contained in the genetic chance model. The model uses the fitness function and the distribution of the genes in the population.

3 Decomposing the fitness function

The fitness value f will be decomposed recursively. First we extract a constant term.

$$f(\mathbf{x}) = \alpha_0 + r_0(\mathbf{x}). \tag{6}$$

Least mean square error of $R_0 = \sum_{\mathbf{x}} p(\mathbf{x}) r_0(\mathbf{x})^2$ gives $\alpha_0 = \bar{f}$.

Next we extract the first order (additive) terms $\alpha_{(i)}(x_i)$ from the residual $r_0(\mathbf{x})$. Each $\alpha_{(i)}(x_i)$ depends only on the value of the i-th locus.

$$r_0(\mathbf{x}) = \sum_{i=1}^{n} \alpha_{(i)}(x_i) + r_1(\mathbf{x}). \tag{7}$$

Minimization of $R_1 = \sum_{\mathbf{x}} p(\mathbf{x}) r_1(\mathbf{x})^2$ gives

$$\alpha_{(i)}(x_i) = \sum_{\mathbf{x}|x_i} p(\mathbf{x}|x_i) r_0(\mathbf{x}) = \sum_{\mathbf{x}|x_i} p(\mathbf{x}|x_i) f(\mathbf{x}) - \bar{f}.$$

We denote this optimal value for $\alpha_{(i)}(x_i)$ as $f_{(i)}(x_i)$. Here $\sum_{\mathbf{x}|x_i}$ means that the allele of the i-th locus is fixed and the summation is taken over all variations of alleles at other loci. By $p(\mathbf{x}|x_i)$ we denotes the conditional probability induced from $p(\mathbf{x})$ under the condition of x_i being fixed. Exactly speaking this conditional probability should be noted as $p(x_1, ..., x_{i-1}, x_{i+1}, ..., x_n|x_i)$. However in order to save the space we use the above notation. Note that $\sum_{\mathbf{x}|x_i} p(\mathbf{x}|x_i) = 1$ holds. The above decomposition is related to first order schemata [5]. $f_{(i)}(x_i)$ is the average fitness of genotypes which belong to schemata $(*, ..., *, x_i, *, ..., *)$.

If $r_1(\mathbf{x}) \not\equiv 0$, we proceed further to extract second order terms from $r_1(\mathbf{x})$:

$$r_1(\mathbf{x}) = \sum_{\substack{(i,j) \\ i<j}} f_{(i,j)}(x_i, x_j) + r_2(\mathbf{x}). \tag{8}$$

Here,

$$
\begin{aligned}
f_{(i,j)}(x_i, x_j) &= \sum_{\mathbf{x}|x_i, x_j} p(\mathbf{x}|x_i, x_j)\, r_1(\mathbf{x}) \\
&= \sum_{\mathbf{x}|x_i, x_j} p(\mathbf{x}|x_i, x_j)\, f(\mathbf{x}) - f_{(i)}(x_i) - f_{(j)}(x_j) - \bar{f}.
\end{aligned}
$$

As before, $f_{(i,j)}(x_i, x_j)$ minimizes $R_2 = \sum_{\mathbf{x}} p(\mathbf{x}) r_2(\mathbf{x})^2$ When we have n loci, we can iterate this procedure $n - 1$ times and finally we get the decomposition of f

$$
\begin{aligned}
f(\mathbf{x}) = \bar{f} + \sum_{i} f_{(i)}(x_i) + \sum_{(i,j)} f_{(i,j)}(x_i, x_j) + \cdots \\
+ \sum_{\substack{(i_1,...,i_{n-1}) \\ i_1<...<i_{n-1}}} f_{(i_1,...,i_{n-1})}(x_{i_1}, ..., x_{i_{n-1}}) + r_{n-1}(\mathbf{x}).
\end{aligned}
$$

Lemma 1 *For all $k = 0$ to $n - 1$*

$$\sum_{\mathbf{x}} p(\mathbf{x}) \, r_k(\mathbf{x}) = 0.$$

Furthermore for all $k = 1$ to $n - 1$ and for all combinations of $(i_1, ..., i_k)$, $i_1 < ... < i_k$

$$\sum_{x_{i_1}, ..., x_{i_k}} p_{(i_1, ..., i_k)}(x_{i_1}, ..., x_{i_k}) \, f_{(i_1, ..., i_k)}(x_{i_1}, ..., x_{i_k}) = 0,$$

Here $p_{(i_1, ..., i_k)}$ is a marginal probability distribution of $p(\mathbf{x})$ on $(x_{i_1}, ..., x_{i_k})$, that is,

$$p_{(i_1, ..., i_k)}(x_{i_1}, ..., x_{i_k}) = \sum_{\mathbf{x} \mid x_{i_1}, ..., x_{i_k}} p(\mathbf{x}).$$

Proof The lemma can be proven by induction. Due to space limitations we have to omit the proof. ∎

Now we formulate several lemmas which are needed for the final theorem. For all of them the assumption of independence of each locus is needed. This condition is called *linkage equilibrium* in the literature of genetics. That is, it is assumed that $p(\mathbf{x})$ is given by

$$p(\mathbf{x}) = \prod_{i=1}^{n} p_i(x_i). \tag{9}$$

Here $p_i(x_i)$ denotes the relative frequency of allele x_i at the i th locus.

The next lemma can be proven by induction similar to lemma 1.

Lemma 2 *For all $k = 1$ to $n - 1$, for all $l = 0$ to k, for all combination of $(j_1, ..., j_l)$, $j_1 < ... < j_l$ and for all fixed values of x_{j_s},*

$$\sum_{\mathbf{x} \mid x_{j_1}, ..., x_{j_l}} p(\mathbf{x}) \, r_k(\mathbf{x}) = 0.$$

For all $k = 2$ to $n - 1$, for all $l = 0$ to $k - 1$, for all combination of $(j_1, ..., j_l) \subset (i_1, ..., i_k)$, $j_1 < ... < j_l$ and for all fixed values of x_{j_s},

$$\sum_{\mathbf{x} \mid x_{j_1}, ..., x_{j_l}} p(\mathbf{x}) \, f_{(i_1, ..., i_k)}(x_{i_1}, ..., x_{i_k}) = 0.$$

Lemma 3 (Orthogonality)

All terms in the decomposition of $f(\mathbf{x})$ are orthogonal to each other, that is,

$$\sum_{\mathbf{xy}} p(\mathbf{x}) p(\mathbf{y}) \, f_{(i_1, ..., i_k)}(z_{i_1}, ..., z_{i_k}) \, f_{(j_1, ..., j_l)}(z_{j_1}, ..., z_{j_l}) = 0 \tag{10}$$

hold unless $k = l$ and $(i_1, ..., i_k) = (j_1, ..., j_l)$ and $z_{i_t} = z_{j_t}$ for all t. For any $k = 1$ to $n - 1$

$$\sum_{\mathbf{xy}} p(\mathbf{x}) p(\mathbf{y}) \, f_{(i_1, ..., i_k)}(z_{i_1}, ..., z_{i_k}) \, r_{n-1}(z_1, ..., z_n) = 0 \tag{11}$$

hold. Here z_{i_t} is x_{i_t} or y_{i_t}, z_{j_t} is x_{j_t} or y_{j_t} and z_t is x_t or y_t.

Proof Without loss of generality we can assume that $k \geq l$, $z_{i_1} \notin \{z_{j_1}, ..., z_{j_l}\}$, and $z_{i_1} = x_{i_1}$. Then taking the sum for the value of x_{i_1} first, we obtain equation (10) by using lemma 2. The proof of equation (11) is similar. ∎

Lemma 4 (Decomposition of Variance)
 The variance of the fitness function f can be decomposed into

$$Var_p = V_1 + V_2 + \cdots + V_{n-1} + V_n. \tag{12}$$

Here V_k for $k = 1$ to $n-1$ are defined as

$$V_k = \sum_{\substack{(i_j,...,i_k) \\ i_1 < ... < i_k}} \sum_{x_{i_1},...,x_{i_k}} p_{(i_1,...,i_k)}(x_{i_1}, ..., x_{i_k}) \, f_{(i_i,...,i_k)}(x_{i_i}, ..., x_{i_k})^2, \tag{13}$$

and

$$V_n = \sum_{\mathbf{x}} p(\mathbf{x}) \, r_{n-1}(\mathbf{x})^2. \tag{14}$$

Proof This decomposition is a direct consequence of the orthogonality described in lemma 3. ∎

The above decomposition is also used in the field of experimental design, factor analysis and analysis of variance. We are now ready to formulate the main theorem.

4 Decomposition of covariance

In order to estimate the regression coefficient, the covariance has to be decomposed also. The result is given in the next theorem.

Theorem 2 *In a random mating genetic population with uniform crossover and in linkage equilibrium, the covariance can be estimated by*

$$Cov_{\bar{p}o} = \frac{1}{2}V_1 + \frac{1}{4}V_2 + \cdots + \frac{1}{2^n}V_n = \sum_{k=1}^{n} \frac{1}{2^k}V_k \tag{15}$$

Proof We recall the definition of the midparent–offspring covariance:

$$Cov_{\bar{p}o} = \sum_{\mathbf{xy}} p(\mathbf{x})p(\mathbf{y}) \left(\frac{f(\mathbf{x}) + f(\mathbf{y})}{2} - \bar{f} \right) \frac{1}{2^n} \sum_{i=1}^{2^n} (f(\mathbf{z}_i) - \bar{f}).$$

Here each element of $\mathbf{z}_i$ is inherited from one of the parents' alleles. Without loss of generality we can assume $\bar{f} = 0$. Because of random mating we have

$$Cov_{\bar{p}o} = \sum_{\mathbf{xy}} p(\mathbf{x})p(\mathbf{y}) \, f(\mathbf{x}) \frac{1}{2^n} (f(\mathbf{z}_1) + \cdots + f(\mathbf{z}_{2^n})).$$

We now compute one of the 2^n elements

$$\sum_{\mathbf{xy}} p(\mathbf{x})p(\mathbf{y})f(\mathbf{x})f(\mathbf{z}_i).$$

These elements can be classified into $n+1$ classes according to the number of alleles (0 to n) which $\mathbf{z}_i$ inherits from $\mathbf{x}$.

For example, let $\mathbf{x}$ and $\mathbf{z}_i$ have one common allele at locus 1, that is, $\mathbf{z}_i = (x_1, y_2, ..., y_n)$. Then applying the decomposition of $f(\mathbf{x})$ and using the orthogonality lemma 3 repeatedly, we get the result

$$\sum_{\mathbf{xy}} p(\mathbf{x})p(\mathbf{y})f(\mathbf{x})f(\mathbf{z}_i) = \sum_{\mathbf{xy}} p(\mathbf{x})p(\mathbf{y})(f_{(1)}(x_1) + f_{(2)}(x_2) + \cdots + r_{n-1}(\mathbf{x}))$$

$$\times (f_{(1)}(x_1) + f_{(2)}(y_2) + \cdots + r_{n-1}(\mathbf{z}_i))$$

$$= \sum_{x_1} p_1(x_1)f_{(1)}(x_1)^2.$$

Now summing over all $\mathbf{z}_i$ which inherit one allele from $\mathbf{x}$, we obtain

$$C_1 = \sum_{\mathbf{z}_i,\, |\mathbf{x} \cap \mathbf{z}_i|=1} \sum_{\mathbf{xy}} p(\mathbf{x})p(\mathbf{y})f(\mathbf{x})f(\mathbf{z_i}) = \sum_i \sum_{x_i} p_i(x_i)f_{(i)}(x_i)^2 = V_1.$$

In general, let $\mathbf{x}$ and $\mathbf{z}_i$ have s common alleles. Without loss of generality let $\mathbf{z}_i = (x_1, x_2, ..., x_s, y_{s+1}, ..., y_n)$ then

$$\sum_{\mathbf{xy}} p(\mathbf{x})p(\mathbf{y})f(\mathbf{x})f(\mathbf{z}_i) = \sum_{i=1}^{s} \sum_{x_i} p_i(x_i)f_{(i)}(x_i)^2$$

$$+ \sum_{\substack{(i,j) \\ i<j}} \sum_{x_1, x_j} p_i(x_i)p_j(x_j)\, f_{(i,j)}(x_i, x_j)^2 + \cdots$$

$$+ \prod_{i=1}^{s} p_i(x_i)\, f_{(1,...,s)}(x_1, ..., x_s)^2.$$

The above equation is a result of the linkage equilibrium. Carefully counting the number of instances of each term and taking the sum of all possible combinations of $\mathbf{x}$ and $\mathbf{z}_i$ which have s alleles in common, we get

$$C_s = \sum_{\mathbf{z}_i,\, |\mathbf{x} \cap \mathbf{z}_i|=s} \sum_{\mathbf{xy}} p(\mathbf{x})p(\mathbf{y})f(\mathbf{x})f(\mathbf{z_i})$$

$$= \binom{n-1}{s-1} V_1 + \binom{n-2}{s-2} V_2 + \cdots + \binom{n-s}{0} V_s.$$

Finally by summing up all C_s from $s=1$ to n, we obtain

$$Cov_{\bar{p}o} = \frac{1}{2^n} \sum_{s=1}^{n} C_s = \frac{1}{2}V_1 + \frac{1}{2^2}V_2 + \cdots + \frac{1}{2^n}V_n \quad \blacksquare$$

From this theorem, we can easily derive the fundamental theorem.

Theorem 3 *In a random mating genetic population with uniform crossover and in linkage equilibrium, the correlation between midparent and offspring and the regression coefficient can be estimated as*

$$Cor_{\bar{p}o} = \sum_{k=1}^{n} \frac{\sqrt{2}}{2^k} \frac{V_k}{Var_p}, \qquad b_{\bar{p}o} = \sum_{k=1}^{n} \frac{1}{2^{k-1}} \frac{V_k}{Var_p}. \qquad (16)$$

Corollary 1 *If the fitness function f is additive, that is, $f(\mathbf{x}) = \sum_i f_{(i)}(x_i)$, then*

$$Cor_{\bar{p}o} = \frac{1}{\sqrt{2}}, \qquad b_{\bar{p}o} = 1. \qquad (17)$$

The fundamental theorem connects the microscopic genetic chance model with macroscopic variables. A severe limitation is the assumption of linkage equilibrium. In the science of breeding estimating the *heritability* plays a crucial role [11]. There are at least three methods to estimate the heritability - the realized heritability, the usual regression coefficient and the regression coefficient derived from the fundamental theorem. The question now arises which estimate is the best prediction for selection experiments? We have to postpone an answer to this question to a forthcomming paper.

5 Examples and comparison with simulations

Numerically decomposing the variance is computationally far too expensive to be of use for the breeder genetic algorithm. Breeders conjecture that the *additive genetic variance* V_1 is the most important factor of the heritability. The higher order interactions will contribute much less to the heritability. We will test in a forthcoming paper if this conjecture is correct. Here we give some simple examples.

5.1 ONEMAX function

Let each gene have n loci, and each locus have 2 alleles 0 and 1. The fitness value is defined by the number of 1s in the gene. This function is totally additive. Hence for ONEMAX function we may use corollary 2.

$$Cor_{\bar{p}o} = \frac{1}{\sqrt{2}}, \qquad b_{\bar{p}o} = 1.$$

Results from simulations using our Parallel Genetic Algorithm Simulator PeGA-suS confirm the above values.

5.2 PLATEAU function

Let the chromosome be composed of n building blocks and each building block have k loci. Each loci has 2 alleles 0 and 1. Then PLATEAU(n, k)(**x**) is defined by the number of blocks which contain only 1's. If this number is s then the fitness value is ks. Here we take PLATEAU(10,3) as an example. We decomposed it under the condition of $p_i(x_i) = 1/2$. Since PLATEAU(10,3) can be described with a 3rd order polynomial, the decomposition of the variance is also up to 3rd order interaction part such as $V_p = V_1 + V_2 + V_3$. We calculated

$$\frac{V_1}{Var_p} = \frac{V_2}{Var_p} = \frac{3}{7}, \frac{V_3}{Var_p} = \frac{1}{7}.$$

The regression coefficient $b_{\bar{p}o}$ is given by

$$b_{\bar{p}o} = \frac{V_1}{Var_p} + \frac{1}{2}\frac{V_2}{Var_p} + \frac{1}{4}\frac{V_3}{Var_p} = 0.68.$$

In this case PeGASuS gives the result $b_{\bar{p}o} \approx 0.65$ for PLATEAU(10,3).

5.3 DECEPTIVE function

DECEPTIVE(n,k)(**x**) is defined on nk loci each with two alleles. For the definition of this function please see [5]. Here we consider DECEPTIVE(10,3). We decomposed it up to 3rd order terms under the condition of $p_i(x_i) = 1/2$ and we got

$$\frac{V_1}{Var_p} = \frac{21}{155} \quad \frac{V_2}{Var_p} = \frac{70}{155} \quad \frac{V_3}{Var_p} = \frac{64}{155}.$$

The estimated value of regression coefficient is $b_{\bar{p}o} = 0.465$. Simulation show a highly oscillating regression coefficient. The average is given by $b_{\bar{p}o} = 0.5$ for DECEPTIVE(10,3).

6 Concluding Remarks

We have derived a formula for calculating the midparent–offspring regression coefficient from the microscopic genetic information of the population. This result was applied to three popular fitness functions. The value calculated by the formula was confirmed by Monte Carlo type simulation.

The usage of this method for the breeder genetic algorithm BGA is under investigation. The numerical implementation of the general decomposition method is prohibitive. It will be useful only if the first term, *the additive genetic variance* V_1 is the main factor contributing to the heritability. This is conjectured in the scientific literature about breeding.

The additive genetic variance is also used in Fisher's well known *Fundamental Theorem of Natural Selection*. It postulates that the heritability which can be exploited by selection only depends on the additive part of the genetic variance[2].

In the literature about genetic algorithm the *schema theorem* is used to connect the microscopic chance model with macroscopic variables [5]. Comparing the schema theorem with the classical fundamental theorem shows the shortcomings of the schema theorem. Extending the fundamental theorem to continuous fitness functions (infinite number of alleles), noisy fitness functions and other crossover operators would be also worthwhile to investigate.

Note: After we had submitted this paper we noticed that Kempthone has derived essentially the same results (Lemma 4, Theorem 2 and 3) in 1950's [7][8].

Acknowledgments

Bill Buckles carefully read the manuscript and gave us helpful comments. This work was done while one of the authors (Hideki Asoh) was at GMD as a guest researcher. He thanks GMD and Electrotechnical Laboratory (ETL) for giving the chance of staying, and also to the Science and Technology Agency of the Japanese government for supporting his stay. This work is a part of the SIFOGA project supported by Real World Computing Partnership.

References

1. Bäck,T. and Schwefel,H.-P. An overview of evolutionary algorithms for parameter optimization, *Evolutionary Computation* 1, 1-24, 1993.
2. Crow,J.F. and Kimura,M. *An Introduction to Population Genetics Theory*, Harper and Row, New York, 1970.
3. Fisher,R.A. *The Genetical Theory of Natural Selection 2nd. Ed.*, Dover Press, New York, 1958.
4. Freedman,D., Pisani,R., Purves,R., and Adhikkari,A. *Statistics* 2nd. Ed., W.W.Norton, New York, 1991.
5. Goldberg,D.E. *Genetic Algorithms in Search, Optimization and Machine Learning*, Addison-Wesley, Readin, 1989.
6. Hartl,D.L. *A Primer of Population Genetics*, Sinauer Associates, Sunderland, 1981.
7. Kempthone,O. The correlation between relatives in a random mating population, *Proc. Roy. Soc. London, B* **143**, 103-113, 1954.
8. Kempthone,O. The theoretical values of correlations between relatives in random mating populations, *Genetics* **40**, 153-167, 1955.
9. Mühlenbein,H. Evolutionary algorithms: Theory and applications, in E.Aarts and J.K.Lenstra (eds.) *Local Search in Combinatorial Optimization*, Wiley, 1993.
10. Mühlenbein,H.and Schlierkamp-Voosen,D. Predictive models for the Breeder Genetic Algorithm, *Evolutionary Computation* 1, 25-49, 1993.
11. Mühlenbein,H. and Schlierkamp-Voosen,D. The science of breeding and its application to the breeder genetic algorithm BGA, *Evolutionary Computation* 1, 335-360, 1994.

Analyzing Hyperplane Synthesis in Genetic Algorithms Using Clustered Schemata

Thang Nguyen Bui[1] and Byung-Ro Moon[2]

[1] Dept. of Computer Science
Pennsylvania State University, Middletown, PA 17057, USA
[2] Dept. of Computer Science and Engineering
Pennsylvania State University, University Park, PA 16802, USA

Abstract. A new type of schema, *c-schema*, is introduced, which emphasizes the inner structure, particularly specific-symbol clusters rather than the defining length. A new type of building block, *c-building block*, is also suggested as a consequence of this. The expected survival probability of a schema based on this new schema model is given as well as a new explanation about how allelic reordering by depth first search can help improve genetic algorithms' search capability. Extensive experimental results are also provided.

1 Introduction

The idea of preprocessing (hyperplane synthesis) for genetic algorithms (GAs) was first proposed in [3] and extensive experimental results on various problems were provided in [2, 4, 5]. The main idea of hyperplane synthesis is to reorder allelic positions before GAs start. The motivation was from Holland's Schema Theorem [10] and the inversion operator [6]. By the Schema Theorem, schemata with short defining lengths have higher probabilities of survival through generations. The objective of preprocessing *was* to decrease the defining lengths of perceived high-quality schemata by pre-reordering alleles rather than using the random reordering suggested by the inversion method. Two types of preprocessing heuristics for GAs on graph optimization problems were given in [3]: one based on breadth first search (BFS) and the other based on depth first search (DFS). The BFS-based heuristic worked well and it could be well explained using solely its effect on the defining lengths of schemata. But for the DFS-based heuristic there was no apparent explanation of its good performance, comparable to that of the BFS-based heuristic, despite the fact that it did not visibly reduce the defining length of schemata. In this paper, we provide a possible explanation for this phenomenon by concentrating on the inner structures of schemata rather than their defining lengths.

DeJong [7] pointed out that the defining length is not necessarily a dominating factor of a schema's survival probability when multi-point crossovers are used. This observation was later extended by DeJong and Spears in [8]. Their work provides us a motivation to concentrate on a schema's specific-symbol clusters. The key property we found in DFS-based Reordering (described in more detail in Section 3.1) is that there are some cases in which we can transform perceived high-quality schemata into counterpart ones with clustered specific-symbol distribution. When this reordering of schemata was applied before the start of a genetic algorithm, it showed a significant performance improvement on certain applications.

In this paper, we use the graph bisection problem as an example and compare the performance of GAs with and without the preprocessing. Let $G = (V, E)$ be a graph on n vertices, where n is even, a *bisection* of G is a partition of the vertex set V into 2 disjoint subsets A and B of equal size. The number of edges having one endpoint in A and the other endpoint in B is called the *cut size* of the bisection. The *graph bisection* problem is the problem of finding a bisection with the minimum cut size. For this problem we use a locus-based encoding. A chromosome is represented by a binary string of length n, where if the ith gene value is 0 (1) then the ith vertex belongs to side A (B). See [2] for implementation details.

We assume that the readers are familiar with basic terminologies of GA: schema, order, specific symbol, defining length, etc. The remainder of the paper is organized as follows. In Section 2, we introduce c-schemata and discuss their survival probability. In Section 3, we provide some combinatorial arguments based on the c-schema model. In Section 4, we show experimental results on the graph bisection problem.

2 C-Schemata

2.1 Building Block Hypothesis and the Schema Theorem

GA's working principle is often explained by the *building-block* hypothesis [10, 9]. According to the building block hypothesis, low-order high-quality schemata are recombined together to construct higher-order high-quality schemata. For a low-order schema to contribute to a higher-order schema, it must be preserved through crossovers. In the single-point crossover scheme, schemata with short defining lengths have higher survival probability through crossovers [10]. Low-ordered high-quality schemata of short defining lengths are called *building blocks*. Building blocks play an important role in genetic space search since genetic algorithms are believed to seek near-optimal performance through juxtaposition of building blocks [9].

Let $P(t)$ represent the population at time t. Denote by $m(H, t)$ the expected number of chromosomes containing a schema H within population $P(t)$. A lower bound on the expected number of chromosomes containing the schema H within population $P(t + 1)$ is given by the following theorem.

Schema Theorem [10] In a genetic algorithm using a proportional selection and single-point crossover, the following holds for each schema H represented in $P(t)$:

$$m(H, t+1) \geq m(H, t)\frac{f(H, t)}{\bar{f}(t)}\left[1 - p_c\frac{\delta(H)}{n-1}\right] \tag{1}$$

where $f(H, t)$ is the average fitness of the chromosomes containing the schema H at time t, $\bar{f}(t)$ is the average fitness of all chromosomes in $P(t)$ at time t, P_c is the crossover rate, $\delta(H)$ is the defining length of the schema H, and n is the length of each chromosome. □

Due to the importance of this theorem, it has been also called the Fundamental Theorem of Genetic Algorithms [9]. Inequality (1) says that short, high-quality schemata have exponentially high survival chance as generations pass.

2.2 Motivation

The analysis of schemas' survival probability based on defining lengths works well on single-point crossover models, but doesn't always work well on multi-point crossover models. DeJong first observed that the survival probability of a 2nd order schema is not necessarily proportional to its defining length when multi-point crossovers are used [7]. Recently, DeJong and Spears extended this to provide a detailed analysis of the survival probabilities of higher-order schemata [8]. Their key observation is that a schema is not disrupted when an even number (including 0) of crossover points fall between the two specific symbols of every pair of adjacent specific symbols. Let the specific symbols of an rth order schema be indexed from 0 (leftmost) to $r-1$ (rightmost). Let L_i be the length between the 0th (leftmost) specific symbol and the ith specific symbol, for $i = 1, 2, \ldots, r-1$; and let n be the length of the chromosome. They provided an approximate recursive equation to calculate $P_{m,even}(k)$, the probability that an even number of crossover points fall between each of the defining positions of the mth order schema (consisting of the 0th specific symbol through the $(m-1)^{st}$ one) by a k-point crossover as follows:

$$P_{m,even}(k) = \sum_{i=0}^{\lfloor \frac{k}{2} \rfloor} \binom{k}{2i} \left(\frac{L_{m-1}}{n} \right)^{2i} \left(\frac{n - L_{m-1}}{n} \right)^{k-2i} P_{m-1,even}(2i) \qquad (2)$$

The above equation assumes that the crossover points are independent of one another (they are actually dependent because no two crossover points can fall onto the same position). But this approximation causes little harm as long as $k \ll n$, which is true in most cases. This equation implies that $P_{r,even}(k)$ is highly dependent on the positions of the specific symbols.

Consider the two schemata H_1 and H_2 of order 8 with the same defining length as follows:

$$\text{***s***s***s***s***s***s***s***s*** } (H_1)$$
$$\text{***sss*s******************s*sss*** } (H_2).$$

We use the character "s" from here on to mark the positions of specific symbols. The specific symbols are evenly distributed on schema H_1, whereas they are highly clustered in schema H_2. If we use a single-point crossover, the survival probability through the crossover is 6/34 for both schemas H_1 and H_2. If we use 2-point crossover, the survival probability of H_1 is $\frac{7\binom{4}{2}+\binom{6}{2}}{\binom{34}{2}} = \frac{57}{561}$, and that of schema H_2 is $\frac{\binom{20}{2}+2\binom{2}{2}+\binom{6}{2}}{\binom{34}{2}} = \frac{207}{561}$. These probabilities are not calculated by Equation (2), but by Equation (3) which will be presented in Section 2.3. The survival probability of clustered schema H_2 is almost four times the survival probability of schema H_1. It is not difficult to guess that this phenomenon will remain with other multi-point crossovers. Defining lengths have little to do with survival probabilities in this context. This suggests that we need a different type of building blocks, *c-building blocks*, when multi-point crossovers are used. In this case, low-order *highly-clustered* schemata should serve as building blocks. The proposed preprocessing transforms perceived important schemata into good clustered forms. A schema can survive even when the above condition for $P_{r,even}(k)$ is not satisfied if all lost specific symbols in a parent are accidentally recovered by the other parent. For simplicity, we ignore such cases in this discussion.

2.3 C-Schemata

In this section we provide another equation for the survival probability of a schema emphasizing the distribution of the specific symbols. We introduce a new type of schema, *clustered schema* or *c-schema*. Define a qth degree c-schema as $D_0 C_1 D_1 C_2 D_2 \ldots C_q D_q$ where $C_i \in \{0,1\}^+$, $i = 1, 2, \ldots, q$, $D_i \in \{*\}^+$, $i = 1, \ldots, q-1$, and $D_0 D_q \in \{*\}^*$. An ordinary schema of order r can be represented by a c-schema of degree q such that $q \leq r$. Define $P_k(D_0 C_1 D_1 \ldots C_q D_q)$ to be the probability that a c-schema $D_0 C_1 D_1 \ldots C_q D_q$ survives through a k-point crossover. For the c-schema to survive, an even number (including 0) of crossover points should fall on each D_i for $i = 1, 2, \ldots, q-1$, and furthermore no crossover point fall within any C_i for $i = 1, 2, \ldots, q$. Let the number of crossover points falling on D_j be $2i_j$. Let i_q be the number of remaining crossover points (i.e., $i_q = k - 2(i_1 + \ldots + i_{q-1})$). The number of all cases where an even number of crossover points fall on every D_i for $i = 1, 2, \ldots, q-1$ is the cardinality of the set $S_{even} = \{(i_1, \ldots, i_{q-1}) | 2i_1 + \ldots + 2i_{q-1} \leq k\}$. For a c-schema to survive through a k-point crossover, it should be the case that $(i_1, \ldots, i_{q-1}) \in S_{even}$ and all remaining crossover points (i_q points) should fall on D_0 or D_q. From the above argument, we have the following non-recursive equation:

$$P_k(D_0 C_1 D_1 \ldots C_q D_q) = \sum_{i_1 + \ldots + i_{q-1} \leq \lfloor k/2 \rfloor} \frac{\binom{|D_1|+1}{2i_1} \cdots \binom{|D_{q-1}|+1}{2i_{q-1}} \binom{|D_0 D_q|}{i_q}}{\binom{n-1}{k}} \quad (3)$$

This probability does take into account the fact that crossover points are dependent variables. The equation reveals an interesting fact: the lengths of $|C_i|$'s have nothing to do with $P_k(D_0 C_1 D_1 \ldots C_q D_q)$ as long as $|C_1 C_2 \cdots C_q|$ is fixed. Any ordinary schema of order r can be also represented by a c-schema of degree q such that $q \leq r$. If $q \ll r$, then the c-schema model provides a much simpler analysis of the survival probability. The smaller q is, the less fragmented the specific symbols are, which we suspect results in a higher survival probability. On the other hand if q is fixed then a c-schema must be such that $|D_1|, |D_2|, \ldots, |D_{q-1}|, |D_0 D_q|$ have a large variance to have a high survival probability (but that may be sufficient to guarantee high survival probability). Fig. 1 shows the relationship between the variance of $|D_i|$'s and $P_k(D_0 C_1 D_1 \ldots C_q D_q)$ on 5-point crossover. Fifth degree c-schemata of order 20 on a chromosome of length 100 were used for the plot.

The preprocessing method called DFS Reordering in the next section effectively uses the above implications. It should be noted that c-schema model has little advantage over an ordinary schema model in analyzing the survival probability when we use single-point crossovers since it is always disrupted if the (unique) crossover point falls within the defining range of the schema unless the other parent has the lost specific symbols.

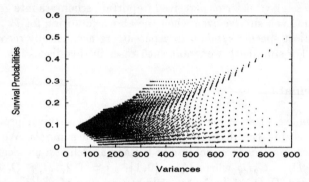

Fig. 1. Relationship between the variance of $|D_i|$'s and the survival probability.

3 Making Use of C-Schemata

3.1 DFS Reordering: A Schema Preprocessing Heuristic

We consider only combinatorial optimization problems on graphs in this paper. We assume locus-based encoding schemes such that every vertex in the graph occupies a fixed corresponding position on chromosomes. In such an encoding, a chromosome can be seen as a linear ordering of vertices with values. A natural order is the one given by its adjacency list or adjacency matrix. DFS Reordering reorders vertices by the visiting order of a depth first search (DFS). A reordering has the effect of transforming every schema into a counterpart schema [3]. We do this only once before the genetic main process begins. DFS Reordering heuristic was proposed in [3] with other heuristics for the purpose of decreasing the defining lengths of high-quality schemata. It was observed that the DFS-based reordering, in general, did not reduce schemas' defining lengths as much as the BFS-based reordering. However, the performance of the GA with DFS Reordering was comparable to that of the GA with BFS Reordering. Thus we need to provide a different explanation for the working of DFS Reordering as the Schema Theorem does not help here.

3.2 How DFS Reordering Helps To Construct Good C-Schemata?

In this section we provide indications why DFS reordering might help creating good c-schemata. We define an *island* to be a connected subgraph forming a cluster with a small number of cross edges (*bridges*) connecting the island to the remainder of the graph. Fig. 2 shows an island of 6 vertices with 4 bridges. In the graph bisection problem, vertices in an island are more likely to belong to the same side than an arbitrary set of vertices in a good solution. In the clique problem, vertices in an island have a larger probability of having a clique or belonging to a clique than an arbitrary set of vertices. This implies that vertices in an island are more likely to form a high-quality schema than an arbitrary set of vertices. Based on this observation, we now think about how a schema consisting of the vertices of an island is transformed into a probabilistically better schema. Consider the schema consisting of vertices in an island; only positions occupied by vertices in the island have specific symbols in the schema. The following proposition says that an island with a small number of bridges is likely to form a good c-schema after a DFS reordering.

Proposition 1. *For an island with k bridges, if the vertices are reordered by the visiting order of DFS, vertices in an island form c-schemata of the form $D_0 C_1 D_1 C_2 D_2 \ldots C_q D_q$ such that $q \leq k+1$.*

Proof. Case 1 (The starting point is outside the island): If a bridge is used as a tree edge in the DFS tree, it acts as an entrance and an exit of the island exactly once. If not, the bridge is not traveled through; consequently it has nothing to do with entrance or exit. Since there are k bridges, we can have a maximum of k entrances and k exits. Each entrance/exit pair has a corresponding set of newly visited vertices in the island. Each set constitutes a set C_i of consecutive specific symbols. There can't be any unvisited vertices left in the island after a maximum of k entrance/exit pairs since this would contradict the fact that DFS visits all vertices. *Case 2 (The starting point is inside the island):* Similar to case 1. In this case, we can have a maximum of $k-1$ entrance/exit pairs each having a corresponding set of new visited vertices in the island except the first exit and the last entrance. Since there may be a set of newly visited vertices before the first exit and after the last entrance, respectively, a maximum of $k+1$ C_i's are possible. □

Although q, the number of C_i's, is bounded by $k+1$, it may be much less than the possible maximum. For each bridge that is classified as a non-tree edge in the DFS, q decreases by 1. The next example hints that q may be considerably less than $k+1$.

In Fig. 2 the left side represents the given indices of the 18 vertices in a given graph. The black vertices in the dotted circle form a cluster and we trace the schema consisting of those vertices. The importance of clustered vertices in graph optimization problems was mentioned at the beginning of the subsection. Using a DFS (the corresponding DFS tree is given in the small rectangle), the vertices are reindexed by the visiting order and the original schema is transformed into another one as shown on the right side of the figure. If we use a single-point crossover, the survival probability of the original schema is $3/17$, and that of the transformed schema is also $3/17$; thus the transformation doesn't improve the survival probability. But if we use a 2-point crossover, the survival probability of the original schema is $\frac{2\binom{5}{2}+\binom{2}{2}+\binom{3}{2}}{\binom{17}{2}} = \frac{3}{17}$, and that of the transformed schema is $\frac{\binom{10}{2}+\binom{3}{2}}{\binom{17}{2}} = \frac{6}{17}$. In the case of 3-point crossover, they are $\frac{64}{680}$ and $\frac{136}{680}$, respectively.

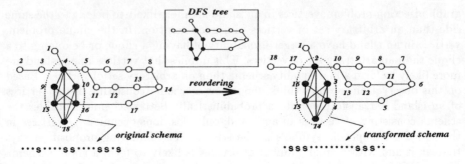

Fig. 2. A schema transformation by DFS Reordering.

Although the defining lengths of the two schemata are the same, the latter has a higher survival probability due to its clustered distribution of specific symbols. This phenomenon is expected to remain for k-point crossover, $k > 3$, by virtue of the discussion in Section 2.3. It is worth noting that the denser the island the fewer the expected number of clusters in the resulting schema. For the example of Fig. 2, since the number of bridges is 4, we expect at most 5 clusters in a schema consisting of those vertices by Proposition 1. However, only 3 of the 4 bridges are used as tree edges, furthermore, it turned out that only two clusters are in the resulting schema after DFS Reordering.

3.3 An Analysis Using A Simple Example

In this section, we provide simple combinatorial arguments with a successful example. Our experiments with the graph bisection problem show that caterpillar graphs and geometric graphs benefit from DFS Reordering. The definition of these graphs are given in Table I later. Among them, we choose caterpillar graphs for our example since they have simple structures, good regularities, and very explicit clustering properties. It is known that caterpillar graphs are very difficult for standard graph bisection algorithms [12]. We assume locus-based encoding as mentioned before, that is, every vertex has its own fixed position on chromosomes.

A caterpillar graph is a graph with sequentially connected articulation points each having the same number of legs. Let a *unit cluster* of a caterpillar graph be a subgraph consisting of an articulation point and its corresponding legs. Fig. 3 shows a caterpillar graph having articulation points with 6 legs. This graph was also used in [3] where it was shown that the expected defining length of a schema of a unit cluster significantly decreases after BFS Reordering, another reordering heuristic that is based on breadth first search. In case of the graph bisection problem, all the components of a unit cluster should belong to the same side, say the left side, in an optimal bisection with few exceptions. We believe that clustered vertices (in a relative sense) are usually more prone to be participants in a high quality schema on a chromosome than an arbitrary set of vertices in most graphs.

Consider a unit cluster U_d consisting of an articulation point with d legs. For brevity we use U_d to refer to both the unit cluster and the corresponding schema

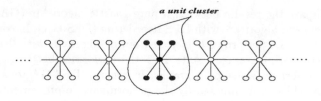

Fig. 3. Caterpillar graph and a unit cluster.

since there is little possibility of confusion. Let's apply DFS Reordering on the caterpillar graph. We ignore the case where the starting point of the DFS (the root of the DFS tree) is inside the cluster since the probability of that happening is very low if $d \ll n$. Index the articulation points from 1 to k, and let the index of the articulation point of the unit cluster under consideration be i. If the first articulation point visited by the DFS has an index greater than i, then a schema consisting of the vertices in the cluster at articulation point i has the following form after reordered by the visiting order of DFS:

$$\ldots.****ss..s****\ldots.****ss..s****\ldots.$$
$$\underbrace{}_{d(i-1)}$$

This is a c-schema of the form $D_0 C_1 D_1 C_2 D_2$ where $|D_1| = d(i-1)$ and $|C_1| + |C_2| = d+1$. If the first articulation point visited by the DFS has an index less than i, then $|D_1| = d(k-i)$, instead of $d(i-1)$. This type of schemata has very high survival probability by the arguments of Section 2. From the above argument and some simple calculations, we obtain the following proposition.

Proposition 2. *If the vertices on the chromosome of a caterpillar graph, that has k articulation points each having d legs, are reordered by the visiting order of a DFS, then a unit cluster U_d forms a c-schema $D_0 C_1 D_1 C_2 D_2$ where $|D_1| \approx \frac{n}{3}$ and $|C_1| + |C_2| = d+1$.* □

This proposition also implies that the defining length of the transformed c-schema is $\approx \frac{n}{3}$ assuming $d \ll n$. In [3] it was shown that the expected defining length of the schema U_d is $\Theta(d)$ if we reorder the vertices by breadth first search (BFS Reordering). This says that DFS Reordering generally makes schemata with quite longer defining lengths than those produced by BFS Reordering. However, experimental results showed that DFS Reordering performed comparable to BFS Reordering on all multi-point crossovers we tried (2, 3, 4, 5, and 9-point crossovers). C-schema model seems to well explain this phenomenon.

4   Experimental Results

Table I shows experimental results on the graph bisection problem. They are updated results from [3] reflecting the latest version of the algorithm. The figures in the table represent the cut size obtained by 1,000 trials on each graph. The column titled "Best Knowns (or Optima)" shows the best known results by the simulated annealing algorithm as given in [11] (for random and geometric graphs) or the optima (for regular, caterpillar, and grid graphs). CPU times are on a Sun SPARC

IPX. We compare the results between a pure genetic algorithm (GA) and those by the same genetic algorithm with DFS Reordering (DFS-GA). In comparing the best results, DFS-GA performed better on 7 out of 40 graphs with degradation in 2 graphs. In comparing average results, DFS-GA performed better on 24 out of 40 graphs, and performed worse on 4 graphs. In general, DFS-GA took some extra time over GA which is dominated by the performance improvement. Since DFS Reordering mainly affects clusters on graphs, graphs without much clusters are not expected to benefit from it; random graphs, regular graphs, and grid graphs are not prone to have clusters due to their rather uniform edge distributions; consequently they did not benefit from DFS Reordering. DFS Reordering even degraded the performance on some grid graphs. In case of the other two types of graphs, caterpillar graphs have explicit clusters and geometric graphs are highly probable to contain clusters; most of them showed dramatic improvement by DFS Reordering. It's also worth mentioning that GA outperformed the simulated annealing algorithm given in [11] in average results even without preprocessing [2].

The significant improvement on caterpillar graphs by DFS-GA (GA preprocessed by DFS Reordering) could be explained by the c-schema model in Section 3.3. We believe that sparse geometric graphs are prone to make clusters which form islands with few bridges as described in Section 3.2. But dense geometric graphs are not expected to have many such islands. Consequently, DFS-GA didn't show such good improvements for dense geometric graphs as opposed to sparse ones (see particularly U500.40). In all of our experiments 5-point crossover was used.

5   Conclusions

We suggested a new type of schemata, c-schemata, to describe the importance of specific-symbol distributions in schemata. Any schema can be represented by a c-schema which provides a convenient way to concentrate on the distribution of specific symbols. A schema associated with a c-schema $D_0 C_1 D_1 C_2 D_2 \ldots C_q D_q$ is most likely to survive well through multi-point crossovers if q is small or the variance of $|D_1|, \ldots |D_{q-1}|, |D_0 D_q|$ is large. DFS Reordering heuristic restructures poor c-schemata into good c-schemata, which helps c-building blocks be easily formed later.

The experimental results on the graph bisection problem is only an example among others. The effectiveness of preprocessing heuristics associated with c-schemata are also shown in the VLSI ratio-cut problem [4] and the traveling salesman problem [5]. Depth first search contributes to genetic algorithms by schema transformations in a quite different way from breadth first search (BFS). BFS Reordering has the tendency to transforms perceived high-quality schemata into counterparts with short defining lengths and consequently can be well explained by traditional analysis. On the other hand, DFS Reordering helps GA by transforming perceived high-quality schemata into good clustered schemata (c-schemata).

Note that the preprocessing uses locus-based encoding's dependence on specific-symbol distribution. Uniform crossover [13] is known to be independent of the distribution of specific symbols. We tried uniform crossover on the same graphs (with $P0 = 0.5$ and $P0 = 0.01$, respectively); the results were worse than those of the DFS-GA, particularly for the graphs which the preprocessing affects much. Finally, Equation (3) is suspected to be simpler to use than Equation (2) in calculating the survival probabilities of schemata. It becomes much simpler when a schema is highly clustered. It would be also worth formally comparing the complexity of the survival probabilities calculations by the two equations.

References

1. T. N. Bui, S. Chaudhuri, F. T. Leighton, and M. Sipser, "Graph Bisection Algorithms with Good Average Case Behavior," Combinatorica, Vol. 7, No. 2, 1987, pp. 171–191.
2. T. N. Bui and B. R. Moon, "A Genetic Algorithm for a Special Class of the Quadratic Assignment Problem," to appear in *The Quadratic Assignment and Related problems*, DIMACS Series in Discrete Mathematics and Theoretical Computer Science.
3. T. N. Bui and B. R. Moon, "Hyperplane Synthesis for Genetic Algorithms," Proc. of the Fifth Int. Conf. on Genetic Algorithms, July 1993, pp. 102–109.
4. T. N. Bui and B. R. Moon, "A Fast and Stable Hybrid Genetic Algorithm for the Ratio-Cut Partitioning Problem on Hypergraphs," Proc. of the 31st ACM/IEEE Design Automation Conference, June 1994, pp. 664–669.
5. T. N. Bui and B. R. Moon, "A New Genetic Approach for The Traveling Salesman Problem," Proc. of the First IEEE Conference on Evolutionary Computation, June 1994, pp. 7–12.
6. D. Cavicchio, "Adaptive Search Using Simulated Evolution," Unpublished Doctoral Dissertation, University of Michigan, 1970.
7. K. DeJong, *An Analysis of The Behavior of A Class of Genetic Adaptive Systems*, Doctoral Thesis, Dept. of Computer and Communication Sciences, University of Michigan, Ann Arbor, 1975.
8. K. DeJong and W. Spears, "A Formal Analysis of The Role of Multi-Point Crossover in Genetic Algorithms," Annals of Math. AI Journal, Vol. 5, 1992, pp. 1–26.
9. D. Goldberg, *Genetic Algorithms in Search, Optimization, and Machine Learning*, Addison-Wesley Pub. Company, 1989.
10. J. Holland, *Adaptation in Natural and Artificial Systems*, University of Michigan Press, Ann Arbor, MI, 1975.
11. D. Johnson, C. Aragon, L. McGeoch, and C. Schevon, "Optimization by Simulated Annealing: An Experimental Evaluation, Part 1, Graph Partitioning," Operations Research, 37, 1989, pp. 865–892.
12. C. Jones, *Vertex and Edge Partitions of Graphs*, Ph.D. Dissertation, Penn. State. Univ., University Park, 1992.
13. G. Syswerda, "Uniform Crossover in Genetic Algorithms," Proc. of the 3rd Int. Conf. on Genetic Algorithms, June 1989, pp. 2–9.

Table 1. Bisections Cut Sizes on 40 Graphs Over 1,000 Trials

Graphs	Best Knowns (or Optima)	Cut Sizes by GA			Cut Sizes by DFS-GA		
		Best	Average	CPU	Best	Average	CPU
G500.2.5	52	**49**	54.15	4.72	50	**53.49**	7.19
G500.05	219	218	222.11	6.63	218	**221.49**	9.78
G500.10	628	626	631.61	11.03	626	**631.16**	14.61
G500.20	1744	1744	1752.52	21.29	1744	**1752.26**	27.60
G1000.2.5	102	96	103.86	13.22	**95**	**101.80**	21.96
G1000.05	451	**445**	458.71	20.06	448	**457.47**	28.24
G1000.10	1367	1363	1376.87	33.83	**1362**	**1376.13**	45.26
G1000.20	3389	3382	3401.98	59.25	3382	**3401.35**	76.09
U500.05	4	2	11.30	6.28	2	**3.04**	9.69
U500.10	26	26	38.76	6.94	26	**29.56**	10.78
U500.20	178	178	182.54	8.32	178	**179.88**	12.41
U500.40	412	412	**412.70**	8.05	412	412.71	11.38
U1000.05	3	8	28.31	19.45	1	**2.31**	25.69
U1000.10	39	39	72.79	20.33	39	**51.14**	35.93
U1000.20	222	222	239.60	23.42	222	**232.57**	34.98
U1000.40	737	737	742.69	27.88	737	**740.09**	38.05
breg500.0	0	0	0.00	1.35	0	0.00	2.11
breg500.12	12	12	12.00	2.39	12	12.00	3.06
breg500.16	16	16	16.00	2.65	16	16.00	3.69
breg500.20	20	20	20.00	2.80	20	20.00	3.88
breg5000.0	0	0	0.00	20.33	0	0.00	38.02
breg5000.4	4	4	4.00	23.49	4	4.00	36.37
breg5000.8	8	8	8.00	26.06	8	8.00	38.10
breg5000.16	16	16	16.00	32.93	16	16.00	52.44
cat.352	1	1	5.82	4.16	1	**1.94**	2.38
cat.702	1	5	11.95	8.61	1	**2.10**	6.56
cat.1052	1	9	18.58	13.74	1	**2.11**	11.58
cat.5252	1	69	98.39	48.23	1	**2.35**	97.97
rcat.134	1	1	1.98	0.36	1	**1.28**	0.52
rcat.554	1	1	4.68	2.01	1	**1.85**	3.35
rcat.994	1	1	7.30	3.77	1	**2.01**	7.13
rcat.5114	1	11	23.00	23.79	1	**2.42**	66.08
grid100.10	10	10	10.00	0.37	10	10.00	0.35
grid500.21	21	21	21.14	3.45	21	**21.00**	2.64
grid1000.20	20	20	20.00	7.59	20	20.00	6.59
grid5000.50	50	50	**50.03**	78.23	50	71.11	69.85
w-grid100.20	20	20	20.00	0.41	20	20.00	0.50
w-grid500.42	42	42	**42.04**	3.44	42	45.39	4.72
w-grid1000.40	40	40	**40.00**	8.53	40	40.03	12.29
w-grid5000.100	100	100	100.00	86.58	100	100.00	56.59

- G$n.d$: a random graph on n vertices with average degree d, see [11].
- U$n.d$: a random geometric graph on n vertices with average degree d, see [11].
- breg$n.b$: a random graph (regular graph) on n vertices with every vertex having degree 3 and the smallest bisection is known to be b with high probability, see [1].
- cat.n : a caterpillar graph, which is a line graph with legs (i.e., paths of length 1), on n vertices and each node has degree 8 (i.e., 8 legs). Similarly, rcat.n denotes a caterpillar graph with n nodes and each articulation point has degree $\sqrt{n}$.
- grid$n.b$: a grid on n vertices and whose smallest bisection has size b and w-grid$n.b$ denotes the same grid but with wrapped around edges.

Convergence Models of Genetic Algorithm Selection Schemes

Dirk Thierens[1] * and **David Goldberg**[2]

[1] Department of Electrical Engineering
ESAT-lab KU.Leuven
Kardinaal Mercierlaan 94
B-3001 Leuven, Belgium
[2] Department of General Engineering
University of Illinois at Urbana-Champaign
104 South Mathews Avenue
Urbana, IL 61801, USA

Abstract. We discuss the use of normal distribution theory as a tool to model the convergence characteristics of different GA selection schemes. The models predict the proportion of optimal alleles in function of the number of generations when optimizing the bit-counting function. The selection schemes analyzed are proportionate selection, tournament selection, truncation selection and elitist recombination. Simple yet accurate models are derived that have only a slight deviation from the experimental results. It is argued that this small difference is due to the build-up of covariances between the alleles – a phenomenon called linkage disequilibrium in quantitative genetics. We conclude with a brief discussion of this linkage disequilibrium.

1 Introduction

Many different genetic algorithm implementations exist and due to the lack of a closed form analytical GA theory it is difficult to compare them objectively. By assuming that the fitness function is normally distributed, we can apply the theory of normal distributions as analysis tool. This kind of analysis is a standard approach in quantitative genetics [2,3] and allows accurate modeling of the GA convergence characteristics.

In [5] a comparative analysis of GA selection schemes was given that modeled the selection behavior in terms of deterministic finite difference equations. The difference equations described the change in proportion of different classes of individuals, assuming fixed and identical fitness function values within each class. Since only selection is used no new fitness values are ever generated. Convergence time is characterized with the takeover time which is the number of

---

* The first author acknowledges the support provided by the Flemish Community under the Concerted Action Project No. 90/94-4. Correspondence can be sent to dirk.thierens@esat.kuleuven.ac.be.

generations needed for the best individual in the population to take over the entire population.

In this paper we take an alternative view by modeling different selection schemes when optimizing a normal distributed fitness function. There are two main advantages of using this approach. First, restricting ourselves to normal distributed fitness functions allows simple yet accurate modeling of the convergence characteristics of selection and recombination together. In order to maintain the normal distribution assumptions as good as possible, we use uniform crossover which maximally decorrelates the alleles. Since there is no epistatic effect between the genes, the population mean fitness does not change after recombination.

Second, the normal fitness distribution modeling allows us to analyze the build-up of covariances between the alleles caused by selection – the so called linkage disequilibrium [2,3]. In previous work we discussed the mixing problem in genetic algorithms [7,10] and since mixing failure is basically an extreme build-up of linkage disequilibrium it is instructive to model the covariance between the genes.

The convergence models predict the proportion of optimal alleles $p(t)$ in the total population as a function of the number of generations t. Experimental results are obtained by optimizing the bit-counting function, which is binomial distributed and can well be approximated with a normal distribution. The population mean fitness at generation t is given by $\overline{f}(t) = l\, p(t)$ and the variance $\sigma^2(t) = l\, p(t)(1 - p(t))$.

The experiments in this paper all use $l = 100$ and $n = 200$. As shown in [6] a population size $n = 2l$ allows reliable decision making for the bit-counting function.

In the next four sections we analyze different GA selection schemes, namely proportionate selection, tournament selection, truncation selection and finally elitist recombination. We conclude with a brief discussion of the allele covariance build-up or linkage disequilibrium.

2 Proportionate Selection

Proportionate selection is the oldest and still best known selection scheme in evolutionary computation and implements the idea that reproduction rates are proportional to the fitness value f [4,8]. The probability of selecting an individual i with fitness f_i and proportion $P_i(t)$ at generation t is given by:

$$P_i(t^s) = P_i(t)\frac{f_i}{\overline{f(t)}}$$

with $\overline{f(t)}$ the mean fitness of the population at generation t.

The increment in population mean fitness can easily be computed:

$$\overline{f(t^s)} - \overline{f(t)} = \sum_{i=1}^{n} P_i(t^s)f_i - \overline{f(t)}$$

$$= \sum_{i=1}^{n} \frac{P_i(t)f_i^2}{\overline{f(t)}} - \overline{f(t)}$$

$$= \frac{1}{\overline{f(t)}}(\overline{f^2(t)} - \overline{f(t)}^2)$$

$$= \frac{\sigma^2(t)}{\overline{f(t)}}$$

Recombination does not change the population mean fitness when optimizing the bit-counting function ($\overline{f(t+1)} = \overline{f(t^s)}$), so the increment of the population average fitness with proportionate selection is proportional to the fitness variance and inverse proportional to the mean fitness.

$$\overline{f(t+1)} - \overline{f(t)} = \frac{\sigma^2(t)}{\overline{f(t)}} \tag{1}$$

Since $\overline{f(t)} = l\, p(t)$ and $\sigma^2(t) = lp(t)(1 - p(t))$ the increase of the proportion $p(t)$ of optimal alleles is given by

$$l(p(t+1) - p(t)) = \frac{lp(t)(1 - p(t))}{lp(t)} = 1 - p(t)$$

Approximating the difference equation with the corresponding differential equation we obtain a simple convergence model expressing the proportion $p(t)$ in function of the number of generations t

$$\frac{dp(t)}{dt} = \frac{1}{l}(1 - p(t))$$

which has as solution

$$p(t) = 1 - (1 - p(0))\, e^{-t/l}.$$

Starting from a random initial population $p(0) = 0.5$ the convergence model becomes:

$$\boxed{p(t) = 1 - 0.5e^{-t/l}} \tag{2}$$

To calculate the convergence speed we compute the number of generations g_{conv} it takes to let the proportion $p(t)$ come arbitrarily close to 1 or $p(g_{conv}) = 1 - \epsilon$

$$g_{conv} = -l \ln(2\epsilon)$$

For $\epsilon = 1/(2l)$ the convergence time is:

$$g_{conv} = l \ln (l) \tag{3}$$

In figure 1 we have plotted the model for a string length $l = 100$ and compared it with experimental results when implementing proportionate selection with stochastic universal sampling. Obviously the model predicts the experimental results very well. The rate of convergence with proportionate selection is extremely slow and it drastically slows down when approaching the solution.

Instead of calculating the convergence speed by computing how long it takes to let the proportion $p(t)$ come arbitrarily close to 1, we might also compute the generation at which the global optimum is expected to be found with a given probability. The probability that at least one of the strings in the population consists of all ones is given by:

$$\text{prob(opt)} = 1 - [1 - p^l(t)]^n$$

From this equation we can calculate the needed allele proportion $p(g_{opt})$ and plug this into equation 2 to obtain the number of generations it takes to find the optimum with given probability prob(opt). For instance in our example with string length $l = 100$, population size $n = 200$ and prob(opt) = 99% we find that $p(g_{opt}) = 0.96$ and $g_{opt} = 260$.

In order to obtain better convergence characterics for proportionate selection one has to use some form of fitness scaling [4]. Instead of scaling the fitness function explicitly it is also possible to use a selection scheme that does not look at the absolute function value but instead performs selection according to the number of individuals in the population that are better or worse.

Examples of this ranked based selection principle are tournament selection, truncation selection and elitist recombination, which we will discuss in the next sections.

3 Tournament Selection

Tournament selection randomly chooses a set of individuals and picks out the best for reproduction. The number of individuals in the set is mostly equal to two but larger tournament sizes can be used in order to increase the selection pressure [10]. Here we consider the case of optimizing the bit-counting function with a tournament size $s = 2$. Under the assumption of a normally distributed function the fitness difference between two randomly sampled individuals in each tournament is also normally distributed with mean $\mu_{\Delta f}(t) = 0$ and variance $\sigma^2_{\Delta f}(t) = 2\sigma^2(t)$. Since we are only selecting the best of the two competing individuals we are actually only looking at the absolute value of the fitness difference. The average fitness difference between two randomly sampled individuals is thus given by the mean value of those differences that are greater than $\mu_{\Delta f} = 0$, which is equivalent to the mean value of one half of the normal distribution truncated at its mean value 0. The mean value of the right half of a standard normal distribution is given by $\sqrt{2/\pi} = 0.7979$.

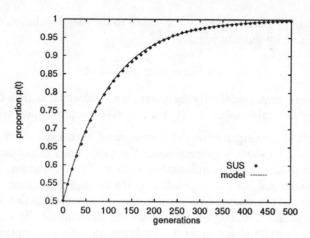

Fig. 1. Convergence model and experimental results of the proportion of optimal alleles when optimizing the bit-counting function with proportionate selection (Stochastic Universal Sampling) and uniform crossover.

Tournament selection selects the best out of every random pair of individuals so the population average fitness increase from one generation to the next is equal to half the mean value of the difference between two randomly sampled individuals:

$$\overline{f(t+1)} - \overline{f(t)} = \frac{1}{2}\ 0.7979\ \sigma_{\Delta f}(t) = \frac{1}{2}\ 0.7979\ \sqrt{2}\ \sigma(t) = \frac{1}{\sqrt{\pi}}\ \sigma(t)$$

or

$$\overline{f(t+1)} - \overline{f(t)} = 0.5642\ \sigma(t) \qquad (4)$$

Since $f(t) = l\ p(t)$ and $\sigma^2(t) = l\ p(t)\ (1 - p(t))$ we get

$$p(t+1) - p(t) = \sqrt{\frac{p(t)(1 - p(t))}{\pi l}}\ .$$

Approximating the difference equation with the differential equation

$$\frac{dp(t)}{dt} = \sqrt{\frac{p(t)(1 - p(t))}{\pi l}}$$

gives us the solution:

$$p(t) = 0.5(1 + \sin{(\frac{t}{\sqrt{\pi l}} + \arcsin(2p(0) - 1)))}\ .$$

For a randomly initialized population $p(0) = 0.5$ the convergence model becomes:

$$\boxed{p(t) = 0.5(1 + \sin{(\frac{t}{\sqrt{\pi l}}))}} \qquad (5)$$

The number of generations g_{conv} it takes to let the population fully convergence is obtained by putting $p(g_{conv}) = 1$

$$g_{conv} = \frac{\pi}{2} \sqrt{\pi l} \tag{6}$$

The convergence time complexity for tournament selection is thus $O(\sqrt{l})$ which compares very favorable to $O(l \ln(l))$ for unscaled proportionate selection.

The proposed convergence model is compared with experimental results in figure 2. The model slightly overestimates the proportion of optimal alleles for tournament selection and recombination with uniform crossover. In a second experiment we recombine the population twice at each generation, so after the usual procedure of tournament selection followed by recombination we randomly shuffle the population and again recombine the individuals. By doing this the alleles of each individual are more decorrelated and the assumptions we made when building the convergence model are less violated. Figure 2 shows that the model now coincides very well with the experimental results, so the slight overestimation is due to the build-up of covariances between the alleles caused by selection. In the last section we will have a closer look at this phenomenon.

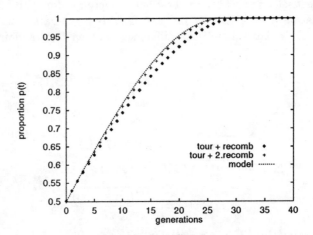

Fig. 2. Convergence model and experimental results of the proportion of optimal alleles when optimizing the bit-counting function with tournament selection and uniform crossover.

4 Truncation Selection

Truncation selection or block selection ranks all individuals according to their fitness and selects the best ones as parents. In truncation selection a threshold

T is defined such that the $T\%$ best individuals are selected. Truncation selection has been used extensively in evolution strategies [1]. It is also often used in quantitative genetics where artificial selection performed by breeders is studied. In [9] a specific genetic algorithm - the Breeder Genetic Algorithm - is proposed that incorporates ideas from breeders to perform parameter optimization tasks, and the convergence model for the bit-counting function has also been computed there.

Block selection [10] is equivalent to truncation selection since for a given population size n one simply gives s copies to the n/s best individuals. Both implementations are identical when $s = 100/T$.

If the fitness function is normally distributed, quantitative genetics defines the *selection intensity* i that expresses the selection differential $S(t) = \overline{f(t^s)} - \overline{f(t)}$ in function of the standard deviation $\sigma(t)$:

$$S(t) = i\ \sigma(t)$$

Using this definition one can easily compute the convergence model:

$$\overline{f(t+1)} - \overline{f(t)} = i\ \sigma(t) \tag{7}$$

Since $f(t) = l\ p(t)$ and $\sigma^2(t) = l\ p(t)\ (1 - p(t))$ we get

$$p(t+1) - p(t) = \frac{i}{\sqrt{l}}\sqrt{p(t)(1 - p(t))}.$$

Approximating the difference equation with the differential equation

$$\frac{dp(t)}{dt} = \frac{i}{\sqrt{l}}\sqrt{p(t)(1 - p(t))}$$

the solution becomes

$$p(t) = 0.5(1 + \sin{(\frac{i}{\sqrt{l}}t + \arcsin(2p(0) - 1)))}.$$

For a randomly initialized population $p(0) = 0.5$ or:

$$\boxed{p(t) = 0.5(1 + \sin{(\frac{i}{\sqrt{l}}t))}} \tag{8}$$

Calculating the number of generations g_{conv} to convergence ($p(g_{conv}) = 1$) is straightforward:

$$g_{conv} = \frac{\pi}{2} \cdot \frac{\sqrt{l}}{i} \tag{9}$$

It is rather remarkable that the convergence models for tournament selection and truncation selection have the same functional form. The only difference is the magnitude of the selection intensity constant i, which can be changed by increasing the truncation threshold or tournament size of the respective algorithms. For the standard tournament selection with tournament size $s = 2$, the selection intensity is $i = 1/\sqrt{\pi} = 0.56$.

Experimental results are shown in figure 3 for a block size $s = 2$ or equivalently a truncation threshold $T = 50\%$, which gives us a selection intensity $i = 0.8$ [2,3,9]. Again the model slightly overestimates the proportion $p(t)$ of optimal alleles and predictions become more accurate when the alleles are decorrelated by repeating the recombination phase.

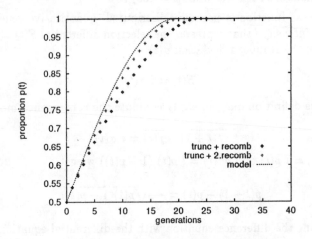

Fig. 3. Convergence model and experimental results of the proportion of optimal alleles when optimizing the bit-counting function with truncation selection and uniform crossover.

5   Elitist Recombination

Recently we have introduced an extremely simple GA implementation [11] where the selection and recombination phases are intertwined. Competition for survival takes place at the level of each family — the mating parents and their offspring — which results in a local elitist selection operator, called elitist recombination. For every mating pair two offsprings are created and the best two of these four individuals go to the next generation, so individuals can only be replaced by other individuals with a higher fitness value. Crossover is applied for every mating pair so there is no need to choose a specific value for the crossover probability parameter p_c.

Elitist Recombination algorithm:

1. initialize population

2. for every generation
   (a) random shuffle population
   (b) for every mating pair:
       - generate offspring
       - keep best two of each family

It is easy to show that - when optimizing the bit-counting function - the best individual of every mating pair will go to the next generation and the worst parent will be replaced by the best of the two offsprings [11]. As a result the population average fitness increase $\overline{f(t+1)} - \overline{f(t)}$ is equal to half the average difference between the worst parent and the best child.

Since the children are basically random samples of a binomial distribution with same parameter $p(t)$ as the parent population, we can compute the population average fitness increase as half the mean fitness difference between two random samples of a normal distribution with mean $\mu = lp(t)$ and variance $\sigma^2(t) = lp(t)(1 - p(t))$.

Obviously this is exactly what we have done when modeling tournament selection so the convergence model for elitist recombination and tournament selection with tournament size $s = 2$ are the same:

$$p(t) = 0.5(1 + \sin\left(\frac{t}{\sqrt{\pi l}}\right)) \tag{10}$$

and

$$g_{conv} = \frac{\pi}{2} \sqrt{\pi l}. \tag{11}$$

Experimental results are shown in figure 4. As with tournament and truncation selection the model slightly overestimates the proportion $p(t)$, and predictions become more accurate when the alleles are decorrelated by repeating the recombination phase. Comparing figure 4 with 2 we note that due to the elitist mechanism the build-up of covariance between the alleles is higher for elitist recombination than for tournament selection and standard recombination.

6 Linkage disequilibrium

The convergence models discussed in the previous sections all assume that the fitness is normally distributed. In practice however there a number of factors - such as a finite population size - that violate this assumption. From the previous experiments it is clear that the most important factor is the build-up of correlations between the alleles. Repeating the recombination phase during each generation made the model predictions significantly more accurate. In this section we will briefly discuss this problem but due to space limitations a detailed analysis is beyond the scope of this paper and can be found in [12].

Selection picks out individuals that are mainly concentrated at the higher level of the fitness distribution. The variance of the population is reduced but

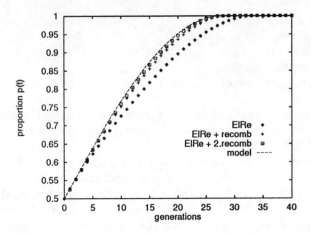

Fig. 4. Convergence model and experimental results of the proportion of optimal alleles when optimizing the bit-counting function with elitist recombination and uniform crossover.

this reduction is not only caused by the change in allele frequency but also by the introduction of covariances between the alleles. If we represent the covariance with σ_{cov} then the variance after selection is given by:

$$\sigma^2(t^s) = \sigma^2(t) + 2\sigma_{cov}(t^s) \tag{12}$$

With truncation selection for instance the variance is reduced with a factor k such that

$$\sigma^2(t^s) = (1 - k)\sigma^2(t) \tag{13}$$

with k given by $k = i(i - x)$ where i is the selection intensity and x is the corresponding deviation of the truncation point from the population mean [3]. The covariance after selection can now be computed from equations 12 and 13:

$$\sigma_{cov}(t^s) = -\frac{k}{2}\sigma^2(t)$$

Crossover decorrelates the genes with a decorrelation factor $\delta = 1 - p_c p_r$ with $p_r = 2p_x(1 - p_x)$ (p_c: crossover probability, p_r: disruption probability and p_x: allele swap probability for uniform crossover). The covariance after selection and recombination is thus given by:

$$\sigma_{cov}(t + 1) = -\delta\frac{k}{2}\sigma^2(t)$$

Using this expression for the covariance we can more accurately calculate the population fitness variance such that the convergence models predict the experimental results even better (for details see [12]).

7 Conclusion

Simple yet accurate convergence models for different selection schemes are derived that allow us to compare the GA selection schemes in terms of their convergence characteristics. The models assume a normally distributed fitness function and predict the proportion of optimal alleles in function of the number of generations. Experimental results for optimizing the bit-counting function show good agreement with the predictions. It is argued that the slight deviations are due to linkage disequilibrium or the build-up of covariances between the alleles which can be included in the models to increase their accuracy.

References

[1] Bäck,T., Hoffmeister,F.,& Schwefel,H.P.(1991) *A Survey of Evolution Strategies.* Proceedings of the Fourth International Conference on Genetic Algorithms, 2-9. Morgan Kaufmann.

[2] Bulmer,M.G.(1985). *The Mathematical Theory of Quantitative Genetics.* Oxford University Press.

[3] Falconer,D.S.(1989). *Introduction to Quantitative Genetics.* Longman Scientific & Technical.

[4] Goldberg,D.E.(1989). *Genetic Algorithms in Search, Optimization and Machine Learning.* Addison Wesley Publishing Company.

[5] Goldberg,D.E.,& Deb,K.(1991). *A comparative analysis of selection schemes used in genetic algorithms.* Foundations of Genetic Algorithms I, 69-93.

[6] Goldberg,D.E., Deb,K.,& Clark,J.H.(1991). *Genetic algorithms, noise, and the sizing of populations.* Complex Systems, 6, 333-362.

[7] Goldberg,D.E., Deb,K.,& Thierens,D.(1992). *Toward a better understanding of mixing in genetic algorithms.* Journal of the Society for Instrumentation and Control Engineers, 32(1),10-16.

[8] Holland,J.H.(1975). *Adaptation in natural and artificial systems.* Ann Arbor: University of Michigan Press.

[9] Mühlenbein,H.,& Schlierkamp-Voosen,D.(1993). *Predictive Models for the Breeder Genetic Algorithm. I. Continuous Parameter Optimization.* Evolutionary Computation 1(1):25-49, MIT Press.

[10] Thierens,D.,& Goldberg,D.E.(1993). *Mixing in Genetic Algorithms.* Proceedings of the Fifth International Conference on Genetic Algorithms, 38-45. Morgan Kaufmann.

[11] Thierens,D.,& Goldberg,D.E.(1993). *Elitist Recombination: an integrated selection recombination GA.* Technical Report ESAT-SISTA/TR 1993-76. To appear in Proceedings of the IEEE World Congress on Computational Intelligence. Orlando, June 1994.

[12] Thierens,D.,& Goldberg,D.E.(1994). *Effects of Linkage Disequilibrium on GA convergence.* Technical Report ESAT-SISTA/TR 1994-41.

Optimal Population Size under Constant Computation Cost

Ryohei Nakano[1], Yuval Davidor[2], and Takeshi Yamada[1]

[1] NTT Communication Science Laboratories, 2, Hikaridai, Seika,
Soraku, Kyoto 619-02, Japan
[2] Department of Applied Mathematics and Computer Science,
The Weizmann Institute, Rehovot 76100, Israel.

Abstract. Optimal setting of genetic algorithm parameters has been the subject of numerous studies; however, the optimality of a population size is still a controversial subject. This work addresses the issue of optimal population size under the constraint of a constant computation cost. Given a problem P to be solved, a GA (genetic algorithm) as a problem solver, and a computation cost C to spend, how should we schedule the problem solving? Under the constant C, there is a trade-off between a population size s and the number r of GA runs. Focusing on this trade-off, the present paper claims there exists the optimal s_{opt} for the given P and GA under the constant C; here, the optimality means maximum of the expected probability of obtaining acceptable solutions. To explain how the optimality comes about we propose the statistical model of GA runs, prove the existence of s_{opt} and get more insight in a specific case. Then experiments were performed using a difficult job shop scheduling problem. The experiments showed the plausibility of the proposed model.

1 Introduction

Among the various GA parameter setting questions, those related to optimal population size seem to be more provocative as they are directly related to the schema theorem and to what Holland called the *implicit parallelism* effect [4]. Traditionally, Holland's much cited $O(n^3)$ estimate of effective schemata processing was used to justify ever increasing population sizes. However, as is well known in the literature, both experimental and theoretical work about this issue suggested different conclusions.

Goldberg in an early note [2] rederived Holland's bound and showed the fallacy of the ever increasing population sizes. Robertson experimentally calculated the optimal population value for some classifier system [7], and Goldberg in the following year extended his original derivation to include varying degrees of parallelism [3]. The above three works assumed maximal schemata processing as the criterion for optimal population size, and raised the issue of defining optimality.

Schaffer, et al. [8] published a comparison study on the parameter setting issue adding few more functions to the original De Jong suite and concluded that Goldberg's '85 original recommendation of optimal population size is too conservative and recommended unnecessarily large population sizes.

Our GA experiences [6, 9] in solving job shop scheduling problems (JSSP), NP-hard optimization problems, has indicated the following two phenomena which have urged us on the present investigation of the population size issue.

Observation 1: *A larger population is likely to produce a better solution, but there seems to be a saturation of the tendency.*
Observation 2: *Repeated runs improve the solution quality.*

When solving a difficult problem such as a JSSP using a GA, a small population, less than 50, seems hopeless in obtaining a solution of high quality, and a larger population size is likely to bring a better solution, but there seems to be a saturation of such tendency when the increased computation effort is facing the law of diminishing return. Furthermore, since most practical GA optimizations are controlled by a trade-off between speed and solution quality, when solving a hard problem, it is necessary to repeat the experiment in order to ensure that the otherwise single GA run did not get trapped in a local optimum.

The above observations might suggest that under the constraint of a constant computation cost there exists a trade-off point between a population size s and the number r of independent GA runs. Working at this trade-off point may maximize the expected probability of obtaining acceptable solution quality. The number s at such a point is called here the *optimal population size* s_{opt}. This paper proposes a statistical model to explain how the optimality comes about, and evaluates the plausibility of the model by doing intensive experiments of GA runs for a JSSP.

2   Statistical Model for Optimal Population Size

We introduce statistical thinking into an analysis of the GA behavior: i.e., we consider a GA run as a random sampling from a certain underlying distribution. For example, Fig. 1 shows a density function estimated from a histogram of solutions[3] obtained from 500 GA runs with $s = 20$ for 10×10 JSSP. Here, a single run can be reasonably considered as a sample taken randomly from the distribution as shown in the figure.

Let $p(x, s)$ be the single-run density function of such distribution, where x denotes a solution obtained from a run with a population size s. The corresponding single-run distribution function $P(x, s)$ can be defined as

$$P(x, s) = \int_{-\infty}^{x} p(z, s)dz. \tag{1}$$

Hereafter, we employ the continuous formalization for convenience, but note that they can be easily transformed into discrete counterparts. Although the solution x takes only discrete values and its distribution may not be smooth, we assume its continuity and differentiability as an approximation to get reasonable insight.

---

[3] In this paper a solution means a cost or fitness of the solution, but the term is used for simplicity.

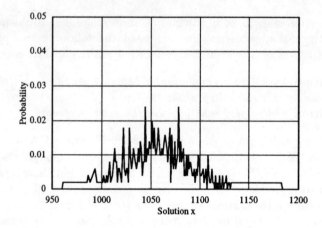

Fig. 1. Single-run density function p(x,s) for 10×10 JSSP (s $= 20$)

We are especially interested in a distribution of the best solution y among solutions x's obtained from r runs, where each x is selected randomly from $p(x,s)$. Let $q(y,s,r)$ be the density function of such distribution. Then the corresponding distribution function $Q(y,s,r)$

$$Q(y,s,r) = \int_{-\infty}^{y} q(z,s,r)dz \qquad (2)$$

is given as a probability of r runs where $x \leq y$ for at least one x. This can be expressed as,

$$Q(y,s,r) = 1 - \left(\int_{y}^{\infty} p(x,s)dx\right)^{r} = 1 - (1 - P(y,s))^{r}. \qquad (3)$$

Especially, with $r = 1$ we have a simple relationship between Q and P:

$$Q(y,s,1) = 1 - (1 - P(y,s)) = P(y,s). \qquad (4)$$

From the above two equations of $Q(y,s,r)$, we get

$$\int_{-\infty}^{y} q(z,s,r)dz = 1 - \left(\int_{y}^{\infty} p(x,s)dx\right)^{r}. \qquad (5)$$

By differentiating both sides with respect to y, we have the following relationship between the two density functions:

$$q(y,s,r) = rp(y,s)\left(\int_{y}^{\infty} p(x,s)dx\right)^{r-1}. \qquad (6)$$

The following condition, which any density must satisfy, can be easily verified:

$$\int_{-\infty}^{\infty} q(y,s,r)dy = 1. \qquad (7)$$

Here the constraint of the constant computation cost is taken into consideration. The constraint means that the computation cost C must satisfy

$$C = s \cdot g(s) \cdot r(s) = const., \tag{8}$$

where $g(s)$ denotes the average number of generations required for convergence and the number of GA runs $r(s)$ now depends on s. Under the constraint, the functions q and Q are rewritten as functions of y and s:

$$q^*(y, s) = q(y, s, r(s)), \tag{9}$$

$$Q^*(y, s) = Q(y, s, r(s)). \tag{10}$$

Now the optimal population size s_{opt} can be defined formally. s_{opt} is defined as the population size which maximizes the expected probability of obtaining acceptable solutions. This is expressed as

$$s_{opt}(\theta) = arg \max_s Q^*(\theta, s), \tag{11}$$

where θ denotes a threshold for acceptable solutions and is chosen to be close to the optimal solution. Note that s_{opt} depends on a threshold θ, meaning it maximizes the expected probability of obtaining solutions better than θ. If θ is equal to the optimal solution, then s_{opt} maximizes the expected probability of obtaining the optimal solutions. In the next we can prove the existence of s_{opt}.

Theorem 1. *Under the constraint of the constant computation cost there exists $s_{opt}(\theta)$ for a fixed θ if the single-run probability $P(\theta, s)$ converges to a certain value $\alpha(< 1)$.*

Proof. We have

$$Q^*(\theta, s) = 1 - (1 - P(\theta, s))^{r(s)}. \tag{12}$$

Maximizing Q^* means minimizing the second term of the right side. Since logarithmic transformation does not change the optimization situation, the optimization problem can be expressed as

$$s_{opt}(\theta) = arg \min_s r(s) log(1 - P(\theta, s)) \equiv arg \min_s f(s). \tag{13}$$

By differentiating the target function $f(s)$ with respect to s, we get

$$\frac{df}{ds} = \frac{dr}{ds} log(1 - P) - \frac{r}{1 - P} \frac{dP}{ds}. \tag{14}$$

Note that we can assume $\frac{dP}{ds} > 0$ and $\frac{dr}{ds} < 0$ for any s. While s is very small, the probability of obtaining acceptable solutions is very close to zero, i.e., $P \approx 0$; thus, $\frac{df}{ds} < 0$. As s gets very large, $\frac{dP}{ds} \approx 0$ (saturation of solution quality) and $log(1 - \alpha) < 0$; thus, $\frac{df}{ds} > 0$. Hence, at a certain point in the middle we have

s_{opt} which satisfies $\frac{df}{ds} = 0$.   Q.E.D.

In a more specific case we can get more insight about s_{opt}. Now assume $g(s)$, the average number of generations required for convergence, is almost constant, meaning virtually independent of s. Although the assumption appears unlikely, it holds at least in our experiments, as will be shown. Then we can calculate a concrete form of P which gives s_{opt} as shown below. That is, from the constraint we get $r(s) = (C/g)/s$. Thus we have

$$\frac{df}{ds} = \frac{C/g}{s^2}\left(-log(1-P) - \frac{s}{1-P}\frac{dP}{ds}\right). \qquad (15)$$

From the equation $\frac{df}{ds} = 0$ we have

$$-log(1-P) = \frac{s}{1-P}\frac{dP}{ds} \qquad (16)$$

By solving this equation we get

$$\overline{P}(\theta, s) = 1 - e^{-cs}, \qquad (17)$$

where c is a positive constant. Thus, when the real distribution $P(\theta, s)$ and its derivative are equal to $\overline{P}(\theta, s)$ and its derivative respectively for a certain s, then such s is s_{opt}. Note that $\overline{P}$ is an exponential curve with freedom of constant c, asymptotically converging to one.

Moreover, in this specific case, it is easily seen that s_{opt} is independent of the computation cost C only by noting that s_{opt} depends solely on the single-run distribution $P(\theta, s)$.

3   Experiments

Experiments are performed to ascertain the plausibility of the proposed model using our GA for a difficult JSSP. The results of the experiments are described below together with short explanations of a JSSP and our GA called GA/GT.

3.1   Job shop scheduling problem

A JSSP has N jobs to be processed on M machines and assumes the following:

- A machine can process only one job at a time.
- The processing of a job, called an *operation*, cannot be interrupted.
- A job consists of at most M operations.
- The *machine sequence* for each job, and the processing time for each operation are given as constraints.
- The *job sequence* on any machine is unknown. A set of the job sequences on all the machines is called a symbolic representation. A feasible symbolic representation is called a *schedule*.

A JSSP is a problem aiming at finding a schedule which minimizes the total elapsed time. In our experiments the 10×10 JSSP (10 jobs, 10 machines) [5] is selected because of its difficulty.

3.2 GA/GT method

GA/GT method [9] is a GA specially tuned for a JSSP. It has a unique crossover called *GT crossover*, which plays an important role in the drastic improvement of performance. GT crossover is embedded in a simple scheduling algorithm which produces a child schedule by referring to two parent schedules (p_0 and p_1), while the scheduling algorithm employs the idea of Giffler and Thompson's active scheduling [1].

GT crossover is outlined as follows:

1. Let o^* be an operation (on machine M_i) with the smallest completion time among all unscheduled operations.
2. Let G be a conflict set obtained by Giffler and Thompson's method. G is a set of operations each of which overlaps its processing with o^* on the same machine M_i.
3. The next operation to be scheduled on M_i is selected from G. Choose randomly one of the schedules $\{p_0, p_1\}$. If p_i is chosen, then the operation among G which is scheduled earliest on p_i is selected and scheduled.
4. Repeat these steps until all operations are scheduled.

3.3 Design of experiments

Two types of experiments are conducted with the aim to obtain reliable statistics of a single-run performance and reliable statistics under the constraint of the constant computation cost. In both cases, a threshold θ is set to be 950, 940, and 930 since we know the optimal solution of 10×10 JSSP is 930. Moreover, in both cases, experiments are designed for the following 11 points of s: 10, 20, 50, 100, 200, 500, 1K, 2K, 5K, 10K, and 20K.

As for the single-run experiments, independent 500 GA runs are done for each s to obtain the good statistics. As for the constant computation cost experiments, the cost C is set to be reasonably high, 10^6, to do experiments for a wide range of s shown above. While conducting the experiments, $g(s)$ was found to be almost equal to 50; thus, $s\ r(s) = 20K$. This means that $r(s)$ decreases as s increases; i.e., $r(10) = 2K$, $r(20) = 1K$, ..., $r(10K) = 2$, and $r(20K) = 1$. The GA runs for each s are repeated independently more than 20 times to obtain reliable statistics for the constant computation cost analysis.

The plausibility of the proposed model is first checked by seeing the results of the constant computation cost experiments, which enables direct verification of the existence of s_{opt}. The plausibility is also checked by comparing the observed $Q^*(\theta, s)$ with the ones estimated using eq.(12). Lastly, since in our application we can assume $g(s) \approx 50$, we can roughly estimate s_{opt} using eq.(17), and compare them with the observed ones.

3.4 Results

Figure 2 shows single-run distribution functions $P(\theta, s)$ using solid lines. Lack of smoothness may be due to the sparseness of sampling points of s. Dotted lines show $1 - exp(-cs)$ of eq.(17) with constants c adequately chosen. Recall that the value and its derivative of the equation express s_{opt}. Thus, by fitting dotted lines to solid ones we can see the following: with $\theta=950$ $s_{opt} \approx 500$ or 2,000, with $\theta=940$ $s_{opt} \approx 500$ or 3,000-4,000, and with $\theta=930$ $s_{opt} \approx 3,000$-4,000.

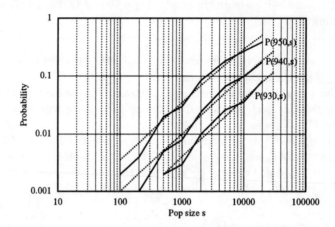

Fig. 2. Single-run distribution function P(x,s) for 10×10 JSSP

Figure 3 shows solution quality of a single run obtained from 500 runs for each s. Here we have remarkably smooth curves which may indicate high reliability of the statistics, where 'sd' denotes standard deviations. Since the x-axis is logarithmically scaled, one can find that the curves have the asymptotic tendency.

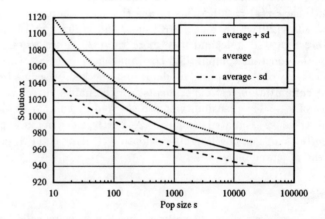

Fig. 3. Solution quality of a single run for 10×10 JSSP

Figure 4 shows constant-computation-cost distribution function $Q^*(\theta, s)$ under the cost of 10^6. The solid lines show the observed Q^*, while the dotted lines show the Q^* estimated using eq.(12). The matching of two lines may verify the plausibility of the model. The figure shows the following: with $\theta=950$ $s_{opt}=2,000$, with $\theta=940$ there exist two peaks at $s=500$ and $2,000$, and with $\theta=930$ the peaks seem to be between $2,000$ and $5,000$. These s_{opt} roughly coincide with those estimated from Fig.2. Note that s_{opt} gradually changes as the threshold θ changes.

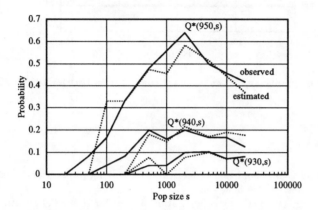

Fig. 4. Distribution function $Q^*(x, s)$ under the constant computation cost for 10×10 JSSP (cost $= 1,000,000$)

Figure 5 shows average solution quality under the same computation cost of 10^6. We see population sizes between $1,000$ and $2,000$ guarantee best averages. Note that we should not jump to a conclusion that the best average point indicates s_{opt}; a larger standard deviation also plays an important role in finding excellent solutions. For example, $s=2,000$ has a slightly larger standard deviation than $s=1,000$.

4 Conclusion

The paper addresses the issue of optimal population size under the constraint of a constant computation cost. We proposed the statistical model to explain how the optimality comes about. Employing the model we can formally prove the existence of the optimal population size and get more insight in a more specific case. The experiments using a job shop scheduling problem revealed that there surely exist such optimal points and showed how they come about, thus showing the plausibility of the model.

Future work includes more experiments to get more insight along the proposed model, and development of a method to find the optimal population size without intensive experiments.

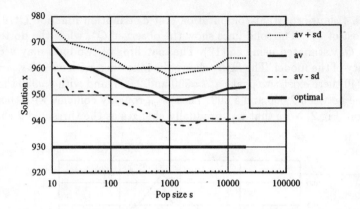

Fig. 5. Solution quality under the constant computation cost for 10×10 JSSP (cost = 1,000,000)

References

1. B. Giffler and G.L. Thompson. Algorithms for solving production scheduling problems. *Oper. Res.*, 8:487–503, 1969.
2. D.E. Goldberg. Optimal initial population size for binary-coded genetic algorithms. Technical Report Report No.85001, TCGA, 1985.
3. D.E. Goldberg. Sizing populations for serial and parallel genetic algorithms. In *Proc. 3rd Int. Conf. on Genetic Algorithms (Arlington, Va.)*, pages 70–79, 1989.
4. J.H. Holland. *Adaptation in natural and artificial systems*. Unuv. of Michigan Press, 1975.
5. J.F. Muth and Thompson.G.L. *Industrial scheduling*. Prentice-Hall, Englewood Cliffs, N.J., 1963.
6. R. Nakano and T. Yamada. Conventional genetic algorithm for job shop poblems. In *Proc. 4th Int. Conf. on Genetic Algorithms (San Diego, CA.)*, pages 474–479, 1991.
7. G.G. Robertson. Population size in classifier systems. In *Proc. 5th Int. Conf. on Machine Learning (Los Altos, CA)*, pages 142–152, 1988.
8. J.D. Schaffer, R.A. Caruane, J. Esheman, L, and R. Das. A study of control parameters affecting online performance of genetic algorithms for function optimization. In *Proc. 3rd Int. Conf. on Genetic Algorithms (Arlington, Va.)*, pages 51–60, 1989.
9. T Yamada and R. Nakano. A genetic algorithm applicable to large-scale job-shop problems. In *Proc. 2nd Conf. on Parallel Problem Solving from Nature (Brussels, Belgium)*, pages 281–290, 1992.

An Evolutionary Algorithm for Integer Programming*

Günter Rudolph

Informatik Centrum Dortmund e.V., Joseph-von-Fraunhofer-Str. 20
D-44227 Dortmund

Abstract. The mutation distribution of evolutionary algorithms usually is oriented at the type of the search space. Typical examples are binomial distributions for binary strings in genetic algorithms or normal distributions for real valued vectors in evolution strategies and evolutionary programming. This paper is devoted to the construction of a mutation distribution for unbounded integer search spaces. The principle of maximum entropy is used to select a specific distribution from numerous potential candidates. The resulting evolutionary algorithm is tested for five nonlinear integer problems.

1 Introduction

Evolutionary algorithms (EAs) represent a class of stochastic optimization algorithms in which principles of organic evolution are regarded as rules in optimization. They are often applied to real parameter optimization problems [2] when specialized techniques are not available or standard methods fail to give satisfactory answers due to multimodality, nondifferentiability or discontinuities of the problem under consideration. Here, we focus on using EAs in integer programming problems of the type

$$\max\{f(x) : x \in M \subseteq \mathbb{Z}^n\} \qquad (1)$$

where $\mathbb{Z}$ denotes the set of integers. Note that the feasible region M is not required to be bounded. Consequently, the encoding of the integer search space with fixed length binary strings as used in standard genetic algorithms (GA) [7, 6] is not feasible. The approach to use an evolution strategy (ES) [13, 14] by embedding the search space $\mathbb{Z}^n$ into $\mathbb{R}^n$ and truncating real values to integers has, however, also its deficiency: As evolution strategies usually operate on real valued spaces they include features to locate optimal points with arbitrary accuracy. In integer spaces these features are not necessary because the smallest distance in ℓ_1-norm between two different points is 1. Therefore, as soon as the step sizes drop below 1 the search will stagnate. Thus, EAs for integer programming should operate directly on integer spaces.

Early approaches in this direction can be found in [4] and [10]. They proposed random search methods on integer spaces in the spirit of a $(1 + 1)$-ES:

---

*This work was done in the BMFT project 'EVOALG' under grant 01 IB 403 A.

Choose $x^{(0)} \in M$ and set $t = 0$
repeat
    $y^{(t+1)} = x^{(t)} + z^{(t)}$
    if $y^{(t+1)} \in M$ and $f(y^{(t+1)}) > f(x^{(t)})$ then $x^{(t+1)} = y^{(t+1)}$
    else $x^{(t+1)} = x^{(t)}$
    increment t
until stopping criterion fulfilled

Here, $z^{(t)}$ denotes the random vector used at step t. Gall [4] and Kelahan/Gaddy [10] used a (continuous) bilateral power distribution with density

$$p(x) = \frac{1}{2 \, k \, a^{1/k}} \, |x|^{1/k-1} \cdot 1_{[-a,a]}(x) \quad , k \in \mathbb{N},$$

to generate random vector z via $z_i = a \cdot (1-2\,u)^k$ with $u \sim U[0,1]$ for each vector component and by truncating these values to integers. The factor a is used to shrink the support of the distribution during the search by a geometrical schedule. Since the support is bounded and its range tends to zero as time increases, the above algorithm is at best locally convergent. Moreover, the truncation of random variables values drawn from continuous mutation distributions to integer values might complicate theoretical investigations. Therefore, the usage of mutation distributions with support $\mathbb{Z}^n$ seems most natural for integer problems (1).

The remainder of the paper is devoted to the construction and test of an appropriate mutation distribution. As there are several candidates for such a mutation distribution we pose some requirements for the desired distribution before using the concept of maximum entropy to guide our final choice. The resulting evolutionary algorithm, which is oriented at a (μ, λ)-ES, is tested for five nonlinear integer problems.

2 Construction of Mutation Distribution

Assume that the current position of the algorithm in the search space is the point $x \in \mathbb{Z}^n$. Since the algorithm does not have prior knowledge of the response surface there is absolute uncertainty about the next step to be taken. In each coordinate direction one might ask the questions: Should we go left or right ? How many steps should be taken in the chosen direction ? The first question has a simple solution: Since we do not have prior knowledge which direction will offer improvement, we should move to the left or right with the same probability. The second question is more difficult to answer: Since we do not know which step size will be successful, we could draw a step size $s \in \mathbb{N}_0$ at random. But which distribution should be used for random variable s ? There are several candidates, for example Poisson, Logseries and geometrical distributions [9]. To select a specific distribution with given mean, say $\theta > 0$, we may use the concept of *maximum entropy*: A distribution with maximum entropy is the one which is spread out as uniformly as possible without contradicting the given information. It agrees with what is known, but expresses maximum uncertainty with respect to all other matters [8]. The usage of this concept to select a distribution usually leads to the task to solve a nonlinear, constrained optimization problem analytically. This will be done in subsection 2.1. The symmetrization of the chosen distribution and its extension to the multivariate case will be considered in subsection 2.2. Finally, we discuss possibilities to control the average step size during the search in subsection 2.3.

2.1 Maximum Entropy

DEFINITION 1

Let p_k with $k \in \mathbb{N}_0$ denote the density of a discrete random variable. Then

$$H(p) = - \sum_{k=0}^{\infty} p_k \log p_k \tag{2}$$

is called the *entropy* of the distribution, provided that series (2) converges[†]. □

PROPOSITION 1

Let X be a discrete random variable with support $\mathbb{N}_0$ and mean $E[X] = \theta > 0$. If the distribution of X is requested to possess maximum entropy, then X must have geometrical distribution with density

$$P\{X = k\} = \frac{1}{\theta + 1} \left(1 - \frac{1}{\theta + 1} \right)^k \quad , \; k \in \mathbb{N}_0 \; . \tag{3}$$

PROOF : The optimal values for p_k can be obtained after partial differentation of the Lagrangian

$$L(p, a, b) = - \sum_{k=0}^{\infty} p_k \log p_k + a \left(\sum_{k=0}^{\infty} p_k - 1 \right) + b \left(\sum_{k=0}^{\infty} k \cdot p_k - \theta \right) .$$

The details are omitted due to lack of space. □

2.2 Symmetrization and Extension to the Multivariate Case

A discrete distribution is symmetric with respect to 0, if $p_k = p_{-k}$ for all k being elements of the support. How this can be achieved ?

PROPOSITION 2   ([12, p. 436–437])

Let X be a discrete random variable with support $\mathbb{N}_0$ and Y a random variable with support $\mathbb{Z} \backslash \mathbb{N}$ and $Y \overset{d}{=} -X$. If X and Y are stochastically independent, then $Z \overset{d}{=} X + Y$ possesses a symmetric distribution with respect to 0. □

Here, X possesses geometrical distribution with $P\{X = k\} = p \cdot (1-p)^k$, so that for Y holds $P\{Y = k\} = p \cdot (1 - p)^{-k}$. The convolution of both distributions leads to the distribution of Z. We distinguish two cases:

[†]Convention: $0 \cdot \log 0 = 0$.

I. Let $k \geq 0$. Then $P\{Z = k\} = P\{X + Y = k\} =$

$$\sum_{j=0}^{\infty} P\{X = j + k\} \cdot P\{Y = -j\} \quad = \quad \sum_{j=0}^{\infty} p \cdot (1-p)^{j+k} \cdot p \cdot (1-p)^{j} =$$

$$p^2 (1-p)^k \sum_{j=0}^{\infty} \left[(1-p)^2\right]^j \quad = \quad \frac{p}{2-p}(1-p)^k .$$

II. Let $k < 0$. Then $P\{Z = k\} = P\{X + Y = k\} =$

$$\sum_{j=0}^{\infty} P\{X = j\} \cdot P\{Y = -j + k\} \quad = \quad \sum_{j=0}^{\infty} p \cdot (1-p)^{j} \cdot p \cdot (1-p)^{j-k} =$$

$$p^2 (1-p)^{-k} \sum_{j=0}^{\infty} \left[(1-p)^2\right]^j \quad = \quad \frac{p}{2-p}(1-p)^{-k} .$$

Thus, the probability function of Z is

$$P\{Z = k\} = \frac{p}{2-p}(1-p)^{|k|} , \quad k \in \mathbb{Z} \tag{4}$$

with $\mathrm{E}[Z] = 0$ and $\mathrm{Var}[Z] = 2\,(1-p)\,/\,p^2$. Next, we consider the multivariate case. Two questions are of special interest: Does the extension to the multivariate case remain symmetric ? What is the expectation and variance of the step size in n-dimensional space ?

DEFINITION 2   ([3])
A discrete multivariate distribution with support $\mathbb{Z}^n$ is called ℓ_1-symmetric if the probability to generate a specific point $k \in \mathbb{Z}^n$ is of the form

$$P\{X_1 = k_1, X_2 = k_2, \ldots, X_n = k_n\} = g(\|k\|_1) ,$$

where $k = (k_1, \ldots, k_n)'$ with $k_i \in \mathbb{Z}$ and $\|k\|_1 = \sum_{i=1}^{n} |k_i|$ denotes the ℓ_1-norm.
□

We shall generate the mutation vector Z by n independent random variables Z_i with probability function (4). Let $k \in \mathbb{Z}^n$ be any point of length $\|k\|_1 = s$, s fixed. Then $P\{Z_1 = k_1, Z_2 = k_2, \ldots, Z_n = k_n\} =$

$$\prod_{i=1}^{n} P\{Z_i = k_i\} \quad = \quad \left(\frac{p}{2-p}\right)^n \prod_{i=1}^{n}(1-p)^{|k_i|} =$$

$$\left(\frac{p}{2-p}\right)^n (1-p)^{\sum_{i=1}^{n}|k_i|} \quad = \quad \left(\frac{p}{2-p}\right)^n (1-p)^{\|k\|_1} .$$

That means that each point with length s is sampled with the same probability. Therefore, the multivariate distribution is ℓ_1-symmetric. To determine the expectation and variance of the step size in n-dimensional space, we require the expectation of random variable $|Z_1|$. Since $P\{|Z_1| = j\} = P\{Z_1 = j\} + P\{Z_1 = -j\}$ for $j \in \mathbb{N}$ and $P\{|Z_1| = 0\} = P\{Z_1 = 0\}$ we obtain

$$
P\{|Z_1| = j\} =
\begin{cases}
\dfrac{p}{2-p} & \text{, if } j = 0 \\[3mm]
\dfrac{2p}{2-p}(1-p)^j & \text{, if } j \in \mathbb{N}
\end{cases}
$$

Straightforward calculations lead to

$$
\mathrm{E}[\,|Z_1|\,] = \frac{2(1-p)}{p(2-p)} \quad \text{and} \quad \mathrm{V}[\,|Z_1|\,] = \frac{2(1-p)}{p^2}\left[1 - \frac{2(1-p)}{(2-p)^2}\right] .
$$

As the random variables $|Z_i|$ are stochastically independent we obtain for vector Z

$$
\mathrm{E}[\,\|Z\|_1\,] = n \cdot \mathrm{E}[\,|Z_1|\,] \quad \text{and} \quad \mathrm{V}[\,\|Z\|_1\,] = n \cdot \mathrm{V}[\,|Z_1|\,] . \tag{5}
$$

It should be noted that (4) could have been derived from the ansatz

$$
P\{Z = k\} = \frac{q^{|k|}}{\displaystyle\sum_{j=-\infty}^{\infty} q^{|j|}} = \frac{q^{|k|}}{1 + 2\displaystyle\sum_{j=1}^{\infty} q^j} = \frac{(1-q)\cdot q^{|k|}}{1+q}
$$

with $q = 1 - p$. Another approach with

$$
P\{Z = k\} = \frac{q^{k^2}}{\displaystyle\sum_{j=-\infty}^{\infty} q^{j^2}} = \frac{q^{k^2}}{1 + 2\displaystyle\sum_{j=1}^{\infty} q^{j^2}} = \frac{q^{k^2}}{\vartheta_3(q,0)} , \tag{6}
$$

where $\vartheta_3(q,x)$ denotes the third Theta function [1, entry 16.27.3], gives exactly the distribution with maximum entropy under the constraints $P\{Z = k\} = P\{Z = -k\}$ for all $k \in \mathbb{Z}$ and $\mathrm{V}[Z] = \sigma^2$ (see Appendix). There are, however, three problems:

1. The multivariate version of (6) is symmetric with respect to ℓ_2-norm.

2. The control of (6) with parameter σ would require the approximate determination of the zeros of a highly nonlinear equation (see Appendix), as soon as parameter σ is altered.

3. There exists neither a closed form of $\vartheta_3(q,0)$ nor of its partial sums, so that the generation of the associated random numbers must be expensive and inaccurate.

While the first point is a matter of taste, the last two points are prohibitive for the usage of distribution (6) in an optimization algorithm. The last two problems do not occur with distribution (4). Firstly, the random variable Z

can be generated by the difference of two geometricly distributed independent random variables (both with parameter p) and a geometric random variable G is obtained as follows: Let U be uniformly distributed over $[0, 1) \subset \mathbb{R}$. Then

$$G = \left\lfloor \frac{\log(1-U)}{\log(1-p)} \right\rfloor$$

is geometricly distributed with parameter p. Secondly, the distribution could be controlled by the mean step size (5), so that one obtains

$$S = n \cdot \frac{2(1-p)}{p(2-p)} \quad \Leftrightarrow \quad p = 1 - \frac{S/n}{(1+(S/n)^2)^{1/2}+1}, \tag{7}$$

where $S = \mathrm{E}[\,\|Z\|_1\,]$.

2.3 Parameter Control

As soon as an probabilistic optimization algorithm approaches the optimum, the step size of the algorithm must decrease to balance the probability to generate a new successful point. There are several ways to control the parameters of the mutation distribution. A simple idea is to decrease the step size s by a deterministic schedule, say $s_t = s_0/t$ or $s_t = \beta^t \cdot s_0$ with $\beta \in (0, 1)$. This is sufficient for problems with only one local (= global) optimum. But for problems with more than one local optimum such a schedule would force the algorithm to approach the closest local optimum. Therefore, it might be useful to offer the chance to increase the step size, too. Evolution strategies employ the following technique [2]: An *individual* consists of a vector $x \in \mathbb{Z}^n$ and a mutation control parameter $s \in \mathbb{R}_+$. Both x and s are regarded as *genes* changeable by genetic operators. First, the mean step size s is *mutated* by multiplication with a lognormally distributed random variable: $s' = s \cdot \exp(N)$, where N is a normally distributed random variable with zero mean and variance $\tau^2 = 1/n$. Thus, the mean step size is decreased or increased by a factor with the same probability and it is likely that a better step size will also produce a better point. Since a mean step size below 1 is not useful for integer problems, the mutated mean step size is set to 1 if the value is less than 1.

Finally, vector x is mutated by adding the difference of two independent geometricly distributed random numbers to each vector component. Both geometric random variables have parameter p depending on the new step size s' via (7).

3 Computational Results

3.1 Sketch of the Algorithm

The evolutionary algorithm to be developed here is basically a (μ, λ)-ES [2] (outlined below). Initially, vector x of each individual is drawn uniformly from the starting area $\mathcal{M} \in \mathbb{Z}^n$, which need not contain the global optimum. The initial value of s is chosen proportional to the nth root of the volume of $\mathcal{M}$. Recombination of two individuals is performed as follows: The step size parameters of the parents are averaged and the new vector x is generated by choosing the vector component of the first or second individual with the same probability. Infeasible individuals are sampled anew.

> initialize μ individuals
> calculate the fitness of the individuals
> repeat
>> do λ times:
>>> select two individuals at random
>>> perform recombination to obtain an offspring
>>> mutate the offspring
>>> calculate the fitness of the offspring
>> od
>> select μ best offspring
> until termination criterion fulfilled

3.2 Test problems

Problem 2.20 (unconstrained) of [14] with $x \in \mathbb{Z}^{30}$: $f_1(x) = -\|x\|_1$ with known solution: $x_i = 0$ with $f(x) = 0$. Starting area $\mathcal{M} = [-1000, 1000]^{30} \subset \mathbb{Z}^{30}$. Initial mean step size $s_0 = 1000/3$.

Problem 1.1 of [14] with $x \in \mathbb{Z}^{30}$: $f_2(x) = -x'x$ with known solution: $x_i = 0$ with $f(x) = 0$. Starting area $\mathcal{M} = [-1000, 1000]^{30} \subset \mathbb{Z}^{30}$. Initial mean step size $s_0 = 1000/3$.

Problem 8 of [5] with $x \in \mathbb{Z}^5$:

$$f_3(x) = (15\ 27\ 36\ 18\ 12)\, x - x' \begin{pmatrix} 35 & -20 & -10 & 32 & -10 \\ -20 & 40 & -6 & -31 & 32 \\ -10 & -6 & 11 & -6 & -10 \\ 32 & -31 & -6 & 38 & -20 \\ -10 & 32 & -10 & -20 & 31 \end{pmatrix} x$$

Best solutions known: $x = (0\ 11\ 22\ 16\ 6)'$ and $x = (0\ 12\ 23\ 17\ 6)'$ with $f_3(x) = 737$. Starting area $\mathcal{M} = [0, 100]^5 \subset \mathbb{Z}^5$. Initial mean step size $s_0 = 50/3$. Derived from problem 9 of [5] with $x_i \geq 0$.

$$f_4(x) = -\sum_{i=1}^{10} x_i \cdot \left[\log\left(\frac{x_i + i}{0.1 + \sum_{i=1}^{10} x_i} \right) - d_i \right] - 6 \cdot (A^2 + B^2 + C^2),$$

with $d = (6.089, 17.164, 34.054, 5.914, 24.721, 14.986, 24.1, 10.708, 26.662, 22.179)$, $A = x_1 + 2\,x_2 + 2\,x_3 + x_6 + x_{10} - 2$, $B = x_4 + x_5 + x_6 + x_7 - 1$ and $C = x_3 + x_7 + x_8 + x_9 + x_{10} - 1$. Best solution known: $x = (3\ 0\ 0\ 3\ 0\ 0\ 0\ 3\ 0\ 0)'$ with $f(x) \approx 150.533$. Starting area $\mathcal{M} = [50, 150]^{10} \subset \mathbb{Z}^{10}$. Initial mean step size $s_0 = 50/3$.

Problem 2 of [11] with $x_i \geq 0$: $f_5(x) = \prod_{i=1}^{15} [1 - (1 - r_i)^{x_i}]$ with constraints $c'x \leq 400$ and $w'x \leq 414$ (see [11] for details). Best solution known: $x = (3\ 4\ 6\ 4\ 3\ 2\ 4\ 5\ 4\ 2\ 3\ 4\ 5\ 4\ 5)'$ with $f_5(x) \approx 0.945613$. Starting area $\mathcal{M} = [0, 6]^{15} \subset \mathbb{Z}^{15}$. Initial step size $s_0 = 2$.

3.3 Results

The evolutionary algorithm was tested with $\mu = 30$ and $\lambda = 100$. The test statistics over 1000 runs for each problem are summarized in tables 1 and 2 below.

	min	max	mean	std.dev.	skew
f_1	106	1519	147.0	96.4	6.68
f_2	115	159	135.6	6.7	0.25
f_3	30	198	107.7	30.5	-0.17
f_4	38	769	94.3	85.9	3.48
f_5	16	49434	582.6	2842.5	9.90

Table 1: Statistics of the first hitting time distribution.

Table 1 shows the minimum, maximum, mean, standard deviation and skewness of the sample of first hitting times (of the global maximum) obtained from 1000 independent runs. Problems f_1 and f_2 only have one local (= global) maximum. Surprisingly, the distribution of the first hitting times is skewed to the right significantly for problem f_1, while the tails of the distribution for problem f_2 are balanced. But as can be seen from table 2 containing the percentiles of the ordered sample, at least 90% of all runs solved problem f_1 in not more than 140 generations. The reasons for these different characteristics are unknown at the moment.

	.10	.20	.30	.40	.50	.60	.70	.80	.90	.95	.97	.99
f_1	118	120	123	125	126	128	131	134	140	276	416	624
f_2	128	130	132	133	135	137	139	141	144	147	149	152
f_3	65	81	94	102	110	118	125	133	145	155	161	173
f_4	46	49	53	57	62	70	82	108	194	260	331	455
f_5	24	26	28	31	34	38	44	84	487	2245	5655	13038

Table 2: Percentiles of the first hitting time distribution

Problems f_3, f_4 and f_5 possess more than one local maxima. Seemingly, problems f_3 and f_4 do not cause difficulties, maybe due to the low dimensionality of the problems. The results for problem f_5 reveal that this problem is solvable for 80% of the runs in less than 100 generations, but there must be local maxima on isolated peaks preventing the population to generate better solutions by recombination, so that mutation is the only chance to move from the top of a locally optimal peak to the global one.

4 Conclusions

The principle of maximum entropy is a useful guide to construct a mutation distribution for evolutionary algorithms to be applied to integer problems. This concept can and should be used to construct mutation distributions for arbitrary search spaces, because special *a priori* knowledge of the problem type may be formulated as constraints of the maximum entropy problem, so that this knowledge (and only this) will be incorporated into the search distribution. The evolutionary algorithm developed here demonstrated the usefulness of this approach. It was able to locate the global optima of five nonlinear integer problems relatively fast for at least 80 percent of 1000 independent runs per problem. Clearly, a test bed of only five problems may not be regarded as a basis to judge the power of the algorithm, but these first results and the 'simplicity' of the mutation distribution are encouraging for further theoretical research.

References

[1] M. Abramowitz and I.A. Stegun (Eds.). *Handbook of Mathematical Functions*. Dover Publications, New York, 1965.

[2] T. Bäck and H.-P. Schwefel. An overview of evolutionary algorithms for parameter optimization. *Evolutionary Computation*, 1(1):1–23, 1993.

[3] K.-T. Fang, S. Kotz, and K.-W. Ng. *Symmetric Multivariate and Related Distributions*. Chapman and Hall, London and New York, 1990.

[4] D.A. Gall. A practical multifactor optimization criterion. In A. Lavi and T.P. Vogl, editors, *Recent Advances in Optimization Techniques*, pages 369–386. Wiley, New York, 1966.

[5] A. Glankwahmdee, J.S. Liebman, and G.L. Hogg. Unconstrained discrete nonlinear programming. *Engineering Optimization*, 4:95–107, 1979.

[6] D.E. Goldberg. *Genetic Algorithms in Search, Optimization, and Machine Learning*. Addison Wesley, Reading (MA), 1989.

[7] J.H. Holland. *Adaptation in natural and artificial systems*. The University of Michigan Press, Ann Arbor, 1975.

[8] E.T. Jaynes. Prior probabilities. *IEEE Transactions on Systems Science and Cybernetics*, 4(3):227–241, 1968.

[9] N.L. Johnson and S. Kotz. *Distributions in Statistics: Discrete Distributions*. Houghton Mifflin, Boston, 1969.

[10] R.C. Kelahan and J.L. Gaddy. Application of the adaptive random search to discrete and mixed integer optimization. *International Journal for Numerical Methods in Engineering*, 12:289–298, 1978.

[11] R. Luus. Optimization of system reliability by a new nonlinear integer programming procedure. *IEEE Transactions on Reliability*, 24(1):14–16, 1975.

[12] P.H. Müller (Ed.). *Wahrscheinlichkeitsrechnung und mathematische Statistik: Lexikon der Stochastik*. Akademie Verlag, Berlin, 5th edition, 1991.

[13] I. Rechenberg. *Evolutionsstrategie: Optimierung technischer Systeme nach Prinzipien der biologischen Evolution*. Frommann–Holzboog Verlag, Stuttgart, 1973.

[14] H.-P. Schwefel. *Numerische Optimierung von Computer-Modellen mittels der Evolutionsstrategie*. Birkhäuser, Basel, 1977.

Appendix: A Family of Maximum Entropy Distributions

The question addressed here is: Which discrete distribution with support $\mathbb{Z}$ is symmetric with respect to 0, has a variance $\sigma^2 > 0$ or a mean deviation s and possesses maximum entropy ? The answer requires the solution of the following nonlinear optimization problem: $-\sum_{k=-\infty}^{\infty} p_k \log p_k \to \max$ subject to

$$p_k = p_{-k} \quad \forall k \in \mathbb{Z}, \tag{8}$$

$$\sum_{k=-\infty}^{\infty} p_k = 1, \tag{9}$$

$$\sum_{k=-\infty}^{\infty} |k|^m p_k = \sigma^2 \tag{10}$$

$$p_k \geq 0 \quad \forall k \in \mathbb{Z}. \tag{11}$$

We may neglect condition (11), if the solution of the surrogate problem fulfills these inequalities. We may therefore differentiate the Lagrangian

$$L(p, a, b) = -\sum_{k=-\infty}^{\infty} p_k \log p_k + a \cdot \left(\sum_{k=-\infty}^{\infty} p_k - 1 \right) + b \cdot \left(\sum_{k=-\infty}^{\infty} |k|^m p_k - \sigma^2 \right)$$

to obtain the necessary condition (9) and (10) and $-1 - \log p_k + a + b |k|^m = 0$ or alternatively

$$p_k = e^{a-1} \cdot (e^b)^{|k|^m} \quad \forall k \in \mathbb{Z}. \tag{12}$$

Exploitation of the symmetry condition (8) and substitution of (12) in (9) leads to

$$\sum_{k=-\infty}^{\infty} p_k = p_0 + 2 \cdot \sum_{k=1}^{\infty} p_k = e^{a-1} \cdot \left(1 + 2 \cdot \sum_{k=1}^{\infty} (e^b)^{|k|^m} \right) = 1. \tag{13}$$

Let $q = e^b < 1$ so that $S(q) := \sum_{k=1}^{\infty} q^{|k|^m} < \infty$ and $q \cdot S'(q) = \sum_{k=1}^{\infty} |k|^m q^{|k|^m}$. Then condition (13) becomes

$$e^{1-a} = 1 + 2 \cdot S(q) = \begin{cases} (1+q)/(1-q) & \text{, if } m = 1 \\ \vartheta_3(q, 0) & \text{, if } m = 2 \end{cases}, \tag{14}$$

where $\vartheta_3(q, z)$ denotes the third Theta function [1]. Substitution of (12) in (10) yields

$$\sum_{k=-\infty}^{\infty} |k|^m p_k = 2 \cdot \sum_{k=1}^{\infty} |k|^m p_k = 2 e^{a-1} \cdot \sum_{k=1}^{\infty} |k|^m q^{|k|^m} = 2 e^{a-1} \cdot q \cdot S'(q) = \sigma^2,$$

so that with substitution of (14) for $m = 2$ one obtains

$$\frac{2 q S'(q)}{\vartheta_3(q, 0)} = \sigma^2, \tag{15}$$

while $m = 1$ gives (7) with $q = 1 - p$ and $s/n = \sigma^2$. The value of q in (15) for given σ can be determined numerically only. Substitution of (14) in (12) gives (6) for $m = 2$ and (4) for $m = 1$.

Long Path Problems

Jeffrey Horn[1], David E. Goldberg[1], and Kalyanmoy Deb[2] *

[1] Illinois Genetic Algorithms Laboratory, University of Illinois at
Urbana-Champaign, 117 Transportation Building, 104 South Mathews Avenue,
Urbana, IL 61801-2996, USA, (e-mail: jeffhorn@uiuc.edu, deg@uiuc.edu)
[2] Department of Mechanical Engineering, Indian Institute of Technology, Kanpur,
UP, PIN 208016, India, (e-mail: deb@iitk.ernet.in)

Abstract. We demonstrate the interesting, counter-intuitive result that
simple paths to the global optimum can be so long that climbing the
path is intractable. This means that a unimodal search space, which
consists of a single hill and in which each point in the space is on a
simple path to the global optimum, can be difficult for a hillclimber to
optimize. Various types of hillclimbing algorithms will make constant
progress toward the global optimum on such long path problems. They
will continuously improve their *best found* solutions, and be guaranteed
to reach the global optimum. Yet we cannot wait for them to arrive.
Early experimental results indicate that a genetic algorithm (GA) with
crossover alone outperforms hillclimbers on one such long path problem.
This suggests that GAs can climb hills faster than hillclimbers by exploiting *building blocks* when they are present. Although these problems
are artificial, they introduce a new dimension of problem difficulty for
evolutionary computation. Path length can be added to the ranks of multimodality, deception/misleadingness, noise, variance, etc., as a measure
of fitness landscapes and their amenability to evolutionary optimization.

1 Introduction

In this paper we present a class of problems designed to be difficult for randomized search procedures that exploit local search space information. In particular,
these problems challenge hillclimbers and mutation algorithms. The problems
are difficult not because they contain local optima that capture the attention of
the search procedure. Indeed, these problems are unimodal and "easy" in the
sense that the simplest hillclimber will always find the global optimum, no matter where in the space it starts searching. Rather, these problems are difficult for
hillclimbers because the only "path" up the hill to the global optimum is very

---

* The first author acknowledges support by NASA under contract number NGT-50873.
The second and third authors acknowledge the support provided by the US Army
under Contract DASG60-90-C-0153 and by the National Science Foundation under
Grant ECS-9022007. We thank Joseph Culberson for pointing us to the literature
on difference-preserving codes. Both Culberson and Greg J.E. Rawlins participated
in early discussions with the second author on hillclimbing hard problems.

long and narrow. The length of the path grows exponentially with the size of the (binary) problem, ℓ.

Constructing hard problems for a class of algorithms is part of a recognized methodology for analyzing, understanding, and bounding complex algorithms. Three types of difficulties for hillclimbers are well-known [3]:
- Isolation or *needle-in-a-haystack* (NIAH)
- Full deception
- Multimodality

All three types of difficulties are also known to pose stiff challenges to genetic algorithms (GAs), and have been used to understand GAs [2, 1].

We propose a fourth type of problem that specifically targets the hillclimber's use of local information. We construct a path that leads a hillclimber to the global optimum, but on a path that is so long that for large problems ($\ell \gg 20$) we simply cannot wait for the algorithm to terminate. We might sit and watch our hillclimber making constant progress for years on an 80-bit problem.

We are motivated to construct and analyze these long path problems by several observations:
- Computational difficulty of an apparently easy problem
- Utility in analyzing hillclimbers and mutation algorithms
- Possible distinguishing problem for GAs versus hillclimbers
- Possible distinguishing problem for crossover versus mutation

These problems represent a dimension of difficulty that has been less obvious than noise, deception, local optima, etc. Unimodal, and with every point on a path to the global optimum, these problems are still intractable for hillclimbers of bounded step size. They might also be intractable for various kinds of mutation algorithms, and for algorithms incorporating recombination, such as GAs with high crossover rates. If they do offer as stiff a challenge to recombinative algorithms as they do to hillclimbers (and apparently to mutation algorithms as well), then we have found yet another class of GA-difficulty. If, on the other hand, the recombinative GA can perform significantly better (faster) on these problems than local-search procedures, then we have found a class of functions that distinguish these two types of algorithms. From this we can learn something about their different strengths and weaknesses relative to each other [6].

2 Definitions: Optima, Paths, and Algorithms

We use the paradigm of a *fitness landscape*, which consists of a search space, a metric, and a scalar fitness function $f(s)$ defined over elements s of the search space S. Assuming the goal is to maximize fitness, we can imagine the globally best solutions (the global optima, or "globals") as "peaks" in the search space. For the purposes of this paper, we define local optimality as follows. We first assume a real-valued, scalar fitness function $f(s)$ over fixed length ℓ-bit binary strings s, $f(s) \in \Re$. Without loss of generality, we assume f is to be maximized. A *local optimum* in a discrete search space S is a point, or region, with fitness function value strictly greater than those of *all* of its nearest neighbors. By "region" we mean a set of interconnected points of equal fitness. That is, we treat as a single optimum the set of points related by the transitive closure of the nearest-neighbor relation such that all points are of equal fitness. This definition allows us to include flat plateaus and ridges as single optima, and to treat a flat fitness function as having no local optima. The "nearest neighbor" relation assumes a metric on the search space, call it d, where $d(s_1, s_2) \in \Re$ is the metric's distance between points s_1 and s_2. Then the nearest neighbors of a point s' are all points $s \in S, s \neq s'$ such that $d(s', s) \leq k$, for some neighborhood radius k. In this paper we use only *Hamming distance* (number of bit positions at which two binary strings differ) as the metric, and assume $k = 1$. Thus a point s with fitness $f(s)$ greater than that of all its immediate neighbors (strings differing from s in only one bit position) is a local optimum.

Although the term "hillclimber" denotes a specific set of algorithms for some researchers, we will use the term more loosely here to describe *all* algorithms that emphasize exploration of a local neighborhood around the current solution. In particular, we assume that our *hillclimber* explores a neighborhood of radius k-bits much better than it explores outside that neighborhood. Therefore, our hillclimber is much more likely to take "steps" of size $\leq k$ than it is to take steps $> k$. Examples of hillclimbers include steepest ascent [12], next ascent [4], and random mutation [10, 1, 8, 9]. GAs with high selective pressure and low crossover rates also exhibit strong local hillclimbing.

A path P of step size k is a sequence of points p_i such that any two points adjacent on the path are at most k-bits apart, and any two points not adjacent on the path are more than k-bits apart:

$$\forall p_i, p_j \in P, \ d(p_i, p_j) \begin{cases} \leq k, \text{ if } |i - j| = 1 \\ \\ > k, \text{ otherwise.} \end{cases}$$

where $d(p_i, p_j)$ is the Hamming distance between the two points and p_i is the ith point on the path P. Thus, our hillclimbing algorithm that takes steps of size $\leq k$ would tend to follow the path without taking any "shortcuts". The step size here is important, because we want to lead the algorithm up the path, but to make the path wind through the search space as much as possible, we will need to fold that path back many times. Earlier portions of the path may thus pass quite closely to later portions, within $k + 1$ bits, so we must assume that our algorithm has a very small, if not zero, probability of taking steps of size $> k$.

3   A Simple Construction: the Root2path

In this section we construct a long path that is not optimally long, but does have length exponential in ℓ, the size (order, or dimension) of the problem, and is simple in its construction. We call it the *Root2path*. Here we choose the smallest step size $k = 1$ to illustrate the construction. Each point on the path must be exactly one bit different from the point behind it and the point ahead of it, while also being at least two bits away from any other point on the path.

The construction of the path is intuitive. If we have a Root2path of dimension ℓ, call it P_ℓ, we can basically double it by moving up two dimensions to $\ell + 2$ as follows. Make two copies of P_ℓ, say copy00 and copy11. Prepend "00" to each point in copy00, and "11" to each point in copy11[3]. Now each point in copy00 is at least two bits different from all points in copy11. Also, copy00 and copy11 are both paths of step size one and of dimension $\ell + 2$. Furthermore, the endpoint of copy00 and the endpoint of copy11 differ only in their first two bit positions ("00" versus "11"). By adding a *bridge point* that is the same as the endpoint of copy00 but with "01" in the first two bit positions instead of "00", we can connect the end of copy00 and the end of copy11. Reversing the sequence of points in copy11, we concatenate copy00, the bridge point, and Reverse[copy11] to create the Root2path of dimension $\ell + 2$, call it $P_{\ell+2}$, and length essentially twice that of P_ℓ:

$$|P_{\ell+2}| = 2\,|P_\ell| + 1 \tag{1}$$

As for the dimensions between the doublings, which are all of odd order, we can simply use the path P_ℓ by adding a "0" to each point in P_ℓ to create $P_{\ell+1}$. If $|P_\ell|$ is exponentional in ℓ, then $|P_{\ell+1}|$ is exponential in $\ell + 1$.

For the base case $\ell = 1$, we have only two points in the search space: 0 and 1. We put them both on the Root2path $P_1 = \{0, 1\}$, where 0 is the beginning and 1 is the end (i.e., the global optimum).

With every other incremental increase in dimension, we have an effective doubling of the path length. Solving the recurrence relation in Equation 1, with $|P_1| = |P_2| = 2$, we obtain the path length as a function of ℓ:

$$|P_\ell| = 3 * 2^{\lfloor (\ell-1)/2 \rfloor} - 1. \tag{2}$$

Path length increases in proportion to $2^{\ell/2}$ or $(\sqrt{2})^\ell$ and thus grows exponentially in ℓ with base ≈ 1.414, an ever-decreasing fraction of the total space 2^ℓ.

Since the path takes up only a small fraction of the search space for large ℓ, the entire Root2path approaches a Needle-in-a-Haystack (NIAH) problem as ℓ grows. We are interested in how long a hillclimber takes to climb a path, not how long it takes to find it. We therefore slope the remainder of the search space (i.e., all points not on the Root2path) towards the beginning of the path. The construction of the Root2path makes it easy to do this. Since the first point on the path is the all-zeroes point, we assign fitness values to all points *off* the path according to a function of *unitation*[4]. The fewer ones in a string, the higher its fitness. Thus, most of the search space should lead the hillclimber to the all-zeroes point, in at most ℓ steps. We call this landscape feature the *nilness*[5] *slope*. Together, the path P_ℓ and the nilness slope form a single *hill*, making the search space unimodal. A deterministic hillclimber, started *anywhere* in the space, is guaranteed to find the global optimum.

---

[3] Thus the point "001" in P_3 becomes "00001" in copy00 and "11001" in copy11.

[4] The unitation $u(s)$ of a string s is equal to the number of ones in s. For example, $u(\text{"0110110"}) = 4$.

[5] The nilness of a string s is simply $n(s) = \ell - u(s)$ (i.e., the number of zeroes in s).

To find the total number of "steps" from the bottom of the hill (the all-ones point) to the top (the global optimum), we add the "height" of the nilness slope, which is simply ℓ, to the path length (Equation 2), and substract one for the all zeroes point, which is on both the path and the slope:

$$\text{Hill-Height}(\ell) = 3 * 2^{\lfloor(\ell-1)/2\rfloor} + \ell - 2 \tag{3}$$

The recursive construction of the Root2path is illustrative, but inefficient for fitness evaluations in our simulations below. In Figure 1 we present pseudocode for a much more efficient *decoding algorithm*[6]. Note that the recursion in the pseudocode is (optimizable) tail recursion. The function *HillPosition* can be used directly as the objective fitness function for optimization (maximization)[7].

```
PathPosition[str] := CASE
        (str == "0")   RETURN 0;  /* First step on path. */
        (str == "1")   RETURN 1;  /* Second step on path. */
        (str == "00—rest-of-string")  /* On 1st half of path.  Recur. */
            RETURN PathPosition[rest-of-string];
        (str == "11—rest-of-string")  /* On 2nd half of path.  Recur. */
            RETURN 3*2^Floor[(Length[str]-1)/2] - 2 -
                PathPosition[rest-of-string];
        (str == "101" OR "1011—all-zeroes") /* At bridge pt. (halfway) */
            RETURN 3*2^(Floor[(Length(str)-1)/2] - 1) - 1);
        OTHERWISE    RETURN false;    /* str is NOT ON PATH. */

HillPosition[str] := IF (PathPosition[str])    /* If str is on path, */
            /* return path position plus problem length (slope). */
            THEN RETURN PathPosition[str] + Length[str];
            ELSE RETURN Nilness[str];  /* Else return position on slope, */
                /*  which is number of zeroes.   */
```

Fig. 1. The decoding algorithm for the Root2path function, $k = 1$.

4 Simulation Results

4.1 The Long Road for Hillclimbers

We restrict ourselves to five simple algorithms, analyzed in [10]:
- Steepest ascent hillclimber (SAHC)
- Next ascent hillclimber (NAHC)
- Fixed rate mutation algorithm (Mut)
- Mutation with steepest ascent (Mut+SAHC)
- Mutation with next ascent (Mut+NAHC)

All five algorithms work with one point, s, at a time. The first point, s_0, is chosen

---

[6] In the literature on coding theory, the development of such algorithms is an important followup to the existence proofs and constructions of long paths [11].

[7] Note that the decoding algorithm assumes $odd(\ell)$.

randomly. Thereafter, s_{n+1} is found by looking at a neighborhood of s_n. With steepest ascent, all of s_n's neighbors are compared with s_n. The point within that neighborhood that has the highest fitness becomes s_{n+1}. If $s_{n+1} = s_n$, then steepest ascent has converged to a local (perhaps global) optimum. Next ascent is similar to steepest ascent, the only difference being that next ascent compares neighbors to s_n in some fixed order, taking the first neighbor with fitness greater than s_n to be s_{n+1}. In our runs, we assume SAHC and NAHC explore a neighborhood of radius one (step size $k = 1$).

Mutation (Mut) flips each bit in s_n with probability p_m, independently. The resulting string is compared with s_n. If its fitness is greater, the mutated string becomes s_{n+1}, otherwise s_n does. Mühlenbein [10], and other researchers, have found that a bitwise mutation rate $p_m = 1/\ell$ is optimal for many classes of problems. The only mutation rate we use here is $1/\ell$.

The other two hillclimbing algorithms we run are combinations of mutation with steepest ascent (Mut+SAHC) and next ascent (Mut+NAHC). These combinations are implemented by simply mutating s_n, and allowing either next ascent or steepest ascent hillclimbing to explore the neighborhood around the mutated string. The resulting string, either the originally mutated string or a better neighbor, is then compared with s_n for the choice of s_{n+1}.

We test on Root2paths of dimension $\ell = 1$ to 20. We only consider paths of step size $k = 1$. In Figure 2, we plot the performance of the five hillclimbers. For each problem size ℓ, we ran each algorithm at random starting points. The plotted points are averages over five runs. We measure performance as the number of iterations (of the hillclimber's main update loop) required to reach the global optimum (i.e., the number of points in the sequence s_n). Note that this is less than the number of fitness evaluations used. For example, since steepest ascent searches a neighborhood of radius one everytime it updates s_n, its number of fitness evaluations is ℓ times the number of iterations.

As Figure 2 illustrates, at least three of the algorithms perform exponentially worse as ℓ increases. Mutation by itself tends to spend a long time finding the next step on the path. Steepest and next ascent tend to follow the path step by step. Steepest ascent with mutation exhibits linear performance, however. The superiority of this hillclimbing variant is explained by its tendency to take steps of size two. Mutation with $p_m = 1/\ell$ takes a single-bit step, in expectation. Steepest ascent then explores the immediate neighborhood around the mutated point. Since the Root2path contains many shortcuts of step size two[8], steepest ascent with mutation is able to skip several large segments of the path.

To force Mut+SAHC to stay on an exponentially long path, we clearly need paths of greater step size. A simple way of building such a path is to extend the construction of the Root2path as follows. For a step size of $k = 2$, we should double the path every *third* increment in dimension. Thus we prepend "111" and "000" to copies of P_ℓ to get $P_{\ell+3}$. We now have a path that grows in length in proportion to $2^{\ell/3}$. We could call these *CubeRoot2paths*. We can generalize to step size k, to get paths that grow as $2^{\ell/(k+1)}$, exponential in ℓ for $k \ll \ell$.

---

[8] For example, the beginning and end of the Root2path are only two bits apart!

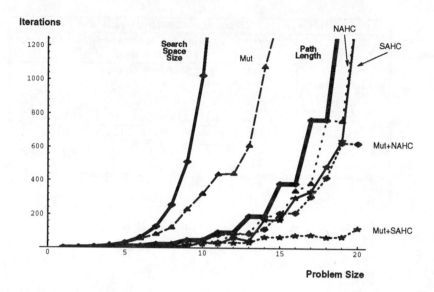

Fig. 2. The performance of five hillclimbing algorithms as a function of the problem size ℓ. Performance is averaged over five runs.

4.2 Crossover's Success

It is not obvious that the long path problems are amenable to recombinative search. From its inductive construction, it is clear that the Root2path has structure. The same basic subsequences of steps are used over and over again on larger scales, resulting in fractal self-similarity. But we do not know if such structure induces building blocks exploitable by crossover [5], as we have not yet applied a schema analysis to these functions. However, certain substrings such as "11" and "1011" (in certain positions) are common to many points on the path. And our first results, summarized in Table 1, indicate that a GA with crossover alone is an effective strategy for climbing long hills in a short time.

In Table 1 we compare three hillclimbers to a GA on three different size Root2path problems (all with stepsize $k = 1$). The GA is a simple, *generational* GA, using single point crossover with probability $p_c = 0.9$, no mutation ($p_m = 0$), binary tournament selection, and the population sizes indicated in Table 1. Random mutation hill climbing (RMHC) is described in [1, 8, 9]. RMHC is like mutation-only (Mut) above, except that one and only one bit flip takes place. Thus, RMHC starts with a random string s_0, and updates s_n by randomly flipping one bit in s_n to form s'_n. If s'_n is better than, or equal to s_n, then s'_n becomes s_{n+1}, otherwise s_n becomes s_{n+1}.

In [1, 8, 9], the authors found that RMHC optimized Royal Road (RR)

PERFORMANCE ON **Root2path**, stepsize $k = 1$			
	Number of Functions Evaluations to Global Optimum mean (std. dev.)		
	problem size		
algorithm	$\ell = 29$	$\ell = 39$	$\ell = 49$
SAHC	1,425,005 (789)	>15,000,000 (0)	>40,000,000 (0)
NAHC	1,359,856 (247)	>15,000,000 (0)	>40,000,000 (0)
RMHC	1,382,242 (112,335)	>15,000,000 (0)	>40,000,000 (0)
GA (Xover only)	25,920 (5830)	75,150 (53,500)	151,740 (140,226)
Pop. size	4000	5000	6000
Height of Hill (path + slope)	49,179 steps	1,572,901 steps	50,331,695 steps

Table 1. GA versus hillclimbers: results from 10 runs of each algorithm.

functions faster than SAHC, NAHC, and the GA. On the Root2path problems, however, the GA[9] seems to outperform the three hillclimbers, and RMHC apparently loses out to the *deterministic*[10] hillclimbers. Comparing the long path problems to the RR functions is not within the scope of this paper[11]. But our early results pointing to superior performance by crossover might be of particular interest to those looking at when GAs outperform hillclimbers [8, 9]. One answer might be "on a hill" (at least, a certain kind of hill).

5 Discussion

5.1 Extension: Longer Paths

It is certainly possible to construct paths longer than the Root2path. A *Fibonacci path* of step size $k = 1$ is constructed inductively like the Root2path. Our inductive step goes as follows. Given a Fibonacci path F_ℓ of dimension ℓ, and a Fibonacci path $F_{\ell+1}$ of dimension $\ell + 1$, we construct a path of dimension $\ell + 2$ by skipping a dimension and then doubling F_ℓ as with the Root2path. But rather than simply adding a single "bridge" point to connect the two copies of

---

[9] For the GA we estimate the number of fitness evaluations (to find the global) as numgens * popsize * p_c, where *numgens* is the number of generations until the global optimum **first** appears. If the GA prematurely converges (i.e., to a non-optimal point), it is restarted **without** resetting *numgens*. Thus *numgens* is cummulative over multiple (unsuccessful) GA runs.

[10] SAHC and NAHC are deterministic in the sense that they are guaranteed to find the global optimum of the Root2path within a maximum time. The GA and RMHC, on the other hand, are stochastic.

[11] It is interesting to note, however, that both landscapes are unimodal (by our definition of local optimality).

F_ℓ, we use the path $F_{\ell-1}$ to connect them. We know we can use $F_{\ell-1}$ to connect the two copies of F_ℓ since $F_{\ell+1}$ is composed of an F_ℓ path coupled with an $F_{\ell-1}$ path.

The formal construction and inductive proof of existence of the Fibonacci path will have to be postponed. The important result to mention here is that the Fibonacci path grows faster in length than the Root2path. The sequence of Fibonacci path lengths, obtained by incrementing ℓ, is the Fibonacci sequence, $\{1,2,3,5,8,13,21,34,55,...\}$, since:

$$|F_\ell| = |F_{\ell-1}| + |F_{\ell-2}|$$

Solving the recurrence relation reveals exponential growth of $\approx 1.61803^\ell$, which has the golden ratio as its base. This base is larger than the base ≈ 1.414 in the exponential growth of the Root2path, but is still < 2. Thus, even the Fibonacci paths will asymptotically approach zero percent of the search space.

The problem of finding a maximally long path with minimal separation has some history, and is known as the "snake-in-the-box" problem, or the design of difference-preserving codes, in the literature on coding theory and combinatorics [7, 11]. Maximizing the length of paths with k-bits of separation is an open problem, even for $k = 1$. However, upper bounds have been found that are $< O(2^\ell)$. Thus the longest paths we can ever find[12] will be $O(2^{\ell/c})$ for some constant $c > 1$. For the Root2path, $c = 2$ for $k = 1$. For the Fibonacci path, $c = 1/(Log_2\Phi) \approx 1.44042$ when $k = 1$, where Φ is the golden ratio.

5.2 Extension: Analysis of Expected Performance

We need both empirical and analytical results for expected performance of various mutation algorithms and recombinative GAs. We wish to explore such apparent tradeoffs as step size k versus length of the path $|P|$. As k increases, $|P|$ decreases exponentially in k, but the number of fitness evaluations required to effectively search a neighborhood of radius k increases exponentially in k. A similar tradeoff involves the mutation rate p_m. As p_m increases, the mutation-only algorithm is more likely to take a larger shortcut across the path, but it is also less likely to find the next step on the path. These kinds of tradeoffs, involving parameters of the search space design and the algorithms themselves, are amenable to analysis of expectation.

5.3 Conclusions

Long path problems are clearly and demonstrably difficult for local searchers (that is, algorithms that search small neighborhoods with high probability, and

---

[12] It is easy to show that maximum path lengths must be $< 2^\ell$, at least for $k \geq 3$: divide the total volume of the search space by a volume $v(k)$ that is a lower bound on the number of off-path points that must "surround" each point on the path. This upper bound indicates that for $k \geq 3$, the optimal path length must approach zero exponentially fast as ℓ increases. This means that for $k \geq 3$, the best growth in path length for which we can hope is x^ℓ, where $x < 2$.

larger neighborhoods with vanishingly small probability). Such algorithms include hillclimbers and the GA's mutation operator. Surprisingly, some of these "intractable hills" can be solved efficiently by GA crossover. The fact that the GA solves problems specifically contrived for hillclimbers lends support to our intuition of GA robustness. Also able to solve long path problems of step size k are hillclimbers of step size $k' > k$. But long path problems of step size k' can be constructed to defeat such hillclimbers. The GA (with crossover) on the other hand *might* scale smoothly with increasing k. Such a result has implications for hybrid algorithms that perform hillclimbing during or after regular GA search: the addition of hillclimbing to the GA could make an "easy" problem intractable. Thus the long path problems reveal to us another dimension of problem difficulty for evolutionary computation; a dimension along which we can characterize, measure, and predict the performance of our algorithms.

References

1. Forrest, S., Mitchell, M.: Relative building-block fitness and the building-block hypothesis. In: L.D. Whitley (ed.): Foundations of Genetic Algorithms, 2. San Mateo, CA: Morgan Kaufmann (1993) 109–126
2. Goldberg, D. E.: Genetic Algorithms in Search, Optimization, and Machine Learning. Reading, MA: Addison-Wesley (1989)
3. Goldberg, D. E.: Making genetic algorithms fly: a lesson from the Wright brothers. Advanced Technology for Developers. 2 February (1993) 1–8
4. Jones, T., Rawlins, G. J. E.: Reverse hillclimbing, genetic algorithms and the busy beaver problem. In: S. Forrest (ed.): Proceedings of the Fifth International Conference on Genetic Algorithms. San Mateo, CA: Morgan Kaufmann (1993) 70–75
5. Holland, J. H.: Adaptation in natural and artificial systems. Ann Arbor, MI: University of Michigan Press (1975)
6. Hoffmeister, F., Bäck, T.: Genetic algorithms and evolutionary strategies: similarities and differences. Technical Report "Grüne Reihe" No. 365. Department of Computer Science, University of Dortmund. November (1990)
7. MacWilliams, F. J., Sloane, N. J. A.: The Theory of Error Correcting Codes. Amsterdam, New York: North-Holland (1977)
8. Mitchell, M., Holland, J. H.: When will a genetic algorithm outperform hill climbing? In: S. Forrest (ed.): Proceedings of the Fifth International Conference on Genetic Algorithms. San Mateo, CA: Morgan Kaufmann (1993) 647
9. Mitchell, M., Holland, J. H., Forrest, S.: When will a genetic algorithm outperform hill climbing? Advances in Neural Information Processing Systems 6. San Mateo, CA: Morgan Kaufmann (to appear)
10. Mühlenbein, H.: How genetic algorithms really work, I. fundamentals. In: R. Männer, B. Manderick (eds.): Parallel Problem Solving From Nature, 2. Amsterdam: North-Holland (1992) 15–26
11. Preparata, F. P., Niervergelt, J.: Difference-preserving codes. IEEE Transactions on Information Theory. **IT-20:5** (1974) 643–649
12. Wilson, S. W.: GA-easy does not imply steepest-ascent optimizable. In: R.K. Belew, L.B. Booker (eds.): Proceedings of the Fourth International Conference on Genetic Algorithms. San Mateo, CA: Morgan Kaufmann (1991) 85–89

Evolution Strategies on Noisy Functions
How to Improve Convergence Properties

Ulrich Hammel and Thomas Bäck

University of Dortmund, Department of Computer Science, LSXI
D-44221 Dortmund, Germany

Abstract. Evolution Strategies are reported to be robust in the presence of noise which in general hinders the optimization process. In this paper we discuss the influence of some of the stratey parameters and strategy variants on the convergence process and discuss measures for improvement of the convergence properties. After having a broad look to the theory for the dynamics of a $(1,\lambda)$-ES on a simple quadratic function we numerically investigate the influence of the parent population size and the introduction of recombination. Finally we compare the effects of multiple sampling of the objective function versus the enlargment of the population size for the convergence precision as well as the convergence reliability by the example of the multimodal Rastrigins function.

1 Introduction

Evolution strategies are claimed to be well suited for experimental optimization [8, 7], where optimal features of a physical system, e.g. the shape of a nozzle [6], are searched for through a series of experiments. Typically a formal model describing the system properties apropriately is not available such that the system has to be viewed as a black box, in the sense that, given a set of parameter values, we observe a corresponding model quality. This complicates the search process, because we can not derive analytical information like gradients directly.

Furthermore the observations are usually disturbed, e.g. due to the limited accuracy of experimentation and observation. An optimization strategie to be of any value in this field must be robust with respect to noise. It is this aspect of evolution strategies that we want to investigate in the following.

We consider only the case of real valued objective functions $f : M \subseteq \mathbb{R}^n \to \mathbb{R}$ with additive normal distributed noise, where we call M the *search space*:

$$F(\mathbf{x}) = f(\mathbf{x}) + \delta , \tag{1}$$

where δ is a random variable with a Gaussian distribution ($N(0, \sigma_\delta)$).

It is the task to find a global optimum point $\mathbf{x}^*$ with

$$\forall \mathbf{x} \in M : f(\mathbf{x}^*) \leq f(\mathbf{x}) , \tag{2}$$

by observations of $F(\mathbf{x})$.

In addition to the deterministic case where we are interested in *convergence reliability* (especially in the case of multimodal functions) and *convergence velocity*, we need to investigate the *convergence precision*, i.e., the exactness with which the optimum is located. Furthermore we will discuss different measures to improve the convergence properties.

For sake of notational clarity we give a broad description of population based evolution strategies sketched in algorithm 1. For details see [2].

Algorithm 1 (The Evolution Strategy)

$$t := 0;$$
initialize $P(t);$
evaluate $P(t);$
while not *terminate* $P(t)$ **do**
    $P'(t) :=$ *recombine* $P(t);$
    $P''(t) :=$ *mutate* $P'(t);$
    evaluate $P''(t);$
    $P(t+1) :=$ *select* $P''(t);$
    $t := t+1;$
od

An individual a consists of two kinds of variables: A vector $\mathbf{x} = (x_1, \ldots, x_n)^T$ of *object variables* denoting a point in the search space and $\mathbf{s} = (s_1, \ldots, s_k)^T$ a vector of strategy variables which affect the evolution process itself. By incorporating the strategy parameters into the individuals the search process is adapted to the underlying topology of the search space. We call this endogenous adjustment of strategy parameters *self-adaptation*.

Consider a parent population $P(t)$ of μ individuals. These μ individuals produce λ offspring by the following process: Two parents p_1, p_2 are randomly selected and give birth to an offspring o of which the ith element o_i is defined as either the ith element of p_1 or the ith element of p_2 with equal propability:

$$o_i = p_{1i} \text{ or } p_{2i} . \tag{3}$$

This scheme of combining parental (genetic) information is called *discrete recombination*. A different scheme, the so called *intermediate recombination*, determines o_i as the average parental information

$$o_i = (p_{1i} + p_{2i})/2 . \tag{4}$$

For both schemes we additionaly introduce *global* variants, where all individuals of the whole population may become parents of one offspring instead of only two, i.e., two individuals are randomly selected from the set of the μ parents independently for each parameter of the offspring instead of only once for each offspring.

In the following we code the recombination operator ρ by a two character string $\rho_x \rho_\sigma$ where ρ_x and ρ_σ stand for recombination on object variables and strategy variables respectively: $\rho_x, \rho_\sigma \in \{\_, d, i, D, I\}$ where d denotes discrete, i intermediate and $\_$ no recombination. Uppercase letters indicate the global variants.

The recombination process is repeated λ times yielding λ offspring.

After recombination an offspring is mutated by adding small normally distributed values to the object variables. The standard deviations of these distributions, also called step sizes, are part of the vector of strategy variables and thus are also subject to mutation and recombination.

Though s might in general consist not only of step sizes (see [1] for details), we restrict our investigation on this case. Therefore we formulate muation as

$$\mathcal{M}(x_1, \ldots, x_n, \sigma_1, \ldots, \sigma_n) = (x'_1, \ldots, x'_n, \sigma'_1, \ldots, \sigma'_n)$$
$$\sigma'_i = \sigma_i \cdot \exp(\tau' \cdot N(0,1) + \tau \cdot N_i(0,1)) \tag{5}$$
$$x'_i = x_i + \sigma'_i \cdot N_i(0,1) \ .$$

The step sizes are mutated by multiplication with two log-normal distributed random factors. A global factor $\exp(\tau' \cdot N(0,1))$ is determined only once for every individual whereas a local factor $\exp(\tau \cdot N_i(0,1))$ is sampled for each σ_i individually.

In some cases it is recommendable to reduce the number of strategy variables to only one single stepsize yielding

$$\mathcal{M}(x_1, \ldots, x_n, \sigma) = (x'_1, \ldots, x'_n, \sigma')$$
$$\sigma' = \sigma \cdot exp(\tau' \cdot N(0,1)) \tag{6}$$
$$x'_i = x_i + \sigma' \cdot N_i(0,1) \ .$$

We denote the number of stepsizes by n_σ.

The so called (μ, λ)-selection is based solely on the value of $F(\mathbf{x})$: The μ best of λ individuals are selected as the parent population of $P(t+1)$. The ratio of μ/λ is called the *selection pressure* which is the critical value for choosing between a path-oriented or volume-oriented search.

Obviously the convergence properties of the ES will depend on the strategy parameters μ, λ, n_σ and the noise level σ_δ. In order to improve the convergence process it might be necessary to base the selection not only on one single observation of $F(\mathbf{x})$, but on the average of t different observations. Therefore throughout this paper we will denote our experiments by a 7-tupel $(\mu, \lambda, n_\sigma, \rho, t, f_i, \sigma_\delta)$ where f_i is the undisturbed objective function.

2 Convergence Velocity, Convergence Precision and the Sphere Model

We start by investigating the behavior of evolution strategies on the *sphere model* f_1:

$$f_1(\mathbf{x}) = \sum_{i=1}^{n} x_i^2 . \tag{7}$$

Though this simple function is not a typical application for evolution strategies it enables us to distinguish the effects of different operators and parameters. On the other hand there are some well known theoretical results for f_1 which will serve as a starting point.

2.1 The Influence of Noise in the Case of a Simple (1,100)-ES.

The following theoretical considerations are allmost entirely taken from a paper of Beyer [4]. For the noisy function f_1 and $n \to \infty$ he gives the following approximation for the dynamics of a $(1,\lambda)$-ES with $n_\sigma = 1$ and no recombination:

$$\frac{dR}{dg} = \sigma^2 \left(\frac{n}{2R} - \frac{2Rc_{1,\lambda}}{\sqrt{\sigma_\delta^2 + (2R\sigma)^2}} \right) . \tag{8}$$

R and g denote the remaining distance to the true optimimum point (0) and the current generation number, respectively. The model is of dimensionality n and $c_{1,\lambda}$ denotes the so called *progress coefficient*, which can be approximated for $\lambda \to \infty$ by:

$$c_{1,\lambda} \sim \sqrt{2 \ln \lambda} . \tag{9}$$

For comparability with our numerical results we have to eliminate the variable σ. Therefore we analyse two special cases:

From (8) we conclude that a $\sigma_\delta \ll \sigma$ will not influence the course of evolution. Neglecting σ_δ results in

$$\frac{dR}{dg} = \frac{n}{2R}\sigma^2 - c_{1,\lambda}\sigma . \tag{10}$$

By differentiating (10) we easily calculate the optimal step size

$$\sigma^* = \frac{R}{n}c_{1,\lambda} . \tag{11}$$

This yields the optimal velocity

$$\frac{dR}{dg}\bigg|_{\sigma=\sigma^*} = -\frac{R}{2n}c_{1,\lambda}^2 \tag{12}$$

$$\frac{df}{dg}\bigg|_{\sigma=\sigma^*} = -\frac{c_{1,\lambda}^2}{n}f . \tag{13}$$

This approximation is depicted in Fig. 1 for $\lambda = 100$. For comparability we generally utilize a population size $\lambda = 100$ in the following, if not otherwise stated.

The second approximation holds for the *steady state* with $dR/dg = 0$ and $\sigma \to 0$:

$$f_\infty = R_\infty^2 = \frac{n\sigma_\delta}{4c_{1,\lambda}} \ , \tag{14}$$

where f_∞ and R_∞ denote the final remaining distance from the true optimum. The tick marks on the right border of Fig. 1 show f_∞ values for different σ_δ.

The remaining curves in Fig. 1 show the outcome of numerical experiments with $(\mu = 1, \lambda = 100, n_\sigma = 1, \rho = \_\_, t = 1, f_1, \sigma_\delta = [1.0, 0.1, 0.01, 0.001])$. Each curve represents the mean fitness of the population averaged over 100 experiments.

As long as the noise level is small compared to $f_1(\mathbf{x})$ the perturbations do not affect the process at all and the convergence velocity is close to the theoretical expectations. The remaining difference can be explained through the fact, that the optimal σ is not known a priori, but has to be adapted throughout the whole search process, implicitly solving a dynamical optimization problem.

When the noise becomes significantly large the process slows down and finally stagnates near the expected f_∞-level.

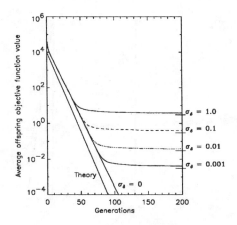

Fig. 1.: Experiments $(\mu = 1, \lambda = 100, n_\sigma = 1, \rho = \_\_, t = 1, f_1, \sigma_\delta = [1.0, 0.1, 0.01, 0.001])$ and corresponding theoretical approximations.

2.2 Improving Convergence Precision.

The Role of the Parental Population Size. For comparability of theory and observation we utilized a rather simple ES variant in the last section. But it is stated [10], that the process of self-adaptation heavily depends on $\mu > 1$ which of course is also a prerequisite for the introduction of recombination. Since up to now there are no theoretical results available we have to rely on numerical experimentation. The left hand side of Fig. 2 shows the outcomes of experiments with $(\mu = [1, 5, 10, 15, 20, 25], \lambda = 100, n_\sigma = 1, \rho = \_, t = 1, f_1, \sigma_\delta = 0.1)$. The noise level is constant while the size of the parent population μ is varied.

The convergence precision is clearly improved with increasing μ due to the fact, that the influence of outliers is reduced. This effect is even more remarkable if we take into account that increasing μ keeps the number of evaluations per generation constant, i.e. this measure introduces no additional costs. Detailed investigations show an optimal μ^* in the interval $10 \leq \mu \leq 20$. In this range the convergence precision is almost independent of variations of μ.

Unfortunately increasing μ reduces the selection pressure μ/λ which is responsible for a linear reduction of convergence velocity.

The Role of Recombination. The introduction of recombination more than compensates the loss in convergence velocity for $\mu > 1$ as Fig. 2 clearly demonstrates, pointing out the importance of recombination in evolution strategies.

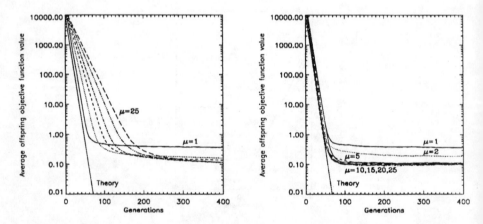

Fig. 2.: Experiments $(\mu = [1, 5, 10, 15, 20, 25], \lambda = 100, n_\sigma = 1, \rho = \_, t = 1, f_1, \sigma_\delta = 0.1)$ (left) and experiments $(\mu = [1, 5, 10, 15, 20, 25], \lambda = 100, n_\sigma = 1, \rho = dI, t = 1, f_1, \sigma_\delta = 0.1)$ (right)

We use discrete recombination for object variables and global intermediate recombination for the step size. Again we conclude $\mu^* \approx 15$ to be an optimal value. This finding corresponds to similar recommendations found in the literatur [9].

Multiple Samplings versus Population Size λ. In order to improve the convergence precision, according to equation (14), we can take two different measures: Enlarging the population size λ or reducing the observation error σ_δ which can be achieved by taking the average over a large number of observations t. The remaining standard deviation of the mean of t observations σ_δ^t depends on σ_δ as

$$\sigma_\delta^t = \frac{\sigma_\delta}{\sqrt{t}} \ . \tag{15}$$

In order to keep the number of evaluations per generation constant and according to (14) we have to evaluate the ratio (16).

$$\frac{n\sigma_\delta}{4c_{1,t\lambda}} \bigg/ \frac{n\sigma_\delta}{4c_{1,\lambda}\sqrt{t}} \ . \tag{16}$$

Thus it is recommendable to increase the population λ as long as the relation

$$1 \leq \frac{c_{1,t\lambda}}{\sqrt{t}c_{1,\lambda}} \tag{17}$$

holds, otherwise we should increase t. Relation (17) holds only for very small values of λ and t. For practical values, e.g. $\lambda = 50$ and $t = 2$ the quotient results in approximately 0.8. This means it is almost allways preferable to increase t rather than λ.

Again (17) is valid only for the simple $(1,\lambda)$-ES without recombination, but we get the same picture through a numerical comparision of the (15,100) strategy including recombination (Fig. 3). For comparability we kept the selection pressure μ/λ constant.

The left Fig. shows the effect of increasing λ whereas on the right side the population is constant but the selection is based on the average of $1 \leq t \leq 20$ observations for each individual. The right picture clearly reflects (15) whereas incrasing the population size yields only small improvements according to (9). Both pictures do not show any significant difference in convergence velocity.

The comparison of these results to earlier investigations on genetic algorithms by Fitzpatrick and Grefenstette [5] show a significant difference. For a similar simple disturbed testfunction in some cases the the GA's performance is much more improved by increasing the population size instead of the number of samples.

3 Convergence Reliablity and Rastrigins Function

Finally we are interested in the convergence reliability of Evolution Strategies in presence of noise. Earlier investigations [3] proved ES to be rather robust against perturbations as long as the level of noise is below a certain threshold depending on the objective function. But how do λ or t affect the convergence reliability?

Of course we can not expect a general answer to this question by experimenting with one single multimodal function. Thus we interpret the following results just as a first hint.

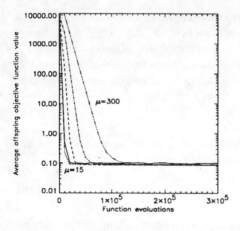 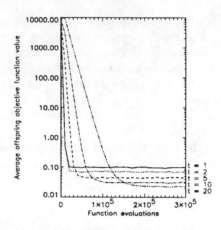

Fig. 3.: Experiments $(\mu = \lambda * \frac{15}{100}, \lambda = [100, 200, 500, 1000, 2000], n_\sigma = 1, \rho = dI, t = 1, f_1,$
$\sigma_\delta = 0.1)$ (left) versus experiments $(\mu = 15, \lambda = 100, n_\sigma = 1, \rho = dI, t = [1, 2, 5, 10, 20, 50],$
$f_1, \sigma_\delta = 0.1)$ (right).

The well known Rastrigins function

$$f_2(\mathbf{x}) = n \cdot A + \sum_{i=1}^{n} \left(x_i^2 - A \cdot \cos(\omega \cdot x_i)\right) \qquad (18)$$

with $n = 30$, $A = 3.0$, $\omega = 2\pi$ and a unique global optimum $f_2(0) = 0$ proved
to be a suitable testcase for Evolution Strategies.

The left hand side of Fig. 4 shows the improvement of the convergence reliability when the number of samples t is increased. The noise level σ_δ is set to 1.
Because the course of evolution heavily depends on the shape of the objective
function we do not show the trajectories of the search process like in Sect. 2.
Instead we depict the distribution of 100 different runs after a fixed number
of generations $g = 1000$, thus getting an estimate for the probability to come
close to the global optimum in a single run. The result is obvious, since by each
doubling of t we just reduced σ_δ^t by a factor of $\sqrt{2}$.

The right hand side sketches the effect of enlarging the population size accordingly, keeping the selection pressure μ/λ constant. Surprisingly the convergence
reliability gets worse with increasing λ. (Please note the different scalings of the
diagrams.) Up to now we do not have a striking explanation for this behavior,
but we conclude that multiple sampling of the objective function in presence of
noise guarantees to reduce the influence of noise and probably will improve the
convergence reliability. In contrast blindly increasing the population size might
even work contra productive.

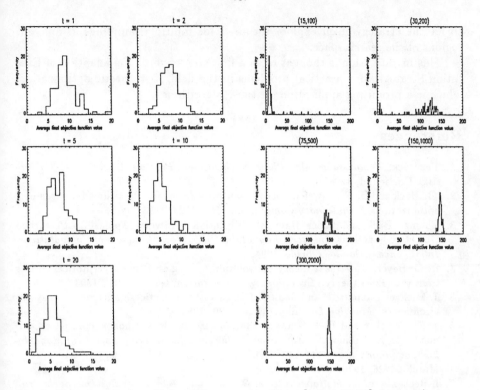

Fig. 4.: Experiments $\left(\mu = 15, \lambda = 100, n_\sigma = n, \rho = dI, t = [1, 2, 5, 10, 20], f_2, \sigma_\delta = 1\right)$ versus experiments $\left(\mu = \lambda \frac{15}{100}, \lambda = [100, 200, 500, 1000, 2000], n_\sigma = n, \rho = dI, t = 1, f_2, \sigma_\delta = 1\right)$.

4   Conclusions

Evolution Strategies have proved to be robust with respect to noise. This paper gives some insight to the role of different strategy parameters and operators.

The right choice of the selection parameter μ is essential for a good localisation of the optimum point, whereas recombination plays a role for the velocity of the process.

Multiple sampling of the objective function reduces the observation error (which is a trivial fact) and therefore improves convergence precision and reliability. The same effect can not be accomplished by solely increasing the population size. This measure may even worsen the result dramatically.

Unfortunately t-times sampling slows down the convergence process by a factor of t reducing the observation error only by $\sqrt{t}$. This way a considerable amount of resources is wasted in regions where the observation error is small compared to the objective function. Therefore the next step will be the incorporation of t as strategy parameter into the algorithm for self-adaptation in order to let the strategy itself explore the need for multiple samplings in different regions of the search space.

This investigation is thought of as a first step towards the adaption of Evolution Strategies for practical problems in the field of stochastic optimization, which is a promising application for those algorithms.

References

1. Th. Bäck. *Evolutionary Algorithms in Theory and Practice*. Dissertation, Universität Dortmund, 1994.
2. Th. Bäck and H.-P. Schwefel. An overview of evolutionary algorithms for parameter optimization. *Evolutionary Computation*, 1(1):1–23, 1993.
3. Thomas Bäck and Ulrich Hammel. Evolution Strategies Applied to Perturbed Objective Functions. In *Proceedings of the IEEE World Congress of Computational Intelligence, Orlando, Florida*, 1994.
4. H.-G. Beyer. Towards a theory of evolution strategies: Some asymptotical results from the $(1 \overset{+}{,} \lambda)$-theory. *Evolutionary Computation*, 1(2):165–188, 1993.
5. J. Michael Fitzpatrick and John J. Grefenstette. Genetic algorithms in noisy environments. *Machine Learning*, (3):101–120, 1988.
6. J. Klockgether and H.-P. Schwefel. Two–phase nozzle and hollow core jet experiments. In D.G. Elliott, editor, *Proc. 11th Symp. Engineering Aspects of Magnetohydrodynamics*, pages 141–148, California Institute of Technology, Pasadena CA, March 24–26, 1970.
7. I. Rechenberg. *Evolutionsstrategie: Optimierung technischer Systeme nach Prinzipien der biologischen Evolution*. Frommann–Holzboog, Stuttgart, 1973.
8. H.-P. Schwefel. *Numerical Optimization of Computer Models*. Wiley, Chichester, 1981.
9. H.-P. Schwefel. Collective phenomena in evolutionary systems. In *Preprints of the 31st Annual Meeting of the International Society for General System Research, Budapest*, volume 2, pages 1025–1033, June 1987.
10. H.-P. Schwefel. Natural evolution and collective optimum–seeking. In A. Sydow, editor, *Computational Systems Analysis: Topics and Trends*, pages 5–14. Elsevier, Amsterdam, 1992.

Modifications and
Extensions to
Evolutionary Algorithms

Selection Schemes with Spatial Isolation for Genetic Optimization

Károly F. Pál

Institute of Nuclear Research of the Hungarian Academy of Sciences
Debrecen, PO Box 51, H–4001, Hungary

Abstract. We tested genetic algorithms with several selection schemes on a massively multimodal spin-lattice problem. New schemes that introduce a spatial separation between the members of the population gave significantly better results than any other scheme considered. These schemes slow down considerably the flow of genetic information between different regions of the population, which makes possible for distant regions to evolve more or less independently. This way many distinct possibilities can be explored simultaneously and a high degree of diversity can be maintained, which is very important for most multimodal problems.

1 Introduction

Living organisms can adapt remarkably well to their environment due to their ability to reproduce themselves in ever varying forms and due to natural selection, which favours the more fit individuals. Genetic algorithms (GAs) use the same principles to solve complex optimization problems. They work on a set of possible solutions, which is called the population. Using members of this set they create new possible solutions in the reproduction process. The most basic operations involved in the reproduction process are crossover, which combines properties of pairs of individuals, and mutation, which makes small random changes on single individuals. Selection pressure is provided by the selection scheme, which controls the evolution of the population. It decides which members of the population may reproduce, which offsprings are accepted and which individuals are rejected and under what circumstances. It ensures evolution by giving more reproductive power to individuals with better values of the function to be optimized.

As the genetic search goes on, good simpler structures, i.e. the best combinations of a few parameters of the problem are multiplied in the population and combined to form good structures of higher complexity. As the worse structures die out, diversity in the population inevitably decreases, and search is confined more and more to the most promising regions of the configuration space. In massively multimodal problems — which are the more interesting cases — too strong selection pressure may cause premature convergence, when the process gets trapped in a not too good local optimum. In some cases there are several very distinct but equally good complex structures that involve the same large subset of parameters. If there is crosstalk between structures corresponding to different sets of parameters, i.e. their contribution is not simply added up in the objective function, it is not enough to have very good structures, we need exactly the ones amongst them that fit to each other the best. In such cases the algorithm must explore and maintain in the population many different possibilities simultaneously. Due to statistical fluctuations one region of the configuration space may seem more promising at some stage of the search than other, possibly even better but least explored regions. If too much efforts are concentrated too soon to that region, there will be no chance to find a really good solution. The selection scheme must be able to maintain diversity.

A problem that shows up the danger mentioned above is the spin-lattice problem considered by Pál [1] to test hybrids of GA and local optimization. Two selection schemes were tried. The one that takes no extra precautions to maintain diversity performed much worse than the one that makes more or less independent evolution possible for different parts of the population by separating them spatially. In the latter case global optima were found with very high probability. Although the hybrid algorithm solves this particular problem easily, its use is not always practical, because it requires a fast local optimization method. Therefore, it is important to find selection schemes that give the best performance in pure GA's for problems with similar difficulties. The requirements here are even higher that in the hybrid algorithm: the best complex structures have to be not only maintained and combined but first they have to be discovered without the help of a local optimization. It takes many generations, so diversity has to be maintained for much longer.

2   The Problem

The test problem we consider here is the same as the one used by Pál [1]. The aim is to find the minimum energy state of a set of 450 four-state spins scattered randomly on a 20 by 30 two-dimensional lattice. The vacancy sites are kept fixed. The spins interact with each other, the energy of the system is given by

$$E = \sum_{i<j} V_{ij} S_i S_j,$$

where S_i is the value of spin i, and V_{ij} characterizes the interaction between spins i and j. If i and j do not occupy neighbouring sites, they do not interact, i.e. $V_{ij} = 0$. The interaction is ferromagnetic between horizontal or vertical neighbours with $V_{ij} = -1$ and antiferromagnetic between diagonal neighbours with $V_{ij} = +1$. S_i can take either of the values $-3/2$, $-1/2$, $1/2$ and $3/2$. Montoya and Dubois [2] considered a similar, but much smaller problem. The number of possible states in our case is 4^{450} and there is an immense number of local energy minima, which is connected to the frustrated nature of the problem. If j is a horizontal and k is a vertical neighbour of spin i, the interactions between i and j and between i and k favour the maximum absolute value with identical sign for all three spins. However, the interaction between j and k tries to force them to take the opposite sign, which means that the plaquette formed by i, j and k is frustrated.

Pál [1] used hybrid algorithms to minimize the energy of the system with a particular arrangement of the vacancy sites. The best states he got had energy -1449. Such states were achieved several times by each method he tried, the best method found one of them in 96% of the attempts. This indicates that they are almost certainly global optima of the system. There are quite a few of them. Examples can be found in the paper of Pál [1]. It is obvious that the problem must have at least two global optima: changing the sign af all spins simultaneously does not alter the energy. In any contiguous region of an optimal lattice there is a striped pattern [1]: all spins have maximum absolute value and their signs alternate either vertically or horizontally. The direction of the stripes may be different in different lattice regions. One type of pattern can join another one around clusters of vacancy sites.

The possible states of the system can be coded by binary strings of 900 bits, with each spin represented by a pair of bits. A combination of n spins correspond to a schema [3] [4] of order $2n$. The performance of schemata corresponding to spin combinations competing with each other in a genetic search can easily be compared: only the interactions between spins that belong to the combination matter. The average of the energy contributions coming from the interactions between spins outside the combination is the same for all competing schemata, and the contributions of the interactions between the two spin groups cancel each other because they have the same value with opposite sign for pairs of representatives of a schema that differ from each other in the sign of the spins outside the combination concerned. From this it is clear that high performance spin combinations must contain interacting spins. The best combination of two spins occupying neighbouring sites in vertical or horizontal direction are the ones with maximum absolute values and identical signs. However, due to the striped structures, in about half of these neighbouring positions the spins have opposite signs in any optimum state, a combination that has the worst performance. This means that some suboptimal combinations can be much fitter than the optimal ones. The same is true for combinations of spins on L-shaped regions of the lattice. However, it does not necessarily mean that the problem is deceptive in the sense as was defined by Goldberg [5]. The above mentioned optimal, but still low performance spin combinations can always be supplemented with a few neighbouring spins in such a way, that the higher order schema corresponding to this enlarged spin combination has high fitness. On contiguous square-shaped lattice regions the best spin combinations are the ones with the striped structure. There are four such arrangements with equal fitness. It is true for any region of the lattice, even for large regions that there are more, very different spin arrangements on them that have similar fitness. However, usually not all of them belong to an optimum state. Schemata corresponding to the best combinations of several spins are almost certainly not represented in the initial population. They have to be discovered by combining smaller spin groups, which itself may not be easy. What is even worse, most of the equally good combinations on each lattice region have to be discovered and maintained in the population, because no algorithm can decide in advance which possible pieces belong to the same optimum state. Lattice regions interact with each other along their borderline, some of them may even overlap. An arbitrary collection of the best pieces gives only a really good state if the pieces fit well to each other. For this reason the algorithm must explore many possibilities simultaneously, and maintain diversity for as long as possible.

3 The Algorithms

In all calculations we present in this paper we created new individuals by using a crossover operation and subsequent mutations. Mutation simulates the effect of occasional errors in transcription. To avoid the disruption of good schemata as much as possible, we used single-point crossover and a tight coding. Single-point crossover swaps those substrings of the parent strings that follow a randomly chosen string position. This way the operation creates two offsprings. If the codes corresponding to two properties of the solutions are close to each other in the string, such a crossover will usually not separate them. To have a good chance that the best spin combinations will not be destroyed, the two-bit units coding interacting spins must not be very far from each other compared to the full length of the string. This can be achieved by ordering the spins as they appear in the lattice row-by-row. This way crossover cuts each parent lattice into two pieces along an almost straight line parallel to the shorter side of the lattice. Such a cut separates relatively few interacting spins. We tried other orderings and other types of crossovers, but — as expected — this method gave the best results with most selection schemes (this was not true in the hybrid algorithm [1]). After crossover we applied a mutation operation on each offspring. The effect of this operation is flipping the value of each bit with a small probability. Goldberg [4] (p. 14) recommends an average of one flip in a thousand bits. After preliminary calculations with mutation rates in this order of magnitude we decided to use a rate of 0.2% in all further calculations. This rate tended to give the best results, although the results were hardly worse with 0.1% or 0.3%.

We considered the following selection schemes.

Scheme A is one of the most traditional schemes. It uses non-overlapping populations: in each generation the whole previous population is discarded. In the selection phase the mating pool is filled up with copies of strings from the current population. The expected number of copies an individual gets is equal to its fitness. We chose fitness to be a linear function of the energy so that the best individual should get about twice as many copies as an average one in each generation (linear fitness scaling [4]). Whenever this scaling gave a negative fitness for some individuals, we reduced the scaling factor so that this should not happen. Each individual surely gets as many copies as the integer part of its fitness. Then the individuals are taken one by one, and each gets one more copy with a probability equals to the fractional part of its fitness, until the mating pool is full (*stochastic remainder selection without replacement* [6]).

The members of the mating pool are arranged into pairs and mated using the reproduction process. The new generation consists of their offsprings.

Scheme B differs from scheme A only in the way the mating pool is filled up. Here pairs are drawn randomly from the current population and a copy of the better individual from each pair enters the mating pool, until the pool is full (*binary tournament selection* [6]). This scheme is simpler than the previous one and it is also more appropriate for parallel processing.

Scheme C is a steady-state scheme, a modified version [7] [1] of Whitley's *Genitor* [8]. In each iteration a random pair is selected as parents, and their offsprings are created. Here each individual has equal chance to be selected. A bias towards better individuals causes faster convergence, but it decreases genetic diversity, which makes the final results worse. An offspring is accepted if it is not identical with any existing member of the population and not worse than the worst individual. In this case the offspring replaces the worst individual in the population. The modification compared to the Genitor is the exclusion of identical individuals from the population. This helps in maintaining a somewhat higher degree of genetic diversity in the final stage of the search, when there would be a danger that a particularly good individual overtakes a sizable proportion of the population.

Scheme D (*deterministic crowding* [9]) was designed by Mahfoud specifically to maintain diversity. He has shown that this scheme is better than any earlier technique in minimizing genetic drift: it is able to continue the search in the neighbourhood of several distinct local optima of a multimodal problem simultaneously. The essence of the scheme is that an offspring may only replace the probably most similar individual: one of its parents. Replacement happens if the offspring is not worse that the parent it competes with. The decision on which offspring will compete with which parent is taken so that the sum of the phenotypic differences between the two parent–offspring pairs should be the smaller. For the problem considered here we calculate phenotypic difference between two individuals by adding up the absolute values of the spin differences on each lattice site.

Scheme E was used by Pál [1] in the hybrid algorithm with excellent results. It introduces a spatial separation between the individuals to make more or less independent evolution possible for distant regions of the population. Mating is restricted to first neighbours. Neighbours are individuals whose indices characterising their position in the memory differs by one. The last and the first members of the population are also considered neighbours. Therefore, the first individual may only mate with the last and the second one, the second one with the first and the third one, and so on. After reproduction one of the offsprings is compared to the parents. The parent that is not better than the offspring is replaced. Whenever the offspring is not worse than either of the parents, the better parent is replaced. (This way we get better results than by replacing the worse or a randomly chosen parent). If the offspring can not compete successfully with its parents, the procedure is repeated with the neighbours of the parents, and so on, until the population is exhausted. Then the other offspring tries to find a place in the population in the same way (it may compete with the first offspring). The experience with this scheme [1] is that the population gradually breaks up into better and worse regions as the search goes on, while the individuals in each neighbourhood become similar to each other. A good offspring will never go far from its parents, consequently it always replaces a similar individual. No individual can settle in any good region, except in the one it was created. The flow of genetic information between different parts of the population is not blocked completely, but it is slowed down considerably, which makes possible for the algorithm to explore distinct possibilities in different regions. We will show that in the pure genetic search the results considerably improve if we further increase the degree of isolation. This can easily be achieved by not allowing the offspring to settle far from its parents. In **scheme E2** the offspring competes only with the parents and with the parents' neighbours, while in **scheme E1** it competes only with the parents. A further advantage of these schemes is that each step requires information only about a very small portion of the population, and that makes them very well suited for parallel processing.

We note that in any scheme where an offspring competes directly with another individual, and their fitness is equal, we accept the offspring. This often happens, as each energy level of the system contains many different states. Our prescription is not the conventional one, but it gives better results. It allows a better exploration of the configuration space by giving a chance to the new individual, and prevents the procedure from getting stuck.

4　Numerical Results and Discussion

The population in our calculations contained 300 individuals. With this choice any possible arrangements of up to 3 spins is expected to have a few representatives in the randomly chosen initial population. We carried out 60 calculations with each selection schemes starting from different initial populations and using different random number sequences. We allowed 500,000 reproductions in each calculations (for schemes A and B 500,100 i.e. 3334 generations).

To compare the rates of convergence for the different schemes, in Fig. 1 we show the averages of the best energies found as functions of the number of reproductions. The statistical error of the average energy at the last reproduction is no more than 7 energy units (90% C.L.) for any set of calculations. Fig. 2 shows the distributions of $d = 100(E_f - E_o)/E_o$, which is the relative difference of the final energy E_f and the probably global optimum $E_o = -1449$ in percents. (The final result is the best solution ever found in the calculation, which is usually not present in the final population for schemes A and B).

Scheme A performes poorly compared to the others. The linear scaling factor 2 we used is about the highest value possible. Diversity can be maintained somewhat better with a lower value, i.e. with a weaker genetic pressure, but it also decreases the rate of improvement in the initial stage. We got definitely worse results in the same number of generations with a scaling factor 1.7, than with 2. Results with the binary tournament selection (scheme B) are much better, but still not very good. A larger population would allow a higher degree of diversity in both schemes, but its advantage would show up only in longer calculations. We repeated the calculations with twice as big populations and half as many generations, and we got worse results.

As far as the initial rate of convergence is concerned, the modified Genitor (scheme C) is the winner. If one wants to get reasonable results fast, this is the scheme to use. However, the rate of improvement slows down very much in the final stage. From the analysis of Goldberg and Deb [10], this is the behaviour we can expect. Genetic diversity is lost too soon, and in the second half of the calculation the evolution is driven almost entirely by mutation, so the method works like a quite ineffective local search. In longer calculations the previous schemes would probably outperform this one.

We can also expect that scheme D, which was designed to maintain diversity, should give better final results than the schemes considered previously, and it does. Convergence is relatively slow at the beginning because no sizable proportion of the population will be attracted fast to explore a relatively good region of the configuration space at that stage. The more cautious approach pays off later. Although our final results are not very much better than with scheme C, the difference would grow in longer calculations. As scheme D uses not only the objective function values, but other information about the solutions as well, one might consider the direct comparison of this scheme with the previous ones unfair.

Scheme E does not use non-payoff information and still gives as good results as scheme D, although the rate of improvement in the final stage is slightly slower. The comparable performance indicates that spatial isolation is not worse at encouraging niche formation and maintaining diversity than the method of scheme D. Furthermore, the degree of isolation can easily be varied, and the results can very significantly be improved by applying a stronger isolation, as it is done by schemes E2 and E1. Although these schemes start very slowly, the energy improves very steadily and by the 500,000th iteration they far overtake the other schemes. The two schemes give very similar results by then, but in longer calculations the initially somewhat slower scheme E1 wins. This scheme is very good at maintaining good competing structures simultaneously in the population, but not as good at mixing good structures corresponding to different properties, which is a drawback. If such structures have been discovered in distant parts of the population, they have a very slim chance to meet. We can improve mixing by allowing distant individuals to mate during the final part of the search. In Fig. 2 the results denoted by E1m were calculated by switching to such a mixing stage for the last 50,000 iterations. In this mixing stage we lift the mating restriction and choose the parents randomly. We note that this strategy is only advantageous, if the problem is such that even distinct good solutions may have structures whose tranfer from one solution to the other can give an even better solution, and if the crossover is able to accomplish such a transfer with a nonnegligible chance. In the initial stages mating between distant individuals should not be allowed. The use of such an operation even only once in

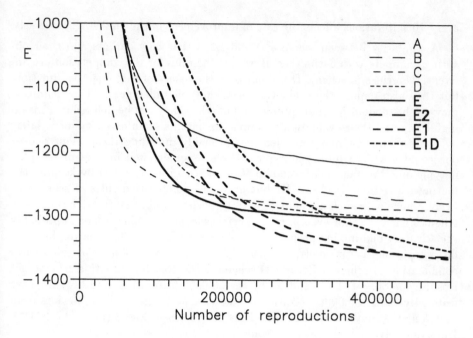

Fig. 1. Convergence of the energy with the different schemes. Each curve represents the average of 60 calculations.

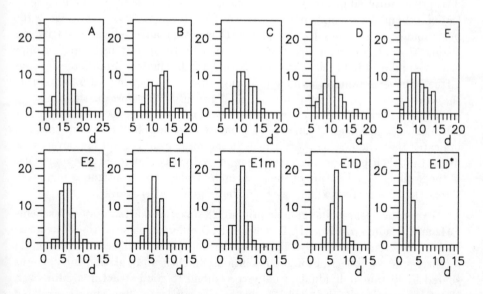

Fig. 2. Distributions of the relative differences of the final energies and the optimum energy in percents after 500,000 (for E1D* 2,000,000) iterations. (Shifts in the scale should be noted).

every 1000 iterations affects the rate of improvement in the final stage adversely.

A similarity between schemes D and E1 is that only parents and their off-springs compete with each other. However, the rules for the competition are different. The rules in scheme D use not only the values of the objective function, but they also require the evaluation of phenotypic differences. Their definition may not be obvious for some problems, but when they can be defined in a meaningful way and their evaluation is simple, we can maintain diversity more safely by using them. For many problems — probably including the present one — one could use the simple genotypic difference equally well instead of the phenotypic one. We can make a combination of schemes E1 and D by keeping the mating restriction of scheme E1 but using the competition rules of scheme D. Convergence with such a scheme is extremely slow, and it never catches up with schemes E1 or E2, not even in much longer calculations. The reason is probably the scheme's bad mixing property. It has a good effect to allow mating between distant parents occasionally, say once in every 200 iterations. We call such a combination of schemes E1 and D scheme E1D. Results with this scheme get close to the ones with E1 and E2 by the 500,000th iteration, and they improve faster. By the 2,000,000th iteration this scheme performs the best. Results from such long calculations with scheme E1D are shown in Fig. 2 (noted by E1D*). Unfortunately, even this method could not find a global optimum.

We also tried single-point crossover with strings that contained the spins in a random order, and uniform crossover [11], which tranfers each bit independently from either of the parents with equal probability. Both operations are very disruptive. Surprisingly, only the first one gave much worse results with each selection scheme than single-point crossover with row-by-row ordering. Only the performance of schemes E2, E1 and E1D was very adversely affected by the change to uniform crossover. The population broke up fast into small groups of very similar individuals. Crossover between individuals from different groups virtually never produced a viable offspring, while the offsprings of parents from the same group hardly differed from their parents. Therefore, if the crossover is unable to transfer useful structures between distinct good solutions, these schemes work like a set of almost independent local searches. However, this also indicates that these schemes can benefit the most from a good crossover. It is likely, that their performance could be improved with a crossover that makes use of the 2-dimensional nature of the problem by transferring contiguous regions of the lattice in a more flexible way than the single-point crossover.

We got the best results (global optimum 28 times in 60 attempts) with scheme E1D and triadic crossover [1]. In scheme E1D different parts of the population evolve almost independently. This way the population will eventually contain a representative collection of good solutions. In such a population bit patterns shared by distant individuals usually correspond to good structures. Moreover, the string positions of the bits belonging to such a pattern often represent related properties (in the present case spin values on a contiguous lattice region). In this case it is advantageous if bits in such positions are inherited together. Triadic crossover achieves just that. Besides the parents, a third individual is chosen from the population randomly. Then the procedure takes the bits in positions where the first parent and the third individual have identical bit values from one of the parents, and the rest of the bits from the other parent. This crossover is completely independent of the ordering of the bits in the string.

Our results demonstrate that the schemes recommended here achieve much better results than other schemes for a massively multimodal optimization problem whose satisfactory solution requires the exploration of many distinct possibilities and the maintainance of a high degree of genetic diversity. However, pure genetic algorithms even with these schemes could not match the performance of the hybrid algorithm [1]. Therefore, if there exists a fast local optimization method for the problem, it is better to use the hybrid algorithm.

References

1. K. F. Pál: Genetic algorithms with local optimization. Submitted to Biol. Cybern.
2. F. Montoya, J.-M. Dubois: Darwinian adaptive simulated annealing. Europhys. Lett. **22** (1993) 79–84.
3. J. H. Holland: Adaptation in natural and artificial systems. The University of Michigan Press, Ann Arbor, 1975.
4. D. E. Goldberg: Genetic algorithms in search, optimization and machine learning. Addison-Wesley, Reading, 1989.
5. D. E. Goldberg: Genetic algorithms and Walsh functions: part II, deception and its analysis. Complex Systems **3** (1989) 153–171.
6. A. Brindle: Genetic algorithms for function optimization. Unpublished doctoral dissertation, University of Alberta, Edmonton, 1981.
7. K. F. Pál: Genetic algorithms for the traveling salesman problem based on a heuristic crossover operation. Biol Cybern **69** (1993) 539–546.
8. D. Whitley: The Genitor algorithm and selection pressure: Why rank-based allocation of reproductive trials is best. In: J. D. Schaffer (ed.): Proceedings of the third international conference on genetic algorithms. George Mason University 1989, pp. 116–121.
9. S. W. Mahfoud: Crowding and preselection revisited. Parallel Problem Solving from Nature **2** (1992) 27–36.
10. D. E. Goldberg, K. Deb: A comparative analysis of selection schemes used in genetic algorithms. In: G. J. E. Rawlins (ed.): Foundations of genetic algorithms. San Mateo, California: Morgan Kaufmann Publishers 1991, pp. 69–93.
11. G. Syswerda: Uniform crossover in genetic algorithms. In: J. D. Schaffer (ed.): Proceedings of the third international conference on genetic algorithms. George Mason University 1989, pp. 2–9.

A Modified Edge Recombination Operator for the Travelling Salesman Problem

Anthony Yiu-Cheung Tang[1] and Kwong-Sak Leung[2]

Department of Computer Science
The Chinese University of Hong Kong
[1] tang028@cs.cuhk.hk
[2] ksleung@cs.cuhk.hk

Abstract. Edge recombination is a crossover operator developed to preserve edge information for the Travelling Salesman Problem. This paper describes a modified version of the operator which converges significantly faster for all the benchmark problems tested.

1 Introduction

The edge recombination crossover is one of the commonly used recombination operators for solving the Travelling Salesman Problem (TSP) using genetic algorithms [8]. This paper describes a new variant of the edge recombination operator which introduces greedy choices to the algorithm. It was found that the modified operator converges significantly faster for all the problems tested.

2 EdgeNN, A New Edge Recombination Operator

An edge recombination operator is an operator that preserves edge information between parent tours. Starkweather et al. [8] described an enhancement (named in [6] as Edge-2) to the edge recombination operator by preserving common edges of the parent tours.

EdgeNN (edge recombination, nearest neighbour) is a variant of Edge-2. It modifies Edge-2 by replacing some non-deterministic steps by a greedy heuristic. The modified edge recombination algorithm is as follows.

1. Identify the two parents as Parent1 and Parent2. Copy a segment of Parent1 to the offspring (The length of this segment is chosen to be 1/4 of the number of cities in the tour and the starting point of the segment is chosen randomly).
2. Construct an edge map using the edge information in Parent2 and the segment of Parent1 not copied to the offspring.
3. Set the last city of the inherited segment in the offspring to be the current city.
4. Remove all occurrences of the current city from all the edge lists.

5. If the current city has elements in its edge list go to step 6; otherwise go to step 8.
6. If there are negative elements (*shared edges*) in the edge list of the current city, choose one to be the current city. Ties are broken at random if more than one shared edge is available. Go to step 4. If there are no shared edges then go to step 7.
7. Determine the city in the edge list of the current city which is *nearest* to the current city. The nearest city becomes the current city. Go to step 4.
8. If there are no remaining unvisited cities, then END. Otherwise, choose an unvisited city which is *nearest* to the current city. Ties are broken at random if the two nearest cities have the same distance from the current city. Go to step 4.

In selecting the next city for the current city, an *edge failure* [6] is said to occur when there are no edges in the edge list of the current city. A new edge has to be introduced that is not found in both parents, such edges are referred to as *foreign edges*.

To illustrate the new algorithm, we use a simple symmetric TSP as an example and its cost matrix is shown in fig. 1 with the upper triangle omitted.

	a	b	c	d	e	f	g	h	i	j	k	l
a	-											
b	3	-										
c	2	9	-									
d	3	2	9	-								
e	7	3	8	1	-							
f	5	1	2	5	7	-						
g	6	6	7	9	4	6	-					
h	2	8	4	2	8	5	1	-				
i	1	7	3	5	5	2	3	9	-			
j	5	3	1	4	3	7	6	1	8	-		
k	8	7	6	3	6	3	4	2	1	7	-	
l	4	5	5	7	9	1	9	3	4	8	8	-

Figure 1. An example cost matrix of a symmetric TSP.

Consider the following tours as parents to be recombined, the tour lengths of Parent1 and Parent2 are 72 and 51 respectively :

```
Parent1 : a b c d e f g h i j k l
Parent2 : f g h c l k j b e i a d
```

The offspring first inherits a fixed segment from Parent1 :

c d e

An edge map is constructed using Parent2 and the remaining subtour of Parent1 (fig. 2). The negative elements are *shared edges* which are present in both parents :

city	edge list
a	l,b,i
b	a,j
c	-
d	-

city	edge list
e	b,f,i
f	-g
g	-f,-h
h	-g,i

city	edge list
i	h,j,a
j	i,-k,b
k	-j,-l
l	-k,a

Figure 2. The edge table.

City *e* is now the current city. Referring to the edge list of city *e*, cities *b, f,* and *i* are the candidates for the next city. City *b* is chosen because the edge {*e,b*} is the shortest. The edge list of city *b* is [*a,j*]. Since edge {*b,a*} and edge {*b,j*} are of the same length, ties are broken at random. Suppose city *j* is chosen. City *k* is then chosen because it is a shared edge. As city *j* has already been selected, the edge list of city *k* now contains only city *l*, hence the new current city is city *l*. The remaining cities are selected by the same process and finally the following tour is formed with a tour length of 54 :

```
c d e b j k l a i h g f
```

3   Experimental Results

3.1   Comparing EdgeNN with Edge-2

Table 1 lists the three problems tested. The data in the column "best known solution" are collected from [2] and [7].

problem	number of cities (n)	best known solution
LIN318	318	42029
PCB442	442	50778
ATT532	532	27686

Table 1. The TSP test bed.

To illustrate the convergence rate of EdgeNN, a genetic algorithm with the following parameters was applied to the test problems :

Population size :	2000
Selection method :	Baker's SUS Selection [1]. Only one offspring is generated by crossing over two parents.
Mutation rate :	0.05
	Mutation is performed by randomly swapping elements within a randomly selected segment of the chromosome.
Generation gap :	0.1
Fitness scaling :	None

Three runs were performed on each problem and the results were averaged (the variances are not significant). A randomly generated initial population was used for each run. For the chosen parameter settings each generation corresponds to 200 recombinations (population size * generation gap = 2000 * 0.1 = 200). The percentage excesses over the best known solution taken after 200,000 recombinations are shown in table 2. The graph for ATT532 is shown in fig. 3, the tour length of the best individual in the population is plotted against the number of generations. The performance of EdgeNN is significantly better.

	LIN318	PCB442	ATT532
Percentage excess over optimal length			
Edge-2	276	459	582
EdgeNN	7	12	14
Edge failures per recombination			
Edge-2	8	12	15
EdgeNN	6	12	10

Table 2. Percentage excess over the optimal solution for Edge-2 and EdgeNN.

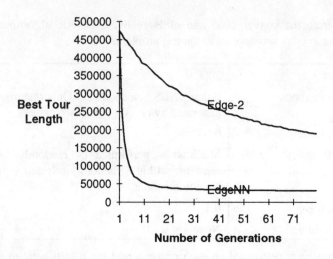

Figure 3. The convergence rate of Edge-2 and EdgeNN on ATT532.

Although EdgeNN produced better results than Edge-2, the comparison is not fair because Edge-2 is a "blind" operator : it uses no local information during recombination. Nevertheless the comparison is made to illustrate the drastic improvement in the rate of convergence by introducing greedy choices to Edge-2.

3.2 Comparing EdgeNN with Edge-3

The Edge-3 operator was designed by Mathias and Whitley [6] which enhances Edge-2 with an additional mechanism to reduce edge failures. Although Edge-3 is also a blind recombination operator, the authors hybridized Edge-3 by a procedure called *2-Repair*, a variant of 2-Opt which compares only the foreign edges produced by edge recombination operators. In view of processing cost and degree of hybridization, EdgeNN is quite similar to the 2-Repair-Edge-3 hybrid.

To compare EdgeNN with Edge-3, an experiment was performed on the problem ATT532. The setting used was chosen to be as similar as possible to that described in their paper. GENITOR [9] with a bias of 1.25 was used with a population size of 2,000. The initial population was created randomly. In the experiment performed by Mathias and Whitley the initial population was first improved by the *1-Pass of 2-Opt procedure*. In our case the initial population was used without any preprocessing because, as shown in fig. 3, the convergence rate of EdgeNN should be sufficiently fast. When 16,000 recombinations had been performed the 1-Pass of 2-Opt procedure was performed on the whole population. The process was then repeated.

Our results were averaged over 30 runs. The average tour length obtained was 28,914 with a best solution of 28,652. These results were slightly better than the average solution of 28,979 with a best of 28,752 obtained by Edge-3 reported in [6].

4 Further Improvement : A heuristic GA using EdgeNN

We agree that "from a function optimization point of view, GAs frequently don't exhibit a 'killer instinct' " [3]. Although a genetic algorithm is good at locating the region containing the global optimum, it may take a very long time to locate the optimal solution. For this reason most attempts to solve TSP using genetic algorithms incorporated some form of hill-climbing heuristics. In this section a genetic algorithm combining EdgeNN and hill-climbing heuristics is presented which produces tours that are within 2 % from the optimal for the problem ATT532.

The heuristics use the k-change operator [5]. The operator improves a tour by deleting k edges of the tour and introducing k new ones such that the tour length is reduced. We used 2-change and 3-change operators. Two objectives guided the design of our algorithm :

Diversity maintenance. If an offspring is *phenotypically* equivalent (i.e. having the same tour length) to either parents, the alleles in a small segment picked randomly are shuffled.

Minimizing the number of local optimizations performed. As the hill-climbing heuristics are CPU-intensive, they are applied under restricted circumstances. The algorithms will stop optimizing a tour after *one* exchange that can reduce tour cost is found. These heuristics are invoked under the following situations :

i) The tour length of an offspring is larger than the average tour length of its parents.
   As it is a waste of time to repair very bad tours, one more constraint is added requiring that the tour length of the offspring must also be shorter than :

$$\text{(mean tour length + minimum tour length) / 2}$$

   The mean and minimum are values with respect to the current population. If these conditions are satisfied, 2-change is applied to the offspring. The fixed segment inherited directly from the parent will not be optimized.

ii) The best tour length so far does not improve after a number of offsprings have been generated.
   We use the population size (*popsize*) as our criterion. When there is no improvement after a *popsize* of offsprings are generated, 3-change is applied to the tour randomly picked from the best ten tours. When there is still no improvement after another 9 * *popsize* offsprings are generated, 2-change will be applied to the best half of the population.

Our algorithm is essentially GENITOR with the following set of parameters :

Population Size	500
Selection Method	Linear ranking with a bias of 1.25
Generation Gap	0.1
Mutation Rate	0
Fitness Scaling	None

The results averaged over 30 runs on ATT532 are shown in table 3. The number of recombinations performed for each run is 250,000. The best tour obtained is within 1% from the optimal and the average tour length obtained is around 2% from the optimal.

Tour length	Best	Mean	SD
	27949	28255	197
average number of 2-changes performed per run	8820		
average number of 3-changes performed per run	1123		

Table 3. Performance of the heuristic GA on ATT532.

5 Discussion

Since EdgeNN selects among the available cities the on nearest to the current city as the next city, the computation cost for EdgeNN will be comparatively higher than that of Edge-2 if there are many edge failures. Fig. 4 shows the averaged accumulated edge failures for the tests on ATT532 described in section 3. The average number of foreign edges produced per recombination was quite high in the beginning but gradually decreased as the tours in the population were becoming more and more similar.

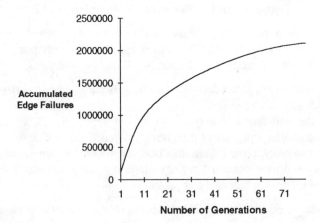

Figure 4. The accumulated number of foreign edges made by EdgeNN for ATT532.

We agree with Grefenstette [4] that for genetic searches "probabilistic choices are usually preferable to deterministic ones." The reason why a part of the offspring is inherited directly from one of the parents is that we do not want too much determinism in our algorithm. Consider the following parent tours :

```
Parent1 : a b c d e f g h i j
Parent2 : f b e i a d j g h c
```

Using EdgeNN, the offspring first inherits a fixed segment from Parent1 :

```
Offspring : c d e f
```

The edge list for city f using Edge-2 is $[b,c,e,g]$. Suppose city c is nearest to city f among these four cities, then EdgeNN will always choose city c if it is available. However, this deterministic behaviour does not always happen. As shown in this example, the edge list for city f using EdgeNN is $[b,g]$ because the fixed segment chosen already includes city c and e.

With regard to foreign edges, suppose city d is the city nearest to city j and that an edge failure occurs in choosing the next city for city j. Since city d has already been added to the offspring, the algorithm has to select a city from the available cities that is nearest to city j. Since the fixed segment is picked randomly, EdgeNN retains some probabilistic choices in selecting foreign edges.

6 Conclusions

The goal of this paper is to present and evaluate the effectiveness of EdgeNN for solving TSPs, and to explore the interactions of EdgeNN with local optimization heuristics. The experimental results show that EdgeNN converges much faster than Edge-2 and produces results similar to a hybridized version of Edge-3. This suggests that any method for solving TSPs can use EdgeNN to generate initial tours of medium quality.

Although satisfactory results are produced for a medium sized problem when local optimizations are combined with EdgeNN, the number of recombinations is a bit too large. Better tour lengths with fewer recombinations may be obtained if more sophisticated local hill-climbing procedures such as the LK algorithm [5] are used.

Remarks. The experiments are constructed using TOLKIEN : *TOoLKI*t for g*EN*etics-based applications, a C++ class library developed by the first author. TOLKIEN is developed as a prototyping tool that enables GA and classifier system applications to be constructed easily. The toolkit is available in /pub/local/tolkien by anonymous ftp access to ftp.cs.cuhk.hk (137.189.4.57).

References

1. Baker, J. (1987). Reducing bias and inefficiency in the selection algorithm. *Genetic algorithms and their applications : Proceedings of the Second International Conference on Genetic Algorithms.* Lawrence Erlbaum Associates, Publishers.
2. Bixby, B., and Reinelt, G. (1990). TSPLIB 1.1.
3. De Jong, K. A. (1993). Genetic algorithms are not function optimizers. *Foundations of Genetic Algorithms 2.* Morgan Kaufmann.
4. Grefenstette, J. J. (1987). Incorporating problem specific knowledge into genetic algorithms. *Genetic Algorithms and Simulated Annealing.* Pitman.
5. Lin, S., and Kernighan, G. W. (1973). An efficient heuristic algorithm for the traveling salesman problem. *Operations Research* 21 : 498-516.
6. Mathias, K., and Whitley, D. (1992). Genetic operators, the fitness landscape and the traveling salesman problem. *Parallel Problem Solving from Nature, 2.* Elsevier Science Publishers B.V.
7. Padberg, M., and Rinaldi, G. (1991). A branch-and-cut algorithm for the resolution of large-scale symmetric traveling salesman problems. *SIAM Review* 33 : 60-100.
8. Starkweather, T., McDaniel, S., Whitley, D., and Whitley, C. (1991). A comparison of genetic sequencing operators. *Proceedings of the Fourth International Conference on Genetic Algorithms.* Morgan Kaufmann.
9. Whitley, D. (1989). The GENITOR algorithm and selection pressure: Why rank-based allocation of reproductive trials is best. *Proceedings of the Third International Conference on Genetic Algorithms.* San Mateo, CA: Morgan Kaufmann.

Step-Size Adaptation Based on Non-Local Use of Selection Information

Andreas Ostermeier, Andreas Gawelczyk, Nikolaus Hansen
Technische Universität Berlin, Fachgebiet Bionik und Evolutionstechnik
Ackerstraße 71-76, D-13355 Berlin
E-mail: {ostermeier,gawelczyk,hansen}@fb10.tu-berlin.d400.de
Phone: 030/31472666

Abstract. The performance of Evolution Strategies (ESs) depends on a suitable choice of internal strategy control parameters. Apart from a fixed setting, ESs facilitate an adjustment of such parameters within a self-adaptation process. For step-size control in particular, various adaptation concepts were evolved early in the development of ESs. These algorithms mostly work very efficiently as long as the relative sensitivities of the parameters to be optimized are known. If this scaling is not known, the strategy has to adapt individual step-sizes for the parameters. In general, the number of necessary step-sizes (variances) equals the dimension of the problem. In this case, step-size adaptation proves to be difficult.

The algorithm presented in this paper is a development based on the derandomized scheme of mutative step-size control. The new adaptation concept uses information accumulated from the preceding generations with an exponential fading of old information instead of using information from the current generation only. Compared to the conventional adaptation scheme, this enables a less locally determined step-size control and allows a much faster adaptation of individual step-sizes without increasing disturbing random effects and without additional evaluations of the fitness function. The adaptation of the general step-size can be improved as well.

Keywords   *evolution strategy, adaptation, self-adaptation, mutative step-size control, step-size, individual step-size, scaling*

Introduction: Step-size Adaptation in ESs

In biology, mutation rates are of essential importance for evolutionary progress. In the case of real-valued continuous parameter optimization with ESs, the biological mutation rate can be interpreted as the standard deviation of mutation steps in the parameter space.

In ESs, there are two common ways of realizing a step-size adaptation. One is Rechenberg´s 1/5-success-rule (Rechenberg 1973). This algorithm works satisfying in most cases but depends on the applicability of an external model of parameter space topology and is only able to adapt one general step-size but no individual step-sizes.

The other method is the mutative step-size control proposed by Rechenberg (1973, 1978) and Schwefel (1977, 1981). This adaptation scheme does not depend on an external model and in principle facilitates the adaptation of individual step-sizes. Here, the strategy parameters (step-sizes) are part of the parameter sets of the individuals and affected by mutation and selection.

Mutative step-size control generally works very well on the adaptation of a general step-size. A corresponding adaptation of individual step-sizes is not possible within simple ESs with small populations, as Schwefel (1987) pointed out. Schwefel favors the use of more complex ESs with larger populations. The problem is, that to enable a reliable individual step-size adaptation the resulting population sizes have to be much larger[1] than necessary concerning the object parameter optimization.

The problem of individual step-size adaptation can be explained from a general point of view by interpreting step-size adaptation as a problem of disturbed optimization (Rechenberg 1994). "Disturbed" means that the fitness value is not exactly measurable.

Derandomized mutative step-size control

Derandomized mutative step-size control (cf. Ostermeier 1994) enables a reliable adaptation of individual step-sizes even in small populations. Basically, the selection of large or small[2] mutations in every generation results directly in a corresponding increase/decrease of the step-sizes. The second, more important difference to conventional mutative step-size control is that the step-size variations passed from one generation to the next are much smaller than the variations within one generation. This reduces the adaptation rate per generation without reducing the step-size variations within the populations. Therefore the information required for a certain step-size adaptation is not gathered in one generation of a large population but in the generation sequence of a smaller population.

Derandomized mutative step-size control using accumulated information

According to the previous section, a sensible adaptation of step-sizes for small populations is only possible in a generation sequence. The adaptation scheme proposed here makes use of this fact. It does not analyze the sizes of the mutations of the last generation only, but the sizes of the variations resulting from adding up the mutations selected in the preceding generations.

Apart from some averaging effects, this method would make no fundamental difference, if the selected mutations in successive generations are uncorrelated. In fact, successively selected mutations are correlated in general: In the case of step-sizes being too large, selected mutations tend to compensate preceding mutations. In effect, the selected mutations are correlated antiparallel in the generation sequence. Correspondingly, too small step-sizes cause parallel correlated mutations.

A parallel correlation of successive mutation steps increases the absolute value of the resulting sum and vice versa. The following algorithm utilizes these correlations - not simply the absolute values of the single mutation steps - by adding up successive mutations. Only the absolute values of the accumulated mutations are evaluated for step-size adaptation.

The adaptation scheme of the individual step-sizes remains formally the same as in the algorithm of derandomized step-size adaptation (Ostermeier 1994). Only the absolute values of the selected mutations have to be replaced by the absolute values of the accumulated selected mutations.

---

[1] Our investigations suggest population sizes about 10*n (n: dimension of the problem). In smaller populations, individual step-sizes that have become small due to stochastic fluctuations perform almost random walks. This leads to long stagnation periods of the optimization if only individual step-sizes but no inclination angles (correlated mutations) are adapted. We interpret the reliable convergence of Schwefel´s strategy variant with correlated mutations only partly as a result of a sensible adaptation process. Its uncritical behaviour mainly results from rotating the mutation ellipsoids almost randomly through parameter space. This ensures the variation of all parameters in spite of some individual step-sizes being arbitrarily small. The inclination angles are uncritical strategy parameters because of their cyclical characteristic: they cannot drift away.

[2] "Large" or "small" refers to the mean variation of the underlying random distribution.

The weighting of the last generation and the lifespan of the information of preceding generations respectively is determined by the newly introduced constant $c \in (0,1]$. The factor $(c/(2\text{-}c))^{1/2}$ normalizes the mean variations of the resulting distributions to one (when no selection takes place). It results from the geometric series of the mean variations of the added mutations:

$$\lim_{m \to \infty} \sqrt{c^2 + \left(c \cdot (1-c)^1\right)^2 + \left(c \cdot (1-c)^2\right)^2 + \dots + \left(c \cdot (1-c)^m\right)^2} = \sqrt{\frac{c}{2-c}}$$

The adaptation scheme of the general step-size uses the convergence of the χ-distribution: $|\vec{z}| = \sqrt{\sum z_i^2} \xrightarrow[n \to \infty]{} N(\sqrt{n}, 0.5)$.

$(1, \lambda)$-ES algorithm with derandomized mutative step-size control using accumulated information

(all multiplications and powers of vectors refer to components)

Creation of λ offspring:

$$\vec{X}^g_{N_k} = \vec{X}^g_E + \delta^g \cdot \vec{\delta}^g_{scal} \cdot \vec{Z}_k \qquad\qquad (k = 1, \dots, \lambda)$$

Selection:

$$\vec{X}^{g+1}_E = \vec{X}^g_{N_{sel}}$$

Accumulation of selected mutations:

$$\vec{\vec{Z}}^g = (1-c)\vec{\vec{Z}}^{g-1} + c\vec{Z}_{sel} \qquad\qquad \vec{\vec{Z}}^0 = \vec{0}$$

Adaptation of general and individual step-sizes:

$$\delta^{g+1} = \delta^g \cdot \left(\exp\left(\frac{|\vec{\vec{Z}}^g|}{\sqrt{n} \cdot \sqrt{\frac{c}{2-c}}} - 1 + \frac{1}{5n} \right) \right)^\beta$$

(absolute value of vector $1/(5n)$ is a correction for small dimensions n.)

$$\vec{\delta}^{g+1}_{scal} = \vec{\delta}^g_{scal} \cdot \left(\frac{|\vec{\vec{Z}}^g|}{\sqrt{\frac{c}{2-c}}} + 0.35 \right)^{\beta_{scal}} {}^{*}$$

(absolute value of components)

Symbols used:

n number of parameters to be optimized (dimension of all vectors used)

$\vec{X}^g_{E/N}$ parameter vector of generation g (**E**: parent / **N**: offspring)

---

* N(0, 1)$^+$-distributed step-sizes $|Z|$ would cause systematically decreasing step-sizes, because the geometric mean of this distribution is less than one. The geometric mean of $(|Z| + 0.35)$ approximately equals one.

It is also possible to transform $|Z|$ by an integral transformation into a logarithmic normal distribution. This solves the problem in an elegant but much more costly way and, corresponding to our tests, does not affect the performance of the algorithm.

δ^g general step-size of generation g

$\vec{\delta}^g_{scal}$ individual step-sizes of generation g $\quad \vec{\delta}^0_{scal} = (1, \dots, 1)$

$\vec{Z} \quad = \quad (z_1, \dots, z_n) \quad$ with z_i $(0, 1)$-normally distributed

sel index of selected offspring of generation g

$c \quad = \quad \sqrt{1/n}$ The factor "**c**" determines how fast the contribution of former generations declines. The loss is about a factor **3** every **1/c** generations. For $n \to \infty$ $(c \to 0)$; $n = 10$ $(c \cong 0.3)$ resp. holds:

$$\left(\lim_{c \to 0} (1-c)^{1/c} = \frac{1}{e} \approx 0.37 \, ; \, (1-0.3)^{1/0.3} \approx 0.3 \right)$$

$\beta \quad = \quad \sqrt{1/n}$

$\beta_{scal} \quad = \quad 1/n$

Adaptation speed and precision depend on these two exponents. Sensible values are in the range $(0, 1)$. Small values facilitate a precise but time-consuming adaptation and vice versa. The given values yield a good compromise. See next section, figure 3. In the case of very difficult problems, a reduction of β_{scal} might be necessary.

Simulations

Tests of the described algorithm have been performed with $\lambda = 10$. Thus, the number of function evaluations equals ten times the number of generations. Simulations have been done on axis-parallel hyper-ellipsoids, Schwefel´s problem, a generalized Rosenbrock´s function, on a sum of different powers and on a Steiner-net.

In order to assess the performance of the derandomized step-size adaptation using accumulated information, results from the derandomized step-size adaptation (without using accumulated information) and from a (8,50)-ES according to Schwefel (1981) are also presented. Schwefel´s strategy with discrete global recombination adapts n individual step-sizes and n(n-1)/2 inclination angles. This means that not only the sizes of the axes of the mutation ellipsoid vary, but it can also be rotated arbitrarily with respect to the coordinate system. A strategy variant that adapts only individual step-sizes and no inclination angles would correspond better to the algorithm presented here, but works - according to our experiments - very unsatisfactorily (cf. also Hoffmeister & Bäck 1991). The simulations with Schwefel´s (8,50)-ES have been carried out with the *Evolution Machine* developed by Voigt, Born and Treptow (1991). Except for the adaptation using accumulated information, all other results are taken from Ostermeier (1994).

Axis-parallel Hyper-Ellipsoids:

Objective function: (*Not to be confused with the considerable different fct.* $\sum i \cdot x_i^2$)

$$F_n(\vec{x}) \quad = \quad \sum_{i=1}^{n} (i \cdot x_i)^2 \quad \Rightarrow \quad minimum \; (=0)$$

$$\vec{x}^0 = (1, \dots, 1), \quad F_{10,30,100}(\vec{x}^0) = 385, \, 9455, \, 338350, \quad F_{stop} = 10^{-10}$$

The simulation results (see figures 1 and 2) show that optimization speeds up considerably with adaptation of individual step-sizes. The feasible speed-up factor (10 ... 100 here) increases with the ratios of the ellipsoid-axes.

The optimization runs shown in figure 1 demonstrate that the step-size adaptation using accumulated information is able to adjust the correct set of individual step-sizes by which the problem is transformed into a hypersphere. After about 3000 function evaluations, the step-sizes are adapted correctly and the convergence rate is as high as with fixed individual step-sizes that are preadjusted correctly.

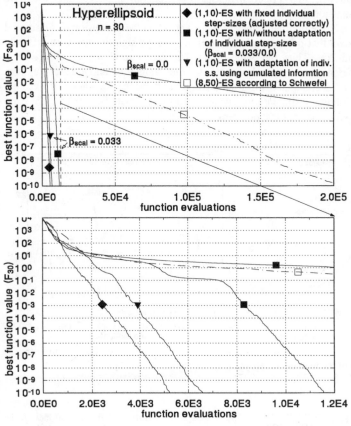

Figure 1

Convergence plots of optimization runs with the hyperellipsoid. The figure below is an enlarged detail of the first 12000 function evaluations of the same optimization runs shown above.

In order to assess the quality of step-size adaptation, an optimization run with the optimal set of (fixed) individual step-sizes is also shown.

In order to clarify the adaptation process, figure 2 - additionally to the fitness values - shows plots of the average ratio of the individual step-sizes to their correct values ($\pi(\delta_{scal})$). In figure 2a optimization runs with and without using accumulated information are compared. The plots of $\pi(\delta_{scal})$ show an acceleration of the step-size adaptation by about a factor three, using accumulated information. Additionally, the adaptation of the correct step-sizes is kept more precisely. The value of $\pi(\delta_{scal})$ stagnates at approximately 1.25 compared to 1.35 without using accumulated information. Figure 2b demonstrates the effect of varying β_{scal}. Reducing β_{scal} (= 0.01) facilitates a more precise but time consuming adaptation. Increasing β_{scal} (= 0.1) causes more stochastic fluctuations of the individual step-sizes.

To find out how to choose β_{scal}, the number of function evaluations needed to reach F_{stop} were measured for different values of β_{scal} (see figure 3). The minima result from the conflict of fast versus precise adaptation. Large values of β_{scal} provoke such stochastic fluctuations that no sensible adaptation is possible. The acceleration of optimization using accumulated information is mainly caused by the faster individual step-size adaptation (cf. also figures 1 and 2). The improvement revealed for $\beta_{scal} = 0$ (no adaptation of individual step-sizes) is caused by the general step-size adaptation. Using accumulated information, the adaptation process acts less locally. In the case of varying curvatures of the quality surface (narrow valleys), this effect increases the general step-size and therefore accelerates the optimization.

According to figure 3, the optimal values of β_{scal} depend on the dimension n. Additional simulations have shown that this dependency does not change significantly with different ratios of the ellipsoid-axes. Thus, the value $\boldsymbol{\beta_{scal} = 1/n}$ seems to be a good choice for a wide range of different problems. Compared to the simple derandomized step-size adaptation, the use of accumulated information does not change the range of sensible values for β_{scal}. All following simulations have been carried out with $\boldsymbol{\beta_{scal} = 1/n}$, that is no special adjustment to the different test problems has been done.

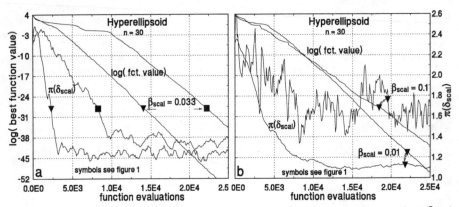

Figure 2   Convergence plots of optimization runs on the hyperellipsoid. The quantity $\pi(\delta_{scal})$ (the average deviation of the individual step-sizes) is defined as follows:

$$\pi(\delta_{scal}) := \exp(\sigma(\ln(\delta_{scal_i} \cdot i)))   \qquad (i=1,...,n \; ; \; \sigma: \text{ mean variation})$$

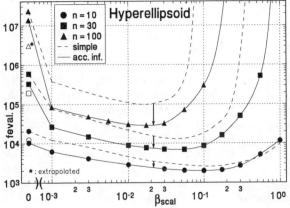

Figure 3   The symbols indicate the number of function evaluations to reach F_{stop} (average of 20 runs). For $\beta_{scal} \geq 0.5$; 0.1 (n=30; 100 resp.) the results of the simulations are influenced by the numerical precision of computation and thus are unreliable. The parameter settings of the derandomized ES with accumulated information are chosen as described above. Only β_{scal} varies. For $\boldsymbol{\beta_{scal} = 0}$ no adaptation of individual step-sizes takes place. So only one general step-size is adapted (Symbols on the left). The dashed lines refer to step-size adaptation without accumulated information (simple). Schwefel´s (8,50) ES (empty symbols) does not depend on the parameter β_{scal}. The results are shown here for comparison merely.

Schwefel´s problem

Objective function:

$$F(\vec{x}) = \sum_{i=1}^{n}\left(\sum_{j=1}^{i} x_j\right)^2 \Rightarrow minimum \ (=0) \ ; \quad n = 20, \ -65 \le x_i^0 \le 65$$

This problem represents - with respect to the coordinate axes - rotated hyperellipsoids. Thus, correlated mutations should be superior to uncorrelated ones. The simulations (figure 4) show that the simple (1,10)-ES with adaptation of only one general step-size is about four times faster than Schwefel´s (8,50)-ES with correlated mutations. This suggests that no actual adaptation of the correlations to the topology of the problem takes place.

By the derandomized adaptation of individual step-sizes, optimization slows down by about 30 %. This is caused by the stochastic fluctuations of the individual step-sizes induced by the adaptation process. Because of the rotation of the ellipsoid axes, the initialization with identical individual step-sizes is optimal or nearly optimal. The acceleration of optimization using accumulated information is caused by an increased general step-size. This is comparable to the axis-parallel hyperellipsoids without adaptation of individual step-sizes.

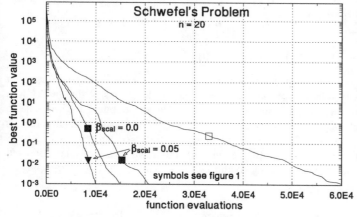

Figure 4
   Convergence plots of optimizations with Schwefel´s problem

■ (1,10)-ES with ($\beta_{scal} = 0.05 = 1/n$) and without ($\beta_{scal} = 0$) adaptation of individual step-sizes
▼ (1,10)-ES with adaptation of individual step-sizes using accumulated information.
❑ (8,50)-ES according to Schwefel

Generalized Rosenbrock Function

Objective function:

$$F(\vec{x}) = \sum_{i=1}^{n-1} 100 \cdot \left(x_{i+1} - x_i^2\right)^2 + \left(1 - x_i\right)^2 \Rightarrow minimum \ (=0)$$

$$n = 30, \ \vec{x}^0 = (0, \ ... \ ,0), \quad F(\vec{x}^0) = 29$$

This problem is characterized by the quadratic association of adjoining parameters. Thus correlated mutations of adjoining parameters should be superior. Schwefel´s (8,50)-ES facilitates a sensible adaptation only in the final stage of optimization (see figure 5). Derandomized adaptation of individual step-sizes accelerates the entire optimization cycle by increasing the step-sizes of adjoining parameters for which variations are of topical relevance.

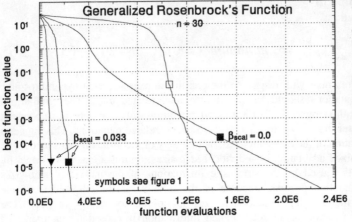

Figure 5
Convergence plots of optimizations with the generalized Rosenbrock function

■ (1,10)-ES with ($\beta_{scal} = 0.033 = 1/n$) and without ($\beta_{scal} = 0$) adaptation of individual step-sizes

▼ (1,10)-ES with adaptation of individual step-sizes using accumulated information.

❑ (8,50)-ES according to Schwefel

Sum of different Powers

Objective function:

$$F(\vec{x}) = \sum_{i=1}^{n} |x_i|^{(i+1)} \quad \Rightarrow \quad minimum \ (= 0)$$

$$n = 30, \quad \vec{x}^0 = (1, \dots, 1), \quad F(\vec{x}^0) = 30$$

This problem cannot be transformed into a hypersphere by an appropriate constant scaling. The sensitivity relations of the parameters (partial deviations of the quality fct.) continuously worsen when approaching the optimum. The derandomized ES is able to adapt the individual step-sizes according to the deteriorating scaling conditions. Its constant progress on the logarithmic scale is shown in figure 6. Schwefel's (8,50)-ES achieves a better quality than the (1,10)-ES without individual step-size adaptation but cannot deal with the deteriorating scaling conditions.

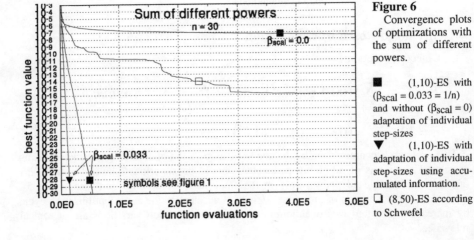

Figure 6
Convergence plots of optimizations with the sum of different powers.

■ (1,10)-ES with ($\beta_{scal} = 0.033 = 1/n$) and without ($\beta_{scal} = 0$) adaptation of individual step-sizes

▼ (1,10)-ES with adaptation of individual step-sizes using accumulated information.

❑ (8,50)-ES according to Schwefel

The Steiner-Net (with fixed topology)

The difficulty with this problem is comparable to the sum of different powers. The optimization problem is to minimize the length of a Steiner-net by finding the optimal positions of the Steiner-points (points of branching). The topology of the Steiner-tree is fixed (see figure 7).

The worsening sensitivity relations of the parameters and premature step-size convergence are caused by the linear dependency of the net-length on shiftings of Steiner-points that are located on "house" positions. The corresponding partial deviations of the quality function stay constantly about +1/-1 while the others converge to zero when approaching the optimum. As a result, the (1,10)-ES with mutative control of only one general step size and Schwefel's (8,50)-ES do not find the optimal Steiner-point positions.

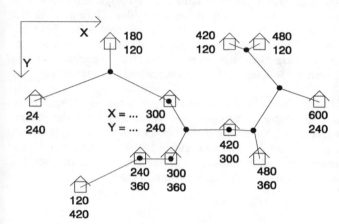

Figure 7
The points to be connected by the Steiner-net are symbolized by houses. The dots represent Steiner-points. The topology of the net is fixed as shown. Only the positions of the Steiner-points are subject to optimization. In the optimal solution, four of the nine Steiner-points are located at "house" positions.

Tests with the algorithm proposed here, have shown that it converges reliably to the optimum without premature step-size convergence. The (1,10)-ES without individual step-sizes and Schwefel's (8,50)-ES mostly converge to nets that are 1 to 10 units longer. Figure 8 shows some optimization runs.

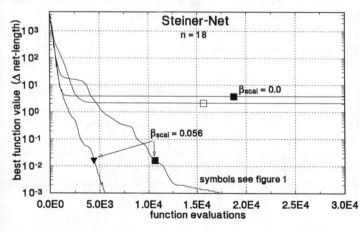

Figure 8
Convergence plots of optimizations runs with the Steiner-Net. The function values plotted are the actual net-length minus 1229.40854 which is the length of the minimal net.

Conclusions

A reliable adaptation of individual step-sizes is of essential importance for the applicability of the ES. Otherwise, the convergence rates can slow down by orders of magnitude for badly scaled problems. Even if the parameter-scaling seems not to be questionable, the lack of an appropriate adaptation of individual step-sizes can cause premature convergence of the general step-size.

Without modifications, mutative step-size control cannot be used for a reliable adaptation of individual step-sizes. Based on the concept of "Derandomized mutative step-size control", which enables a reliable step-size adaptation, the use of accumulated information decreases the locality of the adaptation process. Especially in small populations, the local character of step-size adaptation is disadvantageous because of the poor statistics involved. The additional information utilized by accumulation results from the generation sequence in a very simple way. Only the absolute values of the accumulated selected mutations have to be analyzed. The improvement achieved arises from the implicit use of correlations of the selected mutations in the generation sequence. Consequently, the step-sizes are adapted to such values that successive selected mutations tends to be orthogonal on average. This seems to be characteristical for optimal step-sizes in general.

Simulations show that the adaptation of individual step-sizes is accelerated considerably and becomes more precise and reliable at the same time. The adaptation of the general step-size can be improved as well. This occurs if the topology of the quality function resembles narrow valleys. In such cases the local character of step-size adaptation causes a too small step-size. Proceeding less locally, the use of accumulated information enables the adaptation of larger step-sizes and so accelerates the optimization.

References

Hoffmeister, F. & Bäck, T. (1991). *Genetic algorithms and evolution strategies: Similarities and differences*. In (Schwefel & Männer 1991), pages 455-470.

Ostermeier, A., Gawelczyk, A., Hansen, N. (1994). A Derandomized Approach to Self Adaptation of Evolution Strategies. In *Evolutionary Computation* (to be published).

Rechenberg, I. (1973). *Evolutionsstrategie: Optimierung technischer Systeme nach Prinzipien der biologischen Evolution*. Stuttgart: Frommann-Holzboog.

Rechenberg, I. (1978). Evolutionsstrategien. In B. Schneider and U. Ranft (Eds.), *Simulationsmethoden in der Medizin und Biologie*, Berlin: Springer.

Rechenberg, I. (1994). *Evolutionsstrategie `94*. Stuttgart: Frommann-Holzboog (in print).

Schwefel, H.-P. (1977). *Numerische Optimierung von Computer-Modellen mittels der Evolutionsstrategie*. Volume 26 of *Interdisciplinary systems research*. Basel: Birkhäuser.

Schwefel, H.-P. (1981). *Numerical Optimization of Computer Models*. Chichester: Wiley.

Schwefel, H.-P. (1987). Collective phenomena in evolutionary systems. In *Preprints of the 31st Annual Meeting of the International Society for General System Research, Budapest, 2*: 1025-32.

Schwefel, H.-P. & Männer, R. (Eds.) (1991). *Parallel Problem Solving from Nature*, volume 496 of *Lecture Notes in Computer Science*. Berlin: Springer.

Voigt, H.-M., Born, J. & Treptow, J. (1991). *The Evolution Machine*. Manual. iir, Informatik, Informationen, Reporte.

Strategy Adaptation
by Competing Subpopulations

Dirk Schlierkamp-Voosen * and Heinz Mühlenbein

GMD Schloß Birlinghoven
D-53754 Sankt Augustin, Germany

Abstract. The breeder genetic algorithm BGA depends on a set of control parameters and genetic operators. In this paper it is shown that strategy adaptation by competing subpopulations makes the BGA more robust and more efficient. Each subpopulation uses a different strategy which competes with other subpopulations. Numerical results are presented for a number of test functions.

Keywords: breeder genetic algorithm, strategy adaptation, competition, multiresolution search

1 Introduction

Many evolutionary algorithms depend on a set of control parameters. Often the optimal setting of the parameter depends on the particular application. Moreover the optimal control parameters may be different at the start of the run and at the end where the individuals are very similar to each other.

Basically two approaches have been pursuit to solve the above problem. In the first approach some externally specified schedule is used. The schedule may depend for instance on the time, measured in number of generations. This approach is derived from simulated annealing. The temperature is set at a large initial value, then it is continuously reduced. In genetic algorithms this approach has been tried for changing the mutation rate or the selection [4].

In the second approach the mechanisms of evolution itself are used to adapt the control parameters. The adaptation is not driven by an external schedule but by the internal forces of evolution itself. This approach is successfully used in evolution strategies [3]. In evolution strategies the adaptation of control parameters is done in the same manner as the adaptation of the parameters defining the fitness functions [1].

The crucial question of the second approach concerns the level where the adaptation is done. It may be the level of the individual as it is done in evolution strategies. But also the level of subpopulations or the level of populations can be used. The level implicitly defines the time interval when the adaptation takes place. If for instance populations are used for adaptation, then a minimum

---

* schlierkamp-voosen@gmd.de

number of generations is needed for evaluating the populations. In contrast, individuals are evaluated after each generation.

In this paper we present an adaptation based on subpopulations. It simulates subpopulations competing for the same food. The outline of the paper is as follows. In section 2 the most important control parameters of the breeder genetic algorithm BGA are summarized. In section 3 the competition scheme is explained. The performance of the competition is shown in section 4 for unimodal functions. In section 5 the efficiency and the robustness of the adaptation by competition is demonstrated for multimodal functions.

2 The BGA for Continuous Parameter Optimization

Let an unconstrained optimization problem be given on a domain $D \subset \mathbb{R}^n$

$$\min(F(\mathbf{x})) \qquad a_i \leq x_i \leq b_i \quad i = 1, ..., n \ . \tag{1}$$

The breeder genetic algorithm **BGA** was designed to solve the above problem [6]. The BGA depends on some control parameters which we summarize shortly. The selection is done by *truncation selection*, also called mass selection by breeders. The $T\%$ best of the individuals are selected as parents and then mated randomly.

Discrete recombination
Let $\mathbf{x} = (x_1, ..., x_n)$ and $\mathbf{y} = (y_1, ..., y_n)$ be the parent strings. Then the offspring $\mathbf{z} = (z_1, ..., z_n)$ is computed by

$$z_i = \{x_i\} \ or \ \{y_i\} \tag{2}$$

x_i or y_i are chosen with probability 0.5.

BGA mutation
A variable x_i is selected with probability p_m for mutation. The BGA normally uses $p_m = 1/n$. At least one variable will be mutated. A value out of an interval $[-range_i, range_i]$ is added to the selected variable. $range_i$ defines the *mutation range*. It is normally set to 0.5 times the domain of definition of variable x_i.

Given x_i a new value z_i is computed according to

$$z_i = x_i \pm range_i \cdot \delta \tag{3}$$

The $+$ or $-$ sign is chosen with probability 0.5. δ is computed from a distribution which prefers small values. This is realized as follows

$$\delta = \sum_{i=0}^{k-1} \alpha_i \cdot 2^{-i} \qquad \alpha_i \in \{0, 1\}$$

k is called the precision constant. Before starting the mutation we set $\alpha_i = 0$. Then each α_i is flipped to 1 with probability $p_\delta = 1/k$. Only $\alpha_i = 1$ contributes to the sum. On the average there will be just one α_i with value 1, say α_j. Then δ is given by

$$\delta = 2^{-j}$$

This mutation scheme is discrete. For a number of reasons we now use a continuous mutation scheme where δ is computed as follows

$$\delta = 2^{-k \cdot \alpha} \quad \alpha \in [0, 1]$$

The discussion of this scheme is outside the scope of this paper.

BGA line recombination

The BGA line recombination uses components from both, mutation and recombination. It creates new points in a direction given by the two parent points. The placement of the point is done by the BGA mutation scheme. It works as follows: Let $\mathbf{x} = (x_1, \ldots, x_n)$ and $\mathbf{y} = (y_1, \ldots, y_n)$ be the parent strings with $\mathbf{x}$ being the one with better fitness. Then the offspring $\mathbf{z} = (z_1, \ldots, z_n)$ is computed by

$$z_i = x_i \pm range_i \cdot \delta \cdot \frac{y_i - x_i}{\|\mathbf{x} - \mathbf{y}\|} \tag{4}$$

The $-$ sign is chosen with probability 0.9. The offspring is placed more often in the descending direction.

The rationale behind the three operators is as follows. The BGA mutation operator is able to generate *any* point in the hypercube with center $\mathbf{x}$ defined by $x_i \pm range_i$. But it tests much more often in the neighborhood of $\mathbf{x}$. In the above standard setting, the mutation operator is able to locate the optimal x_i up to a precision of $range_i \cdot 2^{-(k-1)}$. Discrete recombination is a breadth search. It uses the information contained in the two parent points. The BGA line recombination tries new points in a direction defined by the parent points.

In [6] we have proven that a BGA with popsize $N = 1$ (1 parent, 1 offspring, the better of the two survives) using only mutation has approximate *linear order of convergence* for unimodal functions.

Theorem 1. *Given a point with distance $range_i \cdot 2^{-(k-1)} \le r \le range_i$ to the optimum, then the expected progress $E(n, r)$ of the BGA in n dimensions is bounded by*

$$\frac{1}{2kn} \le \frac{E(n, r)}{r} \le \frac{1}{kn} \tag{5}$$

This theorem shows the following problem. The progress depends on k. The larger k, the smaller the progress. But in order to locate the optimum with a given precision ϵ, the value $range_i \cdot 2^{-(k-1)}$ has to be less than ϵ. Therefore a large k may be necessary.

We show the dependence of the BGA on the precision constant k in Fig. 1. The task is to minimize the hypersphere of dimension $n = 100$.

$$F_0(x) = \sum_i^n x_i^2$$

Note that the best fitness is displayed on a logarithmic scale. The simulations have been done with three precision values $k = 4, 8$, and 16. For $k = 16$ one observes for quite a time the predicted linear order of convergence. Small values of k have a better progress at the beginning, but they are able to locate the best fitness to a certain precision only.

Next we summarize the mathematical properties of discrete recombination. A detailed investigation can be found in [7]. Discrete recombination has also *linear order of convergence* in number of generations versus fitness until near the equilibrium. Equilibrium is defined as all genotypes of the population being equal. The fitness value achieved at equilibrium depends on the size of the population and the truncation selection threshold.

In Fig. 2 three simulation runs are shown. One clearly observes the linear order of convergence until near the equilibrium. The rate of progress is larger for a small truncation threshold, but the population converges to a higher fitness value.

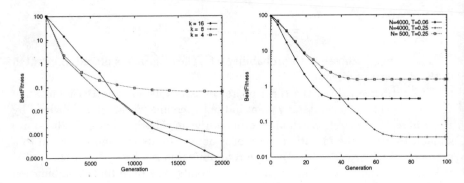

Fig. 1. BGA mutation; hypersphere $n = 100$; precision $k = 16, 8$, and 4.

Fig. 2. Discrete recombination, hypersphere $n = 100$. The gradient of the best fitness achieved depends on the truncation threshold T for selection. For $N = 4000$ $T = 0.25$ and $T = 0.06$ was used.

The computational efficiency of mutation and recombination can be compared by changing the abscissa from number of generations to number of function evaluations. It is easily seen that mutation is by far more efficient. This result indicates that recombination is not an efficient search method to determine the minimum of a quadratic function. We will later show that recombination is an important search operator for determining promising search areas of multimodal functions.

The result of the simulations can be summarized as follows: *The efficiency of the BGA mutation operator depends on the precision constant k. The efficiency of discrete recombination depends on the size of the population and the truncation threshold T.*

The question now arises how to combine recombination and mutation in an optimal way and how to automatically control the precision constant k of the

BGA mutation scheme. We will use for the adaptation the concept of competition between subpopulations. This will be described in the next section.

3 Competition between Subpopulations

The adaptation of parameters controlling evolutionary algorithms can be done on different levels, for example the level of the individuals, the level of subpopulations or the level of populations. Bäck et al. [2] have implemented the adaptation of strategy parameters on the level of the individual. The strategy parameters of the best individuals are recombined, giving the new stepsize for the mutation operator in the next generation. Herdy [5] uses competition on the population level. In this case whole populations are evaluated at certain generations. The strategies of the successful populations proliferate, the strategies of populations with bad performance die out. They are replaced by the successful strategies and afterwards modified by genetic operators. There is no exchange of individuals between populations.

Our adaptation lies between these two extreme cases. The competition is done between subpopulations (groups). The total number of all individuals is fixed whereas the size of a single group varies. Our approach simulates the population changes of species which compete for the same food. Well adapted species increase whereas poorly adapted species decrease. This follows Gausse's principle: *'Two species with identical requirements cannot co-exist in a habitat.'* Occasionally individuals with a good fitness migrate to other groups.

The competition requires a *quality criterion* to rate a group, a *gain criterion* to reward or punish the groups, an *evaluation interval*, and a *migration interval*. The evaluation interval gives each strategy the chance to demonstrate its performance in a certain time window. By occasional migration of the best individuals groups which performed badly are given a better chance for the next competition. The sizes of the groups have a lower limit. Therefore no strategy is lost.

The **quality criterion** is based on the fitness of the best individual of the group. To avoid an inefficient oscillation of group sizes we had to extend the quality criterion. For the evaluation information about the last 10 competitions is used. The group with the best individual gets $best\_ind = 1$, for all other groups $best\_ind$ is set to 0.

The following formula describes the quality of group i. $k = 0$ denotes the current competition, $k = 1$ the previous one, etc.

$$quality(i) = \sum_{k=0}^{9} \left(\frac{10 - k}{10} \cdot best\_ind_k(i) \right) \tag{6}$$

The **gain criterion** defines how to modify the population size of each group according to its quality. The size of the group with the best quality increases, all other groups are decreased.

If group i has the best quality, then

$$N_{t+1}^i = N_t^i + \sum_{j=0, j \neq i}^{G-1} \frac{N_t^j}{8} \tag{7}$$

where N_t^i denotes the size of group i and G denotes the number of groups. All other groups are reduced if their size is greater than the minimal size N_{min}.

$$N_{t+1}^j = N_t^j - \frac{N_t^j}{8} \quad j \neq i \tag{8}$$

This gain criterion leads to a fast adaptation of the group sizes. Each group looses the same percentage of individuals.

The **evaluation interval** is normally set to 4, the **migration interval** to 16.

4   Competition for Unimodal Functions

The behavior of the BGA competition scheme can best be explained with the unimodal hypersphere function. In Fig. 3 four groups with different mutation ranges compete. The mutation intervals are defined in Table 1.

Table 1. Range and mutation steps for precision constant $k = 7$ used.

group	range	max. step	min. step
0	5.120000	10.240000	0.1600000
1	0.160000	0.320000	0.0050000
2	0.005000	0.010000	0.0001560
3	0.000156	0.000312	0.0000049

The different mutation ranges define a multiresolution search. Group 0 is doing large mutation steps and group 3 the smallest. The group with the largest range was initialized with 52 individuals, all the other with the minimum popsize of 4. In the rightmost figure one clearly observes the migration interval which was set to $mig = 32$ for reasons of presentation. At these intervals migration takes place. Therefore the best fitness of the groups becomes equal.

In Fig. 4 the distribution of the population sizes of the four groups is shown. First the group with the largest mutation steps dominates, then the group with the second largest mutation steps takes over and so on. The change of the sizes of the groups correspond to the four waves which can be seen in Fig. 3. In Fig. 5 the quality criterion used for the competition is shown.

In Fig. 6 the competition run is compared to a run without competition. The BGA without competition was initialized with a precision constant of $k = 22$. This precision is comparable to the competition run. Until generation 700 both runs are equally effective. Afterwards the competition run is more effective. This behavior is predicted by the theory.

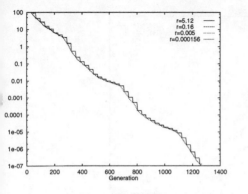 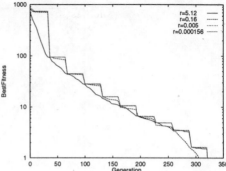

Fig. 3. Competition between 4 groups using different mutation ranges. The precision is $k = 7$.

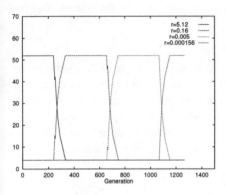 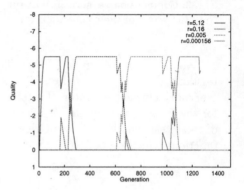

Fig. 4. Distribution of the population sizes; first the group with the largest mutation steps is successful. At the end the group with the smallest mutation steps has taken over.

Fig. 5. Quality criterion which affected the variation of the population sizes shown in Fig. 4.

5 Multiresolution Search for Multimodal Functions

The BGA is intended to solve multimodal optimization problems. In [6] we have shown that the standard BGA using mutation and discrete recombination has also linear order of convergence for some of the popular multimodal test functions. The scaling constants are specific to the fitness function and the precision constant k of the BGA. They are less than for unimodal functions. The reason for this behavior can easily be explained. Most of the test functions have a global structure which is similar to the hypersphere. Therefore the multimodality of the function can be considered as noise for the BGA. The multimodality only reduces the probability of creating better offspring.

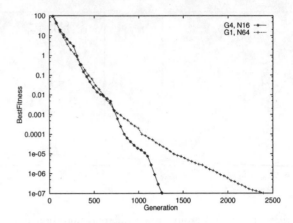

Fig. 6. Competition vs. normal BGA run; For fine tuning competition is more effective. Note the waves of the competition run.

We have pointed out in [6] that the local minima of these test functions are regularly distributed. For these classes of problems discrete recombination is an especially efficient operator. Therefore these test functions are not a challenge for the BGA. For comparisons reason we give some results for the most difficult of these test functions, this is Griewank's function. We will later investigate two functions which we believe are more typical for real life applications.

$$F_8(x) = \sum_1^n \frac{x_i^2}{4000} - \prod_1^n cos\left(\frac{x_i}{\sqrt{i}}\right) + 1 \quad -600 \leq x_i \leq 600 \qquad (9)$$

In Fig. 7 a competition run and a run without competition is shown for Griewank's function of dimension $n = 100$. Both runs used in addition to mutation discrete recombination. The run without competition is slightly more effective. But the BGA with competition is more robust. The BGA without competition converged in 9 of 10 cases to the second minima.

We will now turn to optimization problems where the local minima are distributed more randomly. In [9] these kind of test functions are also proposed as a common benchmark for global optimization problems. We have used the following test function originally proposed by Rechenberg.

$$F_{12}(x) = \sum_{i=0}^{20} \left((100 - i) \cdot \exp\left(- \sum_{k=1}^n \left(\frac{x_k - z_{30 \cdot i + k}}{\sigma} \right)^2 \right) \right) \qquad (10)$$

where $z_j = (32 \cdot z_{j-1} + 13(i+1)) \bmod 31, \quad z_0 = 1, \quad -100 \leq x_i \leq 100$

The function consists of 21 exponential mountains, whose positions are randomly distributed. σ is used to vary the shape of the single hills. Due to limitations of space we have to summarize the simulation results. Competition runs

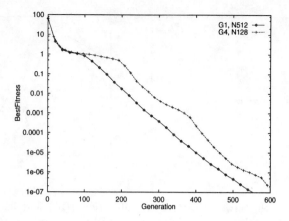

Fig. 7. Griewangk's function (F_8) with and without competition. Both runs consist of 512 individuals. For the competition they were distributed into four groups.

locate the attractor region of the global optimum much faster than runs without competition. The reason is that the group performing large steps is able to locate the attractor regions very fast. In the final stage of the search the group with the smallest steps locates the optimum with high precision.

A real challenge for any continuous function optimization program is to follow a steep curved valley which is only slightly decreasing. An example is the function of Rosenbrock [8]. In [10] the two dimensional function was extended to a n-dimensional function.

$$F_{16}(x) = \sum_{i=1}^{n} \left(100(x_{i+1} - x_i^2)^2 + (1 - x_i)^2\right) \qquad -5.12 \le x_i \le 5.12 \qquad (11)$$

For these kind of functions the BGA mutation scheme is not efficient. Line recombination seems much more promising. With line recombination first the direction is computed, then the mutation step. In Fig. 8 a competition is shown between discrete recombination and line recombination. One observes that first discrete recombination is exploring the search space. For a long time the population stays at the saddle point 1, then after the group using line recombination has taken over, it finally is able to leave the saddle point.

6 Conclusion

Competition between subpopulations using different strategies makes the BGA search more effective and robust. The method presented in this paper is a first step. The strategies have to be defined at the start of the run, only their relative frequency is changed by competition. The user of the BGA has the responsibility to define a set of reasonable strategies for the given problem. The question to

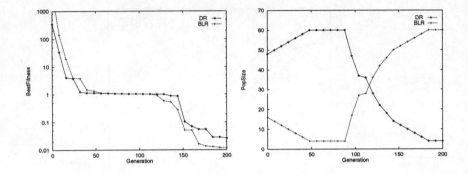

Fig. 8. Competition between discrete recombination (DR) and line recombination (BLR) for Rosenbrock's function of dimension 4. BLR takes over at generation 120.

be investigated in the future is how robust the competition is in respect to the parameters used for the competition. All runs reported in this paper have been done with the same set of parameters.

References

1. Thomas Bäck. Self-Adaption in Genetic Algorithms. In Francisco Varela and Paul Bourgine, editors, *Towards a Practice of Autonomous Systems*, pages 263–271, 1992.
2. Thomas Bäck and Hans-Paul Schwefel. A Survey of Evolution Strategies. In *Proceedings of the Fourth International Conference of Genetic Algorithms*, pages 2–9, San Diego, 1991. ICGA.
3. Thomas Bäck and Hans-Paul Schwefel. An Overview of Evolutionary Algorithms for Parameter Optimization. *Evolutionary Computation*, 1:1–24, 1993.
4. Terence C. Fogarty. Varying the probability of Mutation in the Genetic Algorithm. In J. David Schaffer, editor, *Proceedings of the Third International Conference of Genetic Algorithms*, pages 104–109. Morgan-Kaufman, 1989.
5. Michael Herdy. Reproductive Isolation as Strategy Parameter in Hierarchical Organized Evolution Strategies. In *PPSN 2 Bruxelles*, pages 207–217, September 1992.
6. Heinz Mühlenbein and Dirk Schlierkamp-Voosen. Predictive Models for the Breeder Genetic Algorithm: Continuous Parameter Optimization. *Evolutionary Computation*, 1(1):25–49, 1993.
7. Heinz Mühlenbein and Dirk Schlierkamp-Voosen. The science of breeding and its application to the breeder genetic algorithm. *Evolutionary Computation*, 1(4):335–360, 1994.
8. H. H. Rosenbrock. An automatic method for finding the greatest or least value of a function. *The Computer Journal*, 3(3):175–184, 10 1960.
9. Fabio Schoen. A Wide Class of Test Functions for Global Optimization. *Journal of Global Optimization*, 3(2):133–137, 1993.
10. H.-P. Schwefel. *Numerical Optimization of Computer Models*. Wiley, Chichester, 1981.

Controlling Crossover through Inductive Learning

Michèle Sebag[1] and Marc Schoenauer[2]

[1] LMS, CNRS-URA 317, Ecole Polytechnique, F-91128 Palaiseau
sebag@xela.polytechnique.fr
[2] CMAP, CNRS-URA 756, Ecole Polytechnique, F-91128 Palaiseau
marc@cmapx.polytechnique.fr

Abstract. Crossover may achieve the fast combination of performant building blocks ; but as a counterpart, crossover may as well break a newly discovered building block. We propose to use inductive learning to control such disruptive effects of crossover. The idea is to periodically gather some examples of crossovers, labelled as "good" or "bad" crossovers according to their effects on the current population. From these examples, inductive learning builds rules characterizing the crossover quality. This ruleset then enables to control further evolution : crossovers classified "bad" according to the ruleset are refused. Some experimentations on the Royal Road problem are discussed.

1 Introduction

Various heuristics have been designed to face the central dilemma of genetic algorithms, i.e. the Exploitation of promising regions *vs* the Exploration of new regions [1]. Among these heuristics, see for instance fitness scaling, niching, restricted mating [2]. However, these heuristics must be parameterized by errors and trials, given the lack of theoretical results ; furthermore, these heuristics should be adaptively parameterized : e.g. restricted mating is more adapted to the end than to the beginning of evolution.

This paper focuses on the adaptive control of the crossover operator. Crossover is commonly acknowledged the more powerful engine of evolution, as it enables to combine performant building blocks. But crossover may make a promising parent disappear[3] as well as give birth to a promising offspring. The danger of breaking a building block increases with its length, as shown by the Schemata Theorem [3] : the longer the schema, the more likely a crossover point belongs to its region. But whatever the length of a newly discovered schema, crossover is a danger to it.

This paper investigates the use of inductive learning [7] to prevent using disruptive crossovers ; the idea is to characterize crossovers that are "bad" with respect to the current population, to avoid using them in the next generations. Inductive learning must be periodically redone as the crossover quality heavily

---

[3] Mutation can also destroy it, but with a usually much smaller rate than that of crossover.

depends on the current population.

Section 2 briefly introduces the problem taken as example all along this paper, the Royal Road problem [8] ; on this problem we discuss the kind of knowledge needed in order to control crossover. Section 3 deals with gathering examples of the crossover behavior and evaluating their potentialities for evolving further generations. The proposed frame integrating GA and inductive learning is described in section 4. Last, section 5 presents our first experimental results.

2   Knowledge about Crossover

This section first recalls the Royal Road problem, then discusses the parts respectively devoted to learning and evolving in an integrated scheme.

2.1   Description

The Royal Road problem (RRP) was conceived by M. Mitchell et coll. [8, 5] to study into detail the combined features most adapted to GAs (laying a *royal road...*). Let the problem space be $\Omega = \{0,1\}^P$ and let $H_{i,j}$ denote the schema with i consecutive 1s, beginning at locus j. The first version of the RRP defined on $\Omega = \{0,1\}^{64}$ involves schemas $H_{8,1}, H_{8,9}, H_{8,1+8*k}$, $H_{16,1}, H_{16,17}, H_{16,1+16*l}$, $H_{32,1}, H_{32,33}$ and $H_{64,1}$. The order of a schema is its number of fixed bits ; the fitness of individual x is defined as the sum of the orders of the schemas x belongs to. The authors expected this fitness landscape to be GA-easy because of (a) its building block structure and (b) the reinforcement due to the fact that high-order schemas are composed of low-order schemas.

However, the RRP is definitely *not* GA-easy ; the analysis made by Mitchell and coll. [5] is that the relative failure of GA is due to a "hitchhiking" phenomenon. The idea is that the first individual belonging to a high-level schema, say $H_{32,1}$, will crowd the population ; in the meanwhile, its 32 last bits, "hitchhiked" by the performant first 32 ones may cause any schema concerned with the last 32 bits, such as $H_{8,33}$ or $H_{16,33}$, to disappear. Evolution then goes from scratch regarding the last 32 bits.

2.2   Broad Lines

Let us sketch the behavior required from a "smart" crossover on this problem :

1. No requirement should be put on crossover in the first stages of evolution in order to achieve fast emergence of the low-order building blocks;
2. After a performant building block has emerged i.e. when it comes to have representatives in the population, it should be sequestered according to [5], i.e. crossover should not break it ; e.g. after schema $H_{8,1}$ has emerged, no crossover should break apart the first eight bits in the representatives of this schema.
3. The fact that a crossover is indesirable of course depends on the current population.

Do such requirements make sense in real-world problems ?
They all rely on the assumption that the global fitness function may be decomposed into parts defined on subsets of the search space. These subsets, called *schemas* in a boolean space, can be thought of in a more general frame ; they are called *formae* by Radcliffe [9].

But how are *formae* or *schemas* interrelated ? The answer to this key question should rule the crossover control. To take an example, breaking apart the 5th and 6th bits should be generally forbidden after schema $* * * * \ 1 \ 1 \ * *$ has emerged — if schemas do not overlap ; but what if schema $* * * * \ 0 \ 1 \ 1 \ *$ remains to be discovered ? If two schemas overlap and have different fixed bit values, avoiding to disrupt the firstly discovered schema may prevent to ever discover the other one. Let us call *conflicting fitness* a fitness landscape involving schemas that have different fixed bit values for some bits, and are nevertheless of high average fitness. Then, conflicting and non-conflicting fitnesses must be handled through different kinds of <induction - GA> coupling.

2.3 Learning or Evolving ?

Let us precise the scope of the intended crossover control :

A We may demand that at least one offspring of a representative of a given schema, still belongs to the schema. This requirement ensures this schema is not fleetingly discovered. In this approach, learning precisely rules out *how a given* individual must be combined[4].

B We may demand that a given region is transmitted from any individual to at least one of its offsprings. Patterns existing in this region will thus remain unchanged in the population (except through the selection and mutation effects) ; patterns will evolve in other regions of the search space. What is learned here is something about *how to combine* individuals, whatever the individuals to be crossed.

Option A is clearly more powerful : it applies whatsoever the underlying fitness landscape, be it conflicting or not. In coupling A, induction is devoted to detect the good building blocks discovered so far, while GA provides a smart exploration and combination of these building blocks.

Option B is simpler and more rigid : it forbids some crossover points. Would this control be defined once for all, this option would clearly be inadequate to a conflicting fitness landscape. But what if this control is re-defined periodically ?

On the other hand, our goal in this paper is to study the potentialities of coupling inductive learning and GA. Studying the B coupling on the Royal Road problem[5] may at least tell us if our approach is worth considering any further.

So, though we are well aware of the limitations of our choice, option B will be the only one considered in the sequel of this paper : we tackle the characterization of crossovers that are adapted to a whole population.

---

[4] A still more precise control would concern *who* to combine with a given individual.
[5] The limitations of option B should not be too severe regarding the Royal Road landscape, since it is not conflicting.

3   Learning to Crossover

Since inductive learning needs labelled examples, we must define what representation of crossover we use, and what label, standing for the "desirability" of a crossover, meets our goal of crossover control.

3.1   Representation of a crossover

Let us consider a bit-string representation, and let $\Omega = \{0,1\}^P$ be the search space. A crossover c may then be represented by a *mask* ; let c be given as $(c_1, \ldots c_P)$, $c_i \in \{0,1\}$:

$$\begin{matrix} x_1\, x_2\, ..\, x_P \\ y_1\, y_2\, ..\, y_P \end{matrix} \rightarrow \begin{matrix} x_1'\, x_2'\, ..\, x_P' \\ y_1'\, y_2'\, ..\, y_P' \end{matrix} \text{ with } x_i' = \begin{cases} x_i \text{ if } c_i = 1 \\ y_i \text{ otherwise} \end{cases} \text{ and } y_i' = \begin{cases} y_i \text{ if } c_i = 1 \\ x_i \text{ otherwise} \end{cases}$$

Crossover c may thus be represented by an element of Ω.

In a real-valued representation $(\Omega = R^P)$ a widely used cross-over operator involves barycentric recombination of the parents components [6, 9] :

$$x_i' = \alpha_i x_i + (1 - \alpha_i) y_i \; ; \; y_i' = (1 - \alpha_i) x_i + \alpha_i y_i$$

with α_i in [0,1] or [-.5, 1.5]. A crossover can therefore be represented by vector $(\alpha_1, .. \alpha_P)$, that still belongs to (a subset of) Ω.

3.2   Labelling a crossover

Intuitively, a crossover is *good* if it leads to offsprings with better fitness than that of parents ; it is *bad* if offsprings fitness is worse than that of parents ; otherwise, it is *inactive*.

Choosing good crossovers. The more natural idea is to perform only good crossovers. But a crossover considered good has led to discover a promising individual in the previous generations ; and, since the effects of crossover are reversible, if it is applied on the same individual, it will destroy it. So, a crossover observed to be "good" on a given population is far from being good for ever.

Rejecting bad crossovers. The second natural idea is to reject bad crossovers. Notice that good and bad crossovers evolve quite differently along genetic evolution. A crossover, good at a given step of evolution, may be bad in the very next step. Conversely, if a crossover shows bad, it is because it breaks more useful schemas than it leads to discover ; this fact is likely to persist as long as the population does not change too much. It thus makes sense to characterize the disruptive crossovers by learning rules. These rules enable to reject further disruptive crossovers. This way, the crossover control biases the generation of crossover masks (otherwise random).

Rejecting inactive crossovers. A drawback of inductive learning is that, in order to characterize the class of good or bad crossovers, we need examples of these classes. And, as evolution goes on, the number of good or bad crossovers decreases, and most crossovers become inactive.

But actually, inactive crossovers are still worse than disruptive ones (at least after a given stage of evolution) : with disruptive crossovers evolution goes backwards (hopefully to other promising regions) and the search goes on ; with inactive crossovers, evolution stops. So we ended in deciding to characterize inactive crossovers and to refuse them.

More precisely, we propose the following strategy :

- when less than 70% of the observed crossovers are inactive, phase we denote by *classical*, we refuse disruptive crossovers ;
- when more that 70% of the observed crossovers are inactive, phase we denote by *modern*, we refuse inactive crossovers.

The transition between both phases strongly depends on the niching phenomenon [2]. If only one *species* is to be found, then the population will (in case of success) converge toward a single optimum, i.e. to a uniform population. Long before that, most crossovers would be inactive. Retaining solely active crossovers is equivalent to speeding up the evolution. In opposition, if several *species* are to be found, it is usually irrelevant to cross individuals belonging to different species. Learning and rejecting disruptive crossovers then can play the same role than any niching heuristics (e.g. restricted mating).

4 An integrated frame

This section first describes the GA we use, then give the broad lines of the coupling. Last, the interactions between GA and inductive learning are detailed.

4.1 Genetic Algorithm

The genetic algorithm we use is a lab-made software based on the standards [1] : bit-string encoding, roulette wheel selection with fitness scaling, two-points crossover at a rate of 0.6 with both offsprings replacing the parents, and mutation at a rate of 0.05. The evolution stops either after 1000 generations or when the fitness is constant over the population. The fitness scaling (number of offsprings for the best individual) varies in the experiments (see 5.1).

4.2 Broad Lines of the Coupling

We combine GAs and inductive learning in the following scheme (Fig.1) :

1. A first darwinian period involves N generations of a classical GA ;

2. The next step corresponds to gaining experience about evolution. Examples of crossovers are generated and their behaviors are observed with respect to the current population (section 4.3). A set of rules is built from these examples by inductive learning (section 4.4).

3. Then a "civilized" period involves GA controlled according to the available experience. During M generations (M is called *civilization length*[6]), crossovers classified by the ruleset as disruptive or inactive are refused (section 4.5).

4. After these M generations, the population has evolved and acquiring new experience is necessary. So, the process goes back to step (2).

We call *civilization* the phase of rules induction together with the consecutive M generations obeying these rules.

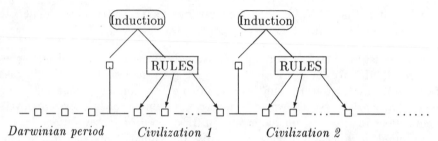

Darwinian period   *Civilization 1*   *Civilization 2*

Figure 1 : Combining GAs and Induction (☐ stands for a generation)

4.3 Gathering crossover examples

Let L be the size of the genetic population. L crossover examples are built as follows :

• A 2-point crossover mask is randomly generated;
• Two individuals are randomly selected in the population;
• These individuals are crossed according to the crossover mask. The mask is labelled as good, bad or inactive, depending on whether the fitness of the best offspring is better, worse or equal to the fitness of the best parent;
• If this mask belongs to a class that includes less than 70% of the L examples, it is added to the example set.

The last condition may result in an never-ended loop if all crossovers belong to the same class. To settle this problem, if the example set is not completed in $5 \times L$ trials, an empty ruleset is considered all along this civilization (that period is therefore darwinian). The current phase is said *classical* if less than 70% of the examples are inactive, and *modern* otherwise.

4.4 Learning rules

We use a star-like algorithm [7], described into detail in [12, 11]. A rule consists of an hypothesis part and a conclusion part. The hypothesis can be thought of as

---

[6] In the following, we take $M = N$.

a schema in the crossover space ; the conclusion here belongs to the set { good, bad, inactive }. A rule is said to cover a crossover mask iff this mask belongs to the schema standing for the hypothesis of the rule.

The induction we use is a bottom-up process : from any example (crossover mask) Ex, we try to find out rules covering Ex and not covering any example belonging to a class other than that of Ex. Among the many solutions, only rules covering the maximum number of examples are retained ; furthermore, we require that a rule covers at least 2 examples. This algorithm does not necessarily provide consistent rules. When an unlabelled crossover is covered by rules of different conclusion, the final decision is determined via a majority vote among these rules.

4.5 Using the rules

A 2-point crossover mask is initialized at random. During the civilized periods, this mask is checked as follows :
• if the ruleset is empty, the mask is accepted.
• if the mask is classified as bad, and the current phase is classical, the mask is refused;
• if the mask is classified as inactive, and the current phase is modern, the mask is refused;
• otherwise, the mask is accepted.

Again, this decision process may result in a never-ended loop if all crossovers are rejected. To prevent this, a gradual relaxation of the ruleset is used :
• rules are weighted ; the weight of a rule is set to the number of learning examples it covers ;
• only rules with weight greater than a threshold s are considered. Threshold s is initialized to 1 (i.e. all rules are considered in the beginning).
• if, on L consecutive trials, less than $\frac{L}{20}$ crossovers are retained, threshold s is incremented of 1.
So, if no crossover is accepted, less and less rules are taken into account.

5 Results and Discussion

5.1 Protocol

Any presented result corresponds to the average result obtained on 30 independant runs. The population size is set to 100, 200 and 500 individuals. The fitness scaling (number of offsprings for the best individual) is set to 1.5 and 2. The civilization length varies from 0 (no learning at all) to 10.

5.2 Results on the Royal Road

The Royal Road problem is modified as in [5] : if $N(i)$ denotes the number of schemas of order i (with i equals 8, 16, 32 or 64) individual x belongs to, the fitness of x is the sum, for all orders i of 0 if $N(i) = 0$ and $i + N(i) \times .2$ otherwise (instead of $N(i) \times i$).

Table 1 shows the number of hits of the global optimum over 30 runs. The mean number of function evaluations needed to hit the optimum is given between parentheses for population size 200 and 500 (meaningless for population size 100).

Pop. Size	100		200		500	
Pressure	1.5	2.0	1.5	2	1.5	2
C. Length						
0	0	0	16 (110.200)	14 (112.400)	30 (255.000)	29 (210.000)
3	1	5	28 (42.400)	23 (44.600)	30 (57.700)	30 (39.240)
5	2	2	28 (36.240)	25 (59.230)	24 (62.920)	18 (79.490)
10	1	1	24 (62.920)	18 (79.490)	30 (54.100)	30 (76.100)

Table 1 : Number of hits (mean nb of evaluations needed)

Note that the results obtained without learning are not identical to those of Mitchell et al. [5], since they never found the optimum in 10^6 evaluations, for a population size of 2000. This difference is due to the fitness scaling mechanism : in [5], the number of offsprings of the best individual is set to the ratio between its fitness and the average fitness over the population.

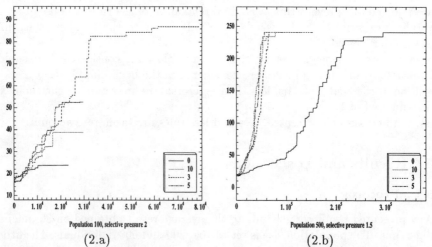

Population 100, selective pressure 2

(2.a)

Population 500, selective pressure 1.5

(2.b)

Figure 2 : Average best fitness function of the number of evaluations

Another criterion of performance is the evolution speed. Fig. 2 (a) plots the mean best fitness obtained for N nb of evaluations, for a population size 100, and a civilization length of 0, 3, 5 and 10. Fig. 2 (b) gives the results corresponding to a population size of 500. Of course, the number of function evaluations includes the number of experiments needed for learning.

5.3 Discussion

A first remark is that, as expected, civilized evolution (i.e. evolution + learning) discovers the global optimum more often than darwinian evolution (Table 1). Furthermore, when both evolutions do reach the optimum, civilized evolution requires less computational effort (Fig. 2.b). On the other hand, when neither evolution does not reach the optimum, civilized evolution goes higher (Fig. 2.a).

Second, it seems that civilized evolution needs a scaling factor smaller than darwinian evolution, of which we propose the following explanation. Selection ensures the survival of performant schemas through duplication of performant individuals. But in civilized evolution, no disruptive crossover is to fear : performant schemas are ensured to survive. Learning thus replaces to some extent, the individual selection by the crossover selection.

Last, we claim that our approach is more general than the heuristic proposed in [5] to overcome the difficulties of the Royal Road problem. Introns are zones of bits not contributing to the fitness [4] ; Mitchell et coll. modify the representation of the Royal Road by separating order-8 schemas by introns of length 24. The use of introns therefore significantly decreases the chances for a crossover to be disruptive : a crossover point may freely arise in an intron zone without disturbing any low-order schema in the current individuals.

However, this heuristic is not easy to use in real-world problems since it requires strong presumptions as to the localization of schemas. In the meanwhile, a learning approach does not require any such a priori information.

6 Conclusion

This paper investigates the coupling of GA and inductive learning according to the following scheme : a first period, called "darwinian evolution" only involves some generations of classical GA ; next periods, called "civilizations", are two-step processes :

• A learning step gathers examples of crossovers and observes their behavior on the current population. These examples enable inductive learning to build a set of rules characterizing relevant crossovers.

• Then, a civilized evolution step consists of M generations, where M is called "civilization length", that differs of classical GA in that that the crossovers selection is biased according to the current ruleset ; only crossovers relevant according to this ruleset, are retained.

In the end of a civilization, the population is significantly different from what it was in its beginning. Another learning phase thus open to a new civilization.

This approach asks a key question : inductive learning provides the evolution with an explicit memory — compared to the implicit memory consisting of the population itself. The implicit memory is safely (if not fast) optimized by GA and modifications of the fitness landscape can lead to powerful optimization strategies [10]. We may then fear explicit memory to disturb the evolution mechanism. Of course, our experiments only considered the artificial problem of the Royal Road, and many more experiments are needed to validate the scope, if any, of our approach.

However, at a very theoretical level, an argument on behalf of explicit memory could be the following. Implicit memory makes few differences between discovery and re-discovery. But this difference is of great importance for the *acceleration of evolution* : an anthropomorphic analogy of the explicit memory we propose to equip the evolution with, is the invention of writing ...

Further research will consider other problems, especially deceptive ones. We also plan to investigate the influence of the civilization length and of the scaling factor on the hybrid evolution we called "civilized" evolution.

References

1. Goldberg D.E. *Genetic algorithms in search, optimization and machine learning.* Addison Wesley, 1989.
2. D.E. Goldberg and Richardson J. Genetic algorithms with sharing for multi-modal function optimization. In J.J. Grefensfette, editor, *Proceedings of ICGA-87*, pages 41–49. Lawrence Erlbaum Associates, 1987.
3. Holland J. *Adaptation in natural and artificial systems.* University of Michigan Press, Ann Arbor, 1975.
4. J.R. Levenick. Inserting introns improves genetic algorithm success rate : Taking a cue from biology. In L. B. Booker R. K. Belew, editor, *Proceedings of ICGA-91*. Morgan Kaufmann, 1991.
5. Mitchell M. and Holland J.H. When will a genetic algorithm outperform hillclimbing ? In *Proceedings of ICGA-93*, 1993.
6. Z. Michalewicz. *Genetic Algorithms + Data Structures = Evolution Programs.* Springer Verlag, 1992.
7. R.S. Michalski. A theory and methodology of inductive learning. In R.S Michalski, J.G. Carbonell, and T.M. Mitchell, editors, *Machine Learning : an artificial intelligence approach*, volume 1. Morgan Kaufmann, 1983.
8. Forrest S. Mitchell M. and Holland J.H. The royal road for genetic algorithms : Fitness landscapes and ga performance. In F. J. Valera and P. Bourgine, editors, *Proceedings of the First European Conference on Artificial Life-93*, pages 245–254. MIT Press/Bradford Books, 1993.
9. N. J. Radcliffe. Equivalence class analysis of genetic algorithms. *Complex Systems*, 5:183–20, 1991.
10. Schoenauer M. and Xanthakis S. Constrained GA optimization. In Forrest S., editor, *Proceedings of ICGA-93*. Morgan Kaufmann, 1993.
11. M. Sebag. Using constraints to building version spaces. In Bergadano F. De Raedt L., editor, *Proceedings of ECML-94, European Conference on Machine Learning*. Springer Verlag, 1994.
12. Sebag M. and Schoenauer M. Incremental learning of rules and meta-rules. In Mooney R. Porter B., editor, *Proceedings of ICML-90, International Conference on Machine Learning*. Morgan Kaufmann, 1990.

Derivative Operators for Preference Predicate Evolution

David H. Lorenz*

Department of Computer Science,
Technion – Israel Institute of Technology

Abstract. This work deals with the problem of function learning by genetic algorithms where the function is used as a preference predicate. In such a case, learning the exact function is not necessary since any function that preserves the order induced by the target function is sufficient. The paper presents a methodology for solving the problem with genetic algorithms. We first consider the representation issues involved in learning such a function, and conclude that canonical representation, relative coding, and search restrictions, are required. We then show that the traditional homologous genetic operators are not appropriate for such learning, and introduce a new configurable analogous genetic operator, named derivative crossover. This operator works on the derivative of the chromosomes and is therefore suitable for preference predicate learning where only the relative values of the functions are important. We support our methodology by a set of experiments performed in the domain of continuous function learning and in the domain of evaluation-function learning for game-playing. The experiments show that indeed using derivative operators increases the speed of learning significantly.

1 Introduction

The problem of function learning has been studied by several researchers in the GA community [6, 9, 3] and is recognized as a difficult problem due to the large space of possible functions. In many cases, however, the learned function is used as a *preference predicate* [10] to compare the relative merit of objects, e.g., states in a search space [9]. In such cases, there is no need to learn the exact function. It is sufficient to learn any function that induces the same order over the set of compared objects.

This work studies the problem of learning functions by genetic algorithms under the following conditions:

1. The target function $f \in \mathcal{F}$ is needed for its use as a preference predicate over $Objects \times Objects$ for comparing objects.
2. A preference predicate over $\mathcal{F} \times \mathcal{F}$, that allows comparing two alternative functions, is supplied.
3. No other fitness measure of functions is available.

---

* E-mail address: david@cs.Technion.AC.IL

The hypothesis space is essentially a set of relations, where a function $f \in \mathcal{F}$ encodes a preorder $\sqsubseteq_f$ over *Objects* × *Objects* such that for all $x, y \in Objects$, $x \sqsubseteq_f y \iff f(x) \le f(y)$. For example, if $\mathbf{S} = \langle s_1, s_2, s_3, s_4, s_5 \rangle$ is an ordered set of objects, the function

$$f(s_i) = [2sin(2i)] \qquad (1)$$

as a preference predicate over $\mathbf{S} \times \mathbf{S}$ encodes the preorder $s_2 \sqsubseteq s_3 = s_5 \sqsubseteq s_1 = s_4$ depicted in Fig. 1.

The learning problem can be represented as an *ordered partitioning problem* as follows: Find and order the equivalent classes induced by the kernel of $\sqsubseteq_f$, f being the target function. The target ordered partition for (1) is:

$$\langle \{s_2\} \sqsubseteq \{s_3, s_5\} \sqsubseteq \{s_1, s_4\} \rangle \qquad (2)$$

Denoting each class in the target partition by a letter from an ordered alphabet $\langle \mathcal{C}, \le_{\mathcal{C}} \rangle$, the learning problem can be represented as the following *classification problem*: Find a classification function *class*: *Objects* → $\mathcal{C}$ such that $x \sqsubseteq_f y \iff$ $class(x) \le_{\mathcal{C}} class(y)$.

In the evolution of classification functions as preference predicates, we allow only a competitive fitness measure [1] to be used in guiding the search in the hypothesis space.

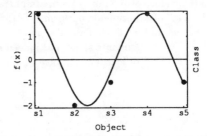

Fig. 1. $f(x) = [2sin(2x)]$ as a preference predicate over $\mathbf{S} \times \mathbf{S}$.

Outline. In the next section we discuss representational issues involved in applying genetic algorithms for such classification problems, considering design and coding decisions. We show that the straightforward vector representation introduces redundancy and therefore increases the size of the hypothesis space unnecessarily, and describe a method for reducing this problem. We proceed with showing in Sect. 3 that the traditional crossover operator is not appropriate for learning preference predicates, and suggest a new analogous configurable *derivative crossover* operator. In Sect. 4 we demonstrate the potential of this new methodology by performing experiments in function learning. Finally, in Sect. 5 we offer conclusions.

2 The Search Space

Each classification function can be represented by a vector over C^l, $l \in \mathbb{N}$, represented by a chromosome $\langle t_1, t_2, \ldots, t_l \rangle$, whose i^{th} element, $t_i \in C$, is the class assigned to the ith object. For example, setting $C = \langle a, b, c \rangle$, the target vector for (2) would be: $\langle c, a, b, c, b \rangle$.

2.1 Vector Representation

Using a vector representation requires two practical decisions:

1. Deciding on the size of the vector, i.e., the chromosome length.
2. Deciding on the size of the alphabet, i.e., the number of classes.

Since it is unreasonable to expect the chromosome length be the total number of objects, we assume that each object is associated with some index (attribute) $1 \leq i \leq l$, $i \in \mathbb{N}$, where l is the length of the chromosome. Therefore, the target preference-predicate is actually a double mapping: Two compared objects $x, y \in Objects$ are first mapped to their corresponding gene locations using a revealed ordering function known to the learner,

$$Index: Objects \rightarrow \mathbb{N} \tag{3}$$

Then $Index(x)$ and $Index(y)$ are mapped to two classes using the learned (concealed) function,

$$f: \mathbb{N} \overset{Chromosome}{\rightarrow} C \tag{4}$$

The object mapped to a higher class is preferred. For the remaining of this paper we assume $Dom(f)$ to be $Range(Index)$, and concentrate in evolving (4).

Deciding a priori on the number of classes, $n = |C|$, can lead to two types of problems. Let n_{optimal} be the size of the partition induced by the target preference-predicate. Either $n < n_{\text{optimal}}$ in which case the representation scheme is too restrictive, or $n > n_{\text{optimal}}$ in which case the representation scheme is too expressive. In both cases the same relation may have multiple representations. For example, setting $C = \langle a, b \rangle$, the target partition (2) cannot be expressed, and yet two distinct vectors might encode the same relation, e.g., $\langle a, a, a, a, a \rangle$ and $\langle b, b, b, b, b \rangle$. Setting $C = \langle a, b, c, d \rangle$, the four vectors $\langle c, a, b, c, b \rangle$, $\langle d, a, b, d, b \rangle$, $\langle d, a, c, d, c \rangle$, and $\langle d, b, c, d, c \rangle$, encode the same partition (2).

To prevent the scheme from being too restrictive, an infinite alphabet,

$$C = \langle \ldots, c_{-2}, c_{-1}, c_0, c_1, c_2, \ldots \rangle \tag{5}$$

is assumed. To prevent coding from being redundant in the sense that the number of possible encodings exceeds the number of classifiers, a canonical representation is used. A *canonical* classification function maps objects *on* a condensed finite subset $\hat{C} \subseteq C$, forcing the entire range of $\hat{C}$ to be used, and setting the first position in the vector to c_0. The vector $\langle d, a, b, d, b \rangle$, for example, is *not* in a canonical form since $\{a, b, d\}$ is not condensed. $\langle c, a, b, c, b \rangle$ is not canonical since its first gene is not 'a'. However, allowing negative gene values, $\langle a, -c, -b, a, -b \rangle$ is a canonical representation for (2). Having decided not cut down the number of classes in $\mathcal{C}$, we perform a qualitative reduction of the search space according to function smoothness characteristics, allowing the number of classes to be determined dynamically.

2.2 Smoothness

In order to make the search space tractable, it is often required to limit the search to a subspace. The supplied index mapping (3) already reduced the search space by partitioning the domain into equivalent classes of objects. Objects that are mapped to the same gene location are considered a priori equally desirable. We farther exploit the knowledge available by (3), and assume that objects that were mapped to adjacent gene locations have similar desirability, and thus should belong to similar classes. This assumption is incorporated by adding a restriction forcing successive genes to be mapped to neighboring or identical classes. The corresponding classification function (4) is hence assumed to be *smooth*.

Given the ordered alphabet (5), define $\|c_i - c_j\| \triangleq |i - j|$. The desired smoothness of the classification function may be imposed by keeping M-bounded slopes:

$$\forall x, y \in Dom(f), \quad \frac{\|f(x) - f(y)\|}{\|x - y\|} \leq M \tag{6}$$

If we denote

$$f'(x) = \frac{\|f(x) - f(x-1)\|}{\|x - (x-1)\|} = \frac{\|f(x) - f(x-1)\|}{1} \tag{7}$$

then having

$$\|f'(x)\| \leq M \quad \forall x \in Dom(f) \tag{8}$$

guarantees M-bounded slopes. Under the smoothness assumption, the search can be focuses on a subspace, $\mathcal{F}_M \subset \mathcal{F}$, of functions with an M-bounded derivative.

3 Configurable Derivative Operators

The traditional homologous-positional one-point crossover does not work well with the suggested representation. The number of classes is never increased, (except perhaps by mutation, which we ignore at this state), requiring the number of classed to be determined in advance. A produced offspring of canonical parents might not be in a canonical form, requiring post-production adjustments. Crossing of two smooth functions, might produce a non-smooth child, spending learning resources on candidates regarded a priori illegal [2]. Lastly, the order between two objects, which both parents agree on, might be scrambled in the child. For example, the two vectors $\langle a, b, c, d, d \rangle$ and $\langle a, a, a, b, c \rangle$ agree that $s_3 \sqsubseteq s_4$. However, $s_3 \sqsupseteq s_4$ in the vector $\langle a, b, c, b, c \rangle$, obtained by crossing these vectors after position 3.

3.1 Motivation

Generalization has an important role in learning systems [8]. Relative operators, as opposed to absolute operators, allows generalization to evolve more naturally. The idea presented is to preserve the order between adjacent genes of the parents. In the above crossover example, for instance, the parents vectors have genes' order $\langle \bullet \sqsubseteq \bullet \sqsubseteq \bullet \sqsubseteq \bullet = \bullet \rangle$ and $\langle \bullet = \bullet = \bullet \sqsubseteq \bullet \sqsubseteq \bullet \rangle$ respectively, thus $\langle \bullet \sqsubseteq \bullet \sqsubseteq \bullet \sqsupseteq \bullet \sqsubseteq \bullet \rangle$ is not a legitimate child.

Example 1. Suppose our domain includes five objects, $\{s_1, s_2, s_3, s_4, s_5\}$, and that the target partition is $\langle \{s_1\}, \{s_2, s_3\}, \{s_4, s_5\} \rangle$. Assume that the following two promising preference predicates have emerged. A chromosome $\langle a, b, b, b, b \rangle$ which succeeded in capturing the precedence of objects s_2, s_3, s_4, s_5 over the object s_1, encoding the partition $\langle \{s_1\}, \{s_2, s_3, s_4, s_5\} \rangle$, and a chromosome $\langle a, a, a, b, b \rangle$ which failed yet to distinguish between s_1 and s_2 but managed to learn an equally significant precedence of objects s_4, s_5 over object s_1, s_2, s_3, and encodes the partition $\langle \{s_1, s_2, s_3\}, \{s_4, s_5\} \rangle$. A positional crossover after position 2, would produce the undesirable chromosome

$$\text{Crossover}(\langle \overbrace{a, b}^{I}, \underbrace{b, b, b}_{II}\rangle, \langle \underbrace{a, a}_{III}, \overbrace{a, b, b}^{IV}\rangle) = \langle \overbrace{a, b}^{I}, \overbrace{a, a, b}^{IV}\rangle$$

encoding the partition $\langle \{s_1, s_3\}, \{s_2, s_4, s_5\} \rangle$. On the other hand, applying an analogous crossover [4] that preserves the *relations* between two neighboring genes rather than their absolute values, could produce the chromosome

$$\text{Crossover}(\langle \overbrace{\bullet \sqsubseteq \bullet}^{I} \underbrace{= \bullet = \bullet = \bullet}_{II}\rangle, \langle \underbrace{\bullet = \bullet}_{III} \overbrace{= \bullet \sqsubseteq \bullet = \bullet}^{IV}\rangle) = \langle \overbrace{\bullet \sqsubseteq \bullet}^{I} = \bullet \overbrace{\sqsubseteq \bullet = \bullet}^{IV}\rangle$$

i.e., $\langle a, b, b, c, c \rangle$, combining this way both parents' information and automatically introducing a third new class, 'c'.

3.2 Derivative Crossover

Let $\mathcal{F}$ be the set of functions $[0, 1] \to \mathbb{R}$. The traditional one-point Crossover can be view as an operator that, given a random crossing point $p \in_R [0, 1]$, returns an operator Crossover_p over $\mathcal{F} \times \mathcal{F}$. Let $f, g \in \mathcal{F}$ be two functions. $\text{Crossover}_p(f, g)$ returns the function combined out of f's part over the interval $[0, p]$ and g's part over the interval $(p, 1]$. For simplicity we assume only one offspring per crossover operation, and consider the other offspring to be $\text{Crossover}_p(g, f)$.

Using a step function $\sigma_p(x) = \begin{cases} 0 & x \le p \\ 1 & x > p \end{cases}$ and using a *lambda expression* $\lambda v.e$, to denote a function whose result is the value of e in an environment where v stands for the argument of the function, we can be express $\text{Crossover}_p(f, g)$ as:

$$\text{Crossover}_p(f, g) = \lambda x. (1 - \sigma_p(x)) f(x) + \sigma_p(x) g(x) \tag{9}$$

The *derivative crossover* performs one-point crossover on the derivatives of the two functions, and then integrates the result to produce the new offspring:

$$Der.\text{Crossover}_p(f, g) = \lambda x. \int_0^x \text{Crossover}_p(f', g') \tag{10}$$

This can be rewritten as:

$$Der.\text{Crossover}_p(f, g) = \lambda x. (1 - \sigma_p(x)) \int_0^x f'(x) + \sigma_p(x) \left(f(p) + \int_p^x g'(x) \right) =$$
$$= \lambda x. (1 - \sigma_p(x)) f(x) + \sigma_p(x) (g(x) + f(p) - g(p)) \tag{11}$$

Both the standard crossover and the derivative crossover can be seen as special cases of a general family of derivative operators defined as follows. Let ρ be a function $\mathbb{R} \to \mathbb{R}$. A derivative crossover using ρ is defined by:

$$Der.\text{Crossover} : (\mathbb{R} \to \mathbb{R}) \to ([0, 1] \to (\mathcal{F} \times \mathcal{F} \to \mathcal{F}))$$

$$Der.\text{Crossover}[\rho]_p(f, g) = \lambda x. (1 - \sigma_p(x)) f(x) + \sigma_p(x) (g(x) + \rho(f(p) - g(p))) \tag{12}$$

The function ρ determines the method of combination at the crossing point, as illustrated in Fig. 2. With $\rho \equiv 0$, (12) become the traditional crossover (9). Using the identity function $\rho(x) = x$, (12) is simply (11). There are many other meaningful combinations worth considering, e.g., $\rho(x) = x + sign(x)$.

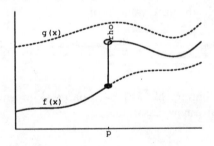

Fig. 2. Derivative Crossover at position p, a schematic view of (12).

The *derivative mutation* performs conventional mutation to the function's derivative, and then integrates the result to produce the mutated offspring:

$$Der.\text{Mutation}_p(f) = \lambda x. \int_0^x \text{Mutation}_p(f') \tag{13}$$

It is interesting to note that (13) may also be seen as a special case of (12), by setting $\rho(x) = x + \mu$, i.e., $Der.\text{Crossover}[\lambda x. x + \mu]_p(f, f)$, μ picked at random. Equation (12) is also applicable for discrete functions, as demonstrated in the next example.

Example 2. Performing a derivative crossover after position 3 of two chromosomes of length 5 over the ordered alphabet $\langle \ldots, -c, -b, a, b, c, \ldots \rangle$ might be:

$$Der.\text{Crossover} \, [\lambda x.x]_3 \, (\langle a, b, c, b, c \rangle, \langle a, b, b, c, d \rangle) =$$
$$= \langle a, b, c, c + (c - b), d + (c - b) \rangle =$$
$$= \langle a, b, c, d, e \rangle$$

Similarly, performing a derivative mutation after position 2 might result in:

$$Der.\text{Mutation}_2 \, (\langle a, b, c, b, c \rangle) =$$
$$= Der.\text{Crossover} [\lambda x.x - 2]_2 \, (\langle a, b, c, b, c \rangle, \langle a, b, c, b, c \rangle) =$$
$$= \langle a, b, c + (0 - 2), b + (0 - 2), c + (0 - 2) \rangle =$$
$$= \langle a, b, a, -b, a \rangle$$

4 Comparative Results

Learning quality and convergence rates were compared between the traditional scheme and the proposed derivative frame. The traditional operators were tested with different sizes of alphabet. The derivative operators were applied on different subspaces $\mathcal{F}_M$, using an infinite alphabet.

The experiments were carried out in the following manner: the population size was kept fixed at 64, the number of generations was 100. Fitness values were assigned according to overall performance. Crossover and mutation were applied with a low probability of 0.1. Rank selection was used.

4.1 Continuous Functions

In a set of experiments, preference predicates were created from continuous functions. The system ability to reveal the concealed function was tested. For this purpose a preference predicate *"better than"* over pairs of preference predicates was defined as follows:

1. Preference predicate $\mathcal{P}$ is said to be *better than* preference predicate $\mathcal{Q}$, if it *wins* more matches in a tournament among the set of competing preference predicates.
2. Preference predicate $\mathcal{P}$ is said to *win* a match against preference predicate $\mathcal{Q}$, if preference predicate $\mathcal{P}$ correctly orders more out of n random pairs of objects, competing against preference predicate $\mathcal{Q}$, letting $n \to \infty$.

In each generation a full tournament was conducted with the chromosomes as the classifiers applied. Two compared chromosomes were independently used to order 500 randomly generated pairs of points. The chromosome that had more correctly ordered pairs $\langle x, y \rangle$, won the match. An ordered pair $\langle x, y \rangle$ was considered correct if $x \sqsubseteq_f y$, where f is the concealed function. The precise identity or quantity of correctly ordered pairs was not revealed to the learner, just as in a real object-space situation.

Figure 3 shows best chromosomes evolved with different genetic schemes for the target function $f(x) = 10 \left[\sin \frac{2\pi x}{50}\right]$. Traditional operators were applied with alphabet sizes 6,12,24, and $Der.\mathsf{Crossover}[\lambda x.x]$ operator was applied over $\mathcal{F}_1$, $\mathcal{F}_2$, $\mathcal{F}_3$. Points represent genes' values. Solid lines represent the target function. Using derivative operators achieved better preference predicates in less generations. Similar results were obtained with more complex functions, as well as with longer chromosomes.

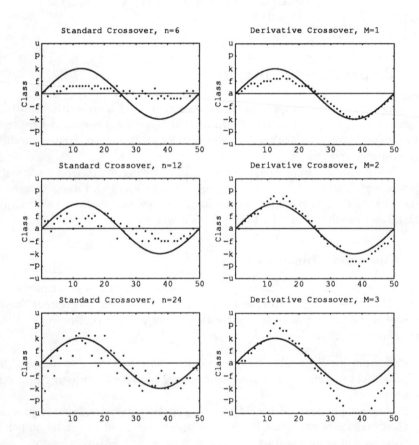

Fig. 3. Best chromosomes using traditional crossover with different alphabet sizes (n) on the left, compared with best chromosomes using derivative crossover over $\mathcal{F}_M$ with different smoothness restrictions (M) on the right, as evolved for the target function $f(x) = 10 \left[\sin \frac{2\pi x}{50}\right]$ after 100 generations using chromosomes of length 50.

4.2 Game Playing

In a second series of experiments the system was tested in a real state-space condition. The domain of game playing was chosen, and the task was to learn the best evaluation function for Checkers, based on a single attribute [7]. Figure 4 shows the performance of best individuals of the first 40 generation, tested against an external player. The benefit of derivative learning compared to learning with the standard genetic operator, is especially important in this domain since calculating the fitness measure requires considerable computing resources.

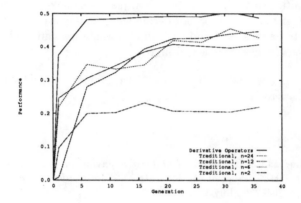

Fig. 4. Learning using traditional operators with different alphabet sizes (n) compared with learning using derivative operators on $\mathcal{F}_1$, in evolving an evaluation function for the game of Checkers.

5 Concluding Remarks

In this paper we study the use of genetic algorithms for learning preference predicates, as follows.

1. We offer a methodology of learning the derivatives of a function instead of the function itself.
2. We introduce a family of configurable *derivative crossover* operators that preserves the relativeness among neighboring genes.

Canonical representation and smoothing restrictions allowed better exploit of the learning resources in the genetic search. In a series of experiments performed with the new operators, the program acquired arbitrary continuous functions and an evaluation function for the game of Checkers, in significant speedup.

In contrast to the traditional operators, the derivative operators are more suitable for order dependent domains. They preserves canonical representation and bounded-slops, and allows the number of classes to be dynamically changed. Gene values are allowed to be negative. Rather than a quantitative limitation of the alphabet, a qualitative smoothness characteristics may be imposed. $\mathcal{F}_M$ is closed under the $Der.\textsf{Crossover}\,[\lambda x.x]$ operator. Objects which both parents agree on their order relative to the cutting position, are kept in the same order in the produced offspring, preserving relativeness of genes rather than absolute values.

An important feature of the derivative operators, yet not common among analogous operators [4, 5], is their compatibility with traditional positional operators. Moreover, different kinds of derivative operators can be applied with different probabilities on the same population, just as crossover and mutation are normally used. A potential user can decide what analogous derivative information is wished to be preserved and with what probability, and apply appropriate derivative crossover operators accordingly.

Acknowledgments I would like to thank Yuval Davidor and Shaul Markovitch for inspiring discussions.

References

1. P. J. Angeline and J. B. Pollack. Competitive envinments evolve better solutions for complex tasks. *Proc. of the* 5th *International Conference on Genetic Algorithms*, pages 264–270, July 17–21, 1993.
2. H. J. Antonisse. A grammer-based genetic algorithm. In G. J. Rawlins, editor, *Foundations of Genetic Algorithms*. Morgan Kaufmann, 1991.
3. M. F. Bramlette. Initialization, mutation and selction methods in genetic algorithms for function optimization. In *Proc. of the Fourth International Conference on Genetic Algorithms*, pages 100–107, San Diego, CA, 1991.
4. Y. Davidor. Analogous crossover. In *Proc. of the* 3rd *International Conference on Genetic Algorithms*, pages 98–103. Morgan Kaufman, 1989.
5. B. R. Fox and M. B. McMahon. Genetic operators for sequencing problems. In G. J. Rawlins, editor, *Foundations of Genetic Algorithms*, pages 284–300. Morgan Kaufmann, 1991.
6. D. E. Goldberg. *GENETIC ALGORITHMS in Search, Optimazation and Machine Learning*. Addison-Wesley, Reading, MA, 1989.
7. D. H. Lorenz and S. Markovitch. Derivative evaluation function learning using genetic operators. In *Games: Planning and Learning, Papers from the 1993 Fall Symposium*, Raleigh, North Carolina, Oct. 22–24, 1993. American Association for Artificial Intelligence, AAAI Press, Menlo Park, California. Technical Report FS9302.
8. T. M. Mitchell. Generalization as search. *Artificial Intelligence*, 18:203 – 226, 1982.
9. L. Rendell. Induction as optimization. *IEEE Transactions on Systems, Man, and Cybernetics*, 20(2):326–338, Mar 1990.
10. P. E. Utgoff and S. Saxena. Learning a preference predicate. In *Proceedings of the* 4th *International Workshop on Machine Learning*, pages 115–121. Morgan Kaufman, 1987.

Adaptive Crossover Using Automata

Tony White
Bell-Northern Research
P.O. Box 3511 Station C
Ottawa, Ontario, CANADA K1Y 4H7
arpw@bnr.ca

Franz Oppacher
School of Computer Science
Carleton University
Ottawa, Ontario, CANADA, K1S 5B6
oppacher@scs.carleton.ca

Abstract. Genetic Algorithms (GAs) have traditionally required the specification of a number of parameters that control the evolutionary process. In the classical model, the mutation and crossover operator probabilities are specified before the start of a GA run and remain unchanged; a so-called static model. This paper extends the conventional representation by using automata in order to allow the adaptation of the crossover operator probability as the run progresses in order to facilitate schema identification and reduce schema disruption. Favourable results have been achieved for a wide range of function minimization problems and these are described.

1.   Introduction

Genetic Algorithms (GAs) have shown themselves to be extremely useful in solving a wide range of optimization problems. Their considerable power arises from the characteristics of survival of the fittest and adaptation achieved through mixing of genetic information using operators such as crossover and mutation. The power of a GA has been analyzed in terms of the Schema Theorem [Holland, 1975] and the Building Block Hypothesis [Goldberg, 1989]. In the schema analysis, search is shown to proceed through identification of highly fit schema, and that such schema are preferentially propagated during the reproductive phase of a GA.

In a classical GA, learning occurs at one level. Namely, object variables change under the influence of the mutation and crossover operators and are guided by selection. Neither the operators, nor the probabilities with which they are applied, change as the algorithm searches for an optimal solution. However, it has been shown that other search mechanisms, such as evolutionary strategies, benefit considerably by being able to adapt control parameters as the search proceeds [Schwefel, 1987].

In the classical GA model, the probability of identifying, and successfully propagating, highly fit schema is proportional to their length. Further, the classical model does not take advantage of information arising from the crossover process;

namely, whether offspring are more or less fit than their parents and what genetic material was exchanged.

The problem, then, in proposing improvements to the classical GA model is to find mechanisms for improved identification of highly fit schema and to reduce the probability with which such schema will be disrupted as GA search proceeds. Stated another way, the probability with which combinations of bits should be exchanged during the crossover phase of a GA should vary as highly-fit schema emerge in the population. This paper proposes an extension to the classical GA wherein the probability of exchanging any particular bit is carried along with the classical bit string representation and varies based upon whether offspring are fitter than one or both of their parents.

This paper consists of five remaining sections. In section two, a review of previous work in the area of adaptive GAs is provided. In section three, a brief introduction to Automata Theory is given. Section four describes the adaptive uniform crossover operator. Section five presents results when using the adaptive uniform crossover operator in a wide range of function optimization experiments. Finally, section six presents the conclusions arising from this work.

2.   Adaptive Operators and Genetic Algorithms

This section provides a brief review of previous work in the area of adaptive GAs. Previous work in this area has included adaptive operator selection [Davis, 1989], adaption in the probability of crossover [Schaffer, 1987] and mutation [Bäck, 1991], [Fogarty, 1989] and several GA parameters using fuzzy techniques [Lee, Takagi, 1993]. In the following two sections, we briefly review the work of Davis and Bäck.

2.1   Adaptive Operator Selection

In the classical GA, the number of operators that can manipulate the bit string is fixed, and the probability with which they can be applied is constant. Further, it is also the case that the operators are applied in a given sequence. It was Davis' [Davis, 1989] observation that different operators are generally required at different stages of the search process and that the GA should adapt and be able to select which operators to apply and in what order. The idea is that adaptation of operator probabilities takes place based upon the performance of the operator's offspring. In short, if the operator produces offspring with a fitness which is superior to that of the parents, then the fitness of the operator should increase. However, if the operator produces offspring with a fitness which is inferior to that of the parents, then the fitness of that operator should decrease. This adaptive operator selection is relevant to this paper in that it *incorporates feedback from the environment* in the adaptive process.

2.2 Adaptive Mutation

An adaptive mutation operator proposed in [Bäck, 1991] encodes mutation operator probabilities directly into the genetic representation of the individuals. Further, mutation rates are also subject to mutation and selection in that they undergo evolution as well as the object variables. Each bit position has an associated mutation probability. The mutation mechanism works by first mutating the mutation rates p_i with mutation probabilities p_i and then using the mutated probabilities p_i' to mutate the object variables themselves. This process is directed by the selection process, which selects good object variable information as appropriate strategy parameter settings. This adaptive operator is relevant to this paper for two reasons. Firstly, the *representation is extended* in order to encode mutation operator probability on a per-bit basis. Secondly, *the representation acts on itself* in order to change the values of the operator probabilities themselves.

3. Automata Theory

Learning automata have been used to model biological learning systems and to determine the optimal action an environment offers. Learning is achieved by the automaton interacting with the environment and processing its responses to the actions that are chosen.

The automaton learning process can be described as follows. The automaton is offered a set of actions by the environment with which it interacts and must choose one of those actions. When an action is chosen, the automaton is either rewarded or penalized by the environment with a certain probability. A learning automaton is one which learns the optimal action i.e. the action which has the minimum penalty probability, and eventually chooses this action more frequently than other actions.

A variable structure stochastic automaton (VSSA) learns by employing a probability updating rule such that the action probability vector at the (n+1)st time instant is computed using the probability vector at the nth time instant in conjunction with the automaton environment interaction at the nth time instant. Hence, if $\mathbf{P}(n)$ is the action probability vector at time n, the VSSA is fully defined by specifying a function H such that: $\mathbf{P}(n + 1) = \mathbf{H}(\mathbf{P}(n), \alpha(n), \beta(n))$, where $\alpha(n)$ is the set of possible actions and $\beta(n)$ is the reward-penalty function.

Studies have centered around two classes of function H, both being linear. In the first class, H is a continuous function allowing $P(n)$ to take any value between 0 and 1. In the second class, H allows $P(n)$ to take a discrete number of values in the range 0 to 1. In the discrete case, linearity is taken to mean that the increments in probability are all equal. This latter class of automata, due to Oommen, have been analyzed using Markov chains, have finite expected convergence time, and appear to have superior accuracy when compared to their continuous counterparts [Oommen, Hansen, 1984].

The automaton of interest in this paper is the two action, discretized linear reward-penalty (DL_{RP}) automaton. The DL_{RP} automaton has N+1 states where N is an even integer. The automaton has a set of states $S = \{s_0, s_1,..., s_N\}$. and associated with the state s_i is the probability i/N that represents the probability of choosing action a_1. Hence the probability of choosing action a_2 is given by $(1-i/N)$. As any one of the action probabilities completely defines the vector of action probabilities, it is possible to consider just $p_1(n)$ with no loss of generality.

In the context of this paper, the $p_1(n)$ correspond to the probability of performing crossover at a specific bit location and $p_2(n)$ is the probability of not performing crossover at that same bit position. The environmental response is determined by the evaluation of the fitness function for a given offspring - a reward being given for a fitter individual, a penalty for an inferior offspring.

4.   Adaptive Crossover Using Automata

GA search has been improved by modifying the search parameters dynamically. This has been achieved by extending the problem representation in order to encode the search parameter and by providing feedback from the environment in order to reward successful operator action. Related work in this area includes [Syswerda, 1992], [Spears, 1992] and [Lee, 1993].

The adaptive uniform crossover (AUX) operator is an extension of the uniform crossover operator [Syswerda, 1989]. The basic idea of the AUX operator is to identify groups of bits within the bit string that should be kept together when crossover occurs. Stated another way, we wish to learn from previous crossover operations in order to minimize highly fit schema disruption in future crossover operations.

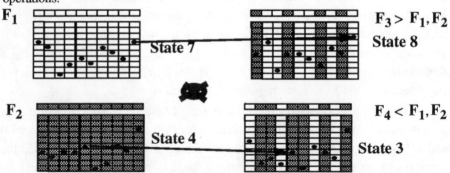

Figure 1   Schematic of adaptive uniform crossover operator

In Figure 1, the basic bit string representation is augmented at each bit position with an automaton, shown as a vertical set of states. The dot associated with each automaton indicates the current state of that automaton. Each state of the automaton maps to a probability of crossover value for that bit string location. State changes occur as a result of feedback from the environment; in this case the environment is provided by the change in value of the fitness of the offspring when compared to the parents.

The principle used here is that bits which were kept together during crossover, and generated superior offspring, should be kept together in future crossover operations. Similarly, bits which were kept together during crossover, and generated inferior offspring, should not be kept together in future crossover operations. Finally, bits which were kept together during crossover, and generated offspring with no discernible fitness change, may or may not be kept together in future crossover operations.

The algorithm used for updating automaton state can be described as:

```
If offspring fitness > Father's fitness then reward bits
which came from Father with probability p_superiorReward.
If offspring fitness > Mother's fitness then reward bits
which came from Mother with probability p_superiorReward.
If offspring fitness < Father's fitness then penalize bits
which came from Father with probability p_inferiorPenalty.
If offspring fitness < Mother's fitness then penalize bits
which came from Mother with probability p_inferiorPenalty.
If offspring fitness = Father's fitness then reward bits
which came from Father with probability p_sameReward or penal-
ize bits which came from Father with probability p_samePenalty.
If offspring fitness = Mother's fitness then reward bits
which came from Mother with probability p_sameReward or penal-
ize bits which came from Mother with probability p_samePenalty.
```

Subject to the limitation $p_{sameReward} + p_{samePenalty} \leq 1$.

A reward is given to an automaton if its fitness exceeds that of a parent by the floating point tolerance value, $f_{tolerance}$. Similarly, an automaton is penalized if its fitness is less than that of a parent by the floating point tolerance, $f_{tolerance}$. Actually, with a non-zero $f_{tolerance}$ value, a dead-band controller has been included in the system. A reward implies that the automaton moves from state i to state i+1. Similarly, a penalty implies that the automaton moves from state i to state i-1. If the automaton is in state n prior to a reward, nothing happens. If the automaton is in state zero prior to a penalty being applied, nothing happens.

From the above algorithm it can be seen that all bits will be rewarded if the fitness of an offspring exceeds the fitness of both of its parents. If the fitness exceeds that of one parent, but is inferior to that of the other, certain bits will be rewarded while others will be penalized. The rewarding and penalizing of an offspring in the situation where its fitness is equal to that of one or both parents is useful in preventing stagnation of the crossover probability at a non-optimal value. The environment gives us incomplete information, in that in certain situations bits will be rewarded which were not the direct cause of improvement. Similarly, for the same reason, bits may be penalized in error. However, over many trials the tendency is for more correct information to be imparted by the environment than incorrect information.

The AUX operator is also modified from that used in the case of the Syswerda uniform operator. In the case of the uniform crossover operator, a random integer from the set $\{0,1\}$ is chosen. If the result is 1, the bits are exchanged; otherwise nothing happens. With the AUX operator, the probability of crossover for the two parents is first obtained using $p^i_{xovr} = P^i(s_i)$ where P^i is the function mapping automaton state to a probability value and s_i is the state of the automaton associated with the ith bit. The function P^i, being a probability, is constrained to lie in $(0,1)$. It is a discrete function, but could be represented by a noisy function if a degree of uncertainty needs to be added to the automaton. The crossover at a particular bit occurs if the following condition prevails: $\sqrt{p\,(mother)^i_{xovr} \cdot p\,(father)^i_{xovr}} \geq rnd\,(0,1)$.

Namely, if the geometric mean of the adaptive crossover probability values exceeds a randomly generated probability value from the uniform distribution, bit exchange occurs. As the geometric mean of two numbers is less than the arithmetic mean, it implies that the adaptive crossover operator is more conservative - exchanging fewer bits - when using the geometric mean.

With the extended representation chosen, the action of mutation now has an effect upon not only the object variable bit but also the associated automaton. If we take mutation of a bit to be the flipping of that bit, then when toggled, the automaton is affected because the automaton state is a function of the value of the bit at that location. If the bit is flipped, logically we lose all information on the state of the automaton and it should therefore be reset. Being essentially unknown, the state is set to a random value.

5.   Experimental setup and results overview

The adaptive uniform crossover operator was tested against all functions in the function test bed - f_1 to f_{24}. The results were compared using equivalent GA search parameters to the uniform crossover operator. A modified version of GENEsYs[1] was

---

1. GENEsYs was obtained from Dr. Bäck (baeck@ls11.informatik.uni-dort-mund.de).

used for all experimental runs. In all GA runs, the same basic parameters were chosen. These are shown in Table 1:

Table 1   Common experimental parameters

Variable	Meaning	Value
P_s	Population size	50
P_m	Probability of mutation (per bit)	0.001
N_e	Number of experiments	100
N_t	Number of trials per experiment	10,000
S	Selection mechanism	Roulette wheel
Coding	How object variable is encoded	Gray coding
l	Length of the object variable..	l = 32n (n being the number of objective function variables)

The crossover probability for the uniform crossover operator was set to 0.5. The geometric form of the crossover exchange operator was used to decide whether bitwise crossover was to take place and P^i had the functional form: $P^i(s) = s/n; s = 0, ..., n$. By choosing this particular functional form, the automata become examples of the DL_{RP} automaton. Initial states were set randomly. The values of the various automata probabilities are shown in Table 2:

Table 2   Adaptive crossover operator parameters

Variable	Meaning	Value
$P_{superiorReward}$	Probability with which an automaton will be rewarded if the offspring is fitter than the parent.	1.0
$P_{inferiorPenalty}$	Probability with which an automaton will be penalized if the offspring is less fit than the parent.	1.0
$P_{samePenalty}$	Probability with which an automaton will be penalized if the offspring is as fit but no fitter than the parent.	0.0
$P_{sameReward}$	Probability with which an automaton will be rewarded if the offspring is as fit but no fitter than the parent.	0.0
$f_{tolerance}$	Floating point tolerance used to decide whether an offspring is more or less fit than its parent(s).	0.0

In the two charts which follow in section 5.1, the best-at-trial[1] fitness is plotted. The y axis is the difference in fitness values of the best solution in the population between the adaptive and non-adaptive runs. The x axis is the trial number. *Therefore, if the curve falls below the x axis, the adaptive run is superior to the non-adaptive run[2].*

---

1. The best-at-trial fitness is the minimum fitness value across the population.
2. As the function optimization problems are minimization problems.

5.1 Discussion

In this study, *naive parameter settings for the various automaton probabilities were chosen in order to test the robustness of the adaptive approach* with the purpose of the study being to achieve better solutions in a given number of trials. Similarly, a simple, linear probability mapping function was chosen. Experiments for 23 functions were performed. Of these, 13 show improvement, 6 show no discernible improvement and 4 are actually worse. While the improvements seen in certain functions are small, in others, such as f_3, f_{11} and f_{17}, they are considerable and statistically significant. Certainly, the belief that more "good" than "bad" information is provided by the environment seems to be supported by the empirical results that the AUX operator is able to produce better solutions than by using the uniform operator alone.

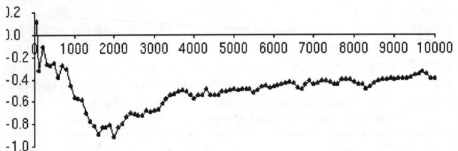

Figure 2 f_3 difference between non-adaptive and adaptive runs

In the above chart, the adaptive run is *initially* worse than the non-adaptive run, due to the fact that the information being fed back from the environment is actually very poor - we are exchanging too many bits in the crossover operation and schema are not being correctly identified. As the run progresses, the value of information being fed back from the environment improves and the DL_{RP} automata converge. *That is, subsets of bits which should be exchanged during crossover begin to emerge.* The value of the feedback from the environment evidently increases rapidly as the adaptive run is superior to the non-adaptive run beyond 200 trials..

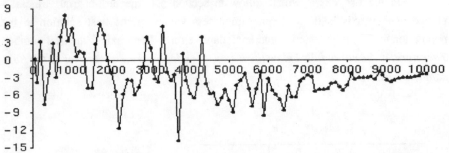

Figure 3 f_{11} difference between non-adaptive and adaptive runs

Figure 3 again clearly shows the same pattern of improvment as seen in Figure 2. In this case, the value of the feedback from the environment is *considerable*, leading to sizeable differences between the non-adaptive and adaptive runs. In the above chart, the adaptive run is clearly superior to the non-adaptive after approximately 4500 trials and is better even at convergence. *So, although the feedback from the environment is initially poor, the automata recover in order to increase the joint access probabilities for bits responsible for improved fitness*

A problem of *stagnation* can occur. The stagnation problem occurs when the automata are in states which map to very high or very low probability values. If, in these situations, fitness improvements are not seen in the offspring, no changes to the automata will be observed and the tendency will be for the same bits to be exchanged in subsequent trials. Obviously, the model described earlier can deal with this problem by setting the $p_{sameReward}$ and $p_{samePenalty}$ probabilities to be non-zero. Similarly, setting $p_{superiorReward}$ or $p_{inferiorPenalty}$ to be values other than one would ensure that the stagnation problem could be monitored by not always rewarding superior or penalizing inferior offspring. By making the various automata transition probabilities non-deterministic we are making the statement that the environment is providing noisy information, which we should treat accordingly.

Using the naive probability settings described earlier, we can see that the feedback from the environment can deceive the automata early in a GA run. This tends to indicate that gradually increasing the reward/penalty probabilities might improve algorithm performance. It should also be noted that in the random initial population, approximately one half of the bits are exchanged during crossover. This is an extremely large number of bits, containing potentially many schema. We would expect that the automata would perform better when fewer bits are exchanged. This implies that initializing the automata such that significantly fewer bits are exchanged early in the run might improve performance as the schema being identified would be smaller.

6. Conclusions and future work

This paper has proposed an adaptive crossover operator (AUX), requiring extensions to the basic representation for any problem wherein an automaton encodes the probability that a given bit will be exchanged with the other parent under the action of the modified uniform crossover operator. From the large number of experiments performed, it has been concluded that the basic adaptive crossover operator shows promise. However, more experiments with other automata parameters are needed.

This paper has considered automata of a single class, whose probability updating rules are discrete in nature. However, the probability updating rules might be modified in such a way as to make them continuous - perhaps depending upon the degree to which the child is inferior or superior to the parent. Another alternative might be to replace the DL_{RP} automaton with the MDL_{RP} automaton as the latter exhibits superior properties in "noiser" environments.

7. References

[Bäck, 1991] Bäck, T., *Self Adaptation in Genetic Algorithms*, Proceedings of the First European Conference on Artificial Life, December 11-13, 1991, MIT Press, pgs 263-271.

[Davis, 1989] Davis, L., *Adapting Operator Probabilities in Genetic Algorithms*, in Proceedings of the Third International Conference on Genetic Algorithms, Morgan Kaufmann Publishers, Inc., Los Altos, CA, pgs.61-69, 1989.

[Goldberg, 1989] Goldberg, D.E., *Genetic Algorithms in Search, Optimization and Machine Learning*, Addison-Wesley, Reading, MA, 1989.

[Holland, 1975] Holland, J., *Adaptation in Natural and Artificial Systems*, University of Michigan Press, 1975.

[Lee, 1993] Lee, M. A., and Takagi, H., *Dynamic Control of Genetic Algorithms using Fuzzy Logic Techniques*, in Proceedings of the Fifth International Conference on Genetic Algorithms, Morgan Kaufmann Publishers, Inc., Los Altos, CA, pgs.76-83, 1993.

[Oommen, Hansen, 1984] Oommen, B.J., and Hansen, E.R., *The asymptotic optimality of two action discetized reward-inaction learning automata*. IEEE Trans. on Systems, Man and Cybernetics. SMC-14, pgs 542-545, 1984.

[Schaffer, 1987] Schaffer, J.D., *An Adaptive Crossover Distribution Mechanism for Genetic Algorithms*, Proceedings of the Second International Conference on Genetic Algorithms, Lawrence Erlbaum, Hillsdale, NJ, pgs. 36-40, 1987.

[Schwefel, 1987] Schwefel, H-P., *Collective phenomena in evolutionary systems*. In 31st Annual Meeting of the International Society for General System Research, Budapest, pgs 1025-1033, June, 1987.

[Spears, 1992] Spears, W. M., *Adapting Crossover in a Genetic Algorithm*, Navy Center for Applied Research in Artificial Intelligence, Naval Research Laboratory Report, #AIC-92-025.

[Syswerda, 1989] Syswerda, G., *Uniform crossover in genetic algorithms*, In Proceedings of the Third International Conference on Genetic Algorithms, Morgan Kaufmann Publishers, Inc. pgs. 2-9, 1989.

[Syswerda, 1992] Syswerda, G., *Simulated Crossover in Genetic Algorithms*, In Foundations of Genetic Algorithms II (FOGA-II), Morgan Kaufmann Publishers, Inc pgs. 239-255.

Controlling Dynamics of GA through Filtered Evaluation Function

Hidenori SAKANASHI, Keiji SUZUKI and Yukinori KAKAZU

Dept. of Precision Eng., Faculty of Eng., Hokkaido Univ.,
North-13, West-8, Sapporo, 060, JAPAN,
Tel: +81-11-706-6445, Fax: +81-11-700-5060
E-mail: {sakana, suzuki, kakazu}@hupe.hokudai.ac.jp

Abstract. As a function optimizer or a search procedure, GAs are very powerful and have some advantages. Fundamental research concerning the internal behavior of GAs has highlighted their limitations as regards search performances for what are called GA-hard problems. The reason for these difficulties seems to be that GAs generate insufficient strategies for the convergence of populations . To overcome this problem, an extended GA, which we name the filtering-GA, that adopts the method of changing the effect of the objective function on the dynamics of the GA, is proposed.

1. Introduction

As a function optimizer or a search procedure, GAs are very powerful and have some advantages [Goldberg89]. Through multi-point search using the population, they can perform robust search, and have been applied to many fields. Moreover, fundamental research has been made concerning their internal behavior. This, however, has revealed the limitations as regards search performance. This kind of problems singled out by such research are known as *GA-hard problems*. In this paper, the GA-hard problems are considered to be types of problem which the simple GA can't easily solve, and include non-stationary problems, problems which have an enormous number of local optima, deceptive problems [Deb93], and so on. Whether they are GA-hard or not, they may be optimized if there is some prior knowledge, but this situation never occurs as it is not necessary to use GAs for problems whose characteristics are already known.

The reason for difficulties seems to be that, for the convergence of populations, GAs generate insufficient strategies. To overcome this problem, in this paper, we proposed an extended GA with a mechanism for controlling the convergence of populations. From the functional point of view, the system consists of three components: the observation of convergence, its force, and the repulsion against it. To realize these functions, the system proposed in this paper uses two GAs and a filter which stores the information showing the trend of convergence.

2. Genetic Algorithms

In the simple GA as a multi-point search procedure, the search points of the objective function F, x_i, are represented in the strings of characters, S_i, and are stored in the population, which is represented as $[[S_i]]^N$ in this paper. Here, supposing that the strings are composed of the binary digit characters $\{0,1\}^l$, N is the population size. Every string is mapped into the search space of the objective function by the decoding function, D. They are tested in the objective function and receive values using the evaluation function, G, and

$$G(S_i) = F(D(S_i)) = F(x_i).$$ (1)

On the basis of those values, *the genetic operators* act on the population and produce the population of the next generation. Through repeated reproduction of the population, strings can receive a larger value from the evaluation function, and the average of those values will increase with each population.

The notion of *the schema* is important for analyzing the behavior of GAs. It consists of the trinary characters {0,1,#}. The character # is called *the don't care mark* and matches both 0 and 1. That is to say, the schema is a set of perfectly matching strings. In contrast to strings in the population that indicate points in the search space, the schemata specify regions thereof. Clearly, schema with a large order are likely to be effected by mutation, and schema with a long defining length will tend to be influenced by crossover. This fact is the essence of *the schema theorem* [Holland75].

GA-hard problems literally mean types of problem which simple GA can't easily solve. Since GAs are known as a robust search procedure applicable to a wide variety of problems, it is felt that such remarkable weak points should be overcome. Hence, much research into GA-hard problems has been presented, and many extended GAs have been proposed. Some of them focus on maintaining adequate diversity of the strings in the population, using sharing [Goldberg87], incest prevention [Eshelman91], crowding [Mahfoud92], introducing ecological frameworks [Davidor93], and so on. Almost all of them aim at solving the specific types of hard problem, and seem to be over-sensitive to parameter settings.

3. Filtering Genetic Algorithm

3.1 Conceptual Dynamics of Filtering-GA

GA-hard problems can be thought of as having a landscape with many static or dynamic local peaks, and we now assume that the objective is to maximize such a multimodal function. Without prior knowledge for solving the problems to which they are being applied, it is difficult for any search procedure to completely avoid the local peaks. To suppress mistaken convergence on the local peaks, the extended GA proposed in this paper, the filtering-GA, repeats its searches many times. In this way, it is possible to repeat the fast evolution of the population, to discover many local optima, and to terminate computation after a certain number of trials in any given local region. Furthermore, if the system can restart from an unexplored region, the search is expected to be more effective, and such search will find the most promising regions sequentially until the search space is completely explored or the system is terminated by an external control.

To reliably locate many peaks in the landscape of a multimodal objective function in one computation, the filtering-GA changes the effect of the objective function on the dynamics of the GA. If the evaluation value around a local optimal area already discovered decreases, the population will move toward another optimal area. In order to realize this mechanism autonomously, we propose the following operations: filtering, covering, and extraction.

3.1.1 Filtering Operation

The first operation of filtering is described here. The filter consists of two sequences of length l, which correspond to the length of the strings, and consist of real numbers, V^0 and V^1. The jth element of the sequence V^h is represented by v_j^h. Using this filter, the string S_i is evaluated by the modified evaluation function, as follows:

$$G_{\text{new}}(S_i) = G(S_i) - \sum_{j=0}^{l} v_j^{s_{ij}}, \tag{2}$$

where s_{ij} is the value $\{0,1\}$ of the jth position of string S_i. As seen in this equation, if v_j^h is large, the strings which have values h (0 or 1) in the jth position will receive a small evaluation value. Then, if v_j^h, in which j and h correspond to the local optima, has a large value, the population will move away from these local optima and is expected to find another local optima. After it has converged on one local optima, the population can be led away to another local optima efficiently if the change of the filter is controlled properly.

Because the system doesn't know what the local and global optima are, it is impossible for the filter values to change when one of the local optima is found. Therefore, the degree of convergence is used for determining the filter values, because the population tends to converge on peaks in the landscape of a problem whether they are optimal or not. Namely, all v_j^h is calculated as:

$$v_j^h = \frac{1}{N} \sum_{i=0}^{N} \left\{ \frac{G(S_i)}{l} \times \text{comp}(h, s_{ij}) \right\}, \tag{3}$$

$$\text{comp}(h, s_{ij}) = \begin{cases} 0, & \text{if } h \neq s_{ij}, \\ 1, & \text{otherwise.} \end{cases} \tag{4}$$

That is, v_j^h is the observed fitness of allele h at position j in the current population. If there are many strings which have value h in the jth position and their evaluation values are large, v_j^h will be large. The filter generated by these equations lowers the evaluation values of strings which have value h in the jth position, in its evaluation of the next generation by **eq. 2**. As a result of this procedure, the population moves away from the region where it has converged (**Fig. 1**).

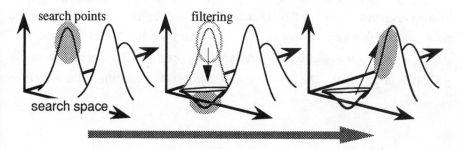

Fig. 1. Image of filtering operation.

3.1.2 Covering Operation

The second operation of the filtering-GA is the covering operation. This operation forces the population to converge in a particular region [Kakazu92]. Consider a schema H as a template of strings which have windows at the position of the don't care marks #s. Then the new string S^{new} is generated by putting this template on one string S. This operation is formalized as follows:

$$S^{new} = \text{cover}(H,S),\tag{5}$$

$$s_j^{new} = \begin{cases} s_j, & \text{if } h_j \neq \#, \\ h_j, & \text{otherwise.} \end{cases}\tag{6}$$

Whether the original string S is or isn't in the region represented by the schema H, the new string S^{new} generated by the covering operation is in this region. If the expected evaluation value of the schema is large, it is quite possible that new strings generated by this mapping will get high evaluation values.

3.1.3 Schema Extraction

The extracted schema is represented by H^{ext}. The values of all its positions are defined by the following equations:

$$h_j^{ext} = \begin{cases} 0, & \text{if } z < 1 - P_{ext}, \\ 1, & \text{if } z > P_{ext}, \\ \#, & \text{otherwise,} \end{cases}\tag{7}$$

$$z = \frac{\sum_{i=1}^{N} s_{ij}}{N}.\tag{8}$$

where P_{ext} is the system parameter named *the extraction threshold*, $0.5 \leq P_{ext} \leq 1$, and z is the mean allele value at position j. **Eq. 7** is named *the extract function*.

3.2 Schematic Structure of Filtering-GA

The filtering-GA consists of two GAs and a filter as shown in **Fig. 2**. One GA is named GA_{str}. This is almost the same as a simple GA except in its evaluation of strings. Systems which consist of several GAs have already been proposed, such as the multi-level GA [Grefenstette86] and so on. The two GAs in the filtering-GA make no hierarchy, and are not equal. They interact with each other and evolve like a co-evolution system [Hillis91, Husbands91]. The strings of GA_{str} are represented as S_i^{str} and the size of the population $[[S_i^{str}]]$ is N_t. Its strings are evaluated through the filtering operation. The other GA is named GA_{sch}, and the members of its population are represented in the form of schemata $\{0,1,\#\}$. Every schema S_i^{sch} in the population $[[S_i^{sch}]]$ of GA_{sch} is evaluated using the covering operation. The population size of $[[S_i^{sch}]]$ is given by N_c. The filter is generated from GA_{sch} and affects the evaluation of GA_{str}.

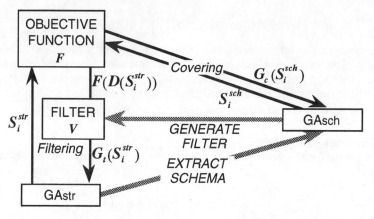

Fig. 2. Schematic diagram of filtering-GA.

3.3 Interaction among Two GAs and Objective Function

3.3.1 Evaluation Functions

The evaluation function of GA_{str}, G_{str}, is given as the next equation, and every string S_i^{str} of GA_{str} is evaluated as follows:

$$G_{str}\left(S_i^{str}\right) = G\left(S_i^{str}\right) - C_e \cdot \sum_{j=0}^{l} v_j^{s_{ij}^{str}} . \tag{9}$$

where G is given in **eq. 1**, s_{ij}^{str} is the value of the jth position of S_i^{str}, v_j^h is the jth value in V^h of the filter, C_e is the system variable, and $0 \le C_e \le 2$. Because the filter stores the tendency of convergence, the population of GA_{str} moves away from the region of convergence. At each generation, the system records the maximum and the average values calculated as G. If the best G value discovered by GA_{str} in a certain generation exceeds the average of all the G values obtained after P_h generations ago, then it would seem that GA_{str} is currently searching the most promising region. Then, to weaken the influence of the filter on GA_{str}, C_e is reduced $2 \times 1/P_h$. The filter never affects GA_{str} when $C_e = 0$. If that condition is not satisfied, the search concerning the region which GA_{str} is currently searching seems to finish or that region is not the most promising region. Then, to strengthen the influence of the filter on GA_{str}, and to cause the population of GA_{str} to move away from that region, C_e is increased $1/P_h$. It is expected that the influence of the filter will reject the convergence of GA_{str} when $C_e = 1$, causing the power to avoid convergence when $C_e > 1$; and when $C_e = 2$, such avoidance power will be negatively coequal to the convergence power of GA_{str} with $C_e = 0$. If it becomes $C_e < 0$ or $C_e > 2$, C_e is resettled at 0 or 2. P_h is named *the history number* and is a parameter of the system.

Every schema of GA_{sch} is evaluated by the following equation:

$$G_{sch}\left(S_i^{sch}\right) = \max_k\left\{G\left(\text{cover}\left(S_i^{sch}, S_k^{str}\right)\right)\right\}. \tag{10}$$

This is the equation for obtaining the expected maximum evaluation values of the schemata. The evaluation values obtained in this way imply the possibility of evolution for the population in those regions. Obviously, a large number of sampling points will ensure accurate estimation. Therefore, all the strings of GA_{str} are utilized in the evaluation of one schema of GA_{sch} using the covering operation.

3.3.2 Generation of Filter
The procedure for the generation of the filter is based on **eq. 3** and is modified as follows:

$$v_j^h = \frac{1}{N_c}\sum_{i=1}^{N_c}\left\{\frac{G\left(S_i^{sch}\right)}{o\left(S_i^{sch}\right)} \times \text{comp}\left(h, s_{ij}^{sch}\right)\right\}, \quad k \in \{0,1\}, \tag{11}$$

where $o(H)$ is the order of the schema H. Based on the definition of the schema, the don't care mark, #, matches both 0 and 1, but it matches neither 0 nor 1 in the function $\text{comp}(h,s)$. The position of #s in each schema never affects the filter, because it has no connection with the convergence of the search.

The population of GA_{sch} evolves and changes according to **eq. 10**, and the filter generated from it varies, in each generation. This means that the evaluation function of GA_{str} given in **eq. 9** changes at each generation. Under the evaluation function, which changes drastically, the population doesn't evolve properly. Hence, the average of all the filters generated after P_h generations ago is used in **eq. 9**. P_h is the history number introduced at **eq. 9**.

3.3.3 Extraction of Schema
To avoid system convergence, we introduce the third interaction between the two GAs, named *the extraction*. This operation is used to estimate where GA_{str} is exploring in the search space, and attracts the attention of GA_{sch} to this region. In practice, the schema which indicates such a region is extracted from the population of GA_{str}, and is joined to the population of GA_{sch}. To determine the evaluation value of the extracted schema, $G_{sch}(H^{ext})$, it is settled as $\max_k G(S_k^{str})$. Then the old schema, which has the lowest fitness value in the population of GA_{sch}, is replaced by this new extracted schema H^{ext}.

4. Computer Simulations
This section examines the search performance of the filtering-GA. The objective functions used here are

$$F_5(S_i) = \begin{cases} 1.2K\dfrac{D_c(S_i)}{l/2}, & \text{if } \sum_{j=1}^{l/2} s_{ij} = 0, \\ K\dfrac{D_c(S_i)}{l}, & \text{otherwise,} \end{cases} \tag{12}$$

where l is the length of the strings, $K = 300$ and $D_c(S_i) = \sum_{j=1}^{l} s_{ij}$, and

$$F_9(S_i) = \sum_{k=1}^{5} F'_{\text{MDF}}(S_i^k),$$ (13)

$$F'_{\text{MDF}}(S_i^k) = \begin{cases} 1 - \left(\left| \frac{l'}{2} - D_c(S_i^k) \right| - \frac{l'}{2} \right), & \text{if } \frac{l'}{2} - \left| \frac{l'}{2} - D_c(S_i^k) \right| \leq 1, \\ 0.8 \times \dfrac{\left(\frac{l'}{2} - \left| \frac{l'}{2} - D_c(S_i^k) \right| \right)}{l'/2 - 1}, & \text{otherwise,} \end{cases}$$ (14)

where $S_i \rightarrow S_i^1 | S_i^2 | \cdots | S_i^5$ shows that a string S_i is divided in to 5 sub-strings of S_i^k and $l' = l/5$ is their length. They are quoted from [Suzuki93] and [Goldberg92], respectively.

The standard parameters used in the simulations are shown in **Table 1**. In $F9$, the maximum generation is set at 10000. These parameters, for both the simple GA and the filtering-GA, do not need to be adjusted for each problem. Therefore, these two GAs may be capable of exhibiting a higher performance than the results shown here.

Fig. 3 reports the performances of the simple GA and the filtering-GA on $F5$. These results were obtained by averaging over 5 independent runs. Although the population of the simple GA completely converged onto a local optimum at 240, the filtering-GA failed optimization only once in 5 trials. This failure was caused by the effect of the scheduling mechanism introduced at **eq. 9**. The accurate acquisition of those schemata is expected to be realized, if C_e is changed in an adaptive way.

In the optimization of $F9$, the filtering-GA could achieve five times as many optima as the simple GA. The filtering-GA could find almost all the global optima under any parameter settings (**Fig. 4**). The ability of the filtering-GA to search in unexplored regions is proven by these results.

	Simple GA	Filtering-GA	
		GAstr	GAsch
population size	500, 1000	30	30
string length	30	30	30
maximum generation	1000	1000	1000
elitist strategy	on	on	off
crossover type	uniform	uniform	two-point
crossover rate	0.8	0.6	0.8
mutation rate	0.03	0.03	0.05
history number	—	10	
extraction threshold	—	0.8	

Table 1. Parameter settings used in simulations.

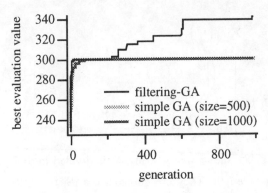

Fig. 3. Search performance of simple GA and filtering-GA on $F5$.

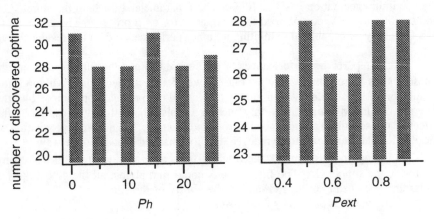

Fig. 4. Change of performance of filtering-GA according to P_h and P_{ext} on $F9$.

5. Discussion

In the simulations of the previous section, the filtering-GA discovered the local optima as fast as the simple GA in the experiments. Moreover, premature convergence never occurred, because it is able to avoid it through using the filtering operation. Thus, the filtering-GA can fast search local optima, using large selection pressure, without convergence of the system.

Concerning computational costs, the filtering-GA offers some new operations, mentioned in section 3, while its two GAs have much smaller populations (30 members) than that of the simple GA (1000 members) and both systems can evaluate a similar number of strings in a generation. When the evaluation begins, the system checks every string position once. That is to say, N *scans* of the strings are necessary each generation in evaluating the members of the population with the simple GA. It is well understood that the selection, mutation and crossover will also require N scans. Therefore, the simple GA necessitates $4N_S$ scans for one generation, and N_S is its population size.

The system must put every schemata of GA_{sch} on all the strings of GA_{str} when the covering operation occurs in the computation of the filtering-GA; and this operation requires N_f^2 scans if the population of GA_{sch} is of equal size, N_f, to that of GA_{str}. Under the same conditions, schema extraction requires N_f scans, because only the strings of GA_{str} are concerned with this operation, and N_f scans are required to generate the filter. The filtering operation necessitates N_f scans, since the system checks every position of the filter at every evaluation in GA_{str}. To add to this, $6N_f$ scans are necessary for the selection, crossover and mutation in both GAs. The costs for the evaluation operations in GA_{sch} and GA_{str} are included in the costs for the covering and filtering operations, respectively. Hence, the filtering-GA requires $(N_f^2 + 9N_f)$ scans of the schemata for one generation.

To equalize the number for the evaluation for one generation, it is reasonable for the population size of the filtering-GA to be set at $N_f = \sqrt{N_s}$. Thus, the cost ratio of the filtering-GA against the simple GA can be calculated as follows:

$$\frac{\text{cost(fGA)}}{\text{cost(sGA)}} = \frac{N_f^2 + 9N_f}{4N_s} = \frac{1}{4} + \frac{9}{4\sqrt{N}}, \tag{15}$$

where N is the number for evaluation for one generation and $N = N_s = N_f^2$. That is to say, the larger N becomes, the faster the filtering-GA will explore the search space of the objective function. In fact, the filtering-GA searches about three times as fast as the simple GA with a population of 1000 members under the parameter settings shown in **Table 1**, and this is nearly equal to **eq. 15**.

6. Conclusions

This paper proposed an extended genetic algorithm (GA), named the filtering genetic algorithm (the filtering-GA), as a multimodal function optimizer. The filtering-GA is intended to solve GA-hard multimodal functions, and to optimize GA-easy problems quickly. It consists of two GAs and a filter. The role of the filter is to smoothen the interaction between the two GAs. Using these three parts, the filtering-GA can search widely throughout the search spaces of problems, and discover many local optima sequentially. Its conceptual and detailed definitions were given, and its functional framework was discussed.

In order to inspect the parameter settings of the mechanisms which are introduced in the filtering-GA, some experiments were carried out. Through them, the filtering-GA exhibited a higher performance than the simple GA. Furthermore its behaviors were observed on several problems, and the mechanisms of the filter and the two GAs were discussed.

References

[Deb93] Deb, K., Horn, J. and Goldberg, D. E., Multimodal Deceptive Functions, Complex Systems, vol. 7, no. 2, pp. 131-153, Complex Systems, (1993).

[Eshelman91] Eshelman, L. J., The CHC Adaptive Search Algorithm: How to Have Safe Search When Engaging in Nontraditional Genetic Recombination, Foundations of Genetic Algorithms, pp. 265-283, Morgan Kaufmann (1991).

[Goldberg87] Goldberg, D. E. and Richardson, J., Genetic Algorithms with Sharing for Multimodal Function Optimization, Genetic Algorithms and Their Applications : Proceedings of The Second International Conference on Genetic Algorithms, pp. 41-49, Lawrence Erlbaum Associates (1987).

[Goldberg89] Goldberg, D. E., *Genetic Algorithms in Search, Optimization and Machine Learning*, p.412, Addison-Wesley (1989).

[Goldberg92] Goldberg, D. E., Deb, K. and Horn, J., *Massive Multimodality, Deception, and Genetic Algorithms*, Parallel Problem Solving from Nature, 2, Proceedings of the Second Conference of Parallel Problem Solving from Nature, pp. 37-45, North-Holland (1992).

[Grefenstette86] Grefenstette, J. J., *Optimization of Control Parameters for Genetic Algorithms*, IEEE tran. on SMC, vol.16, no.1, pp. 122-128 (1986).

[Hillis91] Hillis, W. D., *Co-Evolving Parasites Improve Simulated Evolution as An Optimization Procedure*, Emergent Computation, pp. 228-234, The MIT Press (1991).

[Holland75] Holland, J. H., *Adaptation in Natural and Artificial Systems*, University of Michigan Press (1975).

[Husbands91] Husbands, P. and Mill, F., *Simulated Co-Evolution as The Mechanism for Emergent Planning and Scheduling*, Proceedings of The Fourth International Conference on Genetic Algorithms, pp. 264-270, Morgan Kaufmann (1991).

[Kakazu92] Kakazu, Y., Sakanashi, H. and Suzuki, K., *Adaptive Search Strategy for Genetic Algorithms with Additional Genetic Algorithms*, Parallel Problem Solving from Nature, 2, pp.311-320, North-Holland (1992).

[Mahfoud92] Mahfoud, S. W. , *Crowding and preselection revisited*, Parallel Problem Solving from Nature, 2, pp. 27-36, North-Holland (1992).

[Suzuki93] Suzuki, K., Sakanashi, H. and Kakazu Y., *Iterative Schema Extracting Operation for Genetic Algorithms*, Proc. of Australian and New Zealand Conference on Intelligent Information Systems, p. 517-520 (1993).

A Cooperative Coevolutionary Approach to Function Optimization

Mitchell A. Potter and Kenneth A. De Jong

Computer Science Department, George Mason University, Fairfax, VA 22030, USA
mpotter@gmu.edu

Abstract. A general model for the coevolution of cooperating species is presented. This model is instantiated and tested in the domain of function optimization, and compared with a traditional GA-based function optimizer. The results are encouraging in two respects. They suggest ways in which the performance of GA and other EA-based optimizers can be improved, and they suggest a new approach to evolving complex structures such as neural networks and rule sets.

1 Introduction

Genetic algorithms (GAs), originally conceived by Holland [10], represent a fairly abstract model of Darwinian evolution and biological genetics. They evolve a population of competing individuals using fitness-biased selection, random mating, and a gene-level representation of individuals together with simple genetic operators (typically, crossover and mutation) for modeling inheritance of traits.

These GAs have been successfully applied to a wide variety of problems including multimodal function optimization, machine learning, and the evolution of complex structures such as neural networks and Lisp programs. At the same time, difficulties can and do arise in forcing every problem domain into this traditional GA model. One of the earliest examples of this is the application of GAs to rule learning. Evolving rule sets of varying length and complexity doesn't map neatly into the traditional GA paradigm, resulting in a variety of extensions including Holland's classifier system, Smith's LS system, and Grefenstette's SAMUEL system [11, 14, 7].

In this paper we present an extension of the traditional GA model which appears to have considerable potential for representing and solving more complex problems by explicitly modeling the coevolution of cooperating species. We provide some initial insight into this potential by illustrating its behavior on the well-studied domain of function optimization. We conclude with a brief discussion of work in progress on more complex domains.

2 Cooperative Coevolutionary Genetic Algorithms

The hypothesis underlying the ideas presented here is that, in order to evolve more and more complex structures, explicit notions of modularity need to be introduced in order to provide reasonable opportunities for complex solutions to evolve in the form of interacting co-adapted subcomponents. Examples of this show up in the need for rule hierarchies in classifier systems and subroutines in genetic programming.

The difficulty comes in finding reasonable computational extensions of the GA paradigm for which such substructure "emerges" rather than being pre-specified by the user. At issue here is how to represent such substructures and how to apportion credit to them for their contributions to the problem solving activity. Classifier systems attempt to accomplish this via a single population of interacting rules whose individual fitnesses are determined by their interactions with other rules via a simulated micro-economy [11]. Other extensions have been proposed to encourage the emergence of niches and species in a single population [4, 3], in which individual niches represent competing (rather than cooperating) solutions to the problem.

The use of multiple interacting subpopulations has also been explored as an alternate mechanism for representing the coevolution of species, but has focused primarily on a fixed number of subpopulations each evolving competing (rather than cooperating) solutions (e.g. [8, 2, 15, 16]). The previous work that has looked at coevolving multiple cooperative species in separate subpopulations has involved a user-specified decomposition of the problem into species (see, for example, [12] or [9]).

The system we envision combines and extends these ideas in the following ways: 1) a species represents a subcomponent of a potential solution; 2) complete solutions are obtained by assembling representative members of each of the species present; 3) credit assignment at the species level is defined in terms of the fitness of the complete solutions in which the species members participate; 4) when required, the number of species (subpopulations) should itself evolve; and 5) the evolution of each species (subpopulation) is handled by a standard GA. We call such systems *cooperative coevolutionary genetic algorithms* (CCGAs).

As a first step we have chosen the domain of function optimization as the test bed for our ideas. The choice has several advantages. It is a well-studied area with respect to the use of evolutionary algorithms providing us with a solid frame of reference. It is also the case that there is a natural decomposition of the problem into a fixed number of individual subcomponents, namely, the N parameters of the function to be optimized. This allowed us to defer the most difficult of the five issues listed above (the birth and death of species) and concentrate on designing and testing the remaining four features of the proposed system.

3   Cooperative Coevolutionary Function Optimization

If we think of a solution to a function optimization problem as consisting of specifying the value of N parameters (variables), a natural decomposition is to maintain N subpopulations (species) each of which contains competing values for a particular parameter. One can then assign fitness to a particular value (member) of a particular subpopulation by assembling it along with selected members of the other subpopulations to form one or more N-dimensional vectors whose fitness can be computed in the normal fashion, and using those results to assign fitness to the individual component being evaluated. That is, the fitness of a particular member of a particular species is computed by estimating how well it "cooperates" with other subspecies to produce good solutions.

As a first test of these ideas, the traditional GA shown in figure 1 was extended to the CCGA-1 model given in figure 2.

```
gen = 0
Pop(gen) = randomly initialized population
evaluate fitness of each individual in Pop(gen)
while termination condition = false do begin
        gen = gen + 1
        select Pop(gen) from Pop(gen − 1) based on fitness
        apply genetic operators to Pop(gen)
        evaluate fitness of each individual in Pop(gen)
    end
```

Fig. 1. Traditional GA

```
gen = 0
for each species s do begin
    Pops(gen) = randomly initialized population
    evaluate fitness of each individual in Pops(gen)
end
while termination condition = false do begin
        gen = gen + 1
        for each species s do begin
            select Pops(gen) from Pops(gen − 1) based on fitness
            apply genetic operators to Pops(gen)
            evaluate fitness of each individual in Pops(gen)
        end
    end
```

Fig. 2. CCGA-1

CCGA-1 begins by initializing a separate population of individuals for each function variable. The initial fitness of each subpopulation member is computed by combining it with a random individual from each of the other species and applying the resulting vector of variable values to the target function.

After this startup phase, each of the individual subpopulations in CCGA-1 is coevolved in a round-robin fashion using a traditional GA. The fitness of a subpopulation member is obtained by combining it with *the current best* subcomponents of the remaining (temporarily frozen) subpopulations. This is certainly the simplest form of credit assignment one could imagine. It has some potential problems (such as undersampling and "greediness"), but gives us a starting point for further refinements.

Although this sequential version of the algorithm could be characterized more accurately as quasi-coevolutionary, a fully coevolutionary implementation is also possible (and on our list to explore at a later date) in which each species only occasionally communicates with the other species. Such an asynchronous version of the algorithm would be particularly well suited to a parallel implementation in which each species is evolved on a separate processor.

4   Experimental Results

We evaluated CCGA-1 by comparing its performance with the performance of a standard GA on several function optimization problems. The coevolutionary and standard GA differ only as to whether they utilize multiple species as described in the previous section. All other aspects of the algorithms are equal and are held constant over all experiments. Specifically, the algorithms have the following characteristics:

representation:	binary (16 bits per function variable)
selection:	fitness proportionate
fitness scaling:	scaling window technique (width of 5)
elitist strategy:	single copy of best individual preserved
genetic operators:	two-point crossover and bit-flip mutation
mutation probability:	1/chromlength
crossover probability:	0.6
population size:	100

All the functions used in these experiments have been defined such that their global minimums are zero. The primary performance metric used in evaluating the algorithms is the minimum function value found after a fixed number of function evaluations. Each of the results reported for this metric represents an average computed over fifty runs.

The first set of experiments is performed on four highly multimodal functions that have been used in other experimental comparisons of evolutionary algorithms [13, 6, 1]. We will refer to these functions by the names of the researchers who first proposed them—Rastrigin, Schwefel, Griewangk, and Ackley. The Rastrigin function is defined as

$$f(\mathbf{x}) = 3.0n + \sum_{i=1}^{n} x_i^2 - 3.0\cos(2\pi x_i),$$

where $n = 20$ and $-5.12 \le x_i \le 5.12$. The global minimum of zero is at the point $\mathbf{x} = (0, 0, \cdots)$. The primary characteristic of this function is the existence of many suboptimal peaks whose values increase as the distance from the global optimum point increases. The Schwefel function is defined as

$$f(\mathbf{x}) = 418.9829n + \sum_{i=1}^{n} x_i \sin\left(\sqrt{|x_i|}\right),$$

where $n = 10$ and $-500.0 \leq x_i \leq 500.0$. The global minimum of zero is at the point $\mathbf{x} = (420.9687, 420.9687, \cdots)$. The interesting characteristic of this function is the presence of a second-best minimum far away from the global minimum— intended to trap optimization algorithms on a suboptimal peak. The Griewangk function is defined as

$$f(\mathbf{x}) = 1 + \sum_{i=1}^{n} \frac{x_i^2}{4000} - \prod_{i=1}^{n} \cos\left(\frac{x_i}{\sqrt{i}}\right),$$

where $n = 10$ and $-600.0 \leq x_i \leq 600.0$. The global minimum of zero is at the point $\mathbf{x} = (0, 0, \cdots)$. This function has a product term, introducing an interdependency between the variables. This is intended to disrupt optimization techniques that work on one function variable at a time. The Ackley function is defined as

$$f(\mathbf{x}) = 20 + e - 20 \exp\left(-0.2\sqrt{\frac{1}{n}\sum_{i=1}^{n} x_i^2}\right) - \exp\left(\frac{1}{n}\sum_{i=1}^{n} \cos\left(2\pi x_i\right)\right),$$

where $n = 30$ and $-30.0 \leq x_i \leq 30.0$. The global minimum of zero is at the point $\mathbf{x} = (0, 0, \cdots)$. At a low resolution the landscape of this function is unimodal; however, the second exponential term covers the landscape with many small peaks and valleys.

The graphs in figure 3 show the minimum value found (best individual) as a function of the number of function evaluations averaged over fifty runs using the Rastrigin, Schwefel, Griewangk, and Ackley functions. Both algorithms were terminated after 100,000 function evaluations. In all cases CCGA-1 significantly outperformed the standard GA both in the minimum value found and in the speed of convergence to zero. The statistical significance of these results was verified using a two sample t test.

Recall that CCGA-1 evolves each species (function variable) in a round-robin fashion using the current best values from the other species. This is quite similar in style to the family of numerical optimization techniques which proceed by optimizing one function variable at a time while holding the other variables constant. It is well known that such procedures work well on functions whose variables are reasonably independent, but have difficulties with functions with interacting variables.

On closer inspection, we noticed that CCGA-1 demonstrated slightly less of an advantage over the standard GA on the Griewangk function than on the other three functions. We hypothesize that this due to the interdependencies between the function variables introduced by the Griewangk product term, and selected

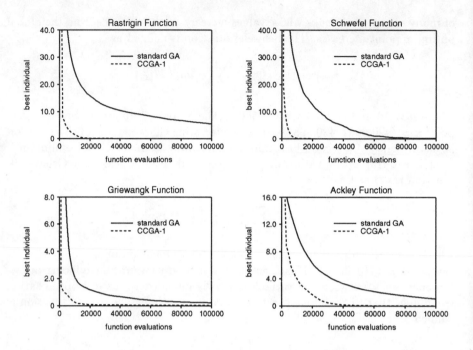

Fig. 3. Comparisons of standard GA and CCGA-1 performance

an additional function (F2) from the original De Jong test suite [5] that has even stronger variable interactions than the Griewangk function. This function is called the Rosenbrock function and is defined as

$$f(\mathbf{x}) = 100(x_1^2 - x_2)^2 + (1 - x_1)^2,$$

where $-2.048 \leq x_i \leq 2.048$. The global minimum of zero is at the point $(1, 1)$. The Rosenbrock function is characterized by an extremely deep valley along the parabola $x_1^2 = x_2$ that leads to the global minimum.

As illustrated in figure 4, CCGA-1 performed much worse than the standard GA on the Rosenbrock function, supporting our hypothesis that interacting variables (product terms) would present difficulties.

We felt that much of the source of this difficulty was due to the simple credit assignment algorithm in CCGA-1. To test this hypothesis, we modified the credit assignment algorithm as follows. Each individual in a subpopulation is evaluated by combining it with the best known individual from each of the other species and with a random selection of individuals from each of the other species. The two resulting vectors are then applied to the target function and the better of the two values is returned as the offspring's fitness.

We evaluated this variant (CCGA-2) on the Rosenbrock and the earlier Rastrigin function to see to what extent performance is improved on interacting

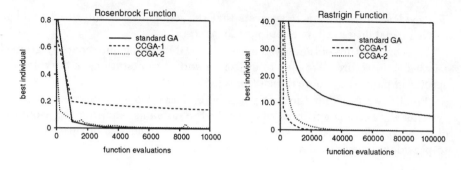

Fig. 4. Comparisons of standard GA, CCGA-1, and CCGA-2 performance

variable problems, and to assess what performance penalty (if any) is observed on a representative of the non-interacting variable problems.

As illustrated in figure 4, CCGA-2 performed as well as the standard GA on the Rosenbrock function, but at the expense of a slight decrease in performance from CCGA-1 on the non-interacting variable problem. These results were tested as before for significance.

Although we have emphasized the number of function evaluations as a measure of cost, the amount of computation required to perform the experiments should also be briefly mentioned. Because the standard GA represents the entire set of function variables in each of its chromosomes while the CCGA algorithms only represent a single function variable in each of their chromosomes, there is much more overhead in a standard GA associated with the genotype to phenotype mapping process. To evaluate each new individual, the standard GA performs a genotype to phenotype mapping on all function variables while the CCGA algorithms only need to apply the mapping to a single function variable. As the dimensionality of the problem increases, this additional overhead becomes considerable. As an illustration, while optimizing the Ackley function of thirty dimensions the standard GA took approximately six times longer to complete a given number of fitness evaluations than the CCGA counterpart.

5   Discussion, Conclusions and Future Work

The results presented here are preliminary in nature, but provide initial evidence of the potential problem solving capabilities of cooperative coevolutionary systems. To make any strong claims concerning their value for function optimization, further refinement of the approach is required as well as additional comparisons with other existing optimization techniques. There are, however, several aspects of this approach that deserve some attention.

First, note that any evolutionary algorithm (EA) can be used to evolve the subpopulations—GAs just happen to be our favorite choice. Hence we encourage others to explore the potential of extending their own favorite EA to a CCEA.

The evidence presented here suggests that the result may be improved problem solving capabilities at lower computational costs.

A second feature of these systems is a natural mapping onto coarsely grained parallel architectures. We plan to utilize networked workstations to coevolve the species in parallel on more difficult problem classes.

Finally, we feel that the real potential of these cooperative coevolutionary systems will become apparent when applied to domains requiring the evolution of more complex structures such as neural networks and sets of rules. We hope to provide such evidence in the near future.

References

1. Bäck, T., Schwefel, H.-P.: An overview of evolutionary algorithms for parameter optimization. Evolutionary Computation 1(1) (1993) 1–23
2. Cohoon, J.P., Hegde, S.U., Martin, W.N., Richards, D.: Punctuated equilibria: a parallel genetic algorithm. Proceedings of the Second International Conference on Genetic Algorithms (1987) 148–154
3. Davidor, Y.: A naturally occuring niche & species phenomenon: the model and first results. Proceedings of the Fourth International Conference on Genetic Algorithms (1991) 257–263
4. Deb, K., Goldberg, D.E.: An investigation of niche and species formation in genetic function optimization. Proceedings of the Third International Conference on Genetic Algorithms (1989) 42–50
5. DeJong, K.A.: Analysis of Behavior of a Class of Genetic Adaptive Systems. PhD thesis, University of Michigan, Ann Arbor, MI (1975)
6. Gordon, V.S., Whitley, D.: Serial and parallel genetic algorithms as function optimizers. Proceedings of the Fifth International Conference on Genetic Algorithms (1993) 177–183
7. Grefenstette, J.J.: A system for learning control strategies with genetic algorithms. Proceedings of the Third International Conference on Genetic Algorithms (1989) 183–190
8. Grosso, P.B.: Computer Simulations of Genetic Adaptation: Parallel Subcomponent Interaction in a Multilocus Model. PhD thesis, University of Michigan, Ann Arbor, MI (1985)
9. Hills, D.W.: Co-evolving parasites improve simulated evolution as an optimization procedure. In C.G. Langton, C. Taylor, J.D. Farmer, and S. Rasmussen, editors, Artificial Life II (1990) 313–324
10. Holland, J.H.: Adaptation in Natural and Artificial Systems (1975)
11. Holland, J.H., Reitman, J.S.: Cognitive systems based on adaptive algorithms. In D.A. Waterman and F. Hayes-Roth, editors, Pattern-Directed Inference Systems (1978)
12. Husbands, P., Mill, F.: Simulated co-evolution as the mechanism for emergent planning and scheduling. Proceedings of the Fourth International Conference on Genetic Algorithms (1991) 264–270
13. Mühlenbein, H.: The parallel genetic algorithm as function optimizer. Proceedings of the Fourth International Conference on Genetic Algorithms (1991) 271–278

14. Smith, S.F.: Flexible learning of problem solving heuristics through adaptive search. Proceedings of the Eighth International Joint Conference on Artificial Intelligence (1983) 422–425

15. Tanese, R.: Distributed genetic algorithms. Proceedings of the Third International Conference on Genetic Algorithms (1989) 434–439

16. Whitley, D., Starkweather, T.: Genitor II: a distributed genetic algorithm. Journal of Experimental and Theoretical Artificial Intelligence **2** (1990) 189–214

A Fuzzy Classifier System Using the Pittsburgh Approach

Brian Carse and Terence C. Fogarty

University of the West of England
Bristol BS16 1QY, UK
b_carse@csd.uwe.ac.uk

Abstract. This paper describes a fuzzy classifier system using the Pittsburgh model. In this model genetic operations and fitness assignment apply to complete rule-sets, rather than to individual rules, thus overcoming the problem of conflicting individual and collective interests of classifiers. The fuzzy classifier system presented here dynamically adjusts both membership functions and fuzzy relations. A modified crossover operator for particular use in Pittsburgh-style fuzzy classifier systems, with variable length rule-sets, is introduced and evaluated. Experimental results of the new system, which appear encouraging, are presented and discussed.

1 Introduction

Fuzzy control has been employed with success in many diverse practical applications: control of a cement kiln [1], 2-dimensional motion control [2], traffic control [3] and temperature control of air streams [4] to name but a few. Based on Zadeh's theory of fuzzy sets [5], a typical fuzzy controller [6] maintains a rule-base of fuzzy rules for mapping real-numbered inputs to outputs. In most existing real application fuzzy controllers, the rule-base is populated with rule-of-thumb relations elicited from human experts who have acquired their knowledge through experience. A good measure of interest is currently being directed at discovering the fuzzy sets and relations automatically using techniques based on machine learning.

In this paper we address the application of genetics based machine learning (GBML) to fuzzy controller design. In particular, we discuss and evaluate a new approach to the fuzzy classifier system based on the Pittsburgh [7] model. Using this model, genetic operations and fitness evaluations apply at the level of the rules-set rather than individual rules.

The fuzzy rule-set representation we have used is based on that described by Parodi and Bonelli [8] which allows the GA to operate on membership functions as well as fuzzy relations. An extension to Parodi and Bonelli's representation which uses variable length rule-sets has been employed. A new crossover operator, based on ordering the constituent fuzzy rules of the rule-base by input membership function centres, is used to encourage coverage of the complete input space. The efficacy of the new operator is compared to that used by Smith [7], and found to produce good results. In particular, fuzzy rule-sets have been evolved which are economical in their coverage of the input space; that is, the density of rules in the input space is automatically adapted by the GA according to the complexity of the input-output mapping in the vicinity of a particular position in the input space.

The paper is organised as follows. Section 2 gives a brief discussion of Pittsburgh and Michigan approaches to learning classifier systems. Section 3 reports on previous research carried out using genetics based machine learning in fuzzy control. In section 4 we discuss our approach to the fuzzy classifier system, and describe a new crossover operator we have devised. Section 5 presents the results of our experiments with the new fuzzy classifier system. Finally, section 6 concludes and suggests areas worthy of further investigation.

2 Pittsburgh and Michigan Approaches to Classifier Systems

These two alternative approaches to classifier systems, named after the universities in which they were devised, have been the source of much debate over recent years. It is not our intention here to enter into that debate, but rather to compare and contrast the two approaches in relation to the fuzzy classifier system we have devised.

The main differences between the two approaches are the level of unit used for genetic manipulation and for credit assignment. In the Michigan approach [9] the units of selection are individual rules. Each rule has an associated strength calculated using some credit assignment technique (for example, the bucket-brigade [10] and, more recently, Q-learning [11]). This strength serves as the rule's fitness when the GA is applied and is also often used in conflict resolution during classifier execution cycles. In contrast, the GA in a Pittsburgh style classifier system operates on complete sets of rules. Each rule-set is assigned a fitness (based on some performance measure) which is used by the GA to navigate through the search space of possible rule-sets. The GA is therefore evaluating individual rules implicitly, in contrast to the Michigan approach which reinforces individual rules explicitly using a credit assignment algorithm.

While it can be argued that the Pittsburgh approach, more closely modelled on evolution in natural systems, places greater emphasis on maintenance of rule structures and cooperation between classifiers, the approach involves much greater computational complexity (in both processing time and memory) compared to the Michigan approach. Wilson and Goldberg [12] argue that a synthesis of the two approaches may be necessary to achieve more flexible learning classifier systems.

3 Previous Work on Genetic Algorithms in Fuzzy Control and Fuzzy Classifier Systems

A number of researchers have addressed the automatic generation of fuzzy rule-sets using evolutionary algorithms. Thrift [13] describes a fuzzy controller for centring a cart on a track. This system learns the relation matrix for a fixed set of membership functions using fitness assignment to complete rule-sets.

Karr [14] describes a genetically adapted fuzzy controller for the cart-pole problem, using a microGA for real-time learning. Fixed rules, set by hand, are used and the GA adapts fuzzy set membership functions. The GA operates at the rule-set level (fixed size rule-sets) with each rule-set allocated a fitness based on mean-squared error during a simulation.

Pham's system [15] also learns fuzzy relations (but not input membership functions) to simulate the step response of a time-delayed second-order plant. In his work he describes the use of parallel Gas to evolve "preliminary designs" (using different initial random seeds) followed by a second stage where a single GA is used to evolve a "detailed design" using the best preliminary designs. The GA operates at the rule-set level (analogous to Pittsburgh style classifiers) using fixed length strings to represent rule-sets.

Valenzuela-Rendon [16] gives the first description of a fuzzy classifier system based on the Michigan approach, with credit assignment to individual rules. Membership functions are fixed and set by hand.

Parodi and Bonelli [8] describe a fuzzy classifier system using a real-numbered representation which simultaneously learns membership functions and fuzzy relations. This system is also based on the Michigan approach, using supervised learning and reinforcement at the level of the individual rule. In their reported experiments in [8], the authors keep the membership function widths fixed (operating on only the centres of membership functions) and do not employ crossover. Real-number creep is used as the mutation operator.

Furuhashi et al. [17] employ multiple stimulus-response Michigan-style fuzzy classifier systems for learning to steer a simulated ship into a goal. Multiple classifier systems are used to suppress excessive fuzziness. The system employs fixed fuzzy set membership functions. Classifier payoffs are assigned by a human supervisor.

4 The Pittsburgh-style Fuzzy Classifier System

In this section we describe the design and implementation of a Pittsburgh style fuzzy classifier system. The representation used for individual rule-sets is based on that described by Parodi and Bonelli [8]. In their system, an individual rule is expressed as:

$$R_k: (x_{c1k}, x_{w1k}); \ldots (x_{cnk}, x_{wnk}) \rightarrow (y_{c1k}, y_{w1k}); \ldots (y_{cnk}, y_{wnk})$$

where each bracketed term represents the centre and width of a particular triangular membership function. We borrow this representation since it allows the GA to operate on both membership functions and as well as relations between them (rules). Rule-set size is allowed to vary under the action of crossover, described below.

A "crisp" input vector $x = (x_1, x_2 \ldots x_n)$ is presented to the system and matched with the fuzzy conditions of the rule-base using the fuzzy AND (min) operator to determine the truth value of individual rules. Output variables are calculated using the centre of mass formula.

The discovery component of our system involves mutation and crossover. The mutation operator is fairly straight-forward and involves the selection of random rules from a rule-set and applying real-number "creep" to either the width or centre of a single randomly selected fuzzy membership function within the rule. In this initial implementation we view mutation as a simple hill-climbing operator for fine-tuning membership functions rather than for introducing radically different genetic structures into the population.

The crossover operator we have used deserves more detailed discussion. In his PhD thesis, Smith [7] describes the need for a modified crossover operator for variable length position-independent rule-sets. (In a production system, fuzzy or otherwise, the position of a particular rule within the rule-set is immaterial to its operation). In particular, the author points out that Holland's schema theorem [18] assumes positional dependence on the structures being manipulated. Smith then goes on to demonstrate how, using the modified crossover operator in conjunction with inversion, high performance combinations of "attributes" within structures will proliferate as a result of selective pressure even with positional independence. The operation of the modified crossover operator is summarised below (for more details, see [7]):

1. Two parent structures $A = a_1...a_n$ and $B = b_1...b_m$ are selected from the population.
2. Alignment points P_A and P_B are selected for A and B from $\{1,...,n-1\}$ and $\{1,...,m-1\}$ respectively.
3. Consider the attributes of A and B indexed in both directions from the alignment points.
   i.e. $A = a_u...a_{-1}a_1...a_v$ and $B = b_{u'}...b_{-1}b_1...b_{v'}$
   A single crossover point x is selected at random from $\{\max(u,u')+1,...,0,...,\min(v,v')-1\}$
4. Two resultant child structures are formed by exchanging the attributes to the right of position x in A and B yielding $a_u...a_xb_{x+1}...b_{v'}$ and $b_{u'}...b_xa_{x+1}...a_v$.

Smith's pioneering work dealt primarily with binary-string representations and discrete input and output variables. No notion of ordering could be applied to the condition parts of individual rules. However, with a fuzzy rule-base operating on a number of continuously varying variables it is possible to introduce a "weak" form of positional dependence by ordering the fuzzy rules according to the centres of their membership functions. Fuzzy rules whose input membership functions overlap (and therefore whose input membership functions are likely to be close together) are epistatically linked since the "crisp" output values over the range of overlap of the inputs is determined by the combined action of all matched rules. A crossover operator which preserves rather than destroying these linkages is likely to be a good one. In this initial implementation of a fuzzy Pittsburgh-style classifier system, we take this observation to its extreme conclusion and order rules on the genome according to input membership function centres. Both Thrift's [13] and Pham's [15] representations for GA-derived fuzzy controllers implicitly exploit this property of "local" epistasis. In the case of the fuzzy classifier system presented here, this characteristic is explicitly utilised through the use of a new crossover operator which is described next.

Two parent rule-sets are selected at random, proportional to fitness. The rules within each rule-set are sorted according to the centre of the membership function for each input variable. For each input variable, a random number within the range of possible values for that variable (we assume this is known). The resultant vector (one component for each input variable) is used to determine the crosspoint for each parent. For example, consider two one-input, one-output rule-sets, each with five rules, having the following centres of membership functions of the input variable:

Parent 1:   0.1   0.3   0.4   0.9   1.5

Parent 2:   0.0   0.05   0.15   0.7   1.0

Suppose the random number 0.35 was chosen as the basis for crossover. The resulting offspring produced by applying the crossover operator would be:

Child 1:   0.1   0.3   0.7   1.0

Child 2:   0.0   0.05   0.15   0.4   0.9   1.5

In the case of n-dimensional input spaces, a crosspoint vector C_i, $i \in \{1..n\}$ is randomly selected. After crossover, Child 1 contains rules from Parent 1 such that $\forall i$, $x_{cik} < C_i$, and the rules from Parent 2 such that $\forall i$, $x_{cik} > C_i$. Child 2 contains the remaining rules from both rule-sets. Care must be taken in the probability distribution used in selecting the components of the n-dimensional crosspoint. For example, choosing each crosspoint component independently using a uniform probability density function between some known limits is not suitable when $n > 1$ since the average "hypervolume" containing rules being crossed over decreases as dimensionality increases. One possibility is to choose a random "hypervolume" in the allowed range, and then to determine individual crosspoint components from this. In the results presented next, this is not a problem since the experiments described pertain to a one-input, one-output mapping.

5 Experimental Results

In this section we describe the experiments and results using the Pittsburgh style fuzzy classifier system. The system was evaluated using a function identification learning task. The function chosen was $y = \sin(20x^2)$. This was selected since it is strongly non-monotonic and the frequency increases with increasing x. We might then expect the system to evolve rule-sets where the density of the centres of rule membership functions in the input space is higher in more "interesting" areas where the input-output mapping is locally more complex.

The system was run using two different crossover operators - a version based on Smith's LS-1 original, outline above, and the new crossover operator described in the previous section. Initially the rule-set size was set at 20 rules, but this was allowed to vary with time (under the action of crossover) up to a maximum of 80, but with a penalty (i.e.reduction in reproductive fitness) applied to all rule-sets with a length greater than 40 with a severity increasing with length. For binary, discrete-valued input Pittsburgh style classifier systems, Smith predicted and observed a tendency for rule-set length to increase without bound in the absence of such a penalty. Interestingly enough we noticed in our experiments that in the fuzzy case this was not so much of a problem, particularly with the new crossover operator.

A fixed population size of 100 rule-sets was used. Each rule-set was seeded with 20 random rules. Input and output membership function centres of rules were chosen randomly from the ranges $-0.2 < x_{cik} < +1.2$ and $-1.4 < y_{cik} < +1.4$. Membership function widths were selected randomly with a mean value equal to twice the inverse of the initial number of rules (i.e. $2.(1/20) = 0.1$) to provide adequate initial coverage.

The genetic algorithm used a "steady-state" replacement strategy, generating two new rule-sets at each generation and replacing the two lowest fitness rule-sets with the new ones. A crossover rate of 0.8 was employed, together with a mutation rate of 0.1. The fitness function used was the scaled mean-square error in the output over the whole input range.

Figure 1 shows a graph of best fitness (averaged over 10 runs with different initial random seeds) against generation number for the two crossover operators. Clearly the new operator is an improvement on the version of Smith's crossover operator that we implemented for this simple one-input, one-output task.

Figure 2 shows a good solution learned by the system. The absolute error is 2.70% (in [8], Parodi and Bonelli report an absolute error of 4.67% for the function $y = \sin(20x)$). This compares reasonably well, particularly considering that the Pittsburgh style system does not employ weights for individual rules. We note the same "staircase" effect as described in [16] and [8], due to the use of non-continuous (triangular) membership functions. Experiments conducted in learning the functions $y = x$ and $y = 4(x-0.5)^2$ over 2000 GA generations produced absolute errors of 1.14% and 3.13% respectively (Valenzuela-Rendon[16] reports 1.79% and 3.76%, Parodi and Bonelli [8] report 1.19% and 3.48% respectively, using Michigan-style classifier systems with approximately the same number of learning cycles).

To investigate how the centres of input membership functions of a good fuzzy rule-base were distributed, we "took the lid off" and looked at the coverage of the individual rules. As might have been expected, many rules were found with the centres of input membership functions clustering around "interesting" areas of the input space, with fewer rules in areas where the input/output mapping varied more slowly. Figure 3 shows the distribution of input membership function centres for the mapping shown in Figure 2.

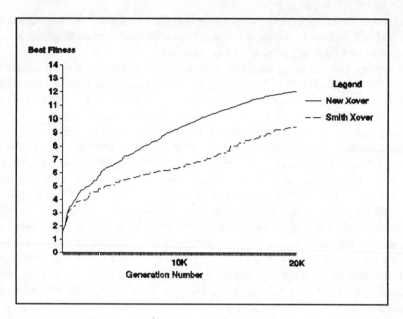

Fig. 1 Performance of the Two Crossover Operators

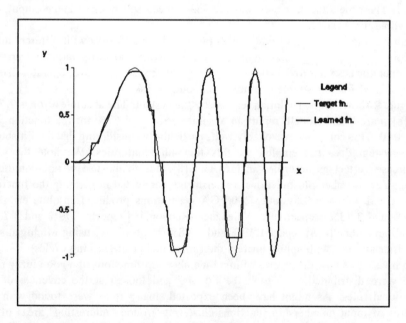

Fig. 2 Identification of the function $y = \sin(20x^2)$

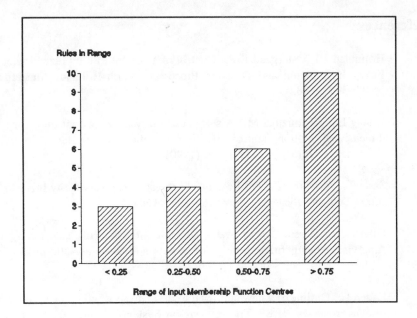

Fig. 3 Distribution of Rule Input Membership Function Centres

6 Conclusions and Further Work

We have described a Pittsburgh style fuzzy classifier system which discovers both membership functions and fuzzy relations. A modified crossover operator based on "weak" positional dependence was introduced. Experiments and results, which appear promising, of applying the new fuzzy classifier system in learning a function identification task have been presented.

This and related work requires further investigation, in particular:

- to test the system's ability to identify more complex functions and functions of more than one variable;
- to investigate the use of a "cover" operator, particularly when the search space is large;
- to explore the use of a lower level operator for rule discovery (e.g. by exchanging membership functions between individual rules); in the system presented here, the only rule discovery mechanism used once the initial random populations have been generated is real-number creep;
- to further investigate improvements to the crossover operator introduced here (e.g. a two-point or uniform version);
- to develop fuzzy classifier systems with internal message passing (all reported fuzzy classifier systems of which the author is aware, including the one presented here, are simple stimulus-response systems).

References

1. Holmblad J.J, Ostergaad L.P.: Control of a cement kiln by fuzzy logic. In: Fuzzy Information and Decision Processes, North-Holland, Amsterdam, pp389-399. (1982)

2. Huang L.J., Tomizuka M.: A self-paced fuzzy tracking controller for two-dimensional motion control. IEEE Transactions on Systems, Man and Cybernetics, 20(5), pp1115-1124. (1990)

3. Saski T., Akiyama T.: Traffic control process of expressway by fuzzy logic. Fuzzy Sets and Systems, 26, pp165-178. (1988)

4. Ollero A., Garcia-Cerezo A.J.: Direct digital control, auto-tuning and supervision using fuzzy logic. Fuzzy Sets and Systems, 30, pp135-153. (1988)

5. Zadeh L.: Outline of a new approach to the analysis of complex systems and design processes. IEEE Transactions on Systems, Man and Cybernetics, SMC-3, pp28-44. (1973)

6. Mamdani E.H.: Applications of fuzzy algorithms for control of a simple dynamic plant. Proceedings of the IEE, 121(12), pp1585-1588. (1974)

7. Smith S.F.: A learning system based on genetic adaptive algorithms. PhD thesis, University of Pittsburgh. (1980)

8. Parodi A., Bonelli P.: A new approach to fuzzy classifier systems. In Proceedings of the Fifth International Conference on Genetic Algorithms, pp223-230, 1993.

9. Holland J.H.: Escaping brittleness: the possibilities of general-purpose learning algorithms applied to parallel rule-based systems. In: Machine Learning, an artificial intelligence approach, volume 2. (1986)

10. Holland J.H.: Properties of the bucket brigade algorithm. In: Proceedings of the First International Conference on Genetic Algorithms, pp1-7. (1985)

11. Roberts G.: Dynamic planning for classifier systems. In: Proceedings of the Fifth International Conference on Genetic Algorithms, pp231-237. (1993)

12. Wilson S.W., Goldberg D.E.: A critical review of classifier systems. In: Proceedings of the Third International Conference on Genetic Algorithms, pp244-255. (1989)

13.   Thrift P.: Fuzzy logic synthesis with genetic algorithms. In: Proceedings of the Fourth International Conference on Genetic Algorithms, pp509-513. (1991)

14.   Karr C.: Design of an adaptive fuzzy logic controller using a genetic algorithm. In: Proceedings of the Fourth International Conference on Genetic Algorithms, pp450-457. (1991)

15.   Pham D.T., Karaboga D.: Optimum design of fuzzy logic controllers using genetic algorithms. Journal of Systems Engineering, 1, pp114-118. (1991)

16.   Valenzuela-Rendon M.: The fuzzy classifier system: a classifier system for continuously varying variables. In: Proceedings of the Fourth International Conference on Genetic Algorithms, pp346-353. (1991)

17.   Furuhashi T., Nakaoka K., Morikawa K., Uchikawa Y.: Controlling excessive fuzziness in a fuzzy classifier system. In: Proceedings of the Fifth International Conference on Genetic Algorithms, pp635. (1993)

18.   Holland J.H.: Adaptation in natural and artificial systems, University of Michigan Press. (1975)

Q-Learning in Evolutionary Rule Based Systems

Antonella Giani, Fabrizio Baiardi and Antonina Starita

Dipartimento di Informatica, Università di Pisa,
Corso Italia 40, 56124 Pisa, Italy

Abstract. PANIC (Parallelism And Neural networks In Classifier systems), an Evolutionary Rule Based System (ERBS) to evolve behavioral strategies codified by sets of rules, is presented. PANIC assigns credit to the rules through a new mechanism, Q-Credit Assignment (QCA), based on Q-learning. By taking into account the context where a rule is applied, QCA is more accurate than classical methods when a single rule can fire in different situations. QCA is implemented through a multi-layer feed-forward neural network.

1 Introduction

The evolution of a population of agents able to solve a given task is one of the most interesting topics of Evolutionary Computation. The paradigms currently under development are the evolution of neural networks [1, 3, 4], Genetic Programming [10], and Evolutionary Rule Based Systems (ERBSs) [15, 6, 7, 8]. In ERBSs the behavioral strategy of an agent is codified by a set of rules. Learning during the lifetime of each individual is allowed. Most ERBSs assign credit to rules through mechanisms inspired by those of Holland's classifier systems [9, 12], namely the Bucket Brigade Algorithm (BBA) [9] and epochal algorithms [6, 7].

This paper presents PANIC (Parallelism And Neural Networks In Classifier systems), an ERBS which introduces a new mechanism, Q-Credit Assignment (QCA), to allocate credit to rules. QCA is based on Q-learning [19], a temporal difference (TD) [16] architecture for reinforcement learning, and it is realised through a neural network (NN). QCA tries to overcome the shared rule problem, posed by traditional credit assignment strategies, by evaluating each rule according to the context where the rule is applied. The module of PANIC which evaluates a set of rules is very similar to Holland's classifier systems: rules can fire in parallel and interact through message passing, using a message list as a short term memory. Therefore, QCA has been defined by adapting Q-learning to the parallel features of the system and to the use of internal messages.

To overcome the large computational load of PANIC, due both to the cost of QCA and to the evaluation of alternative sets of rules, a decentralised and asynchronous parallel model of the Genetic Algorithm (GA) has been developed. Experimental results show that the parallel evaluation of genotypes and the decentralised execution of the genetic operators allow the system to evolve a population of genotypes with high fitness in an acceptable time, as well as a good scalability of the model, with respect to both the evaluation and the time to form genetic groups [5].

The paper is focused on the learning at the individual's level. Section 2 points out some problems of traditional credit assignment mechanisms and proposes QCA. A detailed description of QCA is presented in Sect. 3. Experimental results are presented and discussed in Sect. 4. Finally, Sect. 5 summarises the work and suggests some possible developments.

2 Credit Assignment Issues in Rule based Systems

This section briefly outlines some problems posed by traditional credit assignment methods of rule based systems, namely the BBA [9] and epochal algorithms [6, 7]. The BBA assigns to each rule a scalar value, the strength, which is back propagated along an activation sequence, so that the strength of a rule corresponds to the payoff expected by its use. This method is designed to solve the credit assignment problem in a context of delayed reinforcement learning, where the environmental payoff may be received only after a long sequence of actions. The BBA has several interesting features, i.e. domain independence, incremental learning and parallelism, but it fails if some rules are shared among activation chains leading to different outcomes. An epochal strategy assigns a credit to rules only if and when an environmental reward is received, by distributing the payoff among all the rules activated since the last reward. Such a strategy can assign a correct credit in some situations where the BBA fails, but not in all of them. Consider as an example an agent that interacts with the environment modelled in Fig. 1. The agent can start from either state SI_1 or state SI_2. In SI_1, it can apply the rule R_a, starting an activation sequence leading to final state SF_1 with a reward r_1. In SI_2, the agent takes with R_b a path leading to a reward r_2 ($r_2 < r_1$), whereas with R_a it starts an activation sequence leading to final state SF_3 with no reward. In such a case, the BBA allocates a large strength to R_a, reflecting the reward r_1 expected by its use, causing R_a to win the competition with R_b in state SI_2. An epochal method would overcome this problem if the rule R_a did not appear at the beginning of the sequence, but in the case shown in Fig. 1, R_a will receive a strength larger than R_b, and the system will take the wrong path in SI_2, even if an epochal method is adopted.

Note that epochal algorithms assume a single activation chain during an episode, therefore they cannot handle parallel rule firing. Furthermore, in reinforcement learning tasks as those tackled by ERBSs and classifier systems (CSs), subgoal-reward schemes like the BBA are faster and more accurate than goal-reward schemes like epochal algorithms[1].

As shown by the previous example, a common weakness of both the BBA and the epochal methods is the assignment of a unique credit measure to a rule, independently of the situation where it fires. If a single credit measure is applied

---

[1] For a discussion about this topic see [20]. See also [16] for a more general comparison between temporal difference and supervised methods.

to a rule that can fire in different contexts and with *with different outcomes*, then the measure is wrong in at least one case. On the other hand, rule sharing cannot be avoided if the environment includes a huge number of states. To achieve most advantages of traditional methods, while using a utility measure of rules based on the context, we propose the reinforcement learning architecture Q-learning [19] as the credit assignment mechanism. Q-learning belongs to the Temporal Difference (TD) methods [16], which are widely used in the reinforcement learning field, mainly as an on-line learning scheme in neural networks [11, 17, 18]. Q-learning is a learning architecture to maximise the environmental payoff and it differs from others TD schemes in that it evaluates actions together with environmental states. The following section briefly describes Q-learning and how it can be adapted to a rule based system.

3 QCA: Q-Credit Assignment

3.1 Q-learning Model

Q-learning is a TD reinforcement learning method designed to acquire an optimal policy in Markovian domains by experience, without requiring an exact model of the environment. In this context, the task domain can be modeled as a Markov process, where the agent acts as controller. At each time step, the agent knows the state of the process and executes an action according to an estimate of its consequences in terms of return, i.e. a long-term discounted reward. Then, the estimate is updated according to the immediate reward and to the evaluation of the new state. In such a way, the agent can learn to act optimally by repeatedly experiencing different actions.

More formally, given an action a and a state s, Q-learning has to predict the expected return of the execution of a in s. The prediction is based upon an evaluation function Q of pairs (state, action) and a state evaluation function V, defined as follows:

$$Q(s,a) = r + \gamma V(s')$$

$$V(s') = \max_{k \text{ allowed in } s'} Q(s', k)$$

where s' is the state reached by executing a in s, γ is the discount factor and r is the reward in s'. Thus, the evaluation $V(s)$ of a state s is the best possible outcome from s. The TD error, used to update Q, is the difference between the current prediction $Q(s,a)$ and the value $r + \gamma V(s')$, i.e. the prediction which is currently considered as the correct one, according to the current evaluation function V. The knowledge of $Q(s,a)$ for every a implies that of $V(s)$ and it easily determines the best policy: in the state s the agent has to execute an action a such that $Q(s,a) = V(s)$. To use Q-learning in a rule based system we have to define (a) the meaning of "state" and "action", i.e. to identify the Markov process to be controlled, and (b) how the return prediction has to be computed and updated according to the TD error.

3.2 States and Actions

At each time step, an agent acquires environmental information through the input interface (detectors), codified as messages, and it activates some rules chosen through a bidding competition based mechanism. The system operates on the environment through an output interface (effectors), according to the setting specified by posted messages. In this context, the term "state" usually denotes the collection of external environmental information acquired by the input interface. This definition does not fit the path independence property required by Q-learning, in that the rules to be fired depend on both detector messages and internal ones. This suggests to consider the whole message list as the process state and an "action" as the posting of any message, not only of the effector ones. As a matter of fact, at each time step, messages are posted according to the message list contents, and they modify that contents (process state) because (a) at the next step these messages will form the new list, and (b) they can be effector messages which modify the external environment. To avoid that two lists containing the same messages but in different order are considered two different states, messages in list are ordered according to the binary representation.

While this definition of "process state" does not contrast the classical model [2], it satisfies the path independence property. Finally, since detector messages codify at every step the state of the environment, the reward can be associated unambiguously with the message list contents, i.e. with the process state.

3.3 A Neural Network to Compute the Evaluation Function

The function $Q(s, a)$ is computed by a neural network (NN) that takes as input the message list contents together with a message produced by a satisfied rule. The main motivation of this solution is the complexity of the task domain, i.e. the huge number of possible states and actions to be evaluated. A look-up table representation does not seem feasible, while a NN can store the function in a distributed manner on connection weights. Furthermore, the generalisation capability of a NN provides an inductive mechanism to exploit experiences in evaluating states and actions never seen before, but "similar" to already explored ones. This could increase the ability of the system to discover regularities in the input and to absorb new rules without losing capabilities previously acquired.

In PANIC, Q is implemented by a multi-layer, fully connected feed-forward neural network, with a hidden layer and one output unit. The hidden units activation function is the symmetric sigmoidal function. The output unit is linear and it takes scalar real values corresponding to the Q function evaluation of the input pairs. The input pattern, corresponding to a message list configuration $\{m_1,...,m_n\}$ and to a message m, is the string on $\{-1,1\}$ that is obtained from the string $m_1,..., m_n, m$ by substituting '0' with '-1'. Thus, the number of input units is $l(n + 1)$, where l is the message length and n is the message list size. If the message list is not full, the net input is determined as if any empty position contains the message 0...0. The learning mechanism is implemented by a combination [11, 16] of a TD method and the backpropagation algorithm [14]: the TD error between two successive evaluations is back propagated in the network to update the weights of the network and improve the evaluation function.

3.4 The Problem Solving Cycle

This subsection describes how the QCA mechanism can be embedded in a rule based system. Let be:

s_t the Markov process state, i.e. message list contents, at time t;
$\{a_m\}_t$ the set of messages produced at time t;
$\{a_w\}_t$ the set of messages posted at time t by winning rules;
w_t the weights of the network at time t;
ϵ_t the TD error at time t.

We assume as the basic PS cycle that of a CS [12]. At iteration t:

1. Add all detector messages to s_t;
2. Compare all messages in s_t to all conditions of all rules;
3. For each match, add to $\{a_m\}_t$ the message specified by the action of the satisfied rule;
4. If the size of $\{a_m\}_t$ is larger than that of the message list, establish a competition among messages, according to their utility; then, add winning messages to $\{a_w\}_t$;
5. Produce the current output, according to effector messages in $\{a_w\}_t$; if several external actions are specified, resolve all conflicts according to the utility of the messages, then delete all not winning messages from $\{a_w\}_t$;
6. $s_{t+1}:=\{a_w\}_t$.
7. $t:=t+1$

The environmental reward and the new external state, corresponding to the actions at iteration t, is available at iteration $t+1$. To solve the competition and the conflicts, at step 4 and 5, a utility measure for each rule is required. This measure is computed and updated by the QCA mechanism, by inserting between steps 3 and 4 the following operations:

- Evaluate the set $S = \{Q(s_t, a) : a \in \{a_m\}_t\}$ with network weights w_{t-1}, then compute $V(s_t) = \max S$;
- Compute the TD error $\epsilon_t(a) = \gamma V(s_t) + r_t - Q(s_{t-1}, a)$ for each $a \in \{a_w\}_{t-1}$, with $Q(s_{t-1}, a)$ values computed at iteration $t-1$ with network weights w_{t-1};
- Back propagate the TD errors $\epsilon_t(a)$ in the neural network for each pattern (s_{t-1}, a), $a \in \{a_w\}_{t-1}$, to update the predictions $Q(s_{t-1}, a)$; let the updated network weights be w_t;
- Re-evaluate the current state together with the allowed actions, i.e. the set $S = \{Q(s_t, a) : a \in \{a_m\}_t\}$, with updated weights w_t.

The values $Q(s_t, a)$ are used as utility measures of the messages $a \in \{a_m\}_t$ and $a \in \{a_w\}_t$ in steps 4 - 5.

According to Q-learning, the evaluation of a state $V(s)$ is the maximum value of $Q(s, a)$, where a is any action allowed in s. Thus, the matching phase has to occur before computing $V(s)$. At each iteration, the patterns corresponding to the current state and the allowed actions, are presented to the network twice: at first with old weights, to evaluate the TD error on previous iteration, then with updated weights, to compute the Q values for the current competition.

While Q-learning assumes that only one action can be executed at each iteration, QCA allows several rules to fire in parallel: the TD error is computed for each action and the network learning is applied to the corresponding pattern.

3.5 BBA and QCA: A First Comparison

Like the BBA, QCA is domain independent and incremental, since graceful learning is a feature of TD methods. However, it is not parallel, since a single network evaluates every (s, a) pair. A first advantage of QCA lies in its ability to evaluate the convenience of activating a rule according to the situation. Hence, as shown by the experimental results in Sect. 5, QCA is more appropriate when a rule is shared among several activation sequences. Furthermore, while QCA does not require structural links among rules in order to assign credit to a temporal activation sequence, BBA requires rule coupling to propagate the strength through rule chains back to stage setters.

A drawback of QCA is a large computational cost. At each iteration, it requires $2n$ evaluations, where n is the number of matches, while the number of patterns to be learnt at iteration t is equal to the number of messages produced by the winning rules at iteration $t-1$. Furthermore, the network size grows with the message list and with the message length. Instead, in the BBA the strength of each rule is immediately available and the updating is very simple.

4 Experimental Results

The task domain chosen to test the system is the FSW (Finite State World) [12], where each world is modelled as a finite Markov process. Each world is defined by a set of states, each identified by a number and possibly associated with a non null payoff, and by a transition probability matrix. Each effector message codifies the value for a parameter e, which determines effector settings. The probability matrix P is function of e. This domain allow the modelling of worlds of desired complexity, where rules have to be organised in special structures, like chains or default hierarchies, to obtain the maximum payoff. These structures have been advocated as the basic building blocks to construct more complex knowledge structures [12, 13] and it is essential that the system can both create them and assign them the correct credit.

The experiments reported here concern the credit assignment mechanism only, i.e. an execution corresponds to the evaluation of a set of rules by the

PS module. For a more complete set of tests of PANIC, see [5]. The system is initialised with a set of rules ad hoc for each analysed task, that does not change during the execution. The set includes both rules leading to a reward and wrong ones. The system has to allocate correct credit to the rules and learn how to obtain the maximum payoff.

The performance measure reported in all graphs is the ratio of the obtained payoff to the possible maximum, versus the number of *PS* cycle's iterations. Two measures are considered: an off-line performance P (average on all previous iterations) and an on-line performance Pn (average on the last n iterations).

Because of the random initialisation of the weights of the NN, the initial evaluations of alternative choices may be very different. To allow the exploration to overrule the exploitation in the initial phase of learning, a number K of initial iterations has been fixed, during which the evaluations returned by the NN are altered before competition. The world W1 (Fig. 2), has been used to test how QCA allocates credit to stagesetters at the beginning of an activation sequence. In W1 two actions are allowed, corresponding to the effector settings $e = 0$ and $e = 1$. From the initial state 0, the system can go either to 1, by setting $e = 0$, or to 4, by setting $e = 1$, while from 3 and 6 it always goes to 0. A reward $r = 2$ is associated with 3. The system has been initialised with a set of rules allowing all transition represented by arrows in Fig. 2. Figure 6 shows the performance of the agent in world W1, using the QCA mechanism. The performances in all the graphs are averaged on 10 executions, starting with a different random seed. The used parameters for QCA are a discount factor $\gamma = 0.2$ and a neural network learning rate $\eta = 0.01$. In other experiments with longer paths, the value of K increases. For example, if the length of the paths is 8, the system learns the correct path in 8 executions on 10 with $K = 1000$. The world W2, shown in Fig. 3, has two paths of different lengths, leading to the same reward. The system learned the shortest path, as shown in Fig. 7. Note that, if the difference between the lengths of the two paths is very low, as in W2, the probability of choosing the shortest path increases as γ decreases. In the executions reported in Fig. 7, γ is set to 0.1.

In the world W3, shown in Fig. 4, R is shared between two chains leading to different outcomes. This is a typical situation where the BBA fails, thus we have compared the BBA and the QCA in this environment with the same set of rules. As shown in Fig. 8, the BBA performance sharply falls down to the minimum, while the QCA succeeds in learning the correct path. The QCA performance improves if the competition is biased toward larger evaluation values: this is obtained by raising each prediction value to a constant EPOW before the random competition, so that messages with a higher evaluation are more likely to win the competition.

Finally, the system has been tested in the world W4, shown in Fig. 5, with a set of rules implementing a default hierarchy. As shown in Fig. 9, the QCA assign a correct credit to the rules in the hierarchy. The learning is slower than in other examples because several more patterns are presented to the NN.

5 Conclusions

This paper has presented PANIC, a parallel Evolutionary Rule Based System, whose main feature is the use of an asynchronous and decentralised GA. The analysis of the rule sharing problem in traditional credit assignment algorithms has led us to propose a further mechanism, QCA, embedded in PANIC. QCA is implemented through a neural network and it evaluates rules according to the context where they are applied. As our results show, QCA is able to allocate correct credit to rules and to learn how to obtain the maximum payoff in situations where traditional algorithms fail. The main disadvantage of QCA is a heavier computational load, which is balanced in PANIC by the parallel model of the GA. We argue that PANIC shows the feasibility of the integration of different paradigms, such as rule based systems, neural networks and evolutionary algorithms, to define powerful and robust learning systems.

References

1. P. J. Angeline, G. M. Saunders, and J. B. Pollack. An evolutionary algorithm that constructs recurrent neural networks. *IEEE Transaction on Neural Networks*, 1994.
2. A. G. Barto, R. S. Sutton, and C. J. C. H. Watkins. Learning and sequential decision making. Technical Report COINS 89-95, Comp. and Inform. Sci., Univ. Mass., 1989.
3. R. K. Belew, J. McInerney, and N. N. Schraudolph. Evolving networks: using the genetic algorithm with connectionist learning. Technical Report CSE CS90-174, Comp. Sci. and Engr., Univ. California, 1990.
4. D. J. Chalmers. The evolution of learning: An experiment in genetic connectionism. In *Proceedings of the 1990 Connectionist Models Summer School*, 1990.
5. A. Giani. Un nuovo approccio alla definizione e all'implementazione di siatemi a classificatori. Master's thesis, Dip. di Informatica, University of Pisa, Italy, 1992.
6. J. J. Grefenstette. Credit assignment in rule discovery systems based on genetic algorithms. *Machine Learning*, 3(2-3), 1988.
7. J. J. Grefenstette. A system for learning control strategies with genetic algorithms. In *Proceedings of the Third International Conference on Genetic Algorithms and Their Applications*, 1989.
8. J. J. Grefenstette. Lamarckian learning in multi-agent environments. In *Proceedings of the Fourth International Conference on Genetic Algorithms and Their Applications*, 1991.
9. J. H. Holland. *Escaping brittleness: The possibilities of general-purpose learning algorithm applied to parallel rule-based systems*, volume 2 of *Machine learning: An artificial inteligence approach*. Morgan Kaufmann, 1986.
10. J. Koza. *Genetic programming: On the programming of computers by the means of natural selection*. MIT Press, 1992.
11. L. Lin. Self-improving reactive agents: Case studies of reinforcement learning frameworks. In *From Animals to Animals: Proceedings of the First International Conference on Simulation of Adaptive Behaviour*, 1990.
12. R. L. Riolo. *Empirical studies of default hierarchies and sequences of rules in learning classifier systems*. PhD thesis, University of Michigan, 1988.

13. G. G. Robertson and R. L. Riolo. A tale of two classifier systems. *Machine Learning*, 3, 1988.
14. D. E. Rumelhart, G. E. Hinton, and R. J. Williams. *Learning internal representation by error propagation*, volume 1 of *Parallel Distributed Processing*. MIT Press, 1986.
15. S. F. Smith. *A learning system based on genetic adaptive algorithms*. PhD thesis, University of Pittsburgh, 1980.
16. R. S. Sutton. Learning to predict by the methods of temporal differences. *Machine Learning*, 3, 1988.
17. R. S. Sutton. Reinforcement learning architectures for animats. In *From Animals to Animats: Proceedings of the First International Conference on Simulation of Adaptive Behaviour*, 1990.
18. G. J. Tesauro. Practical issues in temporal difference learning. Technical Report RC 17223, IMB T. J. Watson Research Center, Yorktown Heights, NY, 1991.
19. C. J. C. H. Watkins. *Learning with delayed rewards*. PhD thesis, University of Cambridge, England, 1989.
20. T. H. Westerdale. A defence of the bucket brigade. In *Proceedings of the Third International Conference on Genetic Algorithms and Their Applications*, 1989.

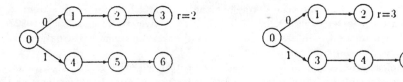

Fig. 1. An environment where both the BBA and epochal methods fail.

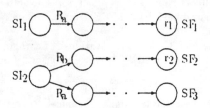

Fig. 2. World W1

Fig. 3. World W2

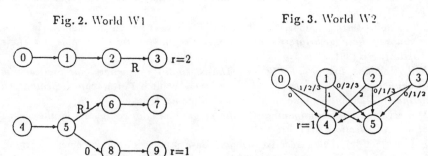

Fig. 4. World W3

Fig. 5. World W4

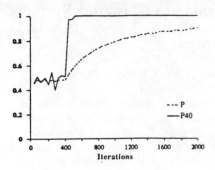

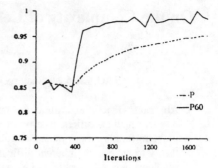

Fig. 6. Off-line and on-line performance of QCA in the world W1 (K = 1000).

Fig. 7. Off-line and on-line performance of QCA in the world W2 (K = 1000).

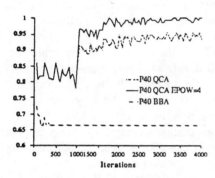

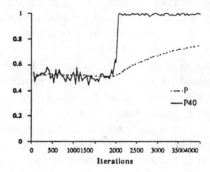

Fig. 8. Off-line and on-line performance of QCA and BBA in the world W3 (K = 1000).

Fig. 9. Off-line and on-line performance of QCA in the world W4 (K = 2000, EPOW = 4).

On the Complexity of Learning in Classifier Systems

U. Hartmann

RAG, ZK 5.21, Shamrockring 1, D-44623 Herne, FRG

Abstract. Genetic algorithms are employed in classifier systems in order to discover new classifiers. The paper formalises this rule discovery or learning problem for classifier systems and uses methods of computational complexity theory to analyse its inherent difficulty. It is proved that two distinct learning problems are NP-complete, i.e. not likely to be solvable efficiently. The practical relevance of these theoretical results is briefly discussed.

1 Introduction

Classifier systems are simple rule based production systems. The basic data structures are binary strings which are matched to conditions, i.e. strings containing wild cards (#). Classifier systems are message passing and work in parallel.

In general, a classifier system only contains a small portion of the possible rules (i.e. classifiers) and even the best of the rules in the system might not achieve much payoff from the environment. The so-called *rule discovery system* generates new classifiers using the existing classifiers in the system. The rule discovery system often employs *genetic operators* as *mutation* or *crossover*. Such genetic algorithms are heuristics which are supposed to generate new, useful rules [2,4,9].

In this paper we use methods of the computational complexity theory in order to analyse the inherent difficulty of learning in classifier systems. Our results do not depend on special (possibly genetic) learning algorithms.

Throughout the paper we assume that the principles of classifier systems are known [2,4,9]. Furthermore we assume that complexity classes NC, P, R (= RP), and NP as well as the concept of NP-completeness and the technique how to prove NP-completeness are known [1,3,5]. However, we will illustrate the ideas of the proofs by examples.

2 Learning in Classifier Systems

We are only interested in analysing the difficulty of learning in classifier systems, hence we do not discuss the performance of the rule based production system of the classifier system.

A message $m_i \in \{0,1\}^\ell$ in a classifier system is a binary string of fixed length ℓ. We will denote the j-th letter of a message m_i by $m_i(j)$ while m_i denotes the i-th message. These messages are collected in a message list $M = (m_1,..,m_m)$ which is a finite list of m messages m_i. A classifier condition $d_i \in \{0,1,\#\}^\ell$ is a string of fixed length ℓ.

A classifier c_i is a production rule containing a fixed number $(d > 0)$ of conditions d_i and one message specification $m_c \in \{0,1,\#\}^\ell$. An arbitrary classifier condition d_i matches a message m_j iff for each q, $1 \leq q \leq \ell$: $d_i(q) = m_j(q)$ or $d_i(q) = \#$.

The message of the classifier c_i is specified by its message specification m_c. If the message m_i matches a certain condition, say d_1, the resulting message is $m_i(j)$ if $m_c(j) = \#$ and $m_c(j)$ else.

Let M be a message list and c_i be a classifier c_i matches a message list M iff each condition d_j $(1 \le j \le d)$ matches at least one of the messages m_q $(1 \le q \le m)$ in the message list.

The main learning task to be solved in a classifier system is to find a set of classifier conditions which agrees with a set of message lists or tasks to be learned. We distinguish positive and negative learning tasks. We state two different learning problems concerning the question whether a classifier agrees with a message list.

Firstly, the set of k classifier conditions has to be consistent with all the positive and negative tasks. According to this learning problem the conditions are required to match exactly the positive training examples; none of the conditions is allowed to match any message given as a negative example. Secondly, the classifier conditions are required to match all of the positive tasks without considering any negative ones. However, we require the classifier to be as specific as possible since the classifier condition which entirely consists of #-symbols matches every message.

3   Learning in Classifier Systems is Hard

At first we will examine a general learning problem for classifier systems. The objective is to find classifier conditions which match each of a set of positive tasks but which do not match any given negative tasks. Such a problem is easily solvable since we can simply check whether one message in each positive task is consistent with all the negative examples. Therefore the trivial solution of this problem consists of p matching classifier conditions where p is the number of positive tasks. However, we require our learning algorithm to find k classifier conditions which are able to distinguish an arbitrary number of positive tasks from an arbitrary number of negative tasks.

Definition 1 *k-DistinguishingClassifierSet (k-DCS)*
Let $P = \{P_0, .., P_p\}$ be a set of positive tasks, $N = \{N_0, .., N_n\}$ be a set of negative tasks where each task N_i, P_i respectively, consists of a set of at most n, p respectively, messages m_j, k a positive number, and $D = \{d_1, .., d_k\}$ a set of classifier conditions.

$k\text{-DCS} := \{ (P, N) \mid \exists D = \{d_1, .., d_k\} : $ *at least one message m of each task P_i in*
P *is matched by a classifier condition in D and no classifier*
condition matches any task N_i in N}

The problem is to decide whether there is a set of classifiers $D = \{d_1, .., d_k\}$ such that each positive task P_i is matched by a classifier condition d_j and no classifier condition matches any negative task N_i.

This formal language turns out to be NP-complete, i.e. there is no effective way to decide whether a given instance is in this language unless NP = R, NP = P respectively.

Theorem 1 *For* $k \geq 2$ *k-DCS is NP-complete with respect to polynomial time reduction.*

Example 1 Existing 2-colouring of a hyphergraph:
The hyphergraph for *HC* is given by $V = \{v_1, v_2, v_3\}$ and $E = \{(v_1, v_3)\}$. Since there are 3 nodes in the graph we construct messages of length *3* and we build one positive example $(P_1, P_2,$ and $P_3)$ for each vertex of the graph. The negative training task N_1 is constructed such that it represents the edge (v_1, v_3):

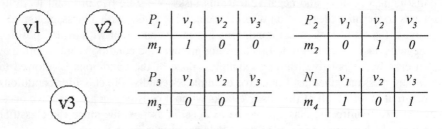

P_1	v_1	v_2	v_3
m_1	1	0	0

P_2	v_1	v_2	v_3
m_2	0	1	0

P_3	v_1	v_2	v_3
m_3	0	0	1

N_1	v_1	v_2	v_3
m_4	1	0	1

Fig. 1. Solvable example for *k-DCS*

A solution of the 2-colouring for this example graph is $\{v_1, v_2\} : \{v_3\}$. The corresponding solution of the 2-DistinguishingClassifierSet problem is *(##0, 00#)*.
Example 2 No existing 2-colouring of a hyphergraph:
We use the same graph as before except that we add hypheredges:

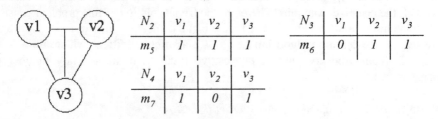

N_2	v_1	v_2	v_3
m_5	1	1	1

N_3	v_1	v_2	v_3
m_6	0	1	1

N_4	v_1	v_2	v_3
m_7	1	0	1

Fig. 2. Unsolvable example for *k-DCS*

There is no 2-colouring of this hyphergraph since we cannot find a set of two vertices which are not connected to each other. Consequently, there is also no solution of the matching classifier problem for $k = 2$.

Proof
Membership *k-DCS* is an element of NP. A nondeterministic one-tape Turing machine guesses a set of *k* classifier conditions $D = \{d_1, .., d_k\}$, and it decides in polynomial time whether the conditions d_i do not match any task in *N* and whether each message list in *P* is matched by a classifier.
Choice *Hypergraph-k-Colourability(HC) = SetSplitting[3]* $\prec_p$ *k-DCS.*

Reduction Let $G = (V, E)$ be a hyphergraph where $V = \{v_1, .., v_p\}$ is a set of vertices and $E = \{e_1, .., e_q\}$ is a set of hypheredges (e_j a subset of V) in an arbitrary instance of *Hyhpergraph-k-Colourability*. The problem is to decide whether there is a assignment of k colours to the vertices in V such that vertices of the same colour are not connected by any hypheredge in E, i.e. each hypheredge contains at least two vertices of different colours.

Set $\ell = p$. Each vertex v_j of HC will be represented by one position $m_i(j)$ of the messages in k-DCS. The value of the number k remains the same for both problems. We construct one positive task for each vertex of the graph. These tasks consist of one single message representing each node of the graph: vertex v_j is represented by a message where $m_i(j) = 1$ and all the other positions are set to 0. Each hypheredge e_j of the graph G is represented by one negative task which contains one single message representing the hypheredge. The values 1 at position $i, j, ..$ indicate that the i-th, j-th,.. vertex is covered by the hypheredge, the values for vertices which are not in the edge are set to 0.

Equivalence Suppose the hyphergraph G is k-colourable. A classifier condition d_i represents a colour of the HC problem where a # at position $i, j, ..$ indicates that the nodes $v_i, v_j, ..$ are of the same colour. Such a classifier condition does not match any task in N because this would represent unconnected vertices of the hyphergraph which are all of the same colour. Each such classifier condition represents a distinct colour and, therefore, matches each of the tasks in P.

Suppose there is a set of k distinguishing classifier conditions. If a matching classifier condition contains a 1 it can only match one represented vertex of G which can be coloured by a distinct colour; if a matching classifier condition contains some # the vertices of G which are represented by the positions containing # can be coloured by another colour. A classifier condition cannot contain # at all the positions which represent connected vertices in G and the set of classifiers has to match each message in P. Therefore a classifier condition represents a possible colouring with k colours; (however, it might propose some possible colours for one vertex). □

Our proof makes use of certain values to specify the reduction. These values give rise to some restrictions for which the problem *k-DistinguishingClassifierSet* remains hard.

Corollary 2 *For $k \geq 2$ k-DCS is NP-complete w.r.t. polynomial time reduction even if*
- each task P_i consists of only one message and
- each task N_i consists of only one message hold.

Note that also the conjunction of the conditions in corollary 2 holds.

Now we will relax the requirements of our loading task in order to examine whether this *easier* task is also easier in the sense of complexity theory. We only request the system to find the most specific classifier conditions which match each positive task.

Definition 2 *MatchingClassifier (MC)*
Let $P = \{P_0, ..., P_p\}$ be a set of positive tasks where each task P_i consists of a set of at most p messages m_1, a positive number k, and a classifier condition d_j.

$MC := \{ (P, k) \mid \exists$ a classifier condition $d_j : d_j$ contains at least k $d_j(h) \neq \#$ and matches each task P_i in P (at least once)$\}$

The problem is to decide whether there is a classifier condition d_j which matches each task P_i (at least once) and which consists of at least k none-# symbols.

It turns out that this problem also is NP-complete, i.e. there is no effective way to solve this decision problem unless NP = R, NP = P respectively.

If we consider the very special case of one single distinguishing classifier condition to be learned the problem k-DCS becomes tractable in a quite strong sense. It was proved to be in the class of problems which are efficiently solvable in parallel, i.e. a member of the complexity class NC [7,8].

Theorem 3 *MC is NP-complete w.r.t. polynomial time reduction.*

Proof in [7].

The above result holds for message lists of length ≥ 3, using a polynomial time reduction of MC to 3-SATISFIABILITY. We proceed to present an improved reduction which utilises the NP-complete problem INDEPENDENTSET in order to prove NP-completeness even for message lists containing only 2 messages.

Theorem 4 *MC is NP-complete w.r.t. polynomial time reduction even if the message list only contains two messages.*

Example 3 Existing independent set of *2* elements:
The graph for *IS* is given by $V = \{v_1, v_2, v_3\}$ and $E = \{ (v_1, v_3), (v_2, v_3) \}$. Since there are *3* nodes in the graph we construct messages of length *3*. The training tasks are constructed such that P_1 represents the edge (v_1, v_3), P_2 represents the edge (v_2, v_3), and P_3 represents the additional task:

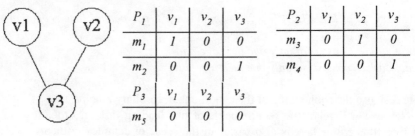

P_1	v_1	v_2	v_3
m_1	1	0	0
m_2	0	0	1

P_2	v_1	v_2	v_3
m_3	0	1	0
m_4	0	0	1

P_3	v_1	v_2	v_3
m_5	0	0	0

Fig. 3. Solvable example for *MC*

A solution of *IP* consists of $\{v_1, v_2\} : \{v_3\}$; the corresponding solution of *MC* is *(00#)*.

Example 2 No existing independent set of *2* elements:
We use the same graph as before except that there is an additional edge (v_2, v_3). Therefore we have to construct another training task P_4 representing the edge (v_2, v_3):

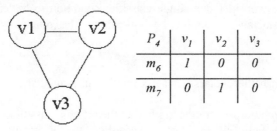

P_4	v_1	v_2	v_3
m_6	1	0	0
m_7	0	1	0

Fig. 4. Unsolvable example for *MC*

There is no solution of *2-IS* since we cannot find a set of two vertices which are not connected to each other. Consequently, there is also no solution of the matching classifier problem for $k = 2$.

Proof
Membership *MC* is an element of NP. A nondeterministic one-tape Turing machine guesses a classifier conditions d_j, and it decides in polynomial time whether d_j matches at least one message of each task in P and whether it contains k positions without wild cards #.
Choice *IndependentSet(IS)[3]* $\prec_p$ *k-DCS*.
Reduction Let $G = (V, E)$ be a graph where $V = \{v_1, .., v_p\}$ is a set of vertices and $E = \{e_1, .., e_q\}$ is a set of hypheredges (e_j a subset of V) in an arbitrary instance of *IS*. The problem is to decide whether there is a set of k vertices in V which are not mutually connected by any edge in E.

Set $\ell = p$. Each vertex v_i of *IS* will be represented by one position of the messages in *MC*. The value of the number k remains the same for both problems. Each edge e_j of the graph G is represented by one task which contains *2* messages: each of the messages represent one of the vertices connected by the edge. The value *1* at position *i* indicates that the i-th vertex is covered by the edge, the values at all the other positions are set to *0*. Now one additional message entirely consisting of *0* is required in order to prevent the solution from containing any *1*.
Equivalence: Suppose there is a independent set of k vertices of the given graph. That is none of the tasks contains two messages matching the positions representing these k vertices. Hence these k positions can be matched by a classifier condition containing *0*'s. The additional task *(P₃)* guarantees that a matching classifier condition consists of *0*'s and *#*'s.

Suppose there is a matching classifier condition consisting of at least k 0's. The vertices represented by these positions are a k-IS since they are not mutually connected. □

In general, learning in classifier systems proved to be hard. Even when we restrict our task to positive examples only it remains NP-complete.

If again we consider one single classifier condition to be learned this problem also becomes tractable in parallel, i.e. a member of the complexity class NC [7,8].

4   Discussion

The question whether a classifier agrees with a message list can be specified in two ways:
1.   The *strong* interpretation is to say that the set of k classifier conditions has to be consistent with all the tasks. According to the strong interpretation the conditions are required to match exactly the positive training examples; given negative examples none of the conditions is allowed to match (k-DCS).
2.   The *weaker* interpretation requires the classifier conditions to match all of the positive tasks without considering any negative ones. However, we require the classifier to be as specific as possible since the classifier condition which entirely consists of #-symbols matches every message (MC).

In practice the *credit assignment system* of a classifier system employs two distinct mechanisms in order to keep the rules as specific as possible: the specificity of the classifier and the bid tax. In complexity theory such optimisation problems are normally formalised as the problem to decide whether there are conditions of a certain length k since an efficient solution for this problem also implies an efficient solution for the optimisation problem. This solution can be achieved in polynomial time using binary search.

Classifier systems are intended to be able to adapt their behaviour in changing environment. In addition such systems have to deal with the difficulty that they have only got an unspecific performance parameter (payoff) and no knowledge whether certain classifiers might possibly be improved.

Like Stephen Judd we will consider fully specified learning tasks [10]. One might object against this strong restriction of the learning task since it does not represent the learning task of classifier systems with all its difficulties. On the contrary we argue that such a restriction is sensible since even this easier task will turn out to be hard. Therefore such a complex learning task would be even harder to solve or require some restrictions on the complexity of the environment.

However, we have not yet discussed why to consider only classifier conditions instead of complete classifiers. In general classifiers of a classifier system possess d conditions. So we do not only consider classifiers which possess one single condition. Classifiers are allowed to send messages which might be used as a memory of the system. When considering a fully specified learning task such a memory is no help at all since the task will only be extended to finding classifiers (or classifier conditions) matching each message list of the task and such internal messages.

In practice such classifiers implementing a memory might be useful in environments with time dependent behaviour. As we argued before this would increase the complexity of the learning problem.

5 Related Results

The computational complexity of learning within resource bounds has been studied first by Leslie Valiant who introduced the model of *probably approximately correct (PAC) learning* [14]. Stephen Judd analysed the so-called *loading problem* in neural networks [10]. Our formalisation of the learning problem is quite close to the loading problem in neural networks.

Leslie Valiant employs Boolean formulae in order to characterise families of learning tasks within his model [14]. The PAC-learning model requires the learning programme to classify correctly a complete domain of Boolean concepts, given a polynomial number of examples. These examples are presented according to a fixed, but unknown probability distribution. However, there might be some bizarre examples which occur with low probability; therefore the learned programme has to agree on most of the distribution but not on all the examples. A sequence of examples which is presented to the learning algorithm might be highly unrepresentative which introduces another source of error. This case is also required to occur with a certain probability. Furthermore the learning programme has to run in polynomial time.

We can interpret a classifier system as a certain normal form of Boolean formulae, if we regard a simple string position in a message as a Boolean variable. All the bits of a message must be matched by one of the classifier conditions, i.e. these Boolean variables are connected by a conjunction. Each message in a message list might be matched by each classifier, i.e. messages are matched by a disjunction of classifier conditions. Each different classifier is allowed to match each message, hence the conjunctions of Boolean k-terms are disjunctive. That is the learned conditions of a classifier system are equivalent to k-term disjunctive normal formulae.

A formula is in k-term disjunctive normal form whenever it is a *DNF*-formula which consists of at most k terms. A formula is in disjunctive normal form (*DNF*) when it is a disjunct of terms and each term is a monomial. A monomial is a conjunction of literals.

k-termDNF are not PAC-learnable [12]. Pitt and Valiant's proof of their theorem on *k-termDNF* is quite similar to our theorem 1 on *k-DCS*. However, we extended the PAC-learning results mentioned above to the slightly stronger proposition that loading in classifier systems is not tractable. The loading problem is *easier* than PAC-learning in the sense that a PAC-learning algorithm is expected to classify correctly the whole domain on the input of randomly chosen examples while a loading algorithm may access each training task. Therefore hardness results on loading are stronger in a practical sense since they prove the *easier* problem to be hard. Of course, there is no such distinction in the terms of complexity theory.

Hans Ros studied randomised Boolean concept learning [13]. He obtained lower bounds on the population size and the number of generations required by a genetic algorithm to approximate a special target function.

Stationary Boolean concept learning by classifier systems has been explored by Liepins and Wang [11]. Using the multiplexor problem they reason that classifier systems are inefficient for stationary Boolean concept learning without actually proving it. In fact, our paper provides the proof of the intractability of Boolean concept learning by classifier systems. Liepins and Wang feel that classifier systems are uniquely well suited for nonstationary concept learning. However, in terms of complexity theory there is no reason to expect efficient solutions for this problem in general.

Hart and Belew worked on the intractability of the optimisation of arbitrary functions by genetic algorithms [6]. That is they proved the intractability of the decision problem whether there is a string in the search space which achieves a higher payoff by a given fitness function of a genetic algorithm. We, however, did not imply any special algorithm or the use of any fitness function. Our results do not depend on any special learning algorithm or class of such algorithms.

As Hart and Belew we consider the inherent difficulty of learning within resource bounds, i.e. we discuss the question whether the learning problem is solvable in practice. We do not study the decidability or computability of learning since exponential time algorithms are not suited for real world problems.

6 Conclusion

We presented our own results on the computational complexity theory of learning in classifier systems. Our results on *k-DistinguishingClassifierSystem* extended Pitt and Valiant's results mentioned above to the slightly stronger proposition that loading in classifier systems is not tractable.

Relaxing the requirement that the classifier condition has to distinguish positive from negative examples we looked for classifiers of a certain specificity which match each of a set of positive tasks. Permitting these positive tasks to consist of sets of messages again we achieve an intractable problem. We proved that it is intractable to find one classifier with a certain specificity which matches such a set of positive message lists.

Two quite restrictive learning problems turned out to be intractable. These results justify the use of genetic algorithms as rule discovery mechanisms since we cannot expect to discover any algorithm which efficiently solves the learning problem for classifier systems. As heuristics genetic algorithms are supposed to achieve good results, however, they do not guarantee to solve the problem at all. Unsurprisingly, classifier systems are not general problem solvers. Hence one should only require reasonable learning tasks (e.g. in restricted domains) to be solved by classifier systems.

References

1. J.L. Balcàzar, J. Díaz, and J. Gabarró. *Structural Complexity I.* EATCS, Monographs on Theoretical Computer Science. Springer-Verlag, Berlin, 1st edition, 1988.
2. L.B. Booker, D.E. Goldberg, and J.H. Holland. Classifier Systems and Genetic Algorithms. *Artificial Intelligence,* 40:235-282, 1989.
3. M.R. Garey and D.S. Johnson. *Computers and Intractability.* Freeman and Company, New York, 1979.
4. D.E. Goldberg. Genetic Algorithmis in Search, Optimizations & Machine Learning. Addison-Wesley Publishing Company, Reading, Massachusetts.
5. A. Gibbons and W. Rytter. *Efficient Parallel Algorithms.* Cambridge University Press, Cambridge, UK, 1988.
6. W.E. Hart and R.K. Belew. Optimizing an Arbitrary Function is Hard for the Genetic Algorithm. In Proceedings of the fourth International Conference on Genetic Algorithms, R.K. Belew, L.B. Booker (eds.), Morgan Kaufmann Publishers, San Mateo, CA, pp. 318 - 323, 1991
7. U. Hartmann. *Computational Complexity of Neural Networks and Classifier Systems.* Diplomarbeit, University of Dortmund, Germany, July 1992.
8. U. Hartmann. Efficient Parallel Learning in Classifier Systems. In Proceedings of the International Conference on Neural Networks and Genetic Algortihms, Insbruck, R.F. Albrecht, C.R. Reeves, N.C. Steele (eds.), Springer-Verlag, Wien, pp. 515-521, 1993.
9. J.H. Holland. *Adaptation.* In R. Rosen and F.M. Snell, editors, Progress in Theoretical Biology IV, pages 263 - 293. Academic Press, New York, 1976.
10. S. Judd. *Neural Network Design and the Complexity of Learning.* Neural Network Modeling and Connectionism. The MIT Press, Cambridge, MA, 1990.
11. G.E. Liepins and L.A. Wang. Classifier System Learning Boolean Concepts. In Proceedings of the fourth International Conference on Genetic Algorithms, R.K. Belew, L.B. Booker (eds.), Morgan Kaufmann Publishers, San Mateo, CA, pp. 318 - 323, 1991
12. L. Pitt and L. Valiant. Computational Limitations on Learning from Examples. *Journal of the Association of Computing Machinery,* 35(4):965-984, October 1988.
13. H. Ros. Some Results on Boolean Concept Learning by Genetic Algorithms. In Proceedings of the third International Conference on Genetic Algorithms, J.D. Schaffer (ed.), Morgan Kaufmann Publishers, San Mateo, CA, pp. 28 - 33, 1989
14. L.G. Valiant. A Theory of the Learnable. *Communications of the ACM,* 27(11):1134-1142, November 1984.

Genetic Programming

A Representation Scheme to Perform Program Induction in a Canonical Genetic Algorithm

Mark Wineberg, Franz Oppacher

Intelligent Systems Lab, School of Computer Science
Carleton University, Ottawa Ontario, K1S 5B6
wineberg@scs.carleton.ca, oppacher@scs.carleton.ca

Abstract. This paper studies Genetic Programming (GP) and its relation to the Genetic Algorithm (GA). GP uses a GA approach to breed successive populations of programs, represented in the chromosomes as parse trees, until a program that solves the problem emerges. However, parse trees are not naturally homologous, consequently changes had to be introduced into GP. To better understand these changes it would be instructive if a canonical GA could also be used to perform program induction. To this end an appropriate GA representation scheme is developed (called EP-I for Evolutionary Programming with Introns). EP-I has been tested on three problems and performed identically to GP, thus demonstrating that the changes introduced by GP do not have any properties beyond those of a canonical GA for program induction. EP-I is also able to simulate GP exactly thus gaining further insights into the nature of GP as a GA.

1 Introduction

In this paper we study the behavior of Genetic Algorithms on the problem of program induction. The Genetic Algorithm (GA) is an adaptive search heuristic which searches a solution space [Holland 75, Goldberg 89]. There have been many attempts to implement the task of program induction using a GA [Cramer 85, Fujiki & Dickinson 87]. The most recent attempt is Genetic Programming (GP) [Koza 92]. GP uses a modification of the GA to breed successive populations of (initially arbitrary) programs until a program that solves the problem emerges.

GP, however, does not follow the GA model exactly. It has a very different "crossover" and uses a variable structured, non-linear chromosome [Koza 92]. Consequently, the behavior of GP is not well understood, and the theoretical underpinnings of the GA model cannot be directly applied to GP [O'Reilly & Oppacher 94]. In order to understand which of the innovations utilized in GP are required to evolve a population of programs towards the correct general solution of a given task, we develop a new GA representation scheme called EP-I. EP-I encodes programs, which GP uses as variable length chromosomes, into linear chromosomes with fixed internal structures. EP-I's underlying canonical GA is then applied to the new chromosomes, and a test suite of program induction problems are solved. The success of the implementation shows that the special crossover used in GP is not necessary to solve program induction using a canonical GA[1].

---

[1] There has been a previous attempt to perform GP-like program induction with a GA [Banzhaf 93]. However in this attempt new genetic operators such as transcription,

2   Genetic Programming

There have been various attempts at using an explicit procedural programming language as a basis for program induction through evolution [Cramer 85, Fujiki & Dickinson 87]. The most recent and powerful of these attempts is Koza's 'Genetic Programming' [Koza 92], which is the current 'state of the art' system. GP processes parse trees using the isomorphically equivalent LISP statements (s-expressions) for its chromosomes.

At the heart of GP lie five basic insights: that it is desirable and feasible to directly manipulate parse trees that are treated as variable length chromosomes; that different problem specific primitives may have to be used for different tasks; and that the primitives should satisfy the property of closure (here closure is a design principle that any operator used in a parse tree should be able to take as input any given atomic expression (i.e., terminals), or the output of any operator). Using these insights helps alleviate the problems of both context sensitive interpretation, and order dependency[2]. The use of parse trees addresses the problem of context sensitive interpretation (at least syntactically). Since a parse tree is fully modular, any change to its structure, as long as the integrity of the tree is kept, will produce valid programs. Order dependencies are alleviated by adhering to the principle of closure in the formation of the primitives. Closure allows changes to be made in the order of the program without destroying its syntactic correctness.

Genetic Programming begins with a set of domain dependent, user-defined operators and terminals, and an initial population of randomly generated solutions. Once the initial population has been created, each program is evaluated, to see how well it operates in comparison with known output. Using the results of the fitness function, programs are selected by a standard GA selection method. Reproduction of the selected programs is done by either copying a program, or mating two programs together using a special crossover operator for parse trees (GP Crossover) . Reproduction continues until the new population is complete. This cycle of evaluation and reproduction continues until an acceptable program is created, or until a maximum number of generations have passed.

GP Crossover exchanges subtrees of two parent parse trees. The crossover points (the location of the subtrees) in the parents are chosen independently of each other. Because of this random choice of the crossover points, the heights of the subtrees are variable. Therefore the heights of the offspring may differ from those of the parents. Since it would be computationally infeasible to allow unrestricted growth in height, a maximum height restriction is imposed on the offspring of GP Crossover. If, as a result of a crossover, an offspring has a tree height that exceeds the maximum, it is rejected.

---

editing and repairing are introduced. This deviation from a canonical GA has to our minds the following disadvantages: it renders the existing GA theory inapplicable to the analysis of program induction, and these new unanalyzed genetic operators prevent a principled analysis of the contribution of GP's innovations.

2   These problems are described by De Jong [De Jong 87] as inherent in any attempt to accomplish program induction using any full programming language. Order dependency occurs when the position of program structures is important. Context sensitive interpretation occurs when the meaning of an expression is affected by changes in another part of the program (this is analogous to epistasis).

3 Evolutionary Programming with Introns: EP-I

While GP is based on GA methods, there are differences. GA has fixed length chromosomes of fixed structure, and GP has non-linear, tree structured, variable length chromosomes. Accordingly GA and GP employ different operators, in particular, GA uses a mutation operator while GP does not, and the GP Crossover differs markedly from its GA counterpart.

The differences between GP, and a canonical GA, should be studied, to see which of the new, or modified, techniques, introduced by GP, are fundamental to the process of program induction through evolution, and which are merely expedient. In particular, is there anything "magical" about the use of GP Crossover that accounts for GP's demonstrated success at program induction?

There are a few other advantages of couching program induction in a canonical GA framework. Two of these advantages are: the extant GA theory becomes applicable to the program induction domain; and techniques thoroughly studied in other GA domains become available to solve problems in program induction.

The reason that GP uses a non-homologous crossover is to accommodate the non-linear structures of the parse trees. The traditional crossovers in GA, such as the 1-point crossover, are defined only for linear chromosomes. A naive application of the traditional crossovers would render the resulting offspring programs completely meaningless. In order to be compatible with the genetic operators used in a canonical GA, a chromosome must, therefore, have the following two properties:

1) the chromosome must be linear
2) after any genetic operator is applied, the resulting chromosome must produce a syntactically correct computer program.

The second property will be called *Syntactic Closure* for the rest of the paper. The proposed approach to program induction, i.e., Evolutionary Programming with Introns, *EP-I* for short, encodes the parse tree in a way that conforms to both of the above requirements.

3.1 Fixing the Tree Height

To simplify the description of EP-I, we shall for the moment restrict ourselves to the case of binary operators[3]. The property of syntactic closure requires the meaning of each locus to be fixed in the chromosome. This allows the crossover operator to exchange genes with their alleles, and not with incompatible genes. Satisfying syntactic closure presupposes the chromosome to have a fixed structure. If the structure were not fixed, the standard crossover operators would blindly cross nodes with incompatible data types. Were the chromosome to be decoded, nonsense would be produced.

As pointed out previously, GP uses a variable structured genotype. It should be noted, however, that the parse trees produced by the creation and reproduction routines have a maximum tree height. If a parse tree is produced with a greater height than the maximum it is rejected.

This suggests a way of using parse trees as the genotype and yet still keep a fixed structure for the chromosome. If one views the genome as a full binary tree,

---

[3] This restriction shall be lifted in section 3.3 below.

expanded out to its maximum depth, with the original parse tree as a subtree, then the length of the genotype is actually unchanging. Therefore the length of the chromosome is now fixed.

3.2 Full Tree Embedding of the Parse Tree

While the above observation allows one to fix the size of the chromosome, it does not determine a fixed structure within the chromosome. An natural way to embed the original parse tree in the expanded tree is at the top, node for node, leaving empty gene loci below the parse tree's terminal nodes. Unfortunately, disconnected tree fragments result if these empty nodes mutate.

A simple observation leads to a slightly different embedding of the parse tree. While the terminals of the parse tree are also its leaves, this is not true for the above embedding of the parse tree in the expanded tree. It is, therefore, intuitive that the terminals should "sink" in the expanded tree, and become leaves there too. In this embedding of the parse tree, all internal nodes are operators, all leaves are terminators, and no empty gene loci are needed. Therefore when crossover is applied, each matched pair of loci will be drawn from the same set. If the pair consists of leaves of the expanded tree, both genes are from the terminal set, otherwise, both genes are from the operator set. The internal structure of the chromosome is now static.

The embedding of the parse tree into the expanded parse tree as defined so far is obviously incomplete. The expanded tree will be mismatched with the parse tree: there will usually be more operator nodes than operators, and more leaves than terminals in the original parse tree. To solve this problem, a small set of related operators, called *selector operators*, are added to the operator set.

A selector operator is a simple function that selects one, and only one, outgoing edge for traversal. In a binary tree there are only two outgoing edges, so there are only two selector functions: selector-0 which selects the left edge, and selector-1 which selects the right edge[4]. These operators can now be used to properly embed the parse tree into the expanded tree.

The basic idea for the embedding is to use the selector operators to route the traversal of the expanded tree "around" areas that do not correspond to any part of the parse tree. Here is a more formal definition.

Let an expanded tree be a full tree with a fixed height that is greater than or equal to the height of the original parse tree. The value of each node in the parse tree must appear in the expanded parse tree. These are called the *corresponding values*. The positioning of the corresponding values in the expanded tree has the following restrictions:

1) If Node B is the kth child[5] of Node A in the parse tree, then the corresponding value of node B must be in the kth subtree of the corresponding value of node A.

2) Node B must be the child of Node A, or a path must exist from Node A to Node B, such that if n_i is an internal node in the path, then, if n_{i+1} is the kth child of n_i and is also in the path, then the value that n_i holds is the operator selector-k. A path that has this property, minus the two end points, will be called a *'selector chain'* (each node on the selector chain holds the selector operator that selects the next node on the selector chain).

---

[4] In case of n-ary trees, we will designate the set of selectors as 'selector-k' , k = 2,..., n.
[5] This definition holds for k-ary trees where $k \geq 2$.

3) The corresponding value of a terminal in the parse tree must be a leaf in the expanded tree.
4) The root of the expanded tree must hold the corresponding value of the root of the parse tree or be a selector operator that is the start of a selector chain that leads to the corresponding value of the root of the parse tree.

The nodes that are not corresponding nodes, nor in a selector chain, can hold any value, as long as the value is from the correct set: leaves must have genes from the terminal set, and internal nodes must have genes from the operator set.

If these properties hold, then the parse tree is properly embedded in the expanded tree (see figure 1 for an example of a parse tree embedded in an expanded tree). When an expanded tree has a parse tree correctly embedded in it, it is called an *expanded parse tree*.

3.3 Introns and N-ary Operators

The terms *intron* and *exon* are borrowed from Genetics [Crick 79]. For our purposes an intron shall mean any genetic material that does not have a phenotypic expression; and an exon, similarly, shall mean any coded genetic material that does have

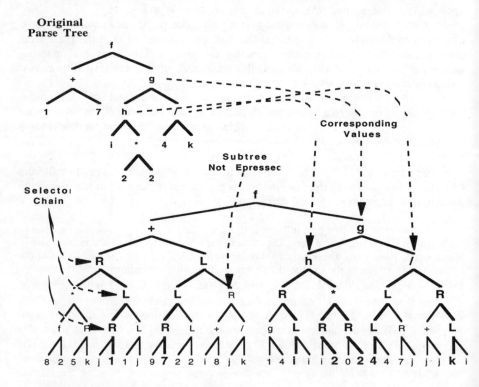

Operator Set, F = {+, -, *, /, f, g, h}
Terminal Set, T = {0, 1, 2, 3, 4, 5, 6, 7, 8, 9, i, j, k}

Figure 1 A Parse Tree Embedded in an Expanded Parse Tree

**Depth-First Encoded
Chromosome**

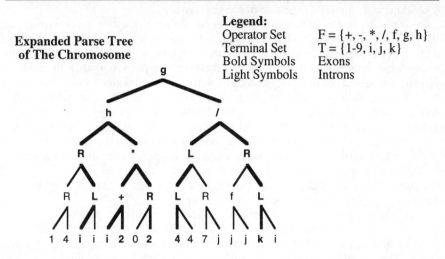

**Expanded Parse Tree
of The Chromosome**

Legend:
Operator Set   F = {+, -, *, /, f, g, h}
Terminal Set   T = {1-9, i, j, k}
Bold Symbols   Exons
Light Symbols   Introns

Figure 2   Example Chromosome with Introns and Exons Detailed

phenotypic behavior. The notion of introns is naturally applicable to EP-I. Like eukaryotic genomes, EP-I has genetic material inside the chromosome that is not expressed when decoded. Subtrees under edges that are not selected by a selector operator, and subtrees under a node set to an operator that does not use all of its parameters, are not included in the decoded s-expression, and so do not have an effect when that s-expression is evaluated by the fitness function. It is natural, therefore, to call these subtrees introns, and all the other nodes, which are expressed in the s-expression, exons. In other words, introns can be thought of as non-selected subtrees in the expanded parse tree. For an example of introns, and exons in a depth first encoded chromosome, see figure 2.

Introns hide genetic code from the selection process. This is both a blessing and a curse. On the negative side, this can be seen as slowing down convergence, since the selection pressures, that drive the system, are not applicable to the hidden code. Such code will not be bred out (except accidentally), even if it is useless or detrimental when expressed, nor recognized and promoted, even if it is beneficial. It is not even a good depository for safekeeping 'good' code; when hidden inside an intron, any schema can still be destroyed by the crossover operator (or the mutation operator if it is allowed to work within introns), which cannot be prevented from selecting crossover points within an intron, since the other chromosome being crossed may have an exon at that locus.

In spite of the above argument, the introns may actually help the search process. An intron can be viewed as an analog of the 'don't care' symbol explicitly expressed in the chromosome. In this respect it is comparable to the Classifier

System's '#' symbol, except that introns affect more than one gene at a time. The intron dynamically blocks out segments of the genotype that are not needed for the ultimate solution. Since this reduces the amount of search space, the introns may actually speed up the convergence process. The positioning of the intron is influenced by selection pressure, and so introns can be seen as a large scale 'gene' that is expressed by blocking out unneeded segments of the genotype.

When an intron is turned into an exon, through mutation or crossover, the intronal material that is activated is frequently the root of a huge subtree, all of which, suddenly, is expressed / hidden. This means mutation, when introns are used in the chromosome, can have a larger effect on the resulting phenotype than in most GA systems. The effects of these large sporadic mutations are unknown.

Before the effects of introns are investigated, it is mandatory that EP-I be shown to work. The positive results reported below are encouraging, and the further exploration of the effects of introns will provide an interesting topic for future work.

Now EP-I with n-ary operators can be easily defined. The first step is to set the fan-out of each node of the tree to equal the maximum number of parameters needed by any operator in the Operator Set. Once this fan-out is found from the Operator Set, and the tree-height is known, a full tree can be created, which can be used as the template for a fixed length chromosome.

While setting the fan-out equal to the maximum number of parameters that any operator can use, fixes the structure of the expanded parse tree, there are still many operators that will take fewer parameters than the maximum. Therefore, the operators at many nodes will be given too many operands. To handle this problem, the operator can be applied to a subset of the values returned by the node's children. In other words they become introns.

3.4 EP-I Genetic Operators

Now that the internal structure of the chromosome is fixed by EP-I, the canonical GA operator can be applied. In figure 3 we show an example of one-point crossover working on a thirty one locus chromosome which encodes an expanded parse tree of height five[6]. Just as with GP's special purpose operators, any manipulation of the chromosome with any canonical genetic operators will lead to a syntactically correct program under EP-I. This can also be seen in the figure, where the children are syntactically correct programs. Since we can now use any traditional GA operator, EP-I opens the doors for using any operators established in other contexts for the purpose of program induction.

3.5 Experiments with EP-I

We have performed a small test suite of three of Koza's program induction problems: symbolic regression, the 6 bit multiplexor, and Fibonacci sequence induction. For a description of these problems see [Koza 92], and for a detailed account of our experiments see [Wineberg and Oppacher 94]. In general, our results using EP-I as a canonical GA are comparable to those achieved using the standard GP algorithm.

---

6   In these figures, Operator Set F = {+, -, *, /, f, g, h}, and Terminal Set T = {0-9, i, j, k}.

Parent 1

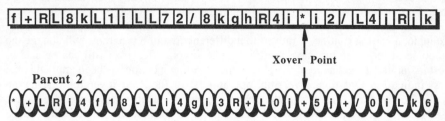

Xover Point

Parent 2

The decoded S-Expressions for Parent 1 and Parent 2 are:
(f (+ 1 7) (g (h i (i i 2)) (/ 4 k))) and (* (+ 4 (- i (g i 3))) (+ 0 (+ 5 j))), respectively.

Child 1

Child 2

The decoded S-Expressions for Child 1 and Child 2 are:
(f (+ 1 7) (g (h i (+ 5 j)) (+ (/ 0 i) k))) and (* (+ 4 (- i (g i 3))) (+ 0 (* i 2))), respectively.

Figure 3 An example of one-point crossover

Furthermore, EP-I can implement the GP crossover and therefore simulate exactly the GP algorithm. As a result of this, it becomes obvious why GP can function without the use of an explicit mutation operator. The primary use of mutation in GA is to re-introduce lost alleles at a given locus when thoses alleles have been prematurely bred out. The GP crossover, when used in EP-I, automatically moves alleles around, and so no locus can permanently be deprived of a valuable gene. Therefore the GP crossover can now easily be seen to incorporate the major effects of mutation.

4 Transposition - A Misunderstood Genetic Operator

In the course of simulating GP crossover in EP-I, we realized that the crossover was in fact moving genetic material around inside the chromosome. This is strongly analogous to a biological process called transposition.

Curiously the tranposition operator actually appears in the GA literature but is mistakenly called 'inversion' [Fujiki & Dickinson 87] or 'permutation' which was considered as a generalization of inversion [Koza 92]. This 'inversion' operator can be applied if the chromosome is built up of blocks of code that retain their meaning when moved to another area of the chromosome. Inversion and transposition are, in fact, very different. While both move code around inside a chromosome, transposition moves meaningful building blocks as opposed to just inverting a sequence of single loci. Furthermore, when using transposition the general phenotype may change since the 'transposon' will have a slightly different effect in the new position. For example, a sorting routine, if moved to a different area of a program, will change the outcome of the program (have a different phenotypic effect) yet still can be said to 'sort its input'. The change of the phenotype after the operator has been applied is the first indication that this 'inversion' operator is, in fact, not inversion. After an application of normal inversion, the phenotype remains unchanged. True inversion is used to bring genes that work well together nearer to each other to reduce the chance of them being disassociated by one point crossover [Goldberg 89]. Transposition, however, behaves in an entirely different manner.

The transposition operator has two potential effects. The first effect, which is usually the design consideration behind its use previously, is to try out a different ordering of the transposons, hoping that a different arrangement will have beneficial phenotypic effects. The second effect is less obvious, but potentially the more potent of the two. The operator affects the distribution of transposons to other positions in the chromosome, where it might also be useful. The new placement in the current chromosome may not be very beneficial, it may even be detrimental, but from that position the transposon will be transferred to other chromosomes by crossover, alleviating the need to develop the code in those positions independently. To be effective in this way, it is imperative that the crossover will not disrupt the transposons.

It is difficult to view the first effect as having a large impact in the evolutionary process. There is no a priori reason for the system to believe that a new ordering would, statistically, have a better effect on the fitness than by inserting new genes through crossover. With crossover in place, it is just a redundant operator in the system. The second effect, however, is far more interesting. The schema being moved has a high probability of being useful, since it is from a highly fit chromosome (otherwise the chromosome it exists in would have probably not been chosen). This method alleviates the need for the same schema segment having to be re-evolved in each location where it is needed. This may be of great benefit for speeding up convergence in a GA.

To implement transposition in EP-I the following algorithm was developed. In a selected chromosome a node is randomly chosen. A second node is chosen in the same chromosome also at random but with the restriction that the new point be at the same level. The subtrees below these nodes are then exchanged, thus effecting the transposition of genetic material.

Experimentation has yet to be done to see whether this transposition method is useful in EP-I.

5 Conclusion and Future Work

To compare EP-I with GP, EP-I was run on a test suite of problems with known performance when solved by GP. Although EP-I traverses the search space of possible programs in a completely different fashion than GP, the published GP results are comparable to the results achieved by EP-I.

The success of EP-I shows that an unmodified GA can perform program induction. This also answers one of our main questions when embarking on this work: determining whether the new operators introduced by GP are uniquely responsible for its success. It is now obvious that the GP Crossover does not have any special properties which are necessary to solve program induction, that a canonical GA lacks. Also, because of EP-I's greater representational flexibility, EP-I can explore many more properties of program induction through evolution than GP. It may even enable greater insights into the process of the GA itself since the task of program induction can now be directly compared to other searching tasks that have been implemented using GAs.

References

[Banzhaf 89] Banzhaf, W., "Genetic Programming for Pedestrians". In Proceedings of the Fiffh International Conference on Genetic Algorithms, 1993, edited by S. Forrest. San Mateo, California: Morgan Kaufmann Publishers Inc., pg. 628.

[Cramer 85] Cramer, N.L., "A Representation for the Adaptive Generation of Simple Sequential Programs". In *Proceedings of an International Conference on Genetic Algorithms and their Applications*, 1985, edited by J.J. Grefenstette. Hillsdale, NJ: Lawrence Erlbaum Associates, 183-187.

[Crick 79] Crick, F., "Split Genes and RNA Splicing" *Science*, Vol. 204 (April 20, 1979): 264-271.

[De Jong 87] De Jong, K. A., "On Using Genetic Algorithms to Search Program Spaces". In *Proceedings of the 2nd International Conference on Genetic Algorithms*, 1987, editor J.J. Grefenstette. Hillsdale, NJ: Lawrence Erlbaum Associates 210-216.

[Fujiki & Dickinson 87] Fujiki, C., and J. Dickinson, "Using the Genetic Algorithm to Generate LISP Source Code to Solve the Prisoner's Dilemma". In *Proceedings of the 2nd International Conference on Genetic Algorithms*, 1987, editor J.J. Grefenstette. Hillsdale, NJ: Lawrence Erlbaum Associates, 236-240.

[Goldberg 89] Goldberg, David E., *Genetic Algorithms in Search, Optimization & Machine Learning.* Reading, Massachusetts: Addison-Wesley Publishing Company, Inc., 1989.

[Holland 75] Holland, John H., *Adaptation in Natural and Artificial Systems.* Cambridge, Massachusetts: MIT Press, 1992; first published University of Michigan, 1975.

[Koza 92] Koza, John R., *Genetic Programming: On the Programming of Computers by means of Natural Selection .* Cambridge Massachusetts: MIT Press, 1992.

[O'Reilly & Oppacher 94] O'Reilly, U.-M., and F. Oppacher, "The Troubling Aspects of a Building Block Hypothesis for Genetic Programming". To appear in *Foundations of Genetic Algorithms 3, 1994.*

[Wineberg & Oppacher 94] Wineberg, M, and F. Oppacher, "A Canonical Genetic Algorithm Based Approach to Genetic Programming" to appear in the proceedings of the ECAI-94 Workshop on Applied Genetic and Other Evolutionary Algorithms, 1994.

Genetic Programming with Local Hill-Climbing

Hitoshi IBA[1]   Hugo de GARIS[2]   Taisuke SATO[1]

[1] Machine Inference Section, Electrotechnical Lab.,
1-1-4 Umezono, Tsukuba-city, Ibaraki, 305, Japan {iba,sato}@etl.go.jp,
[2] Evolutionary Systems Dept., ATR Human Information Processing Research Lab.,
2-2 Hikari-dai, Seika-cho, Soraku-gun, Kyoto, 619-02, Japan. degaris@hip.atr.co.jp

Abstract. This paper proposes a new approach to Genetic Programming (GP). In traditional GP, recombination can cause frequent disruption of building-blocks or mutation can cause abrupt changes in the semantics. To overcome these difficulties, we supplement traditional GP with a recovery mechanism of disrupted building-blocks. More precisely, we integrate the structural search of traditional GP with a local hill-climbing search, using a relabeling procedure. This integration allows us to extend GP for Boolean and numerical problems. We demonstrate the superior effectiveness of our approach with experiments in Boolean concept formation and symbolic regression.

1   Introduction

GAs traditionally use string-based representations in their chromosomes, but this is not always suitable for representing higher-level knowledge. [Koza92] introduced a hierarchical GA approach, where his chromosomes are tree-like expressions that can be recombined by swapping subtrees. Koza labeled his hierarchical version of GA, the "Genetic Programming Paradigm" (called GP). The main difference between traditional GAs and GP, lies in the following graph-theoretical manipulations.

1. **Gmutation**   i.e. changing a node label, or substituting subtrees (Fig.1(a)).

2. **Gcrossover**   i.e. swapping subtrees (Fig.1(b)).

These operations are natural extensions of traditional string-based GA "genetic operators".

It is thought that the effectiveness of traditional GAs is derived from a) the fact that crossover operators construct higher-order schema from lower-order schema by combining useful building-blocks, and b) the fact that mutation operators work by recovering accidentally disrupted schema [Schaffer91]. During the earlier stages of GA processing, chromosome divergence is large due to combination of building blocks that are initially dissimilar, and that the hamming distance between possible early mates is higher. On the other hand, as the GA generations proceed, the convergence of the population leads to a decrease in the hamming distance and to the exploration of a smaller neighborhood. (a type of local search mechanism) [Louis93]. The mutation is a "background" operator, assuring that the crossover has a full range of alleles (i.e. bits) so that the evolution is not trapped on local optima [Holland75, p.111].

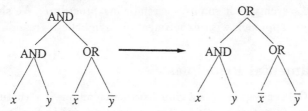

(a) Gmutation (node label change or subtree substitution).

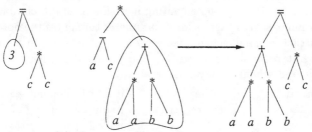

(b) Gcrossover (sub-tree swapping).

Fig.1 Genetic Operators for GP.

This argument is not necessarily true of GP, because building-blocks[1] of structured representations are disrupted so frequently that it is not easy to restore them solely by mutations. To see this, consider the following plausible situations.

1. Genetic operations applied randomly to tree-structures can cause abrupt changes in the semantics of the trees. For instance, the mutation of the root node in Fig.1(a) converts a Boolean function to a totally different function, i.e. from false (i.e. $(x \wedge y) \wedge (\overline{x} \vee \overline{y}) \equiv 0$) to true (i.e. $(x \wedge y) \vee (\overline{x} \vee \overline{y}) \equiv 1$).

2. Randomly chosen crossover points ignore the semantics of the parent trees. For instance, in order to construct the Pythagoras relation (i.e. $a^2 + b^2 = c^2$) from two parent trees (i.e. $c^2 = 3$, $(a-c) \times (a^2 + b^2)$), only one pair of crossover points is valid (see Fig.1(b)). Thus crossover operations seem almost hopeless as a means to construct higher-order building-blocks.

Therefore, traditional GP relies on a large population of chromosomes (for instance, $4000 \sim 16000$ [Koza92]), to maintain population diversity. Recently, a heuristic technique called ADF (Auto Defining Function) has been proposed so as to prevent the disruption of building-blocks by converting a subtree into a single symbol [Koza94].

To solve the above difficulty, this paper proposes a new approach to Genetic Programming when applied to Boolean and numerical problems. This is to supplement traditional GP with a mechanism to recover disrupted building-blocks. More precisely, we augment the traditional structural search of GP with a local

---

[1] In this paper, we define a GP building-block to be a subtree (substructure) useful for constructing a solution tree.

hill-climbing search which employs a relabeling procedure. We show the effectiveness of our approach with experiments in symbolic regression and Boolean concept formation.

2 Fundamental Principles

Traditional GP can regarded as a global search technique in structural (i.e. topological) spaces (e.g. tree structures), and, as discussed in Section 1, results in frequent disruption of building-blocks. To overcome this difficulty, we introduce a new approach to GP, by supplementing it with a local hill-climbing approach. Local hill-climbing search uses as local parameter tuning (of the node functionality) of tree structures, and schema recovery mechanisms, which are equivalent to mutation operators for string-based GA. Our proposed augmented GP paradigm can be considered schematically in several ways:-

augmented GP = global search   + local hill-climbing search
                = structure search   + parameter tuning of
                                       node functionalities
                = topological search + schema recovery

The local hill-climbing mechanism uses a type of relabeling procedure[2], which finds a locally (if not globally) optimal assignment of nodes for an arbitrary tree. Therefore, speaking generally, our new approach can be characterized as:-

augmented GP = traditional GP + relabeling procedure

The augmented GP algorithm is described below:-

Step1 Initialize a population of tree expressions.
Step2 Evaluate each expression in the population.
Step3 Create new expressions (children) by mating current expressions. Apply mutation and crossover to the parent tree expressions.
Step4 Replace the members of the population with the child trees.
Step5 A local-hill climbing mechanism (called "relabeling") is executed periodically, so as to relabel nodes of the trees of the population.
Step6 If the termination criterion is satisfied, then halt; else go to Step2.

As can be seen, Steps1~4 follow traditional GP, where Step5 is the new local hill-climbing procedure. In Step5, parameters (i.e. polynomial coefficients or node functionalities) at non-terminal nodes of a tree are locally tuned by using a statistical method or a label changing mechanism so that the tree outputs local, if not global, optima for a given topology (i.e. the tree structure of input relationships). In our augmented GP paradigm, the traditional GP representation (i.e. the terminal and non-terminal nodes of tree-expressions) is constrained so that our new relabeling procedure can be applied. The sufficient condition for this applicability is that the designed representation have the property of "insensitivity" or "semantic robustness", i.e. changing a node of a tree does not affect

---

[2] The term "label" is used to represent the information (such as a function or polynomial) at a non-terminal node.

the semantics of the tree. In other words, the GP representation is determined by the choice of the local-hill climbing mechanism.

The following two sections show how our augmented GP paradigm can be used to solve both Boolean and numerical problems. We have chosen two vehicles to perform the relabeling procedure, known respectively as ALN and GMDH. The resulting GP variants are called **Boolean GP** and **Numerical GP**, whose characteristics are summarized in the following table:-

	Boolean GP	Numerical GP
Problem Domain	Boolean concept formation	System identification
Tree Type	binary tree	
Terminal Nodes	variables and their negations	variables
Non-terminal Nodes	AND, OR, LEFT, RIGHT	polynomial relationships
Relabeling Process	ALN	GMDH

Table 1 Properties of GP Variants.

3 Boolean GP

Boolean concept learning is an important part of traditional machine learning. The goal is to identify the following function,

$$y = f(x_1, x_2, \cdots, x_n) = \begin{cases} 0, & \text{False value} \\ 1, & \text{True value} \end{cases} \qquad (1)$$

where $x_1, x_2, \cdots x_n$ are binary values (i.e. $\{0,1\}$), from a given set of observable input and output pairs $\{(x_{i1}, x_{i2}, \cdots, x_{in}, y_i) \in \{0,1\}^{n+1} \mid i = 1, \cdots, N\}$. N is number of observations.

We chose the ALN (Adaptive Logic Network) algorithm as our relabeling procedure (Step5 in section 2), and used it to establish the **Boolean GP** variant. The terminal nodes of an ALN tree are the input variables (i.e. $x_1, x_2, \cdots, x_n$) and their negations (i.e. $\overline{x_1}, \overline{x_2}, \cdots, \overline{x_n}$). The non-terminal nodes consist of the following four Boolean functions of two variables: AND, OR, LEFT (which outputs the first input), RIGHT (which outputs the second input). Fig.2 shows an example tree for the following function (called 6-multiplexor – "mx6").

$$y = f(x_1, x_2, x_3, x_4, x_5, x_6) = \overline{x_1}\,\overline{x_2}x_3 \vee \overline{x_1}x_2x_4 \vee x_1\overline{x_2}x_5 \vee x_1x_2x_6 \qquad (2)$$

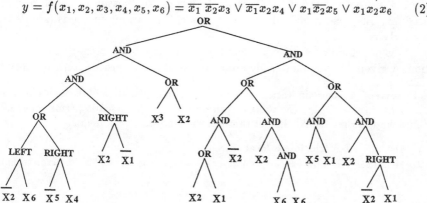

Fig.2 An Adaptive Logic Network (ALN) Tree.

where x_1, x_2 are address variables and x_3, x_4, x_5, x_6 are data variables.

The ALN algorithm gives a good node assignment, which is sometimes globally optimal[3]. Therefore, in Step5 of section2, node functionalities (i.e. AND, OR, LEFT, RIGHT) at non-terminal nodes of a tree are locally tuned by using the ALN algorithm so that the tree outputs local, if not global, optima for a given tree structure of input relationships. Thus **Boolean GP** helps overcome the problem of semantic disruption.

To confirm the effectiveness of **Boolean GP**, we first experimented in learning a simple function mx6 (eqn.(2)). The population size is 40 and the maximum depth limit 8. The probabilities of crossover and mutation are 60% and 3%. We use $\{x_1, x_2, \cdots, x_n, \overline{x_1}, \overline{x_2}, \cdots, \overline{x_n}\}$, as a set T of terminal nodes, $\{AND, OR, RIGHT, LEFT\}$ as a set F of functional nodes. All 64 $(= 2^6)$ input-output pairs are given as the training data. The raw fitness value is the percentage of correct outputs of a given tree. *ALN_Period* parameter is used to designate the period of execution of ALN (i.e. STEP5 of Section 2). Experiments were repeated 10 times with different *ALN_Period*'s. An example of the acquired tree is shown in Fig.2. Fig.3 plots the average number of individuals required to yield a solution (black dots) and their standard deviations (vertical bars) with different *ALN_Period*'s. As can be seen in the figure, the smaller the ALN period is, the fewer individuals are required. Since the maximum depth limit was set to be 8, the maximum number of nodes for this experiment was 128 $(= 2^{8-1})$, which is much smaller than the number required by the original ALN described above.

To compare the performance of **Boolean GP** with traditional GP, we experimented with the learning of more complex functions such as "even 3 parity", "even 4 parity", "even 5 parity", 11-multiplexor [Koza92,94] or Emerald's robot world problem [Janikow93], and confirmed the effectiveness of **Boolean GP**. For example, the average number of individuals to yield a solution for this problem is about 8000. Using traditional GP, this value is about 38400 [Koza94][4]. Since the terminal and non-terminal nodes are different for the two methods, it is not possible to make a direct comparison. However it should be noted that compared to traditional GP **Boolean GP** required 50 times fewer evaluations. We are currently pursuing statistical studies of comparison of our approach to original ALN, traditional GP, and other machine learning methods (see [Iba93b] for early results).

Next we conducted an experiment in learning a nonstationary Boolean function. A given ALN cannot easily adapt to nonstationary situations, because it is

---

[3] Because of the space limitation, we cannot give an explanation of the adaptive process of ALN in this paper. The process is described and discussed in [Armstrong79,91a]. It is known that the ALN algorithm has the following weak points:-

1. An ALN often falls into a local extreme.
2. An initial tree needs a large number of nodes (e.g. up to 60000 [Armstrong91b, p.12]).

---

[4] [Koza94,ch.5] chose as terminal nodes input variables $(x_1, x_2, \cdots, x_n)$ and as non-terminal nodes $\{AND, OR, NAND, NOR\}$.

necessary to construct a new tree from scratch. However, **Boolean GP** retains retain useful building-blocks which enables it to quickly discover non-stationary optima. To confirm this, we used a time-varying environment described below:-

1. The initial target function was mx6 (eqn.(2)).
2. Every 10th generation after the 40th, one of the data variables (x_3, x_4, x_5, x_6) was randomly chosen and negated. For instance, if x_4 was chosen, the new target function would be

$$y = f(x_1, x_2, x_3, x_4, x_5, x_6) = \overline{x_1}\ \overline{x_2}x_3 \vee \overline{x_1}x_2\overline{x_4} \vee x_1\overline{x_2}x_5 \vee x_1x_2x_6 \qquad (3)$$

The other experimental conditions were the same as the previous mx6. In Fig.4 the number of correct outputs (fitness) is plotted against the number of generations. Of course the fitness decreased every 10th generation. Notice that the fitness values quickly rose after these decreases and much more quickly than during the first 40 generations. Therefore **Boolean GP** effectively adapts itself to a time-varying environment.

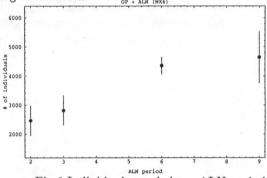

Fig.3 Individuals needed vs. ALN period.

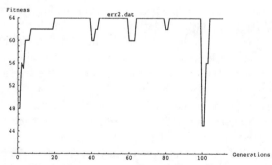

Fig.4 Nonstationary mx6 Experiment.

4 Numerical GP

Numerical GP is aimed at solving a class of numerical optimization problems called "system-identification", which is defined formally as follows. Assume that the single valued output y, of an unknown system, behaves as a function of m real-valued input values, i.e.

$$y = f(x_1, x_2, \cdots, x_m) \qquad (4)$$

Given N observations of these input-output data pairs, i.e. $\{(x_{11}, x_{12} \cdots, x_{1m}; y_1),$ $(x_{21}, x_{22} \cdots, x_{2m}; y_2), \cdots, (x_{N1}, x_{N2} \cdots, x_{Nm}; y_N)\}$, the system identification task is to approximate the true function f with $\overline{f}$. Once this approximate function $\overline{f}$ has been estimated, a predicted output $\overline{y}$ can be found for any input vector $(x_1, x_2, \cdots, x_m)$, i.e.

$$\overline{y} = \overline{f}(x_1, x_2, \cdots, x_m), \tag{5}$$

An example of a binary tree generated by **Numerical GP** is

```
(NODE1
    (NODE2
        (NODE3 (x₁) (x₂))
        (x₃)
    (x₄)))
```

written as a (Lisp) S-expression, where x_1, x_2, x_3, x_4 are the input variables. Non-terminal nodes represent simple polynomial relationships between two descendant (lower) nodes. For example, if we use quadratic expressions for the non-terminal nodes, each node records the information given by the following equations.

$$NODE3 \ : \ z_1 = a_0 + a_1 x_1 + a_2 x_2 + a_3 x_1 x_2 + a_4 x_1^2 + a_5 x_2^2 \tag{6}$$

$$NODE2 \ : \ z_2 = b_0 + b_1 z_1 + b_2 x_3 + b_3 z_1 x_3 + b_4 z_1^2 + b_5 x_3^2 \tag{7}$$

$$NODE1 \ : \ \overline{y_1} = c_0 + c_1 z_2 + c_2 x_4 + c_3 z_2 x_4 + c_4 z_2^2 + c_5 x_4^2 \tag{8}$$

where z_1 and z_2 are intermediate variables, and $\overline{y_1}$ is an approximation of the output. All coefficients $(a_0, a_1, \cdots, c_5)$ are derived from multiple-regression analysis using the least mean square method (see [Iba93a] for details).

The repetition of this multiple regression analysis for the system identification is known as GMDH (i.e. Group Method of Data Handling [Ivakhnenko71]) and we use this method as a relabeling procedure for numerical data. Therefore, in Step5 of section2, polynomial coefficients at non-terminal nodes of a tree are locally tuned by using the GMDH algorithm so that the tree outputs local, if not global, optima for a given tree structure of input relationships. Thus **Numerical GP** helps overcome the problem of semantic disruption.

We applied **Numerical GP** to several problems such as time-series prediction, pattern recognition, and 0-1 optimization. The results obtained were satisfactory. Detailed discussion is given in [Iba93a,94b]. We briefly describe the experiment in solving the "symbolic" regression problem.

The goal of symbolic regression is to discover a set of numerical coefficients for a combination of the independent variable(s) which minimizes some measure of error. In other words, the problem is both the discovery of the correct functional form that fits the data and the discovery of the appropriate numeric coefficients [Koza90, ch.4.3.2]. This problem is closely related to the discovery of various scientific laws from empirical data, such as the well-known BACON system [Langley89]. When applying traditional GP to symbolic regression, it is usual to assign the terminal set $\{T\}$ to the independent variables, and the function set $\{F\}$ to the symbolic operators. However the discovery of the appropriate numeric coefficient is very difficult, because there is no coefficient changing mechanism other than random constant creation.

We experimented with a complex symbolic regression problem of the Heron formula, i.e. the following formula of the area S of a triangle, given the lengths of its three sides (a, b, c):-

$$S = \sqrt{\frac{(a+b+c)(a+b-c)(a+c-b)(b+c-a)}{16}}. \tag{9}$$

The learning of this formula from a set of observations has been studied by [Barzdins93], in which a heuristic enumeration method was used as a traditional machine learning technique. The study showed the difficulty of solving this problem due to complicated terms in the Heron formula. In order to use polynomial symbolic regression, the target formula we used was the square of the area (S^2) with the following parameters.

Population Size	120
Probability of Crossover	60%
Probability of Mutation	3.3%
Terminal Nodes	$\{(0), (1), (2), (3), (sqr1), (sqr2), (sqr3)\}$
Non-terminal Nodes	$\{+, -, \alpha x_1 x_2, \alpha x_1 + \beta x_2\}$
# of Training Data (N)	10

Table 2 Parameters for Symbolic Regression.

Where (1),(2), and (3) indicate the variables a,b, and c respectively. (0) is a virtual variable x_0 for the purpose of representing a constant, i.e. the value of x_0 is always 1. $sqr1$, $sqr2$, and $sqr3$ are square values of a, b, and c. The acquired structure with subexpressions at generation 1105 is shown below (see also Fig.5). This tree gives 100% correct answers to all 10 data.

```
(NODE376268 (NODE370522 (NODE370523 (2) (2)) (sqr1))
  (NODE376269 (NODE375704 (NODE375705 (sqr2) (sqr1))
              (sqr3))
  (NODE376270 (sqr3) (NODE376271 (sqr2) (sqr1)))))
```

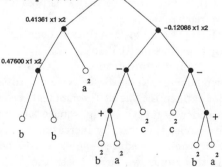

Node	subexpression
NODE376268	$1.26976x_1 + (-0.51711x_2)$
NODE370522	$0.41361x_1 x_2$
NODE370523	$0.47600x_1 x_2$
NODE376269	$-0.12086x_1 x_2$
NODE375704	$-$
NODE375705	$+$
NODE376270	$-$
NODE376271	$+$

Table 3 Subexpressions (Heron).

Fig.5 Acquired Structure.

This final tree expresses the exact formula as follows:-

$$1.26976(0.41361(0.47600 \times b \times b) \times a^2)$$
$$+(-0.51711(-0.12086((b^2 + a^2) - c^2) \times (c^2 - (a^2 + b^2))))$$
$$= 0.24998a^2b^2 - 0.06249(b^2 + a^2 - c^2)^2$$
$$\approx 0.0625\{4a^2b^2 - (b^2 + a^2 - c^2)^2\}$$
$$= \frac{1}{16}(a + b + c)(a + b - c)(a + c - b)(b + c - a) \qquad (10)$$

Thus we regard the complete form as a desired Heron formula (i.e. the square of equation (14)). In NODE370523, *sqrt2* is expanded to $0.47600 \times b \times b$. Therefore, the introduction of square values (i.e. *sqrt1*, *sqrt2*, and *sqrt3*) is not necessary for this experiment. They are used in order to improve efficiency.

For the sake of comparison, we have conducted several experiments and confirmed that **Numerical GP** required about 10 times fewer evaluations than traditional GP for various problems [Iba94a].

5 Discussion and Conclusion

Our augmented GP variants, i.e. **Boolean GP** and **Numerical GP**, overcome the following difficulties with traditional GP in the following ways:-

1. Disrupted schema were recovered using a local-hill climbing technique.
2. Local-extrema problems were solved by using a global search procedure of traditional GP crossover operations.
3. Semantic disruption of a tree by mutation (Fig.1(a)) does not occur, because of our semantically robust representations.

These points were illustrated by the above experiments. The first experiment in Section 3 (Fig.3) showed that the smaller the *ALN_Period*, the better the performance. This means that the hill-climbing search by an ALN algorithm can work well due to its guidance of the crossover operations of traditional GP. On the other hand, both the original ALN (or GMDH) and traditional GP are usually unsuccessful, because they fall into local extrema or suffer from premature convergence. In addition, our tree representations described above are semantically robust (i.e. changing a node of a tree does not affect the semantics of the whole tree) so that it is possible to execute a given hill-climbing search. Moreover, the property of semantic robustness enables to control GP search by MDL (Minimum Description Length) principle, whose effectiveness was shown by experiments [Iba94b].

An important future research is the extension of **Numerical GP** to general symbolic problems. Since **Numerical GP** can only handle polynomial relations for subexpressions at the moment, general symbolic regression (including transcendental functions, e.g. square root function in the Heron formula) are beyond its scope. However, by increasing the types of subexpression, and changing the regression procedures, we expect to be able to cope with more general cases. In this paper, we have chosen the ALN and GMDH algorithms for the relabeling procedures, which in turn, determine the representations for our augmented

GP variants (see Table 1). However these may not be the best choice. We are currently in pursuit of other relabeling procedures for various kinds of problem domain.

Acknowledgment.
We have profitted from discussions with William Armstrong. We also thank John Koza for giving us an opportunity to see the first draft of his new book [Koza94].

References

[Armstrong *et al.*79] Armstrong, W.W. and Gecsei, J. Adaptation Algorithms for Binary Tree Networks, *IEEE TR. SMC*, SMC-9, No.5, 1979

[Armstrong91a] Armstrong, W.W. Learning and Generalization in Adaptive Logic Networks, *Artificial Neural Networks*, (T.Kohonen eds.), Elsevier Science Pub., 1991

[Armstrong *et al.*91b] Armstrong, W.W., Dwelly, A., Liang, J., Lin,D., and Reynolds,S., Some Results concerning Adaptive Logic Networks, unpublished manuscript, Sept. 16, 1991

[Barzdins *et al.*91] Barzdins, J.M., and Barzdins, G.J., Rapid Construction of Algebraic Axioms from Samples, *Theoretical Computer Science*, vol.90, 1991

[Holland75] Holland,J.H. Adaptation in natural and artificial systems, University of Michigan Press, 1975

[Iba *et al.*93a] Iba, H., Kurita, T., deGaris, H. and Sato, T. System Identification using Structured Genetic Algorithms, in *Proc. of 5th International Joint Conference on Genetic Algorithms*, 1993

[Iba *et al.*93b] Iba, H., Niwa, T., deGaris, H. and Sato, T. Evolutionary Learning of Boolean Concepts: An Empirical Study, ETL-TR-93-25, 1993

[Iba *et al.*94a] Iba, H., deGaris, H. and Sato, T. System Identification Approach to Genetic Programming, ETL-TR94-2, in *Proc. of IEEE World Congress on Computational Intelligence*(WCCI94), 1994

[Iba *et al.*94b] Iba, H., deGaris, H. and Sato, T. Genetic Programming using a Minimum Description Length Principle, in *Advances in Genetic Programming*, (ed. Kenneth E. Kinnear, Jr.), MIT Press, 1994

[Ivakhnenko71] Ivakhnenko, A. G. Polynomial Theory of Complex Systems, *IEEE Tr. SMC*, vol.SMC-1, no.4, 1971

[Janikow93] Janikow, C.Z., A Knowledge-Intensive Genetic Algorithm for Supervised Learning, *Machine Learning*, vol.13, 1993

[Koza90] Koza, J. Genetic programming: A paradigm for genetically breeding populations of computer programs to solve problems, Report No. STAN-CS-90-1314, Dept. of Computer Science, Stanford Univ., 1990

[Koza92] Koza, J. Genetic Programming, On the Programming of Computers by means of Natural Selection, MIT Press, 1992

[Koza94] Koza, J. Genetic Programming II: Automatic Discovery of Reusable Subprograms, MIT Press, 1994 (in press)

[Langley *et al.*90] Langley, P., and Zytkow, J. M., Data-driven Approaches to Empirical Discovery, *Artificial Intelligence*, vol.40, 1989

[Louis93] Louis, S.J. and Rawlins, G.J.E., Pareto Optimality, GA-easiness and Deception, In *Proc. of 5th International Joint Conference on Genetic Algorithms (ICGA93)*, 1993

[Schaffer91] Schaffer, J.D. and Eshelman, L.J., On Crossover as an Evolutionarily Viable Strategy, In *Proc. of 4th International Joint Conference on Genetic Algorithms (ICGA91)*, 1991

Dynamic Training Subset Selection
for Supervised Learning
in Genetic Programming

Chris Gathercole and Peter Ross

Department of Artificial Intelligence
University of Edinburgh
80 South Bridge
Edinburgh EH1 1HN
U.K.
{chrisg,peter}@aisb.ed.ac.uk

Abstract. When using the Genetic Programming (GP) Algorithm on
a difficult problem with a large set of training cases, a large population
size is needed and a very large number of function-tree evaluations must
be carried out. This paper describes how to reduce the number of such
evaluations by selecting a small subset of the training data set on which
to actually carry out the GP algorithm.
Three subset selection methods described in the paper are:
Dynamic Subset Selection (DSS),
using the current GP run to select 'difficult' and/or disused cases,
Historical Subset Selection (HSS), using previous GP runs,
Random Subset Selection (RSS).
Various runs have shown that GP+DSS can produce better results in
less than 20% of the time taken by GP. GP+HSS can nearly match
the results of GP, and, perhaps surprisingly, GP+RSS can occasionally
approach the results of GP. GP+DSS also produced better, more general
results than those reported in a paper for a variety of Neural Networks
when used on a substantial problem, known as the Thyroid problem.

1 Introduction

At present, the potential of Genetic Programming (GP) and Genetic Algorithms
(GAs) has been demonstrated in many different problem areas. Generally, these
experiments have involved solving small, relatively neat problems. The future
beckons, however, with large and horribly messy problems, to which the GP
method will have to be scaled up.

With supervised learning, a training set of cases is involved and the aim is
to learn how to classify these known cases and hopefully generalise to be able
to correctly classify all possible cases. Large problems will require large training
sets. In the standard GP algorithm, the entire population of GP function-trees
is evaluated against the entire training data set, and so the number of function-
tree evaluations carried out per generation is directly proportional to both the
population size and the size of the training set.

In this paper, the simple method of Dynamic Subset Selection (DSS) is described. DSS reduces the number of such evaluations that need to be carried out before a satisfactory answer evolves and, in fact, can produce a more general answer. Two other selection methods are described for purposes of comparison: the (even) simpler method of Random Subset Selection (RSS), and Historical Subset Selection (HSS) which uses previous GP runs to select a single training subset. A classification problem involving the Thyroid data set (described below) was used as a token 'large and messy' problem.

2 GP, Code and Parameters

GP [3] involves a population of Lisp-like function-tree expressions, each of which is made up from an allowed set of functions and terminals, all of the same data type. Starting with a randomly generated population of function-trees, the trees which perform best on the problem in question (e.g. classify most training cases correctly) are selected to be the 'breeding stock'. These parent trees are combined (by exchanging subtrees) and mutated (by generating new subtrees) to produce new trees for the next generation of the population which inherit some features from their parents. The next generation of trees is then evaluated against the problem. The best trees are selected to produce the next generation after that, and so on. As with Genetic Algorithms [2, 1], the GP population is evolved to (hopefully) produce function-trees which can perform well on the problem in question.

The allowed function and terminal sets used in this paper are:
{ IFLTE, +, -, *, %, TANH, LOG, MINIMUM_OF_3, NEGATE, SQRT },
and { B1 to B15, F1 to F6, 0, -1 }, where 'B' and 'F' refer to the binary and floating point fields of the Thyroid cases.

The code used for these experiments was adapted from the SGPC code [8], written in C. The parameter settings chosen here were not optimal, by any means, since the main aim was to demonstrate the effect of *Training Subset Selection* and not *Parameter Tweaking*.

3 The 'Large and Messy' Thyroid Problem

The Thyroid data set [6] represents a hard classification problem. The results reported for Neural Networks [4, 5] provide an interesting comparison with the performance of GP, however, the main aim for this paper was to improve the performance of GP on a hard problem.

The data is based upon measurements of the thyroid glands of patients at a hospital. Each measurement vector consists of 15 binary values (0.0 or 1.0) and 6 floating point values (i.e. 21 values in all), and falls into one of three classes. Class 3 signifies a 'normal' thyroid gland and is by far the most common class in both training and test data sets, whilst classes 1 and 2 signify that there were later problems with the gland. To be useful in practise in identifying potential thyroid problems, a classification scheme would have to correctly classify significantly more than 92% of all cases, since over 92% of all patients have a normal (class 3) thyroid gland. There are perhaps between 50 and 100 really difficult cases in the training set and in the test set. So, when attempting to produce a good classification scheme in the range of 97%-100% correct, small improvements are important, and hard to obtain.

There are 3772 cases in the training set and 3428 cases in the test set. Examination of the data in graphical form, e.g. using XGobi [7], reveals that the boundaries between the classes of points are very murky indeed. Points from different classes seem to mingle freely with each other.

In all runs, only the training set is used by the GP to try to evolve its population to classify the thyroid cases into their correct classes. The test set is only used as a check on each generation's best (or fittest) classifier (with respect to the training set), to see how well it generalises to another set of the same kind of data. A run's best classifier is taken to be the one which performs best on the training set. This is not necessarily the one which performs best on the test set.

The setup which generates the fittest classifier with respect to the training set which then performs best on the test set in this way is taken to be the most successful one.

3.1 Modification to Thyroid Problem for this Paper

To make things easier for the GP (after a few initial, unsuccessful runs), the Thyroid problem was reformulated to classifying cases as class 3 or not class 3. This reformulation allowed the GP function-tree's outputs to be treated as boolean (output $\geq 0 \Rightarrow$ class 3, output $< 0 \Rightarrow$ not class 3) .

It proved relatively straight forward, in a separate run, for DSS to produce a function-tree expression which could distinguish between classes 1 and 2 with 100% accuracy on both the training and test sets. If they were to be used in practise, two GP expression trees would have to be used in two phases: First (and most difficult) distinguish between class 3 cases and the others, then, if it is not a class 3 case, distinguish between class 1 and class 2 cases.

Experiments were carried out with three methods of Subset Selection and compared against the baseline performance of the standard GP which uses the entire training set in each generation.

4 Subset Selection Methods

4.1 Dynamic Subset Selection

This simple idea is based upon a few premises and a small amount of hindsight. Firstly, it is of benefit to focus the GP's attention onto the *difficult* cases, i.e. the ones which are frequently mis-classified. Secondly, it is also of benefit to involve cases which have not been looked at for several generations. This leads to the final point that all of the cases in the training set should be looked at, eventually.

The algorithm for DSS involves randomly selecting a target number of cases from the whole training set every generation, with a bias, so that a case is more likely to be selected if it is 'difficult' or has not been selected for several generations.

In each generation, the subset is selected by the following two passes through the full training set.

- In one pass of the entire training set, of size **T**, in a generation, g, each training case, **i**, is assigned a weight, **W**, which is the sum of its current 'difficulty', **D**, exponentiated to a certain power, **d**, and the number of generations since it was last selected (or age), **A**, also exponentiated to a certain power, **a**:

$$\forall i : 1 \leq i \leq T, \quad W_i(g) = D_i(g)^d + A_i(g)^a \tag{1}$$

$$\forall i : 1 \leq i \leq T, \quad D_i(g=0) = A_i(g=0) = 0 \tag{2}$$

The sum of all the cases' weights is also calculated during this first pass.
- Then, in a second pass of the entire training set, each case in turn is given a probability, **P**, of being selected to be in the subset. A case's probability is given by its weight divided by the sum of all the cases' weights and multiplied by the target subset size, **S**:

$$\forall i : 1 \leq i \leq T, \quad P_i(g) = \frac{W_i(g) * S}{\sum_{j=1}^{T} W_j(g)} \tag{3}$$

If a case, i, is selected to be in the subset, then its difficulty, D_i, and age, A_i, are set to 0, otherwise its difficulty remains unchanged, and its age, A_i is incremented. While testing each member of the GP population against each case in the current subset of training cases, the difficulty, D_i, (starting from 0) is incremented each time the case is mis-classified by one of the GP trees.

Giving each case in turn this scaled probability of being selected ensures that, on average, the subset will be of size **S**. However, the subset size will fluctuate around the target size each time a new subset is selected. Other selection methods could easily produce subset sizes of exactly **S**, but it was felt that a varying subset size might contribute more to the efficacy of the GP algorithm.

The current generation of the GP's population is then evaluated against this subset of cases instead of the entire training set.

To use this form of DSS, three parameters have to be set:

- the **Target Number** of cases - subset size
- the **Difficulty exponent** - importance given to difficult cases
- the **Age exponent** - importance given to unselected cases

Currently (and, it seems, as always), choosing useful combinations of parameter settings is somewhat of a black art. For the purposes of the Thyroid data set, a target size of 400 (out of 3772) was quickly chosen as an effective value.

This corresponds to slightly more than the number of *moderately* 'difficult' cases selected by the HSS method, leaving room for a few easy cases to be included.

With the target size set at 400, it was easier to select sensible values for the two exponents. An average difficulty rating for a case, with a population size of 10000, might be around 2000 or so. The most difficult cases would have a rating of 10000 or so. With a target size of 400, it would take at least 10 generations to cover all the 3772 training cases. With this disparity between a very 'difficult' case and an 'old' case, an arbitrary decision was made to keep the difficulty exponent to 1.0 and to set the age exponent to 3.5 . With these exponents, the most difficult cases and cases around 15 generations old would have roughly equivalent weights.

4.2 Historical Subset Selection

Here, previous standard GP runs are used to establish some measure of how difficult each training case is. Over the course of several runs (say, five or so), the cases mis-classified by the best population member in each generation in each run are recorded. These cases then make up the subset used in further GP+HSS runs, and the subset remains static after its initial selection. Due to the rough-and-ready method by which it is selected, the subset contains a mixture of many 'difficult' points and many which are actually quite 'easy' to classify. Even a best-of-generation population member makes some simple mis-classifications early on in its development.

Some simple checks showed different runs producing very similar subsets selected by this method. The statistics almost always agreed on which cases were most often mis-classified, and only disagreed on some of the easier cases. The subset size used in the runs was 545, and included every single case mis-classified during seven previous runs of a standard GP. A core of around 300 cases were mis-classified more than once or twice, and so were considered to be at least *moderately* 'difficult' cases.

4.3 Random Subset Selection

In this form of selection, at each generation, each case in turn is selected to be in the current subset of training cases with an equal probability. This probability is scaled to ensure that the subset selected, on average, is of the target size.

$$\forall i : 1 \leq i \leq T, \quad P_i(g) = \frac{S}{T} \tag{4}$$

As with the DSS method, the subset size fluctuates around the target size with each generation.

5 Results

The results given in this paper come from two groups of runs:

- **Population Size = 10000**

  This population size gave the best results achieved by DSS, but, it was not possible to carry out a reasonable length run of the standard GP with this huge population size because it simply took far too long. For the DSS, HSS and RSS runs, the peak values are shown in Table 1 below.

- **Population Size = 5000**

  These results of the GP, DSS, RSS and HSS runs were included to allow a direct comparison of all four methods. Here, the difficulty exponent was increased to 1.5, to allow for the smaller difficulty values.

  For these four runs, the peak values are also shown in Table 1 below, along with the following three graphs:

  - **Figure 1** shows the DSS run easily outperforming RSS.
  - **Figure 2** shows the standard GP run outperforming HSS, though only due to a surge around generation 48. These two methods often produce similar scores, but HSS achieves them with many fewer function-tree evaluations.
  - **Figure 3** shows DSS matching GP results using only 20% of the number of function-tree evaluations.

Table 1. Best Training and Test Results

Algorithm	Pop. Size	Subset Size	Gener- ations	Tree Evals	Training set % correct	Test set % correct
GP	10000	3772	n/a	n/a	n/a	n/a
GP+DSS	10000	400	69	2.7e+08	99.84	99.27
GP+RSS	10000	400	79	3.2e+08	99.39	98.74
GP+HSS	10000	545	47	2.6e+08	99.20	98.77
GP	5000	3772	60	11.3e+08	99.70	99.00
GP+DSS	5000	400	117	2.3e+08	99.70	99.00
GP+RSS	5000	400	124	2.5e+08	99.10	98.40
GP+HSS	5000	545	57	1.6e+08	99.50	98.70
NN - [4] - Silva and Almeida					99.60	98.45
NN - [4] - Cascade Correlation					100.00	98.48

The best tree produced by the DSS run (with population size = 10000) to distinguish between class 3 and not class 3, was found on Generation 69, giving only 25 errors on the test set. It used only 13 out of the 21 variables available in classifying the Thyroid cases.

5.1 A Quick Summary of Results from Other Runs

Different subset sizes were tried, ranging from 50 to the full training set size of 3772. As the subset size approaches 200 or lower, performance drops off markedly

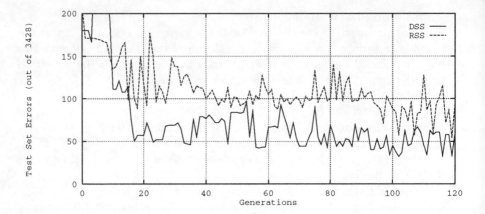

Fig. 1. This figure shows the number of errors made on the test set by the best-of-generation trees produced during a run of the DSS and RSS Methods for each generation.

and fails to match even that of a standard GP. Much larger subset sizes did not appear to boost performance beyond that of the one of around size 400.

Adding in a parsimony factor (i.e. penalising large and 'bushy' trees) speeds up the running of the GP program, since it then uses much less run-time memory to store the whole population of (smaller) trees, and the trees are quicker to evaluate. The standard GP does not perform as well with this restriction as it does without. However, DSS seemed, if anything, to perform slightly better than before.

6 Discussion

The GP + DSS method produces results as good as those of the standard GP and in a much shorter time, on the Thyroid Problem at least. DSS can actually produce better answers, and the population appears to produce a larger variety of solutions in later generations than with standard GP or HSS. The random nature of DSS appears to assist the basic GP algorithm.

At this early stage of investigation, there are strong hints that the method is more widely applicable to general problem solving with GPs and GAs involving large training sets (for time saving), and to difficult problems (for better and more general answers). What is more, DSS is easily added to the basic GP algorithm.

HSS out-performed the standard GP in terms of processing time, and nearly matched it in terms of quality of results. HSS was the main contender for *improvement-of-the-week* until DSS was implemented. One big benefit HSS had

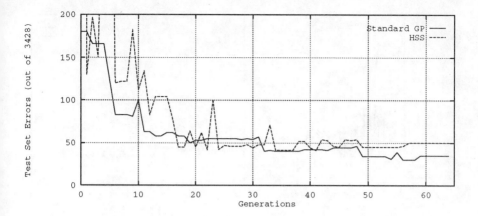

Fig. 2. This figure shows the number of errors made on the test set by the best-of-generation trees produced during a run of the Standard GP and HSS Methods for each generation.

was the ease with which previous standard GP runs could be cannibalised for information to select the subset of difficult cases.

RSS performs surprisingly well, and can match the performance of standard GP in certain situations, in a much shorter time.

The distribution of errors made by the best function-tree was split more or less evenly between problem cases (classes 1 and 2) and no-problem cases (class 3). This could be altered by biasing the GP algorithm to erring on the side of problem cases, i.e. more False-Positive errors and fewer False-Negative errors, which would be more useful in a medical environment.

Looking at the function-trees produced, it was interesting how the best tree used only used 13 out of the 21 variables available to classify most of the cases correctly. This could perhaps lead to some useful savings in data collection costs, or it could help focus attention on some key measurements. It might be possible to make some further measurements and split each key measurement into several different, finer measurements. One advantage of GP over NNs is that it is very difficult to obtain such insights from a trained NN.

When compared with the Neural Network results in [4], the best of which are shown in Table 1 above, the GP+DSS produced a function-tree which generalised better from the training set. To be fair, in splitting up the problem into two phases (class 3 or not, then class 1 or 2), the GP has been presented with an easier problem than was presented to the Neural Networks. This could be taken in different ways: splitting up the problem is mildly cheating, or demonstrating the flexibility of the GP approach.

Possibly one of the more useful aspects of DSS so far has been its ability to

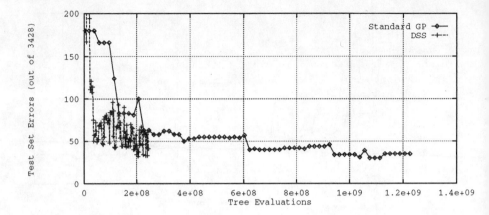

Fig. 3. This figure shows number of errors made on the test set by the best-of-generation trees produced during a run of the Standard GP and DSS methods against the number of tree evaluations carried out.

produce results quickly which, for GP, means that different function sets and parameter settings can be experimented with.

There are myriad lines of investigation to follow up. For instance, how widely applicable is DSS to other problems? How does DSS's randomness influence the behaviour of GP? Would DSS work as well if it was only based on an individual tree's measure of difficulty, e.g. the performance of the best-of-generation tree, or does it need the combined measures from the whole population? Could DSS be applied to other supervised training algorithms, e.g. Neural Networks, where the training cases are continually re-assessed until correctly classified? How sensitive is DSS to its parameter settings?

7   Conclusions

Dynamic Subset Selection added to Genetic Programming performs very well on the large, messy Thyroid problem. It produced equivalent answers with around 20% of the number of function-tree evaluations required by a standard GP, when working with a population size of 5000. Working with a larger population size of 10000, DSS produces better answers than any other method shown here, including those reported for various Neural Networks in [4, 5].

There are strong hints that DSS is more widely applicable to other supervised training problems with GPs and GAs. Benefits include: much less CPU time needed, better generalisation of the answers, a very simple algorithm easily added to a standard GA or GP, allowing GP to be applied to larger supervised learning problems.

Acknowledgments: Thanks are due to Elena Perez-Minana for passing on the Thyroid data and her NN outlook with many helpful discussions, and SERC for PhD grant Number 93314680

References

1. Goldberg, D.E.: GENETIC ALGORITHMS in Search, Optimisation & Machine Learning. Addison-Wesley (1989)
2. Holland, J.H.: Adaption in Natural Selection and Artificial Systems. New edition of the original GA work. The MIT Press (1992)
3. Koza, J.: Genetic Programming: on the programming of computers by natural selection. Contains clear description of a basic Genetic Algorithm as well as a detailed description of Genetic Programming.MIT Press, Cambridge, MA, (1992)
4. Schiffmann, W., Joost, M., Werner, R.: Optimization of the Backpropogation Algorithm for Training Multilayer Perceptrons. University of Koblenz, Institute of Physics, **15** (1992)
5. Schiffmann, W., Joost, M., Werner, R.: Synthesis and Performance Analysis of Multilayer Neural Network Architectures. University of Koblenz, Institute of Physics, **16** (1992)
6. Schiffmann, W., Joost, M., Werner, R.: THYROID training and test data sets. Obtained via electronic mail (1992)
7. Swayne, D., Cook, D., Buja, A.: User's Manual for XGobi, a Dynamic Graphics Program for Data Analysis Implemented in the X Window System (Version 2). Bellcore Technical Memorandum TM ARH-020368 (1992)
8. Tackett, W.A., Carmi, A.: S G P C: Simple Genetic Programming in C. Original source code for GP program used in this paper. Available via FTP at sfi.santafe.edu:pub/Users/tackett (1993)

Genotype-Phenotype-Mapping and Neutral Variation — A case study in Genetic Programming

Wolfgang Banzhaf

Department of Computer Science, Dortmund University
Baroper Str. 301, 44221 Dortmund, GERMANY
banzhaf@tarantoga.informatik.uni-dortmund.de

Abstract. We propose the application of a genotype-phenotype mapping to the solution of constrained optimization problems. The method consists of strictly separating the search space of genotypes from the solution space of phenotypes. A mapping from genotypes into phenotypes provides for the appropriate expression of information represented by the genotypes. The mapping is constructed as to guarantee feasibility of phenotypic solutions for the problem under study. This enforcing of constraints causes multiple genotypes to result in one and the same phenotype. Neutral variants are therefore frequent and play an important role in maintaining genetic diversity. As a specific example, we discuss Binary Genetic Programming (BGP), a variant of Genetic Programming that uses binary strings as genotypes and program trees as phenotypes.

1   Introduction

Historically, there is a long dispute among evolutionary biologists as to the main engine for evolutionary change. Is selection the force that overwhelmingly forms the outcome of evolution? Or is the more influential force that of variation, i.e. events of mutation or recombination of genetic material that provide for the continued progress in evolving generations? Starting with Darwin [1], who already acknowledged the existence of variations selection is not working against, the dispute raged back and forth, with Kimura's neutrality theory of evolution [2, 3] being the most prominent expression of the idea of a variation engine of evolution. Paraphrased, Kimura's theory states that evolution at the molecular level is mainly due to mutations that are nearly neutral with respect to natural selection. Mutation and a resulting random drift of genomes are thus considered main forces behind evolution. Kimura notes that this continuous variation of genetic material, with most of it being neither advantageous nor disadvantageous, is key in understanding natural genetic diversity.

It has become possible in recent years to look in detail at the molecular level of evolution, i.e. the genotypic level where the effects of this neutrality assumption are to be expected. And, indeed, a high variety of genotypes have been shown to exist [4]. In some way, it seems that the mapping from geno-types to phenotypes allows many different genotypes to result in phenotypes of comparable functionality.

The central idea of the present paper is to take this kind of genotype-phenotype-mapping (GPM) into the area of artificial evolution, as it is applied in Evolutionary Computation paradigms like genetic algorithms (GAs), evolutionary strategies or evolutionary programming. We shall be providing ample possibilities for the evolution of neutral variants, since our GPM will by construction be such that many genotypes will map into one phenotype. This is due to the fact that the optimization problem considered is of the class of constrained optimization problems [5]. What we shall not do here, however, and this must be a subject for further study later on, is to consider the important problem of transformation of function. We suspect that in order to include this aspect, an extension of the GPM has to be made that is able to model developmental processes.

The treatment of constrained optimization problems is different from that of unconstrained problems, since a candidate solution is not only judged according to its fitness or quality but also has to obey certain restrictions which exclude entire regions of solution space as unfeasible. Therefore, in constrained optimization two sometimes antagonistic criteria have to be satisfied, (i) quality and (ii) feasibility of a solution. Very often, constraining the solution space leads to local hills or valleys which are difficult to overcome with traditional methods of optimization.

There are several ways to treat constraints in GAs [6] — [8]: One is to include a penalty term in the fitness function. This is called a soft constraint and it is equivalent to allowing the solution to break a constraint by trading solution quality against penalty. In the long run, trading gets more and more difficult until, finally the optimization can only progress by implementing the constraint completely. The other method in order to find good and feasible solutions is a hard constraint. This means to start out with feasible solutions and to restrict search operations in such a way that only feasible solutions are generated during the evolutionary search. Thus, only specially adapted operators may be used that are shown to guarantee feasibility of a transformed solution.

Though in the latter case all solutions are guaranteed to be feasible, the restriction of search operations might lead to solutions that are not optimized. Vice versa, in the former case it might happen that quality improvement by *not* obeying constraints is so large that it is not possible to return to a feasible solution once the algorithms has entered the region of good (but unfeasible) solutions.

A third method based on constraint programming has been proposed to treat constrained optimization problems [9] which makes use of state space search that is enhanced by knowledge of the problem domain.

Another way to optimize problems under constraints is the GPM method proposed here. Search space and solution space are separated, and a mapping between search space (genotypes), where unrestricted search operators can be applied and solution space (phenotypes), where feasibility of solutions is guaranteed, is introduced. Whereas any genotype is allowed in search space, an appropriate GPM provides for feasible solutions in solution space only. It is immediately clear that this requires a mapping of search regions that would lead to otherwise unfeasible solutions, into feasible solutions.

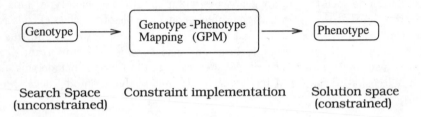

Fig. 1. Functionality of different parts of the algorithm. Unrestricted genotypes scan the search space, GPM provides for an implementation of constraints, solutions are represented by phenotypes in the restricted solution space.

The method used for enforcing feasibility is a two-step process, the first step of which is a raw mapping, with the second being a correction in case the feasibility test is negative. If we now consider a genotype that leads to a feasible solution without being corrected in the second step, we can think of variations that do not change its quality but only remove feasibility. It is those genotypes that will be corrected back by the second step into the nearest feasible phenotype. In other words, some of the information this genotype is carrying is ignored due to the GPM. Needless to say that precisely these are the set of neutral variants that do not influence in any visible way the performance of a phenotypic solution.

The point we are going to make is that the high variability of neutral variants allowed due to GPM permits the algorithms to escape local optima on saddle surfaces. In high dimensional spaces this is the way out of local trapps, and neutral variants are the only way out — apart from appropriate recombination or a lucky but improbable event of just jumping over the barrier. As Eigen [10] has emphasized, a random drift due to the generation of neutral variants broadens the population distribution sufficiently as to secure an escape route with manyfold probability (compared to the fast-decaying spherical distribution around the consensus sequence).

We are going to study one specific example of this phenomenon in Genetic Programming [11], a variant of GAs.

2 Genetic Programming

Genetic Programming (GP) is a variation on the theme of applying artificial selection to structures that are to be optimized [11]. In the context of algorithms, programming languages are the material from which structures are build. Since any kind of language obeys certain grammatical rules, constraints have to be followed by expressions in the respective language.

The GP approach established by Koza starts out from the tree representation of a program. As is well known each expression in a context-free formal language can be stated as a hierarchical tree of nodes of different arity. Arity 0 nodes (leaves) are symbols from a predetermined terminal set. Nodes with arity ≥ 1 are symbols from another set, called functions, which carry a number of arguments. The semantics of these symbols has to be provided by an outside user of the GP system. GP manipulates these symbols by operating on trees and subtrees in order to generate variations or recombinations of already existing trees. The continuous selection of improved trees may lead to algorithms which treat given input/output pairs (fitness cases) correctly. At the outset, the system is seeded with a collection of randomly generated trees, that are guaranteed to obey certain parameter settings (e.g. depth of the tree). The trees are interpreted and evaluated according to the respective choice in functions and terminals, and generate, depending on input data, a certain behaviour in form of algorithmic output.

Because of the presence of grammatical constraints in a programming language, GP is a natural test bed for the ideas developed in Section 1. Figure 2 compares the genotype-phenotype mapping found in Nature with a generic model and an adaption to the needs of evolving algorithms which we call Binary Genetic Programming (BGP). As in Koza's approach, fitness evalution in algorithms is done by comparison of the required output with the actual output of the algorithms.

Whereas Koza evolves phenotypes (program trees) that behave as programs when interpreted with the appropriate system, we evolve genotypes (bit strings). In the spirit of the first method to treat constrained problems mentioned above, in Koza's work only those search operators are used that allow to produce valid program trees. In contrast, we can use any kind of search operator working on bit-strings, since it is the subsequent mapping into program trees, that guarantees fulfillment of the constraints. In order to arrive at correct programs we follow the GPM method of Figure 2c. The main ingredients to this mapping are, first, a coding of pieces of the bit-string into the nodes of a program tree, i.e. into members of the set of functions and terminals, and, second, a correction mechanism that is able to check statements and to transform them into the nearest correct statement if an error was detected. Thirdly, constant pieces of code are added in order to arrive at a working program which can be compiled. The role of the intermediate carrier is to be able to cut out bits encoding parameters without being forced to permanently remove this information from the

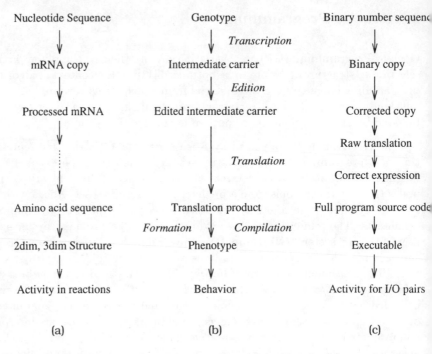

Fig. 2. Sketch of genotype – phenotype mapping; (a) in Nature, (b) generic model, (c) in Binary Genetic Programming (BGP).

bit string. A comparable role exists for messenger RNA (mRNA) in the natural process of expressing genotypes [12], though these mechanisms ar emuch more complex in the natural system than those used here.

One additional twist that GPM gives to a Genetic Programming system is that it allows for varying random numbers. This is due to the freedom that an expression of information gives during the mapping process. We do not intend to compare this new functionality with the more inflexible approach Koza is taking but rather introduce it here as a sideline.

3 Some details of the BGP implementation

GPM expresses genetic information carried by a bit-string in two phases. Phase I takes a bit-string and generates a high-level language construct that is used in Phase II by a regular compiler to generate relocated machine instructions. Whereas Phase II is standard, some details have to be given for Phase I in order to understand the approach.

After drawing a copy from the original bit-string, this copy is processed by scanning it from left to right in 5-bit sections. Each 5-bit section is considered to be a code for a symbol from Table 1 giving either a non-terminal symbol (left side) or a terminal symbol (right side). As we can see, there is a certain amount of redundancy in the coding, with the selection of particular codes for particular nodes rather arbitrary. As in Koza's approach, a decision has to be made as to what sort of functions and terminals are to be used in the application at hand. For the regression application we discuss here, we have chosen numerical functions as the set of non-terminals. On the terminal side we use X, the input to our regression, and $R1...R4$, random numbers generated in different intervals.

Code	Symbol	Code	Symbol	Code	Symbol	Code	Symbol
0 0 0 0 0	PLUS	0 1 0 0 0	PLUS	1 0 0 0 0	X	1 1 0 0 0	X
0 0 0 0 1	MINUS	0 1 0 0 1	MINUS	1 0 0 0 1	R1	1 1 0 0 1	R1
0 0 0 1 0	TIMES	0 1 0 1 0	TIMES	1 0 0 1 0	X	1 1 0 1 0	X
0 0 0 1 1	THRU	0 1 0 1 1	THRU	1 0 0 1 1	R2	1 1 0 1 1	R2
0 0 1 0 0	POW	0 1 1 0 0	POW	1 0 1 0 0	X	1 1 1 0 0	X
0 0 1 0 1	SI	0 1 1 0 1	EX	1 0 1 0 1	R3	1 1 1 0 1	R3
0 0 1 1 0	CO	0 1 1 1 0	RLOG	1 0 1 1 0	X	1 1 1 1 0	X
0 0 1 1 1	EX	0 1 1 1 1	RLOG	1 0 1 1 1	R4	1 1 1 1 1	R4

Table 1. Transcription table of binary strings into functions and terminals. 5-bit coding shown. First bit (category bit) indicates whether a function or a terminal is coded.

The generation of random numbers deserves more discussion: If we would generate a different random number every time, e.g. $R1$ is used in a program, no reliable function could be developed around this random number. Koza solves this problem by defining "random ephemeral constants". These are constants that are generated once and for all at the creation of a program tree. Later they are only combined into different trees, with their value kept fixed. Our approach is different, since we have decided to represent random numbers directly on the bit-string. We use two procedures, one applying intron coding of random numbers, the other applying category bit coding. The former procedure is as follows: Once the scanning process discovers one of the R string-codes, it cuts out the following 2 5-bit sections, i.e. the next 10 bits, for use as a random number. These bits are interpreted as a natural number between 0 and $2^{10} - 1$ and mapped into an interval according to Table 2. The latter method makes use of the fact, that we can look at all the category bits of a string as another (though shorter) bit-string, which might be interpreted differently. Thus, when the code calling for a random number is discovered, the next ten category bits are used to generate the natural number mentioned above. Further treatment is equal in both cases.

The advantage of an explicit representation of random numbers on strings is that their value now becomes susceptible to random mutations and other variations due to genetic operators that are impossible in Koza's scheme. In effect, they have become parameters coded on the string. This additional feature comes at a cost, though. A further processing step of interpreting parameter bits has to be introduced.

Symbol	Interval	Sort
R1	[-1,+1]	Real
R2	[0,1]	Real
R3	[-10,+10]	Integer
R4	[0,10]	Integer

Table 2. Treatment of numbers cut out from the string.

After a string has been scanned and optionally processed, a raw translation of its information is generated which is analyzed for grammatical correctness. If there are not enough terminals supplied on the string, for instance, category bits are changed from right to left until enough terminals are present. The resulting translation is parsed and supplied with parentheses and other necessary characters as well as with unchanging program headers and tails in order to arrive at valid source code of a target language like C or FORTRAN. Finally, a commercial compiler takes over and produces an executable that is run for the predetermined (preferably large number of) test cases of input/output pairs. Due to the fact that we can use compiled code, execution is by orders of magnitude faster than interpreted LISP-code.

4 Numerical simulation for selected regression problems

For this contribution we examined the following two regression problems:

$$y_1 = \frac{1}{2}x^2 \tag{1}$$

$$y_2 = e^{-3x^2} \tag{2}$$

We used 500 fitness cases in the range $x \in [0,4]$. Fitness was defined as the degree to which the above function is approached by an individual from the population. We use the inverse measure of the quadratic deviation

$$e = \sum_{i=1,500} e_i = \sum_{i=1,500} (f(x_i) - y_{1,2})^2 \qquad (3)$$

and try to minimize it. An individual is considered successful if it is able to approach $y_{1,2}$ within a small interval for all the fitness cases:

$$e_i \leq 0.01 \ \forall i. \qquad (4)$$

If the first such individual appears, the population as a whole is considered successful and the simulation is stopped.

Figure 3a-b is the cumulative success probability for 50 runs each. Compared are the two different approaches to implementing random numbers as parameters on the string. From the figures we can see that the category-bit approach is generally better than the intron approach. Also, eq. (1) was not so easily solvable within 50 generations.

As an example, we give solutions for eq. (2) that were achieved by continuing a run that would have stopped for the statistical measurements:

$$f(x) = 0.05^{x^2} \qquad (5)$$

Note that $e^{-3} = 0.0498$. Another solution was

$$f(x) = e^{x^{x-3}} \qquad (6)$$

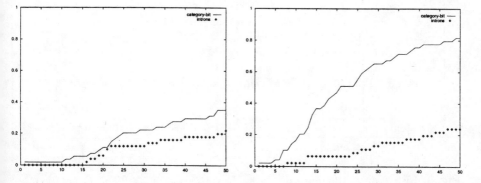

Fig. 3. Success probability for 50 runs of problem (a) eq. (1) and (b) eq. (2).

5 Analysis and conclusion

We shall now take one typical run and analyse it with respect to the question of neutral variations. As a natural distance metric in our search space we take the Hamming distance. Figure 4 - 6 show histograms of Hamming distances from all genotypes to the best genotype. In Figure 4, left, we see that distances are distributed initially around 120 bits, which reflects the fact that the zero-th generation does not yet have any preference in search space (strings have 225 bits).

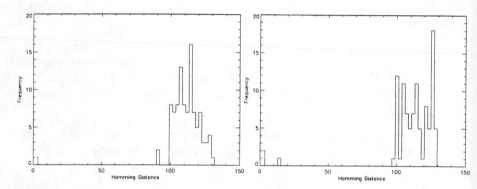

Fig. 4. Histogram of Hamming distances. Left: Generation 0; Right: Generation 7.

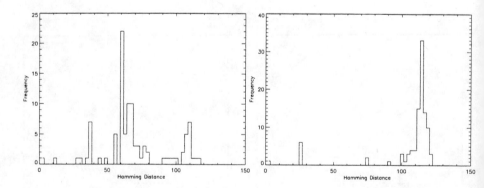

Fig. 5. Histogram of Hamming distances. Left: Generation 15; Right: Generation 19.

The average Hamming distance is smaller in generation 7, since a movement

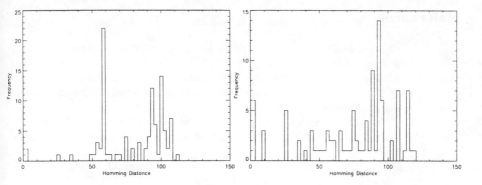

Fig. 6. Histogram of Hamming distances. Left: Generation 22; Right: Generation 25.

towards better solutions has begun. In generation 15 (Figure 5,left), shortly before a correct solution is discovered, the population has an average Hamming distance of appr. 65, concentrating genotypes in more promising regions of the search space. Then a big jump occurs for the best individual, effectively restoring the original distribution of distances.

Figure 6 showns a broadening of the distribution as more and more individuals move into the correct region. Though the deviation e of all individuals is now within 2×10^{-3} of the optimal value, $e = 0$, diversity of genotypes is still remarkable. The reason for this behavior lies in the fact, that part of the genotypic information is not expressed in the phenotype. The unexpressed part may vary arbitrarily, without any consequences for the fitness of the individual.

It is interesting to note further, that program trees that are derived from fixed length binary strings have varying length. Like other bits, the category-bit of random strings is 1 with probability $\frac{1}{2}$. For a translation into binary trees as we use them in our BGP, a function will be at place 1 with certainty. At place 2, a terminal will follow with probability $p_2 = \frac{1}{2}$. For the tree to be complete, a terminal should follow on place 3. This happens with probability $p_3 = \frac{1}{4}$. Thus, one quarter of all randomly generated trees will be very short. It follows that one eighth will contain 2 functions, and so on. A natural tendency toward shorter program trees is therefore built into the algorithm.

The GPM method introduced here is useful in other constraint optimization problems as well. It is hypothesized that the strict separation of search operations (in genotype space) and constraint implementation (in GPM) allows systems of this sort to work more flexible than systems that work with phenotypes only.

References

1. C. Darwin: On the Origin of Species by Means of Natural Selection. London: Murray 1972, 6th Edition
2. M. Kimura: Nature 217, 624 - 626 (1968)
3. M. Kimura: The Neutral Theory of Molecular Evolution. Cambridge: Cambridge University Press 1983
4. T. Mukai: Experimental Verification of the Neutral Theory. In: T. Ohta, K. Aoki (Eds.): Population Genetics and Molecular Evolution. Berlin: Springer 1985
5. G. Reklaitis, A. Ravindran, K. Ragsdell: Engineering Optimization Methods and Applications. New York: Wiley 1983
6. D. Orvosh, L. Davis: Shall we repair? Genetic Algorithms, combinatorial optimization, and feasibility constraints. In: S. Forrest (Ed.): Proc. 5th Int. Conference on Genetic Algorithms, ICGA-93. San Mateo: Morgan Kaufmann 1993
7. H. Fang, P. Ross, D. Corne: A promising GA approach to Job-Shop scheduling, rescheduling, and Open-Shop scheduling problems. In: S. Forrest (Ed.): Proc. 5th Int. Conference on Genetic Algorithms, ICGA-93. San Mateo: Morgan Kaufmann 1993
8. R. Nakano: Conventional GA for job shop scheduling. In: R. Belew, L. Booker (Eds.): Proc. 4th Int. Conference on Genetic Algorithms, ICGA-91. San Mateo: Morgan Kaufmann 1991
9. J. Paredis: Exploiting Constraints as Background Knowledge for Genetic Algorithms: a Case-study for Scheduling. In: R. Männer, B. Manderick (Eds.): Parallel Problem Solving from Nature, 2. Amsterdam: Elsevier Science Publishers 1992
10. M. Eigen: Steps toward Life: a perspective on evolution. Oxford: Oxford University Press 1992
11. J.R. Koza: Genetic Programming. Cambridge (USA): MIT Press 1992
12. M.W. Gray, P.S. Covello: RNA editing in plant mitochondria and chloroplasts. FASEB J. **7** (1993) 64

Genetic L-System Programming

Christian Jacob

Chair of Programming Languages, Department of Computer Science,
University of Erlangen-Nürnberg, Martens-Str. 3, D-91058 Erlangen, Germany
email: jacob@informatik.uni-erlangen.de

Abstract. We present the Genetic L-System Programming (GLP) paradigm
for evolutionary creation and development of parallel rewrite systems (L-
systems, Lindenmayer-systems) which provide a commonly used formal-
ism to describe developmental processes of natural organisms. The L-system paradigm will be extended for the purpose of describing time- and
context-dependent formation of formal data structures representing rewrite
rules or computer programs (expressions).

With GLP two methods gleaned from nature are combined: simulated evolution and simulated structure formation. A prototypical GLP system
implementation is described. Controlled evolution of complex structures is
exemplified by the development of tree structures generated by the movement of a 3D-turtle.

1   L-Systems

The development of an organism may [...] be considered as the execution of a
'developmental program' present in the fertilized egg. The cellularity of higher
organisms and their common DNA components force us to consider developing
organisms as dynamic collections of appropriately programmed finite automata.
A central task of developmental biology is to discover the underlying algorithm
for the course of development.

Aristid Lindenmayer and Grzegorz Rozenberg [6]

Morphogenesis or formation of structures in nature are always the result of complex growth processes. The central idea of L-systems is that structure formation
can be interpreted as the execution of 'programs' or rewrite rules. In nature there
is no blue print for an organism, instead 'rule systems' tell how to build organels
and how to combine these parts to form a complete and functioning organism.
These programs are highly parametrized where the parameters are set by the
environment in which development and interaction processes take place.

Parallel rewrite systems or L-systems [7] provide a useful formal model for the
description of developmental processes in organisms. We will give some rudimentary
definitions for context-free L-systems with stacking capability. As it is in general very
difficult to create an L-system simulating some special growth process we will introduce an evolutionary method (GLP) supporting L-system inference.

1.1 DOL-systems

The context-free D0L-systems[1] are the simplest type of L-systems. Formally a D0L-system can be defined as a triple $G = (\Sigma, P, \omega)$ where $\Sigma = \{s_1, s_2, ..., s_n\}$ is an *alphabet*, P is an endomorphism defined on Σ^*, and ω, referred to as the *axiom*, is an element of Σ^*. P is defined by a *production map* $P: \Sigma \to \Sigma^*$ with $s \to P(s)$ for each $s \in \Sigma$. Whenever there is no explicit mapping for a symbol s the identity mapping $P(s) = s$ is assumed. In a deterministic L-system there is at most one production rule for each symbol $s \in \Sigma$. The word sequence $E(G)$ generated by G is defined as

$$\omega^{(0)} = P^0(\omega), \ \omega^{(1)} = P^1(\omega), \ \omega^{(2)} = P^2(\omega), \ ...$$

where P^i denotes i-fold iteration of P and each string $\omega^{(i+1)}$ is obtained from the preceding string $\omega^{(i)} = \omega_1^{(i)} \omega_2^{(i)} ... \omega_m^{(i)}$ by applying the production rules to all m symbols of the string $\omega^{(i)}$ simultaneously:

$$\omega^{(i+1)} = P(\omega_1^{(i)}) P(\omega_2^{(i)}) ... P(\omega_m^{(i)}).$$

The language of G is defined by $L(G) = \{P^i(\omega); i \geq 0\}$.

1.2 Turtle interpretation of bracketed parametric DOL-Systems

Let us consider the following L-system G:

$$\Sigma = \{F, B, Rl, Rr, P, Pb, Yl, Yr\}$$
$$\omega: \quad F \tag{1}$$
$$P: \quad F \to [F[RlF] F[RrF] F]$$

which generates the following sequence of strings:

Axiom: F

Iteration 1: $[F[RlF] F[RrF] F]$

Iteration 2: $[[F[RlF] F[RrF] F] [Rl[F[RlF] F[RrF] F]] [F[RlF] F[RrF] F]]$
                $[Rr[F[RloF] F[RrF] F]] [F[RlF] F[RrF] F]$

These string sequences describe the fractal growth of an artificial structure. The structure formation process can be easily visualized if we define the following interpretation for the symbols $F, B, Rl, Rr, P, Pb, Yl, Yr$ and [...]. A common interpretation is to let these symbols control the movement of an artificial object (usually known as a 'turtle') which draws lines on its way in 2- or 3-dimensional space :

$F(s_1)$:   move forward with a stepsize of s_1
$B(s_2)$:   move backward with a stepsize of s_2
$Rl(\alpha_1)$:   rotate left for an angle α_1
$Rr(\alpha_2)$:   rotate right for an angle α_2

1. D0 stands for *deterministic* with *no context*.

$P(\alpha_3)$:   pitch for an angle α_3
$Pb(\alpha_4)$:   pitch back for an angle α_4
$Yl(\alpha_5)$:   yaw left for an angle α_5
$Yr(\alpha_6)$:   yaw right for an angle α_6.

In the example system above we have quietly assumed a fixed rotation angle $\alpha_1 = 90$, $\alpha_2 = 60$ and stepsize $s = 0.5$ so we do not have to include these parameters into the strings, however, this was only done in order to keep strings small.

Modular substrings can be marked by the bracket symbols [and]. For each string of the form $s_1[s_2]s_3$ the strings $s_1, s_2, s_3 \in L(G)$ are interpreted in sequence, however, after substring s_2 has been interpreted and before starting to interpret s_3 the turtle is reset to its prior position and orientation after interpretation of s_1. This allows the formation of tree-like structures and branches as the visualization of iterated turtle movement for the example above shows (figure 1).

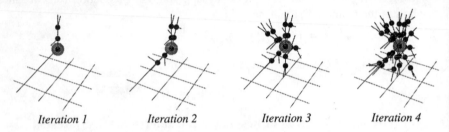

Iteration 1   *Iteration 2*   *Iteration 3*   *Iteration 4*

Fig. 1. Artificial structure generated with DOL-system described in (1). The turtle is oriented upward and its origin is situated at the big spot in the center.

2   L-Systems and Genetic Programming

2.1   Synthesis of L-systems

The inference problem for L-systems involves finding a proper axiom ω and rewrite rules P for a given structure or growth process, i.e. a sequence of structures. For the development of an L-system for a particular (biological) species one usually has to perform the following steps [8]:

1.   analyzation of the biological object,
2.   informal rules definition,
3.   definition of L-system axiom and rules,
4.   computer simulation and interpretation of generated strings,
5.   translation into a graphical output,
6.   comparison of the artificial object with the behavior of the real object,
7.   correction of the L-system and repetition of the steps above (if necessary).

This shows that L-system synthesis is an overall difficult and sometimes tedious process. But what methods do we have at hand for (automatic) generation of L-systems? As P. Prusinkiewicz [9] points out, random modification of production rules generally gives little insight into the relationship between L-systems and the figures they generate. Algorithms reported in the literature up to now are still too limited to be of practical value for complex structure formation [9, p. 39, 62]. Obviously an evolutionary approach is sensible for points 3, 6 and 7. So what we need to support L-system inference on an evolutionary basis is:

- functions to *generate* (possibly codings of) L-systems that are subject to certain constraints (alphabet, iterations, context-sensitivity, parameters etc.),

- *evaluation* functions that return a fitness measure for each interpreted L-system,

- *modification* and *selection* functions which enable interactive L-system editing as well as automatic control through evolutionary techniques.

In the following sections we discuss preliminary ideas about the use of evolutionary techniques for breeding populations of L-systems that describe growth processes which are interpreted in a problemspecific domain and evaluated by a fitness measure with respect to a target growth process.

2.2 Extended GP and GLP

Here we briefly describe what kind of evolutionary algorithm system we use for L-system development and coding. Similar to the genetic programming (GP) paradigm introduced by J. Koza [5] who uses LISP-S-expressions our structures undergoing adaptation are hierarchical, typed expressions (terms).[2]

One of the main differences to the common GP paradigm is the use of higher-order building blocks ('patterns') for expression generation and modification. The coarse structures of problemdependent genotype expressions are generated by combining 'macro-patterns' taken from a predefined pattern pool $Pool = \{p_1, ..., p_M\}$ (see the example patterns around the centered circle in fig. 2). The combinable subexpressions rely on a set of function symbols $F = \{f_1, f_2, ..., f_N\}$ for each of which an arity range $A = \{a_1, ..., a_N\}$ with $a_i = (minarg\,(f_i), maxarg\,(f_i))$ has to be specified.

Each expression from the pattern pool serves as a (possibly partial) descriptions of "organism" genotypes for a problem dependent environment. Only the expression patterns are used for expression generation, i.e. parametrized, possibly constrained, high-level data structures serve as building blocks. Each of these patterns p_i is associated with a set of attributes as e.g. a number of predicates constraining the set of subexpressions that can be 'plugged in'. Another attribute is the pattern rank $r\,(p_i)$ which serves as a kind of fitness measure among patterns that compete for being selected as subexpressions during the expression generation process.[3] This concerns patterns with the same root symbol - as is the case with the recursive and non-recursive version of the *stack*-pattern - as well as with different function symbols within alternatives (fig. 2).

---

2. For an alternative grammar-based approach see [1]. An excellent overview of current extensions and applications of GP can be found in [5]
3. Similar ranks control pattern selection of the genetic operators.

Specialized meta-operators for rank adjustment take care about which patterns enhance the pool and for which patterns focus is increased or decreased through ranks adjustment.

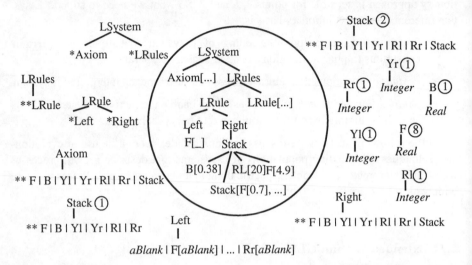

Fig. 2. : Pool of expression patterns. The coarse structure of the L-system description within the centered circle is built by using the depicted expression patterns. *X and **X stand for any single expression or (non-empty) sequence of expressions with head X, respectively. I denotes alternatives. Pattern ranks are depicted within small circles.

2.3 Expression generation

Evolution starts with random generation of an initial population of expressions. Each expression is constructed from a start pattern in a recursive manner by combining expressions from the expression pattern pool, always respecting the pattern constraints as discussed in the previous section.

Generation of an L-system expression might result in the following generation steps[4]:

    LSystem[_Axiom,_LRules]
    LSystem[Axiom[Stack[_F,_RR,_F]],_LRules]
    ...
    LSystem[Axiom[Stack[F[0.8],RR[70],F[1.5]]],_LRules]
    LSystem[Axiom[Stack[F[0.8],RR[70],F[1.5]]],
            LRules[_LRule,_LRule,_LRule]]
    LSystem[Axiom[Stack[F[0.8],RR[70],F[1.5]]],
            LRules[LRule[_Left,_Right],_LRule,_LRule]]
    ...

---

4. Here '_' and '_X' represent formal parameters referring to any expression and expressions with head X, respectively.

LSystem[Axiom[Stack[F[0.8],RR[70],_F[1.5]]],
    LRules[LRule[Left[F[aBlank]]],Right[Stack[RL[110],F[2.],Stack[...],P[50]]],
        LRule[Left[PB[aBlank]]],Right[Stack[B[2.8],Stack[...],RR[70]]], _LRule]]
...

These expressions are decoded into a parametrized bracketed L-system of the following form

ω: F(0.8) RR(70) F(1.5)

P: F($\_$) $\rightarrow$ RL(110) F(2.) [...] P(50)

       PB($\_$) $\rightarrow$ B(2.8) [...] RR(70)

which is then interpreted by a 3D-turtle as demonstrated above.

2.4 Evaluation and reproduction of expressions

The population of L-system genotypes consists of symbolic expressions (data structures) the head symbols of which denote (abstract) data types for which decoding, interpretation and evaluation functions are easily definable by pattern matching mechanisms. This enables simultaneous use of different kinds of L-system genotypes, e.g. merging context-free and context-sensitive L-systems within the same population by introducing a new context-dependent *CLSystem* data type with according interpretation functions. Fitnesses are derived from the L-system interpretation functions so that each L-system genotype receives an associated fitness value.

In order to build the next generation of expressions a genetic operator op_i is chosen from an 'operator pool' $OpPool = \{op_1, ..., op_K\}$ depending on its operator rank $r(op_i)$. Each operator op_i performs a mapping $o(p_i) : G^{a_1(i)} \rightarrow G^{a_2(i)}$ from an $a_1(i)$ - to a $a_2(i)$ -dimensional genotype vector where G is the set of genotype expressions. The individual genotypes are selected according to their fitness values (fitness proportionate, rank-based or other selection schemes). The resulting, possibly modified expressions are entered into the next generation. The selection of genetic operators terminates when the new population is filled up to its maximum size.

2.5 Variations on expressions

Size and shape of the expressions change dynamically during the evolution process through genetic operators. Table 1 gives an overview of operators we currently use. We introduce an alternate selection scheme for subexpressions as arguments for the genetic operators: (possibly constrained) patterns provide templates used for extracting subexpressions for modification or recombination. This enables operators to be applied only within predefined expression contexts where context may vary in the course of the evolution process. For the definition of new patterns and contexts meta-operators (*te*, *ec*) are necessary. Similar to the pattern pool for expression generation there is a pattern pool $Pool_{op_i}$ for each genetic operator op_i; each pattern is associated with a rank number which controls selection among competing patterns. We explain these ideas in detail for the mutation and crossover operators which rely on the templates defined in table 2.

Pattern-Operator		Short explanation ...
Mutation	*mu*	Replace subterms of an expression meeting template constraints by newly generated, equivalent subexpressions.
Crossover	*co*	Exchange subexpressions meeting template constraints between two expressions.
Shrink	*sh*	Delete a subexpression.
Duplication	*du*	Duplicate a subexpression.
Permutation	*pe*	Permute expression arguments randomly, by left or right shift, or by reversion.
Template Extr.	*te*	Extract a template from an expression. 'Successful' templates are inserted into the pattern pools.
Encapsulation	*ec*	Replace a subexpression by a single reference symbol.

Tab. 1 : GP operators collection. For operand selection all the operators rely on operator templates.

GP operator	Rank	Templates for selection of operator agruments
Mutation $T_1(mu)$	3	Axiom[i: *Stack /; Q[i]] *Restrict mutation to expressions with head* Axiom *that have a* Stack *expression complying with a predicate* Q *as their argument.*
$T_2(mu)$	1	*LRules Restrict mutation to expressions with head LRules.
$T_3(mu)$	2	LRule[*Left,Right[**]] Restrict mutation to expressions with head Left appearing within an LRule expression and with a Right term as right context.
Crossover $T_1(co)$	1	*LRule[Left[*], Right[**, Stack[**], **]] Restrict crossover to LRule expressions that contain at least one Stack expression among the Right term arguments.

Tab. 2 : Pattern pool (templates) for GP operators

2.5.1 Pattern Mutation

To perform *pattern mutation* on an individual expression (figure 3a) a mutation template $T_1(mu)$ is selected from the pattern pool $Pool_{mu}$ according to the pattern ranks. Suppose the first template has been selected with predicate Q demanding at least three arguments for the *Stack* term. The subexpression with head

Axiom is then replaced by a newly generated *Axiom* term with a *Stack* argument expression resulting in a modified individual genotype (figure 3b).

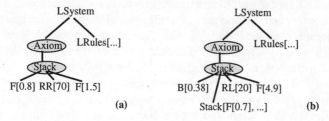

(a) (b)

Fig. 3. : Pattern mutation on an L-system genotype

2.5.2 Pattern Crossover

Pattern crossover is used as a recombination operator which enables exchange of structures of the same type between two individuals. Given the two expressions in figure (4, top) a crossover template $T_1(co)$ is chosen from pattern pool $Pool_{co}$ with according ranking scheme. Subexpressions with head *LRule* meeting the restrictions of template $T_1(co)$ are selected randomly within each expression and exchanged between the two individuals resulting in two modified expressions (figure 4, bottom).

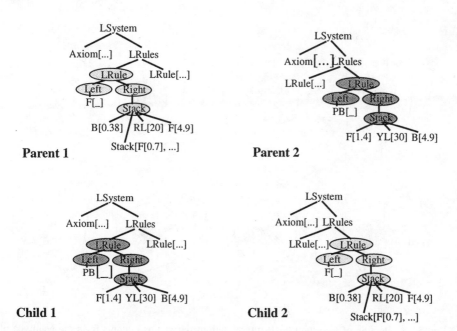

Fig. 4. : Expression recombination: pattern crossover

3   Virtual Genetic L-System Laboratory

In order to test and support problemspecific generation and evolution of expressions within the extended genetic programming paradigm we are designing a virtual GLP laboratory as one part of our genetic programming environment *MathEvolvica*. The following examples should give a brief impression of the surprisingly easy formation of complex structures even with very small populations (between 10 and 20 individuals per generation) and over a short period of generations. The simple problem to be solved was to generate L-systems that form a complex structure (with a number of $0 < b \leq 100$ branches) and with the majority of tree end points (leaves) situated outside the inner cube but within the outer cube boundaries with regard to the horizontal x_1- and x_2-directions (figure 5). The number of L-system iterations was fixed to 3. The axiom and L-rule expressions had to be evolved. The fitness value $f(g_i)$ for each individual L-system genotype g_i, $1 \leq i \leq N$, to be maximized was defined as

$$f(g_i) = b(g_i)^{1 + penalty(g_i)} \quad , \qquad penalty(g_i) = \sum_{k=1,2} penalty(x_k, g_i)$$

where $penalty(x_k, g_i)$ is the portion of x_k leaf coordinates lying within the specified boundaries with each leave having coordinates of the form (x_1, x_2, x_3). The following figures show a collection of interpreted L-systems all derived from a single genotype by applying crossover and mutation over 20 generations. The phenotypes develop to densely packed structures with broad branching.

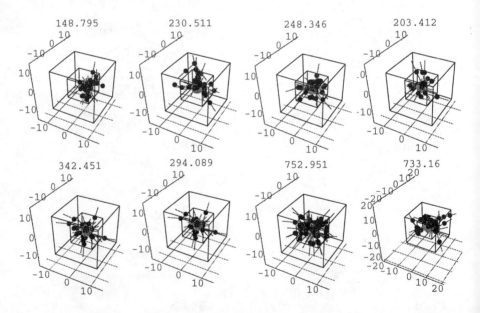

Fig. 5. : Collection of L-system turtle interpretations derived as mutants from the genotype of the first L-system individual (upper left corner). Depicted numbers refer to phenotype fitness.

4 Conclusion and Further Research

We demonstrated how parallel rewrite systems can be designed by evolution processes. Of course, this is only a very limited and rudimentary description of how genetic programming techniques support the design of hierarchical (program or data) structures. Extensions of the GLP/GP laboratory[5] are currently developed and implemented with respect to the following areas:

- using fitness functions that measure similarities among growth processes in order to infer L-systems for (sequences of) target structures,
- including growth functions into fitness evaluation,
- extending the set of interpretation functions,
- extension to context-sensitive, stochastic and table L-systems.

Another important area of research are genetic operators that support hierarchical, modularized expression evolution. A variant of the described GLP system will be used for the design of artificial neural networks.[6]

References

1. Antonisse, H.J., *A Grammer-Based Genetic Algorithm*, in: G. Rawlins (ed.), Foundations of Genetic Algorithms, San Mateo, 1991.
2. Jacob, C., Rehder, J., *Evolution of neural net architectures by a hierarchical grammar-based genetic system*, ICNNGA'93, International Conference on Neural Networks and Genetic Algorithms, Innsbruck, Austria, 1993.
3. Jacob, C., *Typed expressions evolution of artificial nervous systems*, to appear in: ICANN'94, International Conference on Artificial Neural Networks, Sorrento, Italy, 1994.
4. Kinnear, K.E., *Advances in Genetic Programming*, MIT Press, London, 1994.
5. Koza, J.R., *Genetic Programming, On the Programming of Computers by Means of Natural Selection*, MIT Press, London, 1993.
6. Lindenmayer, A., Rozenberg, G. (eds.), *Automata, Languages, Development*, North-Holland, 1975.
7. Lindenmayer, A., *Mathematical models for cellular interaction in development*, Parts I and II, Journal of Theoretical Biology 18, 1968, pp. 280-315.
8. Peitgen, H.-O., Jürgens, H., Saupe, D., *Chaos and Fractals*, New Frontiers of Science, Springer-Verlag, 1993, p. 363.
9. Prusinkiewicz, P., Lindenmayer, A., *The Algorithmic Beauty of Plants*, Springer-Verlag, 1990, pp. 11ff.

---

5. The GP laboratory is implemented in C and *Mathematica*. Currently the user interface is realized through *Mathematica* notebooks and will be extended by a NeXTSTEP based graphical user interface (*Mathematica* is a trademark of Wolfram Research, Inc. NeXTSTEP is a trademark of NeXT Computers, Inc.)
6. Alternative approachs for neural net design with the expression evolution system are described in [2] and [3].

A Genetic Algorithm Discovers Particle-Based Computation in Cellular Automata

Rajarshi Das[1], Melanie Mitchell[1], and James P. Crutchfield[2]

[1] Santa Fe Institute, 1660 Old Pecos Trail, Suite A, Santa Fe, New Mexico, U.S.A. 87501.

[2] Physics Department, University of California, Berkeley, CA, U.S.A. 94720.

Abstract. How does evolution produce sophisticated emergent computation in systems composed of simple components limited to local interactions? To model such a process, we used a genetic algorithm (GA) to evolve cellular automata to perform a computational task requiring globally-coordinated information processing. On most runs a class of relatively unsophisticated strategies was evolved, but on a subset of runs a number of quite sophisticated strategies was discovered. We analyze the emergent logic underlying these strategies in terms of information processing performed by "particles" in space-time, and we describe in detail the generational progression of the GA evolution of these strategies. Our analysis is a preliminary step in understanding the general mechanisms by which sophisticated emergent computational capabilities can be automatically produced in decentralized multiprocessor systems.

1. Introduction

Natural evolution has created many systems in which the actions of simple, locally-interacting components give rise to coordinated global information processing. Insect colonies, economic systems, the immune system, and the brain have all been cited as examples of systems in which "emergent computation" occurs (e.g., see [5, 8]). In the following, "emergent computation" refers to the appearance in a system's temporal behavior of information-processing capabilities that are neither explicitly represented in the system's elementary components or their couplings nor in the system's initial and boundary conditions. Our interest is in phenomena in which many locally-interacting processors, unguided by a central control, result in globally-coordinated information processing that is more powerful than can be done by individual components or linear combinations of components. More precisely, "emergent computation" signifies that the global information processing can be interpreted as implementing (or approximating) a computation [1].

While observations of the behavior of such a decentralized, multicomponent system might suggest that a computation is taking place, understanding the emergent logic by which the computation is performed is typically very difficult. It is also not well understood how evolution creates the capacity for emergent computation in such systems. In this paper we report work addressing both these questions in a simplified model in which emergent computational capabilities in cellular automata are evolved under a genetic algorithm (GA). We apply a framework, called "computational mechanics", for analyzing the emergent logic embedded in the spatiotemporal behavior of spatially-extended systems such as cellular automata [3]. The results demonstrate how globally-coordinated information processing is mediated by "particles" and "particle interactions" in space-time. We also analyze in detail the evolutionary history over which a GA evolved such emergent computation in cellular automata. Though our model is simplified, the results are relevant to understanding the evolution of emergent computation in more complicated systems.

2. Cellular Automata

One of the simplest systems in which emergent computation can be studied is a one-dimensional binary-state cellular automaton (CA)—a one-dimensional lattice of N two-state machines ("cells"), each of which changes its state as a function only of the current states in a local neighborhood. The lattice starts out with an initial configuration of cell states (0s and 1s) and this configuration changes in discrete time steps according to the CA "rule". We use the term "state" to refer to a local state s_i—the value of the single cell at site i. The term "configuration" will refer to the pattern of local states over the entire lattice.

A CA rule ϕ can be expressed as a look-up table ("rule table") that lists, for each local neighborhood, the update state for the neighborhood's central cell. In a one-dimensional CA, a neighborhood consists of a cell and its r ("radius") neighbors on either side. A sample rule (the "majority" rule) for a one-dimensional binary CA with $r = 1$ is the following. Each possible neighborhood η is given along with the "output bit" $s = \phi(\eta)$ to which the central cell is updated. (The neighborhoods are listed in lexicographic order.)

η	000	001	010	011	100	101	110	111
s	0	0	0	1	0	1	1	1

At time step t, the look-up table is applied to each neighborhood in the current lattice configuration, respecting the choice of boundary conditions, to produce the configuration at $t + 1$.

Cellular automata have been studied extensively as mathematical objects, as models of natural systems, and as architectures for fast, reliable parallel computation (for an overview of CA theory and applications, see, e.g., [12, 13]). However, the difficulty of understanding the emergent behavior of CAs or of designing CAs to have desired behavior has up to now severely limited their applications in science and engineering, and for general computation.

3. Details of Experiments

We used a form of the GA to evolve one-dimensional, binary-state CAs to perform a density classification task: the $\rho_c = 1/2$ task [9]. A successful CA for this task will decide whether or not the initial configuration (IC) contains more than half 1s. Let ρ denote the density of 1s in a configuration and let ρ_0 denote the density of 1s in the initial configuration. If $\rho_0 < \rho_c$ ($\rho_0 > \rho_c$), then within M time steps the CA should relax to the fixed-point configuration of all 0s (1s). M is a parameter of the task that depends on the lattice size N.

The CAs in our experiments had $r = 3$, with spatially periodic boundary conditions: $s_i = s_{i+N}$. The $\rho_c = 1/2$ task is nontrivial for a small-radius ($r \ll N$) CA, since density is a global property of a configuration, whereas a small-radius CA relies only on local interactions mediated by the cell neighborhoods. The minimum amount of memory required for the $\rho_c = 1/2$ task is proportional to $log(N)$, since the equivalent of a counter register is required to track the excess of 1s in a serial scan of the IC. In other words, the task requires computation which corresponds to the recognition of a non-regular language. It has been argued that no finite radius CA can perform this task perfectly across all lattice sizes (C. Moore, personal communication), but even to perform this task well for a fixed lattice size requires more powerful computation than can be performed by a single cell or any linear combination of cells, such as the majority rule. Since the 1s can be distributed throughout the CA lattice, the CA must transfer information over large space-time distances ($\approx N$).

The GA begins with a population of P randomly generated 128-bit CA rules, each encoded as a string of the rule-table output bits in lexicographic order of neighborhood patterns. (There are 2^{128} possible rules—far too many for any kind of exhaustive search.) The fitness of a rule in the population is calculated by: (i) randomly choosing I ICs that are uniformly distributed over $\rho \in [0.0, 1.0]$, exactly half with $\rho < \rho_c$ and half with $\rho > \rho_c$; (ii) running the rule on each IC either until it arrives at a fixed point or for a maximum of M time steps; (iii) determining whether or not the final pattern is correct—i.e., N 0s for $\rho_0 < \rho_c$ and N 1s for $\rho_0 > \rho_c$. The initial density ρ_0 is never exactly $1/2$, since N is chosen to be odd. Rule ϕ's fitness $F_I(\phi)$ is the fraction of the I ICs on which ϕ produces the correct final pattern. No partial credit is given for partially correct final configurations.

It should be pointed out that sampling ICs with uniform distribution over $\rho \in [0.0, 1.0]$ is highly skewed with respect to an unbiased distribution of ICs, which is binomially distributed over $\rho \in [0.0, 1.0]$ and very strongly peaked at $\rho = 1/2$. However, preliminary experiments indicated a need for such a biased distribution in order for the GA to make progress in early generations. This biased distribution turns out to impede the GA in later generations because, as increasingly fitter rules are evolved, the IC sample becomes less and less challenging for the GA [9].

The GA works as follows. (i) A new set of I ICs is generated. (ii) $F_I(\phi)$ is calculated for each rule ϕ in the population. (iii) A number E of the highest fitness ("elite") rules is copied without modification to the next generation. (iv) The remaining $P - E$ rules for the next generation are formed by single-point crossovers between pairs of elite rules randomly chosen with replacement. The offspring from each crossover are each mutated m times, where mutation consists of flipping a randomly chosen bit in a string. This defines one generation of the GA; it is repeated G times for one run of the GA. This method is similar to that used by Packard to evolve CAs for the $\rho_c = 1/2$ task [11]. (For a discussion of Packard's experiment, see [10].) Note that F_I is a random variable, since the precise value it returns for a given rule depends on the particular set of I ICs used to test the rule. Thus, a rule's fitness can vary stochastically from generation to generation. For this reason, at each generation the entire population, including the elite rules, is re-evaluated on a new set of ICs.

The parameter values we used were the following. For each CA in the population, $N = 149$ and $I = 100$. Each time a CA was simulated, M was chosen from a Poisson distribution with mean 320 (slightly greater than $2N$). Varying M prevents overfitting of rules to a particular M; see [10]. Allowing M to be larger—up to ten times the lattice size—did not change the qualitative results of the experiments [9]. The chromosomes in the initial population were not chosen with uniform probability at each bit as is common practice, but rather were uniformly distributed over the fraction of 1s in the string. (This restriction for the initial population was made for reasons related to previous research questions; see [10]. A smaller set of subsequent experiments with unbiased randomly generated initial populations indicated that this restriction is not likely to significantly influence the results of the experiments.) We set $P = 100$; $E = 20$; $m = 2$; and $G = 50$ (in some runs G was set to 100; no significant difference in the final results was observed). For a more detailed justification of these parameter settings and the results of parameter-modification experiments, see [9, 10].

CA	Rule Table	$N = 149$	$N = 599$	$N = 999$
Majority	ϕ_{maj}	0.000	0.000	0.000
Expand 1-Blocks	ϕ_{1a}	0.652	0.515	0.503
Particle-Based	ϕ_{1b}	0.697	0.580	0.522
Particle-Based	ϕ_{1c}	0.742	0.718	0.701
Particle-Based	ϕ_{1d}	0.769	0.725	0.714
GKL	ϕ_{GKL}	0.816	0.766	0.757

Table 1: Measured values of $\mathcal{P}_{10^4}^N$ at various values of N for six different $r = 3$ rules: the majority rule, the four rules discovered by the GA in different runs ($\phi_{1a}-\phi_{1d}$), and the GKL rule. The subscripts for the discovered rule tables indicate the pair of space-time diagrams illustrating their behavior in Figure 1. The standard deviation of $\mathcal{P}_{10^4}^{149}$, when calculated 100 times for the same rule, is approximately 0.004. The standard deviations for $\mathcal{P}_{10^4}^N$ for larger N are higher. (This table is similar to that given in [4], where the complete look-up tables for these rules are also given.)

4. Results of Experiments

4.1 Previous Results

We performed 300 runs of the GA with the parameters given above; each run had a different random-number seed. On most runs, the GA proceeded through roughly the same sequence of four "epochs" of innovation, each of which was marked by the discovery of a significantly improved new strategy for performing the $\rho_c = 1/2$ task. As reported in [9, 10], on most runs the GA evolved one of two strategies: (1) Relax to the fixed point of all 0s unless there is a sufficiently large ($\sim 2r + 1$) block of adjacent (or almost adjacent) 1s in the IC. If so, expand that block. (2) Relax to the fixed point of all 1s unless there is a sufficiently large block of adjacent (or almost adjacent) 0s in the IC. If so, expand that block.

A rule implementing strategy (1)—here called ϕ_{1a}—is illustrated in Figure 1(a). The figure gives two "space-time diagrams"—plots of lattice configurations over a range of time steps, with 1s given as black cells, 0s given as white cells, and time increasing down the page. Strategies (1) and (2) rely on the appearance or absence of blocks of 1s or 0s in the IC to be good predictors of ρ_0. For example, high-ρ ICs are more likely to have blocks of adjacent 1s than low-ρ ICs (cf. the bottom diagram in Figure 1(a)). The size of blocks that are expanded was tuned by the GA to be a good predictor of high or low density for $N = 149$ given the distribution of ICs on which the rules were tested.

The block-expanding rules evolved by the GA do not count as sophisticated examples of computation in CAs: all the computation is done locally in identifying and then expanding a "sufficiently large" block. Under F_{100} these strategies obtained fitnesses between 0.9 and 1.0 for different sets of ICs. A more indicative performance measure is "unbiased performance", $\mathcal{P}_I^N(\phi)$, defined as the fraction of I ICs chosen from an unbiased distribution over ρ on which rule ϕ produces the correct final pattern after $2.15N$ time steps. (With an unbiased distribution, most ICs chosen have $\rho \approx 0.5$. These are the hardest cases for any rule to classify.) After each run of the GA we measured $\mathcal{P}_{10^4}^{149}$ for the elite rules in the final generation. The highest measured $\mathcal{P}_{10^4}^{149}(\phi)$ for the block-expanding rules was approximately 0.685. The performance of these rules decreased dramatically for larger N since the size of block to expand was tuned by the GA for $N = 149$. The second row of Table 1 gives $\mathcal{P}_{10^4}^N(\phi_{1a})$ for three values of N. It is interesting to note that one naive solution to the $\rho_c = 1/2$ task—the

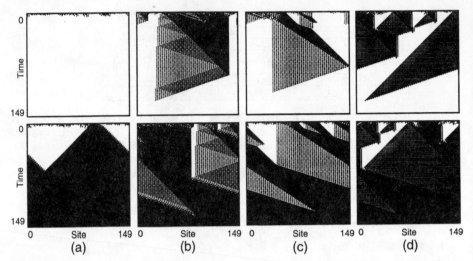

Figure 1: Space-time diagrams for four different rules discovered by the GA. The top diagrams have $\rho_0 < 1/2$; the bottom diagrams have $\rho_0 > 1/2$. Fitness increases from (a) to (d). (a) ϕ_{1a}. (b) ϕ_{1b}. (c) ϕ_{1c}. (d) ϕ_{1d}. Note that the "grey" pattern in (d) consists of alternating 1s and 0s.

$r = 3$ "majority" rule, in which the new state of each cell is decided by a majority vote among the $2r + 1$ cells in the neighborhood—has $\mathcal{P}_{10^4}^{149} = 0$ for all three values of N (first row of Table 1).

Mitchell, Crutchfield, and Hraber [9] described in detail the typical progression of the GA through the four epochs of innovation and the evolutionary mechanisms by which each new strategy was discovered on the way to a block-expanding CA. They also discussed a number of impediments that tended to keep the GA from discovering fitter, more general strategies; primary among them was the GA's breaking of the $\rho_c = 1/2$ task's symmetries in early generations for short-term gain by specializing exclusively on 1-block or 0-block expansion. On most runs this symmetry breaking was an important factor in preventing the GA from progressing to more sophisticated rules.

4.2 The New Strategies Discovered by the GA

Despite the impediments discussed in [9] and the unsophisticated rules evolved on most runs, on seven different runs the GA discovered rules with significantly higher performance and more sophisticated computational properties. Three such rules (each from a different run) are illustrated in Figures 1(b)-(d). For each of these rules—ϕ_{1b}, ϕ_{1c}, and ϕ_{1d}—F_{100} was between 0.9 and 1.0, depending on the set of 100 ICs. Some $\mathcal{P}_{10^4}^{N}$ values for these three rules are given in Table 1. As can be seen, $\mathcal{P}_{10^4}^{149}$ is significantly higher for these rules than for the typical block-expanding rule ϕ_{1a}. In addition, the performances of ϕ_{1c} and ϕ_{1d} remain relatively constant as N is increased, indicating a marked improvement in generalization.

Why does ϕ_{1d}, for example, perform relatively well on the $\rho_c = 1/2$ task? In Figure 1(d) it can be seen that, although the patterns eventually converge to fixed points, there is a transient phase during which a spatial and temporal transfer of information about the density in local regions takes place. This local information interacts with other local information to produce the desired final state. Roughly

ϕ_{1d} successively classifies "local" densities with a locality range that increases with time. In regions where there is some ambiguity, a "signal" is propagated. This is seen either as a checkerboard pattern propagated in both spatial directions or as a vertical black-to-white boundary. These signals indicate that the classification is to be made at a larger scale. Note that regions centered about each signal locally have $\rho = \rho_c$. The consequence is that the signal patterns can propagate, since the density of patterns with $\rho = \rho_c$ is neither increased nor decreased under the rule.

The discovery of these rules was first reported in [4] and methods for understanding their emergent logic were sketched there. In the following we first briefly review the computational mechanics approach to CAs. Using these methods, we then analyze the strategy of ϕ_{1d}—the rule with highest $\mathcal{P}_{10^4}^N$ found in the 300 runs—and describe the generational progression by which it was evolved under the GA.

4.3 Computational Mechanics of Cellular Automata

Like many natural processes that are spatially-extended, cellular-automata configurations often organize over time into spatial regions that are dynamically homogeneous. Sometimes in space-time diagrams these regions are obvious to the eye as "domains": regions in which the same "pattern" appears. In order to understand this phenomenon, and also to deal with cases in which human observation is inadequate or undesired, the notion of "domain" was formalized in [7] by adapting computation theory to CA dynamics. There, a domain's "pattern" is described using the minimal deterministic finite automaton (DFA) that accepts all and only those configurations that appear in the domain. Such domains are called "regular" since their configurations are members of the regular language recognized by the DFA. More precisely, a regular domain Λ is a set of configurations that is temporally invariant ($\Lambda = \phi(\Lambda)$) and whose DFA has a single recurrent set of states that is strongly connected.

Regular domains play a key role in organizing both the dynamical behavior and the information-processing properties of CA. Once a CA's regular domains have been detected, for example, nonlinear filters can be constructed to filter them out, leaving just the deviations from those regularities. The resulting filtered space-time diagram reveals the propagation of domain "walls". If these walls remain spatially-localized over time, then they are called "particles" [3]. Particles are one of the main mechanisms for carrying information over long space-time distances. This information might indicate, for example, the result of some local processing which has occurred at an early time. In this way particles can serve as signals. Logical operations on the information they contain are performed when the particles interact. The collection of domains, domain walls, particles, and particle interactions for a CA represents the basic information-processing elements embedded in the CA's behavior—the CA's "intrinsic" computation.

4.4 The GA Discovery of Particle-Based Computation

In this section we apply the computational mechanics framework sketched above to describe in detail the route by which the GA discovered ϕ_{1d}.

Figure 2(a) plots best fitness (F_{100}) in the population versus generation for the first 50 generations of the run in which ϕ_{1d} was discovered. It can be seen that, before the GA discovers high fitness rules, the fitness of the best CA rule increases in rapid jumps after periods of relative stasis. Qualitatively, the rise in performance can be divided into several "epochs", each beginning with the discovery of a new,

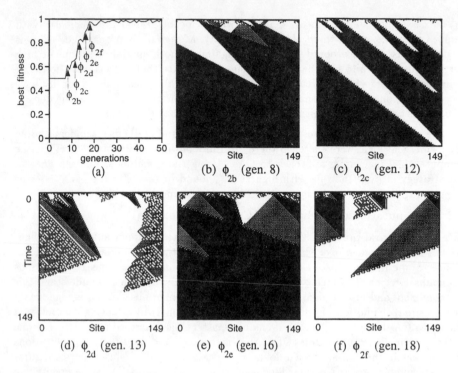

Figure 2: (a) Plot of the fitness of the most fit rule in the population versus generation in the run producing ϕ_{1d}. The arrows in the plot indicate the generations in which the GA discovered each new significantly improved strategy. (b)–(f) Space-time diagrams illustrating the behavior of the best rule at each of the five generations marked in (a).

significantly improved strategy for performing the $\rho_c = 1/2$ task. In Figure 2(a), the initial generations of these epochs are labeled with the name of the best rule found at that generation.

For the first seven generations, the highest F_{100} value equal to 0.5 is achieved by a number of rules that map almost all neighborhoods to the same symbol. Rules in which almost all neighborhoods map to 1 (0) quickly settle to the all 1s (all 0s) configuration irrespective of ρ_0. Such rules are able to correctly classify exactly half of the ICs and thus have a fitness of 0.5.

In generation 8, a new rule (ϕ_{2b}) is discovered, resulting in significantly better performance ($F_{100} \approx 0.61$). Its strategy is illustrated by the space-time diagram in Figure 2(b). ϕ_{2b} was created by a crossover between rule that maps most neighborhoods to 0 and a rule that maps most neighborhoods to 1. A closer inspection of the behavior of this rule reveals that it always relaxes to the all 1s configuration except when ρ_0 is close to zero, in which case it relaxes to the all 0s configuration, yielding $F_{100} > 0.5$. An analysis of particle interactions explains ϕ_{2b}'s behavior. After a very short transient phase, ϕ_{2b} essentially creates three regular domains: 1^* (denoted B), 0^* (denoted W), and $(10)^* \cup (01)^*$ (denoted #). This behavior can be understood readily from ϕ_{2b}'s rule table: out of the 28 neighborhood patterns with five or more 1s

(0s), 27 (22) result in an output bit of 1 (0). Therefore in any IC, small "islands" of length 1, 2 or 3 containing only 1s or 0s in are quickly eliminated, resulting in locally uniform domains. To maintain a $\#$ domain, the neighborhood patterns (1010101) and (0101010) must produce a 1 and 0 respectively, as is done in ϕ_{2b}.

After the B, W, and $\#$ domains are created, the subsequent behavior of ϕ_{2b} is primarily determined by the interaction of the particles representing the domain walls. ϕ_{2b} has three domains and six particles, one for each domain wall type: $P_{BW}, P_{WB}, P_{B\#}, P_{\#B}, P_{W\#}$, and $P_{\#W}$. The velocities of these particles (i.e., the slope of the domain wall corresponding to the particle) are 2.0, 1.0, 3.0, 1.0, −1.0, and −1.0 respectively. There are two annihilative interactions: $P_{BW} + P_{WB} \rightarrow \emptyset_B$ and $P_{B\#} + P_{\#B} \rightarrow \emptyset_B$ (where $\emptyset_B$ indicates a B domain with no particles). Two interactions are reactive: $P_{BW} + P_{W\#} \rightarrow P_{B\#}$ and $P_{B\#} + P_{\#W} \rightarrow P_{BW}$. All these interactions can be seen in Figure 2(b). Several particle interactions never occur as a result of the direction and magnitude of the particle velocities. For example, the particles $P_{\#W}$ and $P_{W\#}$ have the same velocity and never interact. Similarly, although $P_{\#B}$ moves in the same direction as P_{BW}, the former has only half the speed of the latter, and the two particles never have the chance to interact. For similar reasons, the $\#$ domain and its four associated particles $P_{B\#}, P_{\#B}, P_{W\#}$, and $P_{\#W}$ play no appreciable role in the determination of the CA's final configuration. This is easily verified by complementing the output bit of one of the two neighborhood patterns necessary to maintain the $\#$ domain and observing that very little change occurs in the rule's fitness.

Thus, for this epoch we can focus exclusively on the boundaries between the B and the W regions. Because P_{WB}'s velocity is less than that of P_{BW}, P_{BW} soon catches up with P_{WB}. The interaction of these two walls results in a B domain, eliminating the W domain. Therefore when an island of W is surrounded by B domains, the size of the former shrinks until it vanishes from the lattice. Conversely, when an island of B is surrounded by W domains, the B domain grows until it occupies the whole lattice. However, an island of B must occupy at least five adjacent cells in order to expand. Thus if any initial configuration contains a block of five 1s *or* results in the creation of such a block when the rule is applied over subsequent time steps, then the CA inevitably relaxes to the all 1s configuration. Otherwise it relaxes to the all 0s configuration.

The explanation of ϕ_{2b}'s behavior in terms of particles and particle interactions may seem a complicated way to describe simple behavior. But the usefulness of the computational mechanics framework for explicating computation will become clearer as the space-time behavior becomes more complex.

The next four generations produce no new epochs (i.e., no significantly new strategies) but a modest improvement in the best fitness. During this period three changes in behavior were observed, all of which appear in the generation 12 rule ϕ_{2c} (see Figure 2(c)). First, for an island of B to expand and take over the whole lattice, it now must contain at least seven cells. Since a seven-cell island of B is less likely than a five-cell island in low-ρ ICs, more low-ρ ICs are correctly classified. Second, the velocity of $P_{\#W}$ is modified from -1.0 to -3.0, allowing the annihilative reaction: $P_{W\#} + P_{\#W} \rightarrow \emptyset_W$. Thus, unlike in ϕ_{2b}, an island of $\#$ domain when surrounded by the W domain cannot persist indefinitely. Third, the velocity of P_{BW} is decreased to 1.5. Since the velocity of P_{WB} remains constant at 1.0, it now takes longer to eliminate W domains. (This last modification do not result in a significant change in fitness.) Unlike the innovation that resulted in ϕ_{2b}, where crossover played the major role, we find that these modifications (and the ones that follow) are primarily due to the mutation operator.

In generation 13, a new epoch begins with the discovery of ϕ_{2d}, with a sharp jump in F_{100} to 0.82 corresponding to a significant innovation. ϕ_{2d}'s behavior is illustrated in Figure 2(d). Here we use # to refer to an interesting variation of the checkerboard $((10)^* \cup (01)^*)$ domain. While the velocity of P_{WB} is held constant at 1.0, P_{BW} now moves with velocity 0.5 in the same direction. Since P_{BW} cannot catch up with P_{WB}, an island of W can now expand when surrounded by B, with the condition that W has to be at least six cells in length. This means that the rule still defaults to the all 1s configuration, but if there is a sufficiently large island of W in a low-ρ IC (a fairly likely event), the W island expands and the IC is correctly classified. However, misclassification is now possible for $\rho_0 > 0.5$ due to the (less likely) chance formation of an island of W of length six. This aspect of the strategy is similar to the "block-expanding" strategy.

In addition to the above changes, a new interaction is allowed to take place for the first time. The decrease in velocity of the particle P_{BW} to 0.5 not only results in the removal of small islands of B but it also allows $P_{\#B}$ to interact with P_{BW}. The interaction results in the particle $P_{\#W}$ with a velocity of -3.0, creating the necessary symmetry with $P_{B\#}$, which has velocity +3.0. From this juncture the # domain and its four associated particles play a major role in determining the fitness of a CA rule.

After a brief stasis over three generations, two developments result in the improved performance seen in ϕ_{2e}, the best rule in generation 16 ($F_{100} = 0.89$). First, P_{WB} now spontaneously creates a new # domain with two boundaries, one on each side: $P_{W\#}$ moving to the left with a velocity of -1.0, and $P_{\#B}$ moving to the right with a velocity of 1.0 (Figure 2(e)). Since $P_{W\#}$ is moving to the left and can interact with right moving P_{BW} to create $P_{B\#}$, the rule will stop the growth of W domains of length more than 6 cells when surrounded by larger regions of B. This prevents the "block-expanding strategy" error of expanding W blocks when $\rho_0 > 0.5$. This is a major innovation in using particles to effect non-local computation.

Second, the velocity of P_{BW} is further reduced from 0.5 to reduced to 1/3. However, an asymmetry still remains: because P_{BW} is moving to the right with a positive velocity, it takes longer to remove islands of B than to remove islands of W. This asymmetry is rectified by the discovery of ϕ_{2f} in generation 18, in which the velocity of P_{BW} is set to zero (Figure 2(f)), yielding $F_{100} = 0.98$. From generation 19 till the end of the GA run, little change is seen in either the fitness of the best rule in the population or its behavior. ϕ_{2f}'s behavior is almost identical to that of ϕ_{1d} which was discovered later in this run.

Interestingly, ϕ_{1d}'s behavior is very similar to the behavior of the well-known Gacs-Kurdyumov-Levin (GKL) CA, which was invented to study reliable computation and phase transitions in one-dimensional spatially-extended systems [6]. As shown in Table 1, ϕ_{GKL} has higher $\mathcal{P}_{10^4}^N$ than any rule found by the GA, although ϕ_{GKL} and ϕ_{1d} produce the same three domains $B, W, \#$, and also result in identical particles, particle velocities, and particle interactions. The difference in performance results, for example, from asymmetries in ϕ_{1d} not present in ϕ_{GKL} (see [9]); the detailed differences will be described in future work.

5. Conclusion

The results presented here demonstrate how evolution can engender emergent computation in a spatially-extended system. The GA found CAs that used particle-based computation to achieve performance nearly as high as that of the best human-designed rule on a density classification task. These discoveries are encouraging, both for using GAs to model the evolution of emergent computation in nature and for the automatic engineering of emergent computation in decentralized multicomponent systems. In previous work, a number of factors have been identified that limited the GA's performance in our experiments, and suggestions have been made for overcoming these impediments [9]. Even with these impediments, our GA was able to discover sophisticated CAs reliably, though with a low frequency. We expect that these approaches will eventually result in evolutionary-computation methods that discover sophisticated particle-based computation for a wide variety of applications. For example, in work that will be reported elsewhere, the GA discovered CAs that used particle-based computation to rapidly achieve stable global synchronization between local processors.

Acknowledgements. This research was supported by the Santa Fe Institute, under the Adaptive Computation and External Faculty Programs, by NSF grant IRI-9320200, and by the University of California, Berkeley, under contract AFOSR 91-0293.

References

[1] J. P. Crutchfield. The calculi of emergence: Computation, dynamics, and induction. *Physica D*, in press.

[2] J. P. Crutchfield (1994). Is anything ever new? Considering emergence. In G. Cowan, D. Pines, and D. Melzner (editors), *Complexity: Metaphors, Models, and Reality*, 479-497. Reading, MA: Addison-Wesley.

[3] J. P. Crutchfield and J. E. Hanson (1993). Turbulent Pattern Bases for Cellular Automata. *Physica D*, 69:279-301.

[4] J. P. Crutchfield and M. Mitchell (1994). The Evolution of Emergent Computation. Working Paper 94-03-012, Santa Fe Institute, Santa Fe, New Mexico.

[5] S. Forrest (1990). Emergent Computation: Self-organizing, collective, and cooperative behavior in natural and artificial computing networks: Introduction to the Proceedings of the Ninth Annual CNLS Conference. *Physica D*, 42:1-11.

[6] P. Gacs (1985). Nonergodic one-dimensional media and reliable computation. *Contemporary Mathematics*. 41:125.

[7] J. E. Hanson and J. P. Crutchfield (1992). The attractor-basin portrait of a cellular automaton. *Journal of Statistical Physics*, 66(5/6): 1415-1462.

[8] C. G. Langton, C. Taylor, J. D. Farmer, and S. Rasmussen (editors) (1992). *Artificial Life II*. Reading, MA: Addison-Wesley.

[9] M. Mitchell, J. P. Crutchfield, and P. T. Hraber. Evolving cellular automata to perform computations: Mechanisms and impediments. *Physica D*, in press.

[10] M. Mitchell, P. T. Hraber and J. P. Crutchfield (1993). Revisiting the edge of chaos: Evolving cellular automata to perform computations. *Complex Systems*, 7:89-130.

[11] N. H. Packard (1988). Adaptation toward the edge of chaos. In J. A. S. Kelso, A. J. Mandell, and M. F. Shlesinger (editors), *Dynamic Patterns in Complex Systems*, 293-301. Singapore: World Scientific.

[12] T. Toffoli and N. Margolus (1987). *Cellular automata machines: A new environment for modeling*. Cambridge, MA: MIT Press.

[13] S. Wolfram (1986). *Theory and applications of cellular automata*. Singapore: World Scientific.

Simulation of Exaptive Behaviour

Pedro Paulo Balbi de Oliveira

INPE-LAC, Caixa Postal 515
Computing and Applied Mathematics Laboratory
National Institute for Space Research
12201-970, São José dos Campos, SP, Brazil
Email: pedrob@lac.inpe.br

Abstract. Natural selection is such an established fact in evolutionary theory that very often one may be led to think that there are no alternative
evolutionary products rather than the *adaptations*. However, as discussed in
[6], various characters do not have any function at all, the so-called *nonaptations*, while many others, which they call *exaptations*, do have a function,
but their genesis was very likely not directly created through evolution by
natural selection. In evolutionary biology these concepts have already been
taken seriously. This paper aims at bringing them into consideration also by
the research communities of evolutionary computation and of computational
approaches to the evolution of behaviour, which are still overly dominated by
the adaptationist tradition. The background for the presentation is Enact, an
artificial-life world that implements a computational approach for coevolving
exapted behaviours out of sequences of individual nonaptations. A run of
the system is then presented in detail, featuring the onset of a parasite-like
behaviour, whose emergence did not occur through progressive adaptations
of the individuals involved. Discussions are then made regarding the role of
exaptations and nonaptations in the simulation of adaptive behaviour.

1 Introduction

Evolution by natural selection can directly shape up characters for a particular
function; the evolution of the vertebrate eye is usually considered a classical example.
This idea is such an established fact in evolutionary theory that very often one may
be led to think that these products, the *adaptations*, are the only possible outcome
of evolution.

However, as Gould and Vrba ([6]) remind us, there are a number of characters that do not have any function at all, constituting what they call *nonaptations*.
Moreover, and even more importantly, there are phenotypic traits they refer to as
exaptations, that have a current function but whose genesis was not driven towards
this particular function through evolution by natural selection.[1] The authors distinguish two forms of exaptations. First, the characters whose current function is the
cooptation for a new use of a character that was directly due to natural selection
to perform another function. That is, a previous adaptation that is coopted for a
new function; for example, birds' wings were adaptations for thermoregulation, that

---

1 Gould and Vrba ([6]) distinguish between the *functions* of adaptations and the *effects* of
exaptations; but we will not abide by it here.

became exaptations for flight. Second, the cooptation for the current use of a character whose origin cannot be ascribed to having been directly shaped by natural selection. In other words, a previous nonaptation that is coopted for a function; for instance, the sutures in mammalian skulls are thought to have been nonaptations that became exaptations for parturition.

In addition to alleviating the confusion between the criteria of "historical genesis" and "current utility" that permeates the notion of adaptation in evolutionary biology, a further motivation for defining the new concepts comes from the attempt to make explicit the fact that there is much more to explanations in evolutionary theory than the overemphasis on adaptationist explanations suggests. The debate involving exaptationist versus adaptationist explanations is still very active; for example, [17] features a recent debate in the context of the evolution of human language, with both sides fiercely represented. The predominance of the adaptationist programme is precisely the target of the criticisms expressed not only in [6], but also in [5], [11] and [16]. As remarked in [12], it is not that alternatives are not mentioned, but that they are all considered "diversions from the big event, the ascent of Mount Fitness".[2]

More and more, however, important pieces of research have come out contending the hegemony of adaptationism, and vigorously making the case for alternatives. As a whole they identify other sources of order that have been overlooked or even neglected, out of general physical laws, genetic mechanisms and developmental constraints. In particular, we should cite Kauffman's work epitomized by his monograph [8], and the view of evolution by *natural drift* put forward in [20].

While in evolutionary biology exaptations and nonaptations are progressively becoming widely accepted concepts, the research communities of evolutionary computation and of computational approaches to the evolution of behaviour are still overly dominated by the adaptationist tradition. Quite significantly, in the list of 172 references shown in the remarkable review of the field of simulation of adaptive behaviour presented in [9], none of the main articles related to the concepts above can be found. This paper aims at bringing the notions of exaptation and nonaptations into debate within segments of those communities as well, such as the growing field of evolutionary robotics (see [1]).

The background for this presentation is Enact, an artificial-life world that implements a computational approach for coevolving exapted behaviours out of sequences of individual nonaptations; exapted behaviours derived from adaptations cannot be built within Enact. In the next section, the main aspects of the Enact's definition are sketched, and its underlying evolutionary concepts examined in detail. Then, a run of the system is presented featuring the onset of a parasitic behaviour, whose emergence did not occur through progressive adaptations across the generations, but out of a sequence of nonaptations undergone by the individuals involved. Guidelines to be followed by other evolving systems are then suggested that might allow the emergence of that sort of exaptive behaviour. Finally, conclusions are drawn regarding the role of exaptations and nonaptations in the simulation of adaptive behaviour.

---

2 A symptomatic example can be drawn from a recent textbook in evolutionary genetics by a leading researcher in the field. Commenting upon alternative mechanisms of biological heredity known up to that date, the author states that they "... are of less importance, because they are not adaptive ..." ([14, page 12]).

2 Enact, an Artificial-Life World

Overview:
Enact is a family of two-dimensional cellular automata, whose temporal evolution on a periodic background can be described in terms of the metaphor of an artificial-life world where a population of agents undergo a coevolutionary process. During their lifetime, the agents roam around, sexually reproducing, interacting with the environment, and being subjected to a developmental process. Details about the system can be found in [2] and [3].

These artificial-life processes rely upon six categories of states which represent environment (E), the agent's terminals (T), genotype (G), phenotype (P), memetype (K), and an additional category to allow the agents to move (M). The system is programmable by adding *instantiated transitions*, special state transitions that define particular world set-ups. Except for the genotype, all the other cells are subjected to change through environmental interaction during the agent's lifetime.

Individuals in the system have the general form, $\boxed{T \; P \; G \; K_1 \; K_2 \; \cdots \; K_n \; T}$, the leftmost cell being the head, and the rightmost being the tail; the body is the rest. Whenever any of these states is changed into the background state of the world, the agent is killed off; this built-in selection process is activated by means of instantiated transitions that are added to the system, particularly crafted for each world set-up.

Whenever possible Enact's agents move; by design, they move either leftwards or diagonally, and never "bump" into each other. Agents can only "touch" environmental configurations that play the role of interaction sites. By designing specific state transitions to be active only in these sites, it is possible to have specific, controlled interactions taking place between environment and agents. Any agent then interacts with any other in the world through the environment. Since each agent's individual movement may influence the way the other agents move, their developments have a major interdependence through movement.

Selection: Pathways Rather Than Ends
In the standard use of evolutionary computation in optimisation problems, selection is based on the definition of an explicit fitness function. In these cases, its typical role can be allegorically envisaged as the establishing of a set of beacons in the search space, that the search process would then try to reach. As there is no concept of fitness function in Enact, a better image would be the exploration of a space where a set of beacons tells the exploration mechanism where are the forbidden points of the space. So, whereas in, say, genetic algorithms (GAs), selection is bound to rule out most regions of the search space, in Enact selection is not so strict, as most of the space being explored is assumed to be acceptable.

Consequently, selection in genetic algorithms is typically selection *for*: the emphasis is on the environmental interactions preserving the fitter individuals of the population, according to a fitness function predefined for the particular application.

What enables one to refer to selection *for* is either a hindsight analysis of a particular evolved trait, or the previous knowledge of the evolutionary pathway that has to be taken. But in the natural world selection operates *against* features that are incompatible with reproduction and survival; this is the only true statement that can be made in real-time, that is, during the span of time selection is still operating. Such a perspective is the one adopted in Enact, although, for short, we will refer simply to selection, omitting the word "against". In Enact, therefore, the agents that have deleterious features (state configurations) in a particular world set-up are the ones eventually killed off.[3]

This approach to selection stresses the point that, in general, it is not possible to drive evolution in Enact to a predefined end-point. All that is possible is to prevent some evolutionary pathways in advance. Of course, if all evolutionary pathways to a particular end-point are known in advance, it becomes possible to precisely reach that point; however, this is not the general case. Therefore, what matters the most in the system are the pathways, not the ends.

Movement: Enact's Power-House

Movement is the primary source of interaction between the agents. The movement of an agent has a local effect on the movement of its neighbours, and may propagate over the cellular space due to the whole sequence of perturbations of movement to other members of the population in its lifetime. The amount of perturbation that a newborn is able to yield to the organisation of the population depends on the size of the population, the current dynamics of the world, and the size of the cellular space.

Except for ageing, which depends only on the "clock-tick" of the cellular space updating, all the other processes embedded in Enact are powered by movement. Even more importantly, through movement all processes become coupled to each other. Movement is therefore the "power-house" of Enact. Life, death and reproduction of the agents are dependent, through movement, on their being in the right place at the right time.

Genotype: Initial Trend for Development

The head, taking on the states that determine how the agent is going to move at each step of its lifetime, has the ultimate responsibility for an agent's movement. The initial adult state of the head depends on the agent's initial adult phenotypic state, which in turn, depends on the agent's genotype. As development unfolds and the initial adult phenotypic state is replaced, the genotype then becomes ineffective in regard to the individual's movement.

The role of the genotype is then evident: since an agent's movement is coupled to the movement of other members of the population, the genotype cannot fully determine the pattern of movement; it only constrains an individual's movement by providing initial conditions. Hence, it is through the genotype that the *initial pattern of movement* of an agent is established.

Although there is a mapping between genotype and the initial state of the phenotype, there is no mapping between the former and the long-term phenotype of the agent. The reason is that the latter depends much more on the agent's history of interactions than on its genotype.

A similar process happens in relation to the memetype. While there is direct memetic transmission of parental features to the newborn, its long-term status, again, is only constrained by the original memetype; the latest states of the memetype are more dependent on the agent's history of environmental interactions and

---

3 According to [4, page 468], Alfred R. Wallace, the codiscoverer of natural selection, put forward a notion of selection that "differed from Darwin's" in a similar vein; Wallace's idea "was the environment eliminating the unfit, rather than a cut-throat competition among individuals".

its coupled movement with the other members of the population.

Therefore, from the point of view of phenotype and memetype, the role of the genotype is the specification of an *initial trend* in phenotypic and memetic spaces.

Coevolution Without Progressive Adaptation

Depending on the global configuration of the cellular space, and in particular, the actual physical location where the agents are born, the long-term development of two agents may significantly vary, regardless of their having the same genotype; analogously, two agents having distinct genotypes may reach the same long-term developmental state.

Although this lessened role of genotype in development (and consequently, in evolution) is certainly not the common wisdom, it is a central tenet for a minority (though eloquent) group of researchers. Lewontin, for one, has strongly put this point forward in [10], where he discusses the relations between organism, environment and ontogeny; supported by a great number of illustrative examples from biology, he draws conclusions such as that "... there is a many-to-many relationship between gene and organism. The same genotype gives rise to many different organisms, and the same organism can correspond to many different genotypes."

With the inheritance of non-deleterious features playing a minor role in the formation of the agents, and consequent predominance of movement in the determination of the individual's lifetime interactions, for all practical purposes, as a new agent is born its parental lineages are simply discontinued. Hence, there is no room for progressive, phylogenetic improvement of characters to occur.

In Enact there is inheritance of genetic material, even though the variation takes place over a finite and predefined set of alleles. Why then cannot adaptations exist? The factual answer is that, as stated above, the ontogenesis of the agents depends so much on their lifetime interactions. But there is a deeper, conceptual reason, which comes from an usually unspelt-out premise in the theory of natural selection; one that, for having systematically been left implicit, has led too often to a misunderstanding of the theory. The point is that for adaptations to come about, not only some form of "transgenerational stability"[4] is required for the organisms, but also for the environment. We could even say that not only reproduction of organisms are needed, but also of their environment. Very precisely Oyama ([15]) makes this point when writing that "What is required for evolutionary change is not genetically encoded as opposed to acquired traits, but functioning developmental systems: ecologically embedded genomes." Also, in [20] the same idea is expressed when the authors state that "Genes are, then, better conceived as elements that specify what in the environment must be fixed ... In every successful reproduction an organism passes on genes as well as an environment in which these genes are embedded." In a more intuitive way, such an aspect can be readily accepted by imagining what would happen if the fecunded egg of some animal were transplanted into the womb of another animal of a very different species.

Two consequences of the preceding points should be clear so far. First, any evolution in Enact is indeed, *coevolution*, any evolutionary process then becoming the process of coevolving coupled movement among the members of the population. Second, all coevolutionary activity happens without the progressive improvement of

---

4 This term is due to [13].

characters that natural selection induces along organisms' lineages in the form of adaptations. With the latter point in mind, what is the evolutionary process left with? This question is addressed next.

Exapted Characters by Sequences of Nonaptations

In addition to the impossibility of progressive adaptations to be built across the generations, it should be noted that it is also generally impossible for any non-deleterious character to be prevented from becoming deleterious. This results from the fact that in general there is no guarantee that an agent's development has finished. Therefore even if an indidual has developed into a state that might ensure its survival in certain conditions – for example, if it were in isolation from the rest of the population –, that does not mean it will not change into another that would entail its being killed off. Therefore, in the general situation of ongoing developments, i.e., one in which the state of the world is still changing, no exaptation that may have arisen can be preserved. Consequently, all agents' characters – their developmental states – are necessarily nonaptations. Evidently, in all particular cases in which developments are guaranteed to finish, exaptations can be directly observed; but this is not the general case.

However, while in Enact adaptations cannot be built at all by natural selection, exaptations can. Precisely the ones that started as nonaptations. The idea is the following. If a sequence of nonaptations an agent underwent entailed its survival, we can say that the agent acquired an exaptation, or in other words, that it has gone through an exaptive process. The key issue is: even though each nonaptation may have been neutral, the whole sequence was not. But how can the agent's survival be ensured, if there is no guarantee that development has finished? There are two possibilities. Either there has to be a way to detect or enforce the end of the development, at least for the agents that will act as probes into the exaptations; or there has to be a way to "freeze" the developmental process for the amount of time necessary for the exaptation to be probed. The parasitism experiment to be described ahead exemplifies the latter approach.

3 Parasitism without Adaptation

In this section a particular run of Enact is reported, which shows the behaviour of two agents in which one of them has a parasite-like behaviour in relation to the other, without this outcome having been due to an adaptation process. Details of the world set-up and the experiment itself can be found in [2].

According to their pattern of movement here are two kinds of adult agents: one that has a "preferential" movement to the left, and the other which would rather move diagonally. The ageing process – thought of as "loss of energy" due to movement –, is such that the agents can have two distinct ages before being killed off.

The interaction sites are individual environmental cells, as shown in Figure 1 in the form of the various dark, little squares. There are only two agent-environment configurations that support an interaction; at each of them the interaction site itself is not altered, a state change only occurring in the agents, and taking the form of a "feeding" process of the agent. Thus, the situation is one in which the coevolutionary

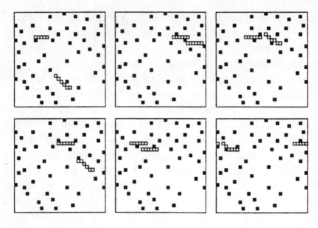

Fig. 1. Main phases of trajectory 0, the one defined by the $\mathcal{D}$-agent while it is interacting with the $\mathcal{L}$-agent. The topmost agent in the top-left picture is the $\mathcal{L}$-agent.

process will reflect the dynamics of the population adjusting itself so as to make a viable use of the "feeding sites".

3.1 The Parasitic Behaviour

We can now turn to the behaviour of the two agents, whose main phases are illustrated in Figure 1. The pictures represent the cellular space punctuated by the environmental (feeding) sites, and the two agents involved. We refer to them as $\mathcal{L}$-agent and $\mathcal{D}$-agent, $\mathcal{L}$ and $\mathcal{D}$ for short, the former being one that preferentially moves leftwards, and the latter, diagonally. In the top-left picture of the figure $\mathcal{L}$ is on the top and $\mathcal{D}$ is on the bottom, both freely moving according to their "nature"; but $\mathcal{D}$ is approaching $\mathcal{L}$. In fact, just when $\mathcal{L}$ is about to pass to the right-hand edge of the space, $\mathcal{D}$ is obstructed by $\mathcal{L}$ and cannot carry on its diagonal movement; therefore it starts following $\mathcal{L}$ and that is the situation depicted in the top-middle picture. Note that, just ahead of $\mathcal{D}$ (which is now moving leftwards) there is an interaction site; it turns out that, a few iterations later, such a site blocks $\mathcal{D}$'s movement which then has no other alternative than to stop, facing that site. As it stops, $\mathcal{L}$ continues to move and soon the way up is free again for $\mathcal{D}$ to re-start its diagonal movement; the top-right picture illustrates the situation, where $\mathcal{D}$ has already moved a few cells up.

Agent $\mathcal{D}$ then moves round, reappearing at the right-hand edge of the space, which is shown in the bottom-left picture; and again, $\mathcal{D}$ is approaching $\mathcal{L}$ from the bottom. The situation now is similar to the one described above, and so it goes until the new configuration is again the first one we started from, and the entire cycle described is re-initiated. Hence, $\mathcal{L}$'s movement to the left is never disturbed by the movement of $\mathcal{D}$. On the other hand, $\mathcal{L}$'s movement interferes twice with $\mathcal{D}$'s behaviour. This cycle defines a trajectory for both agents, which we denote trajectory 0. It can be seen that there are 8 feeding sites at this trajectory, its cycle period lasts 279 iterations, and as such, the $\mathcal{D}$-agent spends, on average, 34.9 iterations without being fed.

In order to evaluate the significance of $\mathcal{L}$ to $\mathcal{D}$'s "life" it is necessary to kill off $\mathcal{L}$ and observe how $\mathcal{D}$'s behaviour is affected. It turns out however that depending on the moment $\mathcal{L}$ is killed off, $\mathcal{D}$ may be affected in different ways. The point here is that, depending on which part of its trajectory the $\mathcal{D}$-agent is at the time $\mathcal{L}$ is killed off, $\mathcal{D}$ will deviate from the original trajectory at different points. There are 23 distinct such *deviation points*.

By killing off $\mathcal{L}$ while $\mathcal{D}$ is at each one of the deviation points, and keeping track of $\mathcal{D}$ until it settles down to a new trajectory, the deviation points can be collapsed into equivalence classes according to the new trajectory for $\mathcal{D}$. We find 5 new trajectories, some of their features being summarized in Table 1.

Trajectory	No. of feeding sites involved	Period (iterations)	Average period without feeding
I	1	93	93
II	1	96	96
III	0	∞	∞
IV	1	94	94
V	2	96	48
0	8	279	34.9

Table 1. The various trajectories and the parasitic relation: if $\mathcal{L}$ is removed from the interaction, the chance of death for $\mathcal{D}$ significantly increases.

Table 1 shows that trajectories I, II and IV lead to an increase in the average period without feeding of nearly three times compared to the case where $\mathcal{L}$ is "alive". Even more dramatic is the case of trajectory III, for which there are no feeding sites. For trajectory V there is an increase in the period without feeding of $\mathcal{D}$, but only by a small amount. It is also interesting to calculate the expected average period without feeding that the agent $\mathcal{D}$ would face, if the agent $\mathcal{L}$ would be killed off by chance. The point here is to work out a weighted average considering that each deviation point encompassed by each trajectory is related to a different number of trajectory positions of the original trajectory. In order to do that we do not consider trajectory III, since it would lead the average to infinity. The value we finally get is 93.6, which is high and in fact a lower bound, since trajectory III was excluded from the calculation. Hence we can conclude that agent $\mathcal{D}$ is definitely taking advantage of the influence that $\mathcal{L}$ has on its behaviour.

This advantage is so clearly defined that it is reasonable to refer to $\mathcal{D}$'s behaviour as parasitic in relation to $\mathcal{L}$. From the perspective of $\mathcal{D}$, its pattern of movement, which leads it to interact with $\mathcal{L}$ and the feeding sites, in the way described above, is an exaptation: it is a cooptation for fitness of the whole sequence of nonaptations $\mathcal{D}$ underwent in its lifetime in the form of a sequence of neutral developmental states.

4 Towards Exaptive Behaviours

In order to allow for the emergence of exaptations out of sequences of nonaptations, and for the possibility of making sense of them, some conditions have to be created. But these will depend on the particular evolving system under consideration. For instance, in a GA-like system, the existence of segments of unused genetic material in individuals that are subject to a developmental process would be an important source for the emergence of nonaptations. There are, however, guidelines that can be identified out of Enact and the parasitism experiment, which may be general enough to be considered in other contexts. They constitute guidelines for enabling, detecting, and interpreting exaptations, which are respectively, described as follows.

Consider evolution as leading to viability rather than optimisation:
Since evolutionary pathways in Enact are not previously specified, the result of the agents' actions, reflected in their development and environmental change, is not previously predefined either; they are indeed the result of a self-organisation process that takes place so as to satisfy the constraints imposed by the selection process.

In the experiment the "advantage" being taken by $\mathcal{D}$ occurs without any a priori concept of optimisation. It happens the way it does just because it is a viable outcome of the world set-up in use.

Shift focus away from adaptations:
Enact takes a radical position in this respect, insofar as adaptations are simply "switched off". For other systems it should suffice to shift the focus of analysis away from the adaptations.

Parasitic behaviours have been reported in the literature in various computer simulations, as in [18], but all of them from a strictly adaptationist perspective. Parasitism was chosen primarily for its simplicity of analysis; but a wealth of other end-configurations have been observed, with high number of agents and wide diversity. For example, an end-configuration suggesting a symbiosis-like behaviour is not a rare occurrence, thus suggesting that other forms of behaviour, say, hyper-parasites, could well be observed. In any case, all the behaviours would have to follow the same characteristic of not being due to adaptation processes.

Find a firm basis upon which to interpret the exaptations:
Making sense of exaptations carries a potential difficulty with it, insofar as an undefined space is opened for the experimenter, in terms of the choice of which domain the interpretations should rely upon. As shown in the experiment, the natural alternative is to describe the outcomes of a run from the perspective of the evolving system itself.

But let us imagine the hypothetical case in which, say, trajectory V entailed agent $\mathcal{D}$ being better off than in trajectory 0. $\mathcal{D}$ would then still be taking advantage of $\mathcal{L}$, although not as much as in the original situation; hence, one would still be inclined to refer to parasitism, although not as decidedly as before. By assuming that agent $\mathcal{D}$ would be better off also in a further trajectory, our conceptualization of the original parasitism would become much looser. By carrying on in this direction, the original parasitism would become even fuzzier, up to the point that eventually it would not make sense to refer to it any more.

This warns us that making sense of the outcomes of animat worlds according to familiar notions such as the parasitism, hyper-parasitism and the like, should be made in a cautious way; first, because the internal coherence of these worlds will not necessarily fit our preconceptions about biological reality; second, because it is too informal, not being able to capture the wealth of subtle changes in behaviours that may come out of a run. In order to avoid these problems, I have performed experiments with world set-ups in which the lifetime interactions of surviving agents is characterised in terms of computable functions, identifiable out of phenotypic and memetic transformations in the agents.

5 Conclusion: Two Traps to be Avoided

The main thrust for Gould and Vrba ([6]) making explicit the notion of exaptation is their belief on the importance of the class of exaptations that began as nonaptations, exactly the type this paper dealt with. As they wrote: "If all exaptations began as adaptations for another function in ancestors, we would not have written this paper. ... the enormous pool of nonaptations must be the wellspring and reservoir of most evolutionary flexibility. We need to recognize the central role of "cooptability for fitness" as the primary evolutionary significance of ubiquitous nonaptation in organisms. In this sense, and at its level of the phenotype, this nonaptive pool is an analog of mutation — a source of raw material for further selection." Just like those authors, we are neither suggesting the demise of adaptations, nor denying the implications of fitness; we are simply making the case for a legitimate supplement to adaptations, whose importance, after all, is the increase of fitness of the individuals.

Considering that natural selection has been under close scrutiny even in evolutionary biology, it is a wise stance to be cautious about its use as the last word in terms of evolutionary mechanisms to be used in computational simulations of adaptive behaviour. In particular, two points should be made. First, when modelling evolving natural systems, we should be aware of the pervasiveness of exaptations, and not fall into the trap of telling facile, "just so" stories ([5]) based on supposed adaptations; enlightening in this respect is the work described in [19] which tested through computer simulations, with positive results, the hypothesis that the neural circuitry, currently subserving the tailflip escape manoeuvre in the crayfish, has a vestigial synapse from a previous epoch in which the circuit was used for swimming instead of flipping. Moreover, note that if the case of parasitism had been shown in the absence of background information about Enact, the reader could very easily be led to the conclusion that it had been the result of an adaptation process; however, as shown, that was not the case.

Second, when performing artificial evolution, there is another trap we can fall into, which is the implicit assumption that there is a fitness scale against which the entire phylogeny of a species can be measured. The more complex a behaviour being evolved, the higher the chance that characters associated with it have to pass through a long sequence of nonaptations, before any change in its fitness can be perceived. Sooner or later, evolutionary roboticists will have to face in their experiments the necessity of "long-jumps" in the associated fitness landscapes, so as to cross these sequences of nonaptations. Even if the resources of time and parallelism of the evolutionary mechanisms may have to be significantly increased! Correctly towards this track (although, ironically, still out of it) seems to be [7], when stating that "There is no universal and objectively set fitness landscape against which bacteria, jellyfish and humans can all have their traits measured for adaptiveness.": after all, if there is no absolute fitness scale across different species, much less should there be across the phylogeny of a single species.

Acknowledgement

I thank Inman Harvey, Phil Husbands, Robert Davidge and Serge Thill for comments on the reported experiment; and Alistair Bray, for proofreading. This work was partially done in England, thanks to the Brazilian institutions, INPE and CNPq.

References

1. D. Cliff; I. Harvey & P. Husbands. "Explorations in Evolutionary Robotics". *Adaptive Behavior*, 2(1):71–104, 1993.

2. Pedro P. B. de Oliveira. "Enact: An artificial-life world in a family of cellular automata." CSRP-248/92, School of Cognitive and Computing Sciences, Univ. of Sussex, Brighton, UK, Sept. 1992.

3. Pedro P. B. de Oliveira. "Methodological issues within a framework to support a class of artificial-life worlds in cellular automata". In: D. G. Green & T. Bossomaier, editors. *Complex Systems: From Biology to Computation*. IOS Press, Amsterdam, pp.82-96, 1993.

4. A. Desmond & J. Moore. *Darwin*. Michael Joseph, London, 1991.

5. S. J. Gould & R. C. Lewontin. "The spandrels of San Marco and the Panglossian Paradigm: A critique of the adaptationist programme." In: E. Sober, editor. *Conceptual Issues in Evolutionary Biology: An Anthology*. Cambridge, MA, MIT Press: Bradford Books, 252–270, 1984.

6. S. J. Gould & E. S. Vrba. "Exaptation — a missing term in the science of form". *Paleobiology*, 8:4–15, 1982.

7. I. Harvey. "The Artificial Evolution of Adaptive Behaviour." DPhil Thesis to appear as: CSRP, School of Cognitive and Computing Sciences, Univ. of Sussex, Brighton, UK, 1994.

8. S. Kauffman. "Origins of Order: Self-Organization and Selection in Evolution." Oxford University Press, 1993.

9. J.-A. Meyer and A. Guillot. "Simulation of Adaptive Behavior in Animats: Review and Prospect". In: J.-A. Meyer and S. W. Wilson, editors. *From Animals to Animats: Proceedings of The First International Conference on Simulation of Adaptive Behavior.*, MIT Press: Bradford Books, Cambridge, MA, USA, pp.2–14, 1991.

10. R. C. Lewontin. "The Organism as the Subject and Object of Evolution". *Scientia*, 118:63–82, 1983.

11. R. C. Lewontin. "Adaptation." In: E. Sober, editor. *Conceptual Issues in Theoretical Biology: An Anthology*, MIT Press: Bradford Books, Cambridge, MA, USA, 234–251, 1984.

12. R. C. Lewontin. "A natural selection". *Nature*, 339:107, 1989.

13. H. R. Maturana & F. Varela. "The Tree of Knowledge: The Biological Roots of Human Understanding". Shambala: Boston, 1988.

14. J. Maynard Smith. "Evolutionary Genetics". Oxford University, New York, 1989.

15. S. Oyama. "The Ontogeny of Information". Cambridge: Cambridge University Press, 1985.

16. M. Piatelli-Palmarini. "Evolution, selection and cognition: From 'learning' to parameter setting in biology and in the study of language". *Cognition*, 31(1), 1989.

17. S. Pinker & P. Bloom. "Natural language and natural selection". *Behavioral and Brain Sciences*, 13:707-784, 1990.

18. Thomas S. Ray. "An approach to the synthesis of life". In: J. D. Farmer, C. Langton, S. Rasmussen & C. Taylor, editors. *Artificial Life II*, 371–408, Addison-Wesley, 1992.

19. D. G. Stork; B. Jackson & S. Walker. ""Non-Optimality" via Pre-adaptation in Simple Neural Systems". In: J. D. Farmer, C. Langton, S. Rasmussen & C. Taylor, editors. *Artificial Life II*, 409–429, Addison-Wesley, 1992.

20. F. Varela; E. Thompson, & E. Rosch. *The Embodied Mind: Cognitive Science and Human Experience*. MIT Press: Cambridge, MA, 1991.

Artificial Spacing Patterns in a Network of Interacting Celloids

Hiroaki Inayoshi

Computation Models Section, ElectroTechnical Lab.(ETL),
1-1-4 Umezono, Tsukuba Science City, Ibaraki, 305, Japan.
tel: +81 298 58 5865;   fax: +81 298 58 5871;   e-mail: inayoshi@etl.go.jp

Abstract. This paper presents artificial synthesis of spacing patterns, as the one example of a project entitled "Celloid for Organismoid". In order to achieve this goal, a new mechanism, called an Artificial Genetic Network (AGN), is introduced, which is inspired from the Genetic Network in nature. A collection of celloids (i.e. artificial cells), each of which interacts according to the same AGN, is compared with a collection of independent celloids, in which each celloid behaves independently from the others. The comparison shows that the former exhibit higher order than the latter. This demonstrates the importance of proper interaction between component parts in organisms.

keywords: artificial life; cell, celloid; organism, organismoid, organization; Genetic Network, Artificial Genetic Network; spacing pattern, bristle; differentiation; interaction; gene, gene expression, regulation;

1 Introduction

The structure, function, and behavior of multicellular organisms is an 'emergent property' that comes from the interaction between its component parts, i.e. cells. I am now working on a project entitled "Celloid for Organismoid", in which I search for artificial synthesis that exhibits this behavior. In other words, the emergence of an artificial organismoid by designing artificial, differentiable celloids [1] as its component parts, collecting them, and letting them interact to organize together. In this paper, one example of this research is presented. The goal of this example is to generate spacing patterns, which are remniscent of ones observed in insects. (When insects produce their bristles, or short stiff hairs, the bristles are spaced in a non-random fashion. New bristles will appear in the largest spaces between the preexisting bristles.) This is a simple example of the general phenomenon of cell differentiation.

A new mechanism, called an Artificial Genetic Network (AGN), which is based on Natural Genetic Networks (i.e. networks of genes), is introduced into the celloids to synthesize the spacing patterns artificially. A collection of celloids, having the same AGN, interact with each other locally, and each celloid makes a dynamical decision whether to have or not to have a bristle, based on this local interaction. The local decisions made by each of celloids give rise to some global

---

[1] This work and the name "cell-oid" are inspired by the "bird-oid" in [Reyn87].

pattern. In spite of the fact that there is no global director determining which celloid should and which should not have a bristle, some degree of order in the spacing pattern emerges. To compare the degree of order in celloids with AGN, a control experiment is done, in which independent cells are collected and each cell makes the same binary decision independently (i.e. without interaction). The comparison shows that the collection of interacting celloids has a higher degree of order than the collection of 'independent cells'. (Note that the goal is *not* in making artificial patterns that mimic exactly natural patterns *but* in generating artificial patterns which have order or regularity. In other words, an emphasis is placed on **order** rather than on **similarity** to nature.)

The remainder of this paper is organised as follows: Section 2 provides a brief description of spacing patterns in insects. Section 3 explains natural and artificial genetic networks. Section 4 presents experiments and their results. Finally, Section 5 provides a conclusion and future directions.

2   Spacing Patterns

Bristles (i.e. short stiff hairs) form a spacing pattern ([Lawr92] p.159). Introducing the metabolization of bristles, this phenomenon can be depicted as Fig. 1.

Note that the binary decision (i.e. to have or not to have a bristle) corresponds to the simplest differentiation, because each cell can take only one of the two states. Therefore, this example provides a basis for the differentiation of cells in general, in which the range of choice will be increased.

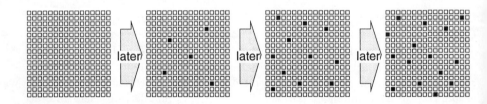

Fig. 1. The spacing patterns of metabolizing bristles: Each small rectangle corresponds to a cell. (Each black rectangle has a bristle, white rectangles have none.)

3   Genetic Networks as a basis for Differentiation

In this paper, **a Genetic Network** refers to **a network of genes** (i.e. **nodes**) which are connected by **regulatory influences** (i.e. **edges**) that affect the expression of other genes. In this section, Natural and Artificial Genetic Networks will be described, after some biological facts are explained.

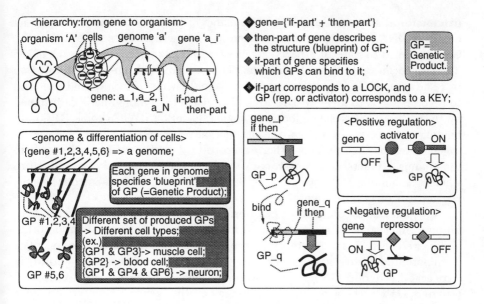

Fig. 2. Hierarchy from gene level to organism level (Left Top), Relation between genome and differentiation of cell (Left bottom), Mechanism of gene regulation (Right), and Two types of gene regulation (Right bottom).

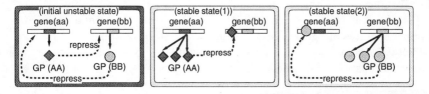

Fig. 3. The simplest Genetic Network composed of two nodes: (exclusive case).

3.1 Natural Genetic Networks ([Alb et al.89])

Every multicellular organism, including a human being, exists as **a collection of cells**. (See Fig. 2:left-top.) And all cells, constituting an organism, have **the same genome**, which is **a collection of genes**. Each gene, constituting a genome, takes either of two states: {**expressed** or **not expressed**} . Here, *to express a gene* means *to produce a* **Genetic Products** (**GPs**, usually proteins, sometimes RNA), *the* **blueprint** *of which is described (specified) in the gene to be expressed.* Produced GPs perform various **functions**. Some GPs act as **enzymes**, others help in **cytoskelton**. But a most important fact is that **some GPs can regulate the production of other GPs**. In other words, they can regulate the expression of genes. This regulation occurs as follows: Each gene has **if-part** and **then-part** ([Inay94b]). (Both parts are described as **one-**

dimensional sequences taken from alphabet of {A,T,G,C}, which are building blocks of DNA.) The then-part of a gene specifies **which GPs to build**. Some GPs can **bind** to some of if-parts of genes (see Fig. 2:right), whereas each of the if-parts specifies **which molecule (or GP) can and which cannot bind to it**. (The sequence in if-part corresponds to a **lock**, while molecules that can bind to it corresponds to **keys to the lock**: The strength of a binding is determined by the **affinity** between the lock and key: cf. [Conr92]) When some GP(s) are binding to a if-part of a gene, the production of the GPs (whose blueprint is specified by the then-part) is either **activated** (= **positive regulation**, where the binding GP acts as an **activator**) or **repressed** (= **negative regulation**, where the binding GP acts as a **repressor**) (See Fig. 2:right-bottom.) Thus, **regulation of gene expression** takes place.

Now, imagine **a collection of nodes**, and suppose each node corresponds to a **gene**. Since some of nodes (=genes) have **potential influences** upon other nodes, we can represent them by **edges**, each of which links two nodes. (The word potential means that influence can occur **only when the gene (node) is expressed (turned ON)**. In other words, so long as the gene is **not expressed (turned OFF)**, the gene has no influence on other genes.) Thus, we obtain a network of genes, which is refered to as a **Genetic Network**, in this paper.

Fig. 3 shows a simple Genetic Network, or a network of **two** genes. Suppose two genes, aa and bb, can produce GPs AA and BB, respectively. If the two GPs, AA and BB, can repress the expression of each other, **exclusive expression** will take place, as in the figure.

Let G be the number of genes in the Genetic Network. Although the number of possible states of "genetic expression" is 2^G, stable states would be a subset of 2^G states, due to the regulations. And this subset gives rise to a set of possible differentiations. (Cf. Fig. 2:left-bottom.)

Note: The Genetic Networks are not exactly the same as Kauffman's **random boolean networks** in [Kauf90]: the latter have only one type of edge, while the former have two, i.e. activative and repressive.

3.2 Artificial Genetic Networks (= AGNs)

An AGN means an **artificial network of artificial genes**. Fig. 4 illustrates **interactions through an AGN**. (The **collection of if-parts** corresponds to the **GSs** (Genetic Switches :cf. [Ptas87]) in the figure, while that of then-parts makes the **list of (producable) GPs**.)

To synthesize the spacing patterns described in section 2, celloids having the same AGN must interact to decide whether to have or not to have a bristle. To achieve this interaction mechanism, I adopt the following AGN, which is called **"linear AGN"**. Let N be the number of genes in this AGN. Genes are supposed to be expressed **only sequentially**, from 1 to N. Therefore, when gene i is expressed, all genes from 1 to N are expressed beforehand. To have or not have a bristle is decided by the number of genes expressed: If more than $N/2$ genes are expressed in a cell, the cell has a bristle. Otherwise the cell does not have. (See Fig. 5:right-bottom.)

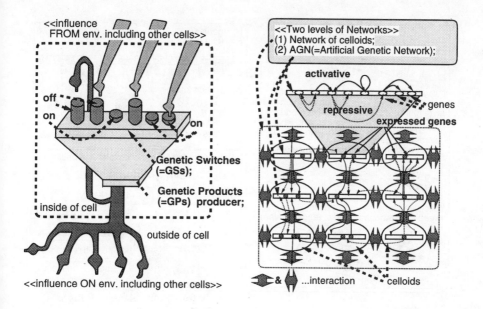

Fig. 4. Interaction between cell and its environment (left), and interaction between cells (right); • Left: The outside world of a cell, i.e. both other cells and environment surrounding the organism, influences upon "genetic state" of the cell, by turning the **GSs** on / off. Then the state of GSs determine which **GPs** to produce, and the produced GPs, in turn, influence back on the **outside world**, including on other cells, as well as on the **internal** state of the cell itself. • Right: Expressed genes in a cell may influence (i.e. activate / repress) upon not only 'genes in *the cell*' but also 'genes in *the neighbor cells*', since all cells share the same AGN. Namely, **target genes to influence upon** exist in all cells. • Both: A different **genetic state** (or, a set of expressed genes) brings the production of a different **set of GPs**, which leads to the **differentiation of cells**.

As for the details of this AGN, see Fig. 5. (Also see [Inay94a].)

4 Experiments and Results

Two experiments are done: One with interaction between celloids ($N = 8$), and the other without it (i.e. control experiment). They are labeled "interaction" and "random" , respectively. Details are as follows. (For the details of the computation in celoids network, see [Inay94a].)

Ten thousand (100*100) celloids, each adjacent to four neighbors, are aligned two-dimensionally. Each celloid dynamically selects one of the two states: { ON (i.e. having a bristle) or OFF (i.e. not having a bristle) }, according to the same rule, the AGN described in the previous sections. As a control experiment, the same number of cells are collected and each of them selects { ON or OFF} *independently from each other*. In other words, in the control experiment, each cell makes a "transition at random" without interaction, as in Fig.6. The probabilities of transition are as follows: P_{ON} is fixed to be $1/2^{10}$, whereas P_{OFF} is

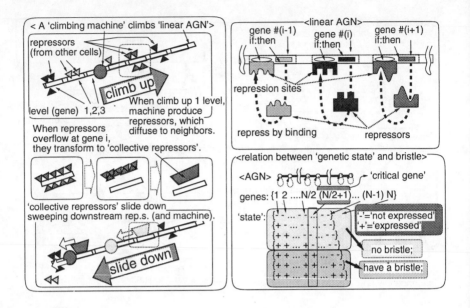

Fig. 5. Gene expression process in each celloid (left) and 'linear AGN' adopted to generate artificial spacing pattern (right). • Left: Gene expression in each celloid is performed by the 'climbing machine' in each celloid. The climbing machine tries to 'climb up' the 'linear AGN', in which network genes from 1 to N are aligned linearly. The machine starts from the outside of the AGN and tries to express gene 1. (To express gene i, expressions of all genes $\{ j; j < i \}$ are required.) The probability of expressing gene i (i.e. of climing up to the i-th level of gene from $(i - 1)$-th level) depends on the number of repressors binding at the gene i. That is, the more repressors are binding at the gene i, the more difficult it becomes to express the i-th gene, when the machine is at $(i - 1)$-th gene. When the machine suceeds in climbing up to the i-th level, (i.e. in expressing the gene i), the machine produces GPs of the gene i, which are repressors to the gene i. (cf. Right.) Produced GPs diffuse to neighbor cells, thus interfere with the climbing processes of the neighbor machines • Left-middle & bottom: When repressors saturate at gene k, they **transform to 'collective repressors'**. This collective repressors slide down to downstream and sweep out everything (e.g repressors) in the downstream. So, if the machine is located at the upstream of gene k, it is not influenced; But if it is at the downstream, all expressed genes are cleared and the machine has to start over the process again.

either $\{ 1/2^5,$ or $1/2^4,$ or $1/2^3 \}$. These three cases are labeled as $\{$ P=(10:5), P=(10:4), P=(10:3) $\}$, respectively in the following figures.

Though each celloid has several adjustable parameters, only one parameter is varied in the experiment. This parameter is Q, the amount of repressors released by each of the gene expressions. Instead of specifying the values of Q, the expected diffusion distance, d, is specified as one of the following values: $\{4, 8, 12, 16, 20\}$. (These are labelled as $\{ d = 4, d = 8, d = 12, d = 16, d = 20\}$, respectively.) Note that the "Manhattan distance" [2] is used and that Q is proportional to $d * d$. Both experiments start from **bald state** (i.e. no bristle at all) and run for several thousands of time steps (or **cycles**).

---

[2] $dist(A, B) = |x_A - x_B| + |y_A - y_B|$, where $A = (x_A, y_A)$ and $B = (x_B, y_B)$.

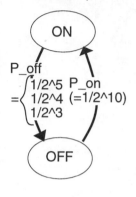

(random transition in each cell)

Fig. 6. Control experiment.

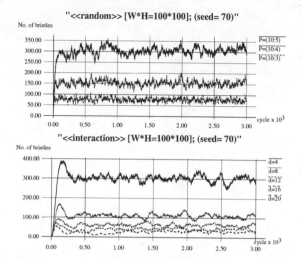

"<<random>> [W*H=100*100]; (seed= 70)"

"<<interaction>> [W*H=100*100]; (seed= 70)"

Fig. 7. No. of bristles vs. cycle in random model (top). and in interaction model (bottom).

Fig.7 shows the relation between the numbers of bristles and the time steps in the "random" (top) and "interaction" (bottom) models respectively. As is seen, the numbers of bristles change with time but the variations remain in certain ranges in both cases. Figs.8 to 11 show two cases of results:

(1) a relatively dense case (i.e. approximately 300 bristles appear in 100*100 celloids.) ... Figs.8 &10.
(2) a relatively sparse case (i.e. approximately 150 bristles appear in 100*100 celloids.) ... Figs.9 &11.

Figs.8 &9. show the snapshots of bristles at three cycles (at cycle # 100, 300, and 500). Each of figs.10 &11 shows the distibution of distances to the nearest bristle from each bristle (at cycle # 100) and compares the interaction model with the random model in two cases, dense and sparse, respectively. (The abscissa stands for the distance between bristles, whereas the ordinate stands for the frequency.) Similar results are obtained when the seeds for the random numbers are changed. In both cases, the following facts are observed:

- In the random model, the distribution of distances between bristles (figs.10 &11) is quite **broad** and **flat**.
- In the interaction model, the distribution of the distance between bristles is **much narrower** and **more peaked**.

A **peaked distribution** reflects **order** in the system, as is seen in Figs.12. Therefore it follows that **the collection of interacting celloids has a higher degree of order than the collection of independent celloids.**

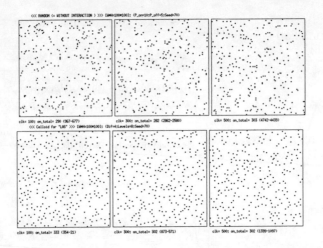

Fig. 8. A relatively dense case: Snapshots of bristles at three cycles (from left, at cycle # 100, 300, and 500). Top= random model; Bottom= interaction model; Each dot in the snaps represents a bristle in 100 * 100 celloids. The exact numbers of bristles in each snap (from left) are 290, 282, 303 (top) and 333, 302, 302 (bottom).

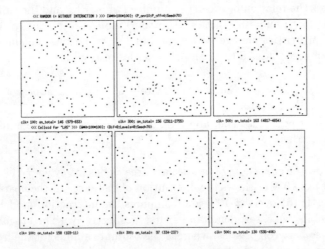

Fig. 9. A relatively sparse case: Snapshots of bristles at three cycles (from left, at cycle # 100, 300, and 500). Top= random model; Bottom= interaction model; Each dot in the snaps represents a bristle in 100 * 100 celloids. The exact numbers of bristles in each snap (from left) are 146, 156, 163 (top) and 158, 97, 130 (bottom).

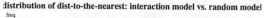

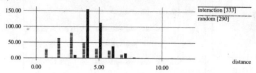

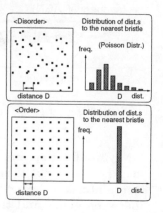

Fig. 10. Comparison of interaction:(d=4) and random:P=(10:5) in relatively dense case;

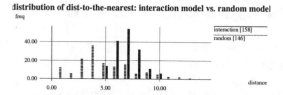

Fig. 12. Comparison of disorder(top) and order (bottom).

Fig. 11. Comparison of interaction:(d=8) and random:P=(10:4) in relatively sparse case;

5 Conclusion

Artificial synthesis of spacing patterns is presented as the one example of a project entitled "Celloid for Organismoid". A new mechanism, Artificial Genetic Network (AGN), is introduced, which is inspired from the Genetic Network in nature, in order to achieve the above goal. A collection of celloids, each of which interacts according to the same AGN, is compared with a collection of independent cells, in which each cell behaves independently from the others. The comparison shows that the former exhibit higher order than the latter. Therefore, the importance of proper interaction between component parts in organisms is demonstrated.

Finally, important future directions are enumerated below:

1. **Generalization of the AGN**: The linear AGN can provide the **sequential / linear** expression of genes. (See Fig. 13:left.) The differentiation with this AGN is based on whether a **critical gene** is expressed or not. But if **branches** are introduced to this AGN, the differentiation into many types can be easily designed. (See Fig. 13:right.)

   Another way to provide differentiation would be to generalize the AGN as in Fig. 4:right. In this case, different **attractors** (i.e. a set of **stable** states of the gene expression) correspond to different types of cells. The number of attractors can change if the AGN can **"mutate"** (e.g. by means of the {generation /deletion} of the {nodes/edges}). This mutatability of the AGN leads to the **evolvability** of celloids with AGN.

2. **Design of the interaction**: The interaction in celloids with the linear AGN is explicit. In other words, all aspects of the interaction are specified explicitly

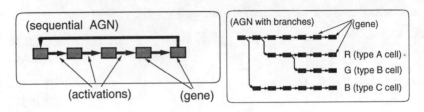

Fig. 13. Linear (or Sequential) AGN (left) and Branchable AGN (right).

by **symbolic mapping**. Instead of using symbolic mapping between genes and their products, (such as the product $\#i$ can repress the gene $\#j$), use of a **template** as in Tierra ([Ray91]) should give rise to **emergent interaction between genes and their products**, which leads to interaction between celloids.

3. **Introduction of cell division and cell death**: In the example shown in this paper, each celloid makes a binary decision whether to have or not to have a bristle. If two other **binary decisions**, for example, **to divide or not to divide** and **to die or not to die**, are introduced into celloids, then an organismoid can **grow**. These decisions will be made based on the local interaction between the celloids, and this local interaction is expected to give rise to **self-organization of celloids**.

References

[Alb et al.89] Alberts B., Bray D., Lewis J., Raff M., Roberts K., and Watson J.D.: "Molecular Biology of the Cell, 2nd ed.", Carland Pub. Inc, (1989).

[Conr92] Conrad M. "Molecular Computing: The Lock-Key Paradigm", in IEEE Computer vol.25, No.11, pp.11-20, (1992).

[Inay94a] Inayoshi H. "Simulating Natural Spacing Patterns of Insect Bristles Using a Network of Interacting Celloids", Proceedings of Artificial Life IV, (1994, in press).

[Inay94b] Inayoshi H. (in preparation).

[Kauf90] Kauffman S.A. "Requirements for Evolvability in Complex Systems: Orderly Dynamics and Frozen Components", in Physica D 42, pp.135-152, (1990).

[Lawr92] Lawrence P.A. "The Making of a Fly", Blackwell Scientific Publications, (1992).

[Ptas87] Ptashne M. "A Genetic Switch: Gene Control and Phage λ (2nd ed.)" Blackwell Scientific Publications, (1987).

[Ray91] Ray T.S.: "An approach to the synthesis of life", in Langton C.,Taylor C.,Farmer J.D.,& Rasmussen S. (Eds.) "Artificial life II", SFI Studies in the Sciences of Complexity, Addison-Wesley, pp.371-408, (1991).

[Reyn87] Reynolds C.W., "Flocks, Herds, and Schools: a Distributed Behavior Model", in Computer Graphics 21(4), pp. 25-34, (1987).

Comparison of Different
Evolutionary Algorithms

Diffuse Pattern Learning with
Fuzzy ARTMAP and PASS

Jorge Muruzábal

Department of Statistics and Econometrics, University Carlos III,
28903 Getafe, Spain

Alberto Muñoz

Department of Applied Physics, University of Salamanca,
37007 Salamanca, Spain

Abstract

Fuzzy ARTMAP is compared to a classifier system (CS) called PASS
(predictive adaptive sequential system). Previously reported results in a
benchmark classification task suggest that Fuzzy ARTMAP systems perform better and are more parsimonious than systems based on the CS
architecture. The tasks considered here differ from ordinary classificatory
tasks in the amount of output uncertainty associated with input categories.
To be successful, learning systems must identify not only correct input categories, but also the most likely outputs for those categories. Performance
under various types of diffuse patterns is investigated using a simulated
scenario.

1 Introduction

Carpenter, Grossberg, Markuzon, Reynolds and Rosen [3] present results in a
letter recognition task indicating that Fuzzy ARTMAP systems perform better
and use fewer resources than the classifier system (CS) schemes considered by
Frey and Slate [5]. In this paper, we propose various pattern learning tasks
and analyze the behavior of Fuzzy ARTMAP and a different CS implementation
called PASS (predictive adaptive sequential system) [7]. The tasks considered
here involve learning the association between a binary input vector and an output
scalar, but they differ from ordinary classificatory tasks in the amount of output
uncertainty associated with input categories. Thus, these patterns reflect more
statistical regularities than function-like assignments.

The patterns we consider can be made increasingly diffuse in various ways.
We first focus on the effect of raising the output uncertainty associated with
input categories. High-uncertainty patterns are interesting in that they reflect
situations in which the output is read with considerable noise and/or the chosen
input vector misses important variance-explaining features or predictors. Patterns can also be diffuse in the sense of presenting a low signal-to-noise ratio.
This will be of interest when only a relatively small fraction of the data is expected to contain useful regularities. Finally, we consider patterns with rather
general (large) input categories, that is, patterns where only a few input coordinates are actually relevant to determine the most likely output. To gain some

initial understanding of the strengths and weaknesses of the two families of systems, each of these three kinds of diffuse patterns will be studied separately in this paper. Future work will study the sensitivity with respect to contamination in the input vectors (a fourth type of diffuseness), as well as mixed cases in which diffuse patterns of different nature are simultaneously present in the data.

The organization is as follows. Section 2 introduces the data-generating mechanism and sets up the language to define each type of diffuseness. Sections 3 and 4 briefly summarize the main aspects of the algorithms. Section 5 reports on the empirical results and presents some preliminary conclusions.

2 The data source

We consider a simple (stochastic) pattern learning task in which data pairs (x, y) are independently drawn from a mixture distribution on the joint sampling space $\{0,1\}^n \times (0,1)$. This distribution involves $c \geq 1$ components (or patterns) specifying particular regularities to be observed from time to time by the systems. Each pattern is defined by a triple (θ, η, v), where $0 < \theta \leq 1$ is the mixing proportion, η is a schema or hyperplane (a subspace formed by fixing the values of some coordinates), and v is a probability distribution on $(0,1)$. A minimum coherency requirement is enforced by considering disjoint η_i only, which also permits straightforward calculation of the optimal level of performance attainable by the systems. For simplicity, v distributions are always taken from the beta family, so they are identified by their parameters α and β. Further, we only consider unimodal densities here (that is, $\alpha, \beta \geq 1$).

If possible, the previous set of patterns is automatically augmented with *noise*; noise is devised as the triple (θ_0, η_0, v_0), where v_0 denotes the uniform distribution over the unit interval and θ_0 and η_0 represent respectively the complement to 1 of the sum of θ_i and the complement of the union of η_i. Thus, the resulting distribution is a particular case of the "signal vs. noise" paradigm.

Sampling proceeds then as follows: a triple is selected at random according to the relative frequencies $\theta_i, (i = 0, 1, \ldots, c)$, x is obtained by either randomly filling up the undefined coordinates in η_i $(i \geq 1)$ or simply choosing a string at random from η_0, and y is taken as an independent realization of v_i. A wide array of situations can be obtained by varying the amount of noise, the number of patterns, the *specificity*[1] of schemata η and the sharpness of distributions v. For example, using the standard "don't care" or "wildcard" symbol #, the pattern defined by $\theta = .7$, $\eta = (00011\#)$ and $\alpha = 8$, $\beta = 1$ is very different from the (rather diffuse) pattern $\theta = .02$, $\eta = (0\#\#\#\#\#)$ and $\alpha = 2$, $\beta = 1$.

---

[1]Defined as the proportion of specified coordinates.

3 Fuzzy ARTMAP

ARTMAP systems are based on the long-introduced Adaptive Resonance Theory (ART) in neural network modelling [2, 4]. Given the present nature of the data, we consider Fuzzy ARTMAP systems only [3].

In a nutshell, Fuzzy ARTMAP systems learn by simultaneously (i) establishing suitable categories in both input and output space (tasks carried out within the so-called A and B modules respectively), and (ii) linking input and output categories according to joint occurrence and predictive success (the linkages being stored in a special unit called the map field or AB module). Modules are made out of fields and fields are made out of neurons (nodes). All categorization and learning are achieved by sequentially modifying three sets of neuron weights, one in each module. The number of weights in the A and B modules are system parameters determining the number and dimension of the weights in the AB module. During training, both x and y are provided as input to the A and B modules, which causes activation to flow from the excited neurons (categories) in A and B into AB, and then (potentially) back from AB into A (see below). During testing, a given input vector typically activates (predicts) a single category in the B and AB modules.

In ARTMAP systems, data can be processed with either natural or complement coding [3, 4]: if natural coding is used, a data item d is processed "as is", otherwise, d is augmented with d^c, the (coordinatewise) complement to 1. Thus, if d is a n-dimensional binary vector x, then the system actually works on a 2n-dimensional binary vector containing n ones and n zeros, whereas, if d is a scalar y, then the vector $(y, 1 - y)$ is supplied. Natural coding introduces an asymmetry in the treatment of zeros and ones which does not correspond with the symmetric role played in the task of interest here. Also, under complement coding, the weight vectors in the A module can be related to schemata like the η_i in section 2.

Within a given A or B module, the tendency of the system to commit new neurons (as opposed to using previously commited neurons) is controlled by the so-called vigilance parameter $0 \leq \rho \leq 1$. When ρ is large, the system tends to commit neurons more easily; otherwise, relatively fewer (and therefore larger) categories are constructed. Vigilance parameters in the A and B modules are denoted by ρ_a and ρ_b respectively.

During training in the A module, a first decision is made on the basis of a similarity measure between the binary input I and the existing categories u_j; this is defined as $\frac{|I \wedge u_j|}{b + |u_j|}$, where $b > 0$ is a system parameter, $\wedge$ is the fuzzy AND operator (defined as coordinatewise minimum), and $|\ |$ stands for the sum of coordinates of its argument. The winning category maximizes this measure. Parameter b controls the degree to which categories that match I exactly tend to win over partial matches.

One of the peculiarities of ARTMAP systems is the fact that the winning category is selected only if a second similarity measure, defined as $\frac{|I \wedge u_j|}{|I|} = \frac{|I \wedge u_j|}{n}$, surpasses ρ_a. Otherwise, the best candidates from the first test are tried out in turn until one succeeds or a fresh neuron is committed.

Let J and K denote respectively the (overall) winning categories in modules A and B. When learning is triggered, the associated weight vector in A (say) is updated as $u_J^{(new)} = (1 - \lambda_a)u_J^{(old)} + \lambda_a(I \wedge u_J^{(old)})$, where $0 < \lambda_a \leq 1$ (all weight vectors are initialized with ones). Thus, under "fast-learning" ($\lambda_a = 1$), the designed schema u_J in module A generalizes to the schema $I \wedge u_J$. Under the "fast-learn/slow-recode" option (recommended for noisy data), $\lambda_a = 1$ only when a node is first committed, thereafter it is fixed and strictly lower than 1. As regards module B, $\lambda_b = 1$ throughout this paper.

If there is disagreement during training between the system's prediction (determined by J) and the observed response category (K), the system revises its prediction by raising the vigilance parameter ρ_a by the minimal amount needed so J no longer passes the second similarity test (and is therefore turned off). The process continues in the A module as described earlier: new winners J' are tested until perhaps an agreement is reached in AB, in which case new learning occurs. Parameter ρ_a returns in either case to its "baseline" value before the next training pair is presented.

During testing, input is fed into the A module, where two things may happen: either a winner J is excited or not. If it is, then the system's predicted category in output space may be read off the associated AB weight vector; otherwise, no prediction is offered and the system issues an "I don't know" flag. Of course, a high baseline value for ρ_a increases the frequency of nonresponse during testing.

4 PASS

We now turn our attention to PASS [7], an experimental prototype designed to test the potential of the simplest classifier system (CS) architecture in a purely statistical problem. Like "fast-learning" Fuzzy ARTMAP, PASS also expresses its predictions as links between schemata in input space and certain regions in output space, yet it does not build categories in output space, only in input space. In output space, it constructs a conditional probability distribution given an input vector. In this paper, however, we simply replace this distribution by its support, so we can compare predictive success on the same grounds.

Like any other CS [6], PASS consists essentially of performance system and learning operators. The performance system is based on an unstructured population of elementary predictive rules called classifiers. Each classifier in PASS has the structure

IF s THEN PREDICT f
(WITH STRENGTH S, RECALLING E)

where s is a schema, f is a predictive density belonging to certain prespecified class Γ, S is a scalar quantity called strength, and E is a small list of observed pairs (x, y). Interpretation of a single classifier is straightforward: if $x \in S$, then expect the associated response to behave according to f. Strength reflects the classifier's previous success (or the confidence the system has in the previous assertion). The exception list E contains a few recent cases where the classifier proved wrong; heuristic operators act on these lists when they reach a (small) threshold length, with the result that new classifiers are formed and/or old ones modified. Thus, PASS classifiers incorporate the additional structures S and E representing two forms of memory not available in ARTMAP systems.

Class Γ should be rich enough for a wide array of behaviors to be possibly described. It should also concentrate on the kind of behaviors that are of foremost interest. In the present case, "interesting" is equated to "distant-from-uniform", so Γ contains only "sharp" densities in this sense. While parametric classes are conceivable, we have chosen a very simple class of histogram densities, namely, those whose class intervals have all the same length and take nonzero values in a "small" number of adjacent intervals only. We sometimes refer to the latter feature by saying that predictions f have bounded, convex supports. The total number of class intervals and the precise meaning of "small" are set by the user.

The rationale for the use of exception lists in general stimulus-response problems is that much can be learned by analyzing what the observations therein contained have in common. To provide some flavor for the underlying reasoning, we sketch here the work of two of the mechanisms acting on filled exception lists. Two key routines return, respectively, whether or not there exist common coordinates in the x vectors (beyond, of course, those in the classifier's schema) and whether or not the responses tend to "cluster"[2]. Now suppose that there are some new common coordinates but responses do not cluster. Then, the current "filtering" schema may be found not sufficiently restrictive, so it can be slightly specialized by negating one of such common coordinates. Conversely, if new common coordinates exist and responses do cluster, then it may be the case that a new regularity has just been detected, which prompts the system to create a new classifier describing it. While these ideas do not extend easily to the general CS architecture, they can be brought about in stimulus-response problems as soon as the response belongs to a some metric space.

Learning in PASS is "slow" in the sense that no crucial decisions on schemata or predictions are made on the basis of single data items, every action is based on accumulated data. On the other hand, classifiers may be (and often are) discarded altogether whenever the system decides to try some other alternatives.

---

[2]No standard clustering algorithm is currently used here. Rather, responses are said to cluster if a sufficiently high number of them are found sufficiently close to one another.

As in Fuzzy ARTMAP, no overall check for consistency or completeness is contemplated, and no provision for the emergence of structure within the population is made explicitly.

Predictions in both PASS and Fuzzy ARTMAP are based on competitive processes (called auctions in CS parlance). A number of winners are selected and predictions follow the opinion of these winners. In PASS, however, winners are considered simultaneously, and the outcome of the competition is stochastic. The elementary predictions read off the winners are combined (weighted by strength) to yield the system's predictive distribution (from which both bounded-length convex and non-convex predictive supports can be formed). PASS enjoys then a potentially higher level of communication among classifiers, at the price that decisions do not necessarily reflect the "best" knowledge currently available in the system.

As in Fuzzy ARTMAP, the specificity D of competing schemata participates explicitly in the auction, this time together with S. Actually, PASS adheres to the traditional auction in which matched classifiers place bids $B = \kappa S D^\gamma$, and effective bids $B^* = B^\phi D^\psi$, the probability of winning being then proportional to B^* (all system parameters are nonnegative). This auction can be made highly dependent on D alone, yet competition is usually (and here in particular) restricted to perfect-matching schemata. The number of winners to draw from the list of matched classifiers, say m, is a critical parameter controlling both the amount of mixing prior to prediction and the relative frequency at which classifiers are tested out.

The auction is just one of the processes where stochasticity is present in PASS. A version of the genetic algorithm performs in the background, though it has not been found to contribute much in its present form [7]. The set of procedures acting on the exception lists contribute more to learning and are partly randomized as well. Reward itself is stochastic: the strength of a "correct" winning classifier is updated as $S^{(\text{new})} = (1 - tax)S^{(\text{old})} - B + R$, where tax is a small fraction of strength usefully collected from matched and not matched classifiers at every time step, and $R = +R_0$ or $-\pi S$ depending on its prediction's "coverage" of the associated pattern distribution(s) v^3. Thus, the recurring presence of stochasticity in PASS is in sharp contrast with the strict determinism found in Fuzzy ARTMAP.

5 Experimental results

We now present a summary of our experiments. We have tried the algorithms just described in three different pattern learning tasks. In each task, we provide the systems with a training sample of size 500. Performance is measured as the proportion of correct predictions on an independent test set of 500 observations

---

[3] The penalty factor π seems useful, particularly during early stages; see [1].

(no voting strategies, as suggested in [4], are considered, although they are probably quite powerful here as well). Data are processed using complement coding in Fuzzy ARTMAP and natural coding in PASS. While no further learning occurs in either system during testing (no new categories or classifiers are created nor old ones modified), strength continues to be updated as usual.

For the sake of comparison, the number of neurons in module A of Fuzzy ARTMAP and the number of classifiers in PASS are both set to a maximum of $\mu = 50$. To understand the full effect of this constraint is an interesting research area in both systems: in ART-based systems, vigilance parameters act critically on the number of categories finally created by the system, while dynamic manipulation of μ (along with m) may promote some form of "knowledge condensation" in CSs and seems useful in PASS (see below). Note that fixing μ does not make the systems equally demanding, as classifiers in PASS require additional memory to implement their exception lists. Also, the bound set by μ in PASS plays more the role of an attractor than a "hard" limit[4].

The systems must also be granted the same scope in their predictive effort. Both Fuzzy ARTMAP and PASS include system parameters that bound the length of their predictions. For our current purpose, a bound of .3 seems appropriate and is used in all runs (the most direct way, though not the only one, of achieving this in Fuzzy ARTMAP is to set ρ_b to .7, preserving the original spirit of the architecture). This bound determines the maximum level of performance attainable by either system at any given task, which provides a useful reference value.

The versions we have investigated differ in system parameters ρ_a, b and λ_a in Fuzzy ARTMAP, and m, μ and the activity rate (w) of the rule-generating procedures in PASS[5]. Results are reported below on the performance of "slow-recode" Fuzzy ARTMAP with (baseline) ρ_a between 0 and .2, b between .05 and .1 and λ_a between .05 and .1. Auction/reinforcement parameters in PASS are $\phi = \psi = \gamma = 1$, $\pi = 10\%$, $tax = 1\%$, $\kappa = .1$, $R_0 = 150$ and an initial strength of 200. Other system parameters are kept at values discussed in previous work [7], although the version used here is different in that (i) the initial strength of most newly-created classifiers is now set to the current median of the population, and (ii) certain modifications are *added* to the population (instead of *replacing* the classifiers that suggested them).

Training in PASS was manually split into two epochs: for the first two presentations (cycles), $m = 5$, $\mu = 50$ and w was "high", while for the remaining

---

[4]Since no classifier is erased until it has been exposed to the data stream for a while, the number of classifiers in the population may occasionally exceed μ, although the system returns to this level as soon as it can.

[5]This activity rate refers, for example, to the probability that a given exception list is analyzed and, therefore, suggestions based on this analysis are incorporated into the population: if w is low, only the strongest classifiers are given a chance. If $w = 0$, no classifiers are modified or new ones introduced.

$$\theta = .15, \quad \eta = (0\#\#1\#00\#0\#\#1), \quad \alpha = 1, \quad \beta = 3$$
$$\theta = .15, \quad \eta = (1\#\#\#01\#\#\#010), \quad \alpha = 1, \quad \beta = 3$$
$$\theta = .15, \quad \eta = (\#00\#\#10\#\#1\#1), \quad \alpha = 1, \quad \beta = 3$$
$$\theta = .15, \quad \eta = (\#\#01\#11\#0\#0\#), \quad \alpha = 3, \quad \beta = 1$$
$$\theta = .15, \quad \eta = (0\#\#01\#1\#11\#\#), \quad \alpha = 3, \quad \beta = 1$$
$$\theta = .15, \quad \eta = (1\#\#1\#0\#10\#\#1), \quad \alpha = 3, \quad \beta = 1$$

Table 1: Task I (optimal performance rate=62.0%)

$$\theta = .08, \quad \eta = (0\#\#1\#00\#0\#\#1), \quad \alpha = 1, \quad \beta = 7$$
$$\theta = .08, \quad \eta = (1\#\#\#01\#\#\#010), \quad \alpha = 1, \quad \beta = 7$$
$$\theta = .08, \quad \eta = (\#00\#\#10\#\#1\#1), \quad \alpha = 1, \quad \beta = 7$$
$$\theta = .08, \quad \eta = (\#\#01\#11\#0\#0\#), \quad \alpha = 7, \quad \beta = 1$$
$$\theta = .08, \quad \eta = (0\#\#01\#1\#11\#\#), \quad \alpha = 7, \quad \beta = 1$$
$$\theta = .08, \quad \eta = (1\#\#1\#0\#10\#\#1), \quad \alpha = 7, \quad \beta = 1$$

Table 2: Task II (optimal performance rate=59.6%)

two, $m = 3$, $\mu = 40$ and w was "low" (in test mode, $m = 3$ and $w = 0$). Four is a "small" number of presentations for PASS, for the system usually benefits from an additional four to six cycles. In contrast, the number of training cycles in Fuzzy ARTMAP varied between 10 and 40. Indeed, Fuzzy ARTMAP's high speed of processing allows for a much larger number of training cycles in considerably less time. However, the ultimate comparison in terms of processing time is hopeless until parallel versions of the algorithms are confronted.

The systems were tested in three (toy) tasks described in Tables 1, 2, 3. Task I presents six high-uncertainty patterns intertwined with noise at a 10% rate; since patterns occur relatively often and their schemata are sharply defined, the main difficulty resides in the slight departure from uniformity. The same schemata define task II, except now noise occurring at a 52% rate makes it hard to detect the otherwise obvious departure from uniformity. In task III, moderate noise joins a moderate departure from uniformity, but the number of irrelevant parameters is large.

We found "fast-learning" Fuzzy ARTMAP not to be competitive in these tasks, which is in contrast with the previously reported success in less diffuse problems [3]. We also found "slow-recode" Fuzzy ARTMAP and PASS to reach comparable levels of performance in tasks I and II (see table 4), a surprising fact given the nature of the architectures and learning mechanisms. The high sensitivity of Fuzzy ARTMAP with respect to ρ_b is also manifest. In Task III, PASS proves somewhat superior. Fuzzy ARTMAP's relative lack of success in Task III suggests a type of regularity that it might find hard to detect in general.

$$\theta = .2, \quad \eta = (0\#\#\#\#\#\#\#0\#\#\#0\#\#), \quad \alpha = 1, \quad \beta = 5$$
$$\theta = .2, \quad \eta = (0\#\#\#\#\#\#\#1\#\#\#\#\#\#), \quad \alpha = 5, \quad \beta = 1$$
$$\theta = .2, \quad \eta = (1\#\#\#\#\#\#\#\#\#\#\#1\#\#), \quad \alpha = 1, \quad \beta = 5$$
$$\theta = .2, \quad \eta = (1\#\#\#\#\#\#\#1\#\#\#0\#\#), \quad \alpha = 5, \quad \beta = 1$$

Table 3: Task III (optimal performance rate=72.6%)

Tasks	Fuzzy ARTMAP ($\rho_b = .7$)	PASS	Fuzzy ARTMAP ($\rho_b = 2/3$)
I (62.0)	56.2 56.6 57.0	55.6 57.5 58.9	59.2 59.4 60.0
II (59.6)	51.8 52.0 52.6	52.5 53.8 55.0	57.2 58.6 59.8
III (72.6)	53.4 53.6 54.0	61.5 64.2 64.8	57.8 58.6 59.2

Table 4: Performance summary. Each cell of the table is based on 5 independent runs; we have just discarded the best and worst figures in each case. Optimal performance figures are provided for each task. While the same version of PASS was used in all three tasks, Fuzzy ARTMAP parameters were slightly tuned in each case. The last column is, of course, not really comparable to the first two, for it refers to a different optimum.

We also note that neither system is completely successful at recovering all defining schemata. It appears that PASS categories tend to be larger than needed (sometimes ingeniously exploiting "hidden" aspects of the set of patterns), whereas Fuzzy ARTMAP categories tend to be finer[6].

Another important difference between the two systems refers to the internal dynamics of the respective knowledge structures. Fuzzy ARTMAP proceeds monotonically in that categories can only evolve in one direction and are never discarded once committed. In adition, new categories are created only when needed. Thus, it seems hard to be more parsimonious than Fuzzy ARTMAP. In contrast, no such features are present in PASS. Actually, provided $w \neq 0$, experiments show that the population of classifiers is perpetually renewed: alternative, nearly equivalent classifiers continuously replace older classifiers, with the result that no classifier is guaranteed a permanent post. However, this apparent lack of stability does not seem to carry serious negative effects on performance. It might be of some value as soon as changes occur from time to time in the data stream (that is, as soon as new patterns develop or old ones disappear). As far as we know, this phenomenon provides a new dimension to the plasticity-stability dilemma that seems worth studying in detail.

---

[6]Under the "slow-recode" option, category interpretation is achieved by "rounding off" weight coordinates to 0, 1 and .5 (or #).

We conclude by pointing out some further directions for research. It seems to us, for example, that the joint election of several winners, along with the associated combination of beliefs, may improve Fuzzy ARTMAP's performance dramatically. It would also be very interesting to develop adaptive schemes for ρ_b (and ρ_a). As regards PASS, automatic manipulation of both the exploration rate (w) and the number of winners (m) during training seems crucial to attain additional stability and convergence; natural heuristics to guide such manipulations may be obtained from the slope of the learning curve.

Acknowledgements. The first author is partially supported by research grants DGICYT PB92-0246 (Spain) and CICYT TIC93-0702-C02-02 (Spain). The second author is grateful to the Neural Network Group at the University of Valladolid (Spain).

References

[1] P. Bonelli, A. Parodi, S. Sen, and S.W. Wilson. NEWBOOLE: A fast GBML system. In *Proceedings of the Seventh International Conference on Machine Learning*, Morgan Kaufmann: San Mateo, CA., 1990.

[2] G.A. Carpenter and S. Grossberg. A massively parallel architecture for a self-organizing neural pattern recognition machine. *Computer Vision, Graphics, and Image Processing*, 37, pp. 54–115, 1987.

[3] G.A. Carpenter, S. Grossberg, N. Markuzon, J.H. Reynolds, and D.B. Rosen. Fuzzy ARTMAP: A neural network architecture for incremental supervised learning of analog multidimensional maps. *IEEE Transactions on Neural Networks*, 3(5), pp. 698–713, 1992.

[4] G.A. Carpenter, S. Grossberg, and J.H. Reynolds. ARTMAP: supervised real-time learning and classification of nonstationary data by a self-organizing neural network. *Neural Networks*, 4, pp. 565–588, 1991.

[5] Frey and Slate. Letter recognition using Holland-style adaptive classifiers. *Machine Learning*, 6, pp. 161–182, 1991.

[6] J.H. Holland, K.J. Holyoak, R.E. Nisbett, and P.R. Thagard. *Induction: Processes of Inference, Learning and Discovery*. MIT Press: Cambridge, MA, 1986.

[7] J. Muruzábal. PASS: A simple classifier system for data analysis. Technical Report WP 93-20, University Carlos III, Statistics and Econometrics Dept., 1993. Submitted for publication.

Different Learning Algorithms for Neural Networks - A Comparative Study

Jochen Heistermann

Siemens AG München
Otto-Hahn-Ring 6
81730 Munich
ZFE ST SN 44
e-mail: Jochen.Heistermann@zfe.siemens.de

Abstract. Neural Networks (NN) are usually trained with gradient search algorithms. Alternative approaches like genetic algorithms (GA) have been proposed before with promising results. In this paper six different training algorithms for NN are compared - two of them based on GA. The algorithms were evaluated with data from practically relevant applications of the Siemens AG.

1 Introduction

A lot of research has been done in the past on training algorithms for Neural Networks. Most of today's algorithms, which are used for applications, are based on error backpropagation [Rum86]. Error backpropagation is a gradient descend method and stems from mathematical optimization theory. One major focus now is to optimize the step size of the backpropagation algorithm. Here, the step size determines how far a step in direction of the gradient will be.

The optimization of NN with GA was discussed before for example by [Müh89], [Whi89a] or [Whi89b]. All these algorithms showed different strength and weaknesses. The approach of [Hei91] was to combine the strength of gradient and genetic search, and to build up hybrid learning algorithms based on this combination.

Two real world examples were choosen from speech and image processing for evaluating different learning approaches. The data were used for practical industrial applications at Siemens [Akt90]. All considered learning algorithms were integrated into the NN simulation environment NNSIM [Nij89]. Many experiments were performed and their results were carefully analyzed.

2 Overview of Data and Algorithms

Each algorithm had the purpose to minimize the error function to zero. By increasing or decreasing the number of training data this exercise could be made more or less difficult.

2.1 The Applications

A phoneme is the smallest significant language unit. The data sets were coded from colloquial language. The german language can be divided into 44 phonemes, which belong to seven phoneme classes. One class for example is the class of nasals, which consists of "em, en, m, n". The analogous data from colloquial language were digitalized at 16 hHz. Each 10 ms a discrete fourier transformation about the last 20 ms was performed to code the short term language signal. The signals were transformed to cepstral coefficients [Akt90], which were represented by a vector of 16 real numbers.

The second application dealt with hand written numbers. The numbers were stored as binary pictures with different size and orientation. To avoid the use of too many neurons the pictures were rastered with 16x16 pixels. The NN's had to identify all those pictures correctly.

Both applications were important for the industrial environment of Siemens. They represent typical NN applications. The diffficulty of the learning task could easily be adjusted by using different training sets. Since each new data set changed the structure of the net and influenced the other patterns it was much more difficult to learn 1000 patterns instead of 10. This feature gave room for exploiting the training algorithms under different circumstances.

The problems were solved by using feed-forward-nets with one hidden layer. The phonemes were trained by 16-16-7 networks with 368 connections and the numbers by 256-25-10 networks with 6650 connections. The objective function added up the squared differences between the actual and the ideal output. To compute the objective function all patterns must be put through the net, what leads to linear growth of the computation time with respect to the problem size. The calculation of the gradient yielded the same amount of runtime as the objective function evaluation.

2.2 The Simulation Environment NNSIM

All learning algorithms were implemented in the simulation environment NNSIM [Nij89]. NNSIM offers high level constructs to build NN. The user had to specify the topology of the net and the transfer functions. Finally, he choosed the learning algorithm for the training phase of the NN. NNSIM was implemented on Apollo WS30 workstations. They had a Motorola 68030-CPU, which is very slow with respect to learning. The use of NNSIM brought up the possibility for a fair comparison between the learning algorithms. The learning algorithms built an own module and were bound to the NN at compile time. The module was enlarged by the code of the algorithms, which were compared in this article. All algorithms have been implemented in C and use the same functions for computing the gradient and objective function.

3 The Algorithms and their implementation

GA + Grad(GA)

Algorithm. GA have its strength in exploring the database in the beginning of the optimization process. They can find promising regions of the search space with high probability. Gradient search algorithms (Grad) are strong dependent on their starting position (in case of a non-convex search space) being strong in fast convergence. It is obvious that an algorithm, starting with GA to find a good starting point and finishing the training session with Grad, will be a promising approach. The strength of both algorithms could thereby combined.

Implementation. Each weight was coded by one real number. The weight matrix between input and hidden layer was stored first, and later on the weights between hidden and output layer were listed. The starting population contained 25 individuals, which created 25 more individuals. The algorithm used was (with some minor changes) the $(\mu + \lambda)$-strategy [Sch77]. When the individual's parameter values (genes) didn't differ more than 1% from each other, then Grad(GA) replaced GA.

Grad(GA)

Algorithm. The optimal step size varies through gradient search from step to step. Optimization theory offers a variety of line search methods. Those methods required a lot of objective function computations - in case of NN they might be very expansive. To solve this problem, a simple GA could help. After having worked out the gradient the objective function was computed using the actual step size. The step size was then mutated to a larger and a shorter value and the two corresponding objective function values were computed. The best of the three values was taken. This method offered a simple, fast and very smooth adaptation to the step size. Practical experiments showed that the optimal step size changed slowly within short time intervals, but dramatically for longer terms.

Implementation. The step size was worked out with a simplified GA. The old step size was mutated twice. The first value ε_{mut1} was computed as ε +

rand$(0, 2\varepsilon)$ and the second value ε_{mut2} as ε - rand$(0, 2\varepsilon)$. The function rand(a,b) computed a uniformly distributed number between a and b. The objective function was computed anew for all three values of ε, where the best of the three was taken and ε being set to the new value.

Grad(const.)

Algorithm. Since many problems are simple and easy to solve, simple methods are often the best. Error backpropagation just calculates the gradient and moves with a constant step size into the gradient direction. The step size can be initialized only once at the starting time of the algorithm.

One of the main characteristics of the simple gradient algorithm is that the objective function never has to be computed. The algorithm moves into the direction of the gradient until it cannot gain further progress. Upon program termination, the objective function is computed.

Implementation. This algorithm implemented the error backpropagation algo-rithm. The gradient was computed and put on the weights multiplied with a small, constant step size.

Grad(rand.)

Algorithm. One drawback of the simple Grad(const.)-algorithm was the possi-bility of cyclic movement around an optimum. This could be avoided by randomly choosen values for the step size from step to step. The algorithm was as simple as Grad(const.) and should be of rather equal quality.

Implementation. The implementation was the same as for Grad(const.) with the exception of the step size varying randomly.

Grad(interpol.)

Algorithm. The step size varies very much at runtime. Optimal step size estimation has been done for example by [Pre88] or [Tro91]. These algorithms need repeated computation of the objective function. One simple approach is quadratic interpolation. One assumes a quadratic form of the objective function and calculates the minimum of a parabola in direction of the gradient. The performance of this algorithm strongly depends on the assumption on the correctness of quadratic interpolation.

Implementation. Using quadratic interpolation, a new step was computed. To compute the parabola an additional objective function value had to be calculated.

Grad(const.) + Grad$_{alt}$(GA)

Algorithm. One additional drawback of error backpropagation is that the current gradient is mostly quite orthogonal to the last one. This leads to an inefficient approximation of an optimum. So called conjugate gradient methods avoid this drawback by taking also the last gradient directions into account. The new search direction is computed by

$$\Xi_{i+1} = \Xi_i + \varepsilon_1 * g_{new}(\Xi_i) + \varepsilon_2 * g_{old}(\Xi_i)$$

with g_{old} as the last gradient direction and ε_1 and ε_2 controlling the influence of the latest and new search direction. $\varepsilon_2 = 0.0$ let the algorithm degenerate to Grad(const.).

Implementation. The values of ε_1 and ε_2 were mutated twice. The best found combination of the two values was taken for further evaluations.

4 Results

All six algorithms had their own strenghts and weaknesses. The question was which algorithm would perform best under specific circumstances.

4.1 Cost Criteria

Four criteria to evaluate the algorithms were identified.

a) Cost
Cost was defined as sum of b) and c).

b) Number of objective fuction calls
Computing the objective function and the gradient took nearly all of the proces-sing time of the algorithm. The genetic operations and construction of the NN were neglectable factors on the runtime.

c) Number of gradient computations
To get the gradient information, one has to run backwards through the net with all patterns. The effort was nearly the same for b).

d) Success
How often was the problem solved?

4.2 Results of Simulation Runs for Small Sized Problems

The classification of 20 phonemes and 40 handwritten numbers was the first problem solved by the algorithms. Figure 1 and 2 show the results. The results and their relations are very similar for both problems. The simplest algorithms lead to the best results. This might look disappointing for more

ambitious researchers, but the problems were simple enough to let simple
gradient search win.

	Cost	Objective function calls	Gradient calculations	Success
Grad(const.)	33,5	2,3	31,2	100
Grad(rand.)	34,3	1,8	32,5	100
Grad(GA)	37,5	25,0	12,5	100
Grad(inter.)	64,5	43,0	21,5	100
GA + Grad(GA)	97,0	90,0	7,0	100
Grad(const.) + $Grad_{alt}(GA)$	184,2	92,1	92,1	100

Fig. 1.   40 numbers (average over 200 runs)

	Cost	Objective function calls	Gradient calculations	Success
Grad(rand.)	33,0	1,6	31,4	100
Grad(const.)	34,3	2,1	32,2	100
Grad(GA)	36,3	24,2	12,1	100
Grad(inter.)	63,0	42,0	21,0	100
GA + Grad(GA)	77,2	66,9	10,3	100
Grad(const.) + $Grad_{alt}(GA)$	148,2	74,1	74,1	100

Fig. 2.   20 phonemes (average over 200 runs)

One result of high interest was the performance of Grad(GA). This
algorithm caused only slightly more cost than the simple methods - but it
needed three times as much computational effort for each learning step.
Grad(GA) found the solution by only 12,1 (12,5) gradient steps, which is

significant better than the 31,4 (31,2) steps needed by Grad(rand) and Grad(const).

The other algorithms performed poorly on the simple problems. They solved them also, but needed much more effort.

4.3 Medium Sized Problems

Rising the problem size by adding more phonemes and numbers lead to different results of the optimization algorithms. Figure 3 and 4 hold the results for 100 phonemes and 200 numbers averaged over 100 simulation runs. The results show Grad(GA) as the best algorithm for both problems. For medium-sized problems it offered the best effort/quality value. The two algorithms without line search follow with some distance, but perform better than the hybrid algorithm GA + Grad(GA).

	Cost	Objective function calls	Gradient calculations	Success
Grad(GA)	100,5	67,0	33,5	100
Grad(const.)	155,5	2,3	153,2	70
Grad(rand.)	159,3	1,9	157,4	80
GA + Grad(GA)	180,9	159,2	21,7	100
Grad(interp.)	441,8	294,6	147,3	20
Grad (const.) Gradalt(GA)	984,3	492,1	492,1	50

Fig. 3. 100 phonemes (averaged over 100 runs)

Grad(GA) seems to be the best solution to problems, which are neither too simple, nor too complicated. The two GA were the only algorithms, which found always a solution. This is not a major advantage, because simple newstart of error backpropagation gives also a high probability of finding an optimum. One result of high interest can be found in figure 5. This figure shows the cost for varying problem size. All algorithms rose in cost with the problem size (of course), the rise stayed almost linear for some time, but got steeper for larger problems. The two GA showed a slower rise than the other algorithms. Probably they might be able to deal with larger problems.

	Cost	Objective function calls	Gradient calculations	Success
Grad(GA)	68,1	45,4	22,7	100
Grad(const.)	83,8	2,1	81,7	80
Grad(rand.)	84,9	1,8	83,1	85
GA + Grad(GA)	140,5	126,5	14,0	100
Grad(interp.)	241,8	161,2	80,6	25
Grad (const.) Gradalt(GA)	303,6	151,8	151,8	50

Fig. 4. 200 numbers (averaged over 200 runs)

4.4 Problems of large size

The best algorithm for medium-sized problems was Grad(GA), a gradient descend technique with genetically controlled step size. The GA based algorithm, which was followed by Grad(GA) after some time did not perform very well for the problems examined so far. It solved all the examples reliable and needed the fewest gradient steps, but the population of the GA required a lot of computation effort. Generally, GA worked for the smaller and medium problems, but without competitive performance.

Figure 6 and 7 show the results for runs with 1000 and 2000 numbers. The algorithms Grad(interp.) and Grad (const.) + $Grad_{old}$(GA) were no longer able to solve the problems and were taken out of the tables. To get the results of these two figures required about six weeks computation time.

The best algorithm was GA + Grad(GA). It found a reasonable starting point with the GA and moved by gradient search with genetically controlled step size smoothly to the optimum. Grad(GA) performed worse and the other algorithms were no longer competitive. The tendency of smaller cost rising of genetic algorithms with varying problem size came to a point, where the other algorithms performed worse. The conclusion of the experiments is to estimate the complexity of the problem first and apply a well-formed algorithm later.

Figure 8 like figure 5 shows the number's cost for varying problem size -

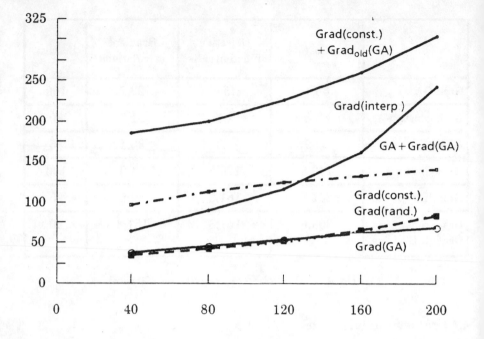

Fig. 5. Number's cost for varying problem size

	Cost	Goal function calls	Gradient calculations	Success
GA + Grad(GA)	420,3	337,8	82,5	100
Grad(GA)	654,3	436,2	218,1	100
Grad(const.)	1004,6	2,5	1002,1	50
Grad(rand.)	1027,8	3,0	1024,8	50

Fig. 6. 1000 numbers (averaged over 10 runs)

with problem size being one magnitude larger. The rise of cost was smallest for the genetic techniques. Only GA were able to solve problems of larger size in a reliable way.

	Cost	Objective function calls	Gradient calculations	Success
GA + Grad(GA)	967,5	746,3	221,1	100
Grad(GA)	1721,1	1147,4	573,7	100
Grad(const.)	3157,6	2,0	3155,6	30
Grad(rand.)	3220,0	2,5	3217,5	20

Fig. 7. 2000 numbers (averaged over 10 runs)

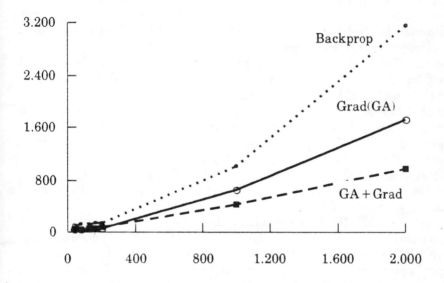

Fig .8. Number's cost for varying problem size

5 Summary and Conclusion

Six different optimization algorithms were evaluated in this paper. Two examples based on data from practical applications were studied for different problem sizes. Larger problems were solved best by a hybrid algorithm, where a GA first found a good starting point for gradient descend. The step size of the gradient search was also controlled by a simple genetic algorithm. If the problems were medium sized, a gradient method with genetic controlled step size outperformed all other algo-rithms. Simple problems were solved easily by all the proposed algorithms. Error backpropagation was the best approach, because it did not calculate the objective function.

6 References

[Akt90] Aktas, A et al.; Classification of Coarse Phonetic Categories in Continuous Speech: Statistical Classifiers vs. Temporal Flow Connectionist Network; Intern. Conf. on Acoustics, Speech, and Signal Processing; New Mexico 1990.

[Hei91] Heistermann, J.: A Parallel Hybrid Learning Approach to Artificial Neural Nets; Proceedings of the third IEEE Symposium on Parallel and Distri-buted Processing; Dallas 1991.

[Müh89] Mühlenbein,H.; Kindermann, J.: The dynamics of evolution and learning - towards genetic neural networks; in Pfeifer, R., Schreter, Z., Fogelman-Soulie, F., Steels, L. (Eds.): Connectionism in perspective; Elsevier 1989.

[Nij89] Nijhuis, J.A.G.; Spaanenburg, L.: NNSIM Internal Structure Reference Version 3.0; Technical Report IMS-TB-07/89; Institut für Mikroelektronik (IMS) Stuttgart 1989.

[Pre88] Press, W.H.; Flannery, B.P.; Teukolsky, S.A.; Vetterling, W.T.: Numerical Recipes in C; Cambridge University Press New York 1988.

[Rum86] Rumelhart, D.E.; Hinton, G.E.; Williams, R.J.: Learning Internal Repre-sentations by Error Propagation; in Rumelhart, D.E.; McCLelland, J.L. (Eds.): Parallel Distributed Processing Vol.1; MIT Press Cambridge Massachusetts 1986.

[Sch77] Schwefel,H.-P.: Numerische Optimierung von Computer-Modellen mittels der Evolutionsstrategie; Birkhäuser Basel und Stuttgart 1977.

[Tro91] Troll, A.: Optimierungsverfahren für die Lernphase bei Neuronalen Netzen; Diplomarbeit an der LMU München, Fachbereich Mathmatik; München 1991.

[Whi89a] Whitley, D., Bogart, C.: The evolution of connectivity: Pruning neural networks using genetic algorithms; Proc. of the 3rd Intern. Joint Conf. on Neural Networks 1989.

[Whi89b] Whitley, D., Hanson, T.: Optimizing neural networks using faster, more accurate genetic search; Proc. of the 3rd Intern. Conf. on Genetic Algorithms 1989.

Program Search with a Hierarchical Variable Length Representation: Genetic Programming, Simulated Annealing and Hill Climbing

Una-May O'Reilly[1] and Franz Oppacher[2]

[1] Santa Fe Institute, Santa Fe, NM, 87505, USA
[2] School of Computer Science, Carleton University, Ottawa, CANADA

Abstract. This paper presents a comparison of Genetic Programming(GP) with Simulated Annealing (SA) and Stochastic Iterated Hill Climbing (SIHC) based on a suite of program discovery problems which have been previously tackled only with GP. All three search algorithms employ the hierarchical variable length representation for programs brought into recent prominence with the GP paradigm [8]. We feel it is not intuitively obvious that mutation-based adaptive search can handle program discovery yet, to date, for each GP problem we have tried, SA or SIHC also work.

1 Introduction

Genetic Programming (GP) [8] is a recent paradigm in the lineage of search techniques for performing program induction [2, 3, 4, 5, 10, 12]. The sources of its effectiveness are: 1) an evolution inspired exploitation and exploration mechanism and, 2) the use of a hierarchical, variable length representation for programs. In the former respect, GP uses fitness proportional selection (á la natural selection) as a basis for choosing which individuals among a population of programs will be the parents of the next generation and a genetics based crossover operation for transforming two parents into two novel offspring. This provides a robust heuristic search approach [7, 6, 8]. Regarding the latter source, the hierarchical representation is supported by a genetic crossover operator which ensures the syntactic closure of all programs and permits programs of different lengths to be generated when two "parent" programs are crossed over. Thus in GP a fixed size and structure of programs in the search space does not have to be *a priori* specified.

One of the goals of this paper is to isolate GP's representation scheme from its evolution-based adaptation to understand the degree to which each is crucial in solving a program discovery problem. Given that a hierarchical variable length representation is used, we would like to obtain a better notion of when GP is the most appropriate paradigm for solving a particular program discovery problem compared with search techniques which traverse with a single point and are not inspired by genetics and evolution. Our approach is to conduct experiments which compare GP to Simulated Annealing (SA) and Stochastic Iterated Hill Climbing (SIHC).

In Section 2 operators which are capable of transforming programs (represented as trees) while permitting program size and length to vary are described. For SA and SIHC we have developed and present a mutation operator "HVL-Mutate", (HVL = Hierarchical Variable Length). Section 3 describes the primitive sets, fitness functions and test suites of the problems we attempt to solve with GP, SIHC and SA. In Section 4 the results of the experiments are presented and discussed.

2 Crossover and Mutation on Programs as Trees

The crossover operator and the hierarchical representation chosen for programs in Genetic Programming are complementary. Hierarchical representation of programs is both intuitive and common. It is helpful in denoting program structure both in terms of specification and execution. A program is represented as a rooted, point-labeled tree with ordered branches. Using LISP as an example the name of the S-Expression is the root of the tree and the arguments of the S-Expression (which may recursively be S-Expressions) are the ordered children of the root. In GP the nodes in each of two parent programs are numbered in a depth first search ordering and then two values, each in the node number range on a parent, are randomly selected as the crossover points. Finally, the two subtrees of the programs, each rooted at the node designated by the crossover point, are swapped. The value of the hierarchical dissection is that the syntax of programs is automatically preserved (i.e. closure is ensured) and programs of different structure and size are generated from parents to offspring.

The GP crossover is clearly an influential element of GP since, as in this experimentation, it often provides the sole means of exploring the search space. Crossover effects the promotion and disruption of partial solutions through the deletion and substitution of subsequences of programs selected on a fitness basis. The selection of crossover points would appear to be a crucial factor in GP because it determines how much "genetic material" (i.e. how much of an S-Expression) will be removed from one program and transplanted to another. The crossover operator introduced by Koza, which we call GP-XO, selects crossover points with a 90% probability bias towards subtrees which are not leaves. The proposed rationale for this bias is robustness and the fact that exchange of leaves is more akin to point mutation than recombination and thus is not explorative enough [8]. The reason for investigating alternative crossover point selection biases is that the actual impact of the 90% probability bias really seems less than clear cut. This is because the process by which programs are initially generated, the blind aspect of crossover and the syntactic constraints of the repertoire of primitives all interact to generate unpredictable leaf to node ratios. In fact, when leaves comprise less than 10% of the size of a tree, GP-XO is actually biased towards leaf selection contrary to the rationale of the bias. As well, presuming that the point mutation of a leaf is a "tweak" or rather small change to a program implies that leaves are constants, variables or simple predicates. In fact they could be functionally complex expressions which simply have no parameters. In this case a point mutation will in fact be "sufficiently" explorative. When the leaves are constants, variables or simple predicates it is also possible that tweaks may be appropriate as localized exploration.

We have devised and experimented with two other crossover operators that only differ in how the crossover point is selected:

- Height-fair-XO groups subtrees of a program by height, with equal probability chooses a group and then randomly selects one subtree of this group as the crossover point. Thus, the root and leaves of a subtree may be chosen with equal probability.
- Fair-XO randomly selects any subtree for swapping.

The objective of experimentation with three different crossover operators is to determine whether crossover point selection (i.e. bias) generally affects convergence rates and whether one crossover point selection scheme is overall superior to the others.

Both SA and SIHC require a mutation operator. Given that a hierarchical representation is chosen, the operator we have designed and used, HVL-Mutate, is inspired from the method for calculating the distance between trees [11]. That approach defines distance as the minimum cost sequence of editing one tree, step by step, to become the other using elementary operations such as substitution, insertion and deletion. In a similar manner, HVL-Mutate changes a program into another by either substituting one node for another (within syntactic constraints), deleting a subtree or inserting one with equal probability. Mutations are intended to be small changes so HVL-Mutate tries to minimize the change to a program within the constraints of supporting a non-binary variable length hierarchical representation. When a subtree is selected as the point above which a new node will be inserted it will always be used as a child of the new node if one is required. All remaining children of the newly inserted node are leaves. In the case of a deletion the node selected for deletion is replaced by the largest of its children. As well, when a leaf is chosen for deletion it is replaced by a different randomly chosen leaf. This algorithm does not guarantee that mutation will not drastically change the size and shape of a tree, but does reduce the probability of that event.

The advantage of HVL-Mutate is that it facilitates search with techniques which are not population based and which do not use the same selection criteria as GP. It permits isolation of the hierarchical variable-length representation aspect of GP from the rest of the GP algorithm.

3 Description of Experiments

We experiment with 3 problems: the 6-bit Boolean Multiplexer (6-Mult), the 11-bit Boolean Multiplexer, (11-Mult), and sorting (Sort-A). The Multiplexer task is to decode address bits and return the data value at the address. 6-Mult uses the primitives IF, OR, NOT, AND which take 3, 2, 1, and 2 arguments respectively. There are 6 variables (i.e. primitives which take no arguments): A0,

A1, D0,...,D3 which are bound before execution to the address bits and data values of a test case. All 64 possible configurations of the problem are enumerated as test cases. A program's raw fitness is the number of configurations for which it returns the correct data value for the given address. 11-Mult is simply a larger scale version of 6-Mult using 3 address bits (A0- A2) and 8 data values (D0-D7). The test suite consists of 2048 test cases.

The task of a program in sorting is to arrange in ascending order the elements in an array. A program is run 48 times, each time with a different array bound to the primitive *array*. The array sizes in the test suite range from 2 to 6 and among the arrays there are 198 elements in total. Among the test suite are 3 arrays which are initially in sorted order and 47 elements initially in their correct positions. The raw fitness of a program is the sum of the number of elements found in the correct position after running the program.

The primitives for Sort-A are Do-Until-False, Swap, First-Wrong, Next-Lowest, and *array* of 1, 3, 1, 2, and 0 arguments respectively. Do-Until-False executes its argument until it returns nil. Swap returns nil if its first argument is not an array. When its first argument is an array, and the second and third arguments evaluate to integers in the range of that array's size it exchanges the elements at the positions corresponding to the integers and returns true. First-Wrong returns nil if its argument is not an array or if the array is sorted. Otherwise it returns the index of the first element which is out of order in the array. Next-Lowest returns nil if its first argument is not an array and its second argument is not an integer within the extent of the array. Otherwise it returns the index of the smallest element in the array after the position indexed by the second argument. At the beginning of each test case the primitive *array* is bound to the array which is to be sorted.

In order to compare the results of GP, SIHC, and SA each run was permitted the same maximum number of evaluations. The GP runs were run with a population of 500 for 50 generations. Both SA and SIHC were given a maximum of 25500 evaluations as this corresponds to the evaluations in GP. The fitness values in the GP runs for all three problems were scaled by linear and exponential factors of 2. Whatever crossover operator used, it was applied 90% of the time with the remaining 10% of individuals chosen by selection being directly copied into the next generation.

The Simulated Annealing algorithm [1] used was basic. Fitnesses were normalized to lie in [0,1] which fitness drops to [0,1]. A starting temperature of 1.5 was always decreased to a temperature over a given number of evaluations according to an exponential cooling schedule. For 6-Mult, 11-Mult,and Sort-A the final temperature was set to 0.0001, 0.0001 and 0.0015 respectively. In SA whenever a mutant is better than its parent it is accepted as the next point from which to move again. The probability with which a mutant with lower or equal fitness than its parent is accepted decreases with the temperature of the system and depending upon the difference in fitness between them according to a Boltzmann distribution.

The algorithm for SIHC is to generate a program at random and apply the mutation operator to it. If the mutant is superior in fitness the search moves to it. Otherwise another mutation on the original point is tried. The maximum number of mutations to generate from a point before abandoning it and choosing a new one at random is a parameter of the algorithm which we call max-mutations. Values of 50, 100, 250, 500, 2500, and 10000 for this parameter were tried. At maximum evaluations or when a perfect solution has been found the algorithm terminates. In our terminology a "step" is the acceptance of a mutant because it is an improvement, a "climb" is a succession of steps and "evaluations" defines the number of mutations performed in a climb.

This experimentation demonstrates that different search strategies can be used with a hierarchical variable length representation. Inevitably, it is also a source of comparison among the strategies in terms of performance. The comparison is expressed in a specific manner however: i.e., there is no "tuning" of a technique to its best potential on a particular problem. For example, in GP, for a given problem and primitive set, while it is known that population size can affect performance, only a fixed population size was used in this experimentation. In SA, for example, the cooling schedule could also have been adjusted to improve effectiveness but was not. Even before experimentation, it seems clear that a greedy hill climbing strategy will never outperform GP or SA because it has no strategy for escaping from local optima.

4   Experiments Results

6-Mult: Table 1 summarizes the GP results obtained for the 6-Mult problem with the 3 different crossover operators. The experiment consisted of a minimum of 30 runs for each crossover operator. Under a t-test [13] with 95% confidence the results show that Height-Fair-XO and GP-XO have a significantly better expected probability of success than Fair-XO. Another significant difference was the average fitness of the population at the end of a run (a run was terminated as soon as a perfect individual was found) where, in contrast to the comparison in terms of probability of success, Fair-XO achieved a significantly better result and GP-XO and Height- Fair-XO were indistinguishable. The two results together might be explained by the fact that Height-Fair-XO is slower to converge because it requires a higher population fitness before it can create an individual fitter than the present fittest in the population. Both Height-Fair-XO and GP- XO needed a significantly less mean number of evaluations than Fair-XO but they did not differ with each other significantly.

Every run of SA to solve 6-Mult was successful and on average SA required 54.2% (7.7%) of available evaluations. After experimentation with various values for the max- mutations parameter (see Table 2) the best result for SIHC occurred when it equaled 10000. With this parameter SIHC solved 6-Mult 77% of the time. On average a successful climb was 9.4 steps and the number of evaluations per step in a successful climb was 7336 resulting in an average of 777.1 evaluations per step. One way of interpreting this value is that it quantifies the local nature of the landscape, i.e., with the given operator, how much effort is required to find

Table 1. GP Crossovers and 6-Mult

6-Mult and Genetic Programming (GP)	Height-Fair-XO	GP-XO	Fair-XO
Percentage of Successful Runs	86.7 (34.0)	79.5 (40.3)	60.9 (49.8)
Confidence Interval (99%, 95%, 90%)	16,12,10	17,13,11	23,18,15
Fittest Individual at End of Run (% of Opt)	98.3 (4.5)	98.0 (4.5)	96.7 (4.6)
Fitness of Population (% of Opt) at End of Run	77.6 (4.6)	78.2 (5.2)	81.6 (3.9)
Evaluations in a Successful Run (% of 25500)	51.4 (15.0)	48.4 (21.4)	57.4 (20.1)
Evaluations Over All Runs (% of 25500)	55.2 (21.9)	55.7 (27.8)	72.0 (26.2)
Tree Height of Successful Programs	7.9 (2.7)	6.9 (3.2)	8.4 (2.3)
Tree Size of Successful Programs	40.4 (18.4)	42.8 (32.0)	48.8 (25.1)

a higher point than the present one. The fact that SIHC was successful implies that there may not be many local optima to stymie the search or that there may be many peaks of optimal height.

Table 2. 6-Mult Hill Climbing

Max Mutations	Prob of Success (%)	Best Fitness (% of opt)	Avg Steps per Climb	Avg Evals per Climb	Evals: Step	Evals: Run (% of 25500)	Successful Runs Evals: Run (% of 25500)
50	10	89.8 (3.1)	2.6	80	30.8	94.0	59.0 (25.9)
100	20	91.4 (3.6)	3.5	165	47	81.7	17.8
250	20	93.5 (3.5)	4.4	425	97	90.0	58.7 (28.2)
500	40	96.6 (2.3)	5.4	855	159	81.8	61.3 (22.0)
10000	77	98.8 (2.8)	9.3	9787	1052	61.5	57.7 (30.2)

Table 3. 6-Mult Comparison of GP, SA and SIHC

6-Mult Search Strategy Comparison	SA	GP Height-Fair XO	SIHC
% Successful Runs	100	86.7	77
Fittest Individual	100	98.3	98.8
Evals of All Runs (% of 25500)	54	77.6	61.5
Evals of Successful Runs (% of 25500)	54	51.4	57.7
Tree Height of Successful Programs	8.6	7.9	5
Tree Size of Successful Programs	58	40.4	23.9

Evidently 6-Mult as a program induction problem is simple because all three of SA, GP (with any of these crossovers), and SIHC were able to solve it. Table 3 compares GP with Height-Fair- XO to SA and SIHC. SA had a significantly superior probabilility of success versus the best performing GP crosssover operator

(Height-Fair-XO) and SIHC. In terms of the evaluations expected over all runs or in successful runs no search technique was statistically superior. Interestingly, SIHC did find successful programs which were significantly shorter (i.e. had less primitives or fewer nodes) and of less depth (i.e. the height of the program trees was less).

11-Mult: Results for the 11-Mult problem are summarized in Table 4. GP could not solve 11-Mult with 25500 evaluations. Regarding the three different crossovers, both Height-Fair-XO and GP-XO obtained significantly better best fitness and population fitness than Fair-XO but they did not differ between themselves significantly. Height-Fair-XO found the fittest program (93.8% of optimal) while the fitness of the best program found by Fair-XO was 87.9% and GP-XO was 87.6%. Only SA among the 3 search techniques was able to obtain

Table 4. GP Crossovers and 11-Mult

11-Mult and Genetic Programming (GP)	Height-Fair-XO	GP-XO	Fair-XO
Percentage of Successful Runs	0	0	0
Best Fitness Found (%)	93.8	87.6	87.9
Fittest Individual at End of Run (% of Opt)	80.9 (5.0)	79.2 (5.5)	76.2 (4.3)
Fitness of Population (% of Opt) at End of Run	74.0 (3.65)	74.1 (4.4)	71.2 (3.9)
Evaluations Over all Runs (% of 25500)	100	100	100

a perfect solution. One solution was a program with tree height of 14 and 1891 nodes. This it accomplished on 3 out of 25 runs. When the number of evaluations was increased by 4500 to 30000 (which effectively slowed the cooling) then 2 more solutions were found. On average SA found a solution which was 93.4% of optimal (adjusted fitness of 1914). The results for SIHC when the maximum mutations parameter was varied from 2500 to 10000 were not significantly different. They are displayed in Table 5. It is interesting to note that a very simple, greedy heuristic that can be coded in less than one page outperforms a complicated and computationally expensive algorithm such as GP.

Table 5. SIHC and 11-Mult

	SIHC					Best Climbs			
Max Mut	Avg Steps per Climb	Avg Evals per Climb	Evals: Step	Avg Best Fitness (%)		Avg Steps per Climb	Avg Evals per Climb	Evals: Step	Best Fitness (%)
50	5.0	107.6	21.5	73.6		20	476	23.8	77.35
100	6.6	229.0	34.5	75.5		32	525	16.4	76.62
250	10.5	637.2	60.8	81.2		60	2273	37.9	87.95
500	15.0	1466.0	97.0	81.6		32.5	2436	74.4	84.38
2500	13.2	3939.0	296.6	74.1		57	12203	214.1	95.31
5000	5.9	2518.9	429.3	88.9 (34.2)		8.4	22093	2630.1	95.31
10000	25.6	21059.0	822.6	88.4 (39.0)		40	25000	625	96.88

Table 6. Comparison of SA, HC, and GP for 11-Mult

11-Mult Search Strategy Comparison	Simulated Annealing	GP Height-Fair-XO	SIHC Max-Mut = 50(
% Successful Runs	16.7	0	0
Best Fitness Found (%)	100	93.8	95.31
Fittest Individual at End of Run (% of Opt)	93.0	80.9	88.9

The 11-Mult problem experiments were interesting because the degree of success of the three search techniques varied. Table 6 compares the performance of GP, SA and SIHC. With the small number of runs it is not possible to conclude that SA is statistically superior to GP or SIHC, however, neither GP nor SIHC ever obtained a perfect solution in 30 runs. When the expected best fitness is compared, GP using Height-Fair-XO (which had the best result) and SIHC when max-mutations = 5000 do not differ statistically significantly. GP is slightly out-performed by hill climbing when the best values are compared: the best fitness ever obtained by GP (with Height-Fair-XO) was 93.8% of optimal and with SIHC it was 96.88% of optimal (max-mutations = 10000).

Sort-A: The first column of Table 7 shows how Sort-A was handled by Simulated Annealing. SA had approximately an 88% probability of success and the expected fitness at 25500 evaluations was very close to optimal (87.4%). This is superior to GP which is shown in the second column. Sort-A required approximately 63% of the allowed evaluations in all runs and about 55% of allowed evaluations in successful runs. This is more than GP with GP-XO. The size and height of the trees of successful programs in Sort-A with SA were less than those obtained with the GP. Table 8 provides the details of SIHC and Sort-A.

Table 7. Sort-A Comparison of GP, SA and SIHC

Sort-A Search Strategy Comparison	Simulated Annealing	GP GP-XO	SIHC (max-mu = 100)
% Successful Runs	88.3	80.0	46.7
Fittest Individual	87.4	49.7	72.6
Evals of All Runs (% of 25500)	62.2	51.3	72.2
Evals of Successful Runs (% of 25500)	54.6	39.1	37.5
Tree Height of Successful Programs	5.64	6.8	6.7
Tree Size of Successful Programs	12.9	25.0	48.3

It is possible to hill climb to a solution in the fitness landscape regardless of the value of the max-mutations parameter. In fact there is no significant difference in the probability of success for the values of the max-mutations parameter we tried. The greedy nature of SIHC seems likely to be responsible for a signicantly lower probability of success when compared to GP or SA. From the details of successful climbs one can see that most climbs take very few steps. It appears that there are many randomly spaced small equally fit peaks.

Table 8. SIHC and Sort-A

SIHC				Successful Climbs		
Max Mut	Prob of Success	Best Fitness (% of Opt)	Evals:Run (% of 25500)	Size	Height	Evals:Run (% of 25500)
50	50	67.6 (47.7)	64.3	52 (7.6)	7.8 (1.3)	28.7 (15.3)
100	46.7	72.6 (40.7)	72.2	48.3 (7.8)	6.7 (1.7)	37.5 (27.6)
250	50	62.1 (55.5)	72.2	64.4 (24.4)	8.2 (1.9)	44.3 (16.7)
500	46.7	63.2 (50.0)	68.2	67.1 (6.8)	7.4 (1.3)	31.1 (25.9)

5   Summary and Future Work

Our first goal was to isolate the variable length hierarchical representation of GP from its neo-Darwinian inspired search strategy. This we did by using that representation and the HVL-Mutate operator with SA and SIHC. A valuable lesson is that a variable length hierarchical representation may be a more fundamental asset to program induction than any particular search technique. We observed mixed or comparable differences between operator and search techniques across different problems. This confirms the notion that the suitability of a search technique depends upon the fitness function and primitives chosen for a particular problem since these influence the nature of the search landscape.

It came as somewhat of a surprise to us that SA and even SIHC are effective on problems in the domain of program discovery. The results clearly suggest something that is somewhat counter-intuitive: that adaptive mutation, with the important qualification is that the programs are represented as trees, is sufficiently powerful to find correct programs in large dimension search spaces. Typically one thinks that programs are so sensitive to context that tweaks are too radical. Since GP swaps sub-trees which are actually sub- programs there is some semantic level exchange of encapsulated function which makes crossover seem more intuitive than mutation. Yet as easily, HVL-Mutate seems to indicate that any intuition that this sort of exchange is necessary is incorrect: the hierarchical representation seems to allow tweaks to explore the search space in a efficient manner.

GP is a kind of Genetic Algorithm (GA). The crossover operator in GAs has been touted as an crucial factor in the power in GAs because of its combinative nature and as one reason GAs may be superior to other search techniques for certain problems (or certain fitness landscapes). Much recent GA research has focused upon finding out for what class of problems GAs are more effective than Hill Climbing and Simulated Annealing. Work in GP which is equivalent to this is very important and we believe this experimentation to a contribution in this respect. It is seems critical that program discovery methods are carefully compared and well understood to avoid premature conclusions regarding superiority. The role of crossover needs to be understood so that it can be determined whether there exist cases where GP is more effective than mutation-based search.

Related work we have in progress is 1) a search for some statistical measures which would indicate the superior technique for a particular problem or the superior crossover operator to choose in GP and 2) finding out how the search techniques compare on larger program discovery problems, i.e. how well do they scale? Automatic definition of functions (ADF) [9] is an important new technique in GP which is claimed to improve performance on big problems. ADF is a technique of representation rather than an operator so it seems likely that HVL-mutate can be modified to support it. We want to find out whether SA or SIHC with the extended HVL-Mutate are sufficiently powerful to handle problems GP with ADF.

References

1. Aarts, E., Korst, J.: Simulated Annealing and Boltzmann Machines. Wiley. 1989
2. Cramer, N. L.: A Representation for the Adaptive Generation of Simple Sequential Programs. Proc of Ist Intl Conf on Genetic Algorithms. Lawrence Erlbaum Assoc. 1985.
3. Friedberg, R.M.: A Learning Machine: Part 1. IBM Journal of Research and Development. 2(1): 2–13 (1958)
4. Friedberg, R.M., Dunham B., North J.H.: A Learning Machine: Part 2. IBM Journal of Research and Development. 3(3): 282–287 (1959)
5. Fujicki, C., Dickinson J.: Using the Genetic Algorithm to Generate LISP Source Code to Solve the Iterated Prisoner's Dilemma. Proc. of the 2nd Intl Conf on Genetic Algorithms. Lawrence Erlbaum Assoc. 1987.
6. Goldberg, D. E.: Genetic Algorithms in search, optimization, and machine learning. Addison-Wesley, 1989.
7. Holland, J. H.: Adaptation in Natural and Artificial Systems: An Introductory analysis with applications to biology, control, and artificial intelligence. 2nd Ed MIT Press,1992. (1st Ed 1978)
8. Koza, J. R.: Genetic Programming; On the Programming of Computers by Means of Natural Selection. Bradford Books, 1992.
9. Koza, J. R.: Genetic Programming II. Bradford Books, 1994.
10. Lenat, D. B: The Role of Heuristics in Learning by Discovery: Three Case Studies. Machine Learning, Eds. R. S. Michalski, J. G. Carbonell and T. M. Mitchell. Tioga Publishing Inc, 1983.
11. Sankoff, S., Kruskal, J.B., Editors: Time Warps, String Edits and Macromolecules: the Theory and Practice of Sequence Comparison. Addison Wesley, 1983.
12. Smith, S., J.: Flexible Learning of Problem Solving Heuristics Through Adaptive Search. Proc of the 8th Intl Joint Conf on Artificial Intelligence. Morgan Kaufmann, 1983.
13. Press, W. H.: Numerical Recipes in C: the art of scientific computing. Cambridge University Press, 1992.

Hybrid Methods

Problem-Independent Parallel Simulated Annealing using Selection and Migration

Per S. Laursen

Department of Computer Science
University of Copenhagen
Universitetsparken 1
2100 Copenhagen Ø, Denmark
e-mail: svalle@diku.dk

Abstract. Parallelization of the Simulated Annealing algorithm is a difficult task, due to its inherent sequential nature. A popular alternative approach has been to perform a number of independent annealings, often augmented by periodic "coordination", the generic strategy being to periodically pick the best current solution as the new starting point for all of the continued annealings.

We have conjectured that a more refined strategy may lead to improved performance. We have sought inspiration from Parallel Genetic Algorithms based on the so-called *island model*. We have implemented three versions of parallel Simulated Annealing; a version without coordination, a version with "traditional" global coordination, and a version with local coordination based on principles from the island model. The experimental results indicate that the proposed local coordination strategy generally outperforms the two other versions.

1 Introduction

A large number of combinatorial optimization problems can presently only be solved to proven optimality if they are of very moderate size, or possess some other special property. This fact motivates the interest for approximation algorithms and heuristics. The former class of algorithms are able to guarantee the quality of the produced (suboptimal) solutions within certain bounds, while heuristics usually only have empirical evidence of their problem solving abilities. Numerous heuristics are tailored to a specific problem type, but some can with little effort be turned into a heuristic for a variety of problems. Belonging to this class is the Simulated Annealing algorithm.

Application of the Simulated Annealing algorithm to a combinatorial optimization problem was first described by Kirkpatrick et al. [Kir82]. Since then, successful application of Simulated Annealing has been reported for a large number of problems. We will henceforth assume the reader to be familiar with the generics of Simulated Annealing. If not, see e.g. Aarts & Korst [Aar89].

The generic Simulated Annealing algorithm has an inherent sequential nature, rendering efficient parallelization non-trivial. Some suggest to perform the parallelization at data level (see e.g. Allwright & Carpenter [All89], Casotto et al. [Cas87]), which is of course a very problem-dependent strategy. Other proposals are more generally applicable, e.g the *division strategy*, which is described in section 2.

The main idea of the division strategy is to perform a number of more or less independent annealings, with the addition that the annealings are "coordinated" from time to time. Prevailing strategies for this are however rather primitive, so it appears likely that more elaborate strategies may improve the performance of the algorithm. An inspiration for such a strategy came from certain types of Genetic Algorithms, namely those based on the *island model*. We describe the island model - and how it may be used as a framework for a division-strategy based algorithm - in section 3.

The quality of the proposed parallel Simulated Annealing algorithm is assessed by comparing it to two other versions based on the division strategy; one which does not employ coordination at all, and one which employs a more traditional (global) coordination strategy. Also, we compare the performance to an equivalent serial algorithm. Results from the experiments are presented and discussed in section 4. Conclusions are finally summarized in section 5.

2 Strategies for Parallelizing Simulated Annealing

The primary motivations for parallelizing Simulated Annealing are either to increase the quality of the solutions produced without increasing the running time, or to preserve a certain solution quality while reducing the running time. As mentioned above, it appears difficult to effectively parallelize the generic Simulated Annealing algorithm, due to its inherent sequential nature. Even so, several strategies for parallelization of Simulated Annealing have been proposed. Below we briefly review a couple of problem-independent strategies.

If a proposed state is rejected in Simulated Annealing, the algorithm stays in its current state. The next state proposed will thus also belong to the neighbourhood of the current state. If the temperature is low, the algorithm may have to generate and evaluate numerous states from the neighbourhood, before a new state is accepted. This fact inspires the following approach: One "master"-processor holds the current state, and distributes this state to the rest of the processors (the "slave" processors). Each slave now generates a neighbouring state, calculates the cost function difference, and decides by the Boltzmann criterion if the new state should be accepted. When some slave processor has found an acceptable state, it forwards this state to the master processor. This new state then becomes the current state, and is thus forwarded to the rest of the slave processors. In case of collisions (more than one accepted state arrive during one iteration), some tie-breaking rule is applied. This strategy is clearly generally applicable. Diekmann et al. [Die92] report efficiencies of above 0.80 when using this parallelization strategy, for up to 64 processors. Other results do however indicate that the performance is somewhat sensitive to the chosen cooling schedule.

A very straightforward strategy is to let each processor perform ordinary, sequential Simulated Annealing on the complete problem, picking the best of the produced solutions as the final solution. Being a probabilistic algorithm, we can expect the algorithm to produce different solutions during multiple runs, rendering this a simple method for improving the solution quality. Instead of performing a number of completely independent annealings, one may choose to periodically "coordinate" the search. This could be achieved e.g. by letting the processors perform some (fixed) number of iterations independently, then collect all the current states, choose one of these states by some criterion (e.g. the state with lowest cost), and use this state as the new starting point for all of the processors during the next period of independent annealing. Exactly how to schedule this coordination is an open question. Aarts & Korst [Aar89] denote parallelization strategies of this type *division strategies*. The strategy presented in this paper aims at improving on the traditional division strategy.

It has also been suggested to combine the above approaches into a hybrid strategy, denoted a *clustering strategy* by Aarts & Korst [Aar89]. Initially, the algorithm is identical to the division strategy, i.e. each processor performs independent iterations. As the temperature decreases, and accepts of new states become more rare, two or more processors "cluster together" and cooperate on a single annealing, in a master-slave fashion as described above. Upon further temperature decrease, the processors form still larger clusters, and ultimately all processors will cooperate on a single annealing, i.e. as described for the first approach. Diekmann et al. [Die92] report good results for such an algorithm as well, using up to 121 processors.

3 An Approach Inspired by Parallel Genetic Algorithms

Consider again the division strategy. If a cooling schedule with a fixed number L of iterations is used, a simple parallelization strategy is then to perform p annealings of length (L/p), one on each of the p available processors. This ought to result in a speedup of about p, depending a bit on how intensely we coordinate the annealings. But what happens to the solution quality? To put it more generally: what is best; one annealing of length L, or p annealings of length (L/p)?

3.1 Optimal Annealing Length

Suppose we discovered that p annealings of length (L/p) did produce better solutions than a single annealing of length L, even without periodic coordination. If no communication during the annealing is involved, we could almost certainly obtain linear speedup by the division strategy. The division strategy will then outperform (or tie) the performance of any strategy that parallelizes the generic Simulated Annealing algorithm, since these algorithms will preserve the solution quality, and can have at most linear speedup. The question of how to trade off solution quality against running time has been examined by Johnson et al. [Joh89], Dodd [Dod90] and Laursen [Lau93], all indicating that there does (for the problems examined, at least) exist some optimal - but problem-dependent - annealing length L_{opt}. The simple division strategy can thus outperform any parallelization of the generic Simulated Annealing algorithm, provided that the individual annealings take at least L_{opt} iterations.

It may however still be that we can improve the solution quality further, by reintroducing the periodic coordination described above. That type of periodic coordination is in our opinion rather crude; all states except one are discarded, and the remaining one is copied onto all processors. This strategy can be perceived as a primitive *Genetic Algorithm*.

3.2 The Island Model

Several researchers have addressed the question of parallelizing Genetic Algorithms efficiently, i.e. how to realize good Parallel Genetic Algorithms (PGAs). Many have been inspired by a concept from evolution theory known as the *island model*.

In the island model, the population is partitioned into subpopulations, each of which live in an area not immediately accessible for members of other subpopulations (an island). Interaction between subpopulations takes place by means of *migration*, i.e. members of a subpopulation travel to the territory of another subpopulation, to compete with its members. Furthermore, a topology is often introduced on the set of islands, implying that any given island will have a number of neighbouring islands, and that individuals may only migrate to neighbouring islands. The interesting property of the island model is that the evolution towards high-quality individuals seems to progress faster than observed for an equivalent single-population model. Also, the island model lends itself very well to rather simple parallelization. Suppose we wish to implement a PGA based on the island model on a MIMD-type p-processor parallel computer, using a population of size P. We then simply maintain a subpopulation of size P/p on each processor. In most applications, the time complexity of a single iteration is linear in the population size, so if we for now omit migration, this strategy - which is obviously very similar to the division strategy for Simulated Annealing - should yield linear speedup.

The pending question is how to realize the migration scheme, i.e. deciding how often migration should occur, how many individuals that migrate, choosing between domestic and immigrated individuals, etc.. These rules are usually found empirically.

3.3 Using Selection and Migration in Parallel Simulated Annealing

Suppose now we modify the division strategy, so that we perform k (say) annealings in parallel on each processor. We thus have a set of states on each processor. Such a set is the analogue of a subpopulation in an island model PGA. The algorithm could then be as follows; let all processors perform l Simulated Annealing iterations on each of the k members of its population. After that, pair each processor with a neighbouring processor (by some definition), and let a number of states migrate to the neighbour. Do selection on each processor, such that k states are left. Perform l new Simulated Annealing iterations on these states, etc.. This algorithm is a sort of hybrid between Simulated Annealing and Genetic Algorithms; between the coordination phases it is Simulated Annealing, but during the coordination phase it is a Genetic Algorithm. The only major decision is how to perform the migration and selection.

During a *rendez-vous* between a pair of processors, migration and selection should take place. There are as mentioned no universal rules for how to do this, so we have chosen a simple strategy: First, each processor copies its complete population of k individuals to the other processor. Both processors now have $2k$ individuals, i.e. both processors have an identical "compound" population. Each processor must now select k out of these $2k$ individuals. There are several possible options for how to do this:

1)   Ordinary selection: Individuals are selected with a probability proportional to their "fitness", where a quantitative definition of fitness could be e.g. $1/c(s)$, where $c(s)$ is the cost function.

2)   Boltzmann selection: The (normalized) Boltzmann probability is calculated for all individuals, and individuals are selected with this probability.

3)   Hard selection: the k best individuals are selected.

4)   Random selection: k individuals are selected at random.

Random selection does not appear to be a viable alternative, since it does not direct the search in any specific direction. Also, 2) can be perceived as a variation of 1), with an alternative definition of fitness. Fitness can be defined in a multitude of ways, so the Boltzmann-inspired definition may be as good as any other definition. We thus decided to choose between Boltzmann selection and hard selection.

A number of tentative experiments were carried out, indicating that hard selection outperformed Boltzmann selection. We found this to be a bit surprising, since Boltzmann selection seemed more "appropriate" in a Simulated Annealing context. Hard selection is on the other hand not as hard as it initially looks. Note that the k best individuals are chosen, meaning that no individual is allowed to appear twice in the same subpopulation. The effect of the hard selection is thus to create two identical new subpopulations on the pair of processors in question, consisting of the k best individuals on these two processors.

3.4 Migration to Alternating Neighbours

It may not be quite evident how this strategy of periodic migration to neighbouring processors is realized in practice. In our case, the target machine is a network of 16 T800 Transputers, connected in a four by four torodial grid topology. Each processor thus has four neighbours; one to the "east", "north", "west" and "south".

As outlined above, a basic "global" iteration consists of performing l Simulated Annealing iterations on each of the k individuals, followed by the migration and selection phase. Since all individuals migrate during each of these phases, each processor must find a target processor to which its individuals can migrate. Since we would like to allow good individuals to influence on the whole population, a static pairing of processors will not suffice. The pairings must thus change dynamically in time. In our specific network, it is quite easy to realize that the processors can be split into two non-connected groups (Red and Green), i.e. the network graph is bipartite. Each processor will thus have four neighbours of the opposite colour.

Suppose now that in some specific iteration, all red processors let their individuals migrate to the green processor to the north, while the green processors all let their individuals migrate to the south. This defines a unique pairing of processors. If all processors then "turn" their direction of communication clockwise in the next phase, we will again have a unique pairing of processors. In graph theoretic terms, we find a perfect matching in the graph during each iteration. This graph thus contains four perfect matchings. It is not hard to show that any d-regular bipartite graph contains d perfect matchings. By shifting from one alternative pairing to another, all processors continuously exchange individuals with alternating processors.

4 Experiments and Results

The algorithm has been implemented in OCCAM on the 16-processor T800 Transputer network described above. The Quadratic Assignment Problem (QAP), the Weighted Vertex Cover Problem (WVCP) and the Graph Partitioning Problem (GPP) have been used as test problems. For all three problem classes, a simple Simulated Annealing algorithm has been implemented, using the standard geometric cooling schedule, and a fixed number of iterations. k - the number of individuals on each processor - was set to five in all experiments.

First, we investigate how the algorithm using the proposed local coordination strategy performs as compared to a version using no coordination at all, and a version using a traditional global coordination strategy, i.e. where all states are gathered, and the best state is copied back to all processors. We use a "standard" parameter choice, i.e. 32 global iterations - denoted g - are performed in total, and 400 local iterations - denoted l - are performed on each individual between each coordination. We apply all three variants of the algorithm to all three test problem classes. For each class, we apply the algorithm to five different problem sizes, five instances of each size, and ten runs on each instance. The results obtained for the version using no coordination are used as a reference case, i.e. all other costs are given relatively to this reference cost. In addition to the parallel versions, we have also implemented a corresponding serial version of the algorithm - i.e. a version that uses $kpgl$ iterations during each run - to ∴ssess the effect of this type of parallelization as such. In the standard case, the serial algorithm thus uses 1,024,000 iterations, since $(k,p,g,l)=(5,16,32,400)$ in that case. The results are displayed graphically on Figure 1 (Figure 1 is the three graphs in the left-hand column of the page containing the graphs). The legend is nc (solid line) for no coordination, lc (dashed line) for local coordination, gc (dotted line) for global coordination and se (dot-and-dash line) for the serial version.

A number of observations can be made from the results presented in Figure 1. For the sake of brevity, we only present the most significant observations here. A more detailed analysis can be found in [Lau94].

First of all, we note that the qualitative structure of the results is similar for all three problem classes. Considering the local coordination strategy first, we observe that this strategy consistently improves on the solution quality produced by the version using no coordination, the smallest WVCPs and GPPs excluded. For the latter problems, the two versions are actually capable of finding the optimal solution in almost all cases, rendering the solution quality almost identical. It also appears that the larger the problem size - i.e. the harder the problem - the more advantageous it becomes to use local coordination.

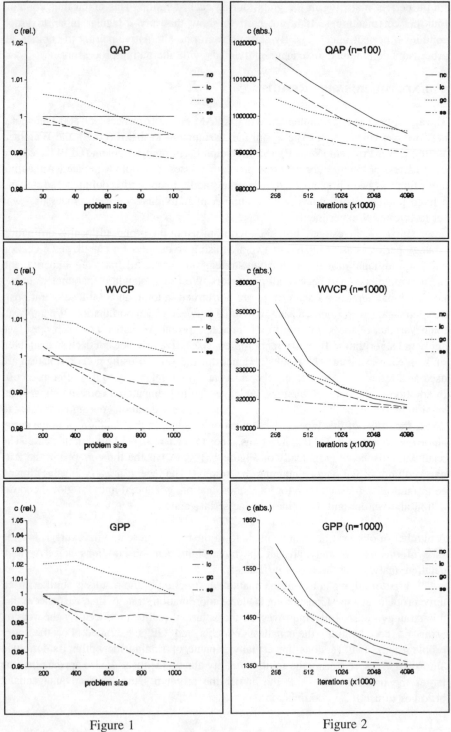

Figure 1   Figure 2

With respect to overhead due to synchronization, local coordination incurs significantly less overhead than global coordination. While local coordination typically only increased the running time by a couple of percent, global coordination caused overhead of typically 10-25 percent. This is due to the fact that global coordination demands that significantly more information must flow through the network. Furthermore, we can expect to maintain the low overhead for local coordination, if we implement the algorithm on a larger distributed system, due to the lack of global control. This will obviously not be the case for global coordination, where the overhead can be expected to grow approximately linear with the number of processors, if strict centralized control is insisted upon.

It also appears that global coordination - at least in the generic form used here - should be used with caution. For the small problems, the solution quality is substantially *worse* compared to omitting coordination. The relative performance of global coordination does however improve as problem size increases. For the WVCP and the GPP, it ties the performance of the no-coordination version for the largest problems, while it actually ties the local coordination strategy for the largest QAPs.

An interesting observation emerges when comparing the results for global coordination and for the serial algorithm. The curves for these two versions look fairly similar, except for a vertical displacement. This could be interpreted as an indication that global coordination (in the form used here) produces a parallel algorithm which behaves similarly to the corresponding serial algorithm. It is however also evident that the global coordination strategy does not produce a genuine parallelization as such of the serial algorithm. The solution quality produced by the serial algorithm is substantially better.

The second experiment has two purposes. First, to examine whether the behavior of the different versions conforms with the tentative conclusions stated above, when other annealing lengths are chosen. Second, to try to quantify the significance of the effects observed. It is not evident how to quantify the significance of the effects; we propose a kind of speedup measure. Speedup in this context is to be understood in a manner different than usually, where it denotes the ratio of wall clock time between a serial and a parallel version of an algorithm. Suppose that the no-coordination version using L iterations is capable of finding solutions of average cost c_{nc}. By including (for instance) local coordination, we may become able to find solutions of average cost c_{lc} ($c_{lc} < c_{nc}$), still using L iterations. The question is then: how much should the number of iterations spent by the no-coordination version be increased, before it is able to find equally good solutions, i.e. solutions of average cost c_{lc}? If the answer is to increase the number of iterations to e.g. $2L$, then local coordination gives us a speedup of 2.

Pinpointing exact speedups would be a formidable experimental task, and not even particularly meaningful due to the inherent noise in the algorithm. Instead, we use the absolute average solution costs for various choices of L. We plot the absolute costs as a function of L, and assume that the solution quality develops linearly (i.e. logarithmically, since the L-axis is logarithmic) between the specific measurement points. The idea is then to choose some absolute cost value - a horizontal line in the graph - and see where the line intersects with the curves for the various strategies.

The experiment is now carried out as follows. We vary the total number of iterations, by varying the parameter l, while keeping g fixed to 32 as in the previous experiment. We try five different values for l, which are $l=(100,200,400,800,1600)$. We only apply the algorithm to the largest test problems from each class. Figure 2 depicts the average absolute solution costs for the various choice of L. (Figure 2 is the three graphs in the right-hand column of the page containing the graphs).

Comparing local coordination to no coordination, we observe that local coordination still appears to be able to enhance the performance of the no-coordination version. Estimation of the "speedup" - as defined before - typically gives speedup values in the region 1.5 to 2, indicating that the positive effect is indeed significant, since the price paid is an increase in running time on just a couple of percent.

It is also evident that the global coordination version produces a drastically deteriorated solution quality, as compared to the serial algorithm. The "slowdown" seems to be at least an order of magnitude. In general, it appears that these types of high-level parallelization strategies are inappropriate in this range of running time and problem size, since the serial version apparently has a significant speedup over even the best of the parallel versions. However, some additional experiments carried out on the *small* test problems gave radically different results. Here the no-coordination version exhibited a significant speedup over the serial version, i.e. quite the opposite of what is observed for the large problems.

The explanation of this phenomenon is most likely tied to the existence of an optimal annealing length L_{opt}. If the number of iterations L carried out by each processor in a no- or local coordination version is much lower than L_{opt} - i.e. $L \ll L_{opt}$, as was probably the case for the larger test problems - then the performance will deteriorate significantly as compared to a serial version, implying that a low-level parallelization of the generic algorithm should be attempted instead. If on the other hand $L \geq L_{opt}$, a high-level parallel version is likely to be superior. Different ranges of running time and problem sizes thus call for different approaches for parallelization.

5 Conclusions

The idea of augmenting a "trivially parallel" version of Simulated Annealing with a coordination strategy inspired by certain types of PGA's appears to be a fruitful one. At the expense of a slight increase in running time, it renders the algorithm capable of finding solutions of a given quality level using about half the number of iterations. Due to the lack of centralized control, good scalability can also be expected.

The experiments also revealed that the traditional global coordination strategy has severe drawbacks. It appears to be the superior choice only in rather extreme regions of running time and problem sizes, and even then only if an efficient low-level parallelization cannot be easily obtained.

On a more fundamental level, the results support the conjecture that different situations call for different strategies for parallelizing Simulated Annealing, if one wishes as efficient an algorithm as possible. The notion of an optimal annealing length seems to be crucial in this respect.

Acknowledgement

This research has been financed by a grant from the Danish Natural Science Research Council (grant no. 11-9833).

References

[Aar89]   E.H.L. Aarts and J. Korst, *Simulated Annealing and Boltzmann Machines*, Wiley, Chichester, 1989.

[All87]   J.R.A. Allwright and D.B. Carpenter, "A distributed implementation of Simulated Annealing for the Traveling Salesman Problem", *Parallel Computing* 10 (1989) 335-338.

[Cas87]   A. Casotto, F. Romeo and A. Sangiovanni-Vincentelli, "A parallel Simulated Annealing algorithm for the placement of macro-cells", *IEEE Transactions on Computer Aided Design* 6 (1987) 838-847.

[Dod90]   N. Dodd, "Slow annealing vs. multiple fast annealing runs - an empirical investigation", *Parallel Computing* 16 (1990) 269-272.

[Die92]   R. Diekmann, R. Lüling and J. Simon, "Problem independent distributed Simulated Annealing and its applications", Technical Report, University of Paderborn, Germany, 1992.

[Joh89]   D.S. Johnson, C.R. Aragon, L.A. McGeoch and C. Schevon, "Optimization by Simulated Annealing: An experimental evaluation; Part I, Graph Partitioning", *Operations Research* 37 (1989) 865-892.

[Kir82]   S. Kirkpatrick, C.D. Gelatt and M.P. Vecchi, "Optimization by Simulated Annealing", IBM Research Report RC 9355, 1982.

[Lau93]   P.S. Laursen, "Simulated annealing for the QAP - Optimal tradeoff between simulation time and solution quality", *European Journal of Operational Research* 69 (1993) 238-243.

[Lau94]   P.S. Laursen, "Parallel Optimization Algorithms - Simplicity vs. Efficiency", Ph.D. Thesis, forthcoming.

Parallel Optimization of Evolutionary Algorithms

Thomas Bäck*

University of Dortmund, Department of Computer Science, Chair XI
D–44221 Dortmund, Germany

Abstract. A parallel two-level evolutionary algorithm which evolves genetic algorithms of maximum convergence velocity is presented. The meta-algorithm combines principles of evolution strategies and genetic algorithms in order to optimize continuous and discrete parameters of the genetic algorithms at the same time (mixed-integer optimization). The genetic algorithms which result from the meta-evolution experiment are considerably faster than standard genetic algorithms and confirm recent theoretical results about optimal mutation rates and the interaction of selective pressure and mutation rate.

1 Introduction

The problem to find optimal settings of the exogenous parameters of a genetic algorithm — with particular emphasis on the mutation rate p_m, crossover probability p_c, and population size λ — constitutes an optimization problem by itself. From a theoretical point of view, only very few results are known which may help to find a useful parameter setting (e.g., a mutation rate $p_m = 1/l$, where l denotes the length of the binary strings, might serve as a starting point [1, 7, 15]). A recent theoretical result, however, clarifies that a universally valid best parameterization of a genetic algorithm does not exist, but the optimal parameter values depend strongly on the particular optimization problem for which the genetic algorithm is applied [12].

Most experimental approaches towards finding guidelines for genetic algorithm parameterization tried to check a range of parameter settings systematically and measured the corresponding genetic algorithm performances over a number of different objective functions (e.g., [13, 18]). In most cases, the online and offline performance [13] was used to assess the quality of a genetic algorithm, and the investigations were restricted to testing the impact and interaction of very few parameters.

A more promising approach tries to evolve optimal parameter settings automatically by applying an optimization algorithm to optimize genetic algorithms. If such a two-level approach utilizes an evolutionary algorithm also on the second level, it is justified to call this a *meta-evolution* experiment. Such an experiment, based on genetic algorithms on both levels, was performed by Grefenstette [11]

---

* baeck@ls11.informatik.uni-dortmund.de

and recently also by Freisleben and Härtfelder [8]. Grefenstette's meta-algorithm searched through a six-dimensional parameter space including population size λ, crossover probability p_c, mutation rate p_m, generation gap, scaling window, and selection strategy (proportional selection in pure or elitist form). The parameter space was discretized also for the continuous parameters, and only a small number (eight respectively sixteen) of different values was permitted for each parameter. Online and offline performance over De Jong's set of test functions [13] were used to measure the quality of genetic algorithms. On the level of the meta-algorithm, standard parameters as suggested by De Jong ($\lambda = 50$, $p_c = 0.6$, $p_m = 0.001$, generation gap 1.0, a scaling window of 7, elitist selection) were used. The meta-evolution experiment resulted in the outcome $\lambda = 30(80)$, $p_c = 0.95(0.45)$, $p_m = 0.01(0.01)$, generation gap 1.0(0.9), a scaling window of 1(1), elitist (pure) selection when online (offline) performance was used.

The experiment of Freisleben and Härtfelder was based on a much larger space of 19 components, split into probabilistic *decisions* and their corresponding parameters. Their "genetic algorithm" worked with real-valued alleles and normally (respectively exponentially) distributed mutations (with fixed standard deviations) and were optimized to solve a particular neural network weight optimization problem. By defining an *indicator function*, five of the 19 variables were identified to have strongest impact on the quality of the evolved algorithms. On the level of the meta-algorithm, the authors simply adopted the currently best second-level parameter settings dynamically after each primary generation [8].

The approach presented here differs from both experiments by using a meta-algorithm which results as a hybrid of genetic algorithms and evolution strategies (see [4] for a comparison) to search in mixed-integer spaces. In addition to continuous parameters, which are evolved as in evolution strategies, discrete parameters (such as selection method, crossover operator, etc.) are evolved as in genetic algorithms. The search space and the parallel meta-algorithm are discussed in section 2 of the paper. Section 3 presents result obtained from an experiment to evolve genetic algorithms of maximum convergence velocity, and some conclusions are given in section 4.

2 The Algorithm

Due to the enormous computational effort required to evaluate a population of the meta-algorithm, a parallel evaluation is desirable. The implementation discussed here is based on a *master-slave* approach, i.e., a global instance (the meta-algorithm) controls a number of worker processes which run in parallel on different processors. The communication between master and slaves is synchronized by the meta-algorithm's generation sequence. In order to evaluate the population of the meta-algorithm (Λ individuals $\mathbf{a}_1, \ldots, \mathbf{a}_\Lambda$), each individual $\mathbf{a}_i$ is interpreted as a description of a genetic algorithm, which runs for a fixed number of function evaluations on a slave processor and delivers a quality information $f(\mathbf{a}_i)$ about its final best solution to the master. The general structure of such an algorithm is outlined in figure 1.

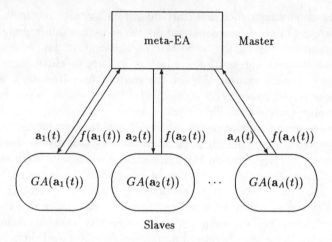

Fig. 1.: Structure of the master-slave implementation of a meta-algorithm, which is running as the master-process. At each generation of the master, each slave evaluates one of the meta-algorithm's individuals by running the genetic algorithm specified by that individual.

2.1 Structure of the Slave Algorithms

The slave algorithms are basically genetic algorithms with a binary representation of individuals. The search space of standard genetic algorithms, however, is extended by some additional selection and recombination mechanisms. More concretely, the genetic algorithms are determined by the following ten parameters:

(1) Crossover probability $p_c \in [0, 1]$.

(2) Mutation rate $p_m \in [0, 0.5]$.

(3) Maximum expected value $\eta^+ \in [1, 2]$ (slope of the linear function) for linear ranking selection [5].

(4) Tournament size $q \in \{1, \ldots, 20\}$ for tournament selection [10].

(5) Parent population size $\mu \in \{1, \ldots, 100\}$ for extinctive selection methods [3].

(6) Offspring population size $\lambda \in \{1, \ldots, 100\}$.

(7) Number of crossover points $z \in \{1, \ldots, 8\}$ for multi-point crossover [13].

(8) Selection operator $s \in \{P, R, T, C\}$ (proportional, linear ranking, tournament, (μ, λ)-selection) [3].

(9) Recombination operator $r \in \{S, U, D, \_\}$ (z-point crossover, uniform crossover [21], discrete recombination [4], none).

(10) Elitist selection flag $e \in \{0, 1\}$ [13].

Notice that the search space consists of continuous as well as discrete parameters. Furthermore, some special relations between variables cause a variation of the true dimension of the search space during the search, since

- p_c is only important if $\mu > 1$ and $r \neq$ _,
- z is only important if $\mu > 1$ and $r = S$,
- η^+ is only important if $s = R$, and
- q is only important if $s = T$.

Due to space restrictions, we cannot give a detailed explanation for each of the possible parameter values but refer the reader to the literature (e.g., [9, 13, 20]).

2.2 Structure of the Meta-Algorithm

The meta-algorithm does not use a binary representation of the parameters (1)–(10) presented in section 2.1. Instead, it utilizes concepts from evolution strategies [20] to mutate the parameters (1)–(6) and self-adapt their standard deviations for mutations. The remaining four parameters (7)–(10) are mutated as in genetic algorithms according to a uniform probability distribution over the set of possible values. In the following, notation is simplified by denoting the i-th parameter from the list given in section 2.1 by x_i. From evolution strategies, the mutation operator for $x_1, \ldots, x_6$ and their corresponding strategy parameters is adapted as follows (see e.g. [4]):

$$
\begin{aligned}
\sigma_i' &= \sigma_i \cdot \exp(\tau' \cdot N(0,1) + \tau \cdot N_i(0,1)) & \forall i \in \{1, \ldots, 6\} \\
x_i' &= x_i + \sigma_i' \cdot N_i(0,1) & \forall i \in \{1, 2, 3\} \\
x_i' &= x_i + \lfloor \sigma_i' \cdot N_i(0,1) \rfloor & \forall i \in \{4, 5, 6\},
\end{aligned}
\tag{1}
$$

where $\lfloor x \rfloor = \max\{i \in \mathbb{Z} \mid i \leq x\}$ serves to get an integer value after mutation. Notice that the strategy parameters σ_i (step sizes) are not exogenously controlled but undergo evolution (by mutation and recombination) as well as the object variables x_i. $N(0,1)$ denotes a realization of a standardized normally distributed random variable, and τ, τ' are "learning rates" for the self-adaptation of strategy parameters (see [4]).

In case of $x_7, \ldots, x_{10}$ the underlying discrete alphabet is of low cardinality, such that uniform mutation is applied to these parameters. The meta-algorithm's mutation rate $\mathcal{P}_m$ for this event is fixed to a value of $\mathcal{P}_m = 0.05$, which turns out in the experiments to be a robust setting (in further work, this should also become a self-adaptive parameter). The remaining exogenous parameters of the meta-algorithm are chosen according to evolution strategies: Discrete recombination on object variables $x_1, \ldots, x_{10}$, intermediate recombination on strategy parameters $\sigma_1, \ldots, \sigma_6$, and a (4,30)-selection strategy (which reflects a technical restriction on the number of processors available for the experiment).

The resulting meta-algorithm represents a new heuristic for searching inhomogenous parameter spaces, i.e., for mixed-integer problems. Although such a combination of concepts from evolution strategies and genetic algorithms seems to be straightforward, no comparable approach was discussed in literature so far. In the following section a first evaluation of the feasibility of this hybrid algorithm is presented.

3 Experimental Results

The main emphasis of this experimental investigation is twofold: First, the principal working mechanism of the hybrid meta-algorithm is evaluated. Second, the experiment intends to check whether the optimal slave algorithm found by the experiments meets or contradicts our expectations. Therefore, the objective function which is optimized by the slave algorithms is chosen to be a simple parameter optimization problem, the sphere model $f(\mathbf{x}) = \sum_{i=1}^{n} x_i^2$, $\mathbf{x} \in R^n$, with $n = 20$ and $-40 \leq x_i \leq 60$. Each object variable x_i is represented by $l_x = 30$ bits, such that the total string length amounts to $l = 600$. Gray coding as described e.g. in [22] is utilized to represent continuous variables as binary vectors.

For the optimization experiments presented here, the meta-algorithm executed 50 generations, i.e., 1504 parameter vectors for genetic algorithms were evaluated. To evaluate the fitness of a genetic algorithm, it was allowed to run for 10^4 function evaluations. The average final best objective function value from two independent runs (with identical genetic algorithm parameters) served as the fitness function for the meta-algorithm. The initial population of all runs of genetic algorithms was identical in order to guarantee a fair comparability of the resulting quality measures.

From the design of this experiment and the quality measure for slave algorithms it is clear that the meta-evolution optimizes for the convergence velocity of genetic algorithms. Since the selection operator (together with the values of μ and λ) has a clear impact on convergence velocity, two different experiments are performed:

(1) The population sizes $\mu = \lambda = 50$ and the proportional selection operator are fixed. Therefore, the search is reduced to the space of standard genetic algorithms (with a dimension of 4–5, depending on the recombination operator).

(2) The complete search space is permitted (with a dimension of 6–10).

The results of both experiments are presented in the following two sections.

3.1 Evolving an Optimal Standard Genetic Algorithm

Table 1 shows the complete initial (left) and final (right) population of the meta-algorithm for experiment (1). For reasons of clarity of the presentation, parameter values which are inactive (according to the rules formulated in section 2.1) are not shown.

The initial population is characterized by a high degree of diversity, and the quality of the genetic algorithms is mainly determined by the mutation rate p_m (a too large mutation rate has disastrous consequences for the performance of genetic algorithms). After 50 generations, however, a well structured and almost homogenous population is evolved by the meta-algorithm. The most important characteristics of the final population are:

- All mutation rates are close to the value $1/l$ ($= 0.001667$), which is exactly the value which was found to be optimal for a $(1+1)$-GA on the counting ones problem [1, 7, 15].

Table 1.: Initial (left) and final population (right) of the meta-evolution experiment using proportional selection with $\mu = \lambda = 50$.

p_c	p_m	z	r	e	Fitness	p_c	p_m	z	r	e	Fitness
0.469	0.02122	—	D	1	$6.43204 \cdot 10^2$	0.969	0.00151	—	U	1	$3.924470 \cdot 10^0$
0.239	0.02183	—	D	1	$6.85113 \cdot 10^2$	0.956	0.00118	—	U	1	$4.784130 \cdot 10^0$
0.975	0.03561	—	_	1	$1.74747 \cdot 10^3$	0.957	0.00153	—	U	1	$5.086330 \cdot 10^0$
0.247	0.04263	8	S	1	$2.42679 \cdot 10^3$	0.956	0.00160	—	U	1	$5.600480 \cdot 10^0$
0.265	0.10329	—	_	1	$3.46830 \cdot 10^3$	0.957	0.00137	—	U	1	$5.616090 \cdot 10^0$
0.424	0.05198	1	S	0	$4.77329 \cdot 10^3$	0.959	0.00151	—	U	1	$5.999380 \cdot 10^0$
0.573	0.10501	—	D	1	$5.10812 \cdot 10^3$	0.957	0.00181	—	U	1	$6.543100 \cdot 10^0$
0.194	0.15447	4	S	1	$5.99915 \cdot 10^3$	0.963	0.00130	—	U	1	$6.615280 \cdot 10^0$
0.442	0.24631	—	_	1	$8.07875 \cdot 10^3$	0.960	0.00144	—	U	1	$7.188730 \cdot 10^0$
0.323	0.35874	6	S	0	$8.39357 \cdot 10^3$	0.964	0.00153	—	U	1	$7.522640 \cdot 10^0$
0.999	0.33714	3	S	0	$8.70468 \cdot 10^3$	0.961	0.00297	—	U	1	$8.227170 \cdot 10^0$
0.283	0.09659	4	S	0	$8.79064 \cdot 10^3$	0.956	0.00142	—	U	1	$8.264990 \cdot 10^0$
0.325	0.26309	—	_	1	$8.79426 \cdot 10^3$	0.958	0.00110	—	U	1	$8.523150 \cdot 10^0$
0.280	0.19972	5	S	0	$8.84707 \cdot 10^3$	0.961	0.00140	—	U	1	$8.546150 \cdot 10^0$
0.764	0.49582	—	U	0	$9.08696 \cdot 10^3$	0.965	0.00134	—	U	1	$9.338230 \cdot 10^0$
0.198	0.49794	—	U	1	$9.16742 \cdot 10^3$	0.964	0.00127	—	U	1	$9.521460 \cdot 10^0$
0.486	0.33294	—	_	1	$9.54032 \cdot 10^3$	0.957	0.00208	—	U	1	$9.761820 \cdot 10^0$
0.233	0.22491	3	S	0	$9.65002 \cdot 10^3$	0.961	0.00184	—	U	1	$1.000500 \cdot 10^1$
0.695	0.43110	—	U	1	$9.80524 \cdot 10^3$	0.960	0.00191	—	U	1	$1.219270 \cdot 10^1$
0.175	0.26968	—	_	0	$9.82232 \cdot 10^3$	0.957	0.00160	—	U	1	$1.238260 \cdot 10^1$
0.135	0.22431	—	D	0	$9.84021 \cdot 10^3$	0.967	0.00141	—	U	1	$1.310300 \cdot 10^1$
0.154	0.28594	—	U	0	$1.01346 \cdot 10^4$	0.968	0.00144	—	U	1	$1.464350 \cdot 10^1$
0.356	0.47504	2	S	1	$1.01738 \cdot 10^4$	0.956	0.00146	—	U	1	$1.589780 \cdot 10^1$
0.143	0.47290	—	U	1	$1.03939 \cdot 10^4$	0.960	0.00130	—	U	1	$1.780140 \cdot 10^1$
0.738	0.38947	—	_	0	$1.03988 \cdot 10^4$	0.956	0.00105	—	U	1	$1.874710 \cdot 10^1$
0.916	0.36282	—	_	0	$1.04819 \cdot 10^4$	0.959	0.00121	—	U	1	$1.893150 \cdot 10^1$
0.446	0.47438	8	S	1	$1.04929 \cdot 10^4$	0.964	0.00119	—	U	1	$1.994610 \cdot 10^1$
0.152	0.45008	5	S	1	$1.08379 \cdot 10^4$	0.961	0.00066	—	U	1	$2.083210 \cdot 10^1$
0.568	0.47423	—	U	1	$1.11591 \cdot 10^4$	0.954	0.00146	—	U	0	$2.172610 \cdot 10^1$
0.044	0.45816	—	U	0	$1.18575 \cdot 10^4$	0.964	0.00164	—	U	1	$2.373870 \cdot 10^1$

- Uniform crossover, applied with a probability $p_c \approx 1$, seems to be important for the search. The concentration on this operator clarifies that highly disruptive operators can be helpful, which was already indicated by other researchers [21, 19].
- The elitist property is invented in order to guarantee that advantageous information is not lost by too disruptive operators and weak selective pressure.

Remaining fitness differences between similar individuals in table 1 can be explained by the fact that the genetic algorithm fitness function is noisy. Normally, it would be necessary to average results from a much larger number of runs — which is currently impossible due to the required computational effort.

3.2 Searching the Complete Space

The final population which is evolved when the complete search space is permitted (experiment (2)) is shown in table 2.

Table 2.: Final population of the meta-evolution experiment using the complete search space.

p_c	p_m	η^+	q	μ	λ	z	s	r	e	Fitness
0.421	0.00383	—	20	7	17	—	T	U	0	$2.164470 \cdot 10^{-6}$
0.421	0.00383	—	20	7	17	—	T	U	0	$2.164470 \cdot 10^{-6}$
0.573	0.00383	—	20	7	17	—	T	U	0	$2.712040 \cdot 10^{-6}$
0.404	0.00383	—	20	7	17	—	T	U	1	$3.473870 \cdot 10^{-6}$
0.570	0.00383	—	20	7	17	—	T	U	0	$3.621860 \cdot 10^{-6}$
0.424	0.00383	—	20	7	17	—	T	D	0	$4.720930 \cdot 10^{-6}$
0.413	0.00383	—	20	7	17	—	T	U	0	$9.608950 \cdot 10^{-6}$
0.414	0.00383	—	20	7	17	—	T	U	0	$1.012210 \cdot 10^{-5}$
0.592	0.00383	—	20	7	19	—	T	U	0	$1.420130 \cdot 10^{-5}$
0.582	0.00383	—	20	7	19	—	T	U	0	$1.420130 \cdot 10^{-5}$
0.418	0.00383	—	20	7	17	—	T	U	0	$1.573790 \cdot 10^{-5}$
0.423	0.00383	—	20	7	17	—	T	U	0	$1.819870 \cdot 10^{-5}$
0.419	0.00383	—	20	7	17	—	T	U	0	$2.168210 \cdot 10^{-5}$
0.417	0.00383	—	20	7	19	—	T	U	0	$2.720590 \cdot 10^{-5}$
0.383	0.00383	—	20	7	17	—	T	U	0	$3.121010 \cdot 10^{-5}$
0.383	0.00383	—	20	7	17	—	T	U	0	$3.249550 \cdot 10^{-5}$
0.571	0.00383	—	20	7	20	—	T	U	0	$4.695690 \cdot 10^{-5}$
0.568	0.00383	—	20	7	17	—	T	U	0	$4.912150 \cdot 10^{-5}$
0.412	0.00383	—	20	7	17	—	T	U	0	$5.726070 \cdot 10^{-5}$
0.416	0.00383	—	20	7	19	—	T	U	0	$7.530270 \cdot 10^{-5}$
0.400	0.00383	—	20	7	20	—	T	U	0	$8.602180 \cdot 10^{-5}$
0.439	0.00383	—	20	7	19	—	T	U	0	$9.137410 \cdot 10^{-5}$
0.415	0.00383	—	20	7	19	—	T	U	0	$9.137410 \cdot 10^{-5}$
0.426	0.00383	—	20	7	17	—	T	U	0	$1.507170 \cdot 10^{-4}$
0.394	0.00383	—	20	7	17	—	T	U	0	$1.610950 \cdot 10^{-4}$
0.593	0.00383	—	20	7	19	—	T	U	0	$7.921950 \cdot 10^{-4}$
0.558	0.00383	—	20	7	17	—	T	U	0	$1.032500 \cdot 10^{-3}$
0.586	0.00383	—	20	7	19	—	T	U	0	$1.736870 \cdot 10^{-3}$
0.424	0.00383	1.330	20	7	17	—	R	U	0	$4.471430 \cdot 10^{-2}$
0.552	0.00383	—	20	7	17	—	M	U	0	$1.720780 \cdot 10^{-1}$

Notice that the fitness of the best genetic algorithm has improved by six orders of magnitude in comparison with the best algorithm evolved by the first experiment. The mutation rate has converged completely, with a final value $p_m = 0.00383$. The fact that p_m is about twice as large as for the first experiment can well be explained by considering the selective pressure. A (7,17)-tournament selection with $q = 20$ is practically identical with $(1,17)$-selection (the selection probability p_1 of the best individual amounts to $p_1 = 0.9542$; see [2]). The resulting strong selective pressure implies an increasing optimal mutation rate and a much larger convergence velocity.

As a consequence of the strong selective pressure, recombination does not play an important role for the evolved genetic algorithms. The predominance of uniform crossover in the population is caused by chance.

3.3 Verification of Results

In order to check the results with a better statistical significance than is afforded with only two runs, the best genetic algorithms obtained from both experiments were also evaluated by running them for $N = 100$ independent experiments and averaging the data. The resulting algorithms $GA_{(1)}$ (first row of the right part of table 1) and $GA_{(2)}$ (first row of table 2) are compared with a "standard" GA ($p_m = 0.001$, $p_c = 0.6$, $\mu = \lambda = 50$, two-point crossover, proportional selection) and the meta-evolution results (from tables 1 and 2) in table 3.

Table 3.: Average final best objective function values from $N = 100$ independent experiments, compared to the corresponding meta-evolution results (from 2 experiments). V_{min} denotes the standard deviation of the results.

Experiment	$\bar{f}_{min}$	V_{min}	Meta-EA, f_{min}
$GA_{(1)}$	$2.331 \cdot 10^0$	$3.328 \cdot 10^0$	$3.924 \cdot 10^0$
$GA_{(2)}$	$7.312 \cdot 10^{-5}$	$1.730 \cdot 10^{-4}$	$2.164 \cdot 10^{-6}$
Standard-GA	$1.032 \cdot 10^2$	$8.289 \cdot 10^1$	—

The mass runs confirm the general quality assessment as obtained from the meta-evolution experiment. It is also interesting to observe that the performance of a standard GA is improved by two orders of magnitude by fine-tuning its parameters with a meta-evolution approach.

4 Conclusions

The meta-algorithm itself, a hybrid of genetic algorithms and evolution strategies, clearly demonstrated its principal effectiveness to tackle mixed-integer optimization problems. As a natural extension of this hybrid, the self-adaptation mechanism can also be applied to the mutation rate(s) of discrete parameters.

Concerning the evolved genetic algorithms, the results on optimal mutation rates and the interaction between selective pressure and optimal mutation rate

[7, 1, 15] are well confirmed by the meta-evolution experiment. This is possible because the continuous parameters (such as p_m) are evolved by evolution strategy methods, such that an arbitrary fine-tuning of parameter values is facilitated.

In the experiments reported here, evolution of convergence velocity was achieved by simply evaluating the slave algorithms according to their potential for improvement within a limited number of function evaluations. Even more interesting, however, is the problem to find parameter settings which favour convergence reliability. The design of an appropriate fitness function to measure convergence reliability of an algorithm is a problem which seems to require the evaluation of a large number of runs in order to obtain a frequency distribution of runs over local optima. Such an approach might be worthwhile due to the fact that almost no empirical knowledge is currently available to guide the search for parameterizations that support convergence reliability.

Acknowledgements

The author gratefully acknowledges support by the DFG (Deutsche Forschungsgemeinschaft), grant Schw 361/5-2.

References

1. Th. Bäck. The interaction of mutation rate, selection, and self-adaptation within a genetic algorithm. In Männer and Manderick [14], pages 85–94.
2. Th. Bäck. Selective pressure in evolutionary algorithms: A characterization of selection mechanisms. In *Proceedings of the IEEE International Conference on Evolutionary Computation*, 1994.
3. Th. Bäck and F. Hoffmeister. Extended selection mechanisms in genetic algorithms. In Belew and Booker [6], pages 92–99.
4. Th. Bäck and H.-P. Schwefel. An overview of evolutionary algorithms for parameter optimization. *Evolutionary Computation*, 1(1):1–23, 1993.
5. J. E. Baker. Adaptive selection methods for genetic algorithms. In J. J. Grefenstette, editor, *Proceedings of the 1st International Conference on Genetic Algorithms and Their Applications*, pages 101–111. Lawrence Erlbaum Associates, Hillsdale, NJ, 1985.
6. R. K. Belew and L. B. Booker, editors. *Proceedings of the 4th International Conference on Genetic Algorithms*. Morgan Kaufmann Publishers, San Mateo, CA, 1991.
7. H. J. Bremermann. The evolution of intelligence: The nervous system as a model of its environment. Technical Report 1, Contract No. 477(17), Department of Mathematics, University of Washington, Seattle, July 1958.
8. B. Freisleben and M. Härtfelder. Optimization of genetic algorithms by genetic algorithms. In R. F. Albrecht, C. R. Reeves, and N. C. Steele, editors, *Artificial Neural Nets and Genetic Algorithms*, pages 392–399. Springer, Wien, 1993.
9. D. E. Goldberg. *Genetic algorithms in search, optimization and machine learning.* Addison Wesley, Reading, MA, 1989.

10. D. E. Goldberg and K. Deb. A comparative analysis of selection schemes used in genetic algorithms. In Rawlins [16], pages 69–93.

11. J. J. Grefenstette. Optimization of control parameters for genetic algorithms. *IEEE Transactions on Systems, Man and Cybernetics*, SMC–16(1):122–128, 1986.

12. W. E. Hart and R. K. Belew. Optimizing an arbitrary function is hard for the genetic algorithm. In Belew and Booker [6], pages 190–195.

13. K. A. De Jong. *An analysis of the behaviour of a class of genetic adaptive systems*. PhD thesis, University of Michigan, 1975. Diss. Abstr. Int. 36(10), 5140B, University Microfilms No. 76–9381.

14. R. Männer and B. Manderick, editors. *Parallel Problem Solving from Nature 2*. Elsevier, Amsterdam, 1992.

15. H. Mühlenbein. How genetic algorithms really work: I. mutation and hillclimbing. In Männer and Manderick [14], pages 15–25.

16. G. J. E. Rawlins, editor. *Foundations of Genetic Algorithms*. Morgan Kaufmann Publishers, San Mateo, CA, 1991.

17. J. D. Schaffer, editor. *Proceedings of the 3rd International Conference on Genetic Algorithms*. Morgan Kaufmann Publishers, San Mateo, CA, 1989.

18. J. D. Schaffer, R. A. Caruana, L. J. Eshelman, and R. Das. A study of control parameters affecting online performance of genetic algorithms for function optimization. In Schaffer [17], pages 51–60.

19. J. D. Schaffer and L. J. Eshelman. On crossover as an evolutionary viable strategy. In Belew and Booker [6], pages 61–68.

20. H.-P. Schwefel. *Numerical Optimization of Computer Models*. Wiley, Chichester, 1981.

21. G. Syswerda. Uniform crossover in genetic algorithms. In Schaffer [17], pages 2–9.

22. A. H. Wright. Genetic algorithms for real parameter optimization. In Rawlins [16], pages 205–218.

Parallel Simulated Annealing and Genetic Algorithms: a Space of Hybrid Methods

Hao Chen & Nicholas S. Flann[1]

Department of Computer Science,
Utah State University,
Logan, UT 84322-4205, U.S.A. flann@nick.cs.usu.edu

Abstract. Simulated annealing and genetic algorithms represent powerful optimization methods with complementary strengths and weaknesses. Hence, there is an interest in identifying hybrid methods (which combine features of both SA and GA) that exhibit performance superior than either method alone. This paper introduces a systematic approach to identifying these hybrids by defining a space of methods as a nondeterministic generating grammar. This space includes SA, GA, previously introduced hybrids and many new methods. An empirical evaluation has been completed for 14 methods from this space applied to 9 diverse optimization problems. Results demonstrate that the space contains promising new methods. In particular, a new method that combines the recombinative power of GAs and annealing schedule of SA is shown to be one of the best methods for all 9 optimization problems explored.

1   Introduction

Simulated annealing (SA) and genetic algorithms (GA) are naturally motivated, general purpose optimization methods that share many similarities. Both methods require little knowledge of the problem to be optimized other than a fitness or cost function. The two techniques initially begin search with random points in the solution space then incrementally generate new points by applying operators. Which points are pursued is controlled by a probablistic decision procedure that guides the method into optimal regions of the solution space.

Although similar, there are some important differences between the two methods. First, SA possess a formal proof of convergence to the global optima, which GA does not have [Ru94]. This convergence proof relies on a very slow cooling schedule of $T_i = \frac{T_0}{\log i}$, where i is bound by the number of iterations [InRo92]. While this cooling schedule is impractical, it identifies a useful trade-off where longer cooling schedules tend to lead to better quality solutions. There is no such control parameter in GA and premature convergence is a significant problem.

Second, GA maintains a population of candidate solutions while SA maintains only one solution. This has many significant impacts on how the solution space is searched. GA can retain useful redundant information about what it has learned from previous search by its representation of schemata or alleles [Jon75] in the individual solutions. These schemata capture critical components of past good solutions, which can be combined together via crossover to form high quality solutions. SA, on the other hand, retains only one solution in the space and exploration is limited to the immediate neighborhood.

Third, SA accepts newly generated solutions probablisticly based on their fitness and only accepts inferior solutions some of the time. This is in contrast to GA, that always accepts new solutions even if they are significantly inferior to older solutions. This characteristic can lead to *disruption*, where good solutions or good schematas are lost or damaged, preventing optimal performance.

Finally, and most significantly, GA is naturally parallel and can easily be adapted to run on massively parallel computers [FoHu91], while SA is an inherently serial algorithm and attempts to parallelize it have lead to relatively small speedups [AaKo89], [Gre90]. Moreover, GA has the potential to exhibit super-linear speedup due to *implicit parallelism* [Hol75] [MG92] caused by the processing of schemata in the solution population.

It is clear from this brief review that GA and SA have complementary strengths and weaknesses. While GA exhibits implicit parallelism and can exploit massively parallel architectures, it suffers from disruption and poor convergence properties. SA, on the other hand, has good convergence properties and is somewhat immune to disruption, but it cannot easily exploit either explicit or implicit parallelism.

A significant task then is to identify *hybrid methods* that combine the strengths of SA and GA, while overcoming the weaknesses. This paper presents a methodology for identifying such hybrids. A space of methods is introduced that contains both SA, GA, existing hybrid methods and new, previously unexplored methods. This space is characterized by viewing SA and GA as special cases of a generic probablistic search method that processes a population of solutions. This generic method comprises of repeated iterations on a population P_i. First, population *modification* is done, where P_i is mapped to a new population $\overline{P_i}$ through the application of operators. Then *control* is applied and a the next population P_{i+1} is formed from P_i and $\overline{P_i}$ based on the fitness of the individuals. The process repeats for some finite number of steps, then the best individual found is output. When the operators are crossover followed by low probability mutation, and the control is selection, we have a standard genetic algorithm [Jon75]. When the neighborhood operator is used and control chooses individuals from P_i or $\overline{P_i}$ based on the Metropolis criteria, we have SA (standard when the population is one, parallel independent when greater than one [HCH91]).

This paper first defines this space of methods as a non-deterministic grammar, where each sentence is a method that describes a unique combinations of population modification and control. Here, 14 simple methods in the space are identified as potentially interesting and described in more detail. Next, a brief review of previous hybrid methods is included, with particular attention given to those methods that are easily described in the space. An empirical study is performed next to determine how well these 14 methods perform on a standard test bed of problems. The paper concludes with an analysis of the results and some identified problems for further study.

2   A Space of Methods

Let P_i represent a population of n individual solutions at iteration i of the method. Each individual solution is denoted $s_{i,j}$, where $1 \leq j \leq n$. A method is defined as some set of *Operators* $\Rightarrow$ *Control*, where *Operators* is some set of operators that map P_i to a new population $\overline{P_i}$ and *Control* is some set of control strategies that produce the next population P_{i+1} from P_i and $\overline{P_i}$. In the fields of SA and GA many varieties of operators and controls have been developed. For this introductory study we choose three operators:

Neighborhood operator N, is used in SA applications where a small, reversable change is made in $s_{i,j}$ to produce $\overline{s_{i,j}}$. In binary string representations, this change involves some small number of bits that are flipped.

Crossover operator plus mutation operator XM, is used in standard GA applications where two individuals $s_{i,j}$ and $s_{i,k}$ are "crossed" to produce two new individuals $\overline{s_{i,j}}$ and $\overline{s_{i,k}}$ such that both new individuals contain some complementary proportion of $s_{i,j}$ and $s_{i,k}$. Then a mutation is performed, usually some small number of bits are flipped with low probability.

Macro Operator XMN is a combination of XM followed by N.

Only two control strategies are explored here:

Selection Control: S, is used in standard GA applications where each member of the population $\overline{s_{i,j}} \in \overline{P_i}$, is evaluated by the fitness function f and selected to be part of the new population P_{i+1} with probability $p_j = f(s_{i,j})/\sum_{k=1}^{n} f(s_{i,k})$.

Temperature Control: T, is used in SA applications with the operator N. In this case a tournament is held between the original individual $s_{i,j}$ and the modified individual $\overline{s_{i,j}}$. First both are evaluated by using f then $\overline{s_{i,j}}$ is selected to be part of the new population P_{i+1} with probability $p_j = e^{\Delta f/T_i}$, where $\Delta f = f(\overline{s_{i,j}}) - f(s_{i,j})$ and T_i is the current temperature. If $\overline{s_{i,j}}$ is not selected, then $s_{i,j}$ is selected.

When the operator is XM or XMN the process is different, since we have two parent individuals and two children. Here we hold 2 tournaments as above, one between $s_{i,j}$ and $\overline{s_{i,j}}$ and the other between $s_{i,k}$ and $\overline{s_{i,k}}$. This technique is described in [MG92].

Using this notation, it is easy to describe the standard method SA as $N \Rightarrow T$, and standard GA as $XM \Rightarrow S$. By trying different combinations, other hybrid methods are easily described. Below 14 simple combinations are enumerated. Where a set is given, such as in $N \Rightarrow T, S$ a non-deterministic choice is intended. Hence, in this method a neighborhood operator is always used, but the new population is produced by choosing either selection S or temperature T. Clearly, this notation is capable of representing and hence generating many possible hybrid methods. This study has focussed on these 14 methods because they are simple and closely related to our original methods.

Temperature Control	Selection Control	Mixed Control
$N \Rightarrow T$	$N \Rightarrow S$	$N \Rightarrow T, S$
$XM \Rightarrow T$	$XM \Rightarrow S$	$XM \Rightarrow T, S$
$XMN \Rightarrow T$	$XMN \Rightarrow S$	$N, XM \Rightarrow T, S$
$XM, N \Rightarrow T$	$XM, N \Rightarrow S$	$N \Rightarrow T, XM \Rightarrow S$
		$N \Rightarrow S, XM \Rightarrow T$
		$XMN \Rightarrow T, S$

There are some hybrids in this space that have been previously introduced and studied. The first method $N \Rightarrow T$ is simply multiple independent runs of SA described in [HCH91] and analyzed in [Sti93]. Of particular interest is $XMN \Rightarrow T$, introduced in [MG92]. This method is known as Parallel recombinative simulated annealing since it only uses temperature for control, but employs both operators as a macro, first performing crossover then a neighborhood operator. Here, the affect of the neighborhood operator was dynamically controlled by temperature; at high temperatures more bits where changed than at low temperatures. A proof is included in [MG92] that demonstrated the method retains the global convergence properties of SA. Also included was a small empirical study that showed the method exhibited good scale-up performance with increased population size, although no comparison was done with SA or GA.

Another existing hybrid method occurs in the space, $N \Rightarrow T, S$ described in [BEE87]. Here, a simultaneous set of running SA algorithms was modified so that selection was periodically used on the population. The authors reported significant improvement compared to standard SA on TSP problems. There have been other hybrids introduced that are not easily included in this space. Of interest is the work by [EAV91] that introduces a generic method similar this one and shows that SA can be viewed as a special case of GA with population size 1 where the only operator is mutation. In [VAL92] a space of hybrid methods is defined as a template where different modules can be inserted producing different methods. In [SiWe87] a genetic operator is described that includes a temperature dependent mutation rate. In [BHS89] a hybrid method that performs a full schedule of SA for each iteration of GA is described. In [LKH91] SA and GA are used in sequence. Here, the initial population for GA is formed by first applying SA to increase its average fitness. In [Gol90] Boltzmann selection is introduced where temperature is used to select the outcome of crossover operators (via a logical acceptance rule), while maintaining a Boltzmann distribution in the population. With the exception of [MG92], none of these previous hybrid methods duplicated SA guaranteed asymptotic convergence, due partly to their obvious complexity. In contrast, many of the hybrids in the space of methods introduced here can be shown to retain the convergence properties of SA. This can be done by adapting the reduction proof included in [MG92]. Such methods include $XM \Rightarrow T$, $XMN \Rightarrow T$ and $XM, N \Rightarrow T$. Methods involving selection are more difficult to analyze.

Now that the space of methods have been introduced and 14 hybrids identified as potentially interesting, an empirical study is described that measures how these methods do in practice on real optimization problems.

3 Experimental Study

The 14 selected methods were implemented and tested on a collection of bench-mark problems. The primary goal of these experiments was to gain insights into *how* well the hybrid methods performed, compared to the standard methods, and to understand *why* such improvements occur. The nature of the space of methods helps in answering this latter question, since many methods vary only by the addition or removal of a control strategy or operator. When a difference in performance is noted between such similar methods, the difference in operator or control can provide an explanation.

The methods were implemented by first implementing the generic method, then instantiating it with different operator and control parameters. To ease coding, all experiments where performed using a modified verion of GENEsYs [Bäck91] running on HP 700 workstations.

The set of optimization problems used in this test are given in Table 1. This set was chosen so as to represent a diversity of different kinds of problems and because it is familiar to the research community. Function f_1–f_5 were used by De Jong in his Ph.D dissertation [Jon75]. The last function, f_{10} is Krolak's 100 city TSP problem, a very difficult optimization problem with many local minima. All these functions differ from each other in some distinct characteristics. The size of the problem set was chosen so as to increase confidence that the results obtained would be both general and unbiased.

Table 1. The 9 optimization problems used for the empirical study.

f_i	Citation	n	Bits	Description	Function
f_1	[Jon75]	30	960	Sphere Model	$f_1(\mathbf{x}) = \sum_{i=1}^{n} x_i^2$
f_2	[Jon75]	2	64	Rosenbrook's	$f_2(\mathbf{x}) = \sum_{i=1}^{n-1}\left(100 \cdot (x_{i+1} - x_i^2)^2 + (x_i - 1)^2\right)$
f_3	[Jon75]	5	160	Step	$f_3(\mathbf{x}) = 6 \cdot n + \sum_{i=1}^{n} \lfloor x_i \rfloor$
f_4	[Jon75]	30	960	Quartic + noise	$f_4(\mathbf{x}) = \sum_{i=1}^{n} i x_i^4 + \text{gauss}(0,1)$
f_5	[Jon75]	2	64	Shekek's Foxholes	$\frac{1}{f_5(\mathbf{x})} = \frac{1}{K} + \sum_{j=1}^{25} \frac{1}{c_j + \sum_{i=1}^{2}(x_i - a_{ij})^6}$
f_6	[Sch81]	20	640	Schwefel's	$f_6(\mathbf{x}) = \sum_{i=1}^{n}\left(\sum_{j=1}^{i} x_j\right)^2 = x^{\mathrm{T}} \mathbf{A} x + b^{\mathrm{T}} x$
f_7	[TöŽi89]	20	640	Rastrigin's	$f_7(\mathbf{x}) = nA + \sum_{i=1}^{n} x_i^2 - A\cos(\omega x_i)$
f_8	[HB91]	30	960	f_1 Changing	$f_8(\mathbf{x}(t)) = \begin{cases} \sum_{i=1}^{n} x_i^2(t) & : \quad t \bmod a \text{ even} \\ \sum_{i=1}^{n}(x_i - b)^2 & : \quad t \bmod a \text{ odd} \end{cases}$
f_{10}	[KFM71]	100	3200	Krolak's 100 TSP	$f_{10}(\mathbf{x}) = \sum_{i=1}^{n} d\big(c_{\pi(i \bmod n)}, c_{\pi((i+1) \bmod n)}\big)$

It is known that both GA and SA are sensitive to fine-tunning of their parameters and it is likely that the hybrid methods are equally sensitive. In this experiment, all the parameters were set either by employing established techniques or employing established values, which have been published. To make the comparison fair, it as decided that the same values or techniques would be used for each method and problem. It is acknowledged that individual improvements may be possible when parameters are specially tuned for each case. The parameters were set as follows:

Termination Criteria: The number of function evaluations for each method was fixed at 5×10^3 for functions f_1–f_8 and 2×10^5 for f_{10}.

Crossover and Mutation XM: Standard two point crossover was used with a crossover probability of 0.72 followed by a bit mutation rate of 0.001.

Neighborhood operator N: The neighborhood operator was defined as a bit mutation where the probability of flipping a bit set at 0.1. Hence, approximately a $\frac{1}{10}$ th of the bits of the encoded string are flipped by each application of the neighborhood operator.

Selection S: Proportional selection with full replacement was used.

Annealing Schedule T: Techniques introduced in [Coh-91] were used to set the initial temperature in a problem dependent way. Here, 1000 operators are applied starting from a randomly generated population and the average uphill cost was computed. The initial temperature is then set such that the initial acceptance probability for an uphill move is 0.95. The final temperature was determined similarly, with the acceptance probability of an uphill move set at 10^{-8}. Temperature was then lowered every n function evaluations, where n was set to equal the population size. The cooling schedule was geometric, where $T_{i+1} = \alpha T_i$ and α set such that the final temperature was reached after the allowed number of function evaluations had been performed.

Population Sizes: Since it is known that GA is sensitive to the population size, a diversity of sizes was used: 6, 12, 24, 50, 100, 150 and 200. Principal results are reported for a population of 50.

4 Analysis of Results

The results of this empirical study is illustrated in Figure 1 and Figure 2. In Figure 1(a) several interesting observations can be made. First, it clear that some methods such as $N \Rightarrow T$; $XM \Rightarrow T$ and $XM, N \Rightarrow T$ are very effective at all problems, while other methods such as $N \Rightarrow S$; $XMN \Rightarrow S$ and $XM, N \Rightarrow S$ are completely ineffective. Second, some problems appear easier to solve than others. For both f_2 and f_5, most methods produce a reasonable solution within the limited number of function evaluations allowed. In contrast, problem f_{10} proved difficult for most methods, with all but $XM \Rightarrow T$ and $XM, N \Rightarrow T$ hardly making any progress in producing a better than random solution in the allocated 2×10^5 function evaluations.

Considering the other cases, where methods perform neither best or worst, it is clear that an understanding can only be gained through careful analysis of both the problem and method. It is here that the space of methods provides an ideal platform for understanding how various operators and control strategies behave and interact. Consider method $XMN \Rightarrow T$ and $XMN \Rightarrow S$, where the only difference is that the former uses temperature control while the latter uses selection control. However, the difference in their performance is stunning, with the method that uses temperature control out performing the one with selection significantly for all problems. It is clear then, that the operator XMN works better in combination with temperature control, rather than selection.

Figure 1(b) shows the top three performing methods for each optimization problem. Note that almost all methods that incorporate temperature either alone, or in combination with selection behaves reasonably well. On the other hand, all methods that uses just selection behave poorly. It becomes more clear when we categorized the methods into three groups, each with a different control strategy, as illustrated in Figure 2. In this case, it is shown that temperature is more effective in general than selection. However, before we eliminate selection as a viable control technique, it must be pointed out that this study has only considered proportional selection and many other more effective selection schemes exists [Gol89].

Among the methods that are shown to be most effective are known methods such as $N \Rightarrow T$[HCH91] and $XMN \Rightarrow T$[MG92]. Of more interest are new methods such as $XM, N \Rightarrow T$ which differs from $XMN \Rightarrow T$ in that the operator is chosed non-deterministically from XM, or N. However, the most interesting result is the impressive behavior exhibited by another new method $XM \Rightarrow T$ that incorporates GA's recombinative power and SA's annealing schedule. Figure 1(b) shows the method finished first on all problems.

Why is the hybrid method $XM \Rightarrow T$ more effective than SA or GA? Many factors contributes to the effectiveness of this method. First, consider a major criticism of GA: the problem of premature convergence. This problem is caused by the loss of genetic diversity, which in turn is caused by oversampling in the selection process. In contrast, when temperature is used as a control instead of selection, a high level of genetic diversity is maintained since no oversampling is performed, yet sufficient control is still present to ensure convergence. Second, consider a major criticism of SA: the problem of slow convergence due to excess function evaluations. Many of these function evaluations are caused by the disruptive behavior of the neighborhood operator which generates many candidates that are rejected. When crossover is used in place of the neighborhood operator, less disruption is caused because new solutions combine parts of existing solutions, resulting in less wasted function evaluations. Furthermore, choosing the crossover operator enables $XM \Rightarrow T$ to inherit the recombinative power of GA so that better solutions can be formed by combining good partial solutions. As a result, the new method formed overcomes significant problems with both GA and SA while inheriting their effective features.

5   Conclusions

The search for superior hybrid methods is motivated by the complementary nature of the strengths and weaknesses of SA and GA. Many previous attempts have produced complex, ad hoc hybrids that are difficult to evaluate and understand (with exception of [MG92]). This paper has taken a different approach by first generalizing the commonalities of SA and GA to produce a generic method, of which SA and GA are special cases. Next, a combinatorial space of methods was identified that represents numerous related hybrid methods. This space then enables a systematic search to be made for useful hybrids.

Fourteen simple methods were identified in the space that are closely related to both SA and GA and an empirical study was performed. In analyzing the results, two principal conclusions can be drawn. First, it was clear that a new hybrid, $XM \Rightarrow T$, when applied to the 9 optimization problems, is superior to all other methods including SA and GA in performance and robustness. Second, the methodology of employing a generative space of methods is very useful in understanding how characteristics of a method affect its performance. For example, when two methods differ by only one characteristic, such as the choice of temperature or selection, it is easy to explain observed differences in performance by known differences in characteristics.

This paper has performed a limited preliminary study of the method space, using only 3 operators and 2 controls. However, this space can easily be extend by introducing new operators and new controls. Hence, the principal contribution here is a *methodology* for generating and studying hybrid SA and GA methods.

References

[AaKo89] Aarts E., & Korst, J. (1989). *Simulated Annealing and Boltzmann Machines: A stochastic approach to Combinatorial Optimization and Neural Computing.* Wiley, Chichester.

[Bäck91] Thomas Bäck (1991). A User's Guide to GENEsYs *University of Dortmund Department of Computer Science Systems Analysis Research Group P.O. Box 50 05 00 D-4600 Dortmund 50 July 1st, 1992*

[BEE87] Boseniuk T., Ebeling W. and Engel A. (1987). Boltsmann and darwin strategies in complex optimization, in *Physics Letters A*, Vol. 125 (6.7).

[BE88] Boseniuk T., and Ebeling W. (1988). Optimization of NP-complete problems by Boltzmann-Darwin strategies including life-cycles. *Europhysics Letters, 6(2)* 107 − −112.

[BE91] Boseniuk T., and Ebeling W. (1991). Boltzmann-, Darwin-, and Haeckel-strategies in optimization problems. *Lecture Notes in Computer Science: Parallel Problem Solving from Nature, 496*, pp. 430-444.

[BHS89] Brown, D. E., Huntley C. L and Spillane A. R. (1989). A parallel genetic heuristic for the quadratic assignment problem. *Proceedings of the Third International Conference on Genetic Algorithms*, pp. 406-415.

[Coh-91] James P. Cohoon, Shailesh U. Hegde, Worthy N. Martin, and Dana S. Richards. Distributed Genetic Algorithms for the Floorplan Design Problem *IEEE Trans. on Computer Aided Design, Vol 10, No. 4, April 1991*, pp. 483-491

[EAV91] Eiben A. E., Aarts E. H. L. and Van Hee K. M. (1991). Global Convergence of genetic algorithms: a Markov chain analysis. *Lecture Notes in Computer Science: Parallel Problem Solving from Nature, 496, 4-12.*

[FoHu91] Fogarty T. C. and Huang R. (1991) Implementing the genetic algorithm on transcomputer based parallel processing systems. In *Lecture Notes in Computer Science: Parallel Problem Solving from Nature*, pp. 145-149.

[Gol89] Goldberg D. E. (1989) *Genetic Algorithms in Search, Optimization & Machine Learning.* Addison-Wesley Publishing Company, Inc. 1989

[Gol90] Goldberg D. E. (1990). A note on Boltzman tournament selection for genetic algorithms and population-oriented simulated annealing. *Complex Systems*, 4, 445 − 460.

[Gre90] Green D. R. (1990). Parallel Simulated Annealing Techniques. *Physica* D 42 293–306.

[HB91] Hoffmeister F. and Bäck T. (1991). Genetic self-learning. In *Proceedings of the First European Conference on Artificial Life, December 11-13*, Paris, France, 1991. MIT Press.

[HCH91] Hoffmann, K. H., Christoph, M. & Hanf, M. (1991). Optimizing simulated annealing. *Lecture Notes in Computer Science: Parallel Problem Solving from Nature, 496*, pp. 221–225.

[Hol75] Holland, J. H. *Adaptation in natural and artificial systems,* Cambridge: MIT Press.

[InRo92] Ingber L. and Rosen B. (1992). Genetic algorithms and very fast simulated reannealing: A comparison. in *Mathematical Computer Modeling*, Vol. 16. Noo. 11. pp. 87–100.

[Jon75] De Jong K. (1975). *An analysis of the behavior of a class of genetic adaptive systems*, PhD. thesis, University of Michigan, 1975. Diss. Abstr. Int. 36(10), 5140B, University Microfilms No. 76-9381.

[KFM71] Krolark P., Felts W. & Marble G. (1971). A man-machine approach to solving the traveling salesman problem. *Communications of the ACM*, 14(4) : 327 − −224.

[LKH91] Lin F. T., Kao C. Y. & Hsu C. C. (1991). Incorporating genetic algorithms into simulated annealing. *Proceedings of the Fourth International Symposium on Artificial Intelligence, 290-297*.

[MG92] Mahfoud S. W. and Goldberg D. E. (1992). Parallel recombinative simulated annealing: A genetic algorithm, in *IlliGAL Report No. 92002*.

[Ru94] Rudolph G. (1994). Convergence properties of canonical genetic algorithms, in *IEEE Transactions on Neural Networks 5 (1)* pp. 96–101, 1994.

[Sch81] Schwefel H. P. (1981). *Numerical Optimization of Computer Models*, Wiley, Chichester, 1981.

[SiWe87] Sirag D. J. and Weisser P. T. (1987). Towards a unified thermodynamic genetic operator. *Genetic algorithms and their applications: Proceedings of the Second International Conference on Genetic Algorithms, 116-122*.

[Sti93] Stiles G. S. (1993). On the Speedup of Simultaneously executed randomized algorithms, in *IEEE Transactions on Parallel and Distributed Systems*, 1993.

[TöŽi89] Törn A. and Žilinskas A., 1989. *Global Optimization*, Volume 350 of *Lecture Notes in Computer Science*. Springer, Berlin, 1989.

[VAL92] Vaessens, Aarts & Lenstra (1992). A local search template, in *Parallel Problem Solving from Nature 2*, North Holland, pp. 65–74.

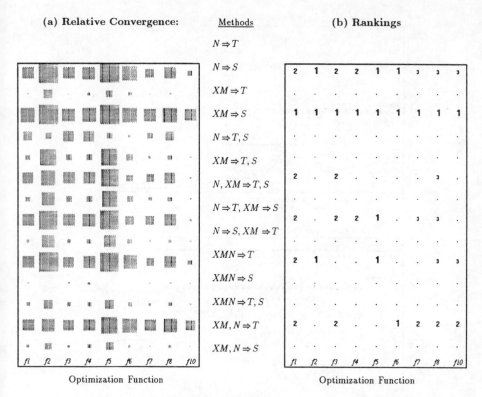

(a) Relative Convergence: Methods   (b) Rankings

Optimization Function   Optimization Function

Fig. 1. Summary of results applying 14 hybrid methods to 9 benchmark function optimization problems. Population size was fixed at 50 individuals. For each function and method, 30 randomized runs were performed and the results averaged. Each run was terminated after a fixed number of function evaluations: 5×10^3 function evaluations for $f1$ through $f8$ and $1 \times 2 \times 10^5$ function evaluations for $f10$. (a) Illustrates the relative convergence of each method applied to each function. The larger the square the closer the best-so-far solution is to the global optimal at termination. (b) Illustrates the best 3 methods for each function as measured by the closeness to the global optimal at termination. Note that some methods are assigned an equal ranking. This was done when their performance was not statistically distinguishable.

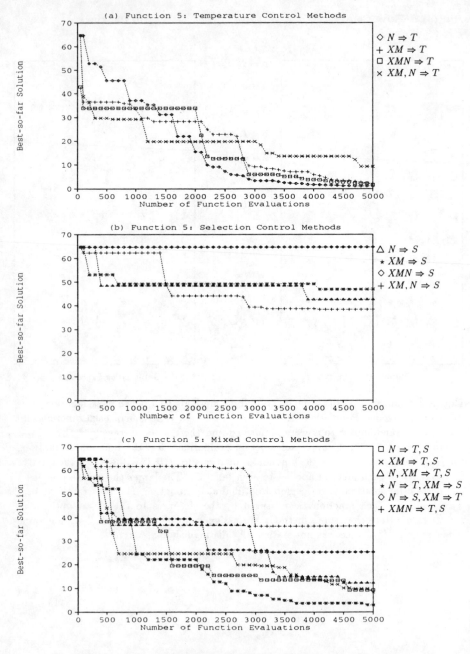

Fig. 2. The best-so-far solution found as the number of function evaluations increases from 50 to 5×10^3 for all 14 methods for $f5$ (Shekel's Foxholes). Population size was fixed at 50 individuals. All runs were repeated 30 times and the results averaged. (a) Illustrates the 4 methods that use only temperature as a control. (b) Illustrates the 4 methods that use only selection as a control. (c) Illustrates the 6 methods that non-deterministicly choose between temperature and selection as control.

Evolutionary Algorithms
for Neural Networks

ENZO-M – A Hybrid Approach for Optimizing Neural Networks by Evolution and Learning

Heinrich Braun and Peter Zagorski

Institute for Logic, Complexity and deductive Systems,
University of Karlsruhe, D-76128 Karlsruhe, Germany,
Internet: braun@ira.uka.de, Tel.: +49-721-608-4211

Abstract. ENZO-M combines two successful search techniques using two different timescales: *learning* (gradient descent) for finetuning of each offspring and *evolution* for coarse optimization steps of the network topology. Therefore, our evolutionary algorithm is a metaheuristic based on the *best* available local heuristic. Through training each offspring by fast gradient methods the search space of our evolutionary algorithm is considerably reduced to the set of local optima.

Using the parental weights for initializing the weights of each offspring both the gradient descent (learning) is speeded up by 1-2 orders of magnitude and the expected value of the local minimum (fitness of the trained offspring) is far above the mean value for randomly initialized offsprings. Thus, ENZO-M takes full advantage of both the knowledge transfer from the parental genstring using the evolutionary search and the efficiently computable gradient information using finetuning.

By the cooperation of the discrete mutation operator and the continuous weight decay method ENZO-M impressively thins out the topology of feedforward neural networks. Especially, ENZO-M also tries to cut off the connections to possibly redundant input units. Therefore ENZO-M not only supports the user in the network design but also recognizes redundant input units.

1 Introduction

Our evolutionary algorithm is a hybrid approach where the selection and reproduction correspond to a genetic algorithm but each offspring is tuned by an efficient local optimization heuristic, before its fitness is evaluated, i.e. in the outer evolutionary loop there is nested an inner optimization loop of the local heuristic. Therefore our approach can be characterized as a metaheuristic (the outer loop) using an efficient local optimization heuristic as a basic operator (the inner loop). By the way, we use the term "evolutionary algorithm", because our algorithm is neither a genetic algorithm [9] nor an evolutionary strategy [11], [16] or program [8], [7], but uses the same common paradigm. This approach has been also successfully applied for other difficult combinatorial optimization problems [1], [2].

For an efficient recombination respectively crossover operator it is crucial that the exchanged substrings (genes) have a similar semantic. Unfortunately, this is not achieved by the standard operators for the strong representation scheme due to the problem of permutable internal representations [4]. That is, two successfully trained networks may extract the same features and use the same internal neural representations in order to solve the given task, but distribute these internal representations in a totally different way among their hidden neurons, i.e. the contributions of the hidden neurons to the overall solution may be internally permuted. Therefore this problem is also referred to as the phenomenon of different structural mappings coding the same functional mapping.

In our former network evolution system ENZO [4], we presented a first successful solution for this problem by additionally optimizing the total connection length in a two dimensional layout. Although this approach was very promising, the global optimum obeying the additional optimization criteria will in general not be the global optimum for the original task, because long connections are avoided although they are sometimes useful. In order to clarify the effects and since the mutation operator is by itself sufficient for an efficient evolutionary search [7], [16] we omitted in ENZO-M the crossover operator and by that circumvented the above mentioned problem.

Additionally to ENZO we use short cut connections for the topology, a faster gradient heuristic RPROP [6] specially adapted to the evolutionary algorithm, weight decay methods for improving the generalization and a more sophisticated mutation operator. The reintroduction of the crossover operator is a current research issue and will be tackled in a forthcoming paper.

For evaluating the performance of our evolutionary approach we tested ENZO-M with three different kinds of applications: (1) three smaller benchmark problems for statistically significant evaluation of the impact our design decisions (a digit recognition problem, the T-C problem and the chess board problem), (2) a real world problem (the classification of medical data for a thyroid gland diagnosis [14], [13]) and (3) a hard touch stone where the best handcrafted network uses a (120-60-20-2-1)- topology with over 5600 connections (a scoring function for the two-player game *Nine Men's Morris* [3]). So at least the last one of them is much more complex than problems considered in publications on comparable topics so far.

2 Optimization of feedforward neural networks

There are two levels of optimization problems. The optimization of the connectivity (design problem) and the optimization of the weights (learning problem). In most applications the learning problem is solved by a gradient descent method, as e.g. backpropagation. But there are some demanding applications, which cannot be solved by gradient descent as e.g. recurrent neural networks. Since evolutionary algorithms use no gradient information, but only a measure for the behaviour (fitness) of each neural network, they can even handle such problems. On the other hand, they are inferior i.e. in particular computationally more expensive, when gradient heuristics already can solve the learning problem sufficiently well.

Evolutionary algorithms which are designed to solve the design problem, has to use a learning algorithm for evaluating the fitness of each offspring. As learning algorithm gradient descent can be used as well as evolutionary algorithms (see above). Since efficient gradient descent algorithms as RPROP [6] solve more efficiently the learning problem for feedforward networks we prefer to use gradient descent for this task. But instead of training the offspring from scratch we propose to use the weight matrix of the trained parent network for constructing the weight initialization. By that both learning is speeded up by 1-2 orders of magnitude and the expected fitness of the offspring is far above the average for its topology.

For the representation of the network there are two types of schemes used: strong and weak. The representation scheme is called strong, if the chromosome is a blueprint of the network i.e. every connection corresponds directly to a substring of the chromosome. Whereas the scheme is called weak, if the chromosome embeds just rules for constructing the network. Obviously, the latter seems to be biologically more plausible, since the natural chromosomes also do not describe the exact connectivity but only the coarse structure. But for most application oriented problems the networks are not so large, that the evolution of the coarse structure suffices. Rather a detailed specified solution is required. Therefore, we use in our approach a strong representation scheme, a linear representation of the matrix of the weights with additional control information for each connection (weight).

As optimization criterion any computable fitness function may be used, e.g.: Learning error, test set error (generalization capability), network size or a weighted sum of several single criteria. Additionally we want to remark that there may be a tradeoff between network size and generalization capability. Although it is widely believed that the smallest network solving the learning task have the best generalization capability, the contrary may be true (e.g. confer our experimental investigations or see [3]).

Moreover, there may be a tradeoff between the accuracy of the fitness function and its efficient computability. Especially, for optimizing the generalization capability as a measure for the expected error on untrained inputs it may be computationally expensive to average about all possible inputs. Therefore, a small, but representative test set has to be used instead. Using a test set can cause overfitting to the test set (*over-evolving* effect) similar to the well-known overfitting to the training set (*over-learning* effect), i.e. the generalization capability can deteriorate due to better fitting the test set caused by the selection pressure for the fitness criterion. In our experimental investigations (cf. section 4.2) we could indeed ascertain that fitting the test set is not the very same as improving the generalization capability, since the test set error decreased significantly faster than the overall error (i.e. the generalization capability). But we could not ascertain an increase of the overall error as an overfitting effect. Since every offspring is tuned only on the training set (totally disjunct from the test set) this possible overfitting on the evolutionary level is much more subtle (cf. fig. 4). Nevertheless, whenever this effect makes trouble, we can use a dynamically changing test set.

Finally, we want to add some remarks on the optimization of feedforward networks. The goal of our system is to provide a powerful design tool for a systematic search for highly optimized neural networks according to user defined specifications. Therefore, the user should be able to constrain the search by specifying both the maximal number of hidden layers and in each layer the maximal number of hidden units. We call the limiting case of this specification the 'maximal network'. Especially, that means the optimization task is to find an optimal subnetwork of this maximal network. This approach has two advantages. Firstly, although the represented neural networks may dynamically grow or shrink, a static representation scheme is possible by using a representation for the maximal network and enhancing the representation of each connection by an 'existing' bit. Secondly, the depth of the network is restricted (by the depth of the maximal network), which may guarantee a fast parallel evaluation.

Furthermore, our system ENZO-M handles networks with short cut connections since this does not slow down the parallel evaluation time but may significantly reduce the network complexity, e.g. the well-known XOR problem can be solved with 1 hidden neuron and 4 connections using short cuts instead of 2 hidden neurons and 6 connections without short cuts.

3 Our Evolutionary Approach

Every heuristic for searching the global optimum of difficult optimization problems has to handle the dilemma between exploration and exploitation. Priorizing the exploitation (as hill-climbing strategies do) bears the danger of getting stuck in a poor local optimum. On the other hand, full explorative search which guarantees to find the global optimum, uses vast computing power. Evolutionary algorithms avoid getting stuck in a local optimum by parallelizing the search using a population of search points (individuals) and by stochastic search steps, i.e. stochastic selection of the parents and stochastic generation of the offsprings (mutation, crossover). On the other hand, this explorative search is biased towards exploitation by biasing the selection of the parents preferring the fitter ones.

This approach has proven to be a very efficient tool for solving many difficult combinatorial optimization problems. A big advantage of this approach is its general applicability. There are only two problem dependent issues: The representation of the candidate solutions as a string (genstring = chromosome) and the computation of the fitness. Even though the choice of an adequate representation seems to be crucial for the efficiency of the evolutionary algorithm, it is obvious that in principle both conditions are fulfilled for every computable optimization problem.

On the other hand, this problem independence neglects problem dependent knowledge as e.g. gradient information. Therefore the pure use of evolutionary algorithms may have only modest results in comparison to other heuristics, which can exploit the additional information. For the problem of optimizing feedforward neural networks we can easily compute the gradient by backpropagation. Using a gradient descent algorithm we can tremendously diminish the search space by restricting the search to the set of local optima.

This hybrid approach uses two time scales. Each coarse step of the evolutionary algorithm is intertwined with a period of fine steps for the local optimization of the offspring. For this approach there seems to be biological evidence, since at least for higher animals nature uses the very same strategy: Before evaluating the fitness for mating, the offsprings undergo a longer period of fine tuning called learning.

Since the evolutionary algorithm uses the fine tuning heuristic as a subtask, we can call it a metaheuristic. Obviously, this metaheuristic is at least as successful as the underlying fine tuning heuristic, because the offsprings are optimized by that. Our experimental investigations will show, that the results of this metaheuristic are not only as good but impressively superior to the underlying heuristic. Furthermore, any improvement of the underlying fine tuning heuristic will improve the whole system. However, there is a tradeoff for the computing time of the local heuristic: more computing time for the local heuristic means less offsprings, as far as the overall computing time is fixed. Therefore we used the fastest gradient heuristic [6] and augmented it with the weight decay and weight elimination techniques in such a way that this augmentation did not augment the computation time unfavourably (e.g. less than double).

In the natural paradigm the genotype is an algorithmic description for developing the phenotype, which seems not to be an invertible process, i.e. it is not possible to use the improvements stemming from learning (fine tuning) for improving the genotype as Lamarck erroneously believed. In our application however, there is no difference between genotype and phenotype, because the matrix of weights, which determines the neural network, can be linearly noted and interpreted as a chromosome (genstring). In this case Lamarcks idea is fruitful, because the whole knowledge gained by learning in the fine tuning period can be transferred to the offsprings (Lamarckism). The strengths of our approach stem mainly from this effect in two ways: Firstly, since the topology of the offsprings is very similar to the topology of the parents, transferring the weights from the parents to the offsprings diminishes impressively the learning time by 1-2 orders of magnitude (in comparison to learning from the scratch with random starting weights). This also implies, that we can generate 1-2 orders of magnitude more offsprings in the same computation time.

Secondly, the average fitness of these offsprings is much higher: the fitness distribution for the training of a network topology with random initial weights will be more or less Gaussian distributed with a modest mean fitness value whereas starting near the parental weights (remind the topology of the offspring is similar but not the same as that of its parents) will result in a network with a fitness near the parental fitness (may be worse or better, cf. section ??). That means, whenever the parental fitness is well above the average fitness (respectively its topology) then the same may be expected for its offspring (in case using the parental weights). Moreover, our experiments have shown for the highly evolved "sparse" topologies that with random starting weights the gradient descent heuristic did not find an acceptable local optimum (solving the learning task), but only by inheriting the parental knowledge and initializing the weights near the parental weights.

Summarizing, our algorithm briefly works as follows (cf. fig. 1). Taking into account the user's specifications ENZO-M generates a population of different networks with a given connection density. Then the evolution cycle starts by selecting a parent, prefering the ones with a high fitness ranking in the current population and by generating an offspring as a mutated duplication of this parent. Each offspring is trained by the best available efficient gradient descent (RPROP [6]) heuristic using weight decay methods for better generalization. By removing negligible weights, trained offsprings may be pruned and then re-trained. Being evaluated an offspring is inserted into the sorted population according to its determined fitness value, thereby removing the last population element. Fitness values may incorporate any design criterion considered important for the given problem domain.

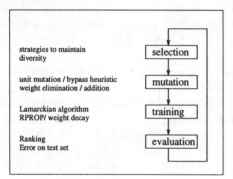

Fig. 1: Evolution cycle of ENZO-M

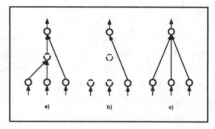

Fig. 2: Bypass algorithm: a) original network b) after deletion of the middle unit c) with added bypass connections

3.1 Mutation

Mutation is the only genetic operator used in ENZO-M. Therefore, we tried to enlarge its sphere of activity. Besides of the widely used link mutation we also realized unit mutation which is well suited to significantly change the network topology, allowing the evolutionary algorithm to explore the search space faster and more exhaustive. Our experiments show that unit mutation efficiently and reliably directs the search towards small architectures.

Within link mutation every connection can be changed by chance. There are two probabilities: p^+ to adding an absent connection and p^- for deleting an existing one. The evolutionary search can be influenced by varying the ratio of p^+ and p^- . Choosing $p^+ < p^-$ speeds-up network dilution leading to sparsely connected networks. On the other hand, the contrary setting $p^+ > p^-$ may be more favourable, since connections are also removed by the local heuristic through the weight decay and pruning operator (see section 3.2).

In contrast to link mutation, unit mutation has a strong impact on the network's performance. Thus we do not mutate each unit itself but change the number of active units by a small amount a. If a is negative, we randomly delete a units prefering units with few connections. Whereas, if a is positive, we insert a units fully connected by small random weights to the succeeding and preceding layers. Changing the number of active units avoids making destructive mutations by deleting a trained and inserting an untrained unit at the same time.

To improve our evolutionary algorithm we developed two heuristics which support unit mutation: the prefer-weak-units (PWU) strategy and the bypass algorithm. The idea behind the PWU-heuristic is to rank all hidden units of a network according to their relative connectivity ($\frac{act.connections}{max.connections}$) and to delete sparsely connected units with a higher probability than strongly connected ones. This strategy successfully complements other optimization techniques, like weight elimination, implemented in ENZO-M.

The bypass algorithm is the second heuristic we realized. As mentioned before, unit mutation is a large disruption of the network topology. So it seems sensible to alleviate the resulting effects. Adding a unit to a well trained network is not very crucial: if this new unit is not necessary, all weights from and to it will be adjusted in such a way, that the network performance is not affected by that unit.

Other than adding an unit, deletion of an unit can result in a network which is not able to learn the given training patterns. This can happen because there are too few hidden units to store the information available in the training set. But even if there are enough hidden units, deleting an unit can destroy important data paths within the network (fig. 2a and b). In opposite to addition of units and connections the effects of deletion can not be repaired by the training procedure. For that reason we restore deleted data paths before training by inserting bypass connections (fig. 2c).

The application of the bypass algorithm significantly increases the proportion of successful networks generated by unit mutation. Both the number of networks with devastated topologies decreases and the generated networks need less epochs to learn the training set, because they are not forced to simulate missing bypass connections by readjusting the weights of the remaining hidden units.

3.2 Training

To train our networks we use a modified gradient descent technique called weight elimination [17]. We add a penalty term accounting for the network complexity to the usual cost function. The new objective function ($E^* = TSS + \lambda * C$) is then optimized by RPROP, a very robust and fast gradient descent method [6]. After training, a part of network weights is close to zero and can be deleted. We delete all weights whose amounts are below a specific threshold (*pruning*). Thereafter the error produced by pruning is minimized by retraining.

The parameter λ is essential for the success of weight elimination. But there is not an universal λ value. Thus we have to adjust λ automatically. Unlike

Rumelhart et. al., we use a very fast algorithms to train the networks, and have only few epochs to find out a suitable λ value. Thus the heuristic to adjust λ recommended in [17] was further developed by adding a dynamic step size adaptation [18].

The heuristic is controlled by monitoring TSS. As long as TSS is sufficiently decreasing, λ as well as the step size $(\Delta\lambda)$ are increased. If λ exceeds its optimal value, as can be seen at TSS, the last growing step is withdrawn and we begin a new growing phase with a smaller $\Delta\lambda$ value.

Weight elimination and mutation cooperate in two ways. Firstly, by setting $p^+ > p^-$ link mutation can add more connections than delete. Thus important connections deleted by weight elimination get a second chance. Secondly, weight elimination is not well appropriate to delete units. This part can be done by unit mutation.

4 Results

We evaluated ENZO-M in two ways. On the one hand, we investigated the impact of our design decisions on small benchmark problems in order to allow a significant statistical evaluation: the effect of Lamarckism (by inheriting parental weights), the overfitting effect (evaluated by meta-cross-validation) and the cooperation of discret unit mutation and the continous weight dacay method (especially, removing redundant input units). On the other hand, we tested ENZO-M on two difficult benchmark problems: Nine Men's Morris - a hard touchstone requiring a high generalization ability given a relatively small training set and the Thyroid gland - a real world problem requiring high classification accuracy given a large training set.

4.1 Digit recognition - The Effect of Lamarckism

The first benchmark we used to test ENZO-M was a digit recognition task. We used a training set of 10 patterns (one per digit) and a second fitness set of 70 noisy patterns to measure the generalization ability of the created networks.

Following the first results obtained with a previous version of ENZO [4] we started our experiments with a 23-12-10-10 topology. ENZO-M was able to minimize the network down to a 20-10 topology without any hidden units showing that this problem is linearly separable. Moreover, ENZO-M disconnected three input neurons from the architecture.

We also used digit recognition to investigate the effects of Lamarckism on the fitness distribution of 100 offsprings generated from one parent network.

From one parent network we generated 100 offsprings by mutation and Lamarckism and then computed the fitness distribution of the networks. We obtained a sharp peak which indicates that the offsprings are not far away from parent network in search space. We compared our results with another 100 networks created from the same parent topology by instantiating all weights randomly (fig. 3). Now the networks are disadvantageous scattered in the search space with a much greater variance and lower mean value of the obtained network fitnesses.

Moreover, other experiments shown that for hard problems the evolved sparse topologies even did not learn the training set after random initialization because the learning procedure get trapped in poor local minima. Thus using Lamarckism is crucial to obtain very small networks. Further, Lamarckism shortens training times by 1-2 orders of magnitude and makes evolutionary search more efficient.

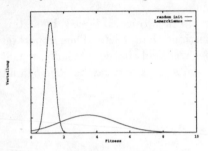

Fig. 3: Comparison of fitness distribution of networks generated by Lamarckism and random initialization. Fitness of parent network was 0.6

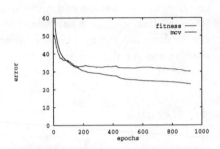

Fig. 4: Error due to the fitness- and meta-cross-validation-sets

4.2 Chess board problem - Overfitting the test set

The second benchmark we used, was a 3*3-chess-board classification problem[1]. It was driven to investigate the effects of overfitting the test set used by the fitness evaluation (*fitness set*). In order to cross-validate the generalization ability we compared the error on this fitness set with the error on a meta-cross-validation set (*MCV-set*) which was disjunct to both the training set and the fitness set. We generated three distinct pattern sets: a training set containing 8 patterns per square, a fitness and a MCV set both containing 32 patterns per square. Fig. 4 shows the error value due to the fitness and MCV sets. As we can see, optimization on the fitness set does not deteriorate the generalization ability.

4.3 TC problem - removing redundant inputs

A third set of experiments was driven to show the effectiveness of the cooperation of the discrete mutation operator and the continuous weight decay method [12]: a 'T' and a 'C' which must be recognized on a 4*4 grid independent of their position or rotation (in 90° steps). Starting with a 16-16-1 architecture (as in [10] described) ENZO-M generated very small networks. Two different 'minimal' solutions were found: a 11-1-1 and a 10-2-1 topology. Both architectures are smaller than solutions obtained by other approaches. Whereas the evolutionary program in [10] removed 79% of the weights and one input unit, ENZO-M surpasses this result significantly by removing 92% of the weights and five input units (i.e. 31% of the input vector).

---

[1] i.e. pixels situated in a black square should be classified with 1 the others with 0

	topology	#weights	classification
start network	16-16-1	288	100%
Mc Donnell	15-7-1	60	100%
ENZO-M	11-1-1	22	100%

4.4 Nine Men's Morris - a hard touchstone

Nine Men's Morris is a benchmark with the largest initial topology (over 5600 connections). In our previous research we investigated networks learning a scoring function for the endgame of Nine Men's Morris in the light of best performance [4]. Now we try to optimize both the networks topology as well as its performance.

The initial topology we used was a 120-60-20-2-1 network. ENZO-M was able to minimize the network to a 14-2-2-1 architecture deleting not only hidden units but also the majority of the input neurons. So ENZO-M can be used to recognize redundant input features and to eliminate them.

The table below shows the performance of three networks: the first network (SOKRATES) was the best handcrafted network developed just by using backpropagation (described in [3]), a second network was generated by ENZO (described in [4]), and a third network we got by ENZO-M.

System	topology	#weights	performance
SOKRATES	120-60-20-2-1	4222	0.826
ENZO	120-60-20-2-1	2533	1.218
ENZO-M	14-2-2-1	24	1.040

Networks optimized by ENZO and ENZO-M show a significantly better performance than the original SOKRATES network. Further, that superior performance is achieved with smaller networks. ENZO network contains the same number of units but fewer connections than the original network whereas ENZO-M network is a radical new and very small topology.

It may be worth emphasizing, that our former system ENZO found a network with a performance slightly surpassing the ENZO-M network but using the full input vector. This difference in performance between ENZO and ENZO-M results from different optimization goals used in each program (performance vs. topology). From that the reader may conclude, that the evolutionarily selected part of the input units by ENZO-M contains the crucial components whereas the remaining bear only little (but not zero) information.

4.5 Thyroid gland - a real world benchmark

The classification of medical data for a thyroid gland diagnosis [14], [13] is a real-world benchmark which requires a very good classification[2]. A further challenge

---

[2] 92% of the patterns belong to one class. Thus a useful network must classify much better than 92%.

is the vast number of training patterns (nearly 3800) which exceeds the size of toy problem's training sets by far. A set of experiments is described by Schiffmann et al. in [14] who compare several algorithms to train feed forward neural networks. They used a constant 21-10-3 topology, which we took as a maximal starting architecture to ENZO-M. We used a population size of 25 individuals and generated 300 offsprings. The resulting network had a 17-1-3 topology, 66 weights and correctly classified 98.4% of the test set.

	topology	#weights	performance
Schiffmann	21-10-3	303	94.8%
ENZO-M	17-1-3	66	98.4%

5 Conclusion

ENZO-M combines two successful search techniques: gradient descent for an efficient local weight optimization and evolution for a global topology optimization. By that it takes full advantage of the efficiently computable gradient information without being trapped by local minima. Through the knowledge transfer by inheriting the parental weights both learning is speeded up by 1-2 orders of magnitude and the expected fitness of the offspring is far above the average for its topology. Moreover, ENZO-M impressively thins out the topology by the cooperation of the discrete mutation operator and the continuous weight decay method. For this the knowledge transfer is again crucial, because the evolved topologies are mostly too sparse to be trained with random initial weights.

Additionally, ENZO-M tries also to cut off the connections to eventually redundant input units. Therefore ENZO-M not only supports the user in the network design but also determines the influence of each input component: for the thyroid gland problem a network was evolved with better performance but 20% less input units and for the Nine Men's Morris problem ENZO-M did even find a network with better performance but only 12% of the input unit originally used.

In spite of our restriction to mutation as the only reproduction operator, ENZO-M has proven to be a powerful design tool to evolve multilayer feedforward networks. Nevertheless, it remains a challenging research issue, to incorporate a crossover operator in order to recombine efficiently complex parental submodules (schema, gene).

References

1. **H. Braun** *Massiv parallele Algorithmen für kombinatorische Optimierungsprobleme und ihre Implementierung auf einem Parallelrechner*, Diss., TH Karlsruhe, 1990
2. **H. Braun** *On solving traveling salesman problems by genetic algorithms*, in: Parallel Problem Solving from Nature, LNCS 496 (Berlin, 1991)

3. **H. Braun, J. Feulner, V. Ullrich** *Learning strategies for solving the problem of planning using backpropagation*, in: Proc. 4th ICNN, Nimes, 1991

4. **H. Braun and J. Weisbrod** *Evolving neural feedforward networks*, in: Proc. Int. Conf. Artificial Neural Nets and Genetic Algorithms, R. F. Albrecht, C. R. Reeves and N.C. Steele, eds. Springer, Wien, 1993

5. **H. Braun and J. Weisbrod** *Evolving neural networks for application oriented problems*, in: Proc. of the second annual conference on evolutionary programming, Evolutionary programming Society, San Diego, 1993, S.62-71

6. **M. Riedmiller and H. Braun** *A direct adaptive method for faster backpropagation learning: The RPROP algorithm*, in: Proc. of the ICNN 93, San Francisco, 1993

7. **D.B. Fogel** *System identifikation through simulated evolution; a machine learning approach to modelling*, Needham Heights, Ginn Press, 1991

8. **L. J. Fogel, A.J. Owens and M.J. Walsh** *Artificial intelligence through simulated evolution*, John Wiley, NY., 1962

9. **J. H. Holland** *Adaptation in natural and artificial systems*, The University of Michigan Press, Ann Arbor, 1975

10. **John R. Mc Donnell and Don Waagen** *Neural Network Structure Design by Evolutionary Programming*, Proc. of the Second Annual Conf. on Evolutionary Programming, San Diego, 1993

11. **I. Rechenberg** *Evolutionsstrategie: Optimierung technischer Systeme nach Prinzipien der biologischen Evolution*, Frommann-Holzboog Verlag, Stuttgart, 1973

12. **D. E. Rumelhart and J. McClelland** *Parallel Distributed Processing*, 1986

13. **W. Schiffmann, M. Joost, R. Werner** *Application of genetic algorithms to the construction of topologies for multilayer perceptrons*, in: Proc. of the int. conf. Artificial Neural Nets and Genetic Algorithms, R. F. Albrecht, C. R. Reeves and N.C. Steele, eds. Springer, Wien, 1993

14. **W. Schiffmann, M. Joost, R. Werner** *Optimization of the backpropagation algorithm for training multilayer perceptrons*, Techn. rep., University of Koblenz, 1993

15. **H. P. Schwefel** *Numerische Optimierung von Computermodellen mittels der Evolutionsstrategie*, in: Interdisciplinary research (vol. 26), Birkhäuser, Basel, 1977

16. **H. P. Schwefel** *Evolutionsstrategie und Numerische Optimierung*, Diss., TU Berlin, 1975

17. **A. S. Weigend and D. E. Rumelhart and B. A. Huberman** *Generalisation by Weight-Elimination with Application to Forecasting*

18. **P. Zagorski** *Entwicklung evolutionärer Algorithmen zur Optimierung der Topologie und des Generalisierungsverhaltens von Multilayer Perceptrons*, Diplomarbeit, Universität Karlsruhe, 1993

Genetic Lander: An Experiment in Accurate Neuro-Genetic Control

Edmund Ronald - Marc Schoenauer

Centre de Mathematiques Appliquees, Ecole Polytechnique, 91128 Palaiseau, France.
Email: {eronald, marc}@cmapx,polytechnique.fr

Abstract. The control problem of soft-landing a toy lunar module simulation is investigated in the context of neural nets. While traditional
supervised back-propagation training is inappropriate for lack of training exemplars, genetic algorithms allow a controller to be evolved without difficulty: Evolution is a form of unsupervised learning. A novelty
introduced in this paper is the presentation of additional renormalized
inputs to the net; experiments indicate that the presence of such inputs
allows precision of control to be attained faster, when learning time is
measured by the number of generations for which the GA must run to
attain a certain mean performance.

1 Introduction to Neuro-Genetic Control

The research presented in this document is part of an ongoing investigation concerning heuristic methods of trajectory planning and control. The underlying
methodology is to control a dynamical system by means of a neural net. As
training exemplars are not available, classical backpropagation [PDP] cannot be
employed to train the net; our solution is to view the matrix of weights as a
vector of real numbers, and to optimise controller performance by means of a
genetic algorithm. The reader will find an overview of evolutionary methods in
neural-net training in [Yao 93].

For our purposes, the basic feasibility of neuro-genetic trajectory planning
was established in [Schoenauer & Ronald 94], a study of genetic net training applied to the truck backer-upper benchmark problem ([Nguyen & Widrow 90]).
Our experimentation with the truck problem indicated that achieving the convergence of the GA to find a controller net requires modest amounts of computer
time,but the GA does not adequtely fine-tune the net for precision control.

Figure 1. shows a typical experiment with our truck-backer upper simulation. It can be seen that the truck makes a very good start at docking, from
many starting positions, but is unable to follow up its good start with a precise
end-manoeuvre. This problem with local fine tuning in neural net training by
GA has been mentioned by Hiroaki Kitano [Kitano 90] who contemplating the
biological implications of this inadequacy believes that "A need for a supplementary scheme for fine-tuning is clear...a cascaded scheme of natural selection,

adaptation and learning is a necessary consequence for survival".

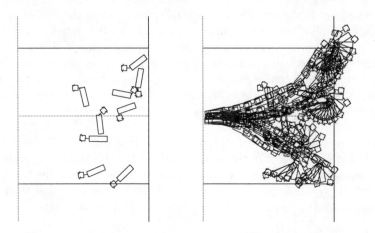

Figure 1: 8 random starting points for truck and ensuing docking traffic.

The methodology we developped for controlling the truck is very similar to that employed for the lunar lander, so we shall review this earlier work. We shall then outline our motives for switching to the simpler and better known lunar lander problem, and define the objective of the numerical experiments which form the core of this paper.

The truck backer-upper problem is fully specified in [Nguyen & Widrow 90]. We can give an abridged description by saying that a driver must back up a truck with trailer system, with the aim of positioning the back of the trailer accurately at a loading dock.

To solve this problem by means of neuro-genetic learning, a neural net controller that "drives" the net was evolved by means of a genetic algorithm. This neural net driver takes the position and orientation of the trailer, as well as the truck/trailer angle as its 4 inputs. The truck is assumed to move backwards by small uniform steps, and so the only output computed by the neural net is the angle of the steering wheels. A population of such "neural drivers" is evolved by means of a GA with the fitness function some combination of docking accuracy and trajectory length.

In the truck study we investigated two possible approaches to neuro-genetic control: On-line learning, and off-line learning.

- In on-line learning, neural net "drivers" are generated on the fly; they only solve the control problem for *one* starting configuration.

– In off-line learning one attempts to train a driver who is able to reach the goal from *any* starting configuration.

It can be seen that off-line learning is extremely time-consuming, as a representative subset of the input space must be trained for. In the case of the truck, on the fly training took a few minutes on a workstation rated at 100 SpecFp 92, while training times exploded to several hours for a driver able to start from 15 predetermined starting positions. Bear in mind that as the dimensionality of the space of staring configurations increases, the cardinality of test ensembles spanning that space increases exponentially. Thus off-line training may lose its appeal due to combinatorial explosion.

As can be seen in Figure 1, the convoluted trajectories of the truck backerupper do not encourage intuitive interpretation of the control strategies adopted by the nets we evolve. In particular, a human operator will find the truck rather hard to dock by hand, and it thus becomes difficult to judge, other than by the numbers, whether a net has a "better" strategy than another net.

For the above reasons, the choice of a simpler problem was deemed preferable, to allow us to investigate ways in which accurate solutions could be syntehsized on the fly in a small number of generations. Ideally, such a speed-up of the learning process would demonstrate the feasibility of using a GA for real-time control.

In the hope of increasing control precision, and perhaps even of gaining a speedup sufficient to demonstrate the feasibility of real-time neuro-genetic control, we decided to tackle a simpler problem than the truck, to wit the lunar lander, which has also been studied in [Suddarth 88]. In our study of lunar lander we introduced a modification in the neural domain of the neuro-genetic method, namely larger nets with input data renormalisation.

Data renormalisation is the the main novelty studied in detail in this paper. This simply entails supplying the controller with redundant, rescaled, copies of its inputs. Although trivial to implement, this technique allowed us to achieve good accuracy with short learning times, for both the truck backer-upper and the lunar lander problems. The experiments reported below show a strong speedup of convergence, yielding much improved results: Convergence to accurate control occurs in fewer generations, mis-convergence occurs more rarely, and the mean accuracy of control improves dramatically.

2   Lunar Lander Dynamics

This paper deals with training a neural net to land a simulated rocket-driven lunar-lander module, under a gravity of 1.5 m/s^2. This simulation has given rise to numerous computer games since the advent of interactive computing, and will be familiar to most readers.

The lunar module is dropped with no initial velocity from a height of 1000 meters. The fuel tank is assumed to contain 100 units of fuel. Burning one unit of fuel yields one unit of thrust. Maximum thrust is limited to 10 units and the variation of the mass of the lunar module due to fuel consumption is not taken into account. The simulation time-slice was arbitrarily fixed at 0.5 seconds.

The input parameters relayed to the neural net once every time-step are the speed, and the altitude. The net then computes the desired fraction of maximal thrust, on a scale from 0 to 1, which is then linearly rescaled between 0 and 10 units.

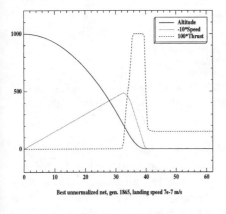
Best unnormalized net, gen. 1865, landing speed 7e-7 m/s

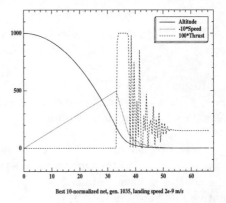
Best 10-normalized net, gen. 1035, landing speed 2e-9 m/s

Figure 2: Best non-normalised
control action in study.

Figure 3: Best overall
control action in study.

A very nice lunar landing effected in this study is shown in Figure 2. This achieved a landing speed of $7\ 10^{-7}m/s$, ie. $0.7mm/s$, hardly enough to mark the lunar surface! Such excellence would hardly be necessary in practice. This result was obtained by straightforward application of neuro-genetic control, with no data renormalization.

It was attained at the price of a long run, namely almost 2000 generations. The control action is also exemplary in the economy of fuel in the deceleration phase: For the main deceleration burst, thrust is pulsed in what amounts to almost a square wave to its maximal permissible value. The remarkable landing softness is attained by means of a long - and very smooth- hover phase which begins immediately after deceleration.

The best landing we achieved in this study is shown in Figure 3. The landing speed of $7\ 10^{-9}m/s$, ie. $0.002mm/s$ is a 2 orders of magnitude improvement over the previous result, and was attained in half as many (1035) generations. This is an achievement of data renormalisation: The net was presented with the two previously cited state inputs, namely speed and altitude, and another pair consisting of the same variables pre-multiplied by a factor of 10.

The interesting features of the best "Armstrong", as displayed in Figure 3, are its surprising precision, and the fact that this precision is attained either in spite of, or more probably, because of the displayed sawtooth shape and roughness of the thrust control. Of course, control by rocket to fit a speed tolerance of 20 Angstroms/s seems rather implausible in reality.

3   The Networks

A classical 3-layered net architecture was employed, with complete interconnection between layers 1 and 2, and 2 and 3. The neural transfer function (non-linear squashing) was chosen to be the usual logistic function $\mathcal{F}$, a sigmoid defined by

$$\mathcal{F}(x) = \frac{1}{1+e^{-\alpha x}}$$

In our work the parameter α was fixed, $\alpha = 3.0$. [1] Each individual neuron j computes the traditional [PDP] squashed sum-of-inputs

$$o_j = \mathcal{F}(\textstyle\sum_i w_i^j x_i)$$

Regarding the sizing of the middle layer, we chose to apply the Kolmogorov model [Hecht-Nieslen 90] which for a net with n inputs and 1 output requires at least 2n+1 intermediate neurons.

Only two net architectures occur in this paper. Both types have only one output (controlling the lunar module's thrust). The canonical method for solving the control problem entails 2 inputs, namely speed and altitude, appropriately normalised between 0 and 1. However, the optimisation by input renormalisation which forms the core of this paper entails adding two inputs to the above cited net, therefore employing 4-input nets. As in both cases we have adhered to the Kolmogorov paradigm, we are studying 2-5-1 and 4-9-1 nets, which respectively have 21 and 55 weights/biases. With the topology fixed, training these nets for a given purpose is a search in a space of dimension 21 or 55. In the neuro-genetic approach, this search is effected by a genetic algorithm.

4   The Genetic Model

The experiments reported in this paper were done with a homebrew general-purpose genetic algorithm package embodying the principles described both in [Holland 75], and [Goldberg 89]. Our genetic algorithm software subjects a small population of nets to crude parody of natural evolution. This artificial evolutionary process aims to achieve nets which display a large *fitness*. The fitness is a positive real value which denotes how well a net does at its assigned task of landing the lunar module. Thus our fitness will be greater for slower landing speeds. The details of the calculation of the fitness are found below.

For the purpose of applying the genetic algorithm, a net is canonically represented by its weights, i.e. as a vector of real numbers. During the course of this work, two distinct homebrew GA software packages were employed. One package

---

[1] An experiment in searching for appropriate values of α is reported in [Schoenauer & Ronald 94]

followed the first methods presented by John Holland in that it uses bit-strings to encode floating-point numbers. The second software package, described below, was a hybridized GA which directly exploits the native floating-point representation of the worktations which it was run on. The hybridization towards real numbers is described in [Radcliffe 91] and [Michalewicz 92]. The results obtained with both programs were consistent, and only the experiments with the floating point package are detailed in this document.

The genetic algorithm progresses in discrete time steps called generations. At every generation the fitness values of all the nets in the population are computed. Then a new population is derived from the old by applying the stochastic selection, crossover and mutation operators to the members of the old population.

- Selection is an operator that discards the least fit members of the population, and allows fitter ones to reproduce. We use the roulette wheel selection procedure as described in [Goldberg 89], with fitness scaling and elitism, carrying the best individual over from one generation to the next.
- Crossover mixes the traits of two parents into two offspring. In our case, random choice is made between two crossover operators: Exchange of the weights beteween parents, at random positions. Or assigning to some of the weights of each offspring a random barycentric combination of its parents' weights.
- Mutation randomly changes some weights by adding some gaussian noise.

The experiments described in the next section used the following parameters in the GA: The net connection weights forming the object of the search were confined to the interval $[-10, +10]$ thereby avoiding overflow conditions in the computation of the exponential. Population size was held to 50 over the whole length of each run, fitness scaling was set to a constant selecetive pressure of 2.0, crossover rate was 0.6, mutation rate 0.2, the gaussian noise had its standard deviation set to half the weight space diameter, ie. 10.0, decreasing geometrically in time by a factor 0.999 at each generation.

5 Results

A spectrum of experiments was carried out with the bit-string and real-number GA's, to determine the effect of various parameter changes on the control accuracy and speed of convergence of the on-line neuro-genetic control method. A single starting point (speed=0m/s, altitude=1000m) was employed across the board.

For all tests, 2 state variables were taken as basis for the inputs to be presented to the net:

$$NormSpeed = Speed/100, NormAltitude = Altitude/1000$$

the fitness of a controller was computed to be

$$fitness = \frac{1}{(0.1 + Speed_{crash}{}^2)}$$

Thus the fitness for a net is some number between 0.0 and 10.0

The following controller architectures were investigated:

- 2-5-1 net. Inputs are *NormSpeed* and *NormAltitude*
- 4-9-1 net. Inputs are *NormSpeed* and *NormAltitude*, and the same renormalized by a factor of 100
- 4-9-1 net. Inputs are *NormSpeed* and *NormAltitude*, and the same renormalized by a factor of 10
- 4-9-1 net. Inputs are *NormSpeed* and *NormAltitude*, and the same renormalized by a factor of 1

The 1-renormalized net gets precisely the same inputs as the 2-input net, only of course, it gets them twice.

In the diagram below the two net architectures are diagrammed. We have denoted by r_i the renormalisation coefficients; the experiments consist of setting r_3 and r_4 to 1, 10, or 100, with r_1 and r_2 set to 1.

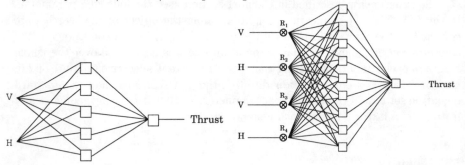

2-input Net   Generalised 4-input Net

A total of 60 GA runs was made for each of these architectures, with the population size set to 50 individuals. For each run, at each generation, the best individual's performance was saved to disk. At the end of each batch of 60 runs, the mean at each number of generations of each architecture's best individuals' performance was computed. The corresponding graph is plotted in Figs 4 and 5, in linear and logarithmic scales:

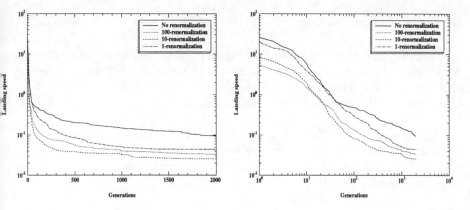

Figure 4: Mean performance,
lin / log scales.

Figure 5: Mean Performance,
log / log scales.

In our opinion, two facets of learning, as evidenced by these graphs, are of interest: Long-term learning, ie. asymptotic behaviour (best observed on the lin / log plot) and on the other hand fast learning ie. in few generations as best observed in the log / log plot.

- The asymptotic behaviour of the mean landing speeds demonstrates the superiority of the renormalised over the non-renormalized nets by the fact that the 4 presented curves are layered, in the order un-normalised / 1 / 100 / 10. In fact, in ultimate mean precision attained over 2000 generations the 10-normalised net wins by half an order of magnitude.
- The close-up, immediate behaviour of the GA demonstrates that this gain carries over to the fast-learning region. A new graph, in which we assess the ratio of the number of generations (normalised/ un-normalised) to reach some speed between 0.1 and 1.0 m/s. Figure 6 shows the speed-up to be truly useful, with computation proceeding faster by a factor of 25 at the speed of 0.1 m/s (4 inches/s).

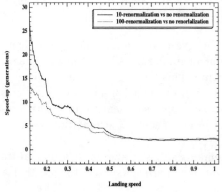

Figure 6: Computational speedup achieved through normalisation.

6 Discussion

The above comparison of computational costs employs the number of generations as a metric. However, in fact the normed nets are larger, (55 vs. 21 weights), and thus slow down the programs by a measured factor of about 2. This is more than offset by the gains in learning performance.

A rather surprising feature can be discerned in the log / log graph: at generation 1, the average best performance per run is already well under 10 m/s for the 1-normalised net. This led us to investtigate more closely the properties of pure random search.

The results are displayed in Figure 7. The "Generations" referred to in the legend correpond to packets of individuals of the same size as the population in the GA.

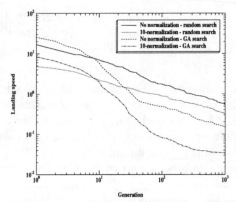

Figure 7: Random search outperforms genetic learning for first "generations".

Pure random search in the space of nets consistently outperforms genetic search for very fast learning, when very approximate precision of control is sufficient. This seemingly counter-intuitive result seems to indicate that random search may supply a basis for real-time control.

In conclusion, we believe that the fine-tuning problem cited by [Kitano 90] can be overcome in control applications by optimising the net architecture specifically for genetic learning. This optimisation can be aided by employing the GA itself to tune the normalisation coeficients [Schoenauer & Ronald 94]. In biological terms, this means we supply supplementary neural pre-adapted for optimal sensitivity at different levels of sensory stimulation.

However, speed remains an issue and as regards real-time control, cascaded random search may yet have its revenge over the sophisticated methods of evolutionary computation.

References

[Angeline, Saunders & Pollack 94] P. J. Angeline, G. M. Saunders and J. B. Pollack, An evolutionnary algorithm that construct recurrent neural networks. To appear in *IEEE Transactions on Neural Networks*.

[Goldberg 89] D. E. Goldberg, *Genetic algorithms in search, optimization and machine learning*, Addison Wesley, 1989.

[Harp & Samad 91] S. A. Harp and T. Samad, Genetic synthesis of neural network architecture, in *Handbook of Genetic Algorithms*, L. Davis Ed., Van Nostrand Reinhold, New York, 1991.

[Hecht-Nieslen 90] R. Hecht-Nielsen, *Neurocomputing*, Addison Wesley, 1990.

[Holland 75] J. Holland, *Adaptation in natural and artificial systems*, University of Michigan Press, Ann Harbor, 1975.

[Kitano 90] Empirical studies on the speed of convergence of neural network training using genetic algorithms. In *Proceedings of Eight National Conference on Artificial Intelligence, AAAI-90*, Vol. 2, pp 789-795, Boston, MA, 29 July - 3 Aug 1990. MIT Press, Cambridge, MA.

[Michalewicz 92] Z. Michalewicz, Genetic Algorithms+Data Structures=Evolution Programs, Springer Verlag 1992.

[Nguyen & Widrow 90] D. Nguyen, B. Widrow, The truck Backer Upper: An example of self learning in neural networks, in *Neural networks for Control*, W. T. Miller III, R. S. Sutton, P. J. Werbos eds, The MIT Press, Cambridge MA, 1990.

[Radcliffe 91] N. J. Radcliffe, Equivalence Class Analysis of Genetic Algorithms, in *Complex Systems* **5**, pp 183-205, 1991.

[PDP] D. E. Rumelhart, J. L. McClelland, *Parallel Distributed Processing - Exploration in the micro structure of cognition*, MIT Press, Cambridge MA, 1986.

[Schaffer, Caruana & Eshelman 1990] J. D. Schaffer, R. A. Caruana and L. J. Eshelman, Using genetic search to exploit the emergent behaviour of neural networks, *Physica D* **42** (1990), pp244-248.

[Schoenauer & Ronald 94] M. Schoenauer, E.Ronald Neuro Genetic Truck Backer-Upper Controller, in *IEEE World Conference on Computational Intelligence* , Orlando 1994.

[Schoenauer & Ronald 94] M. Schoenauer, E.Ronald Genetic Extensions of Neural Net Learning: Transfer Functions and Renormalisation Coefficients, in *submitted to Artificial Evolution 94* , Toulouse 1994.

[Suddarth 88] Steve C. Suddarth, The symbolic-neural method for creating models and control behaviours from examples. Ph.D. dissertation. University of Washington. 1988.

[Yao 93] Xin Yao, A Review of Evolutionary Artificial Neural Networks, in *International Journal of Intelligent Systems* **8**, pp 539-567, 1993.

Effects of Occam's Razor in Evolving Sigma-Pi Neural Nets

Byoung-Tak Zhang

German National Research Center for Computer Science (GMD)
D-53757 Sankt Augustin, Germany
E-mail: zhang@gmd.de

Abstract. Several evolutionary algorithms make use of hierarchical representations of variable size rather than linear strings of fixed length. Variable complexity of the structures provides an additional representational power which may widen the application domain of evolutionary algorithms. The price for this is, however, that the search space is open-ended and solutions may grow to arbitrarily large size. In this paper we study the effects of structural complexity of the solutions on their generalization performance by analyzing the fitness landscape of sigma-pi neural networks. The analysis suggests that smaller networks achieve, on average, better generalization accuracy than larger ones, thus confirming the usefulness of Occam's razor. A simple method for implementing the Occam's razor principle is described and shown to be effective in improving the generalization accuracy without limiting their learning capacity.

1 Introduction

Recently, there has been increasing interest in evolutionary algorithms that use structured representations of variable length rather than linear strings of fixed size [2, 5, 12]. Parse trees or Lisp S-expressions are usually used to represent possible solutions. Since the user-defined expressions can be recursively combined, the method is particularly suited to problems in which some underlying regularity or structure must be automatically discovered. The simplicity and generality of these algorithms have found many interesting applications across a wide spectrum, including problems in artificial intelligence and artificial life [12].

However, the price for the additional flexibility in representation is that solutions may grow arbitrarily large. For example, Kinnear [10] observed in his sorting problem a strong tendency for the individuals in the population to grow without bound. He found almost all of the solutions were so large as to defy any human understanding of them, even after simplifying them in obvious ways.

For this kind of open-ended exploration of solution space, parsimony may be an important factor not just for ease of analysis, but because of a more direct relationship to fitness. Tackett [18] empirically found, in his pattern classification application, a high degree of correlation between tree size and performance; among the set of pretty good solution trees, those with highest performance were usually the smallest within that set. Kinnear [10] also questions the existence of general connection between high evolutionary pressures against increasing size and algorithms of greater generalization ability. However, these studies did not provide a concrete relationship between the complexity of solutions and their generalization accuracy.

The primary objective of this paper is to study the effect of solution size on its generalization performance. We analyze the fitness landscape of the sigma-pi neural networks of variable complexity. The fundamental problem of balancing accuracy and parsimony of solutions is discussed and a general framework to approach the problem is presented. The effectiveness of the method is demonstrated on the synthesis of sigma-pi neural networks for solving parity problems using noisy data.

2   Evolving Sigma-Pi Neural Nets

For concreteness we first describe the problem, i.e. evolving sigma-pi neural networks. In a typical application of neural networks we have a set of data consisting of N input-output pairs:

$$D_N = \{ (\mathbf{x}_c, \mathbf{y}_c) \}_{c=1}^{N}, \tag{1}$$

where $\mathbf{x}_c \in \mathbf{X} \subset \Re^I$, and $\mathbf{y}_c \in \mathbf{Y} \subset \Re^O$. This data set is supposed to implicitly define a functional or statistical relation F between the inputs and the outputs:

$$\mathbf{y} = F(\mathbf{x}), \quad F : \mathbf{X} \to \mathbf{Y}. \tag{2}$$

Neural networks are used to learn the unknown relation F. One of most commonly used architectures is the feedforward network of sigma units. That is, the output of the units in these networks is determined as a function of the weighted sum of inputs

$$u_i = \sum_{j \in R(i)} w_{ij} x_j \tag{3}$$

where w_{ij} is the connection weight from unit j to unit i. The receptive field $R(i)$ denotes the index set of units which is connected to the ith unit. The total input is then transferred to upper layer units by a nonlinear activation function f, e.g. a threshold function:

$$y_i = f(u_i) = \begin{cases} +1 & \text{if } u_i > \theta_i \\ -1 & \text{otherwise} \end{cases} \tag{4}$$

where θ_i is a threshold.

The representational power of this architecture can be extended by allowing pi units as well as sigma units [3]. While a sigma-unit calculates a sum of weighted inputs, a pi-unit builds a *product* of weighted inputs:

$$u_i = \prod_{j \in R(i)} v_{ij} x_j. \tag{5}$$

Here v_{ij} is the connection weight from unit j to unit i and $R(i)$ denotes the receptive field of unit i. The resulting total input is propagated to upper layer units by an activation function chosen depending on applications. By using pi units we can directly build kth-order terms

$$T^{(k)} = f_k \left(\prod_{j=1}^{j_k} v_{kj} x_j \right) \tag{6}$$

which require a number of layers consisting of summation units in conventional neural networks. The higher-order terms can be again used as building blocks which are able to capture a high-order correlational structure of the data. In particular, by building a sigma unit which has as input various higher-order terms $T^{(k)}$, we can construct a higher-order network of sigma-pi units:

$$y_i = f_i(u_i) = f_i \left(\sum_k w_{ik} T^{(k)} \right) = f_i \left(\sum_k w_{ik} f_k \left(\prod_{j=1}^{j_k} v_{kj} x_j \right) \right) \tag{7}$$

Evolutionary algorithms can be used to evolve problem-specific sigma-pi networks [9, 22]. We encode the network as a set of m trees, where m is the number of output units. Figure 1 shows an example of the genotype and its phenotype of a sigma-pi network with one output unit.

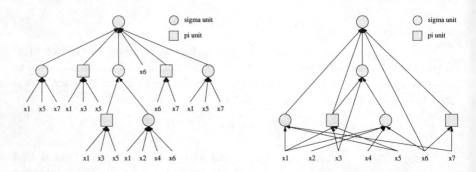

Fig. 1. *The genotype (left) and its phenotype (right) of a sigma-pi network with one output unit*

Each tree has an arbitrary number of subtrees. Each nonterminal node $<Y>$ in the tree represents a sigma or pi unit. Written in the rewrite rule form:

$$<Y> \longrightarrow <U> <r> <\theta> <W>_1 \cdots <W>_r . \tag{8}$$

Here, the variable $<U>$ denotes the type of the unit, i.e. stands for the constant S or P denoting a sigma or pi unit, respectively:

$$<U> \longrightarrow \{ S \mid P \} \tag{9}$$

where the meta symbol | combined with { } denotes exclusive or. Each $<Y>$-node has $r+2$ additional arguments. They are threshold value θ, receptive field size r, and r weights, $w_1, \cdots, w_r$. The integer r is chosen randomly and adapted during evolution. In the genotype the weights w_i are represented as separate nonterminal nodes, each denoted by $<W>$:

$$<W> \longrightarrow W \ <w> \ \{ <Y> \ | \ <X> \}, \tag{10}$$

where constant W stands for the node type. A $<W>$-node has additional two arguments. One is for the weight value w and the other is for pointing recursively to another nonterminal unit $<Y>$ or an external input unit $<X>$. $<X>$ is represented by a constant X followed by an input index i:

$$<X> \longrightarrow X \ <i>. \tag{11}$$

Thus the terminal set is $\{X1, X2, \cdots, Xn\}$, where n is the number of input units which is determined by the problem size. The weights and thresholds are allowed to be binary or integer values.

3 Analysis of the Fitness Landscape

We analyzed the relationship between the average generalization performance and complexity of sigma-pi neural networks. The parity problem of input size $n = 7$ was used in this analysis. We first generated a clean data set B_N of size $N = 2^7$. A noisy training set D_N was then generated from B_N by flipping the output value of each example with 5% probability.

Approximately $M = 20000$ sigma-pi networks of differing size and weights were generated. The performance of each network A_i with weights $\mathbf{w}$ was then measured on the noisy data sets D_N:

$$E(D_N|\mathbf{w}, A_i) = \sum_{c=1}^{N} \sum_{k=1}^{m} (y_{ck} - f_k(\mathbf{x}_c; \mathbf{w}, A_i))^2. \tag{12}$$

where y_{ck} and $f_k(\mathbf{x}_c; \mathbf{w}, A_i)$ are the desired and actual value of the kth output of the ith network given the input pattern $\mathbf{x}_c$. Likewise, the generalization performance $E(B_N|\mathbf{w}, A_i)$ of the network was measured on the test set B_N of N clean examples. Each performance measure was then normalized into the interval $[0, 1]$ by

$$L(i) = \frac{1}{mN} E(D_N|\mathbf{w}, A_i), \tag{13}$$

$$G(i) = \frac{1}{mN} E(B_N|\mathbf{w}, A_i). \tag{14}$$

For each network we also measured its complexity in terms of the number of binary weights:

$$W_i = W(\mathbf{w}|A_i) = \sum_{j,k} w_{jk}^2, \tag{15}$$

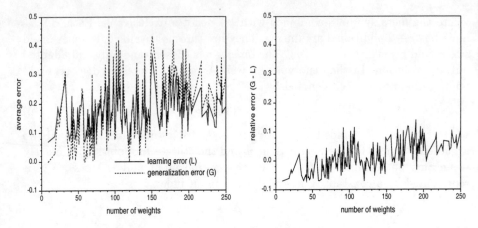

Fig. 2. Effect of number of weights on generalization

where the indices j and k run over all the units in A_i. We then depicted the performance as a function of the network complexity by computing the average training errors $E_L(\omega)$, average generalization errors $E_G(\omega)$ and their difference $E_{G-L}(\omega)$ for each ω:

$$E_L(\omega) = \text{avg}\{L(i) \mid W_i = \omega, \ i = 1, \cdots, M\}, \tag{16}$$

$$E_G(\omega) = \text{avg}\{G(i) \mid W_i = \omega, \ i = 1, \cdots, M\}, \tag{17}$$

$$E_{G-L}(\omega) = E_G(\omega) - E_L(\omega). \tag{18}$$

The resulting fitness landscape is depicted in Figure 2. The graphs are drawn for the ω-points at which more than five W_i-instances have been found in computing (16) and (17).

Similarly we computed the average generalization performance as a function of number of units, ν:

$$U_i = U(A_i), \tag{19}$$

$$E_L(\nu) = \text{avg}\{L(i) \mid U_i = \nu, \ i = 1, \cdots, M\}, \tag{20}$$

$$E_G(\nu) = \text{avg}\{G(i) \mid U_i = \nu, \ i = 1, \cdots, M\}, \tag{21}$$

$$E_{G-L}(\nu) = E_G(\nu) - E_L(\nu). \tag{22}$$

Figure 3 shows the generalization error as a function of the number of units in the network.

The figures show the general tendency that the relative generalization error increases as the network size grows; that is, generalization ability of the network is inversely proportional to network complexity. Note, however, that if we compare some partial regions of the configuration space the tendency may be violated. For instance in Figure 2, the average generalization error for a smaller network consisting of 130 weights is larger than that of a larger network with 190 weights. It is not difficult to imagine that the optimal complexity may differ

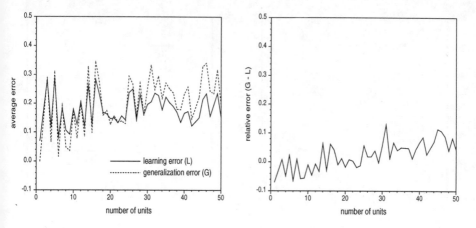

Fig. 3. Effect of number of units on generalization

from one problem to another as well as the task at hand. However, the overall result suggests preference of small networks to larger ones if no information is available about the configuration space, confirming the principles of Occam's razor [1, 21] and minimum description length [16].

4 Effects of Occam's Razor: Simulation Results

The foregoing analysis suggests the necessity of some mechanism to constrain the network size. Parsimony, or simplicity of solution structures, is achievable by adding the tree size or expression length as a component of the fitness function to be minimized [12]. However, too great a penalty for size may lead to early convergence to local minima. A more general case of this multi-objective optimization problem has been discussed by Schaffer [17].

In controlling the accuracy and parsimony of neural networks, it is important that the network be able to approximate at least the training set to a specified performance level. A small network should be preferred to a greater network only if both of them achieve a comparable performance. Otherwise, the algorithm would not reduce the approximation error, preferring smaller networks which can not be powerful enough to solve the task.

We use the following fitness measure

$$F_i \equiv F(D_N|\mathbf{w}, A_i) = \alpha C(\mathbf{w}|A_i) + \beta E(D_N|\mathbf{w}, A_i), \tag{23}$$

where

$$\alpha^{-1} = C_{max}N \text{ and } \beta^{-1} = mN. \tag{24}$$

The first term expresses the complexity penalty of the network. The complexity is defined as

$$C(\mathbf{w}|A_i) = W(\mathbf{w}|A_i) + U(A_i) + 10H(A_i), \tag{25}$$

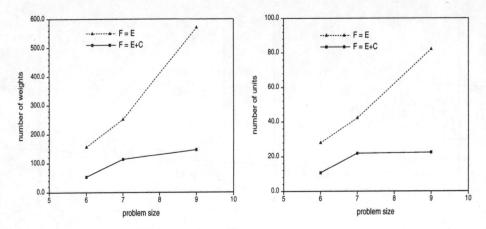

Fig. 4. Effect of Occam's razor on network size

where $W(\mathbf{w}|A_i)$ and $U(A_i)$ are the complexity in terms of weights and units as defined in the last section. Note that the number of layers, $H(A_i)$, appears as an additional penalty term. This is to avoid a deep architecture which requires a large execution time after training. C_{max} in the fitness function is a normalization factor used for the complexity term to be between 0 and 1. The multiplication of the training set size N in $\alpha^{-1} = C_{max}N$ ensures that larger networks are penalized only if their training errors are comparable to smaller ones. In all experiments below we set $C_{max} = 1000$, assuming the problems can be solved by $C(\mathbf{w}|A_i) \leq 1000$.

At the start, the initial population $\mathcal{A}(0)$ of M networks is generated at random. The random initialization includes the type and receptive field of units, the depth of the network, and the values of weights and thresholds. Then, for the gth generation the fitness values $F_i(g)$ of networks are evaluated using the training set of N examples. The best τM networks of gth population are selected into the mating pool $\mathcal{B}(g)$, where $\tau \in (0, 1]$ is the truncation threshold. Each network in $\mathcal{B}(g)$ undergoes a local hillclimbing. Many hillclimbing methods are possible. We use a simple next-ascent hillclimbing procedure: given an individual, a better individual is sought by repeatedly changing the weights until there is no weight configuration found having better fitness in each sweep through the individual.

The hillclimbing produces the revised mating pool $\mathcal{B}(g)$. The $(g+1)$th generation of size M is produced by applying crossover operators to randomly chosen parent networks in the mating pool $\mathcal{B}(g)$. The mutation operation is employed to change the input index of terminal nodes. We also allow a nonterminal symbol S to be mutated by a P and vise versa, i.e. changing the type of neural units. This flexibility ensures that multilayer perceptrons can also be evolved from sigma-pi networks. We use the elitist strategy by replacing the worst fit network A_{worst} in $\mathcal{A}(g+1)$ by the best A_{best} of $\mathcal{A}(g)$. A new population is generated repeatedly until an acceptable solution is found or the variance of the fitness falls below a

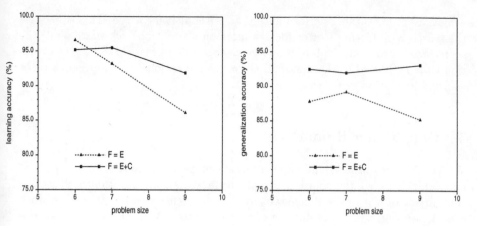

Fig. 5. Effect of Occam's razor on learning and generalization accuracy

specified limit.

The effect of Occam's razor was tested on the parity problem of size $n = 6, 7, 9$. For each problem size n we generated a training set of $2^n/2$ examples which were chosen randomly and inserted noise by changing the ouput value with 5% probability. The generalization performance of the best solution in each generation was tested by the complete data set of 2^n noiseless examples. The population was initialized for every individual to contain sigma and pi units with 50% probability each. The depth of initialized network was limited to 3. The truncation rate was 40%. For each problem size n, the population size and the maximum generation were:

$$M = 100n/2, \quad g_{max} = 10n. \tag{26}$$

For example, $M = 300$ and $g_{max} = 60$ for $n = 6$.

The performance of the method with Occam's razor, i.e. (23), was compared with a method that uses just the error term as the fitness measure, i.e.

$$F_i = F(D_N|\mathbf{w}, A_i) = \frac{1}{mN} E(D_N|\mathbf{w}, A_i). \tag{27}$$

Both methods used the same data. For each method, 10 runs were executed to observe the complexity of the best solution and its training and generalization performance. Figure 4 compares the average network size found at the g_{max}th generation.

Whereas Occam's razor prunes inessential substructures to get parsimonious solutions, without Occam's razor the network size increases without bound. The corresponding learning and generalization performance of both methods are compared in Figure 5. The results show that applying Occam's razor achieves significantly better generalization performance as was expected by the landscape analysis. It is also interesting to note that the evolution with Occam's razor achieved better learning performance than without it for $n > 6$. This is because the search with Occam's razor focuses more on a smaller search space while the search without it may explore too large a space to be practical. Since the evolution time is limited to the maximum of g_{max} generations, using Occam's razor can find a solution faster than without it.

5 Concluding Remarks

We studied the fitness landscape of sigma-pi neural networks to see the relationship between the solution complexity and its generalization ability. The comparison of learning and generalization performance as a function of network complexity suggests the usefulness of Occam's razor. A general method for implementing the principle of Occam's razor is proposed. The simulation results support that significant improvement in generalization ability can be achieved by penalizing the complexity of solutions. While the experiments have been performed in the context of neural networks, the underlying principle of balancing accuracy and parsimony can be applied to a wide variety of applications in which the number of parameters, as well as the parameter values themselves, should be optimized.

Acknowledgement

This work was supported in part by the Real-World Computing Program under the project SIFOGA.

References

1. Y. S. Abu-Mostafa: The Vapnik-Chervonenkis dimension: Information versus complexity in learning. *Neural Computation* 1, 312–317 (1989)
2. T. Bäck and H.-P. Schwefel: An overview of evolutionary algorithms for parameter optimization. *Evolutionary Computation* 1, 1–23 (1993)
3. R. Durbin, D. E. Rumelhart: Product units: A computationally powerful and biologically plausible extension to backpropagation networks. *Neural Computation* 1, 133–142 (1989)
4. C. L. Giles, T. Maxwell: Learning, invariance, and generalization in high-order neural networks. *Applied Optics* 26, 4972–4978 (1987)
5. D. E. Goldberg: *Genetic Algorithms in Search, Optimization & Machine Learning.* Addison Wesley, 1989
6. F. Gruau: Genetic synthesis of Boolean neural networks with a cell rewriting developmental process. Tech. Rep., Laboratoire de l'Informatique du Parallélisme, 1992
7. S. A. Harp, T. Samad, A. Guha: Towards the genetic synthesis of neural networks. In: D. Schaffer (ed.): *Proceedings of the Third International Conference on Genetic Algorithms (ICGA-89).* Morgan Kaufmann, 1985, pp. 360–369

8. H. Iba, T. Kurita, H. de Garis, T. Sato: System identification using structured genetic algorithm. In: S. Forrest (ed.): *Proceedings of the Fifth International Conference on Genetic Algorithms (ICGA-93)*. Morgan Kaufmann, 1993, pp. 279–286

9. H. Kargupta, R. E. Smith: System identification with evolving polynomial networks. In: R. Belew, L. Booker (eds.): *Proceedings of the Fourth International Conference on Genetic Algorithms (ICGA-91)*. Morgan Kaufmann, 1991, pp. 370–376

10. K. E. Kinnear Jr.: Generality and difficulty in genetic programming: Evolving a sort. In: S. Forrest (ed.): *Proceedings of the Fifth International Conference on Genetic Algorithms (ICGA-93)*. Morgan Kaufmann, 1993, pp. 287–294

11. H. Kitano: Designing neural networks using genetic algorithms with graph generation system. *Complex Systems* 4, 461–476 (1990)

12. J. R. Koza: *Genetic Programming: On the Programming of Computers by Means of Natural Selection*. MIT Press, 1992

13. H. Mühlenbein: Evolutionary algorithms – Theory and applications. In: E. H. L. Aarts, J. K. Lenstra (eds.): *Local Search in Combinatorial Optimization*. Wiley, 1993

14. H. Mühlenbein, D. Schierkamp-Voosen: Predictive models for the breeder genetic algorithm I: Continuous parameter optimization. *Evolutionary Computation* 1, 25–49 (1993)

15. I. Rechenberg: *Evolutionsstrategie: Optimierung technischer Systeme nach Prinzipien der biologischen Evolution*. Stuttgart: Frommann-Holzboog, 1973

16. J. Rissanen: Stochastic complexity and modeling. *The Annuls of Statistics* 14, 1080–1100 (1986)

17. J. D. Schaffer: Multiple objective optimization with vector evaluated genetic algorithm. In: J. D. Schaffer (ed.): *Proceedings of the International Conference on Genetic Algorithms and Their Applications*. Erlbaum Associates, 1985, pp. 93–100

18. W. A. Tackett: Genetic programming for feature discovery and image discrimination. In: S. Forrest (ed.): *Proceedings of the Fifth International Conference on Genetic Algorithms (ICGA-93)*. Morgan Kaufmann, 1993, pp. 303–309

19. D. Whitley, T. Starkweather, C. Bogart: Genetic algorithms and neural networks: Optimizing connections and connectivity. *Parallel Computing* 14, 347–361 (1990)

20. B. T. Zhang, H. Mühlenbein: Genetic programming of minimal neural nets using Occam's razor. In: S. Forrest (ed.): *Proceedings of the Fifth International Conference on Genetic Algorithms (ICGA-93)*. Morgan Kaufmann, 1993, pp. 342–349

21. B. T. Zhang, H. Mühlenbein: Evolving optimal neural networks using genetic algorithms with Occam's razor. *Complex Systems* (1994)

22. B. T. Zhang, H. Mühlenbein: Synthesis of sigma-pi neural networks by the breeder genetic programming. In: *Proceedings of the IEEE World Congress on Computational Intelligence (WCCI-94)*. New York: IEEE Press, 1994

Designing Neural Networks by Adaptively Building Blocks in Cascades*

J. Born, I. Santibáñez–Koref, H.–M. Voigt

Technische Universität Berlin
Bionik und Evolutionstechnik
Ackerstraße 71–76 (ACK1), D-13355 Berlin
e–mail:born@fb10.tu-berlin.de

Abstract. We present a novel approach for the structuring of artificial neural networks by an Evolutionary Algorithm. The structuring problem is discussed as an example of a pseudo–boolean optimization problem. The continuous Evolution Strategy is extended by an individual developmental process, in our case a stochastic generation scheme, to allow the use of adaptive genetic operators. On exemplary tests we analyze the performance and evaluate the efficiency of this approach.

1 Introduction

In this paper, we consider the problem of evolutionary designing feed–forward neural networks (FFN, [6]). Informally, the designing problem is: *Find for a given task a FFN-graph which fullfils some optimality criteria.*

The FFN-graph is a directed acyclic graph, thus the problem can be reduced to find a connectivity matrix $C = (c_{ij})$, $c_{ij} \in \{0,1\}, i, j = 1, ..., n$ (with n-number of neurons in the net), for which the FFN performs the required task and fullfils the optimality criteria.

The resulting optimization task is to optimize a pseudo–boolean function (i.e. a real–valued function, depending on binary variables). Since it is known that layered FFN tends to work well, it is possible to assume that the connectivity matrix in most cases will be a block matrix.

In the following, we propose an extension of the continuous Evolution Strategy (ES, [4], [7]) for the solution of block-structured pseudo-boolean problems. Using a parametric model for the generation of connectivity matrices, a stochastic generation scheme (the BBC–Algorithm), we can profit from the capability of the ES to adapt the parameters of the genetic operators used in the evolutionary process.

In section 2 we present details of the evolutionary optimization algorithm, the BBC-EA. Results produced by the BBC–EA for different problems are presented and discussed in section 3. Finally, in section 4, we draw conclusions from the simulations and make some additional remarks on the BBC–EA approach.

---

* Supported by the Bundesministerium für Forschung und Technologie (BMFT) grant SALGON (No. 01 IN 107).

2 Methodology of the BBC–EA

2.1 Recursive Generation of Connectivity Matrices

Kitano [3] has introduced grammatical encoding of FFN. The basic idea is to obtain the connectivity matrix of a FFN by applying a deterministic context-free Graph–L–System to an axiom. A genetic algorithm generates and selects such productions which lead to a graph generation grammar with good task solving properties. This grammar generates within m recursive steps a $(2 \times 2)^m$ connectivity matrix by rewriting word by word in form of (2×2) matrices from an initial (1×1) matrix (axiom).

As in Kitano's paper, our approach is not to manipulate the connectivity matrix itself. Instead of this, a generation scheme for this matrix is manipulated. The initial step consists of generating a directed and labeled tree by rewriting m times an axiom. This tree represents the generation process of the matrix. The next steps of the algorithm consist in changing parts of this tree, which means change some parts of the scheme.

The generation scheme can be imagined as a sequence of cascades of (2×2) blocks which leads to the $(2 \times 2)^m$ connectivity matrix. Therefore, we call the algorithm the "Building Blocks in Cascades"–Algorithm (the BBC–Algorithm).

In [9], we proposed a cyclic scheme with fixed control parameters for the application of the BBC–Algorithm. The following algorithmic version allows the adaptation of the control parameters by an evolutionary process.

2.2 Algorithmic Description of the BBC–Algorithm

Let $G = (K, B)$ be a rooted tree. $K \subseteq \Sigma, \Sigma \neq \emptyset$ is a set of vertices and $B \subset K \times K$ a set of directed edges between vertices from K. All vertices with a distance from the root equal to i are called vertices of the ith level.

Let $SUC(k_0) = \{k_{n+1} \mid \exists b_1, ..., b_n \in B, b_l = (k_l, k_{l+1}), l = 0, ..., n\}$ be the set of successors of $k_0 \in K$.

Let $V = (\Sigma, p, w, m)$ with the axiom $w \in \Sigma$ be a tree generation process , i.e. the root of the tree to be generated.

Let be $p : \Sigma \times \Sigma \times \Sigma \to \Sigma \times \Sigma \times \Sigma$ a generation instruction and m the recursion depth of the generation process.
The generation process is defined as follows:

$G_0 = (K_0, B_0)$ with $K_0 = \{w\}$, $B_0 = \emptyset$

$G_1 = p(G_0) = (K_1, B_1)$ with $K_1 = K_0 \cup \{k_{1,1}, k_{1,2}, k_{1,3}, k_{1,4}\}$,
$B_1 = B_0 \cup \{(w, k_{1,1}), (w, k_{1,2}), (w, k_{1,3}), (w, k_{1,4})\}$

...

$G_i = p(G_{i-1}) = (K_i, B_i)$ with $K_i = K_{i-1} \cup \{k_{i,1}, ..., k_{i,4^i}\}$,

$$B_i = B_{i-1} \cup \{(k_{i-1,j}, k_{i,4(j-1)+k}) \quad j = 1, ..., 4^{i-1}, k = 1, ..., 4\}$$

...

$$G_m = p(G_{m-1}) = (K_m, B_m) \text{ with } K_m = K_{m-1} \cup \{k_{m,1}, ..., k_{m,4^m}\},$$
$$B_m = B_{m-1} \cup \{(k_{m-1,j}, k_{m,4(j-1)+k}) \quad j = 1, ..., 4^{m-1}, k = 1, ..., 4\}$$

Let $A = \{AT : K \to \{0,1\}\}$ the set of mappings which assigns to every node an element from the set $\{0,1\}$ (coloring of the tree) where $\{0,1\}$ is called the set of attributes of the nodes. Then the following functions are defined:

- Let be $flip : \{0,1\} \to \{0,1\}$ with $flip(0) = 1$ and $flip(1) = 0$
- Let $FLIP : K \times A \to A$ with

$$FLIP(k_0, AT)(k) = \begin{cases} flip(AT(k_0)) & k = k_0 \\ flip(AT(k_0)) & k \in SUC(k_0) \\ AT(k) & else \end{cases}$$

be a function which flips the attribute of a node and rewrites the attributes of the successor nodes with this attribute.
- Let $COPY : K \times A \to A$ with

$$COPY(k_0, AT)(k) = \begin{cases} AT(k_0) & k \in SUC(k_0) \\ AT(k) & else \end{cases}$$

be a function which copies the attribute of a node to all successor nodes.

Then the *BBC-Algorithm* can be described as follows:

- *Initial step:*
  Set the recursion depth m.
  Generate a tree with the tree generation process V.
  Choose a coloring AT of the tree.
  Choose the control parameters: determine for every level i , $i = 1, ..., m$ probabilities l_i (probability to change the tree from level i), p_i (probability for the application of the FLIP function) and f_i (probability for the application of the COPY function).
- *BBC step:*
  Choose with probability l_i a level i and perform for the nodes of the ith level:

  Choose with probability p_i a node k and set $AT' = FLIP(k, AT)$.
  Choose with probability f_i a node k and set $AT'' = COPY(k, AT')$.

Set the final connectivity matrix by the attributes of the terminal nodes K_m corresponding to AT''.

2.3   The BBC–Algorithm in an Evolutionary Framework (the BBC–EA)

We embedded the BBC–Algorithm in an evolutionary framework. This is motivated by the general problem of all random search methods (in the presented paper a repetitive use of the BBC–Algorithm) : The efficiency depends on a well–setting or adaptation of the control parameters. An evolutionary framework for the BBC–Algorithm permits a dynamical adaptation of the control parameters.

The evolutionary framework is based on the classical $(\mu + \lambda)$ scheme of the ES (μ – number of parents, λ – number of offspring; see e.g. [4], [7]). The classical scheme is extended by an explicitly realized *individual development*.

The individuals of the initial parent population are generated by using the initial step of the BBC–Algorithm. The encoding, the development, and the evaluation of an individual is done in the following way:

- The *genotype* of an individual contains the control parameters of the BBC–Algorithm (in the following the BBC–Parameters).
- Each individual undergoes a development ("a gene expression") by performing a BBC–step controlled by the BBC–Parameters.
- The gene expression leads to the *preformed phenotype*, which consists of the resulting connectivity matrix, and the tree of its generation scheme.
- By an "adaptation" process, the resulting connectivity matrix is transformed in a directed graph. All nodes and edges are deleted, which are not located on a path between boundary nodes of the graph. The FFN and the corresponding connectivity matrix (in the following "the reduced connectivity matrix") described by this reduced graph is the *adult phenotype*.
- For the adult phenotype the *fitness* is determined by evaluating the graph structure and the performance of the trainined FFN on the required task.

As *genetic operators* we use: Mutation and recombination on genotype level, recombination on level of the preformed phenotypes. Selection is determined by the fitness of the adult phenotype.

The full description of the BBC–EA and the default parameter setting is given in [8].

2.4   The BBC–EA as Universal Network Generator

In order to generate a FFN, the questions arise which structure is "the best", or what is the performance of a special structure ?

We think the best is to give an approach, which can generate a wide variety of such structures: That's why the fitness function can be composed of different functions. We offer in the BBC–EA the possibility to build a fitness criterion by a weighted sum of the following measures of the adult phenotype: Learning–error (mean square error), classification–error, number of iterations for the training of the network, number of connections in the network–graph, minimal path–length in the network–graph, and maximal path–length. (Path–length is the number of vertices between input and output within the network–graph, so that no node occurs twice.)

3   Tests with Selected Problems

In [10], we tested the parity problem of the dimensions 3, 5, 7, and the two spirals problem (see [2]). The relatively good "scaling property" – with regard to the number of generations needed to generate a sub–minimal network – was demonstrated for the parity problem.

First, in this paper we present some results for the 3 dimensional case in order to show the main characteristics of the BBC–EA. The tests were performed by a (20 + 100)–version of the BBC–EA, and we used 10 trials for each problem. The recursion depth of the BBC–Algorithm was 5, i.e. the connectivity matrix had the dimension (32 × 32).

For all tests a modified backpropagation algorithm was used as trainings procedure.

3.1   3-Dimensional Parity Problem with Minimization of the Number of Connections in the Network–Graph (PAR3–CON)

The fitness function for the adult phenotype was computed as the weighted sum of the learning–error and the number of connections in the network–graph. The weight for the learning–error was 0.0 for correctly trained networks, otherwise 1000.0; the weight for the number of connections was 1.0. A trial was stopped if the best individual of the population was represented by an adult phenotype with a correctly trained network, having 10 or less connections.

The results are listed in the following table:

PAR3–CON	best	worst	average
Number of connections	7	10	–
Minimal path–length	1	1	–
Maximal path–length	2	3	–
Number of generations	2	7	4

Figure 1 shows the best connectivity matrix and the corresponding reduced connectivity matrix, generating a network with 1 hidden unit within 1 hidden layer, and 7 connections.

Fig. 1. The best unreduced and reduced connectivity matrix for PAR3–CON.

In this and the next figures of connectivity matrices the following holds: No connection (0) in the upper right triangle is white, a connection (1) is black. The lower left triangle is completely black. Here, and for the following figures of reduced connectivity matrices, a "normed" or "renumbered" reduced connectivity matrix is sketched. This matrix is generated from the reduced connectivity matrix by newly numbering of the nodes and connections from the beginning.

3.2   3–Dimensional Parity Problem with Generation of a Deep–Layered Network with Few Connections in the Network–Graph (PAR3–DEEP)

The fitness function for the adult phenotype was computed as the weighted sum of the learning–error, the (negative) minimal path–length, the (negative) maximal path–length, and the number of connections in the network–graph. The weight for the learning–error was 0.0 for correctly trained networks, otherwise 1000.0; the weight for the minimal path–length was -10.0; the weight for the maximal path–length was -0.5; the weight for the number of connections was 0.005. Each trial was stopped after 100 generations. The results are listed in the following table:

PAR3–DEEP	best	worst	average
Number of connections	105	102	-
Minimal path–length	9	7	-
Maximal path–length	29	25	-
Number of generations	100	100	-

Figure 2 shows the best connectivity matrix and the corresponding reduced connectivity matrix for problem PAR3–DEEP, generating a network with 28 hidden units within 28 hidden layers, and 105 connections.

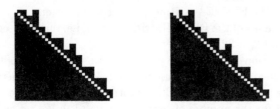

Fig. 2. The best unreduced and reduced connectivity matrix for PAR3–DEEP.

3.3   Solving Problem PAR3–CON – Operating on the Level of the Connectivity Matrix Alone (PAR3–PICK)

We tested the BBC–EA with "pure" operation within the connectivity matrix by fixing the level 5. Only "(1×1)" blocks were free to vary. We stopped each trial after 10 generations. The results are listed in the following table:

PAR3–PICK	best	worst	average
Number of connections	97	139	–
Minimal path–length	1	1	–
Maximal path–length	10	13	–
Number of generations	10	10	–

Figure 3 shows the best connectivity matrix and the corresponding reduced connectivity, generating a network with 16 hidden units within 5 hidden layers, and 97 connections.

Fig. 3. The best unreduced and reduced connectivity matrix for PAR3–PICK.

3.4 The 2–D, Two Spirals Problem with Minimization of the Number of Connections in the Network–Graph (2–SPI–CON)

We present results for the two spirals problem (see [2]) which was used as benchmark for different algorithms.

We used a (6+30)–BBC–EA scheme to solve the problem.

The recursion depth of the BBC–Algorithm was 5, i.e. the connectivity matrix had the dimension (32×32).

The fitness function for the adult phenotype was computed as the weighted sum of the pattern–error and the number of connections in the network–graph. The weight for the pattern–error was 0.0 for correctly trained networks, otherwise 1000.0; the weight for the number of connections was 1.0. We set as lower bound for correctly trained networks a pattern–error of 5% .

We used 10 trials, and each trial was stopped after 10 generations. The results are listed in the following table:

2–SPI–CON	best	worst
Number of connections	44	96
Minimal path–length	1	1
Maximal path–length	8	11
Number of BP–iterations	1,150	4,250

Figure 4 shows the best connectivity matrix and the corresponding reduced connectivity matrix for problem 2–SPI–CON, generating a network with 7 hidden units within 7 hidden layers, and 44 connections.

Fig. 4. The best unreduced and reduced connectivity matrix for 2–SPI–CON.

3.5 Discussion of the Results

Problem PAR3–CON and problem PAR3–DEEP

Both test problems indicate the best–case and worst–case of efficiency (measured by the number of generations) in generating desired topologies of networks.

The main reason of the different efficiency are the different probability of success, i.e. the chance to generate an offspring, having an adult phenotype with a better fitness than the fitness of the parents.

The probability of success is high for problem PAR3–CON at the beginning and during the evolutionary process. Figure 1 shows that in this case the BBC–EA has to operate only with a recursion depth of 3; i.e. a *minimal block–size* of (4 × 4) is sufficient in order to generate the best adult phenotype. Furthermore, figure 1 illustrates that on the level of the preformed phenotype there is a high degree of *redundancy* in order to generate the adult phenotype. Redundancy within the connectivity matrix of the preformed phenotype, concerning the corresponding reduced connectivity matrix of the adult phenotype, means that there are blocks, which can vary without an effect on the fitness. Due to this, the same connectivity matrix of the adult phenotype can be generated by different connectivity matrices of the preformed phenotype.

Both factors - the minimal block size and the redundancy - generate a high probability of success and a high efficiency.

For problem PAR3–DEEP there exists after some few generations a low probability of success, therefore a small rate of convergence follows. As soon as in the connectivity matrix of the preformed phenotype all nodes are connected (the maximization of the path-length is done), all 1–blocks will also emerge in the adult phenotype, and will deteriorate the fitness. Figure 2 may illustrate that at the end of the evolutionary process. A success would only be possible by operating on the 5th level. The minimal block size decreases to (1 × 1), and the redundancy disappears.

Problem PAR3–PICK

The BBC–EA is applied in a strong reduced manner. This version corresponds with an random search algorithm, which flips single elements of the connectivity matrices of the preformed phenotypes. The number of flips is adaptively controlled. Such a "blind pick"–algorithm could be used by an inexperienced person, and is nothing other then to cut and add weights to an existing FFN.

The test results confirm that the complete BBC–EA outperformes such a blind pick–algorithm for this task. The reason is that the blind pick does not profit from the block structure and the redundancy.

Problem 2–SPI–CON

The results confirm that deep layered networks are optimal for this problem (optimal in the sense that we can only operate with a bounded number of nodes).

The BBC–EA was free to generate other then deep layered architectures. A classification–rate of 95% fot training–set was sufficient to stop the training procedure. The number of hidden units ranged from 7 to 10. We refer to other authors who have tested this problem:

Fahlman [1] has summarized some results obtained on this problem. Among the cited results, the most elegant solution is generated by the CASCOR Algorithm by Fahlman and Lebiere. This algorithm is able to solve this problem with a classification–rate of 100% in 1,700 epochs (average over 100 trials). In these trials, the constructed networks ranged from 12 to 19 hidden units, with an average of 15.

4   Conclusions

We have seen that the BBC–EA can be used as an universal network generator. The algorithm generates for different fitness functions structures which fullfil the requirements.

The efficiency of the BBC–EA increases, if it is possible to describe the problem in a redundant manner.

The recursive generation scheme does not make direct use of information from the training procedure (such in other FFN generation schemes, i.e. [1]). The training procedure has only an implicit feedback to the BBC–EA by the fitness function.

Therefore, the BBC–EA offers an efficient search method for pseudo–boolean optimization problems, which are block–structured. For these problems, the BBC–EA performes an adaptive, problem–adequate neighbourhood search.

References

1. S. E. Fahlman, C. Lebiere. The Cascade–Corellation Learning Architecture. In D.S. Touretzky (ed.): Advances in Neural Information Pressing Systems 2. Morgan Kaufmann. 1990.

2. K. J. Lang, M. J. Witbrock. Learning to Tell Two Spirals Apart. In D.S. Touretzky et al. (eds.), Proceedings of the 1988 Connectionist Models Summer School. Morgan Kaufmann. 1988.

3. H. Kitano. Designing neural networks using genetic algorithm with graph generation system. Complex Systems, 4:461–476, 1990.

4. I. Rechenberg. Evolutionsstrategie: Optimierung technischer Systeme nach Prinzipien der biologischen Evolution. Frommann–Holzboog, Stuttgart. 1973.

5. I. Rechenberg. Evolutionsstrategie '94. Frommann–Holzboog, Stuttgart. 1994. (In press.)

6. D. E. Rumelhart, J. L. McClelland. Parallel Distributed Processing. Explorations in the Micro-structure of Cognition. Cambridge, Massachusetts, The MIT Press. 1986.

7. H.P. Schwefel. Numerical Optimization of Computer Models. J. Wiley, Chichester, New York, Brisbane, Toronto. 1981.

8. H. Spielberg. Bushhouse – The documentation to the C – code of the BBC–EA. Internal report, Technical University Berlin, Bionics and Evolution Techniques Laboratory, 1993.

9. H.-M. Voigt, J. Born, I. Santibáñez-Koref. Structuring of Artificial Neural Networks with Generative Grammars. In: M. v.d. Meer (Ed.): Statusseminar des BMFT Neuroinformatik 1992, pages 45–54. DLR, Berlin, 1992.

10. H.-M. Voigt and J. Born and I. Santibáñez-Koref. Evolutionary Structuring of Artifical Neural Networks, Technical Report TR-93-002, Technical University Berlin, Bionics and Evolution Techniques Laboratory, 1993.

Hybrid Adaptive Heuristic Critic Architectures for Learning in Mazes with Continuous Search Spaces

A. G. Pipe[1], T. C. Fogarty[2], A. Winfield[1]

1 Intelligent Autonomous Systems Lab.   2 Bristol Transputer Centre
  Faculty of Engineering   Faculty of Computer Science & Math

University of the West of England
Coldharbour Lane, Frenchay, Bristol BS16 1QY
United Kingdom
email ag_pipe@csd.uwe.ac.uk

Abstract

We present the first results obtained from two implementations of a hybrid architecture which balances exploration and exploitation to solve mazes with continuous search spaces. In both cases the critic is based around a Radial Basis Function (RBF) Neural Network which uses Temporal Difference learning to acquire a continuous valued internal model of the environment through interaction with it. Also in both cases an Evolutionary Algorithm is employed in the search policy for each movement. In the first implementation a Genetic Algorithm (GA) is used, and in the second an Evolutionary Strategy (ES). Over successive trials the maze solving agent learns the V-function, a mapping between real numbered positions in the maze and the value of being at those positions.

1   Background

In attempting to solve problems which involve goal oriented movements through an unknown or uncertain environment the need for a good balance between exploration of the environment and exploitation of the knowledge gained from the exploration has been well established [eg. Thrun 1992]. Such problems are typified by, though not restricted to, mobile robots navigating through 2-dimensional maze-like environments. Much work has been done, embracing a wide range of disciplines. Recently the techniques of Temporal Difference learning, Neural Networks, Genetic Algorithms and "Holland" style Classifier Systems have all been brought to bear with promising results, some researchers using more than one technique to build hybrid systems. The use of Temporal Difference (TD) reinforcement learning algorithms [Barto et al 1989] in action/critic architectures such as the Adaptive Heuristic Critic (AHC) [Sutton 1984, Werbos 1992] and in Q-learning [Watkins 1989], both of which are "on-line" approximations to Dynamic Programming [Barto et al 1991], have shown great promise when applied to maze problems where an agent, such as a mobile robot, attempts to establish an efficient path to a goal state through interaction with its environment.

A good representative example of work in this area has been conducted by Long-Ji Lin. As part of his PhD thesis [Lin 1993] he presented an excellent comparison of these two learning algorithms for two classes of maze solving problem. He used feedforward, and later recurrent, Multi-Layer Perceptron (MLP) Neural Networks to store information about the states (ie. positions) in the maze. It is typical of published work to date in this field [eg. Sutton 1991, Lin 1993, Roberts 1993] that mazes are discretized by dividing the area into a number of states on an equally spaced 2-dimensional grid. It is also typical to restrict the possible actions from any state to a small set of "nearest neighbours" type movements (eg. Lin's "Stochastic Action Selector" [Lin 1993]). Whilst these domains are useful ones in which to establish the efficacy of a learning algorithm they result in some serious limitations for the many "real-world" applications where the requirements of accuracy and range would dictate a very large state space.

If we open up the problem a little and allow the set of possible actions from a state to be linear movements to any other state in the maze then straight line traversals of the open spaces become possible in one movement, thus obviating the need for "close quarters" exploration in those areas which do not require it. However, although this is clearly a very desirable property for the agent to possess, its task of effective exploration at each new position becomes much harder.

If we open up the problem still further we could effectively circumvent our accuracy requirement altogether and allow movements in the maze to be expressed as real valued numbers. We could choose to view our model of this environment as either having states of a size set by the floating point number resolution of the computer we are using or, in the limit, as a continuous environment. As Lin points out towards the end of his PhD thesis [Lin 1993], it is fortuitous that a Neural Network representation of the V-function can make the switch from a discrete input space to a continuous one relatively effortlessly, whereas by contrast a tabular representation cannot. However the question of how to efficiently explore such an environment remains open.

2   Introduction

Below we give an overview of our hybrid architecture.

The two principle components of an Adaptive Heuristic Critic (AHC) architecture are the "action policy" and "critic" parts. Here an Evolutionary Algorithm (EA), either a Genetic Algorithm (GA) or an Evolutionary Strategy (ES), is used directly as the main exploring part of the agent, ie. it forms the "action policy" for each movement in the maze. A Radial Basis Function (RBF) Neural Network is used to store the knowledge gained from exploration and therefore forms the main part of the "critic", using a Temporal Differences (TD) learning algorithm to approximate the V-function (or Utility function) as the search progresses.

At each "movement time step" the EA is restarted with a fresh population and, with the entire maze at its disposal, searches for the best next movement on a "move & return" basis. Here we restrict movements to any straight line traversal of the maze from the current position. Interactions with the environment occur during the search. The fitness function used to rate EA population members is supplied by the RBF Neural Network, which performs a mapping between a given continuous real valued xy-coordinate input and a measure of "value" or "utility" for that position as its output, ie. the V-function as described above.

This process continues through multiple EA generations until either the population has converged or a maximum number of generations has been reached. The highest rated population member is then used to make a "non-return" movement to the next position in the maze. After this a Temporal Difference learning algorithm is executed on the RBF network to change the V-function's shape. Changes are made in the regions of the maze surrounding the movements executed so far in the current trial by distributing a discounted reward or punishment back to them. The amount of this reward/punishment is simply derived from the value of the V-function at the new position. For example if the V-function value at the new position is 255.5 and the value at the previous position was 180.5 then some proportion of the difference (75.0) is added to the previous position's value. According to a simple variant of the standard TD algorithm [Sutton 1991], this process is "daisy-chained" back through time until a "horizon" of backward time steps is reached.

The process described above is then repeated from the new position in the maze until the goal position is reached. This completes one trial. The RBF Neural Network is thus used as an Adaptive Heuristic Critic (AHC) of the EA's every attempt to explore the maze. It learns a V-function which reflects the true value of being in those regions of the maze which have so far been visited, refining the accuracy of the function after every movement in every trial of the maze. Knowledge of the maze is embodied in the Neural Network and all that is inherited in successive trials is the new RBF network weight vector.

We now go on to describe the Critic part of the architecture in more detail, and the maze problem we used to test our implementations. These are common to both implementations. After this we describe our implementations of the Genetic Algorithm (GA) and Evolutionary Strategy (ES) based search policies.

3   The Critic Network

In our application the critic part of an AHC architecture attempts to supply accurate evaluations of "value" or "utility" for new movements proposed by the action policy. Though the environmental model held by the critic may be inaccurate at the beginning of the task, through Temporal Difference learning, it is updated after each action so as to incorporate knowledge about the search so far. As the search progresses the critic's model approaches a more accurate model of the true V-function.

A Neural Network has a number of advantages over tabular methods for storing the V-function. Firstly the function learned is **continuous** in the input space. Secondly a certain amount of data compression can be achieved, though this is variable dependent upon network type.

We chose a gaussian Basis Function RBF Neural Network of the standard form [eg. Poggio & Girosi 1989, Sanner & Slotine 1991] rather than the global learning Multi-Layer Perceptron (MLP) used by Long-Ji Lin [Lin 1993] since this class of Neural Network has certain advantages for real time control applications. Firstly since passes of the learning algorithm affect only weights in the local region the problem of "knowledge drift" in other unrelated parts of the input space is avoided. Secondly learning time for these types of networks can be orders of magnitude faster with no local minima to get stuck in. Most importantly however the characteristic of "local generalisation" which this Neural Network type possesses means that changing the V-function mapping at one point in the input space has a tendency to modify the local region to a gradually diminishing degree as distance from this point increases. This property is very useful here in extracting as much knowledge as possible from each movement through the maze. It translates roughly as, for example, "if a position is a good one then the immediate region around it will also be good".

The Neural Network was modified after each movement using a simple Temporal Differences (TD) algorithm, according to the following update rules;

$$V_{t-1} = V_{t-1} + TDRATE\ ((V_t - PUNISH) - V_{t-1})$$

for the movement prior to the current one then;

$$V_{t-i} = V_{t-i} + TDRATE\ (V_{t-i+1} - V_{t-i}) \qquad \text{for } i = 2 \text{ to HORIZON}$$

Where; V_t = V-function output at time step t; TDRATE = Temporal Difference learning rate between 0 and 1; PUNISH = a small punishment to encourage exploration; HORIZON = TD scope.

If the new value for a V-function output becomes negative it is bounded to zero. The PUNISH factor was included to counteract limit cycles and/or stationary behaviour. Under these circumstances the value of those states will incur a penalty at each time step, thus resulting in the agent eventually breaking out into new areas of the maze.

Clearly the issue of initial off-line training of the Neural Network is an important issue. If the landscape were initially flat everywhere except at the goal state this would cause the critic to provide no useful information except at this final desired position. In our architecture this would cause the action policy, implemented using an Evolutionary Algorithm (EA), to default to random search, which is the best that can be done under the circumstances, and has been much studied in simple state-action space forms elsewhere [eg. Sutton 1991]. However, as mentioned in Barto,

Sutton & Watkins' Technical Report [Barto et al 1989] many "real world" applications allow for some reinforcement to be available as the search proceeds. For example if we consider the case of navigation across a room to a doorway where the path is obscured by obstacles, the agent is still likely to have a sense of distance from its goal, especially if it can "see " over the top of the obstacles. We wish to pursue experiments in this type of environment and therefore off-line pre-trained the Neural Network with a smoothly reducing function of the Euclidean distance from the goal position. However we could have achieved a very similar result by repeatedly letting the agent "loose" from different start positions on a maze with no obstacles. We make no apologies for dong this, in many of the maze problems we used (as here) the agent's possession of such implicit *a priori* assumptions about the nature of its environment can be highly misleading.

4 The Maze Environment

Our maze is set on a unit square. For simplicity we restricted obstacles to straight lines of zero thickness. However they can be at any angle and of any length inside the unit square environment. We experimented with a variety of maze shapes, however the one illustrated below in figures 1 & 2 is typical. We picked this one to show here since it is simple enough to be clear when printed on a small scale but has both "switch backs" and a "dead end".

During the evaluation phase of the action policy each population member of the Evolutionary Algorithm, at each generation, is tested against the environment. The "suggested" new position is tried out on the maze by making the movement and then returning. Any one of these evaluations may cause a Lamarckian interaction with the environment to occur wherein a collision with an obstacle or a wall causes the agent to be halted and placed a small distance removed from the coordinates of collision. When this happens the process of critic evaluation continues, the fitness function used to rate each member of the EA population being supplied by the RBF Neural Network at this new position.

5 Genetic Algorithm

In order to test this architecture, we simplified the action policy by scaling down the resolution of movements in the environment's unit square from full floating point resolution to fixed 9-bit accuracy, ie. the minimum movement size is 1/512. From the perspective of the GA the maze therefore appears as a 512 X 512 square grid, ie. 262144 states. This retains the property of a large search space, but simplifies both modelling of the environment and the required complexity of the GA. However, although the action space is still discrete the environmental model learned by the agent, the Neural Network V-function, retains a real numbered mapping between input coordinates in the unit square to a real numbered V-function output.

Each GA population member is made up of an x-coordinate and a y-coordinate. These are absolute coordinates rather than being relative to the present position purely for computational ease. In all three architectures each GA population member is therefore an 18-bit integer made up of a 9-bit x-coordinate and a 9-bit y-coordinate. Before use as xy-coordinates in the maze it is scaled to the unit square. Though large for maze problems this is quite a small search space for contemporary GAs. A simple implementation was therefore used with a population of 56 individuals. The maximum number of generations was set to 80. The selection method was "Roulette wheel". Crossover and mutation were both 2-point, one in the x-coordinate and one in the y-coordinate. At each new generation the fittest individual from the previous generation is inherited unchanged.

6 The Evolutionary Strategy

Although the Genetic Algorithm described above could be modified and constrained to search real numbered spaces, this is not its natural territory. By contrast the Evolutionary Strategy (ES) [Schwefel 1977, Schwefel 1981] has been specifically designed for searching such environments.

In our simple implementation we followed the guidelines given in Back & Schwefel's paper [Back & Schwefel 1993]. We chose a (μ, λ) selection policy with 8 parents and 56 offspring at each generation, ie. a ratio of 1:7. Each individual is a 2-dimensional object variable vector plus variances for strategy parameters, covariances were not used. We also followed the standard form for mutation of both object and strategy variables. Global discrete recombination was used for the object variables and global intermediate for the strategy variables.

7 Experiments & Results

Many experimental runs were undertaken, here we give a representative set only, one from each of the two implementations. We hope they are sufficient to illustrate the following discussion.

7.1 GA Driven Action Policy

The following maze, GA, Neural Network and TD learning parameters pertain to the results given below.

Maze: (0.1,0.1) is the starting position (the top left corner in figure 1) and (0.78,0.78) is the goal position. Maximum fitness at the goal position is 100. Other off-line trained initial fitnesses calculated by;

$$Fitness_{ij} = 512 \times \left(1 - \left(\frac{\sqrt{(cx_i - goalx)^2 + (cy_j - goaly)^2}}{\text{max.}distance}\right)\right)$$

GA: Crossover probability = 0.9, mutation = 0.01.

RBF: 16 Basis Function centres on each axis, ie. 32 minimum size maze movements between each centre.

TD: TDRATE = 0.7, PUNISH = 8.0, Horizon = 20

Figure 1 illustrates the results of the first trial from start to goal position which took 79 moves to complete. It shows only the final move made from each position in the maze to the next, ie. the GA's "move-and-return" tests are not illustrated. At first glance the exploration looks somewhat

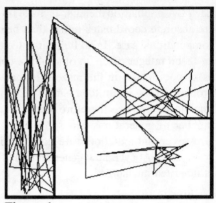

Figure 1

random. However closer investigation reveals an interplay between the GA search, TD learning and off-line pre-training of the V-function network. In the next 5 runs the number of moves required to complete the maze reduced more or less smoothly, mostly spent investigating some small area missed by GA searches in the previous trials or staying still whilst the worth of a position was devalued through the TD learning PUNISH factor. The table below shows the number of moves that the agent took to find the goal position over the first 6 trials.

Trial	No. of Moves
1	79
2	39
3	66
4	46
5	34
6	15

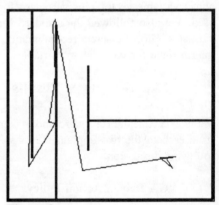

Figure 2

By the 5th trial the top right hand quadrant of the maze ceased to be of any interest to the agent. Figure 2 illustrates the results of the 6th trial. From this trial onwards the path was stable taking 15 or 16 moves to the goal. These moves were mirrored by stable "peaks" in the fitness landscape represented by the V-function Neural Network.

7.2 ES Driven Action Policy

The same maze, Neural Network and Temporal Difference learning parameters were used as in the previous case. The ES parameters were as described above. The results from the first trial are illustrated in figure 3 which took 84 moves to complete. The table below gives the number of moves required to complete the next 5 trials.

Trial	No. of Moves
1	84
2	29
3	44
4	14
5	11
6	14

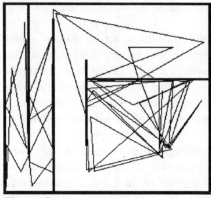

By the 4th trial the "trap" in the top right quadrant was ignored. The path from trial 6 onwards was stable at 11 to 15 moves per trial. Figure 4 shows this path at the 6th trial.

Figure 3

8   Discussion

We found that both architectures presented here were fairly robust to changes in value of the many parameters in the system, such as number of RBF centres, TD learning rate, PUNISH & HORIZON values, GA population size & number of generations, mutation and crossover probabilities etc. Most changes induced a more or less efficient search or affected the convergence behaviour over successive trials rather than resulting in incorrect behaviour. There seemed to be two distinct

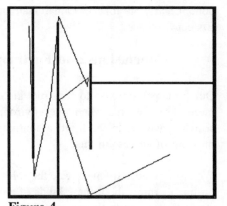

Figure 4

behaviours, first a strongly investigative mode in which large parts of the states space are searched, and then a stable TD reinforced mode which persists until some time variance in the environment occurs.

It is interesting to observe the differing emphasis in the search strategies of the GA and ES. In general, across a number of repeated experiments there is more similarity than contrast in the results, as one would hope. Considering the much larger effective search space that the Evolutionary Strategy had to move around in this is a credit to that action policy. Nonetheless the first trial of each implementation shown in figures 1 & 3 seem to imply that the GA pursues a more thorough search of the maze and appears to be better at "homing in" on the goal, we surmise the following. The former could be due to the better global search characteristics of the GA or due to using too small a population in the ES. The latter may be due to a superior ability on the part of the GA to conduct simultaneous close local and global searches, or again it may be a feature of relative population sizes for the actual differences in problem sizes between these two implementations. Despite these caveats we were greatly encouraged by our experiences with the Evolutionary Strategy (ES).

We tested these action policies against a random search by setting the number of generations to zero for each implementation, ie. the population was randomly initialized only. Under these circumstances, with all other factors the same as before, the random search started with a lower number of movements to solve the maze but convergence was much slower and the best solution discovered consisted of 18 moves, though this was not a stable state.

Although it is claimed in this paper's introduction that the EA performs the exploration whilst the Neural Network performs exploitation, clearly this is an oversimplification. For example the EA uses knowledge gained to date in searching from the current position in the maze at each new generation. The TD learning algorithm presented here clearly shapes the form of exploration because of the PUNISH factor for stationary or cyclic behaviours and any off-line training which is done. Clearly our form of Lamarckian interactions with the environment greatly affect EA convergence.

9　Conclusions and Further Work

Our principal aim was to construct architectures for agents capable of investigating maze-like problems where the environment was characterised by a large discrete search space or, in the limit, a continuous real valued one. We have gained some measure of success in this.

We also intended to investigate the roles of exploration and exploitation in an agent's on-line learning about these kinds of environments. We have found that despite our attempts to separate them our architectures are subtly and multitudinously linked in these respects. However, more experimental and analytical work needs to be done here to fully characterize them.

We are greatly encouraged by the capabilities of the Evolutionary Strategy in this application, but would like to carry out a more focused investigation of the relative abilities of GAs and ESs in optimizing real valued functions of the nature described here.

References

Back T., Schwefel H-P., 1993, 'An Overview of Evolutionary Algorithms for Parameter Optimization', Evolutionary Computation Vol.1 Num.1, pp1-23

Barto A. G., Bradtke S. J., Singh S. P., 1991, 'Real-Time Learning and Control using Asynchronous Dynamic Programming', Dept. of Computer Science, University of Massachusetts, USA, Technical Report 91-57

Barto A. G., Sutton R. S., Watkins C. J. C. H., 1989, 'Learning and Sequential Decision Making', COINS Technical Report 89-95

Belew R. K., McInerney J., Schraudolph N. N., 1990, 'Evolving Networks: Using the Genetic Algorithm with Connectionist Learning', University of California at San Diego, USA, CSE Technical Report CS90-174

Booker L. B., Goldberg D. E., Holland J. H., 1989, 'Classifier Systems and Genetic Algorithms', Artificial Intelligence 40, pp.235-282

Cliff D., Husbands P., Harvey I., 1992, 'Evolving Visually Guided Robots', University of Sussex, Cognitive Science Research Papers CSRP 220

Lin L., PhD thesis, 1993, 'Reinforcement Learning for Robots using Neural Networks', Computer Science School, Carnegie Mellon University Pittsburgh, USA

Poggio T., Girosi F., 1989, 'A theory of Networks for Approximation and Learning', MIT Cambridge, MA, AI lab. Memo 1140

Roberts G., 1989, 'A rational reconstruction of Wilson's Animat and Holland's CS-1', Procs. of 3rd International Conference on Genetic Algorithms, pp.317-321, Editor Schaffer J. D., Morgan Kaufmann

Roberts G., 1991, 'Classifier Systems for Situated Autonomous Learning', PhD thesis, Edinburgh University

Roberts G., 1993, 'Dynamic Planning for Classifier Systems', Proceedings of the 5th International Conference on Genetic Algorithms, pp.231-237

Sanner R. M., Slotine J. E., 1991, 'Gaussian Networks for Direct Adaptive Control', Nonlinear Systems Lab., MIT, Cambridge, USA, Technical Report NSL-910503

Sutton R. S., 1984, PhD thesis 'Temporal Credit Assignment in Reinforcement Learning', University of Massachusetts, Dept. of computer and Information Science

Sutton R. S., 1991, 'Reinforcement Learning Architectures for Animats', From Animals to Animats, pp288-296, Editors Meyer, J., Wilson, S., MIT Press

Thrun S. B., 1992, 'The Role of Exploration in Learning', Handbook of Intelligent Control: Neural, Fuzzy, and Adaptive Approaches, Van Nostrand Reinhold, Ed. White D. A., Sofge D. A.

Watkins C. J. C. H., 1989, PhD thesis 'Learning from Delayed Rewards', King's College, Cambridge.

Werbos P. J., 1992, 'Approximate Dynamic Programming for Real-Time Control and Neural Modelling', Handbook of Intelligent Control: Neural, Fuzzy, and Adaptive Approaches, Van Nostrand Reinhold, Ed. White D. A., Sofge D. A.

Wilson S. W., 1985, 'Knowledge growth in an artificial animal', Proceedings of an International Conference on Genetic Algorithms and their Applications, pp.16-23, Editor Grefenstette J. J.

Mutation Operators for Structure Evolution
of Neural Networks

Uwe Utecht and Karsten Trint

Technical University Berlin, Department Bionics and Evolution Techniques
Ackerstr. 71 - 76, Sekr. ACK 1, D - 13355 Berlin
email: utecht@fb10.tu-berlin.de, trint@fb10.tu-berlin.de

Abstract

The architecture of a neural network can be optimized by structure evolution. The structure evolution is based upon a two-stage evolution strategy (multipopulation strategy): On the population level, the structure is optimized, on the individual level, the parameters are adapted. For the variation of the (discrete) architecture, a mutation operator must be defined. To attain successful optimization, a mutation operator must satisfy two main conditions in the space of structures: First the principle of strong causality must be obeyed (smoothness of the fitness landscape in the space of structure), and second, a transition path between the structures must be guaranteed. In this paper different heuristic mutation operators will be defined and examined on their behavior with respect to strong causality and to neighborhood relation in the space of structures.

1. Introduction

With respect to their function, neural networks are difficult to construct. The functionality of a neural network is determined by the architecture of the net, by the transfer functions of the individual units and by the intensity of the individual connections (the weights). But there is no universal algorithm for designing the architecture, for choosing the transfer function and for adjusting the weights of a neural network for a required task. Lots of different methods have been invented for calculating a set of well-adapted weights for a fixed architecture. Most of these methods are gradient-descent optimization procedures. Generally the architecture itself is heuristically determined. Some new evolutionary approaches try to include the optimization of architecture and transfer function. The main evolutionary algorithms are evolution strategies [Rechenberg '73, Schwefel '77], genetic algorithms [Holland '75, Goldberg '89] and evolutionary programming [Fogel '66, Fogel '94]. As a part of evolution strategies, the structure evolution is a promising algorithm for these kinds of problems.

The structure evolution offers a powerful tool to include the architecture in the process of optimization. As mentioned above, the architecture of a neural network is essential for its functionality. The algorithmical design of the architecture allows to deal with the functionality of a net in a very promising way.

The structure evolution is based on a two-stage evolution strategy, the so-called multipopulation strategy [Rechenberg '89, '94]. The optimization of structure and parameters of a neural network is distributed on two levels [Lohmann '90, '91]. On the upper level - the population level - the structure is optimized by the evolution strategy. This means that the variables of the coded structure, the structure variables, are subject to the process of mutation and selection. In order to evaluate a mutated structure, the weights must be adapted first. This happens on the lower level of the strategy by applying the well-known process of parameter evolution. To give the parameter evolution the opportunity to adapt to the mutated structure, the strategy parameter isolation was created [Lohmann '90]: For a fixed number of generations, the different populations will be optimized separately, subsequently the populations will be qualified and selected.

The multipopulation strategy is described in the formal notation as:

$$[\mu'/\rho' +, \lambda' \, (\mu/\rho +, \lambda)^{\gamma}] \text{ - Evolution Strategy}$$

μ', ρ' and λ' are strategy parameters on the population level (number of parents, recombination number and number of offspring respectively), μ, ρ and λ are strategy parameters on the individual level, γ is the period of isolation.

Applied to neural networks, this results in the separate optimization of architecture and weights. From a mathematical point of view, the architecture of a neural network is the structure which defines the mutual meaning of the weights (parameters) with respect to the quality function. Based upon the method of the two-stage structure evolution, the upper level optimizes the architecture, the lower level adapts the weights to the changed structure. The coding of the architecture by the structure variables has a special significance, because the evolutionary process works on the structure variables. For the mutation of architectures, there exist several ideas:

• *Direct mutation* is often used with genetic algorithms. The mutation is applied directly to the coded structure [e. g. Miller et al. '89]. The coding scheme is very important, because the satisfaction of the strong causality depends on it. A great advantage is the possibility to use the recombination as a convergence speed-up.

• *Genetic programming* or *grammar based systems*, in which an evolutionary process builds a set of a grammar language for the architecture of neural nets. There are logical expressions like, for example, LISP S-expressions [Koza, Rice '91], grammar based systems [Whitley et al. '90, Gruau '93, Jacob, Rehder '93], graph generating or Lindenmeyer-systems [Kitano '90, Born et al. '94] and others.

• *Mutation operators* are applied when using evolution strategies or evolutionary programming for optimizing neural network architectures. Lohmann ['91] applied mutation operators for the development of neural filter structures, Rechenberg et al. ['92] optimized the structure of simple neural networks in order to minimize the connectivity. In the field of evolutionary programming see [Fogel '93, McDonnell, Waagen '93,'94, Maniezzo '94, Angeline et al. '94] for promising approaches of structure optimization of neural networks.

The definition of a mutation operator is the creation of a neighborhood relation in the space of structure. One important condition for the successful optimization of not only discrete problems is the principle of strong causality. Strong causality according to Rechenberg means: a small variation of a quality value is caused by a small variation in the space of parameters. In general, this is obtained for real valued problems by using Gaussian random numbers combined with a stepsize adaptation. Applied to neural networks, this means that the mutation by mutation operators should change the quality of an architecture in a small range.

The main problem is the question for a "small variation of a structure" to satisfy the principle of strong causality. Especially in the field of neural networks, it is widely unknown how a variation of a net architecture effects the quality. Often there are only heuristic hints of a global kind, say the number of layers or hidden units, which may be used for a special problem. What is still missing is a general description of a neighborhood relation for architectures of neural networks.

structuring goals

Another important aspect is the possibility to formulate a lot of different goals for the structure optimization. Basically there are two sets of different structuring goals: *task related* and *net related* goals. The most important structuring goals are: task mastering, generalization, rate of convergence, behavior of convergence, robustness, error tolerance, minimal connectivity, computation time, crossing minimization.

In this report, the task related structuring goal *task mastering* will be considered. This implies that the quality functions on the levels of structure and parameter optimization are identical.

stock of structures

According to Lohmann ['91], the stock of structures describes the set of all valid structures for the respective optimization problem. These are all architectures which satisfy the conditions of the net specification, e. g. number of units and kind of connectivity (feed forward connectivity for example). Another restriction is the inherent fact that a mutual connection between input units and between output units makes no sense and therefore is not permitted.

2. Mutation Operators

In this paragraph, different mutation operators for structure evolution are described. In figure 1, the operators are illustrated in two ways: The variations of the connectivity matrices as well as the effects on the topology are shown. Both representations have advantages, in some cases one or the other way of illustration is easier to understand.

connection-plus-minus. An obvious mutation operator is the connection-plus-minus operator: One connection is either added or removed on any random location. This operator is often used with genetic algorithms, as one bit in the connectivity matrix is changed [e. g. Miller et al. '89].

In the connectivity matrix and in the net topology, it looks like a "small variation of the structure". In the experiment and with a close consideration, it turns out that the behavior in the space of quality can be completely different. Removing a connection can cut important information channels, what results in a high loss of quality.

connection-move. The connection-move operator is similar to the connection-plus-minus operator. In one location, a connection will be removed, and in another location, a connection will be added, but either the source-unit or the destination-unit remains the same. The idea behind this operator is to avoid a large change in quality while removing a connection by creating a new one in the near surroundings.

connection-shift-2-2 & connection-shift-2-3. Both connection-shift operators mutually change the connections between three units. The motivation of this operators is the idea that the careful variation of existing information channels effects the quality only with small variance. Careful variation of information channels means that existing connections between units are varied but not completely deleted or created.

495

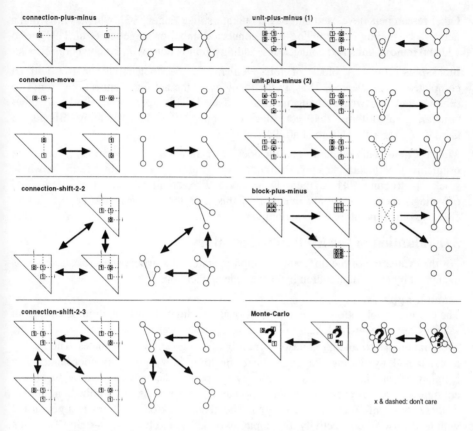

Fig. 1: mutation operators, connectivity matrix and topology

The connection-shift-2-3 operator changes three connection between three units to two connections and reverse. The connection-2-2 operator changes two connections between three units to two other connections, thus, the total number of connections cannot change.

unit-plus-minus (1) & unit-plus-minus (2). The unit-plus-minus operator is a heuristically motivated operator in two versions. Similar to the connection-plus-minus operator, which adds or removes connections, this operator adds or removes units in existing unit sequences. The motivation is the idea that the flow of information will be enlarged or reduced by one calculation unit. It is supposed that the operator will not cause large quality changes because no information channels will be interrupted.

In the connectivity matrix, the operator is presented not very comfortable, as five elements are varied. The topology illustrated in the figure makes clearer what happens with the structure.

The second unit-plus-minus operator is slightly different from the first one. In the first variant, the flow of information will be transferred exactly from two to three connections with an intermediate unit, in the second variant, potential existing connections will be included in the transfer (see figure 1).

Other researchers have used unit based operators, like Fogel ['93], who has modified a network by adding or removing fully connected units, or Angeline et al. ['94], who add and remove units and connections, adding a unit is done without any connections.

block-plus-minus. A block of four elements in the connectivity matrix will be completely set or cleared. Thus, in the topology of the net four connections from two sending units to two receiving units are affected. This operator is similar to other structuring algorithms that act block-orientated like the "Building Blocks in Cascades"-Algorithm [Born et al. '94].

Monte-Carlo. This random operator does not care about considerations of structure or quality. One mutation step is the random drawing of an architecture from the whole stock of structures. Thus, there is no correlation at all between the parent- and offspring-structure. The only intention of this operator is to give the opportunity to compare other operators with random variations.

3. Evaluation of the Mutation Operators

For the evaluation of the different mutation operators, the whole space of structures is examined by total enumeration in an example application.

example application.
The example application is a two dimensional coordinate transformation, known from robotics as backward calculation. The task of the neural network is to calculate the two joint angles α_1 and α_2 of a two joint robot from given xy-coordinates. The quality is calculated by adding the quadratic error from every given xy-coordinate. The solution is ambiguous, because for every point, there exist two valid angle configurations. However, this is not important for the process of optimization, neither of these two configurations is preferred. The given stock of structures is a neural net with feed forward connectivity, two input, two hidden and two output units. The units are processing units according to Rumelhart and McClelland ['86] with a sigmoid transfer function. Thus, there is a maximum number of connections of 13. Every connection may or may not exist, which results in a stock of structures with $2^{13} = 8192$ different architectures.

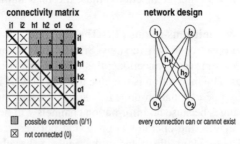

connectivity matrix   network design

□ possible connection (0/1)
☒ not connected (0)

every connection can or cannot exist

Fig. 2: stock of structures

complete examination.
The example application is small enough for a complete enumeration. For the examination of an operator with respect to strong causality, the operator is applied to every possible structure with all allowed transitions. The connection-plus-minus

operator for example is applied to every architecture exactly 13 times, because every existing connection can be deleted and every nonexisting connection can be created.

The quality of the example application is in the range of Q = 12.9 (best solution) and Q = 6400.0 (solution from unconnected net only by adjusting the output-bias). From the application of an operator follows a change in quality Q_δ as the difference of the qualities of the parent and of the offspring:

$$Q_\delta = Q_{parent} - Q_{offspring}$$

Thus, a positive difference Q_δ results from an improvement, a negative difference from a deterioration of quality. The quality differences will be classified and counted for their frequency.

quality difference distribution.

The distribution of the classes is logarithmic and separated by sign. There are the classes (0), (0,1), (1,2), (2,4), (4,8) ... (2048,4096), (4096 and greater) and (0,-1), (-1,-2) ... (-4096 and lower). The class (4,8) for example represents quality differences in the range from 4 to 8. A special class is the (0)-class, a quality difference from exactly zero is improbable, as a noise in the lower level optimization process results in different qualities for equal net architectures [Trint, Utecht '94]. In the (0)-class, all transitions will be counted, which vary the architecture either not or only in irrelevant locations. Irrelevant locations are connections from or to units which carry no information from the input or to the output units.

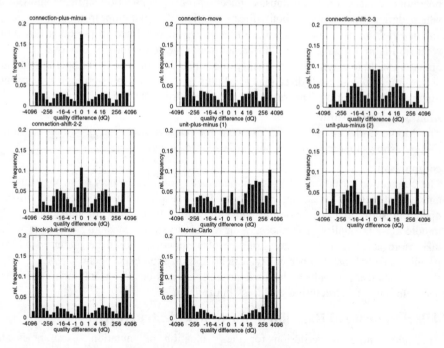

Fig. 3: Quality difference distributions of mutation operators

strong causality

The distribution of the quality differences shows the behavior of an operator with respect to strong causality (figure 3). Strong causality is detected in the diagrams by a high rate of small quality differences: connection-shift-2-3, connection-shift-2-2, unit-plus-minus (1) and unit-plus-minus (2). First of all, it does not matter whether there is an increase or decrease in quality. Correspondingly high rates of large quality variations are not welcome, as this opposes to the principle of strong causality and supports only a weak behavior: connection-plus-minus, connection-move, block-plus-minus and Monte-Carlo.

the (0)-class

Some operators attract attention because of a high number of transitions in the (0)-class. As described above, these are irrelevant transitions which affect the structure of the net only at no information processing locations, for example by adding a connection in a location where no further processing occurs. This happens when the inner structure of the architecture is not considered (e. g. connection-plus-minus, block-plus-minus). Irrelevant mutations are lost mutations, as there is no selection pressure at all.

symmetrical and asymmetrical operators

In figure 3, one can see symmetrical and asymmetric quality difference distributions. This corresponds to the description of the mutation operators (see figure 1). There are operators (connection-plus-minus, connection-move, connection-shift, Monte-Carlo) which define transitions in both directions. Thus, a mutation from a structure to another yielding in a certain quality difference is also defined in the other direction, what results in the same quality difference with reversed sign. It is obvious that these operators yield to a symmetrical quality difference distribution. Other operators do not define transitions in both directions (unit-plus-minus, block-plus-minus), they cannot reverse every transition. This results in an asymmetric distribution.

Monte-Carlo operator

The Monte-Carlo operator is an example for massive violation of strong causality. Figure 3 shows that most transitions cause a large change in quality.

comparison

The connection based operators show poor behavior with respect to strong causality and a high rate of irrelevant mutations. The unit-plus-minus and connection-shift operators show a more favorable behavior with a higher rate of mutations in the middle class of quality differences. With respect to strong causality, operators which take more account of the inner structure of a network, should be preferred as they promise a better convergence behavior in an optimization experiment.

This conclusion should be handled carefully as it is based on only one experiment and with only one structuring goal (task mastering).

4. Neighborhood Relation in the Space of Structures

The other important criterion for the evaluation of mutation operators is the neighborhood relation in the space of structures. To assess the neighborhood relation, every operator will be examined concerning the ability to change structures into other structures. A favorable operator should change by repeated application any given structure into every other structure. This means that the operator should cover the whole space of structures. But it is also possible that the space of structures splits up into several classes of different structures. Structures of one class can be changed into one another by repeated mutations, but members of any other class cannot be reached. The connection-move operator for example cannot change a structure with five connections into a structure with six connections, so structures with five and with six connections belong to different classes. In case of asymmetric operators, two structures belong to the same class if the operator allows a transition between them in both directions.

For the evaluation of the mutation operators, two quantities will be determined, the relative connectivity in space of structures and the average number of possible transitions of every structure. The relative connectivity describes the connectivity of all structures with respect to each other structure. It can vary between zero and one, whereas a value of one represents a complete connectivity (all structures belong to one class), a value of zero represents a complete unconnected space of structures. The relative connectivity is calculated as:

$$rel.\ connectivity = \frac{1}{norm} \sqrt{\sum_{all\ structures} number\ of\ attainable\ structures}$$

An optimal behavior of a mutation operator with respect to neighborhood relation is a high value of relative connectivity.

The average number of possible transitions describes the variability of an operator. A number of 13 for example means that the operator may be applied to every structure on average 13 times, every structure has 13 "neighboring structures".

operator	rel. connectivity	av. number of transitions
connection-plus-minus	1.00	13
connection-move	0.21	13
connection-shift-2-3	0.70	9
connection-shift-2-2	0.19	9
unit-plus-minus (1)	0.002	0.84
unit-plus-minus (2)	0.01	3.38
block-plus-minus	0.72	17.75
Monte-Carlo	1.00	8192

The table shows the quantities described above for the examined mutation operators. Only four operators show a favorable connectivity in the space of structures (connection-plus-minus, connection-shift-2-3, block-plus-minus and Monte-Carlo). Especially both unit-plus-minus operators cannot be used for structure optimization without modification because of very weak behavior in neighborhood relation. An average number of mutations of 0.84 (unit-plus-minus (1) operator) points out that the operator is not practical. This operator can be applied in average once on 84% of all structures!

The neighborhood relation can be improved by the synthesis of different operators, but of course, the effect on strong causality must be considered.

neighborhood relation versus strong causality

The conditions of good neighborhood relation in the space of structures and the satisfaction of the principle of strong causality are, to a large extent, contradictory. Operators with a well connected space of structures (connection-plus-minus, Monte-Carlo) violate strong causality, and operators which obey strong causality have a poorly connected space of structures (unit-plus-minus). An extreme example is the Monte-Carlo operator, it connects the space of structures in a perfect way, every structure is reachable by only one mutation, but strong causality is violated at its most.

The art of designing mutation operators is to create operators with a high connectivity in the space of structures which perform small changes in quality.

5. Conclusion

A number of different, heuristically created mutation operators for structure evolution of neural networks have been presented. They can be divided into two classes, connection-based and unit-based operators. Furthermore, one can distinguish between operators motivated by the inner structure of the network and operators acting on partial structure elements. These operators have been examined in an example application by total enumeration with respect to the principle of strong causality and to the neighborhood relation in the space of structures. It has been shown that operators created with respect to the inner structure obey strong causality in this application to a large extent. In order to achieve a well connected space of structures, a mutation operator must ensure a sufficient transition path between the structures. Unfortunately, these designing goals for mutation operators are contradictory. This points out the importance of a careful design of mutation operators.

Acknowledgement

This research was partly supported by the Bundesministerium für Forschung und Technik (BMFT) under grant SALGON - 01 IN 107 A/1, "Evolutionary Strategic Structuring in Neural Systems".

References

Angeline, P. J., Saunders, G. M., Pollack, J. B.: An Evolutionary Algorithm that Constructs Recurrent Neural Networks; IEEE Transactions on Neural Networks, vol. 5, no. 1, pp. 54-65; 1994

Born, J., Santibáñez-Koref, I., Voigt, H.-M.: Designing Neural networks by Adaptively Building Blocks in Cascades; Proc. of the 3. Conf. on Parallel Problem Solving from Nature; Jerusalem; 1994

Fogel, D. B.: Using Evolutionary Programming to Create Neural Networks that are Capable of Playing Tic-Tac-Toe; IEEE Int. Conf. on Neural Networks, vol. 2, pp. 875-880; San Francisco, CA; 1993

Fogel, D. B.: An Introduction to Simulated Evolutionary Optimization; IEEE Transactions on Neural Networks, vol. 5, no. 1, pp. 3-14; 1994

Fogel, L. J., Owens, A. J., Walsh, M. J.: Artificial Intelligence Through Simulated Evolution; John Wiley & Sons; 1966

Goldberg, D. E.: Genetic Algorithms in Search Optimization and Machine Learning; Addison Wesley; Reading, MA; 1989

Gruau, F.: Genetic Synthesis of Modular Neural Networks; Proc. of the 5. Int. Conf. on Genetic Algorithms; Morgan Kaufmann Publishers; San Mateo, CA; 1993

Gruau, F., Whitley, D.: Adding Learning to the Cellular Development of Neural Networks: Evolution and the Baldwin Effect; Evolutionary Computation, vol. 1, no. 3; The Massachusetts Institute of Technology; 1993

Holland, J. H.: Adaptation in Natural and Artificial Systems; The University of Michigan Press; Ann Arbor, MI; 1975

Jacob, C., Rehder, J.: Evolution of Neural Net Architectures by a hierarchical grammar-based Genetic System; Artificial Neural Nets and Genetic Algorithms; Proc. of the Int. Conf. in Innsbruck; Springer-Verlag; Wien; 1993

Koza, J. R., Rice, J. P.: Genetic Generation of both the Weights and Architecture for a Neural Network; Proc. of the Int. Joint Conf. on Neural Networks, Seattle; IEEE Press vol. 2, pp. 47-56; 1991

Kitano, H.: Designing neural networks using genetic algorithm with graph generating system; Complex Systems, vol. 4, pp. 461-476; 1992

Lohmann, R.: Selforganisation by Evolution Strategy in Visual Systems; in: Voigt, Mühlenbein, Schwefel (ed.): Evolution and Optimization '89; pp. 61-68; Akademie Verlag; Berlin; 1990

Lohmann, R.: Bionische Verfahren zur Entwicklung visueller Systeme; Master thesis, Technical University Berlin, Bionics and Evolution Techniques; 1991

Lohmann, R.: Structure Evolution and Incomplete Induction; Proc. of the 2. Conf. on Parallel Problem Solving from Nature, pp. 175-185; Brussels; 1992

Maniezzo, V.: Genetic Evolution of the Topology and Weight Distribution of Neural Networks; IEEE Transactions on Neural Networks, vol. 5, no. 1, pp. 39-53; 1994

McDonnell, J. R., Waagen, D.: Evolving Neural Network Connectivity; IEEE Int. Conf. on Neural Networks, vol. 2, pp. 863-868; San Francisco, California; 1993

McDonnell, J. R., Waagen, D.: Evolving Recurrent Perceptrons for Time-Series Modeling; IEEE Transactions on Neural Networks, vol. 5, no. 1, pp. 24-38; 1994

Miller, G., Todd, P., Hedge, S.: Designing Neural networks using genetic Algorithms; Proc. of the 3. Int. Conf. on Genetic Algorithms, pp. 379-384; 1989

Rechenberg, I.: Evolutionsstrategie - Optimierung technischer Systeme nach Prinzipien der biologischen Evolution; Frommann-Holzboog; Stuttgart; 1973

Rechenberg, I.: Evolutionsstrategie - Optimierung nach Prinzipien der biologischen Evolution; in: Albertz, J. (ed.): Evolution und Evolutionsstrategien in Biologie, Technik und Gesellschaft; Freie Akademie; Wiesbaden; 1989

Rechenberg, I., Gawelczyk, A., Görne, T., Hansen, N., Herdy, M., Kost, B., Lohmann, R., Ostermeier, A., Trint, K., Utecht, U.: Evolutionsstrategische Strukturbildung in neuronalen Systemen; Statusseminar des BMFT Neuroinformatik, Maurach; ed: Projektträger Informationstechnik BMFT, DLR, pp. 25-34; 1992

Rechenberg, I.: Evolutionsstrategie '94; Frommann-Holzboog; Stuttgart; 1994

Rumelhart, D. E., McClelland, J. L.: Parallel Distributed Processing, Vol. 1 & 2; MIT-Press; Cambridge, MA; 1986

Schwefel, H.-P.: Numerische Optimierung von Computer-Modellen mittels der Evolutionsstrategie; Birkhäuser; Basel, Stuttgart; 1977

Trint, K., Utecht, U.: Methodik der Strukturevolution; Technical Report; Technical University Berlin, Bionics and Evolution Techniques; 1992

Trint, K., Utecht, U.: Selection Mechanisms in Two-Stage Evolution Strategies for Noisy Evaluations; Technical Report TR-94-04; Technical University Berlin, Bionics and Evolution Techniques; 1994

Whitley, D., Starkweather, T., Bogart, C.: Genetic algorithms and neural networks: optimizing connections and connectivity; Parallel Computing, vol. 14, pp. 347-361; 1990

Parallel Implementations of Evolutionary Algorithms

Implementation of Standard Genetic Algorithm on MIMD Machines *

R. Hauser[1], R. Männer[2]

[1] CERN, Geneva, Switzerland
email: rhauser@cernvm.cern.ch
[2] Lehrstuhl für Informatik V, Universität Mannheim, Germany
email: maenner@mp-sun1.informatik.uni-mannheim.de

Abstract. Genetic Algorithms (GAs) have been implemented on a number of multiprocessor machines. In many cases the GA has been adapted to the hardware structure of the system. This paper describes the implementation of a standard genetic algorithm on several MIMD multiprocessor systems. It discusses the data dependencies of the different parts of the algorithm and the changes necessary to adapt the serial version to the parallel versions. Timing measurements and speedups are given for a common problem implemented on all machines.

1 Introduction

In this paper we describe the implementation of a standard Genetic Algorithm [1,2] on a number of different multiprocessor machines. After the discussion of the data dependencies in a straight forward implementation of a GA, the parallelization strategy on each machine is discussed and speedup measurements are presented. No attempt is made to optimize the algorithm for each specific architecture, instead we tried to stay as closely as possible to the original and parallelize in a way which seems natural for an application programmer on such a machine. This includes the use of standard libraries like *Pthreads* if available and e.g. recommended by the vendor as the preferred method of parallelization.

2 Genetic Algorithms

In this section we shortly outline the GA we have implemented on the different machines.

Selection The fitness of each individual in the population is evaluated. The fitness of each individual relative to the mean value of all other individuals gives the probability with which this individual is reproduced in the next generation. Therefore the frequency h_i of an individual in the next generation is given by

---
* This work has been supported by the Deutsche Forschungsgemeinschaft (DFG) under grant Ma 1150/8–1.

$$h_i \propto \frac{f_i}{\bar{f}} \tag{1}$$

where f_i is the fitness of individual i and $\bar{f}$ the average over all fitness values.

Crossover The crossover operator takes two individuals from the population and combines them to a new one. The most general form is uniform crossover from which the so called one–point crossover and two–point crossover can be derived. First two individuals are selected, the first one according to its fitness and the second one by random. Then a crossover mask M_i, $i = 1, \ldots, L$, where L is the length of the chromosome, is generated randomly. A new individual is generated which takes its value at position i from the first individual if $M_i = 1$ and from the second one if $M_i = 0$. The crossover operator is applied with probability P_C.

Mutation Each bit of an individual is changed (e.g. inverted) with probability P_M.

All three steps above are iterated for a given number of generations (or until one can no longer expect a better solution).

3 Parallel Genetic Algorithms

It has long been noted that genetic algorithms are well suited for parallel execution. Parallel implementations of GAs exist for a variety of multiprocessor systems, including MIMD machines with global shared memory [11] and message passing systems like transputers [3,4] and hypercubes [8] as well as SIMD architectures [6,7] like the Connection Machine.

3.1 Dependencies

It is easy to see that the following steps in the algorithm can be trivially parallelized:

Evaluation of fitness function The fitness of each individual can be computed independently from all others. This gives us a linear speedup with the number of processing elements.

Crossover. If we choose to generate each individual of the next generation by applying the crossover operator, we can do this operation in parallel for each new individual. The alternative would be to apply crossover and to put the resulting individual in the existing population where it replaces e.g. a bad solution.

Mutation The mutation operation can be applied to each bit of each individual independently. Besides from the bit value the only information needed is the global parameter P_M.

3.2 Parallelization

It should be noted that it is usually not possible to gain a larger speedup for steps 1) and 2) because of data dependencies between the different steps of the algorithm. This can be seen e.g. for step 2: If the crossover operation selects one of the parents it does this according to its relative fitness. However this can only be done if the fitness values of all other individuals are already computed so that the mean value is available.

In the following we will point out what kind of data each processing element must access to perform the different steps of the algorithm.

Fitness evaluation. Each processing element must have access only to those individuals whose fitness it will compute. In the optimal case (number of processing elements = number of individuals) this is one individual. However the result of this computation is needed by all other processing elements since it is used for computing the mean value of all function evaluations needed in step 2.

Crossover. Each processing element which creates a new individual must have access to all other individuals since each one may be selected as a parent. To make this selection the procedure needs all fitness values from step 1.

Mutation. As in step 1 each processing element needs only the individual(s) it deals with. As mentioned above the parallelization could be even more fine grained as in steps 1 and 2, in which case each processing element would need only one bit of each individual. This could usually only be achieved by a SIMD style machine.

Many implementors of parallel genetic algorithms have decided to change the standard algorithm in several ways.

The most popular approach is the partitioning of the population into several subpopulations [5,9] or introducing a topology, so that individuals can only interact with nearby chromosomes in their neighborhood [3,6,10,12,13]. All these methods obviously reduce the coupling between different processing elements.

Although some authors report improvements in the performance of their algorithm and the method can be justified by biological reasons, we consider it as a drawback that not the original standard GA could be efficiently implemented. The reason is that a genetic algorithm is often a computational intensive task. It often depends critically on the given parameters used for the simulation (e.g. P_M and P_C). There are some theoretical results about how to choose these parameters or the representation of a given problem, but most of them deal with the standard GA only. Even then one often has to try several possibilities to adjust the parameters optimally.

4　The Problem

In the following we present some results of such a parallelization on a number of different multiprocessor systems. We will show that only a small number of properties are required to get an efficient parallel program which implements the standard GA. The systems are all of the MIMD type but range from a special purpose system (NERV) to global shared memory systems (SparcServer, KSR1).

We implemented the same program on all machines. Instead of using some kind of toy problem we decided to use a real application as a benchmark. The task of the GA is to optimize the placement of logic cells in a field programmable gate array (Xilinx). The input is a design file, which is usually created by an external program, as well as a library of user–defined parts and information about the specific chip layout and package. From this input the program creates an internal list of the required logic cells and their connections.

Our test design used 276 logic blocks out of 320 possible on a Xilinx 3090 and 121 I/O blocks. The number of internal connections is in the order of several thousands. Since the chromosomes represent positions for each logic or I/O block, the chromosome length is given by the sum of these two numbers.

The program is completely CPU–bound until it writes the final output file. The big advantage of having a real application is that it does not have the usual problems of benchmarks, like being so small that they fit in the cache of the processor or concentrating the whole computational task in a few lines like in a matrix multiplication. Furthermore we have a simple criterion for comparing the implementations: how fast is the program speeded up by using multiple processors. Since the user may wait for the result of the placement program, measuring the real time to do the task seems to be the most reasonable solution.

5　The NERV multiprocessor system

5.1　The Hardware.

The NERV multiprocessor [14] is a system which has been originally designed for the efficient simulation of neural networks. It is based on a standard VMEbus system [15] which has been extended to support several special functions. Each processing element consists of a MC68020 processor with static local memory (currently 512 kB) and each VME board contains several processor boards. Usually the system is run in a SPMD (Singe Program Multiple Data) style mode, which means that the same program is downloaded to each processing element, while the data to be processed are distributed among the boards.

The following extensions to the VMEbus have been implemented in the NERV system:

A broadcast facility which is not part of the standard VME protocol. It allows each processor to access the memory of all other processor boards with a single write cycle. From the programmer's point of view there exists a region in his address space, where a write access will initiate an implicit broadcast to all other processors. A read from this region will simply return the data in the local memory. For software written in C or C++ a programmer might take advantage of this property in the following way:

A pointer - either to a global variable or dynamically allocated - can be modified in such a way that it points into the broadcast region by a special function called *mk_global()*. Whenever this pointer is dereferenced by a write access an implicit broadcast happens. A read access will return the local data.

Note however that there is no explicit synchronization between the processors. If two processors update the same element, the last one will win.

A second extension on the VMEbus includes a hardware synchronization of all processing elements. The programmer calls a procedure *synchronize()* which will only return after all processors have reached the synchronization point.

5.2 Implementation of the Parallel Genetic Algorithm.

The previous sections suggest the following setup for the algorithm on the NERV system:

The same program is loaded onto each processor. Every processor has a copy of all individuals in his local memory. The current population and the population of the next generation are accessed by two pointers which have been prepared so that they both point into the broadcast region. The same holds for an array which contains the fitness values of all individuals. After each generation the two population pointers are simply exchanged. Let N be the number of processing elements in the system. The general strategy will be to distribute the computational load equally among all processing elements by assigning $\frac{P}{N}$ individuals to each processor.

The parallelization of each GA operator is now straightforward.

Fitness evaluation. Each processor evaluates the fitness of the individuals it has been assigned. The fitness values are simply written into the mentioned array which will automatically initiate a broadcast. Since each processor is responsible for another set of individuals no overlap will occur.

```
int fitness_values[POP_SIZE];
int *fitness;

fitness = mk_global(fitness_values);
for ( i = "first individual"; i <= "last individual", i++)
  fitness[i] = eval(i);
synchronize();
```

Note that the evaluation function uses only the local copy of the population. The access to *fitness[i]* is the (implicit) broadcast.

Crossover. As already mentioned we decided to generate the next generation by looping over all individuals of the new population and either copying an individual from the old one or create a new one by crossover from two parents. Again each processor will be responsible for a part of the population:

```
for ( i =  "first individual"; i <= "last individual"; i++) {
  offspring = &newPopulation[i];
  parent1 = select();
  parent2 = random_select();
  if (random(CROSSOVER_PROB) < CROSSOVER_PROB) {
    k = random(CHROM_LENGTH);
    for(j = 0; j < k; j++)
      offspring[j] = parent1[j];
    for(j = k; j < CHROM_LENGTH; j++)
        offspring[j] = parent2[j];
  } else /* copy individual */
    for(j = 0; j < CHROM_LENGTH; j++)
      offspring[j] = parent1[j];
}
synchronize();
```

After this step $P \cdot L$ elements will have been broadcasted (assuming that we encode e.g. each bit in a separate character) and each processing element will have a complete copy of the new population.

Mutation. The mutation operator is parallelized in the same fashion as the other operators. Again each processor handles $\frac{P}{N}$ chromosomes and broadcasts the results.

```
for(i = "first individual"; i <= "last individual"; i++) {
  individual = &newPopulation[i];
  for(j = 0; j < CHROM_LENGTH; j++)
    if (random(MUTATE_PROB) < MUTATE_PROB)
      individual[j] = !individual[j];
}
synchronize();
```

The broadcast of a bit changed by mutation is done by the assignment to *individual[j]*. Note that the right hand side of this assignment will only access local memory since it is a read access.

5.3 Discussion of NERV implementation

The program will transfer P fitness values (from step 1) and $P \cdot L$ bits for the new population (from step 2) over the common bus. In addition it must transfer the bits which are changed during mutation which may vary in each generation.

This is all communication which will occur. All other values are fetched from local memory. A broadcast facility is the most efficient way to implement this since it does not depend on the number of processors. If we increase the number of processing elements we will decrease the time needed for each step while the communication overhead will stay constant.

6   SparcServer

The SparcServer 2000 is a commercially available shared memory system with up to 16 processors which supports symmetric multiprocessing. All processors have access to a global shared memory. The system runs the Solaris operating system which is responsible for load-balancing.

The normal way to take advantage of the multiple processors in the system is to use the *threads*-library. For synchronizing access to critical regions there are a number of mechanisms like *mutex* and *condition* variables. The thread library is very similar to the POSIX threads interface, although not completely identical.

The same arguments we used for the NERV–system apply here as well. Most parts of the algorithm can be parallelized ideally, but we need a synchronization after each major step. As long as we follow the same programming style as in the NERV–system it is unnecessary to lock data structures on a lower level, since there are no concurrent writes by different threads into the same memory area.

The implementation strategy is therefore to start N worker threads where each one is working on part of the population. The main thread is only responsible for initialization and controlling the synchronization of the other threads.

The synchronization has been implemented on top of the threads library. The GA routine uses only two functions, *thread_init()* and *thread_sync()*. The initialization routine is called once at the beginning of the program. It starts the worker threads and initializes the global mutex and condition variables. The number of worker threads can be given as a program argument. This allows us to vary the maximal number of processors.

7   KSR1

The KSR1 from Kendall Systems Research has some features which distinguish it from the more convential shared memory systems like the SparcServer. Although it looks like a global shared memory system from the programmer's point of view, there is no main memory in the usual sense at all. Instead each processor has a large cache memory of 32 MByte which is backed by mass storage and kept consistent by a cache coherence protocol. The interconnection network is invisible to the programmer, although the latency of memory updates may vary if two distant nodes have to communicate.

Each processor in the system is running an OSF/1 kernel, providing the usual Unix services. The machine can be split in several partitions with a certain number of processors dedicated to a certain program.

For a C program the preferred method of parallelizing a task is to use the POSIX threads library (Pthreads). The functionality is essentially the same as with the Solaris threads library. Therefore the main GA program will be exactly the same, only the *threads_init()* and *threads_sync()* routines had to be adapted.

8   Results

The figures show the speedups which can be achieved by the different systems depending on the number of processors or threads used.

NERV. For the NERV system the programmer has complete control of the system and can decide how many processors he wants to use. The overhead is only marginal, since the necessary functions are directly supported by the hardware. If the number of processors is increased the communication time stays constant. The common bus however sets an upper limit to the extensibility of the sytem—it is not reasonable to consider a system with more than 40 processors in a VME–crate. The speedup is linear although below the theoretical maximum.

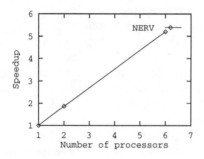

Fig. 1. Speedup vs. nr. of processors on the NERV system.

SparcServer. The SparcServer and the KSR1 are both very similar in that they provide a global shared memory and allow parallelization via a threads package. However, on the Sparc machine the user has no control over the processor resources. He can not specify on how many processors his program will run but must leave this decision to the operating system. The results show that the speedup is only in the order of two for an eight processor system. The system was in multiuser mode although no other computing intensive task was running during the measurements. It is difficult to give a specific reason for this behaviour. The working set of the program is quite large since several hundred net lists must referenced in each fitness evaluation. Therefore the local cache of each processor will usually not suffice to hold all relevant data. If the scheduler does not assign a thread to a specific processor but reschedules them every time they are runnable the situation may get even worse since they have to load their working set from the memory again.

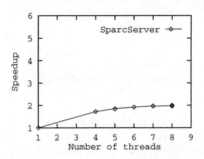

Fig. 2. Speedup vs. nr. of processors on the SparcServer system.

KSR1. The KSR1 allows for more user control over processors. The system is usually configured in a number of partitions with a given number of processors. The program can be run in one such partition and allocate all available processors. The largest usable partition contained 20 processors. The run time decreases as the number of threads is increased as long as we have less threads than processors. Then we can see that the run time starts to increase again. It seems the system overhead for scheduling the threads becomes significantly large at this point.

One major drawback of the KSR1 is the large increase in access time for the different stages of the memory hierarchy. The first-level cache (256 kB) needs two clock cycles, the 32 MByte local cache needs 20 clock cycles and an access to a remote cache needs 140 clock cycles. This is nearly 2 orders of magnitude and our application definitely does not fit into the first-level cache.

Several experience reports [17] about the KSR1 show, that one can achieve a significant speedup if the problem is carefully adapted to the machine specific parameters. However our results are more in line with the report on the port of an existing application [18] whose speedup usually did not exceed a factor of 5.

References

1. J.H. Holland, Adaption in Natural and Artificial Systems (The University of Michigan Press, Ann Arbor, 1975)
2. D.E. Goldberg, Genetic Algorithms in Search, Optimization and Machine Learning, (Addison–Wesley, Reading, 1988)
3. M. Gorges–Schleuter, ASPARAGOS: An Asynchronous Parallel Genetic Optimization Strategy, Proc. 3rd Intl. Conf. on Genetic Algorithms (1989) 422–427

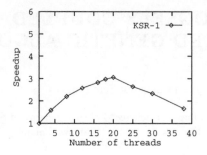

Fig. 3. Speedup vs. nr. of processors on the KSR1.

4. T. Fogarty, Implementing the Genetic Algorithm on Transputer Based Parallel Processing Systems, Parallel Problem Solving from Nature 1 (1991) 145–149
5. J.P. Cohoon, W.N. Martin, D.S. Richards, A Multi–population Genetic Algorithm for Solving the K–Partition Problem on Hyper–cubes, Proc. 4th Intl. Conf on Genetic Algorithms (1991) 244–248
6. R.J. Collins, D.R. Jefferson, Selection in Massively Parallel Genetic Algorithms, Proc. 4th Intl. Conf. on Genetic Algorithms (1991) 249–256
7. P. Spiessens, B. Manderick, A Massively Parallel Genetic Algorithm, Proc. 4th Intl. Conf. on Genetic Algorithms (1991) 279–285
8. C.C. Pettey, M.R. Leuze, A Theoretical Investigation of a Parallel Genetic Algorithm, Proc. 3rd Intl. Conf. on Genetic Algorithms (1989) 398–405
9. R. Tanese, Distributed Genetic Algorithms, Proc. 3rd Intl. Conf. on Genetic Algorithms (1989) 434–439
10. M.G.A. Verhoeven, E.H.L. Aarts, E. v. de Sluis, Parallel Local Search and the Travelling Salesman Problem, Parallel Problem Solving from Nature 2 (1992) 543–552
11. T. Maruyma, A. Konagaya, l. Konishi: An Asynchronous Fine–Grained Parallel Genetic Algorithm, Parallel Problem Solving from Nature 2 (1992) 563–572
12. H. Tamaki, Y. Nishikawa: A Parallel Genetic Algorithm based on a Neighborhood Model and Its Application to the Jobshop Scheduling, Parallel Problem Solving from Nature 2 (1992) 573–582
13. H. Mühlenbein, Parallel Genetic Algorithms, Population Genetics and Combinatorial Optimization; J.D. Becker, I. Eisele, F.W. Mündemann (Eds.): Parallelism, Learning, Evolution, Lect. Notes in Comp. Sci. 565, (Springer,Berlin, 1991) 398–406
14. R. Hauser, H. Horner, R. Männer, M. Makhaniok, Architectural Considerations for NERV—a General Purpose Neural Network Simulation System; in J. D. Becker, I. Eisele, F. W. Mündemann (Eds.): Parallelism, Learning, Evolution, Lect. Notes in Comp. Sci. 565, (Springer, Berlin, 1991) 183–195
15. The VMEbus Specification, Rev. C, VMEbus Int'l Trade Association (1987)
16. R.M. Stallman, Using and Porting GNU CC, Free Software Foundation (1992)
17. R. Schuhmacher (Ed.), One Year KSR1 at the Univerity of Mannheim: Results and Experience, RUM 35/93, University of Mannheim (1993)
18. H. Kredel, Computeralgebra on a KSR1 Parallel Computer, in [17], 26–34

LOOSELY COUPLED
DISTRIBUTED GENETIC ALGORITHMS

Franciszek Seredynski

Institute of Computer Science, Polish Academy of Sciences
ul. Ordona 21, 01-237 Warsaw, Poland

Abstract. Iterated, noncooperative N-person games with limited interaction are considered. Each player in the game has defined its local payoff
function and a set of strategies. While each player acts to maximize its
payoff, we are interested in a global behavior of the team of players measured by the average payoff received by the team. To study behavior of
the system we propose a new parallel and distributed genetic algorithm
based on evaluation of local fitness functions while the global criterion
is optimized. We present results of simulation study which support our
ideas.

1   INTRODUCTION

In recent years, game-theoretic models have been recognized as a useful tool to
study behavior of complex systems. Examples of such systems can be pointed
in many areas of real life: economics, sociology, politics and technology. The
common assumption taken to all these systems considered from positions of
game theory is the assumption that they can be considered as a collection of
individuals acting selfishly and interacting to complete their own goals.

A game-theoretic model which has received lately much attention in the
evolutionary algorithms literature [1, 3, 8] is the prisoner's dilemma [6, 13, 15].
This two-player, non cooperative game has been explored to give an insight
into conditions of cooperating and defecting between players. Extension this
philosophical rather model to more practical N-player models can be expected
in the nearest time.

In the area of Distributed Artificial Intelligence (DAI) game-theoretic models
are also a subject of a current research [4, 8, 9]. Agents of a multi-agent system
are considered as players working on their own selfish goals and taking part in
N-person game. In many applications however, (see, eg. [17]) it is excpected a
global behavior of the multi-agent system, rather than simply a fulfilment of
players' local goals. One of problems which must be solved here is the problem
of incorporating global goals of the multi-agent system into local interests of all
agents.

The paper is motivated by the actual situation in both aforementioned areas. On the one hand we are interested in models of N-person games and their
potential application as a tool of DAI. The model of N-person games with limited interaction which is presented in the next section belongs to the class of

noncooperative games. We show in this section how to incorporate the global goal of the team into local goals of players. While the section discusses static game theory model we are interested in dynamic aspects of the model when players act in the iterated game. On the other hand, the success in applying genetic algorithms (GAs) for the prisoner's dilemma encourage to use them for our problem. In Section 3 we propose a new parallel and distributed GA which we call loosely coupled GAs, to implement our model. Section 4 shows results of experimental study of loosely coupled GAs implementing the model of N-person games. Last section contains conclusions.

2 N-PERSON GAMES WITH LIMITED INTERACTION

We consider a finite game represented by a set N of N players, $N = \{1, 2, \ldots, N\}$; set S_k of strategies for each player $k \in N$; and a payoff function $u_k(s_k, s_{k1}, s_{k2}, \ldots, s_{kn_k})$ which depends only on strategies of a limited number of players: on its own strategy s_k and strategies of its n_k neighbors in the game. Such a model called a game with limited interaction had been primary considered in [18] from positions of learning automata games.

The game with limited interaction can be represented by an oriented graph $G = < V, E >$ called an interaction graph. V is the set of nodes corresponding to the set of players and the set E represents the pattern of interaction between players: arcs incoming to the k-th node define players whose strategies influence the payoff of the player k, and arcs outgoing from the k-th node define players whose payoff depends on strategies of the player k.

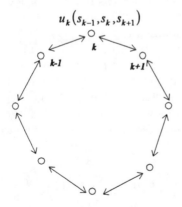

Fig. 1. Interaction graph of a game on a ring

In the paper we will consider a class of games with limited interaction characterized by a regular interaction graph and called homogeneous games. In such games a payoff function is the same for all players. Figure 1 shows the interaction graph of a simple homogeneous game called game on the ring.

Table 1

	s_{k-1} s_k s_{k+1}	$u_k^1(s_{k-1}\ s_k\ s_{k+1})$	$u_k^2(s_{k-1}, s_k, s_{k+1})$
0	0 0 0	20	20
1	0 0 1	0	0
2	0 1 0	0	0
3	0 1 1	0	0
4	1 0 0	0	0
5	1 0 1	50	90
6	1 1 0	0	0
7	1 1 1	70	70

For the game on the ring which will be the subject of our study in the paper we can simplify notation of a payoff function:

$$u_k(s_k, s_{k1}, s_{k2}, \ldots, s_{kn_k}) = u_k(s_{k-1}, s_k, s_{k+1}) \tag{1}$$

The payoff function of any player in the game on the ring depends on its strategy and on strategies of its respectively $k-1$ and $k+1$ neighbors. Assuming that the set S_k of strategies for each player is limited to the set $\{0, 1\}$, the payoff function has 8 entries and Table 1 shows examples of two payoff functions u_k^1 and u_k^2 which will be discussed later.

It is assumed that each player acts in the game independently and selects its strategy to maximize its payoff. The main theorem concerning noncooperative games says [12] that a solution of the game is the Nash equilibrium point. The Nash point is an N-tuple of strategies one for each player, such that anyone who deviates from it unilaterally cannot possibly improve its expected payoff.

The Nash equilibrium point will define payoffs of all players in the game. However, we are not interested in a payoff of a given player, but in some global measure of the payoff received by the team of players. This measure can be e.g. the average payoff $\bar{u}(s)$ received by the team under strategies' combination $s = (s_1, s_2, \ldots, s_N)$, i.e.

$$\bar{u}(s) = \left(\sum_{k=1}^{N} u_k(s) \right) /N, \tag{2}$$

and it is a global criterion to evaluate behavior of the players in the game. The question which arrives immediately concerns the value of the criterion (2) in a Nash point. Unfortunately, this value can be very low.

Analyzing all possible strategies' combinations in the game and evaluating their prices, i.e. a value $\bar{u}(s)$, we can find strategies' combinations with the maximal price and we call them maximal price points. Maximal price points are strategies' combinations which maximize the global criterion (2) of the game, but they can be reached by players only if they are Nash points. A maximal price point usually is not the Nash point and the question which must be solved is how to convert the maximal price point (points) into the Nash point (points).

The solution of the problem for homogeneous games with limited interaction is based [16, 19] on introducing into the game a procedure of local cooperation between players, called a conjugated exchange process. The idea of the conjugated exchange process is based on agreement between players - neighbors in the game to share their winnings in the game. It can be proved that introducing the conjugated exchange process into the homogeneous games transforms maximal price points into the Nash points. For the game on the ring from Fig. 1, the conjugated exchange process simply transforms the payoff u_k of the player k into a new payoff w_k in the following way:

$$u_k \longrightarrow w_k = (u_{k-1} + u_k + u_{k+1})/3. \tag{3}$$

3 LOOSELY COUPLED GENETIC ALGORITHMS

Attempting to apply GAs methodology to the iterated games with limited interaction we face two difficulties: (a) how in a dynamic process of the game to search a solution of the game according to the global criterion (2), i.e. to search a maximal price point, and at the same time (b) how to create GAs model of a player who acts concurrently to maximize its local payoff. If we stand on positions of traditional GAs we should emphasize the first issue, but in this case we lose the concurrent nature of the game. If we emphasize the concurrent behavior of players, it seems that sequential GAs [5, 7] as well as parallel and distributed GAs [2, 10, 11, 14] of both *island* and *diffusion* models are not suitable for our purpose. The common feature of all aforementioned models of GAs is evaluation of a *global fitness* of an individual, despite it belongs to a global population or a subpopulation. For this reason we will call this class of GAs *tightly coupled* GAs. For our purpose, we need GAs with locally evaluated local fitness functions, and at the same time we expect from such a model a global behavior, in the sense of searching a global optimum. We propose such a model below and we call it *loosely coupled* GAs (LCGAs).

The idea of LCGAs implementing the homogeneous game on the ring from Fig. 1 is shown in Figure 2. The algorithm of the LCGAs can be specified in the following way:

#1: create an initial population of solutions of the game
- create randomly for each player an initial population of size n of copies of the player strategies; Fig. 2a shows initial population of the size $n = 4$ of strategies (local individuals) for players $k-1$, k and $k+1$ respectively;
- for each local individual establish randomly links with individuals from neighbor populations in such a way that each individual has only one partner in the neighbor population; chains of individuals create a population of solutions of the game; shadowed individuals from Fig. 2a are the part of some sample solution of the game;

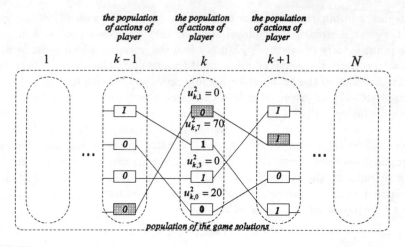

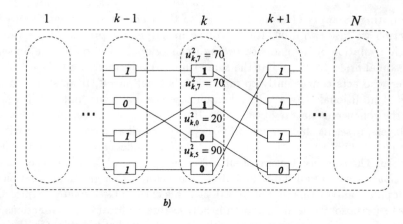

Fig. 2. Loosely coupled GAs:
(a)populations of players' strategies and a population of solution of the game,
(b) reproduction.

- for each local individual (player strategy) of each population (player)
  evaluate its fitness according to the payoff function of the game; if the
  payoff function of the game is e.g. the function u_k^2 from Table 1 then
  the player k obtains for the strategy 0 (Fig. 2a, shadowed box) payoff
  $u_{k,1}^2 = u^2(0,0,1) = 0$;

#2: create a new population of solutions of the game
  - for each population of strategies select probabilistically (wheel roulette
    mechanism) strategies to produce their offsprings;
  - for reproduced strategies of a given player establish old links (high pri-
    ority) with neighbor strategies, or establish links with new random part-

ners, if old partners do not exist in this generation in neighbor populations; Fig. 2b shows that for the player k only strategies 1 and 0 (rows 2
and 4 respectively from Fig.2a) has been reproduced, each receiving two
copies; one of the strategies, the strategy 0 establishes new links, while
the rest maintain the old connections;

- apply a standard operator of mutation for each local individual;
- evaluate the fitness for each local individual.

#3: repeat the step #2 until the termination condition is satisfied.

In the next Section we study the behavior of the presented GA. We will study
its behavior by observation of the global criterion (2) and particularly we will
be interested in the following situations:

- there exists in the game a maximal price point which is at the same time
  the Nash point (payoff function u_k^1 in Table 1);
- there exists in the game a maximal price point which is not the Nash point
  (payoff function u_k^2 in Table 1);
- like above, but players create local coalitions defined by the conjugate exchange process (payoff function u_k^2 in Table 1).

4   SIMULATION RESULTS

Let us analyze the payoff functions u_k^1 and u_k^2 from Table 1 for the game on the
ring (Fig. 1). The game with the payoff function u_k^1 has the maximal price point
$s_{mp} = (1, 1, 1, 1, 1, 1, 1, 1)$. Each player taking part in the game defined by the
vector of strategies s_{mp} obtains payoff equal to $u_{k,7}^1(1, 1, 1) = 70$. The average
payoff $\overline{u}_k^1$ received by the team of players achieves the maximal value equal to
70. The strategy combination s_{mp} is, at the same time, the Nash point. It is easy
to see that for each player there is no reason to change its strategy $0 \rightarrow 1$ and
obtain less payoff equal to $u_{k,s}^1(1, 0, 1) = 50$. We can therefore expect that in
such a game players, according to game theory, will find and play the maximal
price point providing the maximal payoff for the team of players.

The game with the payoff function u_k^2 has the same maximal price point as
the function u_k^1. However, it is not the Nash point because each player changing
its strategy $1 \rightarrow 0$ will obtain higher payoff equal to $u_{k,s}^2(1, 0, 1) = 90$. According
to game theory the players will not use strategies' combination corresponding to
the maximal price point. In this game (as well in the previous one) there exists
the Nash point $s_N = (0, 0, 0, 0, 0, 0, 0, 0)$. There is no reason for any player to
change its strategy $0 \rightarrow 1$ and obtain instead the payoff $u_{k,0}^2(0, 0, 0) = 20$ less
payoff equal to $u_{k,0}^2(0, 1, 0) = 0$. Game theory predicts in such a case that players
will play this Nash point.

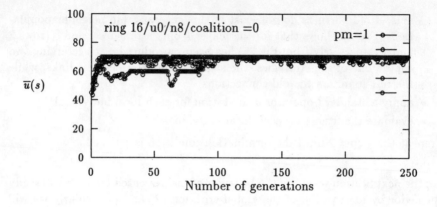

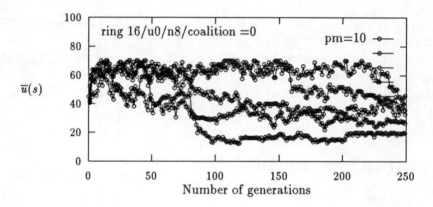

Fig. 3. Behavior of players in the game with the maximal price point being the Nash point

Below we present some results of an experimental study of the game on the ring with the number of players $N = 16$. In such a game the number of possible game solutions (strategies' combinations) is equal to 2^{16}. We will use the payoff functions u_k^1 and u_k^2. Increasing the number of players in the game will result only in that the Nash point and the maximal price point will have 16 0's and 1's respectively. In all experiments we use a population of player strategies equal to $n = 8$, and observe the game during 250 generations. All experiments have been conducted on Sun-classic computer.

Fig. 3 shows behavior of LCGA implementing the game with the payoff function u_k^1 for two mutation probabilities $p_m = 1$ (upper) and $p_m = 10$ (bottom). Each figure presents runs of 5 random samples of the game depicting the dynamics of the iterated game. One can see that the players find quickly strategies corresponding to the maximal price point (being at the same time the Nash point) for values of p_m close to 0 (Fig. 3 upper). Increasing value of the mutation probability acts disruptively on the ability of the global behavior of the team of players (Fig. 3 bottom).

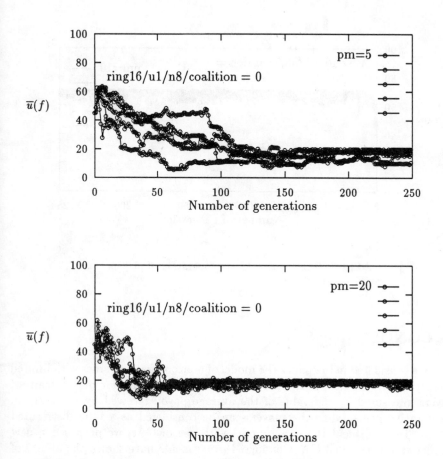

Fig. 4. Game with the maximal price point not being the Nash point (no cooperation)

Fig. 4 shows the behavior of the LCGA in the game with the payoff function u_k^2, without a cooperation between players. Players in the game achieve the Nash point which provides the average payoff $u_k^2 = 20$ for the team of players. The Nash point is achieved by the players for the wide range of values of p_m enough greater than 1.

Fig. 5 shows the behavior of the players in the game with the same payoff function u_k^2 but now the players cooperate according to the rule (3) of the exchange process. One can see that the exchange process in the game with the payoff function u_k^2 transforms the maximal price point into the Nash point. The team of the players is able to find and play the maximal price point providing the maximal payoff for the team. Dependence of this ability on p_m is similar as in the game with u_k^1, but higher p_m is now less disruptive.

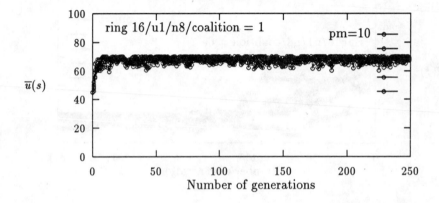

Fig. 5. Game with a local cooperation of players

5 CONCLUSIONS

We have considered in the paper the model of noncooperative games with limited interaction. We addressed the problem of the global behavior of the team of players, measured by the value of the average payoff received by the team in the iterative game, while the players can be considered as a fully distributed system. To implement the game model with use of GAs, we proposed a new parallel and distributed GA. Conducted experiments have shown the ability of this new GA to optimize a global criterion in fully distributed way, on the base of calculation only local fitness functions, depicting at the same time the behavior of the system predicted by the game theory.

ACKNOWLEDGMENTS

This work is supported by the State Committee for Scientific Research (KBN) under Grant N8 S503 025 05.

References

1. R. Axelrod: The Evolution of Strategies in the Iterated Prisoners' Dilemma. In: L. Davis (ed.): Genetic Algorithms and Simulated Annealing. London: Pitman 1987
2. M. Dorigo, V. Maniezzo: Parallel Genetic Algorithms: Introduction and Overview of Current Research. In: J. Stender (ed.): Parallel Genetic Algorithms. IOS Press 1993
3. D.B. Fogel: Evolving Behaviors in the Iterated Prisoner's Dilemma. Evolutionary Computation. vol. 1. N 1 (1993)
4. M.R. Genesereth, M.L. Ginsberg, J.S. Rosenschein: Cooperation without Communication. In: A.H. Bond and Les Geser (eds.). Readings in Distributed Artificial Intelligence. Los Angeles 1988
5. D.E. Goldberg: Genetic Algorithms in Search, Optimization and Machine Learning. Addison-Wesley. Reading. MA 1989
6. D.R. Hofstadter: Metamagical Themas: Questing for the Essence of Mind and Pattern. New York: Basic Books 1985
7. J.H. Holland: Adaptation in Natural and Artificial Systems. Ann Arbor: University of Michigan: Press 1975
8. R. Levy, J.S. Rosenschein: A Game Theoretic Approach to Distributed Artificial Intelligence and the Pursuit Problem. In: E. Werner, Y. Demazeau (eds.): Decentralized A.I.-3. Elsevier 1992
9. B. Lomborg: Game Theory vs. Multiple Agents: the Iterated Prisoner's Dilemma. The 4-th European Workshop on Modeling of Autonomous Agents in a Multi-Agent Word (MAAMAW'92). S. Martino el Cimino Italy 1992
10. B. Manderick, P. Spiessens: Fine-Grained Parallel Genetic Algorithms. In: Proc. of the Third Int. Conf. on Genetic Algorithms 1989
11. H. Muhlenbein, M. Schomisch, J. Born: The Parallel Genetic Algorithms as Function Optimizer. In: Proc. of the Fourth International Conference on Genetic Algorithms 1991
12. J.F. Nash: Equilibrium Points in n-Person Games. Proc. of the National Academy of Sciences USA 36, pp. 48-49
13. P.C. Ordershook: Game Theory and Political Theory: an Introduction: Cambridge University Press 1986
14. C.B. Pettey, M.R. Lutze, J.J. Gretenstette: A Parallel Genetic Algorithm. Proc. of the Second Int. Conference on Genetic Algorithms 1987
15. A. Rapport: Optimal Policies for the Prisoner's Dilemma. Tech. Report N 50. The Psychometric Laboratory: Univ. of North Carolina 1966
16. F. Seredynski: Homogeneous Networks of Learning Automata. Tech. Report N 684. Institute of Computer Science PAS. Warsaw 1990
17. F. Seredynski: Dynamic Mapping and Load Balancing with Parallel Genetic Algorithms. IEEE World Congress on Computational Intelligence. Orlando. Florida. June 26 - July 2 1994
18. M.L. Tsetlin: Automaton Theory and Modelling of Biological Systems. Academic Press. N.Y. 1973
19. V.I. Varshavski, A.M. Zabolotnyj, F. Seredynski: Homogeneous Games with a Conjugate Exchange Process. Proc. of the Academy of Science USSR Techniczeskaja Kibernetika. N 6 (1977)

Applying Evolvable Hardware to Autonomous Agents

Tetsuya Higuchi[1], Hitoshi Iba[1], Bernard Manderick[2]

[1] Electrotechnical Laboratory
1-1-4, Umezono, Tsukuba, Ibaraki, 305 Japan
[2] Erasumus University, Rotterdam

Abstract. In this paper, we describe a parallel processing architecture for Evolvable Hardware (EHW) which changes its own hardware structure in order to adapt to the environment in which it is embedded. This adaptation process is a combination of genetic learning with reinforcement learning. As an example of EHW applications, the arbitration in behavior-based robot is discussed. Our goal by implementing adaptation in hardware is to produce a flexible and fault-tolerant architecture which responds in real-time to a changing environment.

1 Introduction

In the mid-eighties, there was a surge in interest in biological metaphors for computation, adaptation and learning. For example, neural networks (NN) use the brain metaphor and study how knowledge can be represented in NNs. Genetic algorithms (GAs) focus on natural evolution as a metaphor and study its use for optimization, adaptation and machine learning. Recently artificial life (AL) has aimed at a deeper understanding of all phenomena associated with life.

This shift of emphasis from the symbolic processing paradigm in traditional Artificial Intelligence (AI) towards biologically inspired models has led to a "nouvelle" AI. Central to this new paradigm is the importance of building autonomous agents which are situated and embodied in a concrete and ever changing world [2].

Evolvable hardware is a part of this new paradigm. It combines parallelism and two biologically motivated learning techniques, genetic learning [3] and reinforcement learning [11], at the hardware level. We have called the resulting system *Evolvable Hardware* (EHW), since the adaptation process changes hardware architectures. This way, we go one step further than the standard approaches so far, where adaptation only affects software structures. This step is made possible by recent technological developments in software-reconfigurable logic devices, e.g. Field Programmable Gate Arrays (FPGAs) and Programmable Logic Devices (PLDs) [10]. These technologies offer excellent capabilities which make it feasible to build EHW today.

In EHW, adaptation takes the form of direct modification of the hardware structures according to rewards received from the environment. This results in a number of advantages. Adaptation in real-time is feasible due to a speed-up by many orders of magnitude. The system will be flexible and fault-tolerant since EHW can change its own structure in the case of environmental change or hardware error. Our long-term goal is to implement EHW on one chip so that it can be utilized as an "off-the shelf" device.

We have already reported the feasibility of hardware evolution in previous papers; the gate-level hardware evolution [4, 7] and the HDL (Hardware Description Language) level hardware evolution [5] [3]. This paper discusses applying EHW to more practical domain: behavior-based robotics control. We focus on the arbitration problem among behavior modules. The arbitration among such modules becomes a burden to a programmer when the number of modules increases. Arbitration through EHW is discussed, its re-adaptation capability of EHW when some hardware error occurs being of our main concern. Before that, we describe the EHW chip concept where the GA component, the reconfigurable hardware component and the reinforcement component would be integrated into one chip.

2 Evolvable Hardware Architecture

Here, we describe a parallel processing architecture for Evolvable Hardware (EHW). Its adaptation is a combination of genetic learning with reinforcement learning. A first version of the genetic learning component is in place already while the reinforcement learning component is a project for the future.

Nowadays, software-reconfigurable logic devices exist, the architecture of which can be determined by writing a bit string into the device. If the bit string changes, then the architecture and the function of the logic device also changes. This bit string is called *architecture bits*. The basic idea of EHW is to let the architecture bits evolve in order to adapt the function of logic devices to a given environment.

By incorporating both reinforcement learning and genetic learning, EHW can choose by itself a logic device architecture which gives the best performance with respect to the environment.

The genetic learning scheme used is a parallel version of the genetic algorithm (GA) [3]. The GA operates on a population of bit strings, each of which determines the architecture of a software-reconfigurable logic device. Depending on the architecture bit string, the logic device will behave differently. The performance of all these devices for a given task is evaluated in parallel and the resulting performance measure is the fitness of the corresponding architecture of the logic device. The GA gives the better architecture bit strings a higher chance to survive and to recombine. This way, we get a new generation of architecture bit string which might incorporate good features of their parent architectures. This new generation is then fed into the logic devices which will behave accordingly. Performance is again evaluated and the process is repeated.

Reinforcement learning [11] is the second learning scheme to be incorporated in EHW. In reinforcement learning, the response to inputs changes based on the reward following that response. This reward is related to the quality of the response to the given input and it might be delayed. The goal is to maximize

---

[3] The HDL level hardware evolution may be suitable for LSI, but lacks in re-adaptability. In [5], genetic programming is used for HDL evolution. On the other hand, the gate level evolution is suitable for on-line adaptation, but the circuit scale is not large. This paper discusses the gate level evolution.

a positive or minimize a negative reward. There is no teacher or supervisor involved in this learning scheme. In the rest of this section, we describe the overall architecture of EHW.

2.1 Overall EHW Architecture

The schematic of an EHW chip architecture is shown in Figure 1 and consists of the 3 following key components:

1. software-reconfigurable logic devices (RLD)
2. parallel GA hardware (i.e. chromosomes vector registers, vector processing units, and distribution net)
3. reinforcement learning components (RLC)

The architecture functions as follows. Input from the environment enters each RLD via the input interface. Each RLD's architecture is determined by the architecture configuration bits (chromosomes). Therefore, each RLD outputs a value according to the input and its architecture. An RLD is an extension of commercially available Programmable Logic Devices (PLDs), improving on the weakness of current PLDs such as slow downloading and the limit on the numbers of reprogrammings.

The parallel GA hardware receives fitness values from the reinforcement components and performs GA operations according to a new parallel processing scheme. That is, GA operations such as crossover and mutation are executed *bitwise* at each chromosome and this is performed in parallel among all the chromosomes. So far, parallel GAs have not involved the parallelization of the GA operators themselves. In addition to these bitwise parallel operations, fitness evaluations of each chromosome are obtained in parallel as well as in usual parallel GAs.

The vector processing unit, which derives its name from its similarity with vector processing in supercomputers, receives two bits of chromosomes at a time and performs crossover and mutation to these bits. Because this is done in the chromosome registers working in parallel, crossover and mutation are executed at the same time for all the chromosomes in a population. The simple structure of the vector processing as shown in Figure 2 is suitable for VLSI implementation.

The reason to introduce the bitwise parallel processing for GA operations is to cope with GA applications which require real-time performance. For example, if EHW is used for robot control, GA execution time needs to be kept at a minimum because the battery of a robot may run out before the GA converges.

In general, parallel GAs are introduced to speed up fitness evaluation, which is considered to dominate the total GA execution time. However, this is not always true. To see this, suppose that GA execution time is the sum of the fitness evaluation time T_f, and the GA operations time T_g, i.e. mutation, crossover and selection. Using the GAucsd software package, we have found that T_g is about 40 times larger than T_f on the De Jong's test suite of functions. Therefore, for GA problems where T_g dominates the total execution time, the use of a vector processing unit will improve performance significantly. With the reinforcement learning component implemented in hardware, T_f is expected to become much smaller than T_g and this parallel architecture will show the best match.

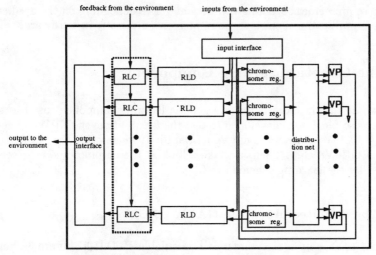

RLC: reinforcement learning component
RLD: reconfigurable logic device
VP: vector processing unit

Fig. 1. A schematic of the VLSI EHW

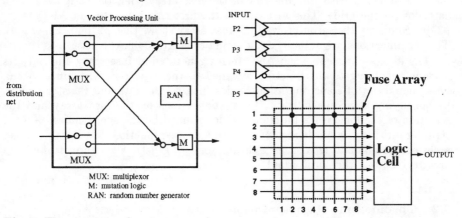

MUX: multiplexor
M: mutation logic
RAN: random number generator

Fig. 2. The structure of vector processing
unit

Fig. 3. A simplified GAL structure

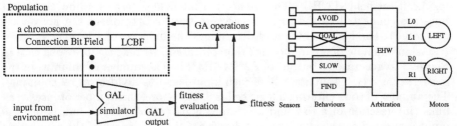

Fig. 4. Overview of the genetic learning scheme

Fig. 5. Modules for *Move-to-Box*
behavior

The reinforcement learning component varies depending on the applications. In simple applications, this can be implemented directly in hardware.

3   The Genetic Learning Component

Here, we discuss in more detail the genetic learning component used in the experiments so far. It was developed to test the feasibility of the EHW-concept and it uses GAL16V8 chips as primitive RLDs. First, we describe the basic hardware of the GAL16V8 chip. Then, we take a look at the chromosome representation followed by the learning scheme itself.

3.1   The Architecture of the GAL16V8 Chip

The GAL16V8 chip is a commercially available PLD [10]. Figure 3 shows the rough structure of GAL16V8 (simplified for explanation). It consists of a *Fuse Array* and *Logic Cells*. The fuse array determines how inputs are connected to a logic cell to generate AND terms. For example, in Figure 3, the inputs p5 and p3 are connected with the first row of the fuse array (the connection is shown as a dot on the grid). This means that the first row generates an AND term, p3*p5. Similarly the second row of the fuse array shows that p2*p4 is generated. These connections are actually a bit string of length 64 in this case.

The logic cell accepts such AND terms generated at fuse array and outputs a value according to the function assigned to the logic cell. The function can be assigned out of some operation modes such as OR gate and register device, by specifying some special bits. Thus, connections on the fuse array and the selection of the logic cell's function are determined by the specification of a bit string, resulting in a hardware device with a desired function. We call this string architecture bits and treat it as a chromosome of genetic algorithms to find the architecture bits that best adapt.

3.2   Chromosome Representation

The chromosome representation used consists of a connection bit field and a logic cell bit field (LCBF). The connection bit field determines how the input lines are connected to the row lines (where the AND terms of the inputs are generated). The logic cell bit field determines the function of a logic cell.

As an example of a chromosome representation, we take the previous case in Figure 3 to generate an output of P2*P4+P3*P5. The number of columns in the fuse array is 8 (i.e. 4 inputs, where each input signal is divided into 2 columns). The number of rows entering a logic cell is 8. Therefore, the number of fuse array links (intersection of a row and a column) is 64 (8 X 8). If the link is on, the input is entered on the row. This number (i.e. 64) is the length of the connection bit field of the chromosome for the EHW. The length of the logic cell bit field is 12 bits including 4 bits to set the the logic cell's function to OR gate function. Thus, the total length of the chromosome for this case is 76 bits.

3.3 Learning Scheme

The genetic learning scheme employed in our experiments is shown in Figure 4. In practice, we simulated the evolution of the GAL chip using software. Instead of rewriting the GAL chip repeatedly, it is written only once, i.e. after the most desirable chromosome is found. We employed this policy at this stage because the current version of GAL chips is not guaranteed for a large number of re-programming sequences. This is one of the weaknesses of current FPGAs as a vehicle for EHW.

First, we prepare an initial population of chromosomes where each chromosome represents a hardware structure implementable on a GAL chip. The GAL simulator in Figure 4 accepts inputs to the GAL, one input at a time, and generates the output according to the structure specified by the chromosome. (The execution time of the GAL simulator is 100 microseconds. If a GAL chip is actually used, the execution time is 10 nanoseconds, i.e. 10,000 times faster.)

Next, the GAL output enters the fitness evaluation module tailored to the specific application. Once the fitness values have been determined, the conventional genetic algorithm operators (selection, mutation, crossover) are applied to the chromosome population in the usual way [3].

4 Experiments with Evolvable Hardware

The advantages of EHW such as its execution speed and its re-adaptability (reconfigurability) may contribute considerably to industorial applications in future. Autonomous agents and pattern recognition are potentially promising candidates for EHW's application domain.

4.1 Subsumption Architecture

Subsumption architecture is a new approach to building behavior-based robots [2]. In such a robot, a goal is attained through interactions among simple modules. For example, to make a robot walk, a module to raise a leg may cooperate with a module to move a leg forward. Adding a new module to a robot leads to improving the performance of a robot. However, in that case, a mechanism is required to arbitrate the interactions between the new module and existing modules. For example, if two modules try to perform opposite goals (i.e. moving forwards and moving backwards), one of the modules should be suppressed (or subsumed) by the arbitration mechanism.

However, as the number of modules increases, the arbitration becomes more difficult. It is almost impossible for programmers to specify all the occasions where arbitration is necessary when the robot contains many modules. This is one of problems associated with the subsumption architecture. Therefore, efforts to implement autonomous arbitration mechanisms are being made, e.g. at Alberta University in Canada [9] and at Sussex University in Britain [8].

EHW is one of the promising candidates to attain this goal. Below we describe the basic idea to solve the arbitration problem with EHW. We use the examples in the Collective Robotic Intelligence Project (CRIP) [9] to illustrate our point.

4.2 Arbitration in *Move-to-Box* task

CRIP aims at a multi-robot system which can perform collective tasks, e.g. multiple robots locate a box and collectively push the box to a destination. To accomplish this example task, multiple robots take the following four behaviors; 1. *Find-Box* 2. *Move-to-box*, 3. *Push-box*, and 4. *Move-to-destination*.

These behaviors are controlled under the subsumption architecture. For example, the *Move-to-Box* behavior consists of the following four behaviors; FIND, SLOW, GOAL and AVOID behaviors. FIND keeps the robot in motion. SLOW reduces the speed of the robot. GOAL is a goal seeking behavior. AVOID is a collision avoidance behavior.

The robot is modelled with two obstacle avoidance sensors, two goal sensors, one collision sensor used to slow the robot, and two motors (left and right wheel motors). As shown in Figure 5, the four modules accept the five sensor outputs, and through the arbitration, motor control commands are generated accordingly. CRIP proposes to solve this arbitration problem by characterizing the behavior output pattern as a mapping problem between sensor outputs and motor commands.

The mapping between sensor outputs and motor commands is defined in Table 1[4]. On the left side of Table 1. the five sensor outputs labelled S_1 to S_5 correspond to *avoid-left, avoid-right, slow, goal-left* and *goal-right* sensor outputs. On the right, there are four motor control bits labelled L_0, L_1 for the left motor and R_0, R_1 for the right motor; each wheel motor has two control bits for stop, half-speed, and full-speed motions as shown in Table 2. Thus, Table 1 defines 32 patterns of arbitration. For example, the entry in row 2 of Table 1 has $S_4 = goal\text{-}left$ ON, resulting in a *move-left* motor command which is implemented by turning the left motor off and the right motor on.

Table 1. Truth table for the arbitration

Dec	S_1	S_2	S_3	S_4	S_5	L_1	L_0	R_1	R_0
0	0	0	0	0	0	0	0	0	0
1	0	0	0	0	1	1	0	0	0
2	0	0	0	1	0	0	0	1	0
⋮			⋮			⋮		⋮	
20	1	0	1	0	0	0	1	0	0
⋮			⋮			⋮		⋮	
31	1	1	1	1	1	0	0	0	1

Table 2. Motor Command

M_1	M_2	Motor
0	0	Stop
0	1	Half Speed
1	0	Full Speed

To learn this mapping, CRIP uses Adaptive Logic Network (ALN) [1], which is a learning network implementable directly on combinatorial logic, having the noise-insensitivity characteristic of neural networks. While CRIP uses ALN, we let EHW learn this task. This difference results in on-line re-adaptation to changing environment. Basically ALN is off-line learning (i.e. ALN is implemented on a combinatorial logic circuit after learning is over), while EHW's learning is on-line and the adaptation result is configured into a new hardware structure on

---

[4] This example was taken from [9].

the spot. This also means that EHW can adapt to unpredictable changes of the environment.

4.3 Experiments

We conducted three experiments for the learning task of the subsumption architecture described in the previous section.

The first experiment concerns the learning of the mapping between sensor outputs and motor commands defined in Table 1. Actually a circuit generating 4 output bits of motor commands is evolved. However, this circuit is a collection of 4 independent circuit, each generating one output bit. Therefore, the evolution of a circuit with one ouput bit is repeated 4 times. Figure 6 shows the result. The Y axis is the correct answer rate. If it reaches 100%, then the harware evolution succeeds; At 1098th generation, the fourth circuit with one ouput bit is successfully obtained (the first circuit at 112th, the second at 250th, and the third at 532nd generation).

The population size is 200, each chromosome has 88 bits. Uniform crossover is executed with a probability of 30%. The mutation rate is 0.5%. Figure 7 is an example of an evolved circuit with one output bit. The circuit consisted of 4 inverters, 3 AND gates and an OR gate.

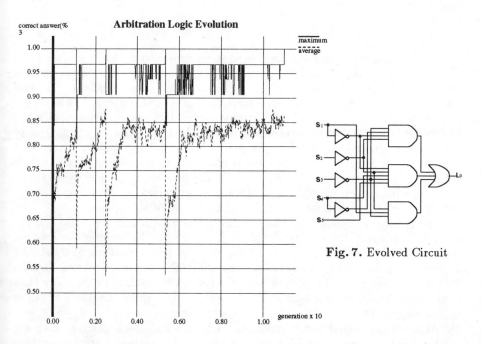

Fig. 7. Evolved Circuit

Fig. 6. Evolution of an arbitration logic

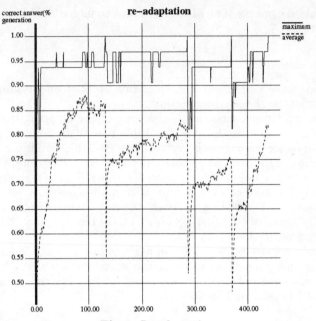

Fig. 8. Re-adaptation

The second experiment was conducted to confirm whether EHW can adapt to environmental change or not. We examined EHW's re-adaptability in a situation where wheel motors become unable to operate at full speed any more and half speed is the only choice. This environmental change corresponds to learning a new truth table where the full speed motor control bits are substituted with the half speed bits in Table 1, starting GA again with the population which already learned the original truth table (Table 1). Figure 8 shows how the hardware evolution goes after the re-adaptation starts (the 0th generation of Figure 8 is equal to the 1098th generation of Figure 6). The learning of the new truth table, i.e. the re-adaptation, completes at the 439th generation, which is significantly better than 1098 generations needed to learn the original mapping.

The third experiment examines further the re-adaptation capability. In the second experiment, the new truth table was learned by EHW after the original truth table was learned. That is, the learning of the new truth table started with an initial population which learned the original truth table. Here we examine the case where the new truth table is learned from the beginning, i.e. starting GAs from an initial population generated randomly, and compare the result with the second experiment.

We have conducted this comparison 15 times, with each different seed for random number generation. If results in the third experiment are always better(faster) than in the second experiment, we could claim that re-adaptation is very effective in responding quickly to environmental changes. However, we could not find that there exist significant differences between these two cases by the Wilcoxon's statistical test.

5 Conclusions

In this paper, we have discussed an application of EHW in the domain of autonomous agents, namely the arbitration in behavior-based robots. We also performed some experiments which confirmed that the idea is sound.

Our current design efforts towards VLSI EHW proceed in two directions. The first is the design of new software-reconfigurable device. The main concern is how to express versatile hardware functions with *less* architecture bits, which directly influences the GA search space. The second is the design of parallel GA hardware [6].

We believe that EHW will be a key component for autonomous agents from the following reasonings:

1. The execution speed of the evolved system will be extremely fast (at least three orders of magnitude faster than a software implementation) because the result of adaptation is the hardware structure itself.
2. Fault tolerant and flexible design is realized because EHW can change its own structure in the case of hardware error or environmental change, utilizing its on-line re-adaptation capability.
3. EHW can implement finite state machines, suggesting the possibility that microprocessor's control programs for animats could be replaced with EHW.

Acknowledgements The authors thank N. Otsu, K. Ohta, T. Niwa, T. Furuya and T. Tanaka for fruitful discussions. GA programming was conducted by R. Sato. They also thank Ronald Kube for his cooperation.

References

1. Armstrong, W., Dwelly, A., Liang, J., Lin, D. and Reynolds, S., "Learning and generalization in adaptive logic networks in artificial neural networks", *Proc. of Intl. Conf. on Artificial Neural Networks*, pp1173-1176, 1991.
2. Brooks, R. "Intelligence Without Reason", *Proc. of IJCAI-91*, 1991.
3. Goldberg, D.E., *Genetic Algorithms in search, optimization and machine learning*, Addison Wesley, 1989.
4. Higuchi, T., Niwa, T., Tanaka, T., Iba, H., de Garis, H. and Furuya, T., "Evolvable Hardware with genetic learning", in *Proc. of SAB conf.*, MIT Press, 1993.
5. Higuchi, T., Niwa, T., Tanaka, T., Iba, H., de Garis, H. and Furuya, T., "Evolvable Hardware – Genetic Based Hardware Evolution at Gate and Hardware Description (HDL) Levels", ETL Tech. Report, 93-4, 1993.
6. Higuchi, T., Niwa, T., Tanaka, T., Iba, H., "A Parallel Architecture for Genetic Based Evolvable Hardware", Proc. of 2nd Workshop on Parallel Processing for Artificial Intelligence, PPAI-93(IJCAI-93 Workshop), 1993.
7. Higuchi, T., Iba, H., Manderick, B., "Evolvable Hardware", in "Massively Parallel Artificial Intelligence", AAAI/MIT Press, to appear in 1994.
8. Harvey, I., "Evolutionary Robotics and SAGA: the Case for Hill Crawling and Tournament Selection", CSRP 222, the University of Sussex, 1992.
9. Kube, C.R., Zhang, H. and Wang, X., "Controlling Collective Tasks With an ALN", *Proc. of IROS 93*, 1993.
10. Lattice Semiconductor Corporation, "GAL Data Book", 1990.
11. Sutton, R.S. (ed.), *Machine Learning, Vol. 8, Numbers 3/4: Special Issue on Reinforcement Learning*, Kluwer Academic Publishers, 1992.

Genetic Algorithms on LAN-message Passing Architectures using PVM: Application to the Routing Problem

F.J. Marin*, O. Trelles-Salazar* and F. Sandoval**

*Dpto. de Arquitectura y Tecnología de Computadores y Electrónica.
**Dpto. de Tecnología Electrónica.
Universidad de Málaga. Plaza El Ejido s/n. 29013 Málaga. Spain.

Abstract In this work we address the Genetic Algorithm parallelization problem, over a LAN-based message passing computer architectures, using PVM 3.1 (Parallel Virtual Machine - Public Domain software) as a software integration tool. The strategy used has been to split the problem into independent functions, most of them running in server processors which perform the work, and report periodically their partial results to a master node which redistributes the information in order to improve the work in each server. The strategy we present here handles all data communications through sockets via PVM calls, in such a way that the communication latency and the overall data-passing load are significantly reduced. In addition, a dynamic load balancing and fault tolerant capabilities are achieved. As an application, we study the Routing problem, which is a classical optimization problem with combinatorial complexity.

1 Introduction

It seems nowadays accepted that parallel computing is the most promising venue for High Performance Computing [6]. Many forms of parallelism exist today, from architectures designed around the idea of bringing together a relatively small number of very tightly-coupled processors, to others where the coupling is relatively loose but the number of processors can scale up to the thousands, getting us into massive parallelism. In general, the practical implementation of any of these parallel computers leads to relatively expensive machines that, presently, seldom exist at the Departmental level.

Recently, two technological breakthroughs have made possible the proposal of another approach to what a parallel computer could be. The availability of very fast processors in modern workstations, besides the widespread utilization of networks, has lead to the suggestion of designing a "virtual parallel computer" bringing together a number of these fast workstations by means of a Local Area Network (LAN), this is what we mean by LAN-based message passing architectures.

A number of approaches to parallel computing of Genetic Algorithms have previously been presented, all of them for multiprocessor architectures. They may be grouped into three general classes:
1.- Migration, which distributes the overall population in a set of subpopulations that

are assigned sequentially to different processors. Periodically, the migration of the best individuals from one subpopulation to another is performed. Depending on the exchange mode, it can be called island model if the individuals migrate to arbitrary subpopulations, often randomly chosen, or stepping stone model, if the migration is limited only to the nearest neighbours. These algorithms have been implemented for T800's transputer mesh (RISC, 32-bits architectures) [7].

2.- Diffusion, where the subpopulations are not isolated, and it is possible to access individuals from other subpopulations; in this way, they will be parents in the recombination process. The strategy used chooses randomly one parent, and the other parent from the fitness distribution of a neighbour subpopulation. This is a fine-grained parallel approach and it is performed synchronously [2] or asynchronously, running in a shared memory parallel machine [9].

3.- Farming, where a master processor manages the overall population and selects its best individuals, which are sent to the server processors. In the server processors these individuals are recombined to create offspring, and evaluated before being sent to the master processor again.

We have developed a mixed farming and migration strategy to parallelize our specific solution to the Routing Problem, using a cluster of workstations running PVM version 3.1 (Parallel Virtual Machine) [4,11,12]. The basic idea of our approach is that the master distributes the population among the servers which periodically report their best partial results to the master. The master assembles these results and re-sends the best partial results to the servers, which use this information to reorient their jobs. A very careful design of the master-server communication strategy has to be achieved in order to make this approach really efficient.

A sequential genetic algorithm has been proposed for the Routing Problem [8] which obtains better results. In this paper we intend to show that the parallelization is open to any application; therefore we have implemented the standard genetic algorithm without considering a specific operator for the application.

2 System and Methods

When studying an architecture of the type of a workstation cluster, the most important aspect to define in detail is how communications among workstations are handled in the cluster. In turn, the cost of the communications depends on a number of aspects, such as the physical bandwidth of the transmission media, the transmission protocols and the integration software used "to create" the parallel computer, the size of the messages to be transmitted, etc [3,10,13].

Our work has been carried out by workstations interconnected via Ethernet running TCP, using the software integration tool PVM release 3.1. PVM is a library of functions addressable either from FORTRAN or from C, providing the means to communicate data among workstations, executing processes remotely, and checking the status of the cluster of workstations as a whole. There are PVM implementations for many different computer architectures, thus making possible the integration of an heterogeneous cluster on workstations into a single virtual parallel computer. PVM has not been developed just for bringing together workstations, but as a general programming tool in different message-passing architectures.

3 Algorithm

As we briefly commented in the Introduction, a simple and cheap design of a LAN-based architecture presents its Achilles heel in the relatively slow data communication bandwidth of the system as a whole. Therefore, for algorithms to be efficiently run in this architecture, it is necessary, that the communications-local computations ratio be low. In other terms, only course grain parallelism is possible over relatively slow data paths. With these considerations in mind, to implement our distributed programs we split the tasks between one "master" processor and a number of "servers" processors, that perform a computational service to the master. The general form of the main loop for the GA, expressed in pseudo-code, is:

```
{ GetParameters();
PerformRequiredInitializations();
do
        {
        if (firtsGeneration)
                CreatePopulation();
        else {
                Selection();
                Crossover();
                Mutation();
        }
        EvaluatePopulation();
        Statistics();
        ReportResults();
        } while (! EndOfJob);
}
```

As we can see, the main loop of the program can work independently, giving an initial population. Then, we can devise a simple strategy in which one master process at the starting time distributes the necessary parameters, so each server can generate its own initial population, and works with it. Every time interval (number of generations), each server reports its best partial results and waits for a response message from the master process. The master process collects the best partial results from each server, selects the best of them and re-sends this result to the servers in order to reorient the servers work. The computation time for one generation in each server will be proportional to the size of the population, so if the population size and the processors are the same in each server, the computation time will be the same too.

The parallelization strategy is the following :

a) The master processor gets the initial parameters, and spawns the server processors, sending them the first message with the following parameters:

* Number of servers (NS).
* Communication interval (T). Time (in number of generations) for each server to report partial results.
* Number best partial results reported by servers (nMS) in each interval T.

* Number best results (nMC) chosen by the master to re-send to the servers.
b) Each server receives the first message and performs the required initialization, the generation of the initial population being the most important. Each server performs its work and for each T generations it sends its nMS best individuals to the master.
c) The master processor has received (NS * nMS) best results from the servers and it selects the nMC best and re-sends to each server.
d) The servers receive the nMC individuals from the master and randomly replace them in their population.
e) When the process reaches its final condition, the master processor sends an end-of-job message to the servers, and the servers exit.

A direct expression in a general message-passing architecture for our approach would then be: Master Process --Routing Problem

Additional parameters in parallel version

NS : Number of servers
T   : Communication interval (in number of generations)
nMS : best partial results sent from each server
nMC : best partial results feedbacked for client
NI : Number of intervals = Total of Generations / T

```
/* Master Process-------------------*/          /* Server Process --------------*/
 {                                               {
 Individual *nbest;
 GetParameters();
 Initialize();
 StartServer(NS,"Nserver");
 Broadcast_first_message(argv, NS);              Initialize();
                                        -----> RECIVE();
                                                PrepareEnvironment(firstMessage);
  while( Van < NI)                               do
   {                                              {
     Van ++;                                        for (i=0; i<T ;i++) Generation();
                                                    Choose_best(Poblacion, nMS);
                                                    message = Prepare_message(nMS);

     for (i=0;i<NS ;i++)  /* Get server messages */
      { RECIVE();                         <- ----   SEND(message);
        for (j=0;j<nMS; j++)
          nbest++ = GetIndividual_from_message();
      }
     Choose_best(nbest, nMC);
     If (Van == NI) c_msj = Prepare_end_message();
          else c_msj = Prepare_message(nMC);
     Broadcast(c_msj, NS);                -----> RECIVE();
                                                GetIndividual_from_message();
                                                Replace(nMC);
   }                                            } while (! eoj);
 Report(nbest);
                                                pvm_exit();
 for (i=0;i<NS;i++) pvm_kill(pinums[i]);        }
 pvm_exit();
}
```

The key points that a parallelization strategy has to address in this particular case are:
1) How the client process initially distributes the data and how we can minimize the communication - computation ratio.
2) How the client process keeps control of the application, allowing for fault tolerance: Centralized control.
3) Portability to general message-passing architectures.

A clear aspect to always be studied in any message-passing architecture is the overall data transmission bandwidth. We are interested in knowing how long it takes for a given piece of information to be transmitted from processor A to processor B. In order to actually measure this bandwidth, we have devised a simple program which occupies the memory with a string of characters of a given length -simulating a message- which is then sent to the other processor a specified number of times. There are two basic procedures that take place during such a transmission, resulting in two different times. The first one is the time that processor A, which we assume is starting the communication, takes to send the information to processor B through a given I/O subsystem -a LAN-associated subsystem. The second time is defined as the total time needed for processor B to be able to process the information sent by A, and it usually involves additional delays in emptying I/O buffers both in A and B, which we are mainly interested. The bandwidth will then be defined as number of bytes that processor A makes available to processor B, over the LAN, per unit of time.

Figure 1 shows the effective bandwidth obtained in a Ethernet-LAN based cluster of seven HP-720's and one HP-705 when the master (a HP-720) broadcasts a message of a fixed length to the seven other servers without waiting for any answer from them. It is clear that for the transmission to be effective, the message length should be in the order of multiples of 4K for this computer platform. Also, in this situation in which there is not processing on the client or on the servers and where servers do not report back anything to the master, the effective bandwidth is in the order of 700 KB. Obviously, as we really map our application on this system, each server has to answer back to the client and the client itself has to do some processing, the effective data bandwidth will be reduced.

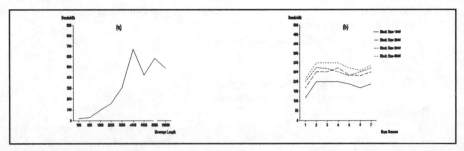

Figure 1. (a) Effective data bandwidth in Kb versus the message block size in bytes for a process involving transmissions with no further processing. (b) Bandwidth in Kb versus number of servers. It is worth noting that this effective bandwidth does not degrade when the number of servers increases, indicating that the proposed approach scales well with the number of processors.

The second aspect refers to how the client process keeps control of the application, allowing for fault tolerance. The master process in each communication interval, checks the status of each server process. If one server has broken for any reason (either, server process failure or server machine failure), it is eliminated from the master-server configuration giving, as result, a robust fault-tolerance procedure.

4 Application to the Routing Problem

The routing problem consists of finding the shortest path between any source node, s, and any destination node, d, of a network, **G**. This network **G**={**N,A**}, is composed of a finite, not empty, set of nodes **N** and a collection of orderly pairs of different nodes, **A**, belonging to **N**. Each pair of nodes (i,j) is called arc or edge. Each arc has a weight, **w**, which is an integer, positive and independent of the other weights. In general, for any two nodes (i,j), it applies $w_{ij} \neq w_{ji}$. The solution to the routing problem is an orderly list of nodes $<n_x(1) \dots n_x(q)>$ which minimizes:

$$\sum_{p=1}^{q-1} W_{p,p+1} \qquad (1)$$

The application of the routing problem to traffic in cities implies: the arcs represent the streets of the city; the nodes represent the intersections of the streets; and the weight of the arc (i,j) depends on the action of parameters such as: the length to be run, the time estimated, the saturation in the arc, the number of vehicles in the route, etc. This is a classical problem of optimization with combinatorial complexity. In an n-nodes fully connected network there are (n-2)! possible paths from any source node to any destination node.

The network under study is composed of 18 nodes (see Figure 2) with are incompletely connected and have bidirectional weights. The connection rate (number of arcs of the network over the total number of possible arcs) is very small.

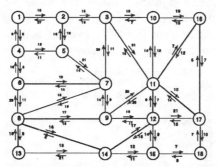

Figure 2. Network under study.

The most important step in the application of GAs to any problem is the choice of a good codification. The speed and the correct running are closely dependent on an appropriate codification. In the routing problem, a codification through a diploide structure (two strings) has been used (see Figure 3). The first string has all the nodes of the network in any order except the first and the last field, which correspond to the source and destination nodes, respectively. The second string has the same number of fields as the first string and it is formed by binary digits 0 and 1, where 0 means that this node does not belong to the path, whereas 1 does.

INDIVIDUAL:

Figure 3. Codification of the problem. Optimal path from node 2 to node 9.

The fitness function is coincident with the relation (1). The selected operator is the Baker's universal stochastic sampling [1]. In this case, the individuals with the lowest fitness values, those that minimize (1), can have a larger number of descendants in the next generation. The solution of the routing problem strongly depends on how the nodes are ordered in the network codification. We need a crossover operator to generate good ordering and we avoid the destruction of sets of nodes that are essential for finding the optimal solution of the problem. In the crossover of two individuals it is necessary that repetitions or omissions of nodes do not appear. We have used a variant of the partially mapped crossover (PMX) [5]. The mutation operator is only concerned with the second string of the diploid structure. This operator changes its binary value with a certain mutation rate.

In all the experiments we need to find the shortest path from node 2 to node 9, with the following values of parameters: crossover rate = 0.7; mutation rate = 0.3. The number of best partial results that each server reports to the master and receives from the master is 10. Each 3 generations the servers report their results to the master. The population size is 1000 individuals, which are distributed in equal chunks to the servers. The number of generations is 300. All the data have been averaged over ten runs. Figure 4 shows the value of the fitness function (performance) versus the number of generations for one server (sequential), two and three servers. The results show that after two intervals of communications the performance improves with the number of servers.

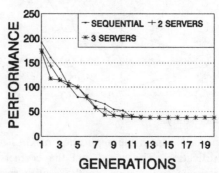

Figure 4. Performance versus number of generations for 1, 2 and 3 servers.

Figure 5 shows the value of the fitness function versus the number of generations for several values of the parameter nMS. nMC is coincident with nMS and 3 servers have been used. Because of the size of the network, there is not an appreciable difference between sending 5 or 10 best partial results from each server.

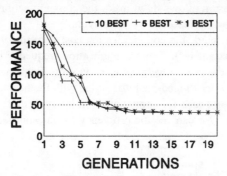

Figure 5. Performance versus number of generations for several values of the parameter nMS.

In Figure 6 the performance versus the number of generations is shown for several values of the interval of communications. The number of servers is three with nMS ten. Since the size of the network is small, the behaviour is practically equal for both three and five intervals of communications.

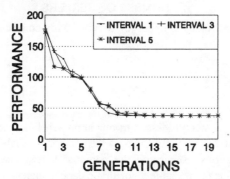

Figure 6. Performance versus number of generations for communications intervals of 1, 3 and 5.

Translating the results obtained in Figure 1 to our application, in which the message length is of 152 bytes for each member (server_id, fitness, 2 * chromosome[Number_of_cities]) , it is clear that transmission of individual members over the LAN would be very inefficient. Therefore, we devised a strategy that changed the problem of transmitting nMS messages into the one of transmitting blocks of members in one message. The size of these blocks is 1520 bytes for 18 cities, 4000 for 50 cities and approximately 8000 for 100 cities, all of them for nMS=10. Conversely, the master also groups its message into blocks, each one containing the results of the processing of the best results from the servers.

We have also measured the communication cost as a function of the number of best results (nMS) reported by the servers. Taking into account the population size we need it is possible to find the best way to communicate these results remembering that the message size should be around a multiples of 4Kb in order to maximize the bandwidth. This criterion allows us to make the communication cost independent of the number of best results reported by the servers.

On the other hand, the communication cost depends on the Communication Interval (given as a parameter). The communication frequency influences the quality of the results; this is the reason we need to choose the frequency as high as possible (shortest interval) in order to feed-back to servers with the best neighbour results. We have measured the worst case for communication intervals of 1, 3 and 5 generations, as shown in Figure 7. We can see the efficiency of our approach is reasonable.

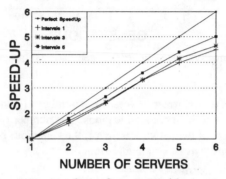

Figure 7. Speed Up versus number of servers with communication intervals as parameters.

5. Conclusions

Considering that the master processor in our approach has a computational load of only between 20%-30%, we would expect the method to scale well for larger size networks of workstations. Regarding the potential heterogeneity of a network of workstations, as well as the possible algorithmic dependencies, a very careful analysis of how the work load is distributed among the different processors as a function of time is mandatory. Our approach provides a simple and direct way to minimize the cost of communications through the sending of blocks of messages. On the other hand, we can expect that the servers work practically synchronized in their jobs; therefore, all of them need the same computation time for a number of generations.

The approach is implemented in such a way that master transmissions stop upon detection of a partial system failure (either, server process failure or server machine failure). The recovery strategy we devised is very simple and powerful: the master process reconfigures the composition of available servers.

The portability of our approach has been tested to be very good, since the communication primitives are implemented as traditional tools in any message-passing architecture. Our approach also is independent of the presence of any special hardware in the parallel system.

The way the Routing Problem is resolved has to be strongly optimized to be able to work in real time. In this work we have studied the different parameters used to parallelize the GA which can be used as a basis of comparison for extrapolating to larger networks.

Acknowledgements. This work has been partially supported by Spanish Comisión Interministerial de Ciencia y Tecnología, Proyect No. TIC92-1325-PB, TIC91-0910-PB and Joint Research UK-189B.

References

1.   Baker, J.E. "Reducing Bias and Inefficiency in the Selection Algorithm", in J.J. Grefenstette, ed., Proceedings of the Second Int. Conf. on Genetic Algorithms and their Appl., Lawrence Erlbaum Associates, pp. 14-22, 1987.

2.   Collins, R.J., Jefferson, D.R., "Selection in Massively Parallel Genetic Algorithms". In R. Belew and L. Booker, ed., Proceedings of the Fourth Int. Conf. on Genetic Algorithms. Morgan Kaufmann, pp. 249-256, 1991.

3.   Fagerholm J., Saarinen S., "Programing in the metacomputer environment PVM", CSC News, APr, 5(1), pp. 21-23, 1993.

4.   Geist G.A., Sunderam V.S., "Network Based Concurrent Computing on the PVM System" US Department of Energy

5.   Goldberg,D.E. and Lingle,R. "Alleles, Loci, and the Traveling Salesman Problem", in J.J. Grefenstette (editor), Proceedings of the First International Conference on Genetics Algorithms and their Applications, 1985.

6.   Helin, J.; "Workstation Clustering at Tampere University of Technology", CSC News, Vol.5 N°1 pp.14-17, April 1993.

7.   Kröger, B.,Schwenderling, P., Vornberger, O., "Parallel Genetic Packing on Transputers", In J.Stender, ed., IOS Press, 1993.

8.   Marin, F.J., Gonzalez, F.J., Sandoval, F. "The Routing Problem in Traffic Control using Genetic Algorithms". 2nd IFAC Symposium on Intelligent Components and Instruments for Control Applications. 1994.

9.   Maruyama, T., Konagaya, A., Konishi, K., "An Asynchronous Fine-Grained Parallel Genetic Algorithm". In R: Männer and B. Manderick, editors, Parallel Problem Solving from Nature, 2, Elsevier Science Publishers B.V., pp. 563-572, 1992.

10.   Miller, P.L., Nadkarni, P.M. and Bercovitz, P.A., "Harnessing networked workstations as a powerful parallel computer", CABIOS, 8(2), 1992.

11.   Sunderam, V.S., "PVM: A framework for parallel distributed computing", Concurrency, Practice and Experience, 2(4), pp. 315-339, 1990.

12.   Sunderam V., Manchek R., Dongarra J., Geist A. Beguelin A. Jiang W., "PVM 3.0 User's Guide and Reference manual". Oak Ridge Nat. Lab. 1993.

13.   Trelles-Salazar O., Zapata E., Carazo J.M., "Mapping Strategies for Sequential Sequence Comparison Algorithms onto LAN-message passing Architectures", High Performance Computing and Networking, 1994.

Applications

GENETIC ALGORITHM BASED DESIGN OPTIMIZATION OF CMOS VLSI CIRCUITS

Anthony M. Hill and Sung-Mo (Steve) Kang

University of Illinois at Urbana-Champaign
Department of Electrical and Computer Engineering and
Coordinated Science Laboratory
1308 W. Main St.
Urbana, IL 61801

Abstract. The proliferation of portable and hand-held electronics combined with increasing packaging costs is forcing circuit designers to adopt low power design methodologies. Low power designs of microprocessors and application specific integrated circuits (ASICs) result in increased battery life and improved reliability. In this paper, we examine the application of genetic algorithms to the low-power design of combinational logic. In particular, we consider the use of genetic algorithms for the optimization of standard cell based designs which account for 20–50% of a typical microprocessor die size. Our algorithm optimizes a user-specified function of delay, power, and area under performance constraints. Empirically, we find that the run time for our algorithm scales linearly with circuit size. In our extensive benchmark suite, this algorithm has reduced power by 17% on the average and as much as 24% on some circuits.

1   Introduction

The current generation of microprocessors and ASIC chips is based upon the complementary-metal-oxide-semiconductor (CMOS) technology. Although CMOS is known as a low-power technology, state-of-the-art fabrication techniques have yielded microprocessor designs containing over three million transistors with the next generation of processors expected to exceed six million transistors per chip [1]. This high packing density has led to increased processor functionality and speed, but it has also resulted in increased power consumption with current state-of-the-art microprocessors consuming up to 30W [1].

Portable and hand-held systems are particularly sensitive to microprocessor power consumption. This class of systems includes laptop computers, personal digital assistants (PDAs), calculators, cellular phones, and their forthcoming derivatives. Current battery technology provides only 20 W·h of energy for each pound of battery weight [2]. Furthermore, projections indicate that at most a 30% improvement in battery performance can be expected over the next five years [3]. Although portable and hand-held systems are driving low-power design, there are other emerging factors that must also be considered.

This research was supported in part by an NSF Graduate Fellowship and Joint Services Electronics Program (JSEP) under contract N00014-93-J-1270.

Increased power dissipation in a logic gate results in increased heat dissipation. As temperature rises, performance degrades and reliability decreases. Hence, more expensive packaging technology must be employed to keep the surface temperature at a reasonable level. Today's computer systems employ relatively inexpensive heat-sinks and fans, but for effective heat removal in future microprocessors, more costly measures will be necessary [4].

In this work we consider power dissipation in logic designed using the standard-cell approach. Due to the enormous integration levels, the design of a modern microprocessor or an ASIC chip requires considerable effort. One popular method employed to reduce design time is the use of standard cells. This design style accounts for 20–50% of the total chip area of a modern microprocessor, and a proportional amount of the power consumption.

In a standard-cell design, a logic circuit is constructed from a standard, pre-designed library of logic primitives, e.g., inverters, AND, and OR gates. Standard cell libraries typically contain multiple versions of the same logic function. We call the set of gates which implement identical logic functions a *logic family*. Each of the gates in a logic family is designed with different transistor sizes, hence each gate will have different delay, area, and power characteristics. Larger transistors provide shorter signal propagation delays, but have larger internal capacitance which results in increased power consumption.

When a logic block is synthesized using the standard-cell approach, we require that the worst-case signal propagation delay through the block meet some delay specification. Furthermore, we may require that the chip area consumed by that logic block be constrained. Under these restrictions, we would like to minimize the power consumption by judicious selection of the logic gates. This problem can most generally be formulated as follows.

$$\text{minimize} \quad f(Area, Delay, Power)$$
$$\text{subject to :}$$
$$Area \leq Area_{max} \tag{1}$$
$$Delay \leq Delay_{max}$$
$$Power \leq Power_{max}.$$

Other researchers have limited their consideration to the special case of minimizing area subject to a delay specification. Chan [5] introduced a non-polynomial run-time heuristic which performed optimal gate sizing, but for reasonable circuit sizes the run time was prohibitive. Lin, Marek-Sadowska, and Kuh [6] have proposed a much faster method at the sacrifice of quality. Their algorithm relies upon iteratively increasing gate sizes until delay specifications are met, then decreasing gate sizes until the specifications are violated. More recently, a suite of additional heuristics have been proposed [7, 8].

To solve the gate-sizing problem, we introduce a genetic algorithm based method. Through utilization of genetic algorithms we are able to obtain a run time efficient algorithm which produces high quality, reproducible results. We have optimized the crossover operator and introduced novel mutation operators which increase the convergence rate of our algorithm.

The remainder of this paper is organized as follows. Section 2 considers models for the performance measures of delay and power. Section 3 presents the proposed algorithm to solve the gate-sizing problem. Section 4 contains results that we have obtained on a suite of benchmarks. Finally, Section 5 summarizes this work.

2 Performance Models

The gate-sizing problem that we consider is for a block of combinational logic. This logic circuit is free of feedback and can be represented by a directed-acyclic-graph (DAG) where vertices correspond to logic gates and edges represent the interconnection of signals between the gates. For each vertex, a logic family is specified (e.g., AND2, a two input logical and gate), but the particular gate from that logic family is not fixed (e.g., AND2-1×, AND2-2×).

To evaluate the performance of a circuit based upon a selected set of gates, we need to evaluate the three performance measures required in (1): area, delay, and power. For a standard cell based design the chip area can be readily measured as the sum of the individual gate areas. However, measurements of delay and power require more intricate calculations.

2.1 Delay Model

Delay through a logic gate can be characterized by a fixed delay in conjunction with a delay linearly dependent on output capacitance. Following the work of previous approaches to delay modeling in standard-cell problems [9], we model the worst-case delay from the inputs of gate i to the output as

$$\tau_i = \max_j (a_{i,j} + b_{i,j} \cdot C_{load} + \tau_j) \tag{2}$$

where C_{load} is the sum of the gate capacitances and any routing capacitance being driven by cell i, j is the set of all inputs associated with cell i, τ_j is the arrival time of the jth. input signal, and the values $a_{i,j}$ and $b_{i,j}$ model the delay from input j to the output of the gate. Since all signal arrival times, τ_j, must be known before the delay at gate i can be evaluated, we need to perform a depth-first traversal of the DAG representing our circuit.

2.2 Power Model

Dynamic power consumption dominates total power dissipation in CMOS circuits. The total power consumption of a circuit is simply the sum of the power consumption for each gate. Dynamic power consumption for a gate is

$$P = \frac{1}{2} \cdot C_{load} \cdot Vdd^2 \cdot f \cdot p_{sw} \tag{3}$$

where C_{load} is the sum of the gate capacitances and any routing capacitance being driven by that gate, f is the frequency of the input signals, and p_{sw} is the probability that a switching event occurs at the output node. We can easily measure capacitance since it is provided for each gate in our library, and Vdd, the power supply voltage, is fixed (usually 5V or 3.3V). The only unknown quantity in (3) is the value of p_{sw}.

For an accurate approximation of p_{sw}, we rely on a method developed by Ghosh et al. [10]. Let p_{one} be the probability that the output node of a gate is logic 1 (corresponding to a high voltage level). Then the probability that the output is logic 0 (corresponding to a low voltage level) is $p_{zero} = 1 - p_{one}$. A switching event can occur on a 1 to 0 transition or on a 0 to 1 transition. Each of these values is numerically equal to $p_{one} \cdot p_{zero}$. Hence, p_{sw} is given by

$$p_{sw} = 2 \cdot p_{one} \cdot (1 - p_{one}). \tag{4}$$

At this point, the power estimation problem reduces to evaluating p_{one}. We approximate p_{one} using a 0-delay model with mutually independent inputs[1]. The best method of illustrating this calculation is through an example. Let p_a, p_b, p_c be the mutually independent probabilities that input signals a, b, and c to a gate are logic 1. Furthermore, let the logic function be defined as $f = \overline{a} \cdot b \cdot c + a \cdot \overline{b} \cdot c + a \cdot b \cdot \overline{c}$ where "+" indicates logical or ($\lor$), "$\cdot$" represents logical and ($\land$), and "$\overline{x}$" represents the negation of variable x. Then p_{one} is

$$p_{one} = [1 - p_a] \cdot p_b \cdot p_c + p_a \cdot [1 - p_b] \cdot p_c + p_a \cdot p_b \cdot [1 - p_c]. \tag{5}$$

To use this method for system-level power estimation, we assume that $p_{one} = 0.5$ for each primary input signal to the circuit. From this boundary condition, a simple depth-first traversal through the circuit will give us the switching probabilities at all gate outputs. These probabilities are constant throughout optimization since they are based upon logic function only, and the logic function of each vertex remains fixed. However, (3) must be recalculated for each solution due to changes in capacitance associated with the different gates chosen for the vertices.

3   A Genetic Algorithm for Gate-Sizing Optimization

3.1   Genetic Algorithm Implementation

Although genetic algorithms are very powerful, they can also lead to slow convergence if designed improperly. We employ several specialized techniques which enable the algorithm to converge very quickly to a neighborhood about the optimal solution. In particular, we employ *rank-based fitness*, *uniform crossover*,

---

[1] A 0-delay model assumes that there is no delay from the inputs to the output of a logic gate. Although this ignores effects such as multiple transitions on nodes due to glitching, it provides an adequate approximation of power consumption at reasonable computational expense. The assumption of mutual independence ignores signal correlation, but also facilitates a good approximation of power.

integer-valued genes, steady-state reproduction, and *specialized mutation operators.* There is a physical basis for using each of these methods which will become apparent in the following description of our algorithm.

In our representation, each chromosome represents a valid solution to our problem, and each gene of our chromosome represents one vertex in the DAG corresponding to our circuit. This gene will be able to take the integer values $\{1, 2, \ldots, n\}$ where n is the number of gates in the logic family specified for that vertex. This representation is very natural, and produces a chromosome length equal to the number of gates in our circuit. To enhance convergence we have experimentally found that steady-state reproduction with only 5% population replacement in each generation produces good results. This allows us to keep track of those solutions which have been discovered to be good and to build off those solutions. This is especially important for the gate-sizing problem where the size of the solution space can approach 10^{1300}.

To improve performance, we have adapted crossover to the gate sizing problem. In our specialized version of crossover, we generate a new solution using the following method.

For each gene in the new chromosome do
    Probabilistically choose a parent from the current population.
    Copy the gene in the parent chromosome to the offspring.

Hence, in our implementation of crossover, every member of the population can participate in the reproduction process for each offspring. Uniform crossover was found to outperform the traditional 2-point crossover and a crossover operator based upon the critical path in the circuit. We hypothesize that this is due to the extremely weak linkage between adjacent genes due to sparse interconnectivity of standard cell circuits.

If crossover is not selected, then our algorithm chooses among three equally probable mutation operators. Each of these operators first probabilistically selects a parent chromosome. This selected chromosome is copied to the new chromosome location where it is modified.

The first mutation operator finds the cell with the highest slack[2] if delay constraints are satisfied and replaces that cell with the next smaller one (areawise) in the library. If delay constraints are not satisfied, this operator selects the cell with the most negative slack and increases the size of that cell. The second mutation operator is designed to reduce area in circuits which meet the delay specifications. This mutation operator randomly selects 1% of the cells to be mutated. If delay is met, the cells selected for mutation are sized downward, otherwise, the cells are sized upward. The third mutation operator is designed to reduce power consumption in chromosomes which meet the delay specifications. It first randomly selects 1% of the cells for mutation. If delay constraints are met, the gates with lowest capacitance in the required logic families are chosen, otherwise, the next largest gates are chosen.

---

[2] The slack for a vertex is the maximum amount the delay can be increased at that vertex such that the circuit-level delays do not exceed specifications [9].

It should be noted that when a new chromosome is generated, it is compared (via a hashing function in conjunction with gene-by-gene comparison for hash table hits) to all other chromosomes in the population. If it is found to be identical to any chromosome, it is discarded. This saves considerably on computational cost and also works to maintain population diversity.

3.2   Cost Function Development

The cost function that we employ in our algorithm assigns a penalty to chromosomes which do not meet delay specifications. This cost function is given by

$$f = \begin{cases} MaxA + Delay, & \text{if } Delay > DelaySpec \\ Power, & \begin{array}{l} \text{if } Power > PowerSpec, \text{ and} \\ Delay < DelaySpec \end{array} \\ Area, & \text{otherwise} \end{cases} \tag{6}$$

where $MaxA$ is the maximum area that a solution can have, $DelaySpec$ is a user-specified worst-case delay, and $PowerSpec$ is a user-specified power consumption. The maximum area can trivially be calculated by assuming each vertex in the circuit is assigned the largest gate in its logic family.

If we wish to minimize area under a delay constraint, we specify the delay constraint and set $PowerSpec = \infty$ effectively removing the power constraint. Solutions which do not satisfy the delay constraint will have higher costs than those which do, and the closer a delay is to the specified constraint, the lower the cost. Solutions which do satisfy the delay constraint are judged solely upon area.

If we wish to optimize power under a delay constraint, we need to specify the delay constraint and set $PowerSpec = 0$. Solutions satisfying the delay constraint will then be judged only on power. Finally, if we wish to minimize delay, we set $DelaySpec = 0$. Under this assignment, the cost function will always correspond to $MaxA + Delay$.

Due to the nature of the gate-sizing problem, the chip area is a much larger quantity than delay and power. To prevent premature convergence to a suboptimal solution, we employ rank-based fitness. Chromosomes are ranked from lowest cost to highest cost and assigned reproduction probabilities based solely upon their ranking. Lower cost chromosomes have higher reproduction probabilities. The need for ranking can be seen by considering (6). Suppose we begin with a population such that delay specifications are not met. Now suppose that we generate one individual which meets the delay specification. This individual will have a much lower cost (by many orders of magnitude) than the other chromosomes. Without rank-based fitness, we can see that premature convergence would result.

Table 1. Performance enhancement for the benchmark circuits.

Circuit		Initial Solution			Minimize Delay		Minimize Power		Minimize Area		Run Time
Name	Gates	Delay	Area	Power	Delay	Ratio	Power	Ratio	Area	Ratio	
C17	8/8	2.87	11408	0.38	2.87	1.00	0.37	0.97	11008	0.96	3
b9	135/162	6.02	227352	7.23	6.02	1.00	5.86	0.81	213328	0.94	11
apex7	261/327	10.95	450712	13.07	10.78	0.98	9.91	0.76	414632	0.92	106
ttt2	268/335	7.40	480768	14.93	7.36	0.99	11.67	0.78	442672	0.92	108
C432	272/325	24.17	433272	10.23	24.03	0.99	8.26	0.81	408744	0.94	148
x1	388/474	6.82	695048	21.87	6.80	1.00	17.46	0.80	636160	0.92	160
alu2	427/525	25.81	721240	16.77	25.54	0.99	13.26	0.79	674360	0.94	164
C880	414/478	17.21	651784	17.59	16.73	0.97	13.70	0.78	607128	0.93	227
C499	519/577	18.59	813760	22.76	18.59	1.00	19.65	0.86	769472	0.95	272
alu4	770/977	27.58	1335592	28.65	27.45	1.00	23.73	0.83	1261824	0.94	287
x3	862/1105	9.41	1648144	53.10	9.33	0.99	40.54	0.76	1498728	0.91	380
C1355	785/803	24.15	1096768	26.03	24.15	1.00	22.00	0.85	1035032	0.94	507
C1908	782/898	26.13	1222176	29.77	26.10	1.00	23.81	0.80	1144392	0.94	570
C2670	868/1029	23.21	1478432	41.80	23.13	1.00	33.68	0.81	1380192	0.93	670
C3540	1222/1511	31.76	2172656	54.82	31.76	1.00	44.37	0.81	2027944	0.93	970
C5315	2272/2608	29.22	3709672	110.88	28.90	0.99	84.02	0.76	3406592	0.92	1720
C6288	3125/3144	94.90	4499336	130.51	94.90	1.00	111.24	0.85	4269736	0.95	2080
i10	2855/3508	35.59	4880872	100.45	35.22	0.99	77.66	0.77	4527560	0.93	2260
des	4451/5688	15.57	8530720	208.98	15.57	1.00	195.83	0.94	8330712	0.98	3770

4 Experimental Verification

4.1 Optimization Environment

The first step in standard cell based design is synthesis. *Synthesis* is the process of implementing complex logic functions by proper combination and interconnection of standard-cell logic gates. To synthesize the benchmark circuits, we employ SIS [11]. The output from synthesis is a circuit which SIS considers to yield minimal delay. The standard cell library employed for synthesis is an augmented version of lib2 from the Microelectronics Center of North Carolina.

For our algorithm, we have found that a standard set of parameters yields uniformly good results. We choose the population size to be 100, and consider 95 of these members to be elite. The number of generations that are considered is allowed to vary for each circuit considered. In general, the number of generations required scales linearly with circuit size.

4.2 Experimental Results

To demonstrate our algorithm, we will optimize the circuits in the following ways: i). minimize delay, ii). minimize power under delay constraints, and iii). minimize area under delay constraints. The delay constraint used in (ii) and (iii) will be the worst case delay in the initial SIS generated circuit.

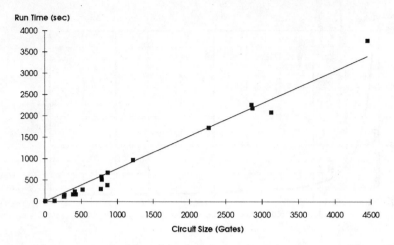

Fig. 1. Experimental run times.

Table 1 contains the results obtained through simulation. All circuits were run through our algorithm 10 times, and the best solution found is reported. All simulated delays are in ns, area is in μm^2, and power is given in $pW/(Vdd^2 \cdot Hz)$ (i.e., normalized to the input frequency and power supply voltage). The column "Minimize Delay" corresponds to the problem of minimizing delay, the column "Minimize Power" corresponds to the problem of minimizing power under delay constraints, and the column "Minimize Area" contains the results for minimizing area under delay constraints. The gate count is given as M/T where M is the number of gates with multiple implementations, and T is the total number of gates in the circuit. Some gates only have a single implementation due to their relative infrequency of use compared to more common gates.

As the table shows, using the largest cells in each logic family in conjunction with a good inverter optimization algorithm allows SIS to produce a circuit with near optimal delay. However, the shortcoming of SIS is that it does not consider smaller gates in other logic families. This is apparent from the amount of excess area that can be removed from the SIS synthesized circuit. The data also clearly indicates that our genetic algorithm based method can significantly reduce the average power consumption for most circuits.

Not only are these performance results important, but since we have employed a genetic algorithm, it is important to determine how the run time scales with problem size. The last column in Table 1 contains the run times observed for these circuits on a SPARCstation 10. Additionally, Fig. 1 shows the run time as a function of circuit size. As this figure shows, run times scale approximately linearly with the circuit size.

In a genetic algorithm we must also determine how the solution quality varies over time. We will consider the case which is of most interest to us, minimizing

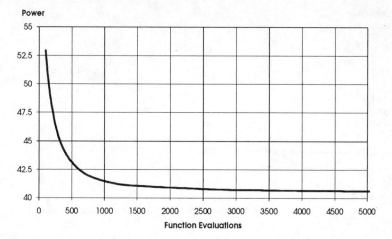

Fig. 2. Solution quality over time for circuit x3.

power consumption. Fig. 2 shows the solution quality of our algorithm over time for circuit x3. This figure shows the average convergence behavior over a series of 10 runs. As indicated, the genetic algorithm converges very quickly to a neighborhood of the optimal solution at which point the convergence rate dramatically decreases as the algorithm begins to rely upon mutation operators. In addition to the average convergence, we need to consider the variation in convergence among different runs. Fig. 3 shows the power consumption during 10 runs for x3. As this figure indicates, there is a very good consistency between runs. Ideally, each group of columns should be flat, however, being within 1% of the best solution is adequate for this application.

5   Conclusions and Open Problems

In this paper we have presented a new genetic algorithm based design optimization method to address the performance-driven gate-sizing problem. Our genetic algorithm achieves circuit design optimization over power, area, and delay. We showed empirically that the run time of our algorithm scaled linearly with circuit size. The results obtained with our algorithm show that performance improvements of up to 9% reduction in area and 24% reduction in power can be achieved utilizing this genetic algorithm.

In future research, more accurate power and delay estimation techniques can be implemented to incorporate glitching effects. Additionally, application of genetic algorithms to more general logic synthesis problems and other VLSI optimization problems should be investigated for the production of designs consuming even less power.

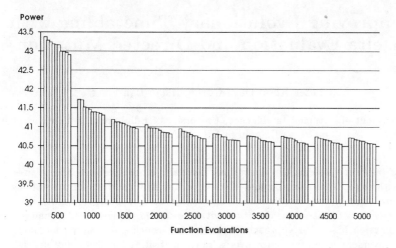

Fig. 3. Solution variation over ten runs.

References

1. Geppert, L. The new contenders. IEEE Spectrum (December 1993) 20–25
2. Bell, T. Incredible shrinking computers. IEEE Spectrum (May 1991) 37–43
3. Eager. Advances in rechargeable batteries pace portable computer growth. Proceedings Silicon Valley Personal Computer Conference (1991) 693–697
4. Bakoglu, H. B. Circuits, Interconnections, and Packaging for VLSI. Reading, MA: Addison-Wesley (1990)
5. Chan, P. Algorithms for library-specific sizing of combinational logic. Proceedings of the 27th ACM/IEEE Design Automation Conference (1990) 353–356
6. Lin, S., Marek-Sadowska, M., Kuh, E. Delay and area optimization in standard-cell design. Proceedings of the 27th ACM/IEEE Design Automation Conference (1990) 349–352
7. Li, W., Lim, A., Agrawal, P., Sahni, S. On the circuit implementation problem. IEEE Transactions on Computer Aided Design of Integrated Circuits and Systems. **12**(8) (1993) 1147–1156
8. Li, W., Lim, A., Agrawal, P., Sahni, S. On the circuit implementation problem. Proceedings of the 29th. ACM/IEEE Design Automation Conference (1993) 478–483
9. Singh, K., Sangiovanni-Vincentelli, A. A heuristic algorithm for the fanout problem. Proceedings of the 27th ACM/IEEE Design Automation Conference (1990) 357–360
10. Ghosh, A., Devadas, S., Keutzer, K., White, J. Estimation of average switching activity in combinational and sequential circuits. Proceedings of the 29th ACM/IEEE Design Automation Conference (1992) 253–259
11. Sentovich, E. et al. Sequential circuit design using synthesis and optimization. Proceedings of the International Conference on Computer Design (1992) 328–333

Improving Evolutionary Timetabling with Delta Evaluation and Directed Mutation

Peter Ross, Dave Corne, Hsiao-Lan Fang

Department of Artificial Intelligence, University of Edinburgh, 80 South Bridge, Edinburgh EH1 1HN, U.K.

Abstract. Researchers are turning more and more to evolutionary algorithms (EAs) as a flexible and effective technique for addressing timetabling problems in their institutions. We present a class of specialised mutation operators for use in conjunction with the commonly employed penalty-function based EA approach to timetabling which shows significant improvement in performance over a range of real and realistic problems. We also discuss the use of *delta evaluation*, an obvious and recommended technique which speeds up the implementation of the approach, and leads to a more pertinent measure of speed than the commonly used 'number of evaluations'. A suite of realistically difficult benchmark timetabling problems is described and made available for use in comparative research.

1 Introduction

Recent research suggests that Evolutionary Algorithms (EAs) are a viable and effective method for addressing timetabling problems [2, 1, 7, 3, 5, 8]. Following the general success shown in these endeavours, the general importance and ubiquity of timetabling problems now warrants systematic attempts to assess the general success of applying EAs to them. That is, there is a need for some standard problem definitions, benchmark problems, benchmark results, and standardised techniques for reference. Towards this end, we discuss a common penalty-function based approach to timetabling, outline a working definition for general timetabling problems, and presents several benchmark problems. In particular some domain-specific operators are described, generally applicable to all timetabling problems, and compared empirically with standard operators on a range of realistic problems.

Our timetabling experiments employ the commonly used (but often *not* used) implementation technique we call *delta evaluation*, whereby the evaluation of a new individual is speeded up by making use of previously evaluated similar individuals. We discuss this for two main reasons: (a) to emphasise and encourage its use as a way of significantly speeding up EA/timetabling applications (especially those involving the direct representation discussed later), and (b) given the use of delta evaluation as standard in this endeavour, it makes sense to record 'machine-independent' indicators of speed in terms other than simply 'number of evaluations', since the speed of an evaluation will vary greatly throughout the process. We hence describe the idea of 'evaluation equivalents' as a useful comparative measure.

We begin in Sect. 2 with a brief description of a common kind of timetabling problem. Section 3 then reviews the basic penalty-function approach, and introduces several new candidate genetic operators, and discusses the use of delta evaluation. Section 4 describes a family of benchmark timetabling problems we are developing, attending mainly to those we use later in experiments. Section 5 describes and records a collection of experiments comparing the performance of the operators described earlier on some of these benchmarks. Finally, Sect. 6 provides some discussion and summary of the paper.

2 Basic Timetabling problems

Timetabling problems involve a set of events $E = \{e_1, e_2, \ldots e_v\}$, and a set of times $T = \{t_1, t_2, \ldots, t_s\}$. Timetablers often also need to take into account a set of places $P = \{p_1, p_2, \ldots, p_m\}$, and/or a set of agents $A = \{a_1, a_2, \ldots, a_n\}$. An *assignment* is a 4-tuple (e, t, p, a) such that $e \in E$, $t \in T$, $p \in P$, and $a \in A$, with the simple interpretation: "event e occurs at time t in place p involving agent a". In a real case, this may for example mean: "The AI lecture starts at 9:00 in room LT-5, given by Minsky".

A timetable is simply a collection of assignments, one per event. The problem is to find a timetable that satisfies, or minimally violates, a (usually large) collection of constraints. The most common such constraint is simply that there should be no clashes; that is, a person should not have to be in two places at once. Considering the relationship with graph colouring problems, we call this an 'edge constraint'. A related and important constraint is what we call an 'event-spread' constraint, which expresses that a person should normally have at least a certain amount of time free between certain of the events in which he or she is involved. There are several other kinds of constraints. The most prominent among them are illustrated in Table 1. This table defines common kinds of constraints in terms of inequalities over assignments (or sets of them). In the table, $t(e)$ refers to the time assignment of event e; an ordering is assumed over the set of times T; e and f are events where, without loss of generality, we assume that $t(e) < t(f)$; and $l(e)$ stands for the duration of event e. Note that from now on in this paper, and for space reasons in Table 1, we will look at problems involving only time assignments, ignoring for now any constraints involving places or agents.

This is a convenience for present purposes, rather than any gross simplification. Place and agent constraints are often easy to handle in exam timetabling problems, for example, and such assignments can be made manually after the harder job of producing the events/times timetable. Also, constraints involving rooms and agents can often be dealt with implicitly via the constraints detailed in Table 1 alone. In many cases, of course, room and agent constraints do make the problem significantly harder; we begin to address this type of problem in [6], for example.

Table 1. Kinds of Timetabling Constraint

Constraint Type	Name	Assignment version
No clash between e and f	Edge	$t(e) + l(e) \leq t(f)$
Spare time s between e and f	Event-Spread	$t(e) + l(e) + s \leq t(f)$
Excluded times S for e	Exclusion	$NOT(t(e) \in S)$
Specified time u for e	Specification	$t(e) = u$
e must be before/after/same-time f	Juxtaposition	$t(e)(<|>|=)t(f)$

3 Timetabling with EAs

The most commonly employed EA approach is the use of a direct representation coupled with a penalty-allocating fitness function. A timetable is represented by a chromosome in which the allele of the ith gene directly represents the time assigned to the ith event; extensions dealing with room and/or agent assignments may be readily imagined. Fitness is simply a weighted sum of constraint violations; ie: high penalties accrue from violations of important constraints, while low penalties are given for soft or unimportant constraint violations. The EA then attempts to mimimise this sum.

It is wise to use *delta evaluation*, in which the computation of a chromosome's fitness is simplified as follows. Consider two timetables, g and h, which differ only in the assignments made to some subset D of the events E. Let $P(t) = \sum_{c \in C} w_c v(c, t)$ be the total penalty accruing to timetable t, where w_c is the weight associated with constraint c and $v(c, t)$ is 1 (0) if constraint c is (not) violated in t. C is the set of constraints. Now, if C_D is the subset of C containing only those constraints which involve one or more events from the subset D of E, then we can easily deduce:

$$P(h) = P(g) - \sum_{c \in C_D} w_c v(c, g) + \sum_{c \in C_D} w_c v(c, h) \tag{1}$$

which expresses P(h) solely in terms of constraints involving the events in D. If the size of C_D is small in relation to C, then this promises to save much time. In general, if h differs from g in k places, then evaluating g needs $2k$ 'constraint-checks'.

We can use of the concept of a 'constraint-check' to form a convenient measure of the speed of an EA/timetabling run. Number of evaluations is no longer a useful measure of this, because the time of an evaluation will vary quite significantly. By summing the total number of constraint-checks, we can thus form more useful cross-comparisons. Further, by noting the constant number of constraint checks that would be needed in a *full* evaluation, we can convert a constraint-checks sum into *evaluation equivalents* (EEs). This gives both a pertinent measure for comparing speed of different configurations, and also enables us to easily see the speedup effect of using delta evaluation.

Applying delta evaluation of timetable h in an EA needs a decision as to which already-evaluated timetable to take as g. A natural choice, which we use, choose g arbitrarily from the parents of h (or just use the single parent, if h was produced via a single parent operator).

3.1 Violation-Directed Operators

Consider the process involved in working out the penalty score for a timetable t; the major part of the process involves checking each constraint in turn. While doing this, extra steps may easily be incorporated which help keep track of the events whose assignments seem to be causing the most difficulty. This might be done as follows. Keep a separate 'violation score' v_i for each event e_i; initially (before evaluation) set $v_i = 0$ for each i. Then, for each constraint c, if $v(c,t) = 1$ (and hence the constraint is violated), add w_c to the violation scores of each event involved in c. At the end of this process, the set of violation scores can be used to infer which events are most problematic in t, and hence inform as to where in the chromosome it would probably be best to direct mutation. We can put this information to use in a variety of ways. the way we examine in this paper is what we call *violation directed mutation* (VDM).

There are two key aspects to VDM; the choice of a gene to mutate, and the choice of allele to mutate it to. Three possibilities for the former are: (a) simply choose the 'best' candidate for mutation, ie: randomly choose one of a set of genes with maximal violation score, or (b) stochastically select one, biased towards genes with higher violation scores, or (c) simply choose one at random (in which case the 'directedness' of the mutation will arise through the later choice of allele).

For allele choice, it is simple to conceive of a directly similar set of possibilities; this needs, though, some analogue of 'violation score' for alleles. This can be done as follows: if the gene chosen for mutation is g, then a violation score for the candidate new allele a is calculated by simply amassing the penalty-weighted sum of violations of constraints involving g which would occur if it was given allele a.

In both cases, the 'stochastic selection' aspect can be done in various ways; in fact we can use almost any standard EA selection scheme. We choose to use straightforward tournament selection for this. A good reason for this choice follows from the added computational complexity associated with the allele-choice operation; rank-based or fitness-based selection, for example, would require us to calculate, every time, a violation score for each possible new allele, which means checking s times through the list of all constraints involved with g (where s is the number of alleles). Using tournament selection with a tournament size of k, however, this only need be done k times at each application of the VDM operator. Notice that we can absorb the extra time complexity of VDM, which only arises significantly when the allele choice component is other than `rand`, into our 'evaluation equivalents' notion by simply recording the number of constraint checks made during the allele choice operation.

We shall refer to variants of the VDM operator as ordered pairs (g,a), where g stands for the gene choice operation, and a stands for the allele choice operation. Instances we look at later will involve rand (random choice), tnK (tournament selection with a given tournament size of K), and best (choose a gene (allele) with a maximal (minimal) violation score).

Finally, we note that very similar operators are described by Eiben *et al*, among others, in [4] for use on graph-colouring and other benchmark constraint satisfaction problems. The differences are that Eiben also considers variants of the operator in which either one, two, or a random number of genes are mutated each time, whereas we only look at single gene mutations here, and Eiben *et al* do not look at variations of bias in the stochastic choice component, and do not look at a best component.

4 Benchmark Timetabling problems

A fully general timetabling problem involves, as we have suggested time, place, and agent assignments along with many and varied kinds of constraints involving, for example, room capacities and teaching loads, as well as those already mentioned. Benchmark problems of this sort are in preparation, but for convenience it makes sense to also investigate a simpler variant of the general problem which is, nevertheless, both realistic and common. Here we will describe one template for such a problem, based on the recurring EDAI[1] multi-departmental modular MSc examination timetabling problem (edai-ett).

The edai-ett involves v events, all of the same duration, and s timeslots spread out evenly over d days. There are four timeslots per day. The problem involves edge constraints, event-spread constraints, and exclusions. The overall event-spread objective is that, whenever a pair of events is edge constrained, these events should also (as well as being in different slots) either be on different days, or have at least one full slot between them. Our edai-ett benchmark set contains the four years' versions of the real problem, coupled with an arbitrarily large collection of randomly generated solvable problems of the same type produced via a problem generator.

Randomly generated problems of the edai-ett type are based on the construction of a random complete timetable T of 50 events within a four-slots-per-day, nine-day timetable structure. A set of edge constraints (each with an accompanying event-spread constraint as above) is then generated which render T's particular partition of events into days, coupled with certain details of its partition of a day's events into slots, as unique in satisfying these edge constraints. A set of exclusion constraints is also generated, which by themselves make T the only solution. A problem itself is then constructed by filtering these edges and exclusions. For example edai-ett-rand(3,40,10) is a problem involving version 3 of T, and containing 40% of the generated edges and 10% of the exclusions.

---

[1] University of Edinburgh Department of Artificial Intelligence

The benchmark set we are developing is much along the lines discussed; for each real timetabling problem it contains, there is also a generator for random variants of problems of the same type. Here we will experiment with a small but useful sample of these problems.

5 Experiments

Two general questions guided the following set of experiments; a) What is the most successful variant of violation-directed mutation on timetabling problems?, and b) How can we generally expect performance to vary as we alter the difficulty of the problem? These are both extremely difficult questions to investigate, owing to the multiplicity of different variations on timetabling problems that can be imagined, to the many distinct (and interacting) ways in which we could alter the so-called 'difficulty' of such a problem, to the many variations possible on violation directed mutation, and also to inevitable restrictions on computational resources. The approach we take is to simplify the questions, and hence the investigation, without, we believe, sacrificing the usefulness of our results. Our investigation thus concentrates on these two issues: (a) How do a reasonable set of variants on violation-directed mutation compare on a typical exam timetabling problem?, and (b) How does performance of the best such variant behave as we vary the number of constraints on a similarly structured problem? To address (a), we investigated several variants of violation directed mutation on `edai-ett-93`, and to address (b) we looked at `edai-ett-rand(1,N,15)` for each of N from 20 to 100 in steps of 20.

5.1 EA Configuration

All experiments shared the following common EA configuration: A reproduction cycle consisted of a breeding step (in which one new chromosome was produced) followed by an insertion step, in which this new chromosome replaced the currently least fit (if strictly fitter itself). With probability 0.2, a breeding step involved the selection of one parent and the simple gene-wise mutation of it with a probability of 0.02 of randomly reassigning the allele of each gene in turn. With probability 0.8, a breeding step involved the selection of one parent (or two, when the operator was uniform crossover)and the application of the given operator. Tournament selection was used with a tournament size of 6, and the population size was always 1,000.

5.2 Variations on Directed Mutation

Several variations on violation directed mutation were explored using the real `edai-ett-93` problem as a benchmark. For each variant of the VDM operator. A trial consists of running the EA for 20,000 reproduction cycles, or until a perfect timetable was found. If convergence occurred to a non-perfect timetable during a trial (the entire population represented the same non-perfect timetable), then a *complete* reinitialisation of the population occurred at the next reproduction step — this counted as 1 reproduction cycle, but 1,000 evaluations (translated further into the appropriate number of evaluation equivalents). For each variation of the VDM operator, 100 trials were performed with a different random seed each time. Eight results are given for each set of trials: the number of trials in which an optimum was found (which, as a percentage, can be taken as a measure of the reliability of the EA variant on this problem), the mean number of constraints violated by the best timetable over all trials, the lowest, mean, and highest number of evaluations recorded to find an optimum over those trials in which an optimum was found, and the lowest, mean, and highest number of EEs recorded to find an optimum over those trials in which an optimum was found.

Table 2. Performance of VDM Variants on edai-ett-93

VDM Variant	No. Perfect Trials	Mean Violations	Evaluations			Eval. Equiv's		
			Lowest	Mean	Highest	Lowest	Mean	Highest
uniform	0	3.8	n/a					
(rand, rand)	3	4.2	18704	19733	19950	1610	1701	1940
(rand, tn3)	80	0.4	10613	13706	17417	3168	4109	5247
(rand, tn6)	92	0.1	7591	10598	15458	3881	5427	7906
(rand, tn9)	98	0.02	6146	8398	11259	4450	6086	8187
(rand, best)	0	29.0	n/a					
(tn3, rand)	5	2.1	17063	17660	18257	1532	1573	1613
(tn3, tn3)	65	1.4	11713	16344	19655	4717	10194	12248
(tn3, tn6)	83	0.3	6752	9160	12090	3603	4796	6190
(tn3, tn9)	93	0.9	5326	8530	19119	4029	6403	15190
(tn3, best)	0	22.4	n/a					
(tn6, rand)	8	2.1	17874	18811	19746	1646	1725	1779
(tn6, tn3)	88	0.20	10463	13930	18644	3175	4335	5687
(tn6, tn6)	82	0.03	6741	9458	13242	3537	4969	7061
(tn6, tn9)	97	0.03	5831	9572	20583	4304	7266	16309
(tn6, best)	0	22.4	n/a					
(tn9, rand)	3	3.1	12120	15756	16044	1237	1419	1554
(tn9, tn3)	77	0.3	10228	14880	18909	3253	4667	6242
(tn9, tn6)	92	0.08	7484	10656	13802	4141	5623	7532
(tn9, tn9)	85	0.19	5359	10684	20771	3875	8186	17121
(tn9, best)	0	23.9	n/a					
(best, rand)	0	20.7	n/a					
(best, tn3)	0	21.5	n/a					
(best, tn6)	0	19.1	n/a					
(best, tn9)	0	13.9	n/a					
(best, best)	0	30.1	n/a					

Clearly enough, it seems that stochastic variations of VDM, in which both the choice of gene to mutate and choice of new allele are biased, stochastic choices, are superior to basic uniform crossover on this problem. Points to note are how reliability varies with the selection pressure for these choices, and also how evaluation equivalents, rather than evaluations, are clearly a more useful indicator of speed than number of evaluations. To see the latter, note how mean EEs rises as we increase selection pressure (because we are performing more computations in, especially, the 'choice of allele' side of the operator), although mean evaluations falls. For example, (rand, tn6) and (tn3, tn9) are closely comparable in reliability on this problem, and a glance at the mean number of evaluations would seem to indicate that (tn3, tn9) is the better of the two owing to its speed. This would be true if we *had to* use full evaluation; using delta evaluation though, it is clear from the mean EEs figures that (rand, tn6) uses significantly fewer constraint checks to achieve similar reliability, and is hence overall the better of the two on this problem.

One clear point is the different degrees to which gene choice and allele choice matter. Looking solely at variations in performance with allele choice fixed, we find there is little difference between, say, (rand, tn3) and (tn9, tn3). Allele choice is rather more significant. For example, (tn3, tn9) is much more reliable than (tn3, rand). Whenever best appears for either allele choice or gene choice however, performance plummets. Another interesting point is that although biased gene choice is better than rand when the allele choice component is rand, it generally leads to slight degradation in reliability when the allele choice component is stochastic.

5.3   Increasingly Hard edai-ett-rand Problems

Some VDM variants were applied to each of 5 randomly generated solvable edai-ett-like problems of increasing constrainedness. The problems addressed were edai-ett-rand(1,N,15) for N from 20 to 100 in steps of 20. Using the same EA configuration as above (except of course for the operator choice), each entry in Table 3 records the number of optima found over 100 trials, and the mean number of EEs over those trials which found an optimum, for the configuration using the operator defined by the row, and on the problem defined by the column. Taking heed of the results discussed above, we look only at variation in bias in biased, stochastic versions of the allele choice component, keeping gene choice fixed at rand.

Table 3 reveals some clear trends. For the simpler problems, with N = 20, 40, and 60, all configurations are 100% reliable at finding an optimum, however the lower bias versions are better simply because they are faster. Again, this is directly attributable to taking advantage of delta evaluation. Number of evaluations actually reduces with increased bias, but the extra constraint checks done during allele choice more than counteract this. Hence, low-biased VDM seems best on simpler problems. As the problem gets harder, the same remains true in the sense that lower-bias versions are generally faster when they find an optimum, although they are rather less reliable. Overall, on the basis that the differences in speed are rather less significant than differences in reliability at finding an

Table 3. Performance of VDM on `edai-ett-rand(1,N,15)` for N from 20 to 100

Operator	Reliability/Mean EEs				
	N=20	N=40	N=60	N=80	N=100
(rand, tn3)	100/844	100/1715	100/3240	33/5007	0/—
(rand, tn6)	100/1212	100/2244	100/3780	100/6534	58/8436
(rand, tn9)	100/1642	100/2839	100/4535	100/7641	97/10154
(rand, tn12)	100/2178	100/3519	100/5349	100/8653	99/11464
(rand tn15)	100/2607	100/4160	100/6199	100/9660	100/12714

optimum, general indications are that higher pressure in the allele choice component is the preferred option for timetabling problems of this type; although not too high, since **best** rapidly decreases in reliability as N increases[2]. The critical region, at which higher bias starts to lose reliability on these problems, has yet to be found.

6 Concluding Discussion

We have shown that realistic timetabling problems can be effectively addressed by an EA whose main operator is VDM, particularly when incorporating a biased, stochastic method for the allele choice component, and either a random or biased stochastic method for the gene choice component. Such an EA is certainly far more effective than a straightforward EA using uniform crossover, achieving, for example 97% reliability on the `edai-ett-93` problem in certain configurations, as opposed to the 0% reliability of uniform crossover. In particular, we have found EA configurations to be very useful and effective on a range of other real timetabling problems in addition to `edai-ett-93` [5, 6].

Looking at the relative effect of different variants of VDM, it seems that the gene choice component may as well be random, while the real power and effect of the operator lies in the allele choice component. This is quite good news for implementation purposes; the combination of delta evaluation with a non-random gene-choice component at least doubles the memory requirement, since the chromosome must carry its gene violation scores around, and also makes the mechanics of delta evaluation more tricky. Results indicate, however, that it is not really necessary to have a non-random gene choice component in VDM, which alleviates these problems.

Many difficult and interesting questions remain in the EA/timetabling research arena. Here we have concentrated on one style of approach, and subsequent enhancements to its performance. General statements on the performance of EAs on timetabling is however complicated by several important factors: first,

---

[2] Space restrictions prevent a fuller presentation of results with other configurations etc . . ., but such is available from the authors.

alternative styles of EA approach are also worth investigating; for example, those in which the chromosome is *indirect*, representing a timetable via a list of instructions, or a particular ordering of events, for later interpretation by a timetable building procedure. EA/timetabling work along these lines is pursued in [8]. Second, there are many more choices of operator possible, including further variants on mutation (single parent operators) and several alternative recombination operators worth investigating. Some of these are looked at in [5]. Third, there is great variation in the space of possible general timetabling problems. We are currently looking for useful landmarks in this space, but for the time being we take the satisficing route of examining EA performance on real timetabling problems we have encountered, and constructing further test problems based on these.

In the interests of further promoting comparative research on this important kind of problem, we encourage researchers to use the benchmarks we have looked at here, and others, which can all be obtained (and explained) via the authors, or directly from the FTP site ftp.dai.ed.ac.uk.

References

1. Abramson D., Abela, J. : A Parallel Genetic Algorithm for Solving the School Timetabling Problem. IJCAI workshop on Parallel Processing in AI, Sydney, August 1991
2. Colorni, A., Dorigo, M., Maniezzo, V.: Genetic Algorithms and Highly Constrained Problems: The Time-Table Case. Parallel Problem Solving from Nature I, Goos and Hartmanis (eds.) Springer-Verlag, 1990, pages 55–59
3. Corne, D., Fang H-L., Mellish, C.: Solving the Module Exam Scheduling Problem with Genetic Algorithms. Proceedings of the Sixth International Conference in Industrial and Engineering Applications of Artificial Intelligence and Expert Systems, Chung, Lovegrove and Ali (eds.), 1993, pages 370–373.
4. Eiben, A.E., Raue, P.E., Ruttkay, Z Heuristic Genetic Algorithms for Constrained Problems. Working papers of the Dutch AI Conference, 1993, Twente, pages 341–353.
5. Corne, D., Ross, P., and Fang, H-L.: Fast Practical Evolutionary Timetabling. Proceedings of the AISB Workshop on Evolutionary Computation, Springer Verlag, 1994, to appear.
6. Ross, P., Corne, D., and Fang, H-L.: Successful Lecture Timetabling with Evolutionary Algorithms. Proceedings of the ECAI 94 Workshop on Applications of Evolutionary Algorithms, 1994, to appear.
7. Ling, S-E.: Intergating Genetic Algorithms with a Prolog Assignment Problem as a Hybrid Solution for a Polytechnic Timetable Problem. Parallel Problem Solving from Nature 2, Elsevier Science Publisher B.V., Manner and Manderick (eds.), 1992, pages 321–329.
8. Paechter, B. Optimising a Presentation Timetable Using Evolutionary Algorithms. Proceedings of the AISB Workshop on Evolutionary Computation, Springer Verlag, 1994, to appear.

Genetic Improvement of Railway Timetables

M.C. van Wezel[1], J.N. Kok[1]
J. van den Berg[2], W. van Kampen[3]

[1]*Department of Computer Science, Utrecht University,
P.O. Box 80.089, 3508 TB Utrecht, The Netherlands.*
[2]*Dutch Railways,* [3]*BSO/AI. Email:* `joost@cs.ruu.nl`

Abstract. We consider how to improve railway timetables. As case we take the Rompnet of the dutch railways, a highly constrained problem, containing both hard and soft constraints. We show how to cast the constraints into the format of the Genocop system. Every train should run every hour at the same time and hence the constraints should be interpreted modulo sixty. This gives a non-convex search space of integer vectors. The Genocop system is designed for convex search spaces, but we show how to adapt the Genocop operators to deal with this non-convex search space. The results of two experiments using the adapted operators are very encouraging.

1 The Rompnet

The Rompnet is a railway system covering most of the real railway system in the Netherlands. The Rompnet case has been used as a test bed by the Dutch Railways, in their research on various scheduling techniques. First we introduce the Rompnet problem.

The Rompnet is a railway system consisting of a number of *railway stations* and a number of *railway sections*, on which a number of *trains* are running. The departure times and halting times of all the trains in a railway system are fixed by a *timetable*. So, a timetable is a *schedule* for a railway system. The quality of a timetable is determined by how good it meets certain requirements. There are a number of "hard constraints" imposed upon a timetable, which will be discussed below, but also a number of "soft constraints". Soft constraints can cause a considerable difference in quality between two timetables which both satisfy all hard constraints. An example of a soft constraint might be minimizing the halting times of the trains in the railway system.

In the Rompnet, every train runs every hour. Distinction is made between different types of trains and railway stations. *Trains* may have one of the following statuses: intercity train, interregion train, slow train, and are marked by the letters IC, IR and AR respectively. The status of a train determines the speed with which it travels, and at which railway stations it halts. *Railway stations* may have one of the following three statuses: IC: an intercity station; all trains halt here, IR: an interregion station; IR and AR trains halt here, AR: a slow train station; only AR trains halt here. The railway stations in the system are connected by railway sections. Of course, the net is not fully connected, so there is no direct connection between *every* pair of railway stations. Not every possible timetable for the Rompnet is valid. A valid timetable has to satisfy a number of hard constraints. Those constraints can be divided into four main groups:

Frequency constraints demand that two trains, which have a part of their route in common, are running in a certain frequency on that common part. An example of a frequency constraint is AR119 AND AR134 ON UT-HAR 13/17. This constraint states that train AR119 and train AR134 have to run between stations UT and HAR min. 13 and max. 17 minutes after one another.

Market constraints enforce good correspondence times between certain trains. An example is UT AR139 ASD AR145 TL 2 8. This constraint has to be interpreted as follows: In railway station UT, stopping train AR139 coming from ASD, has got to give correspondence to train AR145 coming from TL, with min. 2 and max. 8 minutes. This means that train AR139 has got to arrive in UT minimal 2 and maximal 8 minutes before train AR145 is leaving UT.

Sequence constraints enforce each pair of trains using the same section, to keep a minimum time difference of three minutes between them.

Domain constraints are necessary to keep the halting times between reasonable bounds (e.g. between 2 and 8 minutes), and to keep the departure times in the range 0..59.

2   The Genocop System

We discuss briefly the **Genocop** method introduced by Michalewicz and Janikow [Mic92]. The aim of the method is to optimize a function $f(x_1, x_2, \ldots, x_q)$ subject to the following sets of linear constraints: domain constraints: $l_i \leq x_i \leq u_i$, for $i = 1, 2, \ldots, q$, equalities: $Ax = b$, where $x = (x_1, \ldots, x_q)^T$, $A = (a_{ij})$, $b = (b_1, \ldots, b_p)^T$, $1 \leq i \leq p$, and $1 \leq j \leq q$ (p is the number of equations), inequalities: $Cx \leq d$, where $x = (x_1, \ldots, x_q)^T$, $C = (c_{ij})$, $d = (d_1, \ldots, d_m)^T$, $1 \leq i \leq m$, and $1 \leq j \leq q$ (m is the number of inequalities).

Genocop proceeds in two phases. In the first phase, the equalities present in the constraints are used to eliminate the dependent variables in the system. In the second phase, special genetic operators are used to search the resulting search space.

The next step is the reduction of inequalities and domains. This is done by substituting the equations in the reduced equality matrix for all the eliminated variables occurring in the inequalities. This yields a reduced set of inequalities, which are now the only constraints imposed upon the problem.

This set of inequalities can be used to guarantee constraint satisfaction. For example, a feasible interval $[l_i, u_i]$ for the i-th component of a feasible solution $s = (s_1, s_2, \ldots, s_m)$ can be determined dynamically. The values l_i and u_i depend on the other variables' values $s_1, \ldots, s_{i-1}, s_{i+1}, \ldots, s_m$, and the reduced set of inequalities.

The search space that results after the first phase, has to be searched by genetic operators that do not lead to constraint violations. Such operators are called *closed operators*. Michalewicz proposes six closed operators. We only discuss the mutation operators (the reason for this will become clear later on).

Uniform Mutation: a random variable x_i of the chromosome $(s_1, s_2, \ldots, s_m)$ is selected to be mutated. The feasible interval $[l_{x_i}, u_{x_i}]$ for variable x_i is computed, using the values $s_1, \ldots, s_{i-1}, s_{i+1}, \ldots, s_m$ and the constraints. Variable x_i then gets a new value, randomly selected (with uniform probability) from the range $[l_{x_i}, u_{x_i}]$.

Boundary Mutation is very similar to uniform mutation, except that the new value for x_i is either l_{x_i} or , u_{x_i}, instead of a random value in the range $[l_{x_i}, u_{x_i}]$.

Non-uniform Mutation is also very similar to uniform mutation. A random variable s_i of the chromosome $(s_1, s_2, \ldots, s_m)$ is selected to be mutated. The new value for x_i is $x_i + \Delta(t, u_{x_i} - x_i)$ if a random digit is 0 and is $x_i - \Delta(t, x_i - l_{x_i})$ if a random digit is 1. The function $\Delta(t, y)$ returns a value in the range $[0, y]$ such that the probability of $\Delta(t, y)$ being close to 0 increases as t increases. This will cause this operator to perform a uniform search initially, and to search more locally later on in the search process.

3 Improving the Rompnet Timetable

Recall that the Rompnet railway system consists of an number of trains, a number of railway stations, and a number of sections. Let $\mathcal{T}$ denote the set of trains, let $\mathcal{S}$ denote the set of railway stations, and let $\mathcal{B}$ be the set of railway sections present in the Rompnet. A railway station $s \in \mathcal{S}$ is called the *starting station* of a train $t \in \mathcal{T}$, if s is the station where t begins its journey. We now define three functions, one for the halting times of the trains, one for the departure times of the trains, and one for the traveling times of the trains. Define $\mathsf{S} : \mathcal{T} \times \mathcal{S} \mapsto \mathcal{N}$, $\mathsf{D} : \mathcal{T} \mapsto \mathcal{Z}_{60}$, and $\mathsf{R} : \mathcal{T} \times \mathcal{S} \mapsto \mathcal{N}$ as follows. Let $\mathsf{S}(t, s)$ be the halting time of train t at station s, and let $\mathsf{D}(t)$ be the departure time of train t at its starting station. Let $s \in \mathcal{S}$ be a railway station on the route of train t and let B_s^t be the set of all the railway sections encountered by t before arriving at s. Then $\mathsf{R}(t, s)$ is the sum over all $b \in B_s^t$ of the time that train t is traveling on section b.

The value of $\mathsf{R}(t, s)$ is a fixed value, because the traveling times of trains on sections are fixed. The values of $\mathsf{S}(t, s)$ and $\mathsf{D}(t)$ are not fixed; we can manipulate them, within certain bounds, to arrive at a better timetable. By constructing a function S and a function D, we construct a timetable, because the halting times and the departure times of the trains are the only variables in the railway system. Totally, there are 176 trains running in the Rompnet. Altogether, those 176 trains make 240 intermediate stops. An intermediate stop is a stop at a station which is neither the starting station nor the end station of a train. At first sight, the number of stops may seem relatively small. However, the stops are not all stations where a train stops, but they are the stops where trains can pass each other. Moreover, the Rompnet covers only the critical central part of the Netherlands, and many of trains continue outside the Rompnet, making more stops. This yields a total of $176 + 240 = 416$ variables in the Rompnet. Our chromosomes are simply vectors of dimension 416, where the first 176 positions represent the D values of the trains, and the last 240 positions represent the S values. We cast all constraints imposed upon the Rompnet to either an equality constraint or an inequality constraint. This can easily be done, as will be shown below.

All the equality constraints in the Rompnet are produced by some of the *frequency constraints* and some of the *market constraints*.

Frequency constraints: Consider the frequency constraint IC3 AND IC6 UT-AH 30/30. This constraint demands that IC3 and IC6 are running between UT and AH with 30 minutes between them. This implies that IC3 has got to leave station UT half an hour after IC6. Given the departure times of IC3 and IC6, the traveling times of IC6 and IC3 on all railway sections, and the halting times of IC3 and IC6 in all the railway stations encountered before reaching UT, we can generate an equality constraint like D(IC3) - D(IC6) - S(IC6,UT) + S(IC3,UT) - R(IC6,UT) + R(IC3,UT) = 30. Substituting the values of R(IC6,UT) and R(IC3,UT) we rewrite the constraint as D(IC3) - D(IC6) - S(IC6,UT) + S(IC3,UT) = 39. Frequency constraints also generate another type of equality constraints. When two trains have a certain segment of their routes in common, and they are demanded to run in a certain frequency on that common segment, the halting times of both trains on that certain segment will have to be equal. This yields equality constraints of the form S(IR32,ZP) = S(IR33,ZP).

Market constraints: Consider the market constraint RTD TIC1 RLB IC4 ZL 5 5. This constraint demands that train TIC1 gives correspondence to train IC4 in RTD. This means that TIC1 must arrive at station RTD minimal 5 and maximal 5 minutes before IC4 leaves RTD. Using the same method as above, this can be rewritten to an equation. All market constraints with equal minimal and maximal correspondence times can be rewritten to an equation. This yields a total of 2 equations.

Next we discuss the inequality constraints.

Frequency constraints: Consider the frequency constraint AR121/AR122 WITH AR169/AR269 ON AH-ZV 13/17. This constraint demands that trains AR121 passes the segment AH-ZV at least 13 minutes, and at most 17 minutes after train AR169 or train AR269. It also expresses the demand that train AR122 passes the segment AH-ZV at least 13 minutes, and at most 17 minutes after train AR169 òr train AR269, but this is automatically implied by the constraint on AR121, because AR121 and AR122 lie in a 30/30 frequency. So, this gives us the constraint -31 <= D(AR121) - D(AR169) + S(AR121,AH) <= -27 OR -31 <= D(AR121) - D(AR269) + S(AR121,AH) <= -27. All frequency constraints with unequal minimum and maximum "follow-up times" can be transformed into inequalities.

Market constraints: are dealt with as if it were an equality constraint, above, but now yielding an inequality instead of an equality.

Domain constraints: A domain constraint is in fact no more than two inequality constraints, so we treat them as inequality constraints. An example of a domain constraint is 2 <= S(IR39,UT) <= 5.

Sequence constraints: express the demand that there is a minimum difference of 3 minutes between any pair of trains on any section at any time. Suppose we want to generate a sequence constraint for two trains $t1, t2 \in \mathcal{T}$, on section $b \in \mathcal{B}$. If $t1$ and $t2$ are driving with the same speed on section b, they must arrive at the beginning of section b at least 3 minutes apart from one another to satisfy the sequence constraint. If there is a difference in speed, they have to arrive at least so far apart that, at the end of the section, there will still be a 3 minutes difference between them, without $t1$ having passed $t2$ or vice versa. Suppose that $t1$ is the faster train. In this case, $t1$ has to arrive at section b at least 3 minutes *before* $t2$, or at least $3+c$ minutes *after* $t2$. Here, c is the number of minutes that $t2$ is slower than $t1$ on section b.

After we have constructed the inequalities, they are rewritten using the equality matrix. This yields a new set of inequalities, which are then the constraints imposed upon the Rompnet.

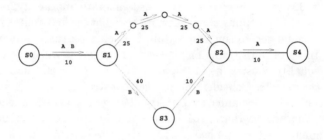

Fig. 1. A (part of a) railway system.

As we have seen, all constraints of the Rompnet can separately be cast to either an equation or an inequality constraint. Remember that every train departs every hour in the Rompnet. This poses a problem. Consider figure 1. We see a part of a railway system here. Suppose that the following constraints are imposed upon this railway system: one market constraint, demanding that train B gives correspondence to train A in station S2, with a minimum of 2 minutes, and a maximum of 8 minutes. This is the constraint S2 B S1 A S4 2 8. This constraint can be rewritten to -48 <= D(A) + S(A,S2) + S(A,S1) - D(B) - S(B,S3) - S(B,S1) <= -42. Assume one frequency constraint S1 WITH S2 ON S0-S1 13/17. This constraint demands that train A leaves station S0 at least 13, and at most 17 minutes after train B. This is expressed by 13 <= D(A) - D(B) <= 17.

Suppose S(A,S2) = S(A,S1) = S(B,S3) = S(B,S1) = 0, and D(A)=10. We can now compute a valid interval for D(B) from the two constraints. The market constraint yields: -58 <= D(B) <= -52 and the frequency constraint yields: 3 <= D(B) <= 7. This is obviously a non-satisfiable set of constraints. However, if we rewrite all the numbers modulo 60, we obtain the constraints: 2 <= D(B) <= 8 AND 3 <= D(B) <= 7 which *can* be satisfied.

Consider the constraints 40 <= X <= 20, 10 <= X <= 50. Obviously, both constraints are satisfied if 10 <= X <= 20 OR 40 <= X <= 50. Disconnecting the lower bounds and the upper bounds of the constraints in order to compute the maximum lower bound and the minimum upper bound would yield four separate inequality constraints: X <= 20, X <= 50, X >= 10, X >= 40, which is a non-satisfiable set of constraints. However, we can still compute the intersection of all the "intervals" generated by the constraints. Suppose we want to compute the intersection of the intervals yielded by A <= X <= B and C <= X <= D. This can be done using the function f that gives a list of intervals:

$$f([A, B], [C, D]) = \begin{cases} [A, B] \cap [C, D] & \text{if } A \leq B \wedge C \leq D \\ f([A, 59], [C, D]) \bullet f([0, B], [C, D]) & \text{if } A > B \\ f([A, B], [C, 59]) \bullet f([A, B], [0, D]) & \text{elseif } C > D \end{cases}$$

This function returns a "list of intervals", which captures the notion of the intersection of a number of "intervals in $\mathcal{Z}_{60}$". The bullet denotes concatenation.

The implication of the above is that our search space becomes divided into a number of small "feasible parts", as opposed to the convex search space in the original Genocop system. The problem is that, with such a search space, the original Genocop operators loose their closedness. Therefore, we will have to adjust the Genocop operators so that closedness is preserved.

Uniform mutation can be used if we allow uniform probability mutations to the integers in the valid intervals. We showed how to compute a list of feasible intervals. To perform a uniform mutation on a variable, we compute a list. Next, one of the list elements is chosen. The probability of a certain list element being chosen depends on the number of integers it constrains relatively to the other intervals in the list. Finally, the variable is assigned a new value, which is chosen at random, with uniform probability, among the integers in the list.

Boundary mutation can not be implemented, because we do not have a single feasible interval $[l, u]$ with only two bounds l and u, but we (may have) a number of such intervals $[l_1, u_1], \ldots, [l_n, u_n]$. Instead of a normal boundary mutation, we now select one of the n intervals $[l_c, u_c]$ at random with uniform probability, and assign one of the values l_c, u_c.

Non-uniform mutation can also be implemented. First, a list of intervals is computed in the manner described above. Next, the interval in this list containing the current value is determined. In this interval, a normal non-uniform mutation is then performed. The new value is rounded to the nearest integer value within the interval.

The adjusted operators described above, were implemented in a program called **GOP** (Genetic Optimization Package). Next we roughly describe the operation of the program. GOP starts with reading the constraints, the population size, and the frequencies of the operators from a file. The equalities are used to produce a new set of inequality constraints, which are brought together in one matrix. One initial chromosome is read from file. This initial chromosome, or initial point, satisfies all the constraints.

The next step in the operation of GOP, is to create the initial population, consisting 'tt popsize' copies of the initial point, where tt popsize is the population size. After this preprocessing, GOP is ready to start the evolutionary process. The number of generations is also specified in the input file.

The fitness function we used is directly derived from our objective: minimizing the halting times and the correspondence times of the trains in the Rompnet.

Generally, we can say that inequality constraint i, represented by row i of the inequality matrix, is satisfied by chromosome x iff the predicate "InBounds(i,x)" is satisfied, where InBounds(i,x) is defined as follows. Let l_i and u_i denote the lower bound respectively the upper bound of inequality constraint i, and $I_i(x)$ denotes the sum in inequality constraint i. Define $l'_i = mod60(l_i)$ and

$$u'_i = \begin{cases} mod60(u_i - 1) & \text{if } mod60(l_i) = mod60(u_i) \land l_i \neq u_i \\ mod60(u_i) & \text{otherwise.} \end{cases}$$

The predicate InBounds(i,x) is true if the intersection $f([v,v],[l'_i,u'_i])$, where $v = mod60(I_i(x))$, is not a sequence consisting of only empty sets.

Minimizing the halting times and the correspondence times now becomes a matter of finding a chromosome x, such that the sum of the all the halting times and correspondence times are minimized. Each halting time has an upper bound and a lower bound, which are represented by a domain constraint. This domain constraint is represented by a row in our inequalities matrix. The lower and upper bounds of the correspondence times in the Rompnet are generated by market constraints. Each market constraint is represented by one or two rows in our inequalities matrix.

We can mark the rows of the inequalities matrix representing domain constraints on halting times and market constraints by a boolean array `TARGET`. If, for an arbitrary row i of the inequalities matrix, `TARGET[`i`]` = TRUE, this means that the lower bound l_i is the "target value" when evaluating $mod60(I_i x)$.

We can now define a fitness function for a chromosome x

$$f(x) = \frac{C}{\displaystyle\sum_{i:\text{TARGET}[i]=TRUE} \text{diff}60(mod60(I_i x), mod60(l_i))}$$

where C is some large constant for preventing truncation errors. We took the value of C to be 1000. The function $\text{diff}60(y,z)$ for $y,z \in \mathbb{Z}_{60}$ returns the value we have to add to z to obtain y, i.e. $\text{diff}60(y,z) = z + 60 - y$ if $z < y$ and equals $z - y$ if $z \geq y$. This fitness function f can be used for roulette wheel selection, but in order to keep the variance of the fitness values high, we subtracted a value $B = \tau.f_{min}$ from every fitness value $f(x)$. Here, f_{min} is the minimal fitness value over all chromosomes in the current population, and τ is a system parameter, for which we took the value 0.9. This leads to the fitness function $g(x) = f(x) - B$. Using this fitness function, chromosomes with smaller halting times and better correspondence times have more chance of being selected for reproduction and mutation. If a chromosome x is selected for mutation, a variable x_i is selected to be mutated at random. The program then looks in the inequalities matrix which rows represent constraints in which x_i occurs. Next, a list of feasible intervals is computed and a mutation is performed, in the way described above.

4   Results

We did two separate experiments: a first one with all the equality constraints, and all the inequality constraints, except for the sequence constraints. The second one contains all the equality constraints and all the inequality constraints, except for the inequality constraints for segments with one or four parallel sections. This covers the greater part of the Rompnet. Scheduling on four section segments is easier, because if we put the fast trains going in one direction on one section, and the slow trains going in that direction on the other section, we do not have to deal with big speed differences. On the one section segments, there relatively few trains running, so this should not pose a big problem either.

In the left of figure 2, we see the number of generations on the x-axis, and the sum of the halting times and the correspondence times for the best chromosome of the population on the y-axis. In this run, we used the small constraints set (without sequence constraints). This sum is 837 minutes for the initial point. The GOP program reduced it to 353 minutes.

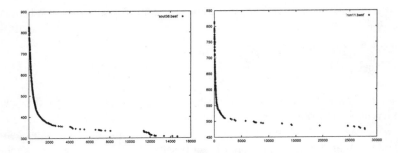

Fig. 2. Sum of halting and correspondence times (in minutes) against the generation number for the first and second experiment.

In the right of figure 2, we used the second set of constraints. The sum that has to be minimized has an initial value of 837 minutes, and it is reduced to 473 minutes. In table 1 we give the results for different runs for the first and the second constraint sets. In all runs, a population size of 150 individuals was used.

In figure 3, we see the initial timetable, the timetable produced by GOP using the small constraints set, and the timetable produced using the second constraints set respectively. Those graphs may seem rather pointless, but we can see from them that the halting times are significantly smaller in the timetables produced by GOP. The halting times are represented by the last 240 variables in the chromosomes.

#	Best	Average	Worst		#	Best	Average	Worst
1	384	402.239	436		1	473	483.673	508
2	379	395.946	411		2	477	487.100	517
3	385	400.733	418		3	486	497.366	538
4	374	387.459	402		4	487	497.366	521
5	353	363.706	385		5	489	501.306	527

Table 1. Results for the two constraints sets.

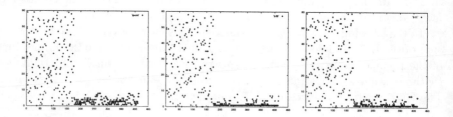

Fig. 3. The initial point and the best point found for the first and the second constraints set.

5   Evaluation

We have shown that it is possible to have good results on improving solutions for heavily constrained non-convex problems like the Rompnet problem using a new variant of the Genocop system. Although a lot of work has been done for timetabling, for example for job shop scheduling, for assigning teachers to classes ([BUM91], [CLS91], and also for scheduling trains ([AMP93], [GBH91]) we have not seen the requirement that every hour the schedule should be the same. As outlined before, this causes the search space to become non-convex. Usually when non-convex search spaces are encountered one uses filter or repair algorithms to remain in the valid search space. For the Rompnet it is possible to calculate intervals in which the search can take place.

Our experiments start from an initial valid point. If such a point is not available one can use two sets of constraints, of which one is the set of "target constraints", and the other is a set of "current constraints". The program would then begin with very relaxed "current constraints", which would have to be satisfied by the wole population. The "current constraints" could then be adjusted dynamically as the population gets fitter and fitter, and in the end, we hope that the population satisfies all "hard constraints".

An important advantage of the method (compared to more standard operations research) is that during the whole evolutionary process, the population consists of valid timetables. This means that at any stage, we can look how the timetables in the population are developing. This is particularly useful if the fitness function contains more than one term, and the terms frustrate one another. In this case, the weights of the terms can easily be adjusted with an interactive tool during runtime, so that the desired balance between the terms of the fitness function can be found. This way, we can make a "wish" more or less important during runtime. This opens many possibilities for the construction of intelligent planning tools.

Another advantage is that heuristic methods (including those of operations research and of artificial intelligence) can easily be incorporated in the genetic algorithm, if we are able to express them as crossover or mutation operators on the strings we used.

References

[AMP93] Abramson, D., Mills, G. Perkins, S. *Parallelisation of a Genetic Algorithm for the Computation of Efficient Train Schedules* Proceedings of the 1993 Parallel Computing and Transputers Conference, IOS Press, 1993.

[BUM91] Bagchi, S., Uckun, S., Miyabe, Y. & Kawamura, K. *Exploring Problem-Specific Recombination Operators for Job Shop Scheduling.* Proceedings of the Fourth International Conference on Genetic Algorithms, pp. 11-17, Morgan Kaufmann, 1991.

[CDM90] A. Colorni, M. Dorigo, and V. Manezzo. Genetic algorithms and highly constrained problems - the time-table case. In H.P. Schwefel and R. Männer, editors, *Proceedings First Conference on Parallel Problem Solving from Nature,* pages 55–59, 1990.

[CLS91] Cleveland G.A. & Smith, S.F. *Using Genetic Algorithms to Schedule Flow Shop Releases.* Proceedings of the Fourth International Conference on Genetic Algorithms, pp. 161-169, Morgan Kaufmann, 1991.

[Dav91] L. Davis. *Handbook of Genetic Algorithms.* Van Nostrand Reinhold, 1991.

[GBH91] Gabbert, P.S., Brown, D.E., Huntley, C.L., Markowicz, B.P. & Sappington, D.E. *A System for Learning Routes and Schedules with Genetic Algorithms.* Proceedings of the Fourth International Conference on Genetic Algorithms, pp. 430-436, Morgan Kaufmann, 1991.

[Mic92] Z. Michalewicz. *Genetic Algorithms + Data Structures = Evolution Programs.* Springer Verlag, 1992.

[MJ91] Z. Michalewicz and C.Z. Janikow. Handling constraints in genetic algorithms. In *Proceedings of the fourth international Conference on Genetic Algorithms.* Morgen Kaufmann Publishers, 1991.

[TN93] S.R. Thangiah and K.E. Nygard. Schoolbus routing using genetic algorithms. In *Proceedings SPIE, Applications of Artificial Intelligence X - Knowledge based systems,* volume 1707, pages 387–398, 1993.

[WSS90] D. Whitley, T. Starkweather, and D. Sharon. Using simulations with genetic algorithms for optimizing schedules. In *Proceedings Computer Simulation Conference,* pages 288–293, 1990.

Using a Genetic Algorithm to Search for the Representational Bias of a Collective Reinforcement Learner

Helen G. Cobb[a] and Peter Bock[b]

[a] Naval Research Laboratory, Code 5514, Navy Center for Artificial Intelligence, 4555 Overlook Ave., SW, Washington, D. C., USA 20375-5337; cobb@aic.nrl.navy.mil

[b] Department of Electrical Engineering and Computer Science, The George Washington University, 2020 K Street, NW, Suite 300, Washington, D. C., USA 20052

Abstract. In reinforcement learning, the state generalization problem can be reformulated as the problem of finding a strong and correct representational bias for the learner. In this study, a genetic algorithm is used to find the representational bias of a stochastic reinforcement learner called a Collective Learning Automaton (CLA). The representational bias specifies an initial partition of the CLA's state space, which the CLA can strengthen during learning. The primary focus of this study is to investigate the usefulness of the very strong representational biases generated by the system. The study compares the accuracy of an inexperienced learner's bias to the accuracy of an experienced learner's bias using *PAC*-like measures of Valiant. The results presented in the paper demonstrate that, in general, it cannot be assumed that a representation that is part of an experienced learner's solution to a problem will provide an accurate learning bias to an inexperienced learner.

1 Introduction

In recent years, several researchers have studied *inductive biases* in the context of concept learning and concept formation (*e.g.*, [21, 26, 13, 7]). During the inductive process of concept learning, a learner forms a hypothesis that goes beyond the instances observed ([21], pp. 3). Thus, for any generalization to take place, the learner must have some preference that enables the learner to form or select one hypothesis over another during hypothesis formation. These preferences are called inductive biases [21].

Biases not only exist in concept learners; they also exist in other learners such as reinforcement learners. In general, biases can exist in deductive as well as inductive inference, and the forms of a bias can be both *representational* and *procedural*. In concept learners, a representational bias exists in selecting the learner's hypothesis language (*i.e.*, a language bias); in reinforcement learners, a representational bias exists in selecting the organization of the learner's associative memory. Procedural biases include the methods the learner employs for modifying its hypotheses (or memory contents) over repeated instances (or trials), exploring the environment, and taking advantage of available knowledge. *A learner's bias* is defined here to be any persistent preference the learner has for organizing and using information while learning. *Inher-*

ited biases are defined to be those biases that exist in the learner at the time the learner is instantiated. In addition, the learner may also periodically restructure or redefine itself as a result of learning: such biases are defined to be *learned biases*.

Researchers in concept learning and in learning theory consider two important qualities of bias: *strength* and *correctness* [26]. In concept learning, a stronger language bias corresponds to a smaller cardinality of the language hypothesis space. Based on this definition, more concise languages are stronger languages. In reinforcement learning, a stronger representational bias corresponds to a smaller associative memory. A correct bias enables learning, whereas an incorrect one prohibits learning. From a probabilistic point of view, one measure of the correctness of a bias is its *accuracy* [7, 17].

It is especially important in reinforcement learners that solve sequential decision problems to consider the size of the state space. If we assume that states correspond to the stimuli sensed by a reinforcement learner, then even for seemingly moderately sized problems, the number of states the learner needs to consider grows quickly as we increase either the resolution of the stimuli or the number of sensors. Basic reinforcement learners using tabular types of memories, such as Watkins' tabular Q-learner [27], and Bock's Collective Learning Automaton (CLA) [4], do not generalize over stimuli. The primary objective of such reinforcement learners is to infer a correct stimulus-response mapping, given a predefined stimulus domain. Without using a representation that provides some form of state or input generalization, the reinforcement learner's ability to learn in large state spaces may be severely limited.

Researchers have defined the problem of finding a representation for a reinforcement learner in different ways. For example, Sutton refers to the problem as a *structural credit assignment problem* [24]; Whitehead and Ballard consider the problem in terms of *perceptual aliasing* [28]; Chapman and Kaelbling refer to the problem as an *input generalization problem* [5], and Lin refers to the problem as the *state space generalization problem* [17]. Because the learning process of a standard reinforcement learner does not include state space generalization, this meta-level problem can be considered to be an example of the general problem of *finding a strong and accurate representational bias* for the learner.

Most of the researchers that have studied state generalization have focused on searching for a representational bias while the learner accumulates experience. In these systems, a *bias adjustment mechanism* changes the bias of the learner periodically.[1] Two general approaches for adjusting bias are discussed in the literature. One approach is to directly employ either a bias weakening (divisive) or a bias strengthening (agglomerative) technique that essentially performs a directional search [5, 18, 19, 30]. The bias adjustment mechanism periodically strengthens (or weakens) a bias to form a new bias, depending on changes in the learner's performance or on observed inconsistencies in perceptual state information.[2] Most of this research examines the bias search problem for Q-learners [27] or learners using Temporal Difference methods [24]. Another general approach for finding a strong and correct representational bias is to use

---

1. Most authors of papers on reinforcement learning do not use learning bias terminology.

2. This technique is also referred to as *active bias adjustment* [13].

the implicitly parallel search of a Genetic Algorithm (GA). Several researchers have explored hybrid systems that use a GA to search for the representation of a reinforcement learner [15, 16, 29, 30]. However, only a few of these systems try to find minimal (*i.e.*, strongest) representations [29, 30]. In these GA-based systems, there is typically a high degree of two-way communication between the GA and a learner (for classifiers) or a population of learners (for generational GAs). This Lamarckian transfer of knowledge from the current generation to the next effectively means that the system accumulates learning experience over the generations. In effect, the GA operators perform bias adjustment. It is important to note that without incorporating some kind of learned information in the evolutionary process, the computation time needed to evolve representations for large learning systems can take *years* ([16], pp. 214).

The results of these studies generally show that there is a significant improvement in performance with successive learning trials whenever a system uses a bias adjustment mechanism in conjunction with learning. Most of the research does not focus on the usefulness of the learned representation as a bias to be applied to an inexperienced learner (*i.e.*, the accuracy of the learned bias). In other words, it is not clear to what extent the usefulness of the learned representation depends on the experiences of the reinforcement learner. By analogy, consider for a moment two types of information resources: one is a small reference manual and the other is a more verbose tutorial. Both resources explain how to repair a washing machine, but the usefulness of each resource depends on who is using it. An experienced repairman may be able to interpret the reference manual, because he can fill in missing details from his experience, but an inexperienced repairman may require the tutorial in order to succeed in repairing a machine. The bias represented by the reference manual is only accurate in a narrow sense: it is accurate for the experienced repairman, but not for the inexperienced one.

The primary focus of this study is to investigate the accuracy of the representational biases generated by a hybrid system called SPARCLE (State Partitioning Collective Learning System), in which a generational GA searches for the representational bias of a population of CLA reinforcement learners.[3] All of the CLAs in the population are identical except for their representational biases, so only the biases are expressed in the genes. The objective of SPARCLE is to search for a minimal representational bias that consistently permits a CLA to successfully learn a task. At the beginning of each generation, each CLA in the population inherits a representational bias, which has the effect of partitioning the CLA's state space. Using the inherited bias, the CLA performs a task to the best of its ability. While learning, however, a CLA may reduce the size of its inherited bias by permanently forgetting parts of the representation that are used very infrequently. Upon halting, the CLA sends the GA a reduced (learned) representational bias along with the CLA's evaluation of its own performance. Depending on the reliability of the performance estimate required, the GA may re-evaluate the bias for several additional CLA life-spans with the CLA's forgetting mechanism temporarily deactivated. After the evaluating all of the members in the population, the GA calcu-

---

3. A CLA is considered to be *collective* because it modifies its memory only upon receiving a delayed, summary evaluation from the environment. This evaluation reflects the quality of the entire learning episode, called a *stage,* and not just the value of the goal state.

lates each bias' fitness based on the final size of the bias and the median performance using that bias.[4] Biases that permit the CLA to perform well, along with the CLA's memory contents, are saved off-line for subsequent analysis. The net effect is that SPARCLE combines an evolutionary search for representational biases with a bias strengthening technique based on forgetting in the learner.

Because the GA uses the current generation's learned biases to generate inherited biases for the next generation, SPARCLE also uses Lamarckian evolution. However, each new generation of CLAs starts out as inexperienced learners so that a representation is tested in terms of its desirability as an inherited bias. Thus, SPARCLE's architecture emphasizes an evolutionary search for strong and accurate inherited biases, rather than considering the large number of possible bias adjustment mechanisms that learners could use to compensate for initially incorrect biases.

The accuracy of the resulting biases can be examined using Valiant's PAC-learning[5] framework [17, 7]. In this framework, the learner's goal is to develop a hypothesis of the target concept, or a classification rule, L_h, that approximates the actual target concept, L_T. If $D(L_h, L_T)$ is the probability that L_h and L_T produce a different classification of an instance that is drawn iid,[6] then the goal of the learner is to produce L_h such that

$$Pr\{ [D(L_h, L_T) \leq \varepsilon] \} \geq 1 - \delta. \qquad \text{(Eqn 1)}$$

Increasing the size of the sample increases the confidence in the error estimate, $D(L_h, L_T)$, so that the probability that L_h approximates the target concept within ε is $1 - \delta$ [7]. Notice that Eqn 1 applies to deterministic, passive learners that draw instances iid. Given the same instance distribution, the classification accuracy of a resulting L_h should not vary significantly from one instantiation of the learner to the next, where each instantiation uses a different pseudo-random number stream. Thus, finding a L_h that has a reliably low classification error implies the learner's biases are accurate. For active learners that do not store instance information, however, the resulting L_h can vary significantly with the actual sampling sequence, even though the underlying distribution remains the same between instantiations. Only trials of the entire learning process are known to be independent and identically distributed examples of the learner's behavior.[7] For such learners, the PAC-learning framework can be used to evaluate bias accuracy if we move sampling up a level to examine the learning process as a whole.

In reinforcement learning (a type of active learning that summarizes experiences), the probability that the learner's approximate steady-state performance is close to the optimal performance is analogous to the probability that the classification of an instance using L_h is within ε of the target concept. We consider a solution to be ε-optimal if the normalized deviation in the average performance from the optimal one over the

---

4. The performance distribution is not Gaussian.

5. Angulin first used the acronym PAC-learning (*Probably Approximately Correct* learning) to describe Valiant's learning framework [7].

6. identically and independently from the same distribution

7. One way to overcome this problem would be to design a PAC reinforcement learner.

last stages of the learner's life-span is less than ε. Based on this formulation, if a solution is ε-optimal for some large fraction of independently repeated trials of the learner's life-span, then the bias is accurate. Thus, repeatedly finding an accurate solution, A_s, implies an accurate bias, A_b (*i.e.*, $A_s \Rightarrow A_b$). The experiments in this paper demonstrate that an experienced learner's bias may not always be successfully applied to a novice learner as an inherited bias (*i.e.*, if S is a learned bias used in an optimal solution, $S \not\Rightarrow A_b$). This analysis suggests a bias found using some form of dynamic bias adjustment in an active learner needs to be tested repeatedly to ensure the bias' accuracy.[8]

The remainder of the paper is organized as follows: Sections 2 and 3 provide an overview of the CLA and GA components of the system, respectively. The standard generational GA is well documented, so only important modifications to the algorithm are discussed.[9] Section 4 describes the test problems explored in the study; Section 5 provides an outline of the experimental methodology and then presents the results of the experiments, and Section 6 presents the conclusions.

2 The Collective Learning Automaton

The CLA's representational bias consists of a set of points within the stimulus domain called *stimulants*. The CLA translates the bias it inherits from the GA into an internal representation using a built-in function that maps incoming stimuli into stimulants. In general, the purpose of the stimuli-to-stimulant mapping is to partition the stimulus domain into non-overlapping regions which act as the internal, perceptual states of the learner [28]. The automaton uses the stimulants to develop a probabilistic Stimulant-Respondent mapping (S-R mapping) for performing a task. In the current implementation, the mapping uses a nearest neighbor Euclidean distance measure so that each stimulant acts as a centroid of a region, where all of the stimuli mapping into a region elicit the same probabilistic response behavior from the CLA. This many-to-one mapping creates an approximate (discrete) Voronoi tessellation of the parts of the state space visited by the learner.[10]

At its simplest level, the CLA maintains a two-way *interaction* with the environment. After performing a stimulus-to-stimulant mapping, the CLA selects a response for the given stimulant, and then sends the outgoing response to the environment. This interaction continues over an interval called a *stage*, the length of which is task dependent. The environment marks the end of a stage by sending an evaluation to the CLA, which the CLA then transforms into an internal reinforcement called a *compensation*. The CLA uses the compensation in several ways: to update the probabilities in its S-R

---

8. Notice that testing the bias is not the same as testing the bias adjustment mechanism.

9. The GA of SPARCLE is a modified version of GENESIS, Version 5.0, written by J. Grefenstette [14].

10. A stimulant in the CLA serves the same purpose as the antecedent of a rule in a simple production system. However, unlike a rule, each stimulant may be associated with all possible responses (consequents) rather than having one explicit "then" part. Instead of learning a rule strength that reflects the degree of association between a rule's pre-condition and its specified post-condition, the CLA develops a probability density over the possible responses.

mapping, to update the stimulant probabilities (used by the forgetting mechanism), and to compute an estimate of the learner's own performance. The CLA's performance is the running average of the compensation values over a *final run* of stages. The CLA stops when either the value of the CLA's compensation remains the same for the final run (whether the solution is optimal or not), or the current number of stages exceeds the number of stages the automaton is permitted to run. Upon stopping, the CLA reports its performance to the GA, regardless whether or not the CLA has converged. At the same time, the CLA also reports the final stimulant set. (See [6] for details.)

The CLA periodically activates its forgetting mechanism after the first 200 stages to determine which stimulants should be retained. Unlike a typical forgetting mechanism that would use some "forgetting constant" to increase the likelihood of forgetting relatively inactive stimulants, the CLA's forgetting mechanism uses the learner's compensation to update a stimulant's probability of being useful. During each activation, stimulants are sorted by their probabilities in descending order, and a cumulative probability distribution is formed. Those stimulants whose cumulative probability exceeds 0.999999 are marked for possible elimination. If the same set of stimulants remain unmarked for three consecutive activations of the forgetting mechanism, then the CLA retains unmarked stimulants and forgets (or eliminates) marked ones.

3 Evolving a Representational Bias

In SPARCLE, each member of the population consists of a variable number of integer-valued, n-dimensional points, where each of the n dimensions corresponds to one of the CLA's sensors.[11] The variable length representation is similar in some ways to the representations used in other systems [23, 8, 10, 12, 15]. Each set has a maximum number of randomly selected points which is typically much smaller than the number of points in the stimulus domain.

SPARCLE's GA goes through the standard generational cycle of evaluating population members, selecting members for reproduction, cloning selected members, and generating a new population from the clones using crossover and mutation operators. In SPARCLE, however, all of the population members are evaluated before calculating fitness values. To calculate fitness, population members are first ranked using the accuracy criterion of the representation (CLA performance), and then secondarily ranked using the strength criterion (size of stimulant set). Fitness values are calculated, starting with the highest ranking member, using a linear combination of these two criteria. The accuracy and length of each member is normalized by the accuracy and length of the current generation's highest ranking performer. In particular, the fitness for population member i is

$$fitness(i) = penalty \times \left[\frac{\beta \times (accuracy)(i)}{accuracy(best)} \right] \times \left[\frac{length(best)}{length(i)} \right], \qquad \text{(Eqn 2)}$$

---

11. These points are interpreted as stimulants by the CLA. The representation also includes a fixed-length set of integer-valued, m-dimensional points that are interpreted as respondents by the CLA, where each of the m dimensions represents one of the CLA's effectors. Here, respondents are the same as responses.

where β is the coefficient used to determine the relative weight of the accuracy to the strength criterion (currently, $\beta = 2$), and *penalty* is the coefficient used to adjust fitness values. Whenever the ranking is violated, a penalty is applied so that the resulting fitness values are consistent with the original ranking; otherwise, *penalty* = 1. After computing fitness values, the GA reproduces members using proportional selection, with the objective of maximizing fitness values. By forcing fitness values to be consistent with the ranking of population members, the GA effectively uses a selection mechanism that has some of the characteristics of both rank-based selection [3] and proportional selection.

The GA next applies the *similarity crossover* operator to create new offspring from the clones of selected population members. Similarity crossover has some of the same characteristics as Davidor's *analogous crossover* [8]. In some sense, the similarity crossover is a generalization of 2-point crossover. Instead of exchanging substrings, similarity crossover exchanges points that lie in the same region of an n-dimensional space. Fig 1 illustrates the similarity crossover operator for a two-dimensional stimulus space. The dot and cross symbols represent the points making up the (cloned) parents A and B, respectively. To begin crossover, the operator randomly selects one of

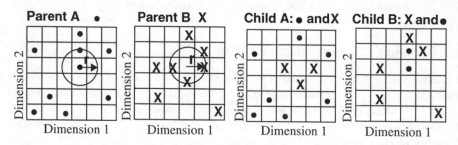

Fig. 1. Similarity crossover for a two-dimensional stimulus space

the points in parent A and the number of points to be crossed over, K. Using the selected point as the center of an n-dimension (discretized) hypersphere, the operator locates a region in parent A that includes K neighboring points. If the region within the defining radius covers more than K points, then K is expanded to include these additional points. The radius encompassing the neighborhood in parent A is then used to select K' neighboring points from parent B that lie in the same region of the space. The K or more points of parent A are exchanged with the K' points of parent B to form children A and B. If there are no points in parent B to cross over (*i.e.*, $K' = 0$), then child A is the same as parent A, and child B obtains a copy of parent A's K points. Those population members not participating in crossover are subjected to low levels of *incremental mutation* [9, 25].

4 Example Problems

This paper examines two problems: a simple maze problem introduced by Sutton [27] while studying his Dyna system, and the well-known pole-balancing problem described by Michie and Chambers [20]. A complete description of the pole-balancing problem used in this study can be found in [1].

The learning objective for the maze problem is to find a shortest path from the start state, S, to the goal state, G. As indicated in Fig 2, there are four overlapping optimal solutions to the problem. There are 47 legal states within the maze. Even though the state space is small, the problem is difficult in the sense that the learner can cycle through the maze before finally reaching state G. The state information (stimulus) is the current position of the learner in the maze (*e.g.*, [0, 3] is state S); the possible control decisions (responses) are to move North (N), South (S), East (E) or West (W).

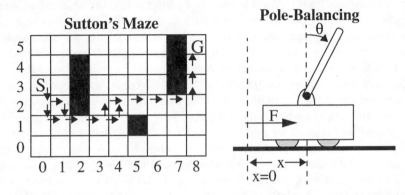

Fig. 2. Two example problems: A simple maze and the pole-balancing problem

The learning objective for the pole-balancing problem is to maintain the upright position of the pole by applying a positive or negative force of magnitude of 10 Newtons parallel with the plane. A failure condition occurs whenever the cart is displaced from the zero position by more than 2.4 meters in either direction, or the angle of the pole with the vertical axis exceeds 12 degrees in either direction. The initial position of the pole is randomly selected between -0.1 and 0.1; the initial angle is randomly selected between -6 to 6 degrees. The state information consists of the position of the cart (x), the cart's velocity, ($\dot{x}$), the angle of the pole (θ), and the angular velocity of the pole ($\dot{\theta}$); the control decision consists of two values: a negative or positive force. The state variables are quantized into *equally sized* intervals (based on an analysis of the unevenly sized quantization intervals reported in the literature). The three variables x, ranging from -2.5 to 2.6, $\dot{x}$ ranging from -1.6 to 1.7, and $\dot{\theta}$ ranging from -151 to 152 are all quantized into 3 intervals. The state variable θ, ranging from -12 to 12, uses a higher resolution: 24 intervals. This quantization results in a total of 648 discrete states from which the GA can form subsets as representational biases.

5 Experimental Design and Results

To ensure that SPARCLE finds accurate biases, the GA needs to repetitively test each bias during the population evaluation cycle.[12] The focus of this paper, however, is to demonstrate that $S \neq A_b$. To do so, it is only necessary to find a representation that, when combined with a learned S-R mapping and learned stimulant probabilities, reliably permits the CLA to find an optimal solution, but when used as a bias for an inexperienced CLA, does not reliably permit the CLA to find an optimal solution. To generate a pool of biases that can be tested, several runs of SPARCLE are made (*e.g.*, 30 runs of 60 generations of pole-balancing).[13] During each run, the five best performing solutions (a solution consists of a stimulant set, a learned S-R mapping, and learned stimulant probabilities) are saved off-line for further evaluation. These solutions represent trials where the CLA converges to an optimal solution during one CLA life-span.

After competing the runs, unique biases of different sizes are extracted from the saved files for testing. Before testing the accuracy of the biases, their associated solutions are tested first for robustness under minor perturbations. Only biases that are part of solutions where the CLA is within $\varepsilon \leq 0.05$ of the optimal solution for at least 98 out of 100 trials are selected for additional testing. Selected biases are tested again for 100 trials, but this time, the CLA's forgetting mechanism is turned off, the CLA's S-R mapping is initialized to indicate random selection, and the stimulants are initialized to be equally probable. At the end of each trial, SPARCLE records the average performance over the final run of the CLA's life-span along with other statistics. A cumulative frequency distribution of the fractional difference of the CLA's performance from the optimal performance is made for each bias to examine the bias' degree of accuracy.

The extraction process produced a total of 111 biases for the maze problem, ranging from 4 to 9 stimulants, and 44 biases for the pole-balancing problem, also ranging from 4 to 9 stimulants in size. Fig 3 shows four examples of the cumulative performance distributions. The plots emphasize that biases having the same strength (*e.g.*, 6 stimulants for the maze problem) can have differing degrees of accuracy. For the pole-balancing problem, the more accurate bias is noisy: the CLA achieves $\varepsilon \leq 0.05$ for 66% of the trials. The second bias produces sub-optimal performance so that the CLA only achieves $\varepsilon \leq 0.60$ with the same reliability. For the maze problem, the better bias is fairly accurate: the CLA achieves $\varepsilon \leq 0.10$ for 97% of the trials. The less accurate bias produces some sub-optimal performance: the CLA achieves $\varepsilon \leq 0.25$ with a 71% reliability. Fig 4 shows scatter plots for each problem that summarize the distributions in terms of their standard deviations and median values. The biases for the maze problem are generally more accurate than those for the pole-balancing problem, probably due to the maze problem having an inherently discrete problem domain.

---

12. The GA's evaluation of a CLA's bias is noisy, but the distribution of performance values is not Gaussian. For this reason, the results of Fitzpatrick and Grefenstette do not apply [11].

13. The parameter settings for the GA's operators are typical: the crossover rate is 0.6; the probability of applying incremental mutation to a stimulant's dimension is 0.001. Other parameters are set as a function of the problem domain and task. For the maze problem, the population size is 30, the run length of the GA is 25 generations, the bias has a maximum of 30 stimulants, the total number of CLA stages is 3500, the final run length is 250 stages, and the maximum number of interactions per stage is 200. For the pole-balancing problem, the population size is 40, the run length of the GA is 60 generations, the bias has a maximum of 120 stimulants, the maximum number of CLA stages is 10,000, the final run length is 1000, and the maximum number of interactions per stage is 10 (*i.e.*, the CLA receives an evaluation after 10 interactions, or fewer, should the CLA fail to balance the pole, similar to Osella's pole-balancing CLA[22]). Given these parameters, the CLA must balance the pole perfectly for 1,000 stages in order for the CLA to have a successful run of 10,000 interactions with the environment.

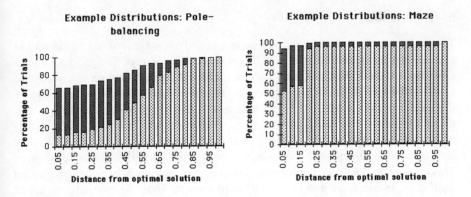

Fig. 3. Examples of bias accuracy distributions for the two problems

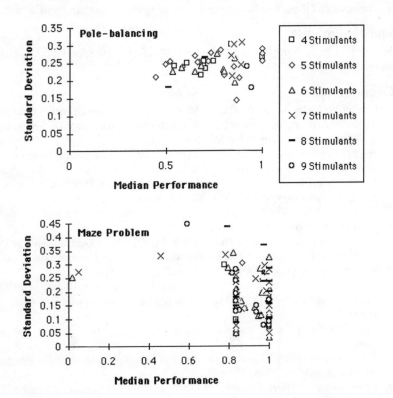

Fig. 4. Scatter plots for median and standard deviation of the bias distributions

6 Conclusions

This paper describes how a GA-based system, called SPARCLE, searches for strong and accurate representational biases of a CLA reinforcement learner. The paper also demonstrates that the representational bias of a successful learner is not necessarily useful to an inexperienced learner. If a learner uses its representation to perform a task and if the learner performs dynamic bias adjustment of that representation while learning, then there may be an interaction between the final representational bias and the knowledge acquired by the learner. As the learner gains experience, the representation may be reduced to complement the knowledge stored in the learner's associative memory. This interaction can result in a solution that is extremely accurate even though the bias itself is not (when applied to an inexperienced learner). Thus, the reduced accuracy of a bias may not be simply due to the stochastic nature of the learner. Nevertheless, from the GA's perspective, the evaluation of a CLA's bias is noisy. To increase the likelihood of finding an accurate bias for a reinforcement learner such as the CLA, the GA needs to perform some amount of repetitive testing of the biases during its search. The authors believe that these results are generalizable to other problem domains and tasks.

Acknowledgments

We would like to thank Diana Gordon and Alan Meyrowitz for their editorial comments on earlier drafts of this paper.

References

1.   Charles W. Anderson and W. Thomas Miller, III (1990). Challenging Control Problems. In *Neural Networks for Control* (eds. W. Thomas Miller, III, Richard S. Sutton, and Paul J. Werbos), pp. 184. Cambridge, MA: MIT Press.

2.   Peter J. Angeline and Jordon B. Pollack (1992). Coevolving High-level Representations. *LAIR Technical Report 92-PA-COEVOLVE*, Lab. for AI Research, Ohio State University.

3.   James Edward Baker (1989). *An Analysis of the Effects of Selection in Genetic Algorithms*. Doctoral Dissertation, Vanderbilt University.

4.   Peter Bock (1993). *The Emergence of Artificial Cognition: an Introduction to Collective Learning*, Singapore: World Scientific.

5.   David J. Chapman and Leslie Pack Kaelbling (1991). Input Generalization in Delayed Reinforcement Learning: An Algorithm and Performance Comparisons. *Proc. of the Twelfth Intern. Conf. on Artificial Intelligence*, pp. 726 - 731.

6.   Helen G. Cobb (Forthcoming). *Toward Understanding Learning Biases in a Collective Reinforcement Learner.* D.Sc. dissertation, The George Washington University, Washington, DC.

7.   Lonnie Chrisman (1989). Evaluating Bias During PAC-Learning. *Sixth International ML Workshop.*

8.   Yuval Davidor (1990). *Genetic Algorithms and Robotics: A Heuristic Strategy for Optimization.* Singapore: World Scientific.

9.   Lawrence Davis (1989). Adaptive Operator Probabilities in Genetic Algorithms. *Proc. of the Third Intern. Conf. on Genetic Algorithms.* pp. 61-69. San Mateo, CA: Morgan Kaufmann.

10.   K. De Jong, W. M. Spears, and D. Gordon (1992). Using Genetic Algorithms for Concept Learning. *Machine Learning.* Vol. 13, pp. 161-188. Boston, MA: Kluwer Academic.

11. J. Michael Fitzpatrick and John J. Grefenstette (1988). Genetic Algorithms in Noisy Environments. *Machine Learning 3*, pp. 101-120. The Netherlands: Kluwer Academic.

12. David E. Goldberg (1991). Don't Worry, Be Messy. *Proc. of the Fourth Intern. Conf. on Genetic Algorithms*, pp. 24 - 30. San Mateo, CA: Morgan Kaufmann.

13. Diana F. Gordon (1990). Active Bias Adjustment for Incremental, Supervised Concept Learning. (Dissertation) *Technical Report UMIACS-TR-90-60*. Univ of Maryland.

14. John J. Grefenstette (1984). GENESIS: a system for using genetic search procedures. *Proc. of a Conf. on Intelligent Systems and Machines*, pp. 161-165. Rochester, MI.

15. John J. Grefenstette (1988). Credit Assignment in Rule Discovery Systems based on Genetic Algorithms. *Machine Learning 3*, (2/3), pp. 225-245. Boston, MA: Kluwer Academic.

16. Frédéric Gruau and Darrell Whitley (1993). Adding Learning to the Cellular Development of Neural Networks: Evolution and the Baldwin Effect. *Evolutionary Computation* 1 (3), pp. 213-233. Cambridge, MA: MIT Press.

17. David Haussler (1988). Quantifying Inductive Bias: AI Learning Algorithms and Valiant's Learning Framework. *Artificial Intelligence*, **36**, pp. 177-221.

18. Long-Li Lin (1992). Self-Improving Reactive Agents Based on Reinforcement Learning, Planning and Teaching. *Machine Learning 8*, pp. 293-321. Boston, MA: Kluwer Academic.

19. S. Mahedevan and J. Connell (1991). Automatic programming of behavior-based robots using reinforcement learning. *Artificial Intelligence.* Vol 55, pp. 311-365. Elsevier.

20. D. Michie and R. A. Chambers (1968). BOXES - an experiment in adaptive control. *Machine Intelligence II*, pp. 137-152. London: Oliver & Boyd.

21. Tom M. Mitchell (1980). The Need for Biases in Learning Generalizations. *Technical Report CBM-TR-117*. Dept. of Computer Science, Rutgers University, New Brunswick, NJ.

22. Stephen A. Osella (1989). Collective Learning Systems: a Model for Automatic Control. *Proceedings IEEE International Symposium on Intelligent Control,* pp. 393-398.

23. S. F. Smith (1983). *A learning system based on genetic adaptive algorithms*, Ph.D. Thesis, Dept. Computer Science, Univ. of Pittsburgh.

24. R. S. Sutton (1990). First Results with Dyna. In *Neural Networks for Control* (eds. W. Thomas Miller, III, Richard S. Sutton, and Paul J. Werbos), pp. 184. Cambridge, MA: MIT Press.

25. David M. Tate and Alice E. Smith (1993). Expected Allele Coverage and the Role of Mutation in Genetic Algorithms. *Proc. of the Fifth Intern. Conf. on Genetic Algorithms*, pp. 31-37. San Mateo, CA: Morgan Kaufmann.

26. Paul E. Utgoff (1986). Shift of Bias for Inductive Concept Learning. *Machine Learning: An Artificial Intelligence Approach, Vol. II*, Chapter 5, pp. 107-148. Michalski *et al* (ed.). Los Altos, CA: Morgan Kaufmann.

27. C. J. C. H. Watkins (1989). *Learning with Delayed Rewards*, Doctoral Dissertation, Cambridge Univ. Psychology Department, England.

28. Steven D. Whitehead and Dana H. Ballard (1991). Learning to Perceive and Act by Trial and Error. *Machine Learning 7*, pp. 45-83. Boston, MA: Kluwer Academic.

29. D. Whitley, T. Starkweather, and C. Bogart (1990). Genetic algorithms and neural networks: optimizing connection and connectivity. *Parallel Computing*, Vol. 14, pp. 347-361.

30. B. Zang and Heinz Mühlenbein (1993). Genetic Programming of Minimal Neural Nets Using Occam's Razor. *Proc. of the Fifth Intern. Conf. on Genetic Algorithms*, pp. 342-349. San Mateo, CA: Morgan Kaufmann.

An Evolutionary Algorithm for the Routing of Multi-Chip Modules

Jens Lienig[1] and Holger Brandt[2]

[1] Concordia University, Dept. of Electrical and Computer Eng., Montreal, Quebec, Canada
Email: jensl@ece.concordia.ca

[2] Dresden University of Technology, Institute of Electronics Technology, Dresden, Germany

Abstract. The routing of a multi-chip module is the process of designing the layout of the electrical interconnections between the components of this multi-chip module. We present an evolutionary algorithm as a novel approach for this optimization problem. The representation scheme of the routing structures and the operators associated with the proposed algorithm are described. The performance of the algorithm is tested on different multi-chip modules and it is shown that the quality of our routing results outperforms heuristically achieved routing structures of these multi-chip modules.

1 Introduction

Multi-chip modules are special hybrid circuits which combine several bare integrated chips to one compact module. The electrical interconnections of these chips (called nets) are realized on several layers which are situated between the chip layer and a ceramic substratum (see Figure 1).

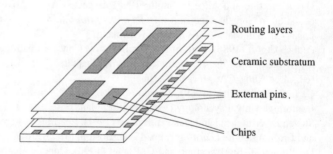

Routing layers

Ceramic substratum

External pins.

Chips

Fig. 1. Multi-chip module.

The routing of multi-chip modules is the process of designing the layout of these interconnections by connecting pins of the same net subject to a set of routing constraints. The routing quality is crucial to the electrical performance of the multi-chip module. The routing problem of multi-chip modules is considered as NP-complete and therefore, there is no known deterministic algorithm that produces an optimal routing solution in polynomial time.

Evolutionary algorithms are a new class of heuristic search methods based on the biological evolution model. During the last years, evolutionary algorithms have been applied more and more successfully to find good heuristic solutions to NP-complete optimization problems in various fields [1], [5].

So far, evolutionary algorithms for routing have been applied only to the channel and switch-box routing problem of integrated circuits [2], [3], [9], [10], [11], [12]. To the best of our knowledge, our paper is the first one that applies an evolutionary algorithm to multi-chip module routing. The contributions of this paper are:

- To provide an evolutionary algorithm that is capable of handling the routing problem of multi-chip modules.
- To compare the performance of our evolutionary algorithm with a conventional heuristic approach.
- To show the effect of some specific characteristics of our algorithm on the achieved routing results.

2 Problem Definition

In this paper we focus on the type of multi-chip module shown in Figure 1. The bare chips are placed on the top layer called the chip layer. The interconnections are formed on a certain number of layers including the chip layer. The external pins are situated on the edges of the ceramic substratum.

The multi-chip module routing problem is as follows. Given a set of rectangular routing regions with z_{max} routing layers and a set of nets $\mathcal{N}$. The pins[3] that belong to the same net $n \in \mathcal{N}$ have to be connected subject to certain constraints and quality characteristics. The connection has to be made on the routing area of any of the layers z with $1 \leq z \leq z_{max}$.

The interconnections are associated with the following constraints:

- Different nets cannot cross each other on the same layer and must respect a minimum distance rule.
- A net may change from one layer to another layer using a contact window called *via*.

Three quality characteristics are used in this work to asses the quality of the routing result:

- number of routing layers,
- routing length and
- number of vias.

---

[3] The term "pin" describes both a pin of a chip as well as an external pin.

3 Description of the Algorithm

3.1 Survey

Evolutionary algorithms are optimization strategies that imitate the biological evolution process. An overview of the evolutionary algorithm presented in this paper is shown in Figure 2.

```
generation = 0
create initial population Π = (i₁, i₂, ..., iₙ)
fitness calculation (Π)
while (generation ≤ max_generation)
{
  generation = generation + 1
  while (no_offspring ≤ max_no_offspring)
  {
    no_offspring = no_offspring + 1
    mate α = selection(Π)
    mate β = selection(Π)
    descendant = crossover(α, β)
    if mutation then descendant = mutation(descendant)
  }
  fitness calculation (descendants)
  include descendants in Π
  reduction(Π)
  fitness calculation (Π)
}
optimize best individual
```

Fig. 2. Outline of the algorithm.

3.2 The Representation Scheme

The multi-chip module is represented in a three-dimensional lattice (see Figure 3). The dimension in z-direction is equal to the number of routing layers. Two horizontal adjacent lattice points represent the minimal distance between two adjacent different routing connections on the multi-chip module.

Each individual is encoded in one lattice. Lattice points are occupied with coding numbers of the routing connections and pins. The representation must distinguish between routing connections that can be shifted or erased during the evolutionary process and fixed pins. Thus, we choose the following encoding:

Let (x, y, z) be a position in the lattice, $L(x, y, z)$ be the value of the lattice position and (x', y', z') be the corresponding coordinate on the multi-chip module.

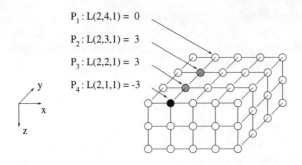

$P_1 : L(2,4,1) = 0$

$P_2 : L(2,3,1) = 3$

$P_3 : L(2,2,1) = 3$

$P_4 : L(2,1,1) = -3$

Fig. 3. Representation scheme of the routing structure.

- If $L(x, y, z) = 0$, the multi-chip module is not occupied at (x', y', z') (e.g., P_1 in Figure 3).
- If $L(x, y, z) > 0$, the multi-chip module is occupied with a routing connection at (x', y', z') (e.g., P_2, P_3 in Figure 3). This routing connection can be shifted or erased. $L(x, y, z)$ represents the net number of this routing connection.
- If $L(x, y, z) < 0$, the multi-chip module is occupied with a pin at (x', y', z') (e.g., P_4 in Figure 3). This pin cannot be shifted or erased. $|L(x, y, z)|$ represents the net number of this pin.

This representation enables a simple monitoring of the routing constraints directly in the representation scheme.

3.3 Creation of an Initial Population

The initial population is constructed from randomly created routing structures, i.e. individuals.

First, each of these individuals is assigned a random initial number of layers z_{ind}.

Let $\mathcal{S} = \{s_1, ...s_i, ...s_k\}$ be the set of all pins of the multi-chip module which are not connected yet and let $\mathcal{T} = \{t_1, ...t_j, ...t_l\}$ be the set of all pins having at least one connection to another pin. Initially $\mathcal{T} = \emptyset$. A pin $s_i \in \mathcal{S}$ is chosen randomly among all elements in $\mathcal{S}$. If $\mathcal{T}$ contains pins $\{t_u, ...t_j, ...t_v\}$ (with $1 \leq u < v \leq l$) of the same net n, a pin t_j is randomly selected among them. Otherwise a second pin of the net n is randomly chosen from $\mathcal{S}$ and transferred into $\mathcal{T}$. Both pins (s_i, t_j) are connected with a so-called "random routing". The random routing is performed by a fast heuristic line-search algorithm [6] with random locations of the extension lines. If the random routing of (s_i, t_j) is not feasible, an additional layer z_i with $1 < z_i < z_{max}$ is introduced at a random position and the routing of (s_i, t_j) is repeated. After connecting s_i and t_j, s_i is transferred into $\mathcal{T}$. The process continues with the next random selection of $s_i \in \mathcal{S}$ until $\mathcal{S} = \emptyset$.

The creation of the initial population is finished when the number of completely routed multi-chip modules is equal to the population size $|\Pi|$. As a consequence of our strategy, these initial individuals are quite different from each other and scattered all over the search space.

3.4 Evaluation of Fitness

The fitness of each individual is evaluated to judge the quality of the individual according to the quality characteristics mentioned earlier. This evaluation is needed for both the selection of mates for crossover and the decision on which individuals survive into the next generation.

First, we introduce a cost function C_i, which analyzes the routing length and the number of vias and layers of each individual i:

$$C_i = (C_{length} * \sum_{n=1}^{N_{net}} L_n + C_{via} * N_{via}) * (C_{layer} * N_{layer}) \tag{1}$$

where N_{layer} = the number of layers,
N_{net} = the number of nets,
N_{via} = the number of vias,
L_n = the routing length of net n,
C_{layer} = the cost factor of the number of layers,
C_{length} = the cost factor of the routing length, and
C_{via} = the cost factor of the number of vias.

An average cost value of the initial population $C_{initial}$ is calculated once to enable us to normalize C_i:

$$C_{initial} = \frac{\sum_{i=1}^{N_{indiv}} C_i}{N_{indiv}} \tag{2}$$

where N_{indiv} is the number of individuals of the initial population.

The fitness F_i of an individual i can now be calculated according to

$$F_i = \frac{C_{initial}}{C_i} \tag{3}$$

After the evaluation of F_i for all individuals of the population Π these values are scaled linearly as described in [4], in order to control the variance of the fitness in the population.

3.5 Selection Operator for Crossover

The mate α is randomly selected with a probability that is proportional to its fitness value F_α. In other words, any mate $\alpha \in \Pi$ is selected with a probability

$$\frac{F_\alpha}{\sum_{i \in \Pi} F_i}$$

The mate β is randomly chosen among all individuals, independent of its fitness value.

An individual may be selected any number of times in the same generation for crossover.

3.6 Crossover Operator

During the crossover, the genetic materials of the mates α and β are combined to create a descendant.

First, all nets in α are evaluated according to

$$Q_n = \frac{1}{C_{segment} * \frac{N_{segment}}{N_{pin}} + C_{length} * \frac{L_n}{L_{opt}}} \tag{4}$$

where N_{pin} = the number of pins of net n,
  $N_{segment}$ = the number of segments of net n,
  L_n = the routing length of net n,
  L_{opt} = the optimal routing length of net n in Manhattan metric,
  C_{length} = the cost factor of the routing length, and
  $C_{segment}$ = the cost factor of the number of segments.

The initial number of layers of the descendant is equal to the number of layers of α.

The descendant acquires 60 % of its nets from the mate α. These nets are chosen randomly in α with a probability that is proportional to their quality Q_n. In other words, any net $n \in \mathcal{N}$ of the mate α is selected with a probability

$$\frac{Q_n}{\sum_{i \in \mathcal{N}} Q_i}$$

Layers of the descendant that are not occupied with any net segments are deleted.

The remaining nets are transferred from the mate β to the descendant in a random order. If the transferred net from β does not satisfy the constraints, e.g., it causes a net crossing or requires more layers than given in the descendant, the segment(s) of the transferred net that cause(s) the violation is (are) excluded from the transferring process. Both end points of this (these) segment(s) are connected using our random routing strategy (see Section 3.3). If the connection is not possible, (an) additional layer(s) is (are) inserted until a valid connection can be created.

3.7 Mutation Operator

The descendants are subject to a mutation operator with a low probability. The mutation operator changes randomly parts of the routing structure of these descendants.

A rectangle with random sizes is defined at a random layer of the descendant. All routing structures inside this rectangle are deleted. The remaining net points on the edges of this rectangle are connected again in a random order with our random routing strategy.

3.8 Reduction Operator

To ensure a constant population size $|\Pi|$, we apply a deterministic reduction operator. This operator enables high quality individuals to survive as many generations as they are superior. The operator chooses the $|\Pi|$ fittest individuals of the combined set of Π and the descendants to survive as Π into the next generation.

3.9 Optimization of the Best Individual

A final heuristic local optimization strategy is applied to improve the best individual that results at the end of the evolution process. Our optimization strategy simply sequentially reroutes each net with a shortest path algorithm [7]. If the net achieves a better quality according to equation (4), the rerouting is accepted. Otherwise, the previous net layout is left intact.

4 Experimental Results

The algorithm has been implemented in the C programming language. The size of the source code is approximately 6000 lines.

Due to the numerous technological constraints of multi-chip modules, there do not exist universal routing benchmarks in literature. In the following, we compare our results with those heuristically achieved for multi-chip modules in [8].

4.1 Measurement Conditions

The algorithm was executed 10 times (with different initializations of the random number generator) for each of the multi-chip modules. We always terminated the program after 200 generations.

The values of the other parameters are as follows:

Population size $|\Pi|$ = 50
$no\_offspring$ = 50
Mutation probability [4] = 0.00002

4.2 Routing Results

Table 1 lists the best and the average results achieved with our algorithm in 10 program executions for each of the multi-chip modules TEST, S6009, MC29 and TU1. They are compared with results obtained with a heuristic multi-chip module router presented in [8]. It can be seen that the quality of our results outperforms the heuristically achieved routing structures in all cases.

	TEST	S6009	MC29	TU1
Number of chips	6	21	27	17
Number of pins	54	481	374	368
Number of external pins	9	133	112	112
Number of nets	15	169	126	120
Size of the module [mm²]	50x35	50x50	50x50	35x35
Best results with heuristic algorithm [8]				
Routing length [mm]	1352	4646	4017	4106
Number of vias	129	1297	945	934
Number of layers	2	4	4	4
Best results with evolutionary algorithm				
Cost factors $C_{length} : C_{via} : C_{layer}$	1:1:1	1:3:1	1:1:1	1:1:1
Routing length [mm]	1347	4507	3885	3812
Number of vias	125	1203	942	927
Number of layers	2	4	4	4
Average results with evolutionary algorithm				
Cost factors $C_{length} : C_{via} : C_{layer}$	1:1:1	1:3:1	1:1:1	1:1:1
Routing length [mm]	1347	4581	3998	3901
Number of vias	125	1253	943	933
Number of layers	2	4	4	4

Table 1: Experimental results.

---

[4] Our mutation probability is the probability with which any lattice position (x, y, z) in the representation scheme is subject to the mutation operator.

Our average results of the 10 program executions differ from the best results due to our decision to stop the execution always after 200 generations. It must be noted that the best results can be always achieved if the number of generations is not limited.

According to the priority of the different quality characteristics, the cost factors C_{length}, C_{via} and C_{layer} have to be changed. Table 1 shows the cost factors with which we obtain the best proper balance of our quality characteristics - routing length, number of vias, and number of layers.

4.3 Effect of the Quality of the Initial Population

The results in Table 1 were obtained with randomly created *non-optimized* individuals in the initial population. For practical applications of our algorithm, it is interesting to investigate on how the existence of already-heuristically-optimized routing structures in the initial population effects characteristics such as the convergence behavior and quality of the routing result.

In Table 2, we show the effect of the initial population on the number of generations needed to achieve our best results of Table 1. Each initial population is a combination of randomly routed individuals and individuals produced by the heuristic multi-chip module router proposed in [8]. As can be seen from the table, the total size of the initial population is always 50. The "Min.", "Avg." and "Max." entries are, respectively, the minimun, average and maximum number of generations in 100 program executions needed to achieve the best result.

| Initial population | | Generations needed to achieve the best result of Table 1 | | | | | |
| randomly created | heuristically optimized | TEST | | | MC29 | | |
		Min.	Avg.	Max.	Min.	Avg.	Max.
50	0	28	38	63	112	298	703
48	2	12	28	53	101	241	641
46	4	12	27	53	111	312	904
40	10	10	48	112	208	834	4702

Table 2: Effect of the number of generations needed to achieve the best result of Table 1 with different initial populations.

From our experiment we conclude that the existence of a very small percentage of optimized individuals in the initial population can speed up the convergence behavior, especially for large problem sizes. This indicates that a practical implementation of an evolutionary routing algorithm for multi-chip modules could include heuristic strategies to improve its efficiency.

5 Conclusions

In developing this algorithm, the following conclusions have been reached:

- A problem-specific three-dimensional representation scheme allows an efficient monitoring of the numerous technological constraints related to multi-chip modules.
- A sufficient diversity within the population (including the initial population) is crucial to the robustness of an evolutionary algorithm for a design problem.
- Since our crossover operator cannot guarantee that high quality mates produce high quality descendants, we allow high quality individuals, irrespective of whether they are mates or descendants, to survive as long as they are superior.
- From our results we believe that evolutionary algorithms are promising tools for solving the routing problem of multi-chip modules and other optimization tasks in the physical design of electrical circuits.

References

1. Bäck, T., Schwefel, H.-P.: An Overview of Evolutionary Algorithms for Parameter Optimization. Evolutionary Computation 1 No. 1 (1993) 1-23
2. Chen, Y.-A., Lin, Y.-L., Hsu, Y.-C.: A New Global Router for ASIC Design Based on Simulated Evolution. Proc. International Symposium VLSI Technology, Systems, and Applications, Taipei, Taiwan, (1989)
3. Geraci, M., Orlando, P., Sorbello, F., Vasallo, G.: A Genetic Algorithm for the Routing of VLSI Circuits. Euro Asic '91 (1991) 218-223
4. Goldberg, D. E.: Genetic Algorithms in Search, Optimization, and Machine Learning. Reading, MA: Addison-Wesley Publishing Company (1989)
5. Goldberg, D. E.: Genetic and Evolutionary Algorithms Come of Age. Communications of the Association for Computing Machinery (CACM) 37 No. 3 (1994) 113-119
6. Hightower, D. W.: A Solution to Line-Routing Problems on the Continuous Plane. Proc. of IEEE Design Automation Workshop (1969) 1-24
7. Lee, C. Y.: An Algorithm for Path Connections and its Applications. IRE-Trans. on Electronic Computers (1961) 346-365
8. Lienig, J., Thulasiraman, K., Swamy, M. N. S.: Routing Algorithms for Multi-Chip Modules. Proc. of the European Design Automation Conference (1992) 133-136
9. Lienig, J., Thulasiraman, K.: A Genetic Algorithm for Channel Routing in VLSI Circuits. Evolutionary Computation 1 No. 4 (1994) 293-311
10. Lin, Y.-L., Hsu, Y.-C., Tsai, F.-S.: SILK: A Simulated Evolution Router. IEEE Trans. on Computer-Aided Design 8 No. 10 (1989) 1108-1114
11. Prahlada Rao, B. B., Hansdah, R. C.: Extended Distributed Genetic Algorithm for Channel Routing. Proc. of the Fifth IEEE Symposium on Parallel and Distributed Processing (1993) 726-733
12. Rahmani, A. T., Ono, N.: A Genetic Algorithm for Channel Routing Problem. Proc. of the Fifth International Conference on Genetic Algorithms (1993) 494-498

System Design under Uncertainty: Evolutionary Optimization of the Gravity Probe-B Spacecraft

Samuel P. Pullen
Bradford W. Parkinson

Department of Aeronautics and Astronautics, Stanford University
Stanford, CA. 94305 U.S.A.

Abstract. This paper discusses the application of evolutionary random-search algorithms (*Simulated Annealing* and *Genetic Algorithms*) to the problem of spacecraft design under performance uncertainty. Traditionally, spacecraft performance uncertainty has been measured by *reliability*. Published algorithms for reliability optimization are seldom used in practice because they oversimplify reality. The algorithm developed here uses random-search optimization to allow us to model the problem more realistically. Monte Carlo simulations are used to evaluate the objective function for each trial design solution. These methods have been applied to the *Gravity Probe-B* (GP-B) spacecraft being developed at Stanford University for launch in 1999. Results of the algorithm developed here for GP-B are shown, and their implications for design optimization by evolutionary algorithms are discussed.

1 Introduction

Design for reliability has always been a critical concern for spacecraft developers because spacecraft, once launched, cannot be repaired after a serious failure without incurring extreme expense. As a result, all spacecraft are analyzed for *reliability*, or the probability of meeting the mission success criteria over time. Because spacecraft reliability calculations must be based on inaccurate failure rate data and questionable assumptions, these numbers are generally used only to show that they meet arbitrary specifications set by the customer.

This paper uses the flexibility of evolutionary optimization methods to overcome these obstacles. Traditional reliability optimization can make only simplified trade-offs between reliability and cost or weight, but global-search methods can handle any optimization function. Furthermore, since simulation can generate arbitrary function evaluations and since gradients are not required, we can adopt a more realistic model of component and subsystem reliability.

Variants of two well-known evolutionary methods are developed here for a general reliability design problem. The *simulated annealing* approach uses one trial solution which "evolves" in the search process, while the *genetic algorithm* maintains a population of solutions that evolve according to the concept of natural selection. Results for the former method for two different objective functions are discussed in detail, while a framework for genetic algorithm evolution is presented along with some preliminary conclusions. The results presented here already show significant improvements over traditional reliability optimization methods and suggest new paradigms for spacecraft reliability analysis.

2   Traditional Reliability Analysis

As mentioned above, reliability analysis is an established field, and it can form the basis for design optimization under uncertainty. Since the U.S. Government is a major customer, the handbooks it has published or influenced contain the generally accepted methods of reliability analysis [1,2,3]. These methods are based on the *exponential* failure distribution in which reliability is given by

$$R(t) = \exp[-\lambda t] \tag{1}$$

where λ is a constant failure rate found in tables [1,2]. This distribution is *memoryless*; the probability of failure over a given interval of time is independent of the length of time that has already passed. This assumption is often questionable, but the exponential distribution continues to be used because of its simplicity.

Most spacecraft contracts use (1) and the data in [1] to compute reliability predictions for the components of their design. Redundancy is usually built in to avoid *single-point failure modes*, which are events that by themselves cause mission failure. Using (1) to compute component reliability, series and parallel network reliability can be computed using the standard equations in [3] which assume that all failure modes are *independent*. The result is a system reliability prediction over the mission time line that must meet user specifications.

Since spacecraft are to a large degree unrepairable after launch, reliability is a key concern, but most systems engineers distrust handbook data and the assumptions present in the traditional model despite being obligated to do the computations. As a result, spacecraft tend to be overdesigned to "ensure" adequate reliability. This guarantees that the reliability specifications are met, but it does not help engineers make informed risk-based trade-off decisions.

3   New Spacecraft Reliability Model

The first step toward improving the traditional reliability model is to use a *Weibull* failure distribution that allows failure rates to vary with time. It is a generalization of the exponential distribution, and its success probability is given by

$$R(t) = \exp[-t^\beta/\alpha] \tag{2}$$

Here, α is the *scale* factor that expresses mean time-to-failure, and β is the *shape* factor that varies the effective failure rate over time ($\beta = 1$ gives the exponential distribution). In [4], actual spacecraft failure data is fitted to this failure model, and estimates for α and β for various spacecraft mission types are given. For spacecraft, β is around 0.12 (< 1), which indicates that spacecraft are more likely to fail early in a mission as design or manufacturing flaws become apparent. Failure rates decrease over time, as units that pass through this "burn in" period are more likely to last.

The uncertainty inherent in the handbook failure rates is another concern. Previously, we have created a model that assigns variances to failure rates for various components [5]. Using the data from [4], an algorithm for simulation-based reliability predictions has been developed. For each trial, an exponential failure rate is sampled from a Normal distribution with the mean published failure rate and the assigned variance. It is transformed to the Weibull distribution, and the component reliability is computed using (2) for that trial only. A significant number of samples are thus needed to obtain the resulting uncertainty distributions.

4   Optimization by Simulated Annealing (SA)

Simulated annealing (SA) is one of the simpler evolutionary-type algorithms used for global optimization. SA generates a random variant of the current trial solution and evaluates its objective function value. If the new value is superior, the new solution is accepted in place of the old one. If not, the new solution will still be accepted with a probability given by

$$P_{accept} = \exp\left[-\Delta V/T\right] \tag{3}$$

where ΔV is the difference in objective values and T is an "annealing temperature" that slowly decreases. Higher temperature increases the acceptance probability, so the algorithm is less likely to accept "backward" steps as time goes on [6,7,8].

The SA algorithm used in this study has a unique method of generating a new solution. Trial solutions are specified by a collection of "genes" that give the number of units of each component type to be included. In the spacecraft case, the solution (a string of integers) is broken down into functional subsystems (as shown in Table 3). Each time a new solution is generated, at least one of the changeable subsystems (all but the first two) is randomly selected for modification. Those not selected retain the same values as in the last solution.

For each component in a subsystem to be changed, a pair of staircase functions is computed based on the current number of units (nc) and the minimum and maximum number allowed for that component (m and M respectively). The minimum number is the number needed for mission success, and the maximum for a given case is the *lesser* of two quantities: $2\,nc$ or the absolute maximum number allowed. The probability function for the number of units in the new solution is

$$
\begin{aligned}
P[\text{new} = nx \mid \text{old} = nc] &= 2.5\big/\{2(M-m)\} && \text{for } nx = nc \\[2mm]
&= \frac{1 - 2.5\big/\{2(M-m)\}}{\displaystyle\sum_{i=1}^{M-nc+1} i}\, nx && \text{for } M \geq nx > nc \\[2mm]
&= \frac{1 - 2.5\big/\{2(M-m)\}}{\displaystyle\sum_{i=1}^{nc-m} i}\, nx && \text{for } nc > nx \geq m
\end{aligned}
\tag{4}
$$

Equation (4) creates a "stairstep" distribution that peaks when $nx = nc$. Retaining the current number of units is thus quite probable. The more different a new number is, the less likely it is to be selected. Note that there is an equal probability of the new number being either higher or lower than nc. This probability function clearly makes large changes unlikely; so new solutions take on an "evolutionary" character.

As noted above, the use of an arbitrary probability model requires *Monte Carlo simulations* to evaluate the objective function for each new design solution. Each simulation step consists of a time simulation of a mission given the system reliability model. Since the unit reliabilities are unknown random variables with the distributions discussed in Section 3.0, these must be re-sampled from a random number generator and the mission reliability recomputed.

Using the canonical SA algorithm in [7], Table 1 gives the parameters used for this research. Note that adaptation as discussed in [6] for continuous objective functions is not used. The convergence tolerance in Table 1 represents a comparison between "evolving" evaluations of a solution that has not been replaced in at least one constant-temperature period (300 new solutions). If this occurs, a new simulation evaluation of the current solution is conducted, and its new evaluation is the weighted average of new and old evaluations. For example, if the solution has not changed in the last 3 temperature iterations (900 new solutions), the new evaluation will be:

$$new\ evaluation = \{\ 3\ (old\ evaluation)\ +\ new\ simulation\ result\ \}\ /\ 4 \qquad (5)$$

When the new evaluation differs from the old by less than the convergence tolerance, the algorithm prints the best solution found thus far and exits. The algorithm also exits when the current temperature falls to a point (10 times the tolerance) at which acceptance of any lower-evaluation solution becomes exceedingly unlikely.

SA Parameter	Value	Notes	GA parameter	Value	Notes
Initial temp.	2×10^6	$V_{max} = 15 \times 10^6$	Population size	25	duplic. poss.
Num. temp.	300	# iter. for given T	Crossover rate	0.6	after reprod.
Temp. mult.	0.90	dec. after 300 iter.	Mutation rate	0.01	use eq. (4)
No. simulations	500	per. function eval.	No. simulations	500	per func. eval.
Converge tol.	0.003		Converge tol.	0.01	

Table 1: Simulated Annealing Parameters   **Table 2:** Genetic Algorithm Parameters

5   Optimization by Genetic Algorithms (GA)

In the canonical genetic algorithm (GA) format [9], chromosomes, or members of a population of trial solutions, are expressed as binary numbers (0-1), and the standard genetic evolution operators are designed for this type of population. For the system design application, however, the format used for the SA algorithm in the previous section is much more natural. Thus, variants of the GA operators for this genetic format must be developed. The current versions of these operators are discussed here. Testing of these operators is progressing, and results along with updated operators will be given in a future paper.

Previous research on using Monte Carlo simulation to evaluate the objective function (or *fitness*) of population members has provided insight into the GA design parameters used here [10]. These are given in Table 2. The revised operators are:

Reproduction: Roulette wheel selection is used to choose solutions for the next generation (before crossover). Since the evaluations tend to be similar, the fitnesses are linearly normalized from best to worst by multiplying the difference between the best fitness and a given fitness by 10. The best solution is always reproduced into the next generation (*elitism*), and the weighted-average equation (5) is used when applicable to update (rather than replace) the fitness of the best solution [9].

Crossover: Subject to the crossover rate in Table 2, after reproduction, two solutions are "mated" together to produce *one* offspring. The two parents simply average their unit numbers for each component type within a randomly selected (using the procedure for selecting subsystems in SA) crossover window to give the number of units in the offspring (randomly rounded up or down if $n.5$). The crossover rate determines the ratio of offspring to reproduced strings in the next generation, as N_{cr} (= 0.6 N) solutions are crossed over in N_{cr} combinations to produce N_{cr} offspring.

Mutation: Each gene (number of units for a given component) is subject to random mutation with a probability given in Table 2. If a gene is mutated, the current number of units is replaced according to the SA probability equation (4). This function has a high probability of retaining the same number of units; so the mutation rate is inflated to compensate.

Population Convergence: The convergence test is conducted after fitness evaluation but before the next generation is reproduced. If the average fitness of the population differs from that of the best solution in the population by less than the tolerance given in Table 2, the algorithm stops and outputs the final solution population.

Given these operators, the similarity of SA and GA for this application is clear. The two key differences are "evolving" one solution as opposed to many solutions, and using the SA random-perturbation search with acceptance function (3) as opposed to using the genetic-based operators, which search the objective function by *hyperplanes*.

6   The *Gravity Probe-B* Spacecraft and Objective Functions

While the algorithms detailed above are generally applicable to design optimization problems, the results published here focus on the *Gravity Probe-B* (GP-B) spacecraft being developed by Stanford University under a NASA contract. By orbiting a spacecraft in polar low-earth orbit and using drag-free control to remove disturbances caused by particle impacts, gravity gradients, and the like, it is possible to monitor two relativistic effects on bodies in orbit around a massive object [11]. Since these effects are tiny compared to Newtonian disturbances, extremely precise gyros and readout sensors, a science telescope for precise inertial reference, and an extremely accurate drag-free attitude controller are required [12,13].

The GP-B satellite is divided into two sections. The *experimental payload* is built around the *probe*, which contains the gyros, sensors, proof mass, telescope, gas lines, and electronics, and the *dewar*, which surrounds the probe with superfluid helium to keep its temperature in the cryogenic range needed by the sensors. This equipment has never flown before; so its reliability is uncertain. The *spacecraft bus*, which supports payload operations in space, is being developed separately by Lockheed Missiles and Space Company (LMSC). Figure 1 shows a drawing of the GP-B spacecraft.

Our work uses the separation between payload and bus to focus on spacecraft bus optimization given the uncertain reliability of the launch system and the payload

spacecraft bus   *dewar*   *telescope*

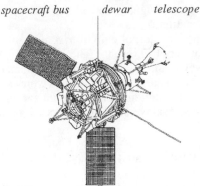

Figure 1: GP-B Spacecraft

(which LMSC cannot control). It is thought that the bus should be made very simply and reliably to not add unnecessary failure modes to an already high-risk situation. This logic will be tested by the optimization carried out here.

The optimal design is driven by the form of the objective function used to model the *utility*, or relative values of outcomes, of the decision maker. The objective function for LMSC is assumed to be the fee, or profit as a percentage of the spacecraft bus cost, it is to receive depending on the outcome of the mission. To represent constraints, *penalty functions* are applied which subtract costs that for exceeding spacecraft weight, volume, and power constraints. This can be expressed as follows:

$$LMSC\ value\ =\ award\ fee + cost\ fee + on\text{-}orbit\ fee - penalty\ costs \qquad (6)$$

The Stanford objective function is instead focused only on achieving a successful science mission, so it is dominated by on-orbit performance:

$$Stanford\ value = on\text{-}orbit\ value + cost\ savings - penalty\ costs \qquad (7)$$

For LMSC, the on-orbit fee percentage of the baseline bus cost of \$ 100 million is given by the following equation, assuming a spacecraft bus failure ends the mission. If there is no failure, LMSC gets the maximum of 6%. If a launch or payload failure ends the mission, the LMSC fee percentage is zero unless at least six months of success are obtained, in which case this equation for the maximum fee (MPF) is used:

$$MPF = \left[\frac{(tm-6)^5}{216|tm-6|} + 6 \right] PFF - 6 \qquad (8)$$

where tm is the number of months of successful science data-taking, and PFF is an independent, subjective performance evaluation made by NASA. This equation is also used for the Stanford on-orbit fee except that the result is normalized to one by dividing by 6% (the best possible result), since it is the only driving factor.

For LMSC, NASA regulations set the minimum overall fee to 0% and the maximum to 15% (even though (6) can give a wider range of values). Note that changing the redundancy of the spacecraft bus design primarily changes the on-orbit value, unit costs, and penalty only. Since much of the LMSC award fee is independent (for our purposes) of the bus design, it seems that greater improvement can be expected for the Stanford function.

Also note that these functions do not employ *risk aversion* to express nonlinear preferences for very good or very bad results. The functions (6) and (7) are based on *expected values* only. However, Stanford places a much greater penalty on a mission that produces no useful science data. LMSC must also worry about the consequences of a spacecraft failure to its reputation. Future optimization runs will experiment with how exponentially scaled risk-averse values affect the optimal solutions.

7   Design Optimization Results

Optimal design runs using both the LMSC and Stanford objective functions and the SA algorithm have been conducted. Attempts have also been made to determine which input parameter changes show the most sensitivity in the optimal results.

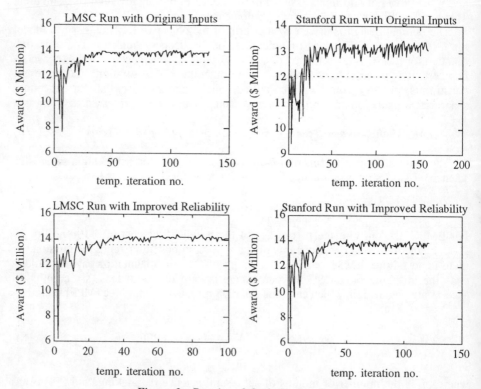

Figure 2: Results of Optimization Runs

Figure 2 shows the evolution of the LMSC and Stanford objective values for two typical runs. The dashed line represents the initial evaluation of the LMSC baseline design. Each evaluation point represents the value of the current SA solution at the end of each constant-temperature iteration. The last points on these plots represent the latest evaluations of the best solutions found. The upper plots are for runs with the "best guess" reliability models for launch and payload operations, both of which (mean reliability of 0.93) are considerably worse than for the baseline spacecraft bus design (0.975). The lower plots are for runs in which the launch and payload models were improved and uncertainty was reduced. In these latter cases, we expect the resulting value uncertainty to decrease, although there is less room to improve over the baseline result. Convergence appears rapid, but the time scale is misleading, since the termination tolerance is deliberately made small to run more reliability simulations and study the steady-state variance of the optimal design values.

Table 3 contains the minimum numbers of working components, the LMSC baseline design, and the best solutions for the "original reliability" case (L = LMSC, S = Stanford). The algorithm was initialized with the baseline solution, so it is to be expected that the objective value would drop as the SA algorithm explores a range of options. Table 4 has mean result values that show 5.1% improvement over the basic baseline design for the LMSC case and 9.2 % improvement for the Stanford case. The greater improvement for the Stanford cases reflects the greater optimization focus on on-orbit performance in that case. Running on a Sparc-10 workstation, "official" convergence was obtained in about 10-18 hours, but as noted above, the tolerance could have been increased (stopping the runs earlier) with little change in the results.

Component	Min.	L base	L opt.	S opt.	Component	Min.	L base	L opt.	S opt.
Structure	1	1 (nc)	1	1	telem. proc.	1	2	3	4
Thermal	1	1 (nc)	1	1	remote proc.	1	2	4	2
SA string	92	96(nc)	96	96	flight comp.	1	2	2	3
power reg.	1	2	1	3	solid-st. rec.	1	2	1	1
NiCd batt.	1	2	1	1	P/Y gyro as.	1	2	1	1
pwr. cont.	1	1 (ir)	2	2	star tracker	1	2	3	2
omni ant.	1	4	1	3	R/Y gyro as.	1	2	1	1
circ. switch	1	2	2	1	thrusters	16	18	24	22
RF switch	1	2	1	4	ATC elect.	1	2	2	2
trans. sw.	1	2	1	1	mass trim	1	2	2	1
trnspond.	1	2	4	3	SA release	4	4 (ir)	8	7
cmd. proc.	1	2	3	4	SA separ.	1	1 (ir)	2	1

(nc) cannot be changed   (ir) internally redundant

Table 3: GP-B Spacecraft Optimal Design Results

Note in Table 3 that the optimal designs show some consistent patterns when compared to the baseline solution. While the baseline has the same redundancy for all components, the SA-generated solutions remove redundancy from less-risky or cost-effective components and add redundancy to components that have high failure rates and/or failure rate uncertainties. This is not surprising, and it points out the potential sub-optimality of the traditional method of allocating redundancy. The use of penalty functions works well, as no "invalid" solutions were accepted after the first 30 iterations. For certain components, the optimal redundancy changes significantly from one run of the SA algorithm to the next, and there are places where a human designer could adjust the results using his own qualitative design knowledge. Interestingly, attempts by the authors to do this have not yet been able to achieve a higher objective value. This suggests that the objective function is *insensitive* to components whose optimal unit numbers vary noticeably between optimization runs.

However, the Monte Carlo function evaluation uncertainty needs to be addressed. Using the Central Limit Theorem (CLT), the simulated function evaluations can be considered to be approximately Normally distributed. From Figure 2, we see that convergence around a limited range of result values is typically obtained after about 30 iterations. Table 4 contains the mean values (μ) and standard deviations (σ) of the objectives for all four cases. This level of variability does not seem to confuse the SA algorithm since convergence around the mean result is not lost after it is acquired.

Case	μ ($ M)	σ ($ M)	% Imp.	Case	μ ($ M)	σ ($ M)	% Imp.
LMSC orig.	13.81	0.143	5.14	Stan. orig.	13.12	0.185	9.23
LMSC imp.	14.13	0.141	3.62	Stan. imp.	13.75	0.172	6.01

Table 4: Summary of Optimization Results

One approach to handling the variability question would be to monitor the statistics in Table 4 in "real time" and to stop the Monte Carlo evaluations when sufficient certainty is attained. This idea is developed for GA's in [14]. The measure of statistical certainty could be based on a measure of risk aversion to the variability of the award result. This approach will be examined in follow-on research.

Since the SA procedure gives good results and is flexible enough to adapt to a wide variety of design problems, our work on the separate genetic algorithm approach is attempting to compare and contrast the two methods as adapted to this reliability design problem. While the SA approach chooses subsystem groups in which to make random modifications, the GA crossover operator, since it searches by hyperplanes at the component level, may be better able to isolate the individual components that are critical to overall performance. Better search-by-component might avoid the differences between unit numbers seen in different runs of the SA procedure. However, the GA approach will consume more computer time per solution evaluation and may not give significantly better results. Even so, our ability to modify the canonical SA and GA approaches to fit a given design problem or apply domain-specific knowledge suggests that various mixes of operators from both algorithms may give the best results.

8   Summary and Conclusions

The results shown here seem to justify the use of global optimization for this spacecraft design problem. Using simulated annealing, improvement can be obtained relative to the LMSC baseline design even though the objective functions are only partially sensitive to changes in component redundancy. Convergence of the global search did not take very long considering the complexity of the reliability analysis and the variance of the Monte Carlo simulations. The smooth pattern of convergence demonstrates that evolutionary global search is a useful way of conducting reliability optimization based on the new reliability model. Although the variance of the objective values is significant, it does not prevent the algorithm from converging.

The usefulness of this type of design optimization algorithm is threefold. First, it allows search of the design space to globally optimize an *arbitrary* value function based on an arbitrary system performance model. Second, it demonstrates the flexibility of evolutionary global optimization using simulation evaluations, since it accommodates domain-specific modifications to canonical SA and GA that improve search efficiency. Lastly, it is a design tool that allows the user to complement the computerized search by making manual variations to the optimal result in an attempt to gain further improvement.

The genetic algorithm-based optimization procedure is now beginning testing using the same reliability model. Other areas of follow-on work include simulation variance monitoring and reduction methods and applying risk aversion to the objective function evaluation. This application of evolutionary search strategies to optimal design under uncertainty should be very useful for a wide range of real-world projects.

References

1. *Reliability Prediction of Electronic Equipment* (MIL-HDBK-217E). Washington, D.C.: Department of Defense, October 1986
2. *Nonelectric Parts Reliability Data 1991* (NPRD-91). Rome, N.Y.: Reliability Analysis Center, 1991
3. *Reliability Modeling and Prediction* (MIL-STD-756B). Washington, D.C.: Department of Defense, November 1981
4. H. Hecht, M. Hecht: "Reliability Prediction for Spacecraft" (AD/A164-747). Los Angeles, CA.: SoHar Inc., December 1985
5. S. Pullen, B. Parkinson: "A New Approach to Spacecraft Reliability Analysis Using Tabulated Failure Rates". Stanford Univ., Unpub. Manuscript, June 1993
6. D. Vanderbilt, S.G. Louie: "A Monte Carlo Simulated Annealing Approach to Optimization over Continuous Variables". *Journal of Computational Physics*, 56, 259-271 (1984)
7. A. Karimi, A.V. Sebald, S. Isaka: "Use of Simulated Annealing in Design of Very High Dimensioned Minimax Adaptive Controllers". In: *Asilomar Conference on Signals, Systems, and Computers*. Pacific Grove, CA. 1989, pp. 116-118
8. W. Press, S. Teukolsky, W. Vetterling, B. Flannery: *Numerical Recipes in C: Second Edition*. New York: Cambridge University Press 1992
9. L. Davis (ed.): *Handbook of Genetic Algorithms*. New York: Van Nostrand Reinhold 1991
10. J. Grefenstette, J.M. Fitzpatrick: "Genetic Search with Approximate Function Evaluations". In: *Proceedings of the First International Conference on Genetic Algorithms*. Pittsburgh, PA. 1985, pp. 112-120
11. C.W.F. Everitt: "Gravity Probe B: I. The Scientific Implications". In: H. Sato, T. Nakamura (eds.): *Proceedings of the Sixth Marcel Grossmann Meeting on General Relativity*. Singapore: World Scientific 1992, pp. 1632-1644
12. D. Bardas, *et. al.*: "Gravity Probe B: II. Hardware Development; Progress Towards the Flight Instrument". In: *Ibid.*, pp. 382-393
13. Y.M. Xiao, *et. al.*: "Gravity Probe B: III. The Precision Gyroscope". In: *Ibid.*, pp. 394-398
14. A.N. Aizawa, B.W. Wah: "Dynamic Control of Genetic Algorithms in a Noisy Environment". In: *Proceedings of the Fifth International Conference on Genetic Algorithms*. Urbana-Champaign, IL. 1993, pp. 48-55

Soft Selection in D-optimal Designs

Iwona Karcz-Dulęba

Institute of Engineering Cybernetics
Technical University of Wrocław,
Janiszewskiego 11/17,
50-372 Wrocław, Poland

Abstract. A new algorithm generating the D-optimal experimental designs, based on an evolutionary search with soft selection, is presented. An efficiency of the numerical algorithm is compared with classical exchange algorithms. Preliminary results are promising and encourage more detailed investigations.

1 Introduction

In conventional optimization algorithms the best solution found so far becomes the basepoint for the further search. This approach is effective in local optimization but fails when the global optimum has to be found. A class of optimization procedures effective in global optimization is being developed currently. Authors claim that these algorithms resemble the natural optimization processes - the theory of evolution (e.g. molecular evolutionary optimization [3] or Genetic Algorithms [9]) and the thermodynamics (Simulated Annealing [11]). What these methods have in common is another strategy of basepoints selection, which might be called *soft selection*. In the soft selection better solutions are prefered but worse solutions also have a chance to be selected as search bases. The good global optimization properties of these *natural computation* methods induce their applications in many domains.

An *evolutionary search with soft selection* [6] is one of the natural computation methods. It has been derived from a simple stochastic model of asexual evolution. The method might be considered as a cross between Genetic Algorithms (similar selection rule) and Evolutionary Programming [5] (similar mutation rule). The effectiveness of this algorithm was usually tested on relatively simple tasks - continuous, regular, few dimensional adaptive landscapes. In this paper an attempt to apply the soft selection method to the discrete D-optimal experimental designs, which is a more complex optimization problem, is reported.

The discrete experimental designs task is an example of difficult optimization problem with multiple optima and multidimensional search space [2]. The aim of the experimental designs is to find the best localization of measuring points for identification purposes. When a large number of experiments might be executed, well known and reliable continuous design methods are usually applied. Often, technological or economical considerations severely reduce the possible number of measurements to just a few. In such cases the so called discrete design should be used (e.g. to plan observations of wildlife habitats density [12]). The optimal arrangement of a small, fixed number of measuring points proves to be a difficult problem. While few extremely simple cases can be solved analytically, numerical procedures are used to deal with practical problems. Presently, there exists a number of competitive algorithms among which Mitchell's DETMAX [12] is often considered as the best the D-optimal discrete designs procedure. However powerful, the existing algorithms do not work satisfactorily in more complex cases. Attempts to create more effective methods are continuing. The application of the natural computation method is an obvious try. Presented results of evolutionary search with soft selection in D-optimal designs seem to be promising.

2   D-optimal Designs for an Experiment Task

An object with inputs $x_1, x_2, \ldots, x_p$ and an output y, under influence of a random noise z is considered. A model of the object for an input x from a closed and limited design region $\Omega \subset R^p$ with exactness to a parameter b_j is expressed by the formula:

$$y = \sum_{j=1}^{k} b_j \cdot f_j(x_1, x_2, \ldots, x_p) + z \; ; \tag{1}$$

where linearly independent and continuous on Ω functions f_j $(j = 1, ..., k)$ are known. The identification task requires evaluating k values of b_j based on the observation y in N input (measuring) points $\mathbf{x} \in \Omega$. A relation between the output and inputs is given by the following regression function:

$$\mathbf{Y} = \mathbf{X}\beta + \xi \tag{2}$$

where:

$\mathbf{X} = \{f_j(\mathbf{x}_i)\};$ $i = 1, 2, \ldots, \mathbf{N}; \; j = 1, 2, \ldots, k$ - the design matrix (of independent variables)

$\mathbf{x}_i = [x_{i1}, x_{i2}, \ldots, x_{ip}];$ $i = 1, 2, \ldots, \mathbf{N}$ - values of inputs for following observations

$\mathbf{f} = [f_1, f_2, \ldots, f_k]^T$ - the vector of given functions, depending on an assumed model

$\mathbf{Y} = [y_1, y_2, \ldots, y_N]^T$ - the vector of observations

$\beta = [b_1, b_2, \ldots, b_k]^T$ - the vector of parameters to be estimated

$\xi = [z_1, z_2, \ldots, z_N]^T$ - the vector of errors (uncorrelated random variables identically distributed, with the mean zero and the constant variance σ^2)

The least squares estimate of the parameters vector β can be expressed as follows:

$$\hat{\beta} = (\mathbf{X}^T \mathbf{X})^{-1} \cdot \mathbf{X}^T \mathbf{Y} \; . \tag{3}$$

The $\mathbf{X}^T\mathbf{X}$ matrix is called the *information matrix* of design. An actual response y at an input point x is predicted by $\hat{\mathbf{y}}$:

$$\hat{\mathbf{y}}(x) = \mathbf{f}(x)^T \cdot \beta \ . \tag{4}$$

The variance of $\hat{\mathbf{y}}$ is given by:

$$\mathbf{v}(x) = \mathbf{f}(x)^T (\mathbf{X}^T\mathbf{X})^{-1} \cdot \mathbf{f}(x) \cdot \sigma^2 \ . \tag{5}$$

Finding the optimal setting of N measuring points in the design region is the purpose of discrete experimental design. The N-point exact design is called *D-optimal* if its information matrix determinant $|\mathbf{X}^T\mathbf{X}|$ is maximal on Ω.

The D-optimal discrete designs are usually obtained by applying "exchange algorithms" based on the procedure developed by Fedorov [4]. In this approach, a current N-point design is modified by exchanging design points in order to obtain increase in a value of the information matrix determinant. Mitchell's DETMAX algorithm [12] seems to be the most popular. In this procedure a design point with the minimal variance (5) is exchanged with a point from the design region having the maximal prediction variance. DETMAX algorithm has already had many modifications ([8], [10]). Other methods use different optimization strategies, e.g. the "branch and bound" search [15].

3　Evolutionary Search with Soft Selection

The method of evolutionary search with soft selection might be regarded as randomizations of Eigen's model of macromolecular evolution [3]. A search is performed by a population of m individuals (trials). An individual is characterized by a n-coordinate vector (a type), describing its location in an adaptive landscape (a search space), and by a fitness (a quality index). The random selection and modification are used to construct offspring generations. Each individual can be chosen as a parent (a base trial) with probability proportional to its quality: the higher the quality, the bigger the chance of being selected. The probability of the modification from type to type depends on the distance between these types. The evolutionary (optimization) process can be defined by probabilities of selection (6) and modification (7):

$$P[e'He'' \mid e' \in G(k),\ e'' \in G(k+1)] = \frac{q(u(e'))}{\sum_{e \in G(k)} q(u(e))} \tag{6}$$

$$f(x'' \mid e'He'',\ u(e') = x',\ u(e'') = x'') = g(x', x'') =$$

$$(\sqrt{2\pi\sigma^2})^{-n} \prod_{k=1}^{n} \int_{-\infty}^{\infty} \exp[-\frac{1}{2\sigma^2}(x_k' - x_k)^2]dx_k \tag{7}$$

where:

$e', e'' \in E$	- individuals (trials) in a process E;
$G(k)$	- k-th generation of individuals;
$e'He''$	- relation: individual e'' is based on individual e';
$x', x'' \in R^n$	- types of individuals;
$u : E \to R^n$	- identification of types function;
$q : R^n \to R^+$	- the quality function;
$g : R^n \times R^n \to (0,1)$	- probability of types modification.

Computer simulations [6], [7] have demonstrated that while individuals tend to be concentrated around local optima, the population is able to cross saddles between neighbouring optima - hopefully finding the global one. The ability of saddle crossing makes the process useful in global optimization but its local optimization properties are worse - it localizes the optimum approximately.

4 Algorithm with Soft Selection in the D-optimal Designs

In the D-optimal designs task the precise value of optimal design is required. The poor effectiveness of the evolutionary search with soft selection in local optimization implied its linking with a local search procedure. Two versions of local optimization have been considered: A1 - a hard selection: a new generation consists of modified offsprings of the best individual found so far; A2 - a best selection: there is no population, only one - the best individual, is reproduced. An application of the first version increases the probability of finding the optimum (a simultaneous search in m random directions). An application of the second version decreases a number of criterion function evaluation thus speeds up computations.

To express the discrete optimal design problem in terms of the evolutionary search with soft selection it is enough to interpret:

- one individual as a N-point design;
- the type of an individual as a $N \times p$ coordinate vector;
- a quality index q given by a value of the information matrix determinant;
- the population as a group of m-individuals (designs).

The soft selection algorithm proceeds in following steps:

Step 1: the initial population of the design points is randomly distributed in the design region Ω, using uniform distribution;

Step 2: quality indices of individuals (i.e. the information matrix determinants) are calculated;

Step 3: base designs for the next generation are selected using the inverse distribution method:

   1. relative quality indices r_i are attributed to individuals:

$$r_i = \left(\sum_{j=1}^{i} q_j\right) \Big/ \left(\sum_{j=1}^{m} q_j\right) \quad ; \quad i = 1, \ldots, m$$

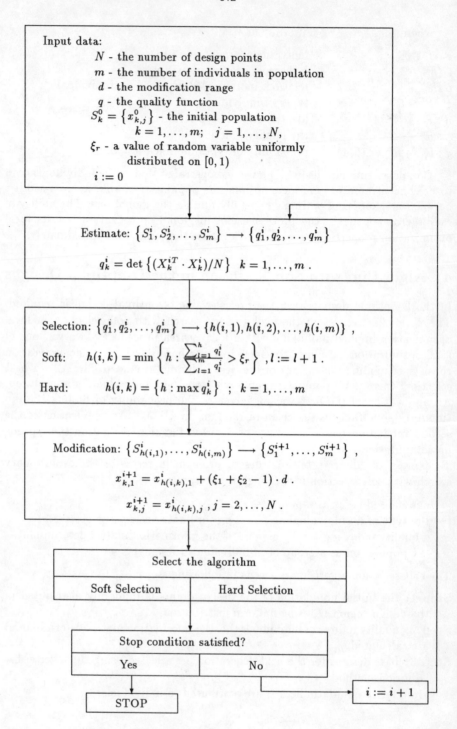

Fig. 1. A flow diagram of soft selection algorithm (version A1) in D-optimal designs

2. a random value, uniformly distributed on the interval $[0, 1)$ is generated;
3. the first individual with r_i greater than the random value is selected as the base design;

the above process is repeated m times and the base generation of designs is created;

Step 4: one point of selected base design, randomly chosen, is modified; every coordinate is changed by a random value, triangular distributed around 0 and with a range d;

Step 5: goto Step 2 unless stop condition is satisfied.

In order to speed up and simplify computations a few alternations of the original algorithm have been undertaken:

- only one of N design points (randomly selected) is modified at each "reproduction" cycle;
- in the case when a quality index q equals to zero design points are modified (as in Step 4);
- the triangular distribution is used in modification;
- if a new coordinate gets value out of the Ω the boundary value is taken.

A flow diagram of the algorithm (version A1) is presented in Fig. 1.

5 Results

The effectiveness of the D-optimal algorithm with soft selection has been examined on six tasks taken from [1], [10] (Table 1).

	$f^T(x)$	Design region
1.	$(1, x, x^2, x^3, x^4, x^5)$	$\Omega = \{x : -1 \leq x \leq 1\}$
2.	$(1, x_1, x_2, x_3, x_4)$	$\Omega = \{x : -1 \leq x_i \leq 1 , i = 1, ..., 4\}$
3.	$(1, x_1, x_2, x_1^2, x_2^2)$	$\Omega = \{x : -1 \leq x_i \leq 1 , i = 1, 2\}$
4.	$(1, x_1, x_2, x_1 \cdot x_2, x_1^2, x_2^2)$	$\Omega = \{x : -1 \leq x_i \leq 1 , i = 1, 2\}$
5.	$(1, x_1, x_2, x_3, x_1 \cdot x_2, x_2 \cdot x_3, x_1 \cdot x_3, x_1 \cdot x_2 \cdot x_3)$	$\Omega = \{x : -1 \leq x_i \leq 1 , i = 1, 2, 3\}$
6.	$(1, x_1, x_2, x_1 \cdot x_2, x_1^2, x_2^2, x_1 \cdot x_2^2, x_1^2 \cdot x_2, x_1^2 \cdot x_2^2)$	$\Omega = \{x : -1 \leq x_i \leq 1 , i = 1, 2\}$

Table 1.

During the soft selection procedure the modification range has been given the value $d = 0.2$ and during the local search it has been successively decreased from $d = 0.2$ to $d = 0.0013$. Populations of 2, 4, 8 elements for the A1 version of algorithm and 4, 8 elements for the A2 version have been tested. Increasing of the average quality during 40 generations has been treated as an approach to a local optimum and the local optimization procedure has been switched on. A lack of progress in the average quality has been treated as process trapping in the local optimum and then the soft selection has been triggered. Computations have been stopped when a value of information matrix determinant exceeded 99% of the best results from [10].

Both versions have been compared with algorithms: Fedorov's, modified Fedorov's, k-exchange, Mitchell's and Wynn-Mitchell's (see Table 2).
In Table 2 the following data concerning the soft selection algorithm, for $m = 4$, are given:
I - the average number of criterion computations ($Eval$) from five runs of the algorithm;
II - the minimum number of criterion function evaluation;
III - the best quality index.
Comparative data concerning the other algorithms are taken from [10].
As shown in Table 2 results obtained are promising. A number of criterion func-

Algorithm		Task					
		1		2		3	
		N=8		N=9		N=9	
		QC	Eval	QC	Eval	QC	Eval
1. Fedorov		6.17 e-8	1576	9.02 e-1	15597	9.76 e-3	9036
2. Mod. Fedorov		6.44 e-8	2031	9.02 e-1	7826	9.76 e-3	4205
3. k -exchange		6.40 e-8	988	9.02 e-1	4007	9.76 e-3	2392
4. Mitchell		6.31 e-8	2203	9.02 e-1	3808	9.75 e-3	22953
5. Wynn - Mitchell		6.32 e-8	611	9.02 e-1	1955	9.33 e-3	1233
6. soft - selection v. A1	I	6.38 e-8	3555	8.93 e-1	13742	9.66 e-3	972
	II	6.41 e-8	968	8.99 e-1	2632	15.80 e-3	580
	III	6.44 e-8	1872	8.99 e-1	13352	21.95 e-3	3840
7. soft - selection v. A2	I	6.38 e-8	1308	8.93 e-1	4903	9.66 e-3	809
	II	6.40 e-8	610	8.95 e-1	1372	16.20 e-3	670
	III	6.44 e-8	837	9.00 e-1	5304	17.20 e-3	730
Algorithm		4		5		6	
		N=10		N=14		N=15	
1. Fedorov		9.46 e-3	9851	7.28 e-1	21372	6.82 e-6	27591
2. Mod. Fedorov		9.46 e-3	8950	7.28 e-1	5951	6.82 e-6	8083
3. k -exchange		9.43 e-3	2558	7.28 e-1	2548	6.82 e-6	3225
4. Mitchell		9.44 e-3	10706	7.28 e-1	2858	6.82 e-6	3335
5. Wynn - Mitchell		9.41 e-3	1735	7.28 e-1	1715	6.79 e-6	2883
6. soft - selection v. A1	I	9.37 e-3	2187	7.20 e-1	17624	6.75 e-6	6928
	II	9.44 e-3	1584	7.27 e-1	5912	6.79 e-6	2880
	III	9.46 e-3	1892	7.27 e-1	5912	6.82 e-6	13520
7. soft - selection v. A2	I	9.37 e-3	3823	7.20 e-1	16918	6.75 e-6	36059
	II	9.37 e-3	678	7.22 e-1	11832	6.76 e-6	2331
	III	9.46 e-3	2407	7.24 e-1	23670	6.82 e-6	69198

Table 2.

tion evaluations is comparable with other competitive algorithms; in one task
the number is smaller than in other methods while in one task is bigger than
all but the Fedorov's method. In the task No. 3 the quality index obtained is
much better than obtained in [10]. The A2 version is more efficient for first four
tasks while the A1 version for last two tasks which seem to be more difficult. An
application of the idea taken from the exchange algorithms, i.e. modification of
the point with minimal variance, has not led to any significant improvement in
the soft selection procedure.

6 Summary

The new algorithm finding the D-optimal experimental designs has been presented. The method is based on the stochastic algorithm of evolutionary search
with soft selection. The obtained results of computations seem to be promising.
In some tasks the algorithm is faster or gives better quality index than well
known and widely used classical D-optimal algorithms.
It should be emphasized that experiments are at the preliminary stage. Answers
for the questions of the range of parameters, the class of tasks in which the
method is effective, the soft-local switching rule and making the stop condition
more versatile will be the subject of our future research.

References

1. R. Cook, C. Nachtsheim: A comparison of algorithms for constructing exact D-
   optimal designs. Technometrics 22, No. 3, pp.315-324 (1980)
2. Y. Dodge, V. Fedorov, H. Wynn: Optimal design of experiments: an overview.
   In: Y. Dodge, V.V. Fedorov, H.P. Wynn (eds.): Optimal design and analysis of
   experiments. Elsevier Science Publishers B.V., North-Holland (1988)
3. M. Eigen: Self-organization of matter and the evolution of biological macromolecules. Naturwissenschaften 58, pp. 465-523 (1971)
4. V. Fedorov: Theory of optimal experiments. Preprint No. 7, Publ. Moscow State
   University, Moscow (1969)
5. L.J. Fogel: Autonomous automata. Industrial Research 4, pp. 14-19 (1962)
6. R. Galar: Handicapped individua in evolutionary processes. Biol. Cybern. 51, pp.1-
   9 (1985)
7. R. Galar: Evolutionary search with soft selection. Biol. Cybern. 60, pp.357-364
   (1989)
8. Z. Galil, J. Kiefer: Time- and space-saving computer methods, related to Mitchell's
   DETMAX, for finding D-optimum designs. Technometrics 22, No. 3, pp. 301-313
   (1980)
9. J. Holland: Adaptation in natural and artificial systems. Ann Arbor, Univ. of
   Michigan Press (1975)
10. M.E. Johnson, C.J. Nachtsheim: Some guidelines for constructing exact D-optimal
    design on convex design space. Technometrics 25, No. 3, pp. 271-277 (1983)
11. S. Kirkpatrick, C.D. Gellat, M.P. Vecchi: Optimization by simulated annealing.
    Science 220, No. 4598, pp.671-680 (1983)

The Weighted Graph Bi-Partitioning Problem: A Look at GA Performance

Hiroaki Inayoshi and Bernard Manderick

[1] Computational Models Section, ETL, Japan
[2] Computer Science Dept., EUR, The Netherlands

Abstract. We assess the performance of the GA on the weighted graph bi-partitioning problem which is an NP-complete problem. The assessment is done in two ways. First, the GA is compared with other search techniques and second, the fitness landscapes to be optimized are quantified in different ways and these data are related to the GA-performance.

1 Introduction

The genetic algorithm (GA) offers the promise of a widely applicable, robust global search strategy [Gol89, Dav91]. Good GA-performance is a matter of finding a proper balance between exploitation and exploration. This in its turn is affected by GA-parameters like the selection strategy, the genetic operators and their corresponding rates.

Although a lot of theoretical and empirical knowledge has been accumulated, there is still little insight in the proper role of each of the components of the GA and how they interact to achieve effective search. Moreover, theory and practice seem to be at odds at certain points. For instance, what is the proper role of mutation? Is it merely a background operator whose main role is to recover lost alleles [Gol89] or is it a much more important operator than previously thought as many experiments show, e.g. [SCED89]. Or consider crossover disruption. The schema theorem seems to indicate that it should be minimized. But why then does uniform crossover perform so well on many problems while it is so highly disruptive [Sys89, LES89]. As a last example, consider the royal road functions which is a class of functions defined in such a way that the global optimum should be discovered easily by crossover [FM]. Consequentially, it is hard to understand why random mutation hill-climbing outperforms the GA by one order of magnitude.

The GA can only be a competitive optimization technique for a whole range of problems if we have a clear understanding of the specific role of each of its components and how they interact synergetically.

We are convinced that such an understanding is impossible without a detailed analysis of the fitness landscape to be optimized [MdWS91]. We expect that the landscape will reveal when the GA effectively searches the whole space and when it gets stuck in local optima or faces other difficulties.

This is the first paper of a series where we take a bottom up approach and analyze empirically the contribution of the different components in the overall search, and this is done for qualitatively different fitness landscapes. Our goal is to end up with a number of guidelines telling us for which landscapes the GA is a competitive optimization technique and how to tune it to obtain maximal performance. This way, we hope to contribute to transform GAs from an art, which it very much still is, into a well understood technique.

In this paper, we assess the GA-performance on the weighted graph bi-partitioning or GBP-problem in two ways. First, it is compared with a number of other search techniques: three hill-climbing techniques [FM], iterative improvement using the Kernighan-Lin heuristic [KL70], simulated annealing [OvG89] and a hybrid technique combining the GA with the Kernighan-Lin heuristic. And second, fitness landscape corresponding with this problem is analyzed. In particular, we look at the distribution of local optima in the search space and investigate its impact on the efficiency of different search strategies especially the GA.

The GBP-problem was chosen for a number of reasons. First, it is an important combinatorial optimization problem known to be NP-complete [GJ79]. Second, a powerful heuristic, called the Kernighan-Lin heuristic, exists which finds high quality local optima with a high frequency [KL70]. This heuristic serves as a bench mark for the other techniques. Third, the difficulties the GBP-problem poses can be tuned easily by changing parameters like the mean graph connectivity.

And finally, solutions can be encoded as bit strings and the distance between these strings can be calculated easily. This makes the GBP-problem a perfect candidate for the genetic algorithm. This is not the case for other well-known combinatorial optimization problems like the traveling salesman problem and job-shop problems where permutations are a more natural genetic representation. Different distances can be defined on the set of all permutations and this gives raise to qualitatively different fitness landscapes for the same problem instance. Some of these distances are also difficult to calculate. Moreover, there is multitude of genetic operators which further complicates the picture.

The rest of the paper is organized as follows. First, we describe the optimization problem. Second, we describe how we quantify the fitness landscape to be optimized. Third, we compare the different search techniques considered. And finally, we conclude.

2 The Optimization Problem

The problem studied in this paper is a weighted graph bi-partitioning problem (or GBP-problem) with an even number $2N$ of nodes, $2N = 200$ in our case. The objective is to divide the nodes in two equal disjoint sets $A = \{a_1, a_2, \cdots a_N\}$ and $B = \{b_1, b_2, \cdots b_N\}$ ($\#A = \#B$) such that the total sum of weights $w_{i,j} > 0$, where $w_{i,j}$ connects the nodes $a_i \in A$ and $b_j \in B$, is minimized, i.e. the cost function $C(\{A, B\}) = \sum_{a_i \in A} \sum_{b_j \in B} w_{i,j}$ associated with the partition $\{A, B\}$ is minimized.

This minimization problem can be transformed in an equivalent maximization problem by defining the fitness function $f(\{A, B\}) = C_{max} - C(\{A, B\})$. Depending on the search technique, either the cost function C is minimized or the fitness function f is maximized.

The instances we have studied are characterized by the following tunable parameters:

1. The mean connectivity μ_p of the graph: for small μ_p the graph is sparsely connected while for large μ_p it is densely connected.
2. The standard deviation σ_p of the connectivity.
3. The distribution of the weights: In the experiments, the weights are distributed according to an exponential distribution. Other possibilities are normal and uniform distributions.

2.1 Search Space

In the following, each graph bi-partitioning (GBP) $\{A, B\}$ consisting of 2 equally sized node sets is called a bi-graph **b** and if the graph contains $2N$ nodes, then **b** is represented by a bit string of length $2N$ as follows: First, all $2N$ nodes are numbered from 1 to $2N$. If one of these nodes belongs to the subset A then the corresponding bit is set to 1, otherwise it is set to 0. Vice versa, each $2N$ bit string with an *equal* number of 0s and 1s represents a bi-graph **b**. Therefore, we call this a bi-graph bit string or simply bi-graph and the set of all such strings is called the bi-graph space **B**. From now on, depending on the context **b** denotes a bi-graph or its bit string representation.

This problem gives rise to the search space denoted by $\mathbf{B}_N$ (N is the dimension of the space) as follows: Two search points **b** and **b**' are said to be neighbors if and only if **b** can be transformed into **b**' by exchanging one 0 and one 1, i.e. one 0-1 exchange. It is clear that the mapping $d_B(\mathbf{b}, \mathbf{b}')$ defined for all $\mathbf{b}, \mathbf{b}' \in \mathbf{B}_N$ as the minimum number of 0-1 exchanges to transform **b** into **b**' is a distance in the usual sense. If **b** and **b**' differ in $2M$ of the $2N$ bits then $d_B(\mathbf{b}, \mathbf{b}') = M$.

In Table 1, we contrast the search space $\mathbf{B}_N$ of the bi-graphs with the space $\mathcal{Z}_2^{2N}$ of all bit strings of length $2N$ in which it is embedded: $\mathbf{b} \in \mathbf{B}_N$ when **b** contains an equal number of 0s and 1s. For $N = 200$, the size of the search space is $\#\mathbf{B}_N \approx 9.1 \times 10^{58}$ which is about 5.5% of the size of $\mathcal{Z}_2^{2N}$.

Finally, we get the fitness landscape by assigning each $\mathbf{b} = \{A, B\} \in \mathbf{B}$ the associated fitness $f(\mathbf{b}) = C_{max} - C(\mathbf{b})$.

3 Fitness Landscape Analysis

The methodology to analyze fitness landscapes is borrowed from [Kau93]. Fitness landscapes can be quantified in a number of different ways.

1. The number of local optima and the size of their region of attraction is estimated.

	B	$\mathcal{Z}_2^{2N}$
Size	$\frac{(2N)!}{N!N!}$	2^{2N}
Neighbors	N^2	N
Diameter	N	$2N$
Density	$\frac{1}{\sqrt{\pi N}}$	1

Table 1. The search space B with the d_B-distance compared with the bit string space $\mathcal{Z}_2^{2N}$ in which it is embedded with the usual Hamming distance d_H.

2. The relation between the size of the region of attraction and the fitness of local optima is determined to see if there is a correlation.
3. The distribution of these optima over the search space is determined.
4. The autocorrelation function of the landscape and the correlation coefficients of the search operators are determined [MdWS91].

Together these measures give us a good picture of the difficulties a landscape might pose for a search technique and how the used search operators explore the landscape. This paper only concerns the distribution of optima.

In Figure 1, we show the distribution of local optima of a 200-node instance. The X-axis shows the cost of a local optimum and the Y-axis shows the distance from the optimum to the best local optimum that we have found. This figure clearly shows that the high quality local optima tend to be close to each other.

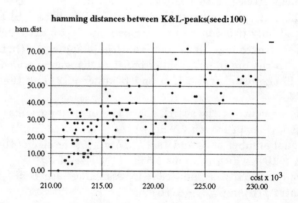

Fig. 1. The distribution of the local optima of a 200-node instance of the GBP-problem.

In Figure 2, we display the neighborhood of 2 bi-graph partitions (BGPs): one is a local optimum and the other is a random BGP. The X-axis corresponds with a node of the first subgraph and this node is then exchanged with each of the nodes of the second subgraph. The cost change is plotted in the Y-direction. This figure indicates that the landscape is quite smooth. The typical change in cost around a local optimum is about 7 % of cost of that GBP while it is about 2 % for a random GBP. A surprizing fact is that the mean connectivity μ_p of the graph to be partitioned has almost no effect on the fitness landscape: sparsely and densely connected graphs give rise to similar fitness landscapes. For instance, the autocorrelation function was the same for all landscapes.

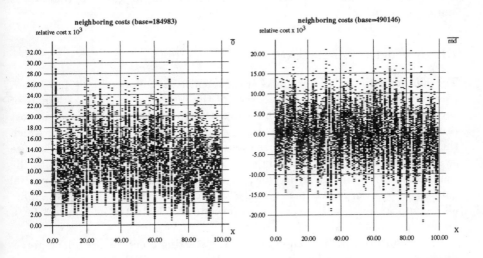

Fig. 2. The neighborhood around the global optimum (left) and a random GBP (right) of the GBP-instance in the previous figure. The cost of the global optimum and the random GBP are 184,983 and 490,146, respectively – see text for more details.

4 Comparison of Search Techniques

We have compared the following search techniques: three hill-climbing techniques [FM], iterative improvement using the Kernighan-Lin heuristic [KL70], simulated annealing [OvG89], Hopfield network [HT85] and a hybrid technique combining the GA with the Kernighan-Lin heuristic.

To apply each of these techniques one has to define: 1) a search space, 2) a move set that can be used to modify a search point and which defines a neighborhood relation and distance on that space, and 3) a fitness function. Together, they define a fitness landscape.

For all techniques, the search space and the fitness function were the space and the corresponding fitness function defined in Section 2.1. For all techniques but the Lin-Kernighan heuristic, the move set consists of the immediate neighbors of the current search point. As a result, all techniques are optimizing the same fitness landscape. The hillclimbers, the Hopfield net and simulated annealing are searching the immediate neighborhood while the Kernighan-Lin heuristic and the crossover operator can move further away from the current search point.

In this paper, we only consider iterative improvement using the Kernighan-Lin heuristic, the GA and a hybrid GA. For more details we refer to [Ina92]. Suffice it to say that the hybrid GA outperformed the other techniques and that it was very consistent in the sense that almost always the global optimum was found.

4.1 Kernighan-Lin heuristic

The KL-heuristic for the graph GBP problem is as follows: Let $\{A, B\}$ be a partition of the graph where A consists of the nodes $\{a_1, a_2, \cdots a_N\}$ and B of the nodes $\{b_1, b_2, \cdots b_N\}$. Swap the nodes a_{i_1} and b_{j_1} for which gain g_1 in cost is maximal. Then, swap the nodes $a_{i_2} \in A \setminus \{b_{j_1}\}$ and $b_{j_2} \in B \setminus \{a_{i_1}\}$ for which the additional gain g_2 is maximized and this is continued until all nodes are swapped. Of course, the total gain $G = \sum_{i=1}^{N} g_i = 0$ since we end up with the same GBP as we started with. Now, we determine the k for which the partial gain $G_k = \sum_{i=1}^{k} g_i$ is maximal. Finally, the new GBP is obtained by swapping all a_{i_l} and b_{j_l} for $l = 1, \cdots, k$. This procedure is illustrated in Figure 3 for a 10-node graph.

The resulting GBP is then used as a new starting point for the above procedure and this is repeated until $g_1 < 0$. In this case, the GBP is a local optimum for the KL-heuristic. This heuristic is a very powerful one which finds high quality solutions with a high probability [KL70].

4.2 The Genetic Algorithm

The genetic algorithm (abbreviated as RGA) used has the following parameters: 1) the population size is ranging from $N = 40$ to $N = 100$, and 2) rank-based selection [Whi89] is used since it combines two properties: First, the selection pressure remains constant during the search and second, the pressure can be tuned easily by changing the selection probabilities assigned to each rank. We used linear rank-based selection only. The usual genetic operators for bit strings are adapted in such a way that the offspring is again a bi-graph bit string.

Mutation of a bi-graph string $\mathbf{b}$ consists of one 0-1 exchange. The resulting string is one of its N^2 neighbors.

The crossover is a variant of uniform crossover. Take two parents $\mathbf{b}$ and $\mathbf{b}'$ and suppose that $d_B(\mathbf{b}, \mathbf{b}') = M$, i.e. $\mathbf{b}$ has at M locations a 0 where $\mathbf{b}'$ has a 1, and at M different locations $\mathbf{b}$ has a 1 where $\mathbf{b}'$ has a 0. At the remaining $2N - 2M$ locations both strings are equal.

Offspring is generated as follows: The $2M$ locations where the parents differ are filled at random with an equal number of zeros and ones, each other location

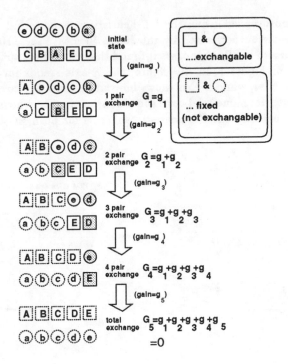

Fig. 3. The Kernighan-Lin heuristic for a 10 node GBP-problem. Given the partition $\{\{a, b, c, d, e\}, \{A, B, C, D, E\}\}$.

inherits the common value shared by the two parents. The resulting offspring is again a bi-graph and its mean d_B-distance to each of its parents is $M/2$.

4.3 The Hybrid Genetic Algorithm

The hybrid GA (HGA) is the same as the GA above except that after each generation, the KL-heuristic is applied to all members of the population. This way, we get an improved generation consisting of local optima for the KL-heuristic which is then used by the GA to produce the next generation. This cycle continues for an number of generations.

4.4 Comparison

We have done 300 runs for 8 different instances of the GBP-problem. The GA-performance was quite poor on these instances. All other techniques that we have considered performed significantly better than the GA – cfr. the left part of Figure 4. The basic difference is that all the other techniques do some kind of hillclimbing and this seems to be important for smooth landscapes.

Iterative improvement using the KL-heuristic is a powerfull technique but it was consistently outperformed by the HGA. In most cases, HGA found the global optimum and in all other cases it found the second best optimum – confer the right part of Figure 4. In this figure, the X-axis stands for the best cost obtained in one trial, while Y-axis shows how many times the cost has obtained out of 300 trials. Here, one trial corresponds to a search in which less than 500 points are improved by the KL-heuristic and this for both HGA and iterated KL.

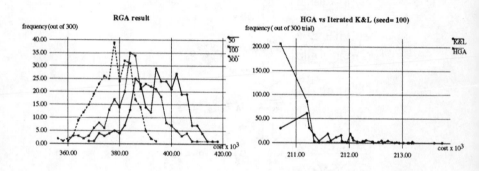

Fig. 4. Comparison of the GA-performance with that of the hybrid GA.

Our experiments indicate that crossover is a useful operator on the GBP-problem and Figure 1 explains why. The best local optima tend to be close to each other. As a result, genotypes located at high quality optima which are recombined might generate some offspring in the region of attraction of even better optima. And, that offspring will move to the better optimum due to hillclimbing. The distribution of local optima provides in a sense a "royal road" towards the global optimum.

5 Conclusions and Future Work

The results of our experiments presented here can be summarized as follows:

- Search combining the GA and local search is better than either technique alone. Moreover, this combination proved to be the best of the compared techniques.
- Crossover is a useful operator as a consequence of the distribution of the optima: the better optima tend to be in each neighborhood. Note that this usefulness has nothing to do with the lack of crossover disruption. Since it is randomly decided whether two nodes are connected or not, building blocks will have a large defining length on average and therefore they will be susceptible to crossover disruption.

Acknowledgments

While working on this project, Bernard Manderick stayed at ETL as a Science and Technology Agency Fellow.

References

[Dav91] L. Davis, editor. *Handbook of Genetic Algorithms*. Van Nostrand Reinhold, New York, 1991.

[FM]   S. Forrest and M. Mitchell. Relative building-block fitness and the building-block hypothesis.

[GJ79]   M.R. Garey and D.S. Johnson. *Computers and Intractability: A Guide to the Theory of NP-completeness*. W.H. Freeman and Company, San Francisco, 1979.

[Gol89] D. E. Goldberg. *Genetic Algorithms in Search, Optimization, and Machine Learning*. Addison-Wesley, Reading, 1989.

[HT85]   J.J. Hopfield and D.W. Tank. Neural computations of decisions in optimization problems. *Biological Cybernetics*, 52:141–152, 1985.

[Ina92] H. Inayoshi. *Simulations and Optimizations of Networks/Systems*. PhD thesis, Tsukuba University, 1992. In Japanese: Nettowa-ku sisutemu no simyure-syon to saitekika.

[Kau93] S.A. Kauffman. *The Origins of Order: Self-Organization and Selection in Evolution*. Oxford University Press, Oxford, 1993.

[KL70]   B.W. Kernighan and S. Lin. An efficient heuristic procedure for partitioning graphs. *Bell Systems Technical Journal*, 49(2):291–307, 1970.

[LES89] R. Caruana L. Eshelman and D. Schaffer. Biases in the crossover landscape. In J. D. Schaffer, editor, *Proceedings of the Third International Conference on Genetic Algorithms*. Morgan Kaufmann, San Mateo, 1989.

[MdWS91] Bernard Manderick, Mark de Weger, and Piet Spiessens. The genetic algorithm and the structure of the fitness landscape. In R. K. Belew and L. B. Booker, editors, *Proceedings of the Fourth International Conference on Genetic Algorithms*. Morgan Kaufmann, San Mateo, 1991.

[OvG89] R.H.J.M. Otten and L.P.P.P van Ginneken. *The Annealing Algorithm*. Kluwer Academic Publishers, Boston, 1989.

[SCED89] J. D. Schaffer, R. A. Caruana, L. J. Eshelman, and R. Das. A study of control parameters affecting online performance of genetic algorithms for function optimization. In J. D. Schaffer, editor, *Proceedings of the Third International Conference on Genetic Algorithms*. Morgan Kaufmann, San Mateo, 1989.

[Sys89] G. Syswerda. Uniform crossover in genetic algorithms. In J. D. Schaffer, editor, *Proceedings of the Third International Conference on Genetic Algorithms*. Morgan Kaufmann, San Mateo, 1989.

[Whi89] D. Whitley. The GENITOR algorithm and selective pressure: Why rank-based allocation of reproductive trials is best. In J. D. Schaffer, editor, *Proceedings of the Third International Conference on Genetic Algorithms*. Morgan Kaufmann, San Mateo, 1989.

Software Tools for Evolutionary Computation

RPL2: A Language and Parallel Framework for Evolutionary Computing

Patrick D. Surry and Nicholas J. Radcliffe

Edinburgh Parallel Computing Centre, King's Buildings
University of Edinburgh, Scotland, EH9 3JZ

Abstract. The Reproductive Plan Language RPL2 is an extensible, interpreted language for writing and using evolutionary computing programs. It supports arbitrary genetic representations, all structured population models described in the literature together with further hybrids, and runs on parallel or serial hardware while hiding parallelism from the user. This paper surveys structured population models, explains and motivates the benefits of generic systems such as RPL2 and describes the suite of applications that have used RPL2 to date.

1 Motivation

As evolutionary computing techniques have acquired greater popularity and have been shown to have ever wider application, a number of trends have emerged. The emphasis of early work in genetic algorithms on low cardinality representations is diminishing as problem complexities increase and people find it more convenient and effective to use more natural data structures. There is now extensive evidence, both empirical (Davis, 1991; Michalewicz, 1993) and theoretical (Mason, 1993; Radcliffe, 1991, 1994), that the arguments for the superiority of binary representations (Holland, 1975; Goldberg, 1989, 1990) were at least overstated. As the fields of evolution strategies (Baeck *et al.*, 1991), genetic programming (Koza, 1992) and evolutionary programming (Fogel, 1993) come together with genetic algorithms, an ever increasing range of representation types is becoming commonplace.

During the last decade, as interest in evolutionary algorithms has increased, there has been the simultaneous development and wide-spread adoption of parallel and distributed computing. The inherent scope for parallelism evident in evolutionary computation has been widely noted and exploited, most commonly through the use of *structured population models* in which mating probabilities depend not only on fitness but also on *location*. In these structured population models each member of the population (variously referred to as a chromosome, genome, individual or solution) has a site—most commonly either a unique coordinate (e.g. Gorges-Schleuter, 1990) or a shared island number (e.g. Norman, 1988)—and matings are more common between members that are close (share an island or have neighbouring coordinates) than between those that are more distant. Such structured population models, which are described in more detail in section 2, have proved not only highly amenable to parallel implementation, but also in many cases computationally superior to more traditional *panmictic* (unstructured) models in the sense of requiring fewer evaluations to solve a given problem (Gordon & Whitley, 1993). Despite this, so close has been the association between parallelism and structured population models that the term *parallel genetic algorithm* has tended to be used for both. It is a minor objective of this paper to encourage the adoption of the term *structured population model* when it is this aspect that is referred to.

The authors of this paper both work for Edinburgh Parallel Computing Centre, which makes extensive use of evolutionary computing techniques (in particular, genetic algorithms) for both industrial and academic problem solving, and wished to develop a system to simplify the writing of and experimentation with evolutionary algorithms. The primary motivations were to support arbitrary representations and genetic operators along with all population models in the literature and their hybrids, to reduce the amount of work and coding required to develop each new application of evolutionary computing, and to provide a system that allowed the efficient exploitation of a wide range of parallel, distributed and serial systems in a manner largely hidden from the user. RPL2, the second implementation of the *Reproductive Plan Language*, was produced in partnership with British Gas plc to satisfy these aims. This paper outlines the main benefits of exploiting such a system, focusing in particular on the population models supported by RPL2 (section 2), its support for arbitrary representations (section 3), the modes of parallelism it supports (section 4) and the applications for which it has been used (section 5).

RPL2 takes the form of an interpreted language with some specialised data structures and functions designed to simplify drastically the task of implementing and experimenting with evolutionary algorithms. Example *reproductive plans* are given in the appendix. Both parallel and serial implementations of the run-time system exist and will execute the same plans without modification.

2 Population models

Structured populations fall into two main groups—fine-grained and coarse-grained. In the fine-grained models, also known variously as *diffusion* (Muehlenbein *et al.*, 1991) or *cellular* models (Gordon & Whitley, 1993), it is usual for every individual to have a unique coordinate in some space, typically a grid of some dimensionality with either fixed or cyclic boundary conditions. In one dimension, lines and rings are most common, while in two dimensions regular lattices, tori and so forth dominate. More complex topologies in higher dimensions are also certainly possible. Individuals mate only within a neighbourhood called a *deme* and these neighbourhoods overlap by an amount that depends on their size and shape. Replacement is also local. This model is well suited to implementation on so-called Single-Instruction Multiple-Data (SIMD) parallel computers (also called array processors or, loosely, "data-parallel" machines). In SIMD machines a (typically) large number of (typically) simple processors all execute a single instruction stream synchronously on different data items, usually configured in a grid (Hillis, 1991). Despite this, some of the earlier implementations were by Gorges-Schleuter (1989), who used various distributed memory machines. It need hardly be said that the model is of general applicability on serial or general parallel hardware.

The characteristic behaviour of such fine-grained models is that in-breeding within demes tends to cause speciation as clusters of related solutions develop, leading to natural niching behaviour (Davidor, 1991). Over time, strong characteristics developed in one neighbourhood of the population gradually spread across the grid because of the over-lapping nature of demes, hence the term *diffusion* model. As in real diffusive systems, over time there is of course a tendency for the population to become homogeneous, but this happens less quickly than in panmictic models. This population model tends to help in avoiding premature convergence to local optima. Moreover, if the search is stopped at a suitable stage the niching behaviour allows a larger degree of coverage of different optima to be obtained than is typically possible with unstructured populations. Both this and the alternative coarse-grained models are illustrated in figure 1. Other papers describing the variants of the diffusion model include Manderick & Spiessens (1989), Muehlenbein (1989), Spiessens & Manderick (1991), Davidor (1991), Baluja (1993), Maruyama *et al.* (1993) and Davidor *et al.* (1993).

RPL2 supports fine-grained population models by allowing populations to be de-clared as arbitrary-dimensional structures with fixed or cyclic boundaries and provides the `structfor` loop construct, which allows (any part of) a reproductive plan to be executed over such a structured population in an unspecified order, allowing the system to exploit parallelism if it is available. A deme structure must also be specified for fine-grained populations. Demes are specified using a special class of user-definable operator (of which several standard instances are provided), and indicate a pattern of neighbours for each location in the population structure.

The other principal structured population model is the *coarse-grained* model, prob-ably better known as the *island* model. In this, several panmictic populations are allowed to develop in parallel, occasionally exchanging genomes in migration steps. In some cases, the island to which a genome migrates is chosen stochastically and asynchronously (e.g. Norman, 1988), in others deterministically in rotation (e.g. Whitley *et al.*, 1989), while in still others the islands themselves have a structure such as a ring and migrations only occur between neighbouring islands (e.g. Cohoon *et al.*, 1987); this last case is sometimes known as the *stepping stone* model. The largely independent course of evol-ution on each island again encourages niching (or *speciation*) while ultimately allowing genetic information to migrate anywhere in the (structured) population, and again this helps to avoid premature convergence and encourages covering if the algorithm is run with suitably low migration rates.

Coarse-grained models are typically only loosely synchronous, and work well even on distributed systems with very limited communications bandwidths. They are sup-ported in RPL2 by special declarations and use of the `structfor` loop construct and migration operators. There is sufficient flexibility included to allow arbitrary hybrid models also, for example, an array of islands each with fine-grained populations or a fine-grained model in which each site has an island (which could be viewed as a gen-eralisation of the stepping stone model). Other papers describing variants of the island model include Petty & Leuze (1989), Cohoon *et al.* (1990) and Tanese (1989).

Unstructured (panmictic) populations are also, of course, available using simple variable-length arrays, which may be indexed directly or treated as last-in-first-out stacks.

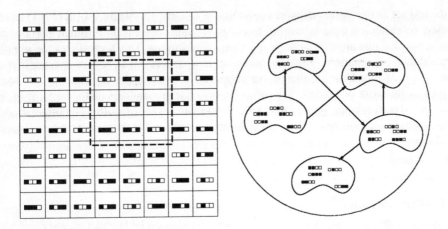

Fig. 1. The picture on the left illustrates a so-called *fine-grained* (*diffusion* or *cellular*) population structure. Each solution has a spatial location and interacts only within some neighbourhood, termed a deme. Clusters of solutions tend to form around different optima, which is both inherently useful and helps to avoid premature convergence. Information slowly diffuses across the grid.

The picture on the right shows the coarse-grained *island* model, in which isolated subpopulations exist on different processors, each evolving largely independently. Genetic information is exchanged with low frequency through migration of solutions between subpopulations. Again this helps track multiple optima and reduces the incidence of premature convergence.

3   Representation Issues

It was stressed in section 1 that a major design aim for RPL2 was that it should impose no constraints on the data structures used to represent solutions. This is achieved by including a generic pointer in the genome data structure that references a user-definable data structure, together with fields that are (potentially) relevant to all problems. A distinction is then made between *representation-independent* operators, whose action depends only on the standard fields of a genome (such as fitness measures), and *representation-dependent* operators, which may manipulate the problem-specific part. Examples of representation-independent operators include selection mechanisms, replacement strategies, migration and deme collection. All "genetic" operators (most commonly recombination, mutation and inversion) are representation-dependent, as are evaluation functions, local optimisers and generators of random solutions. This breakdown strongly promotes code re-use as domain-independent operators can form generic libraries. Even representation-dependent operators may have fairly wide applicability since many different problems may share operators at the genetic level: it is only evaluation functions that invariably have to be developed freshly for new problem domains. RPL2 is equally suited to all modes of evolutionary computing, but most of the applications built to date have used genetic algorithms.

Some evolutionary algorithms have been developed that employ more than one representation at a time. A notable example of this is the work of Hillis (1991), evolving sorting networks with a parasite model, where the evaluation function evolves to change the test set as the sorting networks improved. Similarly, Husbands & Mill (1991) have used co-evolution models with different populations optimising different parts of a process plan that are then brought together for arbitration. This necessitates the use of multiple representations. There are also cases in which control algorithms are employed to vary the (often large number of) parameters as an evolutionary algorithm progresses, such as the work of Davis (1989) adapting operator probabilities on the basis of their observed performance. RPL2 caters for the simultaneous use of multiple representations in a single reproductive plan, which greatly simplifies the implementation of such schemes.

4 Parallelism

Evolutionary algorithms that use populations are inherently parallel in the sense that— depending on the exact reproductive plan used—each chromosome update is to some extent independent of the others. There are a number of options for implementation on parallel computers, several of which have been proposed in the literature and implemented. As has been emphasised, population structure has tended to be tied closely to the architecture of a particular target machine to date, but there is no reason, in general, why this need be so.

Parallelism is supported in RPL2 at a variety of levels. Data decomposition of structured populations can be achieved transparently, with different regions of the population evolving on different processors, possibly partially synchronised by inter-process communication. Distribution of fine-grained models tends to require more interprocess communication and synchronisation so their efficiency is more sensitive to the computation-to-communications ratio for the target platform.

Task farming of compute intensive tasks, such as genome evaluation (e.g. Verhoeven *et al.*, 1992; Starkweather *et al.*, 1990), is also supported using the `forall` loop construct. This indicates that a set of operations is to be performed on all members of a population stack in no fixed order. This is particularly relevant to real-world optimisation tasks, for which it is almost invariably the case that the bulk of the time is spent on fitness evaluation. (For examples of this, see section 5, which discusses applications.) User operators may themselves include parallel code or run on parallel hardware independently of the framework, giving yet more scope for parallelism (e.g. George, 1994). In the unlikely event that none of these modes of parallelism is appropriate, RPL2 provides a convenient mechanism for performing multiple independent runs on parallel machines or distributed workstation networks.

RPL2 will run the same reproductive plan on serial, distributed or parallel hardware without modification using the minimum degree of synchronisation consistent with the reproductive plan specified. It uses (and makes available) the Marsaglia pseudo-random number generator (Marsaglia *et al.*, 1990), which as well as producing numbers with much better statistical distributions allows identical results to be produced on different processor architectures provided that they use the same floating point representation.

5 Applications

Applications that have currently been tackled using RPL2 include optimising a gas pipeline network with British Gas using a variable-cardinality integer representation (Boyd *et al.*, 1994), the Travelling Sales-rep Problem using a permutation representation with Random Assorting Recombination (Radcliffe, 1994) and data mining using a hierarchical genetic algorithm to evolve interesting sets of rules concerning data (Radcliffe & Surry, 1994). Trivial test problems using binary representations have also been implemented. Applications that used the prototype RPL system include optimising a retail network for Ford cars using an evaluation function that was a spatial interaction model running on a Connection Machine with a set representation (George, 1994), stock market tracking with a hybrid scheme based on a set-based representation (Shapcott, 1992) and neural network topology optimisation (Dewdney, 1992).

Several libraries of operators and representations are provided with the RPL2 framework. Constructing new operators and representations is a simple matter of writing standard ANSI C functions with return values and arguments corresponding to RPL2 data types. A preprocessor generates appropriate wrapper code to allow the operators to be called dynamically at plan run-time. New libraries of operators may optionally include initialisation and exit routines, start-up parameters, and check-pointing facilities. A library of representation-independent operators need include nothing further, while a new representation must define several routines that can be used by the framework to pack, unpack and deallocate the user-defined component of a genome. The packing and unpacking routines are necessary to allow genomes to be passed between processors cleanly, but may be null for serial applications.

Customised versions of the framework are built by linking together whatever combination of operator libraries and representations is desired, allowing locally developed operators to be tested in the context of existing libraries, maintained in some central location. RPL2 is distributed freely. Inquiries are welcomed by electronic mail at rpl2-support@epcc.ed.ac.uk. A wide range of serial and parallel hardware platforms is supported.

Acknowledgements

The serial prototype of RPL2 was implemented by Claudio Russo (1991), who developed many of the ideas with Radcliffe. The parallel prototype was developed by Graham Jones (1992). Mark Green and Ian Boyd from British Gas worked together with Patrick Surry on the design and implementation of RPL2.

References

Thomas Bäck, Frank Hoffmeister, and Hans-Paul Schwefel, 1991. A survey of evolution strategies. In *Proceedings of the Fourth International Conference on Genetic Algorithms*. Morgan Kaufmann (San Mateo).

Shumeet Baluja, 1993. Structure and performance of fine-grain parallelism in genetic search. In Stephanie Forrest, editor, *Proceedings of the Fifth International Conference on Genetic Algorithms*. Morgan Kaufmann (San Mateo).

Ian D. Boyd, Patrick D. Surry, and Nicholas J. Radcliffe, 1994. Constrained gas network pipe sizing with genetic algorithms. Technical Report EPCC–TR94–11, Edinburgh Parallel Computing Centre.

J. P. Cohoon, S. U. Hegde, W. N. Martin, and D. Richards, 1987. Punctuated equilibria: a parallel genetic algorithm. In *Proceedings of the Second International Conference on Genetic Algorithms*. Lawrence Erlbaum Associates (Hillsdale, New Jersey).

J. P. Cohoon, W. N. Martin, and D. S. Richards, 1990. Genetic algorithms and punctuated equilibria. In H. P. Schwefel and R. Manner, editors, *Parallel Problem Solving From Nature*, pages 134–144. Springer-Verlag.

Yuval Davidor, Takeshi Yamada, and Ryohei Nakano, 1993. The ECOlogical framework II: Improving ga performance at virtually zero cost. In Stephanie Forrest, editor, *Proceedings of the Fifth International Conference on Genetic Algorithms*. Morgan Kaufmann (San Mateo).

Yuval Davidor, 1991. A naturally occurring niche and species phenomenon: The model and first results. In *Proceedings of the Fourth International Conference on Genetic Algorithms*, pages 257–263. Morgan Kaufmann (San Mateo).

Lawrence Davis, 1989. Adapting operator probabilities in genetic algorithms. In *Proceedings of the Third International Conference on Genetic Algorithms*. Morgan Kaufmann (San Mateo).

Lawrence Davis, 1991. *Handbook of Genetic Algorithms*. Van Nostrand Reinhold (New York).

Nigel Dewdney, 1992. Genetic algorithms for neural network optimisation. Master's thesis, University of Edinburgh.

David B. Fogel, 1993. Evolving behaviours in the iterated prisoner's dilemma. *Evolutionary Computing*, 1(1).

Felicity A. W. George, 1994. Using genetic algorithms to optimise the configuration of networks of car dealerships. Technical Report EPCC–TR94-05, Edinburgh Parallel Computing Centre.

David E. Goldberg, 1989. *Genetic Algorithms in Search, Optimization & Machine Learning*. Addison-Wesley (Reading, Mass).

David E. Goldberg, 1990. Real-coded genetic algorithms, virtual alphabets, and blocking. Technical Report IlliGAL Report No. 90001, Department of General Engineering, University of Illinois at Urbana-Champaign.

V. Scott Gordon and Darrell Whitley, 1993. Serial and parallel genetic algorithms as function optimisers. In Stephanie Forrest, editor, *Proceedings of the Fifth International Conference on Genetic Algorithms*. Morgan Kaufmann (San Mateo).

Martina Gorges-Schleuter, 1989. ASPARAGOS: an asynchronous parallel genetic optimization strategy. In *Proceedings of the Third International Conference on Genetic Algorithms*, pages 422–427. Morgan Kaufmann (San Mateo).

Martina Gorges-Schleuter, 1990. Explicit parallelism of genetic algorithms through population structures. In H. P. Schwefel and R. Männer, editors, *Parallel Problem Solving from Nature*, pages 150–159. Springer Verlag (Berlin).

W. Daniel Hillis, 1991. Co-evolving parasites improve simulated evolution as an optimization procedure. In Stephanie Forrest, editor, *Emergent Computation*. MIT Press (Cambridge, MA).

John H. Holland, 1975. *Adaptation in Natural and Artificial Systems*. University of Michigan Press (Ann Arbor).

Philip Husbands and Frank Mill, 1991. Simulated co-evolution as the mechanism for emergent planning and scheduling. In *Proceedings of the Fourth International Conference on Genetic Algorithms*. Morgan Kaufmann (San Mateo).

Graham P. Jones, 1992. Parallel genetic algorithms for large travelling salesrep problems. Master's thesis, University of Edinburgh.

John R. Koza, 1992. *Genetic Programming: On the Programming of Computers by Means of Natural Selection*. Bradford Books, MIT Press (Cambridge, Mass).

B. Manderick and P. Spiessens, 1989. Fine-grained parallel genetic algorithms. In J. David Schaffer, editor, *Proceedings of the Third International Conference on Genetic Algorithms*, pages 428–433, San Mateo. Morgan Kaufmann Publishers.

G. Marsaglia, A. Zaman, and W. W. Tsang, 1990. Toward a universal random number generator. *Statistics and Probability Letters*, 9(1):35–39.

Tsutomo Maruyama, Tetsuya Hirose, and Akihiko Konagaya, 1993. A fine-grained parallel genetic algorithm for distributed parallel systems. In Stephanie Forrest, editor, *Proceedings of the Fifth International Conference on Genetic Algorithms*. Morgan Kaufmann (San Mateo).

Andrew J. Mason, 1993. Crossover non-linearity ratios and the genetic algorithm: Escaping the blinkers of schema processing and intrinsic parallelism. Technical Report Report No. 535b, School of Engineering, University of Auckland.

Zbigniew Michalewicz, 1993. *Genetic Algorithms + Data Structures = Evolution Programs*. Springer Verlag (Berlin).

Heinz Mühlenbein, M. Schomisch, and J. Born, 1991. The parallel genetic algorithm as function optimiser. In *Proceedings of the Fourth International Conference on Genetic Algorithms*, pages 271–278. Morgan Kaufmann (San Mateo).

H. Mühlenbein, 1989. Parallel genetic algorithms, population genetics and combinatorial optimization. In *Proceedings of the Third International Conference on Genetic Algorithms*, pages 416–421. Morgan Kaufmann (San Mateo).

Michael Norman, 1988. A genetic approach to topology optimisation for multiprocessor architectures. Technical report, University of Edinburgh.

Chrisila C. Petty and Michael R. Leuze, 1989. A theoretical investigation of a parallel genetic algorithm. In *Proceedings of the Third International Conference on Genetic Algorithms*. Morgan Kaufmann (San Mateo).

Nicholas J. Radcliffe and Patrick D. Surry, 1994. Co-operation through hierarchical competition in genetic data mining. Technical Report EPCC–TR94–09, Edinburgh Parallel Computing Centre.

Nicholas J. Radcliffe, 1991. Equivalence class analysis of genetic algorithms. *Complex Systems*, 5(2):183–205.

Nicholas J. Radcliffe, 1994. The algebra of genetic algorithms. *To appear in Annals of Maths and Artificial Intelligence*.

Claudio V. Russo, 1991. A general framework for implementing genetic algorithms. Technical Report EPCC–SS91–17, Edinburgh Parallel Computing Centre, University of Edinburgh.

Jonathan Shapcott, 1992. Genetic algorithms for investment portfolio selection. Technical Report EPCC–SS92–24, Edinburgh Parallel Computing Centre, University of Edinburgh.

Piet Spiessens and Bernard Manderick, 1991. A massively parallel genetic algorithm: Implementation and first analysis. In *Proceedings of the Fourth International Conference on Genetic Algorithms*, pages 279–286. Morgan Kaufmann (San Mateo).

T. Starkweather, D. Whitley, and K. Mathias, 1990. Optimization using distributed genetic algorithms. In H. P. Schwefel and R. Manner, editors, *Parallel Problem Solving From Nature*, pages 176–185. Springer-Verlag.

Reiko Tanese, 1989. Distributed genetic algorithms. In *Proceedings of the Third International Conference on Genetic Algorithms*. Morgan Kaufmann (San Mateo).

M. G. A. Verhoeven, E. H. L. Aarts, E. van de Sluis, and R. J. M. Vaessens, 1992. Parallel local search and the travelling salesman problem. In R. Männer and B. Manderick, editors, *Parallel Problem Solving From Nature, 2*, pages 543–552. Elsevier Science Publishers/North Holland (Amsterdam).

Darrell Whitley, Timothy Starkweather, and Christopher Bogart, 1989. Genetic algorithms and neural networks: Optimizing connections and connectivity. Technical Report CS-89-117, Colorado State University.

Appendix: Example RPL2 plans

Panmictic example

```
% This is a simple panmictic (unstructured) example that illustrates how
% parallelism can be applied to such problems (the forall construct)
% The plan is based on a population/cache model with generational update.

plan(PanmicticExample)

use      StdInst, Binary(128);        % parameterised by string length
string   sFile;
bool     bMaxIsBest;

int      iCounter, nGenerations, i, nPopsize;

genome   gNew,gChild,gParentA,gParentB;
gstack   gsPop, gsCache, gsParents;    % population, cache, and parents

sFile := "stdout";                     % direct output to the terminal
nPopsize := 200;                       % population size
nGenerations := 100;                   % number of generations
bMaxIsBest := TRUE;                    % maximise the evaluation function

Randomize(0);                          % pseudo-random initialisation

for iCounter := 1 to nPopsize          % create initial population
        gNew := RandomGenome();
        Push(gNew,gsPop);
endfor

forall gChild in gsPop                 % parallel evaluation of population
        EvalOneCount(gNew);            % number of 1s in string
endforall

for i := 1 to nGenerations             % generational update scheme

        Empty(gsCache);                % empty the stack for next generation
        Empty(gsParents);             % empty the array of parents

        ScaleRanked(gsPop, bMaxIsBest, 0.0, 1.0);        % scale on ranking
        SelectScaledSUS(gsPop, 2 * nPopsize, gsParents); % choose all parents

        for iCounter := 1 to nPopsize  % create new generation of genomes
                gParentA := Pop(gsParents); % do 3pt crossover,
                gParentB := Pop(gsParents); % with 20% clone rate
                gChild := CrossNpt(gParentA, gParentB, 3, 0.8);
                Push(gChild,gsCache);
        endfor

        forall gChild in gsCache       % mutate and evaluate in parallel
                Mutate(gChild, 0.01);  % bit-wise mutation rate of 1%
                EvalOneCount(gChild);
        endforall

        Swap(gsPop, gsCache);          % swap the new generation for the old

        StatsPrint(i,10,gsPop,sFile);  % collect population statistics
endfor
endplan
```

Hybrid population structure example

```
% In this more complex plan, the population is a set of islands,
% each of which contain a fine-grained population.  Each generation is
% formed by crossing the best and a random genome at each point.

plan(CombinationExample)

% Declare the population structure and defines the deme.  Cyclic (toroidal)
% and no-wrap boundaries are indicated by '@' and ':' respectively.

use StdInst, Set(200);                 % use a 200 element set representation
structure [5:island, 5:island, 10@fine, 10@fine] deme Taxicab(2);

int      iGeneration, nGenerations;
bool     bMaxIsBest;

% These correspond to the entire population structure (5x5x10x10 elements)
gstack  [*,*,*,*]       gsTmp;
genome  [*,*,*,*]       gPop, gMate, gSelf;

% These correspond only to the island axes of the population (5x5 elements)
gstack  [*,*,-,-]       gsImmigrants;
genome  [*,*,-,-]       gBestImmigrant, gEmigrant;

nGenerations := 100;
bMaxIsBest := FALSE;
Randomize(0);                          % pseudo-random initialisation

structfor [*,*,*,*]                     % loop over everything
        gPop := RandomGenome();         % generate a random initial population
        Squash(gPop);                   % simple evaluation function
endstructfor

for iGeneration := 1 to nGenerations    % generational update scheme

        structfor [*,*,-,-]             % loop over the island axes

                structfor [*,*]         % loop over remaining fine-grained axes

                        DemeCollect(gsTmp,gPop);        % collect neighbours
                        gSelf := SelectRawTournament
                                (gsTmp, bMaxIsBest, 2, 0.7, FALSE);
                        gMate := SelectRandom(gsTmp);
                        gPop := rarw(gSelf, gMate, 1);  % RAR-1 operator
                        Mutate(gPop, 0.02);             % set mutation
                        Squash(gPop);                   % evaluate population

                endstructfor

                % possibly migrate the best member of each island randomly
                % and replace a random member with the best immigrant

                gEmigrant := ReduceRawBest(gPop, bMaxIsBest);
                MigrateRandom(gsImmigrants, gEmigrant, 0.1);
                gBestImmigrant := SelectRawBest(gsImmigrants, bMaxIsBest);
                ProjectRandom(gPop, gBestImmigrant);

        endstructfor
endfor
endplan
```

Subject Index

Lecture Notes in Computer Science

For information about Vols. 1–792
please contact your bookseller or Springer-Verlag

Vol. 830: C. Castelfranchi, E. Werner (Eds.), Artificial Social Systems. Proceedings, 1992. XVIII, 337 pages. 1994. (Subseries LNAI).

Vol. 831: V. Bouchitté, M. Morvan (Eds.), Orders, Algorithms, and Applications. Proceedings, 1994. IX, 204 pages. 1994.

Vol. 832: E. Börger, Y. Gurevich, K. Meinke (Eds.), Computer Science Logic. Proceedings, 1993. VIII, 336 pages. 1994.

Vol. 833: D. Driankov, P. W. Eklund, A. Ralescu (Eds.), Fuzzy Logic and Fuzzy Control. Proceedings, 1991. XII, 157 pages. 1994. (Subseries LNAI).

Vol. 834: D.-Z. Du, X.-S. Zhang (Eds.), Algorithms and Computation. Proceedings, 1994. XIII, 687 pages. 1994.

Vol. 835: W. M. Tepfenhart, J. P. Dick, J. F. Sowa (Eds.), Conceptual Structures: Current Practices. Proceedings, 1994. VIII, 331 pages. 1994. (Subseries LNAI).

Vol. 836: B. Jonsson, J. Parrow (Eds.), CONCUR '94: Concurrency Theory. Proceedings, 1994. IX, 529 pages. 1994.

Vol. 837: S. Wess, K.-D. Althoff, M. M. Richter (Eds.), Topics in Case-Based Reasoning. Proceedings, 1993. IX, 471 pages. 1994. (Subseries LNAI).

Vol. 838: C. MacNish, D. Pearce, L. Moniz Pereira (Eds.), Logics in Artificial Intelligence. Proceedings, 1994. IX, 413 pages. 1994. (Subseries LNAI).

Vol. 839: Y. G. Desmedt (Ed.), Advances in Cryptology - CRYPTO '94. Proceedings, 1994. XII, 439 pages. 1994.

Vol. 840: G. Reinelt, The Traveling Salesman. VIII, 223 pages. 1994.

Vol. 841: I. Prívara, B. Rovan, P. Ružička (Eds.), Mathematical Foundations of Computer Science 1994. Proceedings, 1994. X, 628 pages. 1994.

Vol. 842: T. Kloks, Treewidth. IX, 209 pages. 1994.

Vol. 843: A. Szepietowski, Turing Machines with Sublogarithmic Space. VIII, 115 pages. 1994.

Vol. 844: M. Hermenegildo, J. Penjam (Eds.), Programming Language Implementation and Logic Programming. Proceedings, 1994. XII, 469 pages. 1994.

Vol. 845: J.-P. Jouannaud (Ed.), Constraints in Computational Logics. Proceedings, 1994. VIII, 367 pages. 1994.

Vol. 846: D. Shepherd, G. Blair, G. Coulson, N. Davies, F. Garcia (Eds.), Network and Operating System Support for Digital Audio and Video. Proceedings, 1993. VIII, 269 pages. 1994.

Vol. 847: A. L. Ralescu (Ed.) Fuzzy Logic in Artificial Intelligence. Proceedings, 1993. VII, 128 pages. 1994. (Subseries LNAI).

Vol. 848: A. R. Krommer, C. W. Ueberhuber, Numerical Integration on Advanced Computer Systems. XIII, 341 pages. 1994.

Vol. 849: R. W. Hartenstein, M. Z. Servít (Eds.), Field-Programmable Logic. Proceedings, 1994. XI, 434 pages. 1994.

Vol. 850: G. Levi, M. Rodríguez-Artalejo (Eds.), Algebraic and Logic Programming. Proceedings, 1994. VIII, 304 pages. 1994.

Vol. 851: H.-J. Kugler, A. Mullery, N. Niebert (Eds.), Towards a Pan-European Telecommunication Service Infrastructure. Proceedings, 1994. XIII, 582 pages. 1994.

Vol. 852: K. Echtle, D. Hammer, D. Powell (Eds.), Dependable Computing - EDCC-1. Proceedings, 1994. XVII, 618 pages. 1994.

Vol. 853: K. Bolding, L. Snyder (Eds.), Parallel Computer Routing and Communication. Proceedings, 1994. IX, 317 pages. 1994.

Vol. 854: B. Buchberger, J. Volkert (Eds.), Parallel Processing: CONPAR 94 - VAPP VI. Proceedings, 1994. XVI, 893 pages. 1994.

Vol. 855: J. van Leeuwen (Ed.), Algorithms - ESA '94. Proceedings, 1994. X, 510 pages.1994.

Vol. 856: D. Karagiannis (Ed.), Database and Expert Systems Applications. Proceedings, 1994. XVII, 807 pages. 1994.

Vol. 857: G. Tel, P. Vitányi (Eds.), Distributed Algorithms. Proceedings, 1994. X, 370 pages. 1994.

Vol. 858: E. Bertino, S. Urban (Eds.), Object-Oriented Methodologies and Systems. Proceedings, 1994. X, 386 pages. 1994.

Vol. 859: T. F. Melham, J. Camilleri (Eds.), Higher Order Logic Theorem Proving and Its Applications. Proceedings, 1994. IX, 470 pages. 1994.

Vol. 860: W. L. Zagler, G. Busby, R. R. Wagner (Eds.), Computers for Handicapped Persons. Proceedings, 1994. XX, 625 pages. 1994.

Vol: 861: B. Nebel, L. Dreschler-Fischer (Eds.), KI-94: Advances in Artificial Intelligence. Proceedings, 1994. IX, 401 pages. 1994. (Subseries LNAI).

Vol. 862: R. C. Carrasco, J. Oncina (Eds.), Grammatical Inference and Applications. Proceedings, 1994. VIII, 290 pages. 1994. (Subseries LNAI).

Vol. 863: H. Langmaack, W.-P. de Roever, J. Vytopil (Eds.), Formal Techniques in Real-Time and Fault-Tolerant Systems. Proceedings, 1994. XIV, 787 pages. 1994.

Vol. 864: B. Le Charlier (Ed.), Static Analysis. Proceedings, 1994. XII, 465 pages. 1994.

Vol. 865: T. C. Fogarty (Ed.), Evolutionary Computing. Proceedings, 1994. XII, 332 pages. 1994.

Vol. 866: Y. Davidor, H.-P. Schwefel, R. Männer (Eds.), Parallel Problem Solving from Nature - PPSN III. Proceedings, 1994. XV, 642 pages. 1994.

Vol 867: L. Steels, G. Schreiber, W. Van de Velde (Eds.), A Future for Knowledge Acquisition. Proceedings, 1994. XII, 414 pages. 1994. (Subseries LNAI).

Vol. 868: R. Steinmetz (Ed.), Multimedia: Advanced Teleservices and High-Speed Communication Architectures. Proceedings, 1994. IX, 451 pages. 1994.

Vol. 869: Z. W. Raś, Zemankova (Eds.), Methodologies for Intelligent Systems. Proceedings, 1994. X, 613 pages. 1994. (Subseries LNAI).

Vol. 870: J. S. Greenfield, Distributed Programming Paradigms with Cryptography Applications. XI, 182 pages. 1994.

Vol. 871: J. P. Lee, G. G. Grinstein (Eds.), Database Issues for Data Visualization. Proceedings, 1993. XIV, 229 pages. 1994.